◎Harden's

In association with **RÉMY MARTIN** FINE CHAMPAGNE COGNAC

The Heart of Cognac

UK Restaurant Guide
2009

"Restaurant lovers bible" Daily Mail

Survey-driven reviews of over 1750 restaurants, pubs and cafés

RÉMY MARTIN
FINE CHAMPAGNE COGNAC

The Heart of Cognac

Celebrating emerging excellence

The Harden's guide is unique because it is the UK's only fundamentally 'democratic' restaurant guide. It starts with no preconceptions as to the sorts of establishments people 'ought' to be interested in, and its content simply reflects the views expressed in a wide-ranging national survey of regular restaurant-goers. This survey has been conducted annually for the past 11 years.

In its own way, Rémy Martin also strives to stand out: by only selecting eaux-de-vie from the two finest crus regions in Cognac, we ensure our cognacs have an aromatic profile and depth of flavour that exceed every expectation and set us apart from others. Our revolutionary Coeur de Cognac adds further weight to our epicurean philosophy.

What unites Rémy Martin and Harden's is a passion for great food and drink, and for shared experience. Whilst culinary excellence has always been taken for granted in France, the restaurant scene in the UK has been a work-in-progress for many years. London has now emerged as a dining capital of note on a worldwide scale, and the rest of the UK is raising its game too. Rémy Martin are proud to be involved with this guide which – led by the ordinary regular restaurant-goer – is charting this evolution.

The Rémy Martin awards are committed to highlighting and encouraging new talent emerging in the thriving UK restaurant scene whilst bringing you the highest quality restaurant information. We raise a glass of our finest – be it V.S.O.P, XO or Coeur de Cognac – to the UK restaurant scene, and to the golden age of UK restaurants. Long may it continue.

The Heart of Cognac

For nearly three centuries, Rémy Martin has been passionate about producing the finest cognacs of exceptional quality and taste. There are three main characteristics which distinguish Rémy Martin from other cognacs: the harmony between the complexity of the aromas and the sweetness of the flavours; the elegant richness of the aromas and palate; and the length of the finish which leaves a lasting impression on the taste buds.

It remains the only large cognac house still in family ownership and is the only house that uses grapes grown from the region's best vineyards found in the heart of Cognac (Grande and Petite Champagne). Made from a blend of over 240 eaux-de-vie, this dedication to quality has seen Rémy Martin become the worldwide leader in the premium cognac category.

The Centaur Brand

The Sagittarius Centaur — a symbol of the alliance of man and nature was adopted by the Rémy Martin family in 1870. Not only is Sagittarius the star sign of Rémy Martin's founding father, Paul-Émile Rémy Martin, but it is also representative of many of the values that the family upholds – courage, energy, audacity and generosity.

Artist and Artisan

The role of the cellar master commands huge respect. It demands a special combination of skills: knowledgeable viticultualist, skilled wine maker, master blender, and expert taster, all whilst never losing sight of the house style. Thanks to the skilled craftsmanship of generations of cellar masters, Rémy Martin has been able to anticipate the evolution of consumer tastes and adapt and innovate accordingly.

Spirit for Life

Much more than a digestif, Rémy Martin has a cognac to suit every mood and occasion from celebrations to moments of solace. Throw out the rule book: aperitif, digestif, cocktail or frozen, Rémy Martin captures the spirit for living.

Rémy Martin V.S.O.P

This is the world's favourite V.S.O.P (Very Superior Old Pale) cognac and the benchmark by which all other V.S.O.Ps are measured. Rémy Martin V.S.O.P shows near perfect balance of the three cornerstones of great cognac: floral, fruity and spice. Blended from over 240 eaux-de-vie, the result is a wonderfully balanced and smooth V.S.O.P.

Much more than simply a traditional digestif, the versatility of Rémy Martin V.S.O.P means it is perfect for many occasions. Create a cocktail muddled with ginger ale and orange zest as the ideal way to start a party or settle down, put your feet up and enjoy it neat at the end of the day.

Or why not try our new concept and impress friends by pulling a bottle out of the freezer and serving it chilled? Traditionally served at room temperature, freezing the cognac gives it a different dimension. The superior aromatic intensity which is characteristic of Rémy Martin V.S.O.P intensifies and concentrates to create an entirely new delicious drink with a smooth, richer viscosity. Every serve has a powerful depth of flavour creating a fuller, rounder taste and works particularly well with smoked fish such as salmon.

The pleasure of Rémy Martin V.S.O.P can make any moment special.

RÉMY MAR

FINE CHAMPAGNE C

V.S.O.

Fondée en 172

PRODUCT OF FRA

Coeur de Cognac

Through expert blending, Rémy Martin has created a fruit-driven and succulent spirit – Coeur de Cognac. Fresher and lighter than traditional cognacs, the predominant flavours are ones of apricot, honey and vanilla. The first taste is like biting into a succulent, juicy peach whilst the nose bursts with ripe summer fruits and the palate is rich and soft - without the fiery finish usually associated with cognac.

Coeur de Cognac is intended for sheer drinking pleasure to be enjoyed anytime, anywhere. Try it over a little crushed ice that will help to reveal all its complex flavours. It is ideal as an aperitif, sipped throughout dinner or as the perfect end to your meal.

Developed with people who appreciate fine food and dining in mind, it is a natural accompaniment to many types of canapés as well as sweet and savoury dishes such as smoked salmon, sweet potato cakes, fillet of beef, chocolate and desserts with apricots and peaches. Here is a chocolate canapé recipe that serves 24 to get you started.

Individual Chocolate Puddings with Clotted Cream and Strawberries

170g 6oz dark chocolate
110g 4oz unsalted butter, cut into small chunks
170g 6oz caster sugar
55g 2oz flour, sifted
2 eggs, beaten
2tsp vanilla extract

To serve
1 pack of strawberries
1 pot of clotted cream

1. Preheat the oven to 170 C / 325 F / gas mark 3.
2. Butter some individual silicone moulds or mini muffin tins and dust with cocoa powder, set aside.
3. Melt the butter and chocolate in a bowl over a pan of simmering water. When the mixture has melted, remove the bowl from the heat and allow the chocolate to cool.
4. Add the sugar and vanilla extract to the chocolate, stir through then beat in the eggs and fold in the flour.
5. Place a heaped teaspoon of the mixture into each mould. Bake for 15 minutes and allow the puddings to cool slightly before removing them from the tins.

Recipe by Celia Francis

www.coeurdecognac.com

RÉMY MARTIN
FINE CHAMPAGNE COGNAC

The Heart of Cognac

Rémy Martin XO

Sophisticated and beautifully balanced, Rémy Martin XO
Excellence (Extra Old) combines aromatic richness and
complexity with a wonderful velvety texture. The nose yields
hints of jasmine, ripe fig and candied orange and the palate
shows notes of cinnamon and freshly baked brioche.

Rémy Martin XO is aged for up to 37 years in Limousin oak cask
to achieve its maturity and balance.

XO is a wonderful digestif and the perfect partner to rich
hazelnut and cinnamon desserts. Rémy Martin XO truly is the
taste of extravagance.

FINE
CHAMPAGNE
COGNAC

RÉMY MARTIN
FINE CHAMPAGNE COGNAC

XO
EXCELLENCE

A.O.C. FINE CHAMPAGNE COGNAC

Enjoying Rémy Martin

Not only are Rémy Martin Fine cognacs the ideal choice to round off a wonderful meal, but Rémy Martin can also be enjoyed as a long drink before dinner or as the perfect accompaniment to fine food.

Rémy Martin Melon Rouge

2oz Rémy Martin V.S.O.P
4 pieces of fresh watermelon
3/4 oz gomme syrup

Muddle ingredients. Add ice and strain twice into a martini glass.

Centaur Spice

A refreshing long drink, combining Rémy Martin V.S.O.P with a hint of orange and bitters, lengthened with ginger ale. A simple but stunning drink – ideal for dinner parties.

Method:

Fill a glass with ice
Add 2 dashes of Angostura bitters
Twist a sliver of orange peel over ice and drop into glass
Add a shot of Rémy Martin V.S.O.P
Top with ginger ale
Gently stir

Rémy Martin Strawberry Elixir

2oz Rémy Martin V.S.O.P
4 fresh strawberries
3/4 oz Gomme syrup
1/4 cup fresh pomegranate juice
1 oz pressed apple juice
Garnish: sliced strawberries

Muddle and strain 4-5 strawberries. Add juice with gomme syrup, pomegranate juice and pressed apple juice in a cocktail shaker. Add Rémy Martin V.S.O.P and ice. Shake well and strain into an ice-filled high ball glass.

2009 Rémy Martin Restaurant Awards

Now in its seventh year, the Rémy Martin Restaurant Awards recognise the new restaurants across the UK which have achieved outstanding levels of excellence. This award will help you to recognise food and service quality.

There are 11 awards, 4 in London and 7 regional winners.

WINNER 2009
RÉMY MARTIN

● **Two Fat Ladies at the Buttery**
Glasgow

● **Barn Asia**
Newcastle Upon Tyne

● **Highwayman**
Kirkby, Lonsdale

● **Nut Tree Inn**
Murcott

● **Walnut Tree Inn**
Abergavenny   ● *LONDON

● **Hotel TerraVina**
Woodlands

● **2 Fore Street**
Mousehole

*L'Anima
Pearl Liang
Ristorante Semplice
Texture
London

One restaurant has additionally been awarded the ultimate accolade – the Rémy Martin Excellence Award. This award is given to the restaurant which has shown itself as the true outstanding rising star of the UK restaurant scene in the last 12 months.

Winner Of The Excellence Award

L'Anima, City of London

L'Anima, meaning 'the soul' in Italian, is the brainchild of renowned chef Francesco Mazzei. Housed in a space designed by famed architect Claudio Silvestrin, the restaurant serves contemporary Italian cuisine in a chic minimal setting. The design of the restaurant bordering the City and Shoreditch took three years and as a result the interior is magnificent.

An open and inviting space with a glass frontage, extensive use of white limestone, brown porphyry and marble reflect the sophistication and quality, yet simplicity of Francesco's menu.

Inspired from his childhood in Calabria, Italy, where food is considered an expression of love and tradition, Francesco opened his first restaurant at 18. He has since worked at famed establishments such as The Dorchester, Hakkasan and most recently St Alban.

Reflecting the long-hours City culture, the restaurant serves breakfast, lunch and dinner plus an all-day menu served in the bar, with seasonal daily specials and typical Italian fare. In the restaurant, Francesco creates dishes with bold yet clean and distinct flavours. Signature dishes include tube-shaped pasta served with soft spicy salami, capers, anchovies and oregano in a tomato sauce with fried aubergine and grated hardened ricotta cheese. The bar serves stylish cocktails, a selection of Prosecco and a wide range of Italian wines by the glass and bottle.

London

Pearl Liang, Paddington

The theory behind this classy contemporary Chinese is that a well prepared Chinese dish should appeal to more senses than just the sense of taste. Its colour should be pleasing to the eye, and there should be evenly contrasting textures and tastes within the meal – crispy and smooth, spicy and gentle, yin and yang. Its sumptuous décor – black marble bar, floor-to-ceiling bamboo poles, giant wooden abacus and purple padded thrones – gives it a fantasy-land feel. The menu is long and varied, excelling in traditional Chinese cuisine. Both manager Humphrey Lee and Chef Paul Ngo previously worked at the Mandarin Kitchen, but in Pearl Liang have created a unique Chinese restaurant.

Ristorante Semplice, Mayfair

This sumptuous osteria is co-owned by chef Marco Torri and manager Giovanni Baldino with business partner Marino Alberto. In the past, Torri has worked at The Halkin Hotel, Locanda Locatelli and Stefano Cavallini. Inside the luxuriously decorated interior, with golden walls and leather chairs, the focus is on simple Italian ingredients that stand out from the crowd – free-range rabbit, cheeses flown in daily from Caserta, Sarawak pepper and home-made egg pasta. Dishes that have gained high praise are the octopus starter and the main course risotto of clams and cime de rapa. The restaurant also boasts an impressive all-Italian wine list served.

Texture, Marylebone

Texture is the brainchild of chef Agnar Sverrisson and master sommelier Xavier Rousset. Sverrisson, originally from Iceland met Rousset, a former head sommelier at Hotel du Vin, whilst they were both working under Raymond Blanc at La Manoir Aux Quat' Saisons. Thanks to their combined expertise, they have created a restaurant where light healthy food and exquisite wines are accorded equal importance. The cuisine is modern European and, as the name suggests, focuses on combining and emphasising different consistencies. Signature dishes include Icelandic lamb with broth, barley and root vegetables, and chargrilled Anjou pigeon with sweetcorn, shallot, bacon popcorn and red wine essence.

UK

2 Fore Street, Mousehole

Having trained under Raymond Blanc, owner Joe Wardell has transformed an uninspiring café into a chic and stylish French bistro-style restaurant. Set in the picturesque fishing village of Mousehole on the south coast of Cornwall, 2 Fore Street is passionate about good food. The menu changes regularly to reflect the freshest of local produce and boasts an array of crowd-pleasers, from local steamed mussels and hand-cut

RÉMY MARTIN
FINE CHAMPAGNE COGNAC

The Heart of Cognac

chips to half grilled lobster with herb butter, plus daily fish specials landed that day in Newlyn. In addition to a special children's menu, dietary requirements are also carefully considered: the homemade chocolate and almond cake is wheat and gluten free.

TerraVina, Woodlands

Set in the beautiful New Forest, TerraVina is a wine and food enthusiast's dream. The brainchild of Gerard Basset MW, one of the UK's leading wine experts, and his wife Nina, TerraVina is a triumphant combination of intimate warmth and first-rate service. Head chef, David Giles, offers unaffected, flavouresome food with a Californian wine county style that makes the best use of local produce. The open kitchen is a feature of the restaurant, along with a wood-burning stove and wine cellar on view to customers. The kitchen dishes up mouth-watering delicacies using locally-sourced and organic produce. A melt-in-the-mouth cep mushroom tart may be followed by roast wild bream or aged rib-eye of beef. To enhance the vinous experience, TerraVina has two state-of-the-art Enomatic machines (for dispensing wines by the glass).

The Highwayman, Kirkby Lonsdale

Following a £1.2 million renovation, The Highwayman opened in its present guise in April 2007. Originally an 18th century coaching inn, legend states that it was the midnight haunt of Lancashire's notorious highwaymen. It now offers a 21st century version of 'the local', serving British classics reflecting the seasons and regional specialties. Craggy stone floors, warm solid wood furniture, crackling log fires in winter and fabulous walled gardens to lounge in for summer alfresco dining ensure the restaurant is always welcoming. The menu inspired by Nigel Haworth, Chef Patron of nearby Northcote, is a tribute to traditional specialties of the area, including wild Cumbrian rabbit pie and heather-reared Bowland lamb Lancashire hotpot.

Nut Tree Inn, Murcott

Situated in a quaint 16th century country inn, the Nut Tree Inn is full of character with low-beamed ceilings and a log-burning stove. Owned by Mike North, one of the youngest ever Michelin-starred chefs, the restaurant serves pub food at its finest. The aim of the kitchen is to be self-sufficient and plans are ambitious. With seven pigs in the garden, a home made smokery and over an acre set aside for a vegetable garden, the

RÉMY MARTIN
FINE CHAMPAGNE COGNAC

The Heart of Cognac

dishes on offer reflect the high quality of the fresh ingredients. Highlights include confit belly of Oxfordshire pork with salt and vinegar potatoes, celeriac puree and apple gravy, and oil-poached fillet of halibut with herb risotto.

Walnut Tree Inn, Abergavenny

The renowned Walnut Tree Inn re-opened this year in a joint venture between Shaun Hill, the former chef-owner of Ludlow's Merchant House, and local hotelier William Griffiths. Shaun Hill has transformed this legendary restaurant and the menu is an eclectic mix, based on personal taste and sound cooking techniques. Whilst an Italian influence is still noticeable, the style is otherwise modern British. A unifying feature is the core of excellent ingredients, local where feasible, and carefully chosen. The menu changes weekly and could include skate with shrimps and dill beurre blanc, or loin of Berkshire pork, pigs cheeks and black pudding.

Two Fat Ladies at the Buttery, Glasgow

The Buttery, one of Glasgow's oldest and most celebrated restaurant sites, now provides a perfect home for the locally celebrated Two Fat Ladies concept (which started off at an address with '88' in it, hence, in bingo-speak, the name). With its unique traditional interior of oak panelling, stained-glass, and mahogany and marble bar, the site has always been known for its relaxed and welcoming atmosphere. The new restaurant offers such great local specialties such as tian of Orkney crab, avocado and Bloody Mary jelly, and Estate of Mey fillet of beef, shallot confit and red wine reduction.

Barn Asia, Newcastle

Situated in a stylish square, Barn Asia is the newest addition to the locally-celebrated 'Barn' chain of restaurants. Offering a fantastic new twist on the China Town experience, the restaurant brings together the French influenced cuisine of Vietnam with dishes from other Far Eastern countries, specialising in tapas-style dishes such as scallops with pork and peanut caramel, tempura of salt and chilli soft shell crab and Korean barbeque beef. Huge prints of artwork from the region and real Vietnamese memorabilia contribute to a truly authentic experience. Owner Mark Lagun even travelled to the region with his chef to research the dishes for a true Asian flavour.

Search online hardens.com

© **Harden's Limited 2008**

ISBN 978-1-873721-82-7

British Library Cataloguing-in-Publication data: a catalogue record for this book is available from the British Library.

Underlying UK map images ©MAPS IN MINUTES™/Collins Bartholomew (2008).

Printed in Italy by Legoprint

Research assistants: Samantha Hawkins; Jonathan Drew; Jaclyn Allen; Sarah Ashpole; Jane Riley

Editorial assistants: Syreeta Jun Searle; Alexandra Woodward

Harden's Limited
14 Buckingham Street
London WC2N 6DF

The views expressed in the editorial section of this guide are exclusively those of Harden's Limited

Would restaurateurs (and PRs) please address communications to 'Editorial' at the above address, or ideally by email to: editorial@hardens.com

The contents of this book are believed correct at the time of printing. Nevertheless, the publisher can accept no responsibility for errors or changes in or omissions from the details given.

CONTENTS

Amaya 40

Pearl Liang 92

RATINGS & PRICES

We see little point in traditional rating systems, which generally tell you nothing more than that expensive restaurants are 'better' than cheap ones, as they use costlier ingredients and attempt more ambitious dishes. You probably knew that already. Our system assumes that, as prices rise, so do diners' expectations.

£ Price
The cost of a three-course dinner for one person. We include half a bottle of house wine, coffee and service (or a 10% tip if there is no service charge).

Food
The following symbols indicate that, *in comparison with other restaurants in the same price-bracket*, the cooking at the establishment is:

 Exceptional

 Very good

Some restaurants are worth a mention but, for some reason (typically low feedback) we do not think a rating is appropriate. These are indicated as follows:

 Tip

We also have a category for places which attract a notably high proportion of adverse comment:

 Disappointing

Ambience
Restaurants which provide a setting which is very charming, stylish or 'buzzy' are indicated as follows:

 Particularly atmospheric

Restaurant Rémy awards
 A Restaurant Rémy symbol signifies this year's winners – see front colour section

Small print

Telephone number – All numbers in the London section are (020) numbers.
Sample dishes – these dishes exemplify the style of cooking at a particular establishment. They are merely samples - it is unlikely that these specific dishes will be available at the time of your visit.
Details – the following information is given where relevant:
Directions – to help you find the establishment.
Website – if applicable.
Last orders time – at dinner (Sun may be up to 90 mins earlier).
Opening hours – unless otherwise stated, restaurants are open for lunch and dinner seven days a week.
Credit and debit cards – unless otherwise stated, Mastercard, Visa, Amex and Maestro are accepted.
Dress – where appropriate, the management's preferences concerning patrons' dress are given.
Children – if we know of a specified minimum age for children, we note this.
Accommodation – if an establishment has rooms, we list how many and the minimum price for a double.

FROM THE EDITORS

To an extent we believe to be unique, this guide is written 'from the bottom up'. That is to say, its composition reflects the restaurants, pubs and cafés which people across the country – as represented by our diverse reporter base – talk about. It does not, therefore, concentrate on hotel restaurants (as does one of the major 'independent' guides whose publisher also does big business in paid-for hotel inspections). Nor does it 'overweight' European cuisines. Most restaurants in this country fall in the category usually called 'ethnic', but most guidebooks would lead you to think that such places are generally unworthy of serious commentary. It seems to us that this approach is positively wrong-headed in a country where the diversity of restaurant types is one of the most notable (and positive) features.

The effects of London's restaurant revolution of the '90s are now apparent across the whole of the UK. Most major conurbations, for example, now have several ambitious restaurants good enough to be of note to visitors. The areas that are still truly 'culinary deserts' are becoming both smaller and more dispersed. Much as this is to be applauded, it does not make our task any easier, and we are keenly aware – as any honest publisher must acknowledge – that all guide books are imperfect. There will be deserving places missing, and opinions will be repeated that the passing of time has rendered redundant. However, we believe that our system – involving the careful processing of tens of thousands of reports – is the best available.

We are very grateful to each of our thousands of reporters, without whose input this guide could simply not have been written. Many of our reporters express views about a number of restaurants at some length, knowing full well that – given the concise format of the guide – we can seemingly never 'do justice' to their observations. We must assume that they do so in the confidence that the short – and we hope snappy – summaries we produce are as fair and as well-informed as possible. You, the reader, must judge – restaurant guides are not works of literature, and should be assessed on the basis of utility. This is a case where the proof of the pudding really is in the eating.

Given the growing scale of our task, we are particularly grateful for the continuing support we have received from Rémy Martin Fine Champagne Cognac in the publication of this guide. With their help, this is now well on the way to becoming the most comprehensive – as well as the most democratic and diverse – guide available to the restaurants of the UK.

All restaurant guides are the subject of continual revision. This is especially true when the restaurant scene is undergoing a period of rapid change, as at present. **Please help us to make the next edition even more comprehensive and accurate: sign up to join the survey by following the instructions overleaf.**

Richard Harden   Peter Harden

How This Book Is Organised

This guide begins in London, which, in recognition of the scale and diversity of its restaurant scene, has an extensive introduction and indexes, as well as its own maps. Thereafter, the guide is organised strictly alphabetically, without regard to national divisions – Ballater, Beaumaris, Belfast and Birmingham appear together under 'B'.

For cities and larger towns, you should therefore be able to turn straight to the relevant section. Cities which have significant numbers of restaurants also have a brief introductory overview, as well as entries for the restaurants themselves.

In less densely populated areas, you will generally find it easiest to start with the map of the relevant area at the back of the book, which will guide you to the appropriate place names.

How This Book Is Researched

This book is the result of a research effort involving thousands of 'reporters'. These are 'ordinary' members of the public who share with us summary reviews of the best and the worst of their annual dining experiences. This year, more than 8,000 people gave us some 85,000 reviews in total.

The density of the feedback on London (where many of the top places attract several hundred reviews each) is such that the ratings for the restaurants in the capital included in this edition are almost exclusively statistical in derivation. We have, as it happens, visited almost all the restaurants in the London section, anonymously, and at our own expense, but we use our personal experiences only to inform the standpoint from which to interpret the consensus opinion.

In the case of the more commented-upon restaurants away from the capital, we have adopted an approach very similar to London. In the case of less-visited provincial establishments, however, the interpretation of survey results owes as much to art as it does to science.

In our experience, smaller establishments are – for better or worse – generally quite consistent, and we have therefore felt able to place a relatively high level of confidence in a lower level of commentary. Conservatism on our part, however, may have led to some smaller places being underrated compared to their more visited peers.

How You Can Join The Survey

Register on our mailing list at www.hardens.com and you will be invited, in the spring of 2009, to participate in our next survey. **If you take part you will, on publication, receive a complimentary copy of Harden's Restaurant Guide 2010.**

LONDON
INTRODUCTION &
SURVEY RESULTS

LONDON INTRODUCTION

What makes London special?

Until recently, most people would have said that it was the internationalism of London's restaurants that was their most eye-catching feature. Indeed, the joke was that if you were going to eat well, the only certainty was that you wouldn't – except for breakfast, perhaps – be eating English.

That's no longer really true: as a complement to the hotch-potch of cuisines which remains a key strength of the city – there aren't many cuisines you can't eat here well – there are now some definably English restaurants of real note too.

Of non-indigenous cuisines, the ones in which London, as a legacy of empire, excels are those of the Indian subcontinent. Indeed, the concentration of diverse restaurants within this category within a relatively small area makes London arguably the world's leading 'Indian' restaurant city. (The poorest-served cuisine until recently was Chinese, but – even here – there are now signs of progress.)

Which is London's best restaurant?

As in most major cities the 'best' restaurants are still by and large French, and the best grand French restaurant in town, currently by a fair margin, is Marcus Wareing's *Pétrus*. Also at a very high level is the Chelsea flagship of the UK's best-known chef, *Gordon Ramsay*, and – if you're looking for the sort of dinner Escoffier might recognise as such – *Le Gavroche*. The best all-round mid-price restaurants are *Chez Bruce* (again Londoners' favourite destination this year) and its sibling *The Ledbury*.

For further best restaurant suggestions, consult the double-page spread on pages 32 and 33.

What's 'in' at the moment?

The days when the scene was small enough to have only a handful of 'in' restaurants have passed. Nowadays, the question is rather: 'in' with whom? For the Dolce Vita crowd, the place of the moment is still – whatever its other failings – *Cipriani*. The media still regard *The Ivy* as something of a canteen, but *Scott's* is starting to establish itself as the all-purpose see-and-be-seen destination. The fashion world is still somewhat taken with *Sketch* and *Momo*. *The Wolseley* is the 'café' to be seen at (especially for breakfast). *J Sheekey* – and in particular *Le Caprice* – are 'in' with people who feel that being 'in' is trying a bit too hard.

For younger City and international types, the all-round appeal of orientals such as *Zuma*, *Roka*, *Hakkasan* and *Yauatcha* remain very strong.

I'm not fussed about 'scenes' – where can I get a good meal at reasonable cost?

The best tip of all – and this may become even more so if recession bites – is to lunch rather than dine. If you do, they don't come much grander than *Le Gavroche* – for less than many lesser restaurants charge for dinner.

One of the greatest successes of recent times has been *Arbutus* – right in the heart of Soho – where the formula has always been conceived with good value in mind. Some other Gallic restaurants – pre-eminently *Galvin Bistro de Luxe* and *Racine* – offer a top-quality product, but at prices which leave the customer happy.

For sheer upper-middle market value, the family of restaurants put together by Nigel Platts-Martin is impossible to beat. *Chez Bruce* has made itself into a modern legend, and *La Trompette*, *The Glasshouse* and *The Ledbury* – all a little way from the centre – are worthy stablemates to it. If you're looking for decent upper-middle market value in the West End, names worth considering include *Le Caprice*, *Clos Maggiore* and *Latium*.

The names above, however, are just the beginning. Look through the Area Overviews beginning on page 120. These should enable you to find value – wherever in town you're looking and whatever your budget – for any occasion.

And for the best of British tradition?
As we suggested earlier, British food, until quite recently, was largely reserved for tourists. The Roast Beef of Old England still is. If that's what you're looking for, head for *Simpson's-on-the-Strand* for the full tourist experience, or *Rules* for a rather more agreeable one.

In just the last few years, though, restaurants with more intelligent and wholehearted roots in native culinary traditions have become very fashionable. (This is often painted as some kind of renaissance, but in truth there never was a golden era of British Restaurant Cooking.)

The pioneer establishment of the new-wave Brits – which long seemed to be crying in the wilderness – was *St John*. But over the last few years the trend – often conflated with 'gastropub' cooking in many people's minds – has become mainstream. Restaurants proper which may be said to be strongly influenced by the style include *Magdalen*, *Great Queen Street*, *Hereford Road* and – most recently and most modishly – *Hix Oyster Bar & Grill*.

Isn't London supposed to be a top place for curry?
London, as noted above, has a reasonable claim to being the world's top Indian restaurant city. At the top end, leading lights such as *Rasoi Vineet Bhatia*, *Amaya*, *The Painted Heron*, *Benares* and *Zaika* are pushing back the frontiers, but – perfectly reasonably – charge the same as equivalent restaurants with European cuisines. What's therefore more exciting in terms of value is the vast range of subcontinental restaurants where you can still have a knock-out meal for the sort of prices you're hardly ever likely to find if you eat European-style. Two of the

best of the budget subcontinentals – both, in fact, Pakistani – are *New Tayyab* and the *Lahore Kebab House*.

You said diverse: what about other cuisines?
A major hit of recent times has been the cuisines of North Africa and the Eastern Mediterranean. These cuisines lend themselves well to good budget experiences. London was traditionally notably deficient in Mexican (and Latin American) restaurants, but this has been something of a buzz area in the last few years, with openings such as Crazy Homies, Green & Red Bar & Cantina.

There's supposed to be a recession coming. Any tips?
● The top tip, already noted, is to lunch not dine. If you're a visitor, you'll find that it's better for your wallet, as well as your digestion, to have your main meal in the middle of the day. In the centre of town, it's one of the best ways you can be sure of eating 'properly' at reasonable cost.

● Think ethnic – for a food 'experience' at modest cost, you'll almost always be better off going Indian, Thai, Chinese or Vietnamese (to choose four of the most obvious cuisines) than French, English or Italian. The days when there was any sort of assumption that ethnic restaurants were – in terms of comfort, service and décor – in any way inferior to European ones is long gone.

● Try to avoid the West End. That's not to say that, armed with this book, you shouldn't be able to eat quite well in the heart of things, but you'll almost certainly do better outside the Circle Line. Many of the best and cheapest restaurants in this guide are easily accessible by tube. Use the maps at the back of this book to identify restaurants near tube stations on a line that's handy for you.

● If you must dine in the West End, try to find either pre-theatre (generally before 7.30 pm) or post-theatre (generally after 10 pm) menus. You will generally save at least the cost of a cinema ticket, compared to dining à la carte. Many of the more upmarket restaurants in Theatreland do such deals.

● Use this book! Don't take pot luck, when you can benefit from the pre-digested views of thousands of other diners-out. Choose a starred restaurant, and you're very likely to eat much better than if you walk in somewhere on spec. And once you have decided that you want to eat within a particular area, use the Area Overviews (starting on p120) to identify the restaurants that are offering top value.

● Visit our website, www.hardens.com, for the latest reviews, and restaurant news.

SURVEY MOST MENTIONED

These are the restaurants which were most frequently mentioned by reporters. (Last year's position is given in brackets.) An asterisk* indicates the first appearance in the list of a recently-opened restaurant.

1	J Sheekey (1)
2	Chez Bruce (2)
3	The Wolseley (3)
4	Hakkasan (5)
5	Gordon Ramsay (6)
6	Bleeding Heart (4)
7	Scott's (24)
8	Pétrus (12)
9	Le Gavroche (11)
10	The Ivy (7)

Pétrus

11	La Poule au Pot (9)
12	La Trompette (18)
13	Arbutus (13)
14	Oxo Tower (8)
15	Galvin Bistrot de Luxe (16)
16	Le Caprice (15)
17	Andrew Edmunds (10)
18	Zuma (22)
19	The Square (26)
20	Gordon Ramsay at Claridge's (14)

Galvin Bistrot de Luxe

21	Yauatcha (19)
22	The Anchor & Hope (27)
23	Wild Honey*
24	The Cinnamon Club (23)
25	Locanda Locatelli (20)
26	Benares (-)
27	Tom Aikens (25)
28	maze (21)
29	Le Café Anglais*
30	L'Atelier de Joel Robuchon (32)

Yauatcha

31	Roka (-)
32	Moro (29)
33	The River Café (32)
34	Amaya (28)
35	The Ledbury (-)
36	The Don (30)
37	Roussillon (40)
38	St John (36)
39=	St Alban (35)
39=	Zafferano (-)

Amaya

LONDON - HIGHEST RATINGS

These are the restaurants which received the best average food ratings (excluding establishments with a small or notably local following).

Where the most common types of cuisine are concerned, we present the results in two price-brackets. For less common cuisines, we list the top three, regardless of price.

British, Modern

£45 and over		Under £45	
1	Chez Bruce	1	Lamberts
2	Bacchus	2	The Anglesea Arms
3	The Glasshouse	3	Tom Ilic
4	Petersham Nurseries	4	Phoenix Bar & Grill
5	Notting Hill Brasserie	5	Inside

French

£45 and over		Under £45	
1	Pétrus	1	Upstairs Bar
2	Gordon Ramsay	2	Galvin Bistrot de Luxe
3	La Trompette	3	Fig
4	Le Gavroche	4	Cellar Gascon
5	The Ledbury	5	Rosemary Lane

Italian/Mediterranean

£45 and over		Under £45	
1	Assaggi	1	Latium
2	Quirinale	2	A Cena
3	Enoteca Turi	3	Il Bordello
4	Locanda Locatelli	4	Oliveto
5	Riva	5	Spacca Napoli

Indian

£45 and over		Under £45	
1	Rasoi Vineet Bhatia	1	New Tayyabs
2	Amaya	2	Babur Brasserie
3	Zaika	3	Bombay Palace
4	The Painted Heron	4	Kastoori
5	Veeraswamy	5	Hot Stuff

Chinese

£45 and over
1. Kai Mayfair
2. Yauatcha
3. Hunan
4. Princess Garden
5. Hakkasan

Under £45
1. Mandarin Kitchen
2. Pearl Liang
3. The Four Seasons
4. Yming
5. Singapore Garden

Japanese

£45 and over
1. Zuma
2. Roka
3. Umu
4. Sumosan
5. Ubon

Under £45
1. Jin Kichi
2. Dinings
3. Sushi-Say
4. Pham Sushi
5. Kurumaya

British, Traditional
1. St John
2. Scott's
3. The Anchor & Hope

Vegetarian
1. Kastoori
2. Roussillon
3. The Gate

Burgers, etc
1. Ground
2. Haché
3. Eagle Bar Diner

Pizza
1. Il Bordello
2. Oliveto
3. Pizza Metro

Fish & Chips
1. Two Brothers
2. Golden Hind
3. Fish Club

Thai
1. Sukho Thai Cuisine
2. Amaranth
3. Churchill Arms

Fusion
1. Ubon
2. Tsunami
3. Archipelago

Fish & Seafood
1. One-O-One
2. J Sheekey
3. Mandarin Kitchen

Greek
1. Vrisaki
2. Daphne
3. Retsina

Spanish
1. Barrafina
2. Moro
3. Cambio de Tercio

Turkish
1. Mangal Ocakbasi
2. Cyprus Mangal
3. Gem

Lebanese
1. Fresco
2. Beirut Express
3. Al Sultana

SURVEY - NOMINATIONS

Ranked by the number of reporters' votes.

Top gastronomic experience

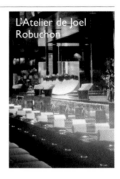
L'Atelier de Joel Robuchon

1. Gordon Ramsay (1)
2. Chez Bruce (2)
3. Pétrus (4)
4. Le Gavroche (3)
5. La Trompette (9)
6. Tom Aikens (5)
7. L'Atelier de Joel Robuchon (6)
8. The Square (-)
9. maze (7)
10. J Sheekey (-)

Favourite

The Wolseley

1. Chez Bruce (1)
2. Le Caprice (5)
3. J Sheekey (3)
4. La Trompette (6)
5. The Wolseley (2)
6. The Ivy (4)
7. Moro (7)
8. Pétrus (-)
9. Galvin Bistrot de Luxe (9)
10. Gordon Ramsay (8)

Best for business

Rhodes 24

1. The Wolseley (1)
2. The Don (3)
3. Bleeding Heart (2)
4. The Square (6)
5. 1 Lombard Street (5)
6. Coq d'Argent (4)
7. The Ivy (9)
8. The Goring Hotel (-)
9. Galvin Bistrot de Luxe (-)
10. Rhodes 24 (10)

Best for romance

Bleeding Heart

1. La Poule au Pot (1)
2. Andrew Edmunds (2)
3. Bleeding Heart (3)
4. Chez Bruce (4)
5. Clos Maggiore (9)
6. Le Caprice (5)
7. Oxo Tower (Rest') (7)
8. Pétrus (-)
9. Café du Marché (6)
10. J Sheekey (-)

OPENINGS AND CLOSURES

Restaurants in bold are included in the London section of this guide – for the full selection, see Harden's London Restaurants 2009 (£11.99), available in all good bookshops.

Openings

Aaya
L'Absinthe
Ambassade de L'Ile
L'Anima
Apsleys
L'Autre Pied
Balfour
Baozi Inn
Beach Blanket Babylon EC2
Beehive
Bel Canto
The Betjeman Arms
Bianco Nero
Bincho Yakitori W1
Bob Bob Ricard
Bord'Eaux
The Botanist
Le Bouchon Breton
The Boundary
Brasserie James
Brasserie St Jacques
Buddha Bar
Bumpkin SW7
Butcher & Grill
Byron
The Carpenter's Arms
Catch
Cha Cha Moon
Chicago Rib Shack
Cinnamon Kitchen
The Clissold Arms
Commander
Côte
Cruse 9
D Sum 2
Da Scalzo
Dehesa
Devonshire Terrace
Dexters SW4
Diner NW1
The Duke Of Sussex
Eastway
Eco W4
The Electric Birdcage
The Establishment
54 Farringdon Road
The Fox and Anchor
Franco Manca
Gazette SW12
Giaconda Dining Room
Giusto
Green Door Bar & Grill EC3
Grille
Haché SW10
Haozhan
Hélène Darroze
Hix Oyster & Chop House
Inamo
Iznik Kaftan

Jimmy's
Jom Makan
Kazan EC3
Khoai N12
Knaypa
Kyashii (The Kingly Club)
Landau
Ma Cuisine
Mango & Silk
Mango Tree
Manicomio EC4
Marco
Market
maze Grill
Mela SE24
The Mercer
Min Jiang
Mint Leaf EC2
Missouri Angel
Modern Pantry
Monty's SW6
Murano
Napket W1 (x2)
1901
The Normanby
Number Twelve
Osteria Emilia
Osteria Stecca
The Pantechnicon Rooms
Pho W1, WC1
Pinchito
The Prince Of Wales
Princess Victoria
The Queens Arms
Rock & Rose
Saf
Sagar W1
Salade W2, EC4
Sheekey Oyster Bar
St James's Hotel & Club
Tart
Tendido Cuatro
Terranostra
The Three Bridges
Tom Ilic
Urban Turban
Vanilla Black
Vanilla
Vapiano
Vivat Bacchus SE1
Water House
York & Albany

Closures

Amici SW17
Angela Harnett
Arkansas Café
Aurora EC2
The Aviary
Babes 'n' Burgers
Bar Capitale EC4
Blandford Street
Brasserie Pierre
Brian Turner
Bush Garden Café
C Garden
Casale Franco
Crescent House
Dish Dash SW10
Eco SW9
Eriki NW8
Fishmarket EC2
Florians
The Food Room
Frock's
Garden Café
Gili Gulu
Hara the Circle Bar
Hugos SW7
Ikkyu
Jaan
Kaz Kreol
Khyber Pass
Kobe Jones
Lanesborough/Conservatory
Lavender SW9
Leadenhall Italian Restaurant
Lou Pescadou
Louvaine
Lundums
Ma Goa SW6
Miyabi
Mocotò
Molloys
Morel
No. 77
La Noisette
O'Conor Don
The Oratory
Oriental City Food Court
Page in Pimlico
Le Palais du Jardin
La Piragua
Randall & Aubin SW10
Ravioli
Redmonds
Rosmarino
Rudland & Stubbs
La Saveur
Sea Cow N16, SW4
Shimo
Shish W2
Silks & Spice
Soho Spice
Standard Tandoori
Susie Wong
Tabaq
Tenth Restaurant
Terminus
Upper Glas
Wakaba
Zaytouna
Zen Central
ZeNW3

LONDON
DIRECTORY

A Cena TW1 £40 Ⓐ ⭐
418 Richmond Rd 8288 0108
Locals "absolutely love" this "comfortable" St Margaret's Italian, near Richmond Bridge – "the food just gets better", and you get a "great welcome" too. / **Details:** *www.acena.co.uk; 10.30 pm; closed Mon L & Sun D; booking: max 6, Fri & Sat.*

Aaya W1 £52 Ⓐ ⭐
66-70 Brewer St 7319 3888 2–2D
From Alan Yau's brother Gary, a path-breaking restaurant, bringing high-quality Japanese fare (including top-quality sushi) and striking design values to Soho; it's no bargain, but standards on our early-days visit were uniformly very high. / **Details:** *www.aaya.com; 11.30 pm, Sun 10.30 pm.*

L'Absinthe NW1 £35 Ⓐ
40 Chalcot Rd 7483 4848
Jean-Christophe Slowik's "busy" new bistro may have finally broken the jinx on this Primrose Hill corner site (most recently, the Black Truffle, RIP); it serves up ultra-traditional Gallic fare at very keen prices. / **Details:** *10.30 pm, Sun 9.30 pm; closed Mon.*

Adams Café W12 £26
77 Askew Rd 8743 0572 6–1B
"A favourite local haunt", in Shepherd's Bush, especially notable for its "friendly" service; by day, it's a greasy spoon, but at night it transforms into a BYO Tunisian café, serving "an interesting array of N African dishes" (including "delicious tajines"). / **Details:** *11 pm; closed Sun.*

Addie's Thai Café SW5 £26 Ⓐ ⭐
121 Earl's Court Rd 7259 2620 4–2A
Near Earl's Court tube, an "authentic" café, hailed by its small fan club as a "top value-for-money Thai". / **Details:** *www.addiesthai.co.uk; 11 pm; closed Sat L & Sun L; no Amex.*

Agni W6 £28 ⭐
160 King St 8846 9191 6–2C
"Amazing, fresh, clean Indian" dishes – "as cheap as chips" – win many fans for this "stark" outfit, opposite Hammersmith Town Hall; there's a vague feeling, though, that it's "gone downhill" of late. / **Details:** *www.agnirestaurant.com; 11 pm; D only.*

Al Sultan W1 £39 ⭐
51-52 Hertford St 7408 1155 2–4B
No one doubts that this Shepherd Market Lebanese is an "authentic" spot, and the food is "good" too – "you do pay Mayfair prices for it", however, and the décor is "terrible". / **Details:** *www.alsultan.co.uk; 11 pm.*

Al-Waha W2 £33 ⭐
75 Westbourne Grove 7229 0806 5–1B
A "cosy" Bayswater Lebanese attracting steady praise for its "delicious" food and "unvarying" standards. / **Details:** *www.alwaharestaurant.com; 11.30 pm; no Amex.*

Alain Ducasse
Dorchester W1 £104
53 Park Ln 7629 8866 2–3A

"Not nearly up to Paris or Monte Carlo…" – the Gallic über-chef's Mayfair opening has *"fallen woefully short of expectations"*; the food *"tries hard to be flash"*, but just ends up *"seriously underpowered"*, and it comes at *"wild"* prices too.
/ **Details:** www.alainducasse-dorchester.com; 10 pm; closed Mon, Sat L & Sun; jacket.

The Albemarle
Brown's Hotel W1 £67
Albemarle St 7493 6020 2–3C
Rocco Forte Hotels rarely seem to get their dining rooms spot-on, and this newly-revamped "traditional" bastion, in Mayfair, is no exception; its "spacious" layout is "great with clients", but while fans praise its "perfect British fare", rather too many critics think it "a waste of money". / **Details:** www.roccofortecollection.com; 10.30 pm.

Alisan HA9 £29
The Junction, Engineers Way, Wembley 8903 3888

"Impressive" dim sum comes at a notably "low cost", at this "spacious and airy" modern Cantonese, right by Wembley Stadium.
/ **Details:** www.alisan.co.uk; Mon-Thu 11 pm, Fri & Sat 11.30 pm, Sun 10.30 pm.

Alloro W1 £50
19-20 Dover St 7495 4768 2–3C
Cooking that's "well-polished" and "not too expensive" makes this "very professional" Italian restaurant (and bar) a "dependable" Mayfair destination, especially for a business lunch.
/ **Details:** www.alloro-restaurant.co.uk; 10.30 pm; closed Sat L & Sun.

Amaranth SW18 £25 ⭐

346 Garratt Ln 8874 9036

This "simple Earlsfield BYO" is always "packed" ("you need to book most evenings"), thanks to its "real" Thai food at "unbeatable-value" prices. / Details: 10.30 pm; D only, closed Sun; no Amex.

Amaya SW1 £56 Ⓐ⭐⭐

Halkin Arc, 19 Motcomb St 7823 1166 4–1D

"Cutting-edge", "exotic" and "subtle" Indian cuisine elicits waves of rave reports on this "swish" Belgravia hot spot; "the tapas format could seem faddish, but here it really works". / Details: www.amaya.biz; 11.15 pm, Sun 10.15 pm.

Ambassade de l'Ile SW7 £90

117/119 Old Brompton Rd 7373 7774 4–2B

Offshoot of a starry restaurant in Lyons, this ambitious South Kensington newcomer (on the site of Lundum's, RIP) is a puzzling affair in every way; our early-days lunchtime visit found notably up-and-down food, and décor – black shag-pile and all – so bizarre that it was impossible to work out who the place is supposed to appeal to. / Value tip: set weekday L £51 (FP). Details: www.ambassadedelile.com; 10 pm; closed Sun.

Anarkali W6 £28 ⭐

303 King St 8748 1760 6–2B

"Not much changed over many years" – this "friendly", if slightly "gloomy", Hammersmith veteran is "still a cut above many Indians". / Details: www.anarkalirestaurant.co.uk; midnight, Sun 11.30 pm.

The Anchor & Hope SE1 £35 ⭐⭐

36 The Cut 7928 9898

"The Holy Grail of gastropubs" – this "mobbed" Waterloo boozer strikes the "perfect balance" between "wonderfully earthy" British cooking and "unpretentious, even ordinary surroundings"; the wait can admittedly be "excruciating", but it's "worth it". / Details: 10.30 pm; closed Mon L & Sun D; no Amex; no booking.

Andrew Edmunds W1 £38

46 Lexington St 7437 5708 2–2D

"Rickety" but "wonderfully snug", this Soho townhouse "has a certain je-ne-sais-quoi" that makes it unbelievably popular, especially for a "dream date"; the "simple" food is "no gastronomic tour de force", but – like the "fascinating wine list" – it offers "great value". / Details: 10.30 pm; no Amex; booking: max 6.

Angelus W2 £60

4 Bathurst St 7402 0083 5–2D

Ex-sommelier Thierry Tomasin's Bayswater pub-conversion hasn't quite lived up to the launch "hype" – fans do find it a "sophisticated" sort of place with "fabulous" wine, but critics note only "cramped" conditions and "average" standards overall. / Details: www.angelusrestaurant.co.uk; 11 pm; closed Mon.

The Anglesea Arms W6 £38

35 Wingate Rd 8749 1291 6–1B

"It's worth waiting for a table", at this "superb" gastropub "classic", near Ravenscourt Park, where the "freshly-chalked" menu delivers "mouthwatering" dishes; incredibly – for those who remember the bad old days – service "is actually pretty good" too. / Details: Tue-Sat 10.30 pm, Sun & Mon 10 pm; no Amex; no booking.

Anglo Asian Tandoori N16 £24

60-62 Stoke Newington Church St 7254 3633

In Stoke Newington, a "good-quality Indian of long standing"; attractions include "great food" and "staff who never forget a face". / Details: www.angloasian.co.uk; 11.45 pm.

L'Anima EC2 £52

1 Snowden St 7422 7000

WINNER 2009

RÉMY MARTIN

For our money, one of the best openings of recent times – this Italian newcomer, behind Broadgate, offers deft cooking (from Francesco Mazzei, ex-St Alban) in a minimalist setting of a design-quality rarely seen in London; in the early days, service was charming too. / Value tip: set weekday L £38 (FP). Details: www.lanima.co.uk; 10.30 pm; closed Sat & Sun.

Annie's £37

162 Thames Rd, W4 8994 9080

36-38 White Hart Ln, SW13 8878 2020

"Boudoirish" décor has helped these "casual" and "obliging" west London hang-outs win quite a following; brunch is "always reliable", but, more generally, the food "lacks wow-factor". / Details: W4 10 pm, SW13 11 pm.

Apostrophe £14 Ⓐ ⭐
16 Regent St, SW1   7930 9922   2–3D
10 Grosvenor St, W1   7499 6511   2–2B
20/20 Opt' Store, 216 Tott' Ct Rd, W1   7436 6688   1–1C
23 Barrett St, W1   7355 1001   2–1A
40-41 Great Castle St, W1   7637 5700   2–1C
215 Strand, WC2   7427 9890   3–2D
42 Gt Eastern St, EC2   7739 8412
3-5 St Bride St, EC4   7353 3704
*With their "ultra-fresh sarnies" and "outstanding coffee" – not to
mention "the best hot chocolate" – these "pricey alternatives to Pret"
still "take some beating". / **Details:** www.apostropheuk.com; L & afternoon
tea only, Barrett St 8pm; no Amex; no booking.*

Apsleys
Lanesborough Hotel SW1 £75
1 Lanesborough Pl   7333 7254   4–1D

*The conservatory of Hyde Park Corner's landmark luxury hotel emerged
this year from a lavishly OTT revamp (from leading US designer Adam
Tihany); despite its new Anglo-Saxon name, the food is rustic Italian,
and – though competent enough – rather overshadowed by the setting
and the service. / **Value tip:** set always available £45
(FP). **Details:** www.apsleys.co.uk; 11 pm; booking: max 12.*

Arancia SE16 £31 Ⓐ ⭐
52 Southwark Park Rd   7394 1751
*"A totally unexpected cosy oasis, in deepest Bermondsey" –
this "fantastic" and "personal" Italian serves up "honest" food
at "ridiculously cheap" prices. / **Value tip:** set weekday L £20
(FP). **Details:** www.arancia-london.co.uk; 11 pm; closed Mon & Sun D.*

Arbutus W1 £42 ⭐
63-64 Frith St   7734 4545   3–2A
*"An utterly winning formula"; "adventurous" and "hearty" cooking and
"fabulous wine sold in 25cl carafes" – all at "fair" prices – make this
"confident" Soho two-year-old one of the West End's top foodie hot
spots; the "bustling" setting, though, suffers from "awkward"
proportions. / **Value tip:** set weekday L £27
(FP). **Details:** www.arbutusrestaurant.co.uk; 10.45pm, Sun 9.30 pm.*

Archipelago W1 £49 Ⓐ ⭐
110 Whitfield St   7383 3346   1–1B
*A "most bizarre" menu (including "zebra, locust, gnu, peacock and
scorpion") is only part of the "truly memorable" – and "romantic" –
formula of this "Bohemian-quirky" den, near the Telecom Tower;
the food is "not just strange for the sake of it", though – indeed,
it's often "brilliant". / **Details:** www.archipelago-restaurant.co.uk; 10.30 pm;
closed Sat L & Sun.*

Ark Fish E18 £35 ⭐

142 Hermon Hill 8989 5345

"It's worth the wait for a table", say fans of this South Woodford chippy, which offers "tasty" fare in "huge" portions.
/ **Details:** www.arkfishrestaurant.co.uk; Tue-Thu 9.45 pm, Fri & Sat 10.15 pm, Sun 8.45 pm; closed Mon; no Amex.

Asia de Cuba
St Martin's Lane Hotel WC2 £82 Ⓐ

45 St Martin's Ln 7300 5588 3–4C

"It certainly has a pulse", but that's the only real plus nowadays of this once-oh-so-trendy dining room, on the fringe of Covent Garden – service is so-so, and its "Asian-Cuban, sharing" cuisine can come out "weird instead of interesting". / **Details:** www.stmartinslane.com; midnight, Thu-Sat 12.30 am, Sun10.30 pm.

Assaggi W2 £59 ⭐⭐

39 Chepstow Pl 7792 5501 5–1B

"The best Italian in London, bar none"; implausibly located above a pub, this "plain" Bayswater dining room may be "noisy" and "cramped", but Nino Sassu's "fabulous" food, and the "wonderful" service make it one of the hottest tickets in town. / **Details:** 11 pm; closed Sun; no Amex.

L'Atelier de Joel Robuchon WC2 £80 Ⓐ⭐

13-15 West St 7010 8600 3–2B

"Wow!"; most reporters are still "blown away" by the "extraordinary" (if "tiny") dishes and the "sexy" décor of the famous French chef's Theatreland jewel; service of late has been very "average", though, and bills can be "apocalyptic". / **Details:** www.joel-robuchon.co.uk; 10.30 pm.

The Atlas SW6 £34 Ⓐ⭐

16 Seagrave Rd 7385 9129 4–3A

"Gourmet pub food" draws a big fan club to this backstreet boozer, near Earl's Court 2; it's also a "cosy" place (and has "a great terrace for summer days"). / **Details:** www.theatlaspub.co.uk; 10.30 pm; closed Sun D; no booking.

Atma NW3 £41 ⭐

106c Finchley Rd 7431 9487

New owners seem to have done nothing to dent the appeal of this "unsung hero", in Belsize Park – it is "on a different level from most Indian restaurants in terms of quality and presentation".
/ **Details:** www.atmarestaurants.com; 11 pm; closed Mon.

Aubergine SW10 £98

11 Park Wk   7352 3449   4–3B

What's up at this suddenly "fading" Chelsea dining room? – there are still many fans who acclaim William Drabble's food as "sublime", but there are also reports of "a sad decline", and of "surprisingly bad" service. / Value tip: set weekday L £54 (FP). **Details:** *www.auberginerestaurant.co.uk; 11 pm; closed Sat L & Sun; no jeans or trainers.*

Aurora W1 £36 Ⓐ

49 Lexington St   7494 0514   2–2D

Can't get into Andrew Edmunds (opposite)? – this "pretty little place" (complete with cute courtyard) is also supremely "charming" and likewise well-suited to romance; it also offers "good-value" fare from "an interesting short menu". **/ Details:** *Mon & Tues 10 pm, Wed - Sun 10.30 pm; closed Sun.*

L'Autre Pied W1 £52 ✪

5-7 Blandford St   7486 9696   1–1A

"A great addition to Marylebone eating" – this offshoot of Pied à Terre serves up "adventurous" and often "stunning" dishes; it has, however, inherited the awkward former Blandford Street (RIP) site, and can similarly seem "devoid of atmosphere". / Value tip: set weekday L £35 (FP). **Details:** *www.lautrepied.co.uk; 11 pm, Sun 9.30 pm.*

L'Aventure NW8 £53 Ⓐ✪

3 Blenheim Ter   7624 6232

"For that special meal", Catherine Parisot's "traditional" St John's Wood charmer – with its "cosy interior in winter and lovely summer terrace" – makes a famously "romantic" choice; its Gallic fare is "delicious" and "unfussy" too. / Value tip: set weekday L £34 (FP). **Details:** *11 pm; closed Sat L & Sun.*

Awana SW3 £52 ✪

85 Sloane Ave   7584 8880   4–2C

In the heart of Chelsea, this "modern and glamorous" Malaysian restaurant has gathered quite a following for its "tasty" fare; some reporters, though, feel that "unless you've got money to burn, the only way to enjoy it is one of those half price-offers". / Value tip: set weekday L £30 (FP). **Details:** *www.awana.co.uk; Mon-Wed 11 pm, Thu-Sat 11.30 pm, Sun 10.30 pm.*

Babur Brasserie SE23 £32 Ⓐ✪✪

119 Brockley Rise   8291 2400

"You just don't expect restaurants of this quality deep in SE London suburbia" – this "classy" modern Indian, in Honor Oak Park, offers "wonderfully original" cuisine and "exceptional" service. / Details: *www.babur.info; 11.30 pm.*

Babylon
Kensington Roof Gardens W8 £61 Ⓐ

99 Kensington High St   7368 3993   4–1A

"Visit on a spring day, and stroll around the gardens" – on the 8th floor! – to catch this "beautiful" Kensington eyrie at its best; service "means well but lacks polish", however, and the food varies. / Value tip: set Sun L £42 (FP). **Details:** *www.virgin.com/roofgardens; 11 pm; closed Sun D.*

Bacchus N1 £82 ⭐
177 Hoxton St 7613 0477
*"El Bulli comes to London", at this "daring", year-old pub-conversion; Nuño Mendes "doesn't get the press he deserves" for his "really exciting" creations, that are "experimental without being pretentious" – perhaps it's got something to do with the "dodgy" Hoxton location. / **Details:** www.bacchus-restaurant.co.uk; midnight; D only, closed Sun.*

Back to Basics W1 £42 ⭐⭐
21a Foley St 7436 2181 1–1B
*A "cramped" Fitzrovia bistro which "never fails to please", thanks to its "brilliant" fish and seafood, served "in unusual combinations" – "get there early for the best choice". / **Value tip:** set always available £27 (FP). **Details:** www.backtobasics.uk.com; 10.30 pm; closed Sun.*

Bam-Bou W1 £45 Ⓐ
1 Percy St 7323 9130 1–1C
*"There's always a good buzz", at this "dark" and "decadent" Fitzrovia townhouse, which is decked out in "French Indo-Chinese" style; its oriental fare is "fresh and extremely tasty", but the "superb cocktails" are arguably an even greater attraction. / **Details:** www.bam-bou.co.uk; 11 pm; closed Sat L & Sun; booking: max 6.*

The Banana Leaf Canteen SW11 £30 Ⓐ⭐
75-79 Battersea Rise 7228 2828
*"An absolute gem"; this "oriental canteen", in Battersea, wins a loud cheer from reporters as an "excellent cheap and cheerful option". / **Details:** 11 pm; need 6+ to book.*

Banners N8 £32 Ⓐ
21 Park Rd 8348 2930
*The "absolutely massive breakfasts" at this "buzzy", "fun" and "child-friendly" Crouch End hang-out are something of an institution; at other times it offers an "eclectic" menu, and an experience that's "not always cheap but definitely cheerful". / **Details:** 11.30 pm, Fri midnight; no Amex.*

Bar Italia W1 £18 Ⓐ
22 Frith St 7437 4520 3–2A
*The food will never win any awards, but fans say this "lively" 24/7 "classic" does "London's best espresso"; it's "a great spot for watching Italian football matches", or to see "Soho low-life" passing by. / **Details:** open 24 hours, Sun 3 am; no booking.*

Barrafina W1 £42 Ⓐ★★

54 Frith St 7813 8016 3–2A

"Faultless!… except they need more seats!" – the Hart brothers' year-old Barcelona-inspired tapas bar may be *"cramped"* and *"busy"*, but its *"awesome"* dishes have made it one of the top survey raves of recent years; *"it's worth the wait"*. / **Details:** www.barrafina.co.uk; 11 pm; closed Sun; no booking.

Basilico £30 ★

690 Fulham Rd, SW6   0800 028 3531
26 Penton St, N1   0800 093 4224
515 Finchley Rd, NW3   0800 316 2656
175 Lavender Hill, SW11   0800 389 9770
178 Upper Richmond Rd, SW14   0800 096 8202
"Standard-to-exotic toppings" – plus *"very thin and delicious bases"* – make the pizzas of this popular chain *"by far the best of the take-aways"*. / **Details:** www.basilico.co.uk; midnight; no booking.

Bayee Village SW19 £32

24 High St   8947 3533
"A fine Chinese restaurant", in the heart of Wimbledon Village; it can seem a mite *"overpriced"*, and some regulars say last year's refurb *"robbed it of character"*, but fans find the new style *"lovely"*, *"quiet"* and *"relaxed"*. / **Details:** www.bayee.co.uk; 11 pm.

Beach Blanket Babylon £65 Ⓐ✗

45 Ledbury Rd, W11   7229 2907   5–1B
19-23 Bethnal Green Rd, E1   7749 3540
Stick to the "divine" cocktails, at these "stunning" Gothic hang-outs (now in Shoreditch, as well as Notting Hill) – try to eat, and you risk "clueless" service and nosh that's "disappointing" and "hugely overpriced". / **Details:** 11 pm.

The Beehive W1 £32 ★

126 Crawford St   7486 8037   1–1A
In Marylebone, an interesting re-working of the gastropub concept – more like an informal continental restaurant – by leading restaurateur Claudio Pulze; the food was good on our early-days visit, but it's difficult to predict how this hard-to-categorise venture will prosper. /

Beirut Express £35 ★

65 Old Brompton Rd, SW7   7591 0123   4–2B
112-114 Edgware Rd, W2   7724 2700   5–1D
The name says it all, at this "great" and "quick" Lebanese chain, where you get an "overload" of "delicious" kebabs, salads and juices, all at "unbelievable" prices. / **Details:** W2 2am, SW7 midnight; W2 no credit cards.

Bellamy's W1 £62
18-18a Bruton Pl 7491 2727 2–2B
Gavin Rankin's "posh" Mayfair mews brasserie has a "personal feel"
and "charming" staff, even if – for such a "smart" location – seating
is quite "cheek-by-jowl"; critics find the food "expensive and unexciting",
but the more general view is that it's "very enjoyable".
/ **Details:** www.bellamysrestaurant.co.uk; 10.15 pm; closed Sat L & Sun.

Belvedere W8 £50 Ⓐ
Holland Pk, off Abbotsbury Rd 7602 1238 6–1D
"A wonderful setting among the peacocks" is not the only plus point
of this "beautiful" and "glamorous" Art Deco-styled favourite, within
Holland Park – generally speaking, food and service are "hard to fault"
too. / **Details:** www.belvedererestaurant.co.uk; 10 pm; closed Sun D.

Benares W1 £65 ✪
12 Berkeley Hs, Berkeley Sq 7629 8886 2–3B
Thanks to his "fantastically subtle" cuisine, Atul Kochar's "sophisticated"
Mayfair Indian is "going from strength to strength" – it also offers
"efficient and helpful" service, in a "beautifully-designed" (if "slightly
impersonal") space. / **Value tip:** set weekday L £28
(FP). **Details:** www.benaresrestaurant.com; 10.30 pm.

Benja W1 £44 ✪
17 Beak Street 7287 0555 2–2D
"Set over a number of small floors", this dinky Soho yearling has
a "lovely atmosphere", and serves some "very good" Thai food too.
/ **Details:** www.benjarestaurant.com; 10.45 pm; closed Sun.

Bentley's W1 £61 ✪
11-15 Swallow St 7734 4756 2–3D
"The oyster-bar has a great buzz", say fans of Richard Corrigan's revived
Mayfair stalwart, and it makes a "fun" venue for some "classic seafood"
(not least at the al fresco tables on the newly-pedestrianised street);
service can "lapse", though, and the relatively "subdued" and "pricey"
first-floor dining room attracts more mixed reports. / **Value tip:** set
weekday L £43 (FP). **Details:** www.bentleysoysterbarandgrill.co.uk; midnight;
booking: max 12.

Best Mangal W14 £24 Ⓐ✪
104 North End Rd 7610 1050 6–2D
"It may look like an ordinary Turkish place, but you often have to book",
at this "friendly" establishment, near West Kensington tube; it serves
"unbeatable" kebabs, "freshly cooked on a charcoal BBQ in front
of you". / **Details:** midnight; no Amex.

Bibendum SW3 £67 Ⓐ
81 Fulham Rd 7581 5817 4–2C
This "very comfortable" and "lovely" first-floor Brompton Cross veteran
– which "looks at its best for lunch" – has "sharpened up its act"
of late; its modern Gallic cuisine, however, is still somewhat eclipsed
by the "brilliant" (if "pricey") wine list. / **Value tip:** set brunch £46
(FP). **Details:** www.bibendum.co.uk; Mon-Fri 11 pm, Sat 11.30 pm,
Sun 10.30 pm; booking: max 12.

Bincho Yakitori £34 Ⓐ⭐
16 Old Compton St, W1   7287 9111   3–2A
Oxo Tower, Barge House St, SE1   7803 0858
*"Forget the 8th-floor 'Oxo Tower'" – "for half the money, you get double
the satisfaction", on the second floor of the South Bank landmark; it's a
"crowded but fun" venue with "amazing" views, and serving "succulent"
Japanese skewers (and other "tapas-like" dishes); the new Soho offshoot
seems the palest of imitations. /*

Blakes
Blakes Hotel SW7 £104 Ⓐ❌
33 Roland Gdns   7370 6701   4–2B
*"Dark", "decadent", "discreet"… and "ridiculously overpriced",
this datedly luxurious South Kensington basement is still – for its small
fan club – "the most romantic place in town"; standards are "variable",
though, and it inspires much less interest than once it did.
/ Details: www.blakeshotels.com; 10.45 pm.*

Bleeding Heart EC1 £49 Ⓐ⭐
Bleeding Heart Yd, Greville St   7242 8238
*"Hidden-away in an historic courtyard", near Holborn, this amazingly
popular "all-rounder" – which comprises tavern, bistro and restaurant –
is a "surefire winner" for business or romance; its "veeeery French" staff
deliver "admirable" dishes and "splendid" wine in "dimly-lit" and "rustic"
surroundings. / Details: www.bleedingheart.co.uk; 10 pm; closed Sat & Sun.*

Blue Elephant SW6 £52 Ⓐ
4-6 Fulham Broadway   7385 6595   4–4A
*"For the full Thai experience" ("orchid for the lady, and all"), you can't
beat this "beautiful theme park" – complete with "bridges, streams,
and foliage" – lurking "behind a dull facade" on Fulham Broadway;
the cooking "has slipped in recent years… but I still don't see how any
date could fail to be impressed". / Value tip: set weekday L £36
(FP). Details: www.blueelephant.com; midnight, Sun 10.30 pm; closed Sat L
(except Stamford Bridge match days).*

Blue Jade SW1 £31
44 Hugh St   7828 0321   1–4B
*"Totally reliable" and "always welcoming" – a useful Thai corner spot,
hidden-away in the back streets of Pimlico. / Details: 11 pm; closed
Sat L & Sun.*

La Bodeguita del Medio W8 £38 Ⓐ
47 Kensington Ct   7938 4147   4–1A
*There are "tasty" Cuban tapas – "a nice change from the familiar
Spanish range" – and "the Mojitos are fab", at this improving Latino
bar/restaurant, in a cute alley off Kensington High Street.
/ Details: www.bdelmlondon.com; 11 pm.*

Boisdale SW1 £65 Ⓐ
13-15 Eccleston St   7730 6922   1–4B
*"For a boisterous, big-eating, big-drinking meal" – complete with "great
steaks", "a fab selection of whiskies", "super jazz" and "a sensational
cigar terrace" – this "clubby", Scottish-themed Belgravia haunt may well
be the place… if you can overlook the fact that it's "a wee bit overpriced", that is. / Value tip: set dinner £41 (FP). Details: www.boisdale.co.uk;
11.15 pm; closed Sat & Sun.*

Bombay Bicycle Club £35
128 Holland Park Ave, W11   7727 7335   5–2A
3a Downshire Hill, NW3   7435 3544
95 Nightingale Ln, SW12   8673 6217
For a "smart curry", the "still very atmospheric" Wandsworth original
of this Indian chain has long been "worth a trip"; all branches inspire
positive reports, however, not least for their "superb take-aways"; as this
guide was going to press, the chain was acquired by Tiffinbites.
/ Details: www.thebombaybicycleclub.co.uk; 11 pm; D only ex NW3, Sun open
L & D.

Bombay Brasserie SW7 £55
Courtfield Close, Gloucester Rd   7370 4040   4–2B
One of London's path-breaking quality Indians – this Raj-scale South
Kensington institution was still achieving "first-rate" standards when
it closed for a major refurb in mid-2008 – we trust that it will re-emerge
stronger than ever. / Details: www.bombaybrasserielondon.com; 11.30 pm.

Bombay Palace W2 £44
50 Connaught St   7723 8855   5–1D
"Shame about the setting" – "a big box of a room with hotel décor";
this "seriously under-rated" venture, north of Hyde Park, has "charming
and professional" service, and its "classic" Indian cuisine has been
"consistently fantastic over many years".
/ Details: www.bombay-palace.co.uk; 11.30 pm.

Bord'Eaux
Grosvenor House Hotel W1 £50
Park Ln   7399 8460   2–3A
With its "confused menu" and "aircraft hangar" proportions, this new
Gallic brasserie is a perfect example of just how 'wrong' hotel-
restaurants can be; bizarrely, the food and service are actually quite
*good, so the place has its uses as a Mayfair business rendezvous. / **Value***
***tip:** set pre theatre £34 (FP). **Details:** www.bord-eaux.com/; 10.30 pm, 11 pm*
Fri & Sat.

Il Bordello E1 £42
75-81 Wapping High St   7481 9950
"Huge and fabulous portions of every kind of Italian food" –
not least "unbeatable pizzas" – help win the usual rave reviews for this
notably "professional" Wapping fixture, which is "always packed" and
"buzzing". / Details: 11 pm; closed Sat L.

Boudin Blanc W1 £50
5 Trebeck St   7499 3292   2–4B
"Just like a little piece of France" – this "super" bistro in Shepherd
Market offers "fantastic" food, in a "crowded" and "noisy" setting with
"bags of atmosphere"; nicely-located outside tables make it "great
outdoors in summer" too. / Details: www.boudinblanc.co.uk; 11 pm.

Brasserie James SW12 £38
47 Balham Hill   8772 0057
Near Clapham South, an extremely competent new local restaurant
from a former head chef of Quaglino's, offering no-nonsense Gallic fare
that – on our early-days visit – almost invariably satisfied; it was already
pretty busy too. / Details: www.brasseriejames.com.

Brew Wharf SE1   **£41**   Ⓐ
Brew Wharf Yd, 1 Stoney St   7378 6601
*A South Bank beerhall – occupying an impressively "light and airy"
series of railway arches – where "simple well-cooked food" is "matched
by great beer". / Details: www.brewwharf.com; 9.30 pm; closed Sun D.*

Brula TW1   **£43**   Ⓐ
43 Crown Rd   8892 0602
*This "very Left Bank" bistro describes itself as a 'restaurant du quartier',
and – with its "lovely" staff, and its "more-than-competent" Gallic food –
"the inhabitants of this part of St Margarets are indeed lucky to have
it". / Details: www.brula.co.uk; 10.30 pm.*

Brunello
Baglioni Hotel SW7   **£70**
60 Hyde Park Gate   7368 5900   4–1B
*The departure of the former chef seems to have had no effect on this
wackily-luxurious Kensington design-hotel – for Italian fare that's
no more than "decent", however, it remains a "dizzyingly expensive"
place to eat. / Details: www.baglionihotellondon.com; 10.45 pm.*

Buddha Bar WC2   **£ –**
8 Victoria Embankment   3371 7777   1–2D
*Opening under Westminster Bridge (near the Savoy) as this guide goes
to press, a lavish oriental offshoot of a perennially-popular Parisian
bar/restaurant. / Details: www.buddhabar-london.com.*

Buen Ayre E8   **£39**   ⒶⒶ
50 Broadway Mkt   7275 9900
*"Authentic, unreconstructed and unpretentious" – this "happy and
buzzy" Argentinean 'parillada', in Hackney, "pulls in punters from far
and wide", thanks to its "tremendous" steaks, served "at a fraction
of the typical London price". / Details: www.buenayre.co.uk; 10.30 pm; closed
weekday L.*

Bumpkin   **£43**   ⒶⒶ
102 Old Brompton Rd, SW7   4–2B
209 Westbourne Park Rd, W11   7243 9818   5–1B
*This "rustic" Notting Hill hang-out – a "crowded" brasserie, plus "cosy"
upstairs restaurant – is "as much like a real country place as Harrods
is like a farm shop"; its "funky" style and "sturdy" comfort fare are
winning over the critics, though, and a South Kensington offshoot opens
in late-2008. / Details: www.bumpkinuk.com.*

Busaba Eathai   **£28**   ⒶⒶ
106-110 Wardour St, W1   7255 8686   2–2D
8-13 Bird St, W1   7518 8080   2–1A
22 Store St, WC1   7299 7900   1–1C
*"The queues out the door tell their own story"; these "superior versions
of Wagamama" are "cool" places, which offer "fresh" and "strongly-
flavoured" Thai dishes at large communal tables – let's hope the formula
survives the dreaded national 'roll out', scheduled to commence in late-
2008. / Details: 11 pm, Fri & Sat 11.30 pm, Sun 10 pm; W1 no booking;
WC1 need 12+ to book .*

Byron W8 £26 Ⓐ
222 Kensington High St   7361 1717   4–1A
*With its "mouthwatering" burgers (and "yummy courgette chips too"),
this "posh" new diner, by the entrance to Holland Park, has been
a "welcome" addition to Kensington; its "cleverly-designed interior" helps
create "a real buzz", too. / Details: www.byronhamburgers.com; Mon-Thu
11 pm, Fri-Sat 11.30, Sun 10.30 pm.*

Café 209 SW6 £23 Ⓐ
209 Munster Rd   7385 3625
*"Joy lives up to her name" – and is "a real giggle" too – at the "tightly-
packed" Fulham BYO Thai over which she presides; "the food's not top
class, but you can guarantee a good night". / Details: 10.30 pm; D only,
closed Sun, closed Dec; no Amex.*

Le Café Anglais
Whiteley's W2 £48
8 Porchester Gdns   7221 1415   5–1C

*It's been "much-hyped", but Rowley Leigh's large new Art Deco-style
brasserie is undoubtedly an "elegant" and "airy" space that's given
"a very necessary culinary boost to Bayswater"; service is often "inept",
though, and realisation of the long and enticing menu is somewhat up-
and-down. / Details: www.lecafeanglais.co.uk.*

Café du Marché EC1 £45 Ⓐ★
22 Charterhouse Sq   7608 1609
*This "tucked-away" Smithfield stalwart is, as always, "hard to fault
on any level"; "top-notch, French provincial cooking", "friendly but
efficient" staff and its "lovely, rustic style" make it "a tip-top choice for
business or romance". / Details: www.cafedumarche.co.uk; 10 pm; closed
Sat L & Sun; no Amex.*

Café Japan NW11 £29 ★★
626 Finchley Rd   8455 6854
*You don't go to this "cramped" café, opposite Golder's Green station,
for its looks, but for its "sensational sushi" at "amazing prices" –
even so, "it'd be nice if they revamped". / Details: www.cafejapan.co.uk;
10 pm; closed Mon, Tue, & Wed L-Fri L; no Amex.*

Café Spice Namaste E1 £44 ★★
16 Prescot St   7488 9242
*A "marvellous and subtle range of textures, spicing and flavours" has
long been the hallmark of Cyrus Todiwala's east-City Indian, still
frequently nominated as "the best in London"; "warm and efficient
service" helps add charm to its "bright and quirky" interior.
/ Details: www.cafespice.co.uk; 10.30 pm; closed Sat L & Sun.*

Caffé Vergnano £ 8
62 Charing Cross Rd, WC2   7240 8587   3–3B
Royal Festival Hall, SE1   7921 9339   1–3D
Coffee "worthy of Milan" and "wonderful hot chocolate" are the twin
highlights of this emerging chain – everything else is by the bye. /

Cambio de Tercio SW5 £46
161 Old Brompton Rd   7244 8970   4–2B
"You can't go wrong", at this "fun" Earl's Court Spaniard, where the
"authentic but innovative" food is amongst the "best in town", certainly
of its type; it's matched by a "really interesting" wine list too.
/ Details: www.cambiodetercio.co.uk; 11.30 pm.

Il Cantuccio di Pulcinella SW11 £29
143 St John's Hill   7924 5588
"A very good, no-nonsense Italian", in Wandsworth, with a particular
reputation for pizza... and, "with Mama always sitting in the corner",
you feel this is "the genuine article" too.
/ Details: www.ilcantucciodipulcinella.co.uk; 11 pm; Mon-Thu D only, Fri-Sun open
L & D; no Amex.

The Capital Restaurant
Capital Hotel SW3 £82
22-24 Basil St   7589 5171   4–1D
Eric Chavot's "beautifully-realised" cuisine "can be compared with the
best in London", but the atmosphere of this small and "quiet"
Knightsbridge hotel dining room divides reporters – fans find it "discreet"
and "personal", but for critics it's just rather "austere"; "outstanding
value lunch". / Value tip: set weekday L £51
(FP). Details: www.capitalhotel.co.uk; 10 pm; no jeans.

Le Caprice SW1 £55
Arlington Hs, Arlington St   7629 2239   2–4C

The "sheer class" of this resurgent '80s "classic", near the Ritz, still
"ticks all the boxes" for its army of fans; the service
is "the slickest in town", the food is "simply great" ("with no gimmicks"),
and the décor, though rather dated, "somehow still looks sophisticated".
/ Details: www.caprice-holdings.co.uk; midnight.

Caraffini SW1 £42
61-63 Lower Sloane St   7259 0235   4–2D
An "honest" and still-"vivacious" Italian old-timer, near Sloane Square,
which – thanks to its "exceptional" service and "no-frills", "classic"
cooking – maintains a huge fan club. / Details: www.caraffini.co.uk;
11.30 pm; closed Sun.

The Carpenter's Arms W6 £38
91 Black Lion Ln   0871 8741 8386   6–2B
It's already hard to get a booking at this gastropub newcomer, hidden-away in an obscure bit of Hammersmith; fans say it has been "a great addition to W6", but there's also a school of thought that it's "over-rated" – "decent, but not as good as others nearby". / Details: 11 pm, Sun 9.30 pm; no Amex.

Cây Tre EC1 £31 ★
301 Old St   7729 8662
Redecoration has led to improvements across the board at this "great local Vietnamese", near Hoxton Square, which continues to offer "amazing food at incredibly cheap prices". / Details: www.vietnamesekitchen.co.uk; 11 pm, Fri-Sat 11.30 pm, Sun 10.30 pm.

Cecconi's W1 £55 Ⓐ
5a Burlington Gdns   7434 1500   2–3C
Not only a hit "with the hedge fund set" – Nick Jones's "bustling" Italian brasserie is becoming a truly "useful" linchpin of modern Mayfair life (from breakfast onwards); the food – perhaps surprisingly – "is quite good too"! / Details: www.cecconis.co.uk; 1am, Sun midnight.

Cellar Gascon EC1 £38
59 West Smithfield Rd   7600 7561
This "budget version of Club Gascon" is a "cool" bar with a "very buzzy" style; its food, though, inspires less excitement than the "hard-to-beat" list of SW France wines. / Details: www.cellargascon.com; midnight; closed Sat & Sun.

Centrepoint Sushi WC2 £23 Ⓐ★
20-21 St Giles High St   7240 6147   3–1B
"Extremely fresh, tasty and good-value sushi" makes it worth seeking out this "friendly" operation, above an oriental supermarket, right by Centrepoint. / Details: www.cpfs.co.uk; 10.30 pm; closed Sun.

Le Cercle SW1 £45 Ⓐ★★
1 Wilbraham Pl   7901 9999   4–2D
"Grazing is taken to a new level", at Club Gascon's groovy Belgravia basement offshoot – its "absolutely thrilling French tapas and beautifully matched wines" are now even better than its famous City-fringe sibling's. / Details: www.lecercle.co.uk; 11 pm; closed Mon & Sun.

Cha Cha Moon W1 £18
15-21 Ganton St 7297 9800 2–2C

From Wagamama-creator Alan Yau, a hotly-awaited new oriental 'format', of which this elegantly-styled Soho canteen is the first example; at launch prices – £3.50 for every dish, mainly noodles and dim sum – it was a bargain, but it's not clear how long this pricing will last.
/ Details: 11.30 pm.

Champor-Champor SE1 £43
62 Weston St 7403 4600
"Down a dingy sidestreet behind Guy's Hospital", a "fabulously eccentric" destination – with its "sweet" staff, and "Malay-fusion" cuisine that's "packed full of flavours", it can make a "wonderful" discovery for first-time visitors. / Details: www.champor-champor.com; 10.15 pm; closed Mon L, Tue L, Wed L, Sat L & Sun; booking: max 12.

Chapter Two SE3 £40
43-45 Montpelier Vale 8333 2666
"Worth a trip to Blackheath" – this "classy" basement operation offers "rich and sophisticated cooking at unusually low prices"; it's "getting better" too, and supporters say it's "catching up with its Bromley sibling, Chapter One". / Details: www.chaptersrestaurants.co.uk; 10.30 pm, Fri-Sat 11 pm.

Chelsea Bun Diner SW10 £25
9a Lamont Rd 7352 3635 4–3B
"Huge menu, great prices... you can't go wrong" – London's top "hang-over-cure" breakfast maintains the high profile of this "American diner-style" greasy spoon, at World's End; BYO. / Details: www.chelseabun.co.uk; midnight, Sun 10 pm; no Amex; no booking, Sat & Sun.

Chez Bruce SW17 £56
2 Bellevue Rd 8672 0114
"Relaxed, not a temple" – that's the whole joy of Bruce Poole's "unpretentious" foodie Mecca, by Wandsworth Common, which is yet again Londoners' No. 1 favourite haunt; "unshowy, but beautiful" food and "wonderful" wine are served up by "unbelievably helpful" staff, and all "without an OTT price tag". / Value tip: set Sun L £41 (FP). Details: www.chezbruce.co.uk; 10.30 pm; booking: max 6 at D.

Chez Marcelle W14 £26
34 Blythe Rd 7603 3241 6–1D
"Like Fawlty Towers, but with great food"; Marcelle's "one-woman show", behind Olympia, is a "delightfully chaotic" place, where "lovingly-prepared" Lebanese fare is served up for "a pittance". / Details: 10 pm; closed Mon, Tue-Thu D only,Fri-Sun open L & D; no credit cards.

China Tang
Dorchester Hotel W1 £75
53 Park Ln 7629 9988 2–3A
"Shame the food doesn't keep pace" with the "gorgeously opulent", "'30s-Shanghai" décor of David Tang's "decadent" Mayfair basement; it comes at "absurd" prices too. / **Value tip:** set always available £30 (FP). **Details:** www.thedorchester.com; midnight.

Chisou W1 £40 ⭐
4 Princes St 7629 3931 2–1C
The setting's "nondescript", but this "handily-located" Japanese café, near Oxford Circus, serves up "beautiful sushi", and a range of other "exciting" dishes, in a "wonderfully charming" way.
/ **Details:** www.chisou.co.uk; 10.30 pm; closed Sun.

Chor Bizarre W1 £43 🅐⭐
16 Albemarle St 7629 9802 2–3C
It's "as much an experience as a meal" to eat at this "wackily-furnished" Mayfair Indian; the "imaginative" cuisine is an attraction in itself, though, making it all the more undeserved that the place sometimes "seems empty". / **Details:** www.chorbizarre.com; 11.30 pm; closed Sun L.

Churchill Arms W8 £20 🅐⭐
119 Kensington Church St 7792 1246 5–2B
"You always know what to expect", at this "wonderful" annex to a "traditional Notting Hill pub" – "heaving plates of Thai food", served in a "cosy", if "cramped" and "chaotic", setting; "how do they do it so cheaply?" / **Details:** 10 pm; closed Sun D.

Chutney SW18 £26 ⭐
11 Alma Rd 8870 4588
"A gem in the heart of Wandsworth" – this "fantastic" curry house wins praise for its "lovely" service, and for its "delicious" (if "not especially creative") cooking. / **Details:** 11.30 pm; D only.

Chutney Mary SW10 £54 🅐⭐
535 King's Rd 7351 3113 4–4B

"Lovely modern Indian food with amazing spices" keeps this famous Chelsea-fringe "subcontinental pioneer" in London's foodie front-line; recently revamped, it has "very attractive" décor throughout, but "the conservatory is the best place to sit".
/ **Details:** www.realindianfood.com; 11.15 pm, Sun 10 pm; closed weekday L; booking: max 12.

Ciao Bella WC1 £31 Ⓐ
86-90 Lamb's Conduit St 7242 4119 1–1D
"A terrifically good-value old-fashioned Italian", in Bloomsbury, offering
"huge" portions to *"locals and tourists alike"*, in *"very crowded"*
conditions – *"don't expect the best food in the world"*, but otherwise
"it's a riot". / *Details:* www.ciaobellarestaurant.co.uk; 11.30 pm, Sun 10.30 pm.

Cibo W14 £42 ★
3 Russell Gdns 7371 6271 6–1D
*Sometimes seeming "quiet" nowadays, this once-fashionable Olympia
Italian is still a firm favourite for its diehard fans, who praise its
"high standards" and "reasonable prices".*
/ *Details:* www.ciborestaurant.net; 11 pm; closed Sun D.

The Cinnamon Club SW1 £60 Ⓐ★
Old Westminster Library, Great Smith St 7222 2555 1–4C
"Wonderfully delicate" Indian cuisine has won renown for this former
library – a much-needed *"haven"* of gastronomy in under-served
Westminster; it's a *"lovely"* and *"impressive"* place, albeit in a style
that's fairly *"businessy"*. / *Value tip:* set dinner £39
(FP). *Details:* www.cinnamonclub.com; 10.45 pm; closed Sun; no trainers.

Cinnamon Kitchen EC2 £
9 Devonshire Sq
*First offshoot of the celebrated Cinnamon Club – this large new Indian
restaurant is scheduled to open in late-2008, in the Devonshire Square
development, near Liverpool Street. / Details:* www.cinnamonkitchen.co.uk.

Cipriani W1 £75 ⊗
25 Davies Street 7399 0500 2–2B
*"WAGs", "B-listers", "obnoxious Russians and their nieces", "surgery-
addicted women", "extreme Euros"…* – the cavalcade of *"people-
watching"* at this otherwise *"astonishingly bad"* and *"wildly overpriced"*
Mayfair Venetian is *"impossible to beat"*. / *Value tip:* set weekday L £51
(FP). *Details:* www.cipriani.com; 11.45 pm.

Clarke's W8 £63 ★
124 Kensington Church St 7221 9225 5–2B
"Assured" cooking with *"a high-quality, low-key simplicity"* has long been
the *"ethos"* of Sally Clarke's Californian-inspired HQ, near Notting Hill
Gate; of late, however, it has *"slipped a little"*.
/ *Details:* www.sallyclarke.com; 10 pm; closed Sun; booking: max 14.

Clifton E1 £22 ★
1 Whitechapel Rd 7377 5533
"One of the best Brick Lane Indians" – *"a cut above in terms of both
food and atmosphere"*. / *Details:* www.cliftonrestaurant.com; midnight, Sat &
Sun 1am.

The Clissold Arms N2 £38
115 Fortis Grn 8444 4224
"The décor's a bit run-of-the-mill", but this newly-refurbished boozer –
linked with the glory days of The Kinks – is *"a good all-round gastropub"*
that's all the more welcome in the thin area around Muswell Hill.
/ *Details:* 10 pm, Sun 9 pm; no Amex.

Clos Maggiore WC2   £55   Ⓐ ✪

33 King St 7379 9696 3–3C

*"A perfect romantic haven in the midst of tourist-trap Covent Garden";
it's the "lovely" conservatory and "phenomenal" wine list ("like 'War &
Peace'") which are the special attractions, but the food can
be "excellent" too.* / **Value tip:** *set weekday L £39
(FP).* **Details:** www.closmaggiore.com; 10.45 pm, Sat 11.15 pm, Sun 10 pm;
closed Sat L & Sun L.

Club Gascon EC1   £60   ✪

57 West Smithfield 7796 0600

"Paradise for foie gras lovers" – this *"casual"* foodie hot spot,
by Smithfield Market, is the place for a *"hugely indulgent"* meal
of *"sumptuous and heart-stoppingly rich Gascon dishes"*, served tapas-
style; there's *"a fascinating wine list from SW France"* too.
/ **Details:** www.clubgascon.com; 10 pm, Fri & Sat 10.30 pm; closed Sat L & Sun.

Le Colombier SW3   £47   Ⓐ

145 Dovehouse St 7351 1155 4–2C

*Thanks to its "no-nonsense" Gallic fare, this "civilised" bistro, by Chelsea
Square, is "always packed"* – or perhaps it has more to do with the
"helpful and professional" service, and the quiet and notably *"attractive"*
terrace. / **Value tip:** *set weekday L £35
(FP).* **Details:** www.lecolombier-sw3.co.uk; 10.30 pm, Sun 10 pm.

Comptoir Gascon EC1   £46   Ⓐ ✪ ✪

63 Charterhouse St 7608 0851

*Discover "France on your doorstep", at this "uncannily good" spin-off
from Club Gascon* – with its *"hearty"* fare and *"unstarchy"* setting,
it *"mixes bistro simplicity with the refinement of its parent"*.
/ **Details:** www.comptoirgascon.com; 10 pm, Thu & Fri 11 pm; closed
Mon & Sun.

Coq d'Argent EC2   £58

1 Poultry 7395 5000

"The roof garden is fantastic on a summer evening", at the D&D group's
6th-floor bar/restaurant, by Bank (and it enjoys some *"stunning"* views
too); it's a venue that *"works well for business"*, despite *"boring"* food
and sometimes *"disorganised"* service. / **Value tip:** *set always available £45
(FP).* **Details:** www.coqdargent.co.uk; 10 pm; closed Sat L & Sun D.

Cork & Bottle WC2   £35   Ⓐ

44-46 Cranbourn St 7734 7807 3–3B

*A supremely "cosy" and "timeless" basement "oasis", just off "seedy
Leicester Square"; the food "doesn't seemed to have changed a jot since
the '70s"* – its main virtue is to *"provide an excuse"* to order from the
"phenomenal wine list". / **Details:** www.corkandbottle.net; 11.30 pm;
no booking after 6.30 pm.

Costa's Fish Restaurant W8   £23   ✪

18 Hillgate St 7727 4310 5–2B

"As friendly as ever" – this veteran, Greek-run chippy near Notting Hill
Gate wins a consistent thumbs-up from its small local fan club.
/ **Details:** 10 pm; closed Mon & Sun; no credit cards.

Crazy Bear W1 £55 🅐⭐

26-28 Whitfield St   7631 0088   1–1C

"Top-notch oriental-fusion food" and a *"cosy"* and *"opulent"* setting make for an ultra-*"romantic"* experience at this *"fun and fashionable"* oriental bar/restaurant, hidden-away in Fitzrovia; (in their different ways, the *"manic"* bar and *"mirrored loos"* are *"great"* too).

/ **Details:** www.crazybeargroup.co.uk; 10.30 pm; closed Sat L & Sun; no shorts.

Crazy Homies W2 £35 🅐⭐

127 Westbourne Park Rd   7727 6771   5–1B

Tom Conran's *"buzzy Mexican local"*, where *"scatty"* staff serve up *"truly authentic food"*, and *"lethal margaritas"*; it's *"always great fun"*. / **Details:** www.crazyhomieslondon.co.uk; 10.30 pm; closed weekday L; no Amex.

Cyprus Mangal SW1 £25 ⭐

45 Warwick Way   7828 5940   1–4B

An *"excellent, no-frills"* kebab house, with *"prompt and friendly"* service, in the heart of Pimlico. / **Details:** Sun-Thu midnight, Fri & Sat 1 am; no Amex.

D Sum 2 EC4 £40

14 Paternoster Row   7248 2288

"A good choice of dim sum" helps this shiny newcomer near St Paul's live up to its name; initial reports are few, but for *"business lunches or an after-work dinner"*, the place already has its fans.

/ **Details:** www.dsum2.com; 11 pm; closed Sat & Sun L.

Dalchini SW19 £31 🅐⭐

147 Arthur Rd   8947 5966

An *"interesting"* menu – *"Indian with a Chinese twist"* – and *"friendly"* service make this Wimbledon Park fixture a *"good bet"*; *"sit upstairs if you can"*. / **Details:** www.dalchini.co.uk; 10.30 pm, Fri & Sat 11 pm; no Amex.

Daphne NW1 £31 🅐

83 Bayham St   7267 7322

A *"homely"* and *"genuine"* Camden Town taverna of long standing, which still offers *"reasonably-priced"* Greek food and *"a good night out"*; *"nice roof terrace, too"*. / **Value tip:** set weekday L £20 (FP). **Details:** 11.30 pm; closed Sun; no Amex.

Daphne's SW3 £48 🅐⭐

112 Draycott Ave   7589 4257   4–2C

"Cosy", *"friendly"* and *"atmospheric"*, this Knightsbridge Italian is much better for being less trendy than it once was – you get *"surprisingly good food nowadays…* and you can generally get a table". / **Value tip:** set weekday L £31 (FP). **Details:** www.daphnes-restaurant.co.uk; 11.30 pm, Sun 10.30 pm; booking: max 12.

Daylesford Organics SW1 £40 🅐

44B Pimlico Rd   7881 8060   4–2D

"Lady Bamford knows her design", and reporters 'dig' the *"beautifully-finished, white marble and glass"* look of her Pimlico deli-café; it's at its best for breakfast or a cake – otherwise prices can seem *"unjustified"*; a Notting Hill sibling is expected to open in late-2008.

/ **Details:** www.daylesfordorganic.com; 8 pm, Sun 5 pm.

Defune W1   **£68** ⭐⭐

34 George St   7935 8311   2–1A

*"Truly exquisite" food (especially sushi) and "very gracious" service help
offset the "completely soulless" ambience of this Marylebone stalwart;
"take your trust fund", though – even fans say it's "way overpriced".*
/ **Details:** 11 pm.

Dehesa W1   **£43** Ⓐ⭐

25 Ganton St   7494 4170   2–2C

*It's not just the "lovely" interior which makes this "cool" spin-off from
Salt Yard a "fantastic addition" to Soho – its "affordable" and
"very enjoyable" Italian/Spanish tapas, and "delicious" wines too,
have transplanted very well.* / **Details:** www.dehesa.co.uk; 11 pm; closed
Sun D; no booking.

Delfina Studio Café SE1   **£45** ⭐

50 Bermondsey St   7357 0244

*An airy Bermondsey "art gallery-cum-restaurant", where it's "a pleasure
to eat", and where the "well-spaced" tables are well suited to business-
lunching; the "excellent" food has "a Kiwi slant", and is matched by an
"imaginative" and "good-value" wine list.* / **Details:** www.thedelfina.org.uk;
10 pm; L only, except Fri when open L&D, closed Sat & Sun.

Dinings W1   **£30** Ⓐ⭐⭐

22 Harcourt St   7723 0666

*"Incredible"; make sure you "book ahead", if you want to sample this
"delightful" Japanese, where the "amazing" sushi somehow transcends
the location in a "weird" Marylebone "bunker".* / **Details:** 10.30 pm;
closed Sat L & Sun.

The Don EC4   **£47** Ⓐ⭐

20 St Swithin's Ln   7626 2606

*Near Bank, an "oasis of quality", widely tipped as "the best place for
business in the City", thanks to its "relaxed" style, "well-executed" food,
"superb" wine, and "attentive" staff; the cellar bistro
is "more atmospheric" than the (recently-extended) upstairs.*
/ **Details:** www.thedonrestaurant.com; 10 pm; closed Sat & Sun; no trainers.

Donna Margherita SW11   **£40** Ⓐ⭐⭐

183 Lavender Hill   7288 2660

*"An authentic neighourhood Italian for the Lavender Hill mob" –
this "casual" Neapolitan wins particular praise for its "fantastic pizza
and pasta".* / **Details:** www.donna-margherita.com; 11 pm, Sat & Sun
10.30 pm.

Dorchester Grill
Dorchester Hotel W1   **£80**

53 Park Ln   7629 8888   2–3A

*"How can they get it so wrong?"; since a "ridiculous", "mock Scottish"
revamp a couple of years ago, this once-splendid Mayfair chamber has
gone from bad to worse – service is lacklustre, and its "forgettable" food
comes at "blistering" prices.* / **Value tip:** set weekday L £46
(FP). **Details:** www.thedorchester.com; 11 pm, Sun 10 pm; no trainers.

Duke Of Sussex W4   £35
75 South Pde   8742 8801   6–1A
Fans hail a "wonderful restoration" of this Chiswick boozer, applauding its "wholesome", "Spanish-influenced" food, "knowledgeable" staff and "glorious back garden"; it doesn't wow everyone, though – the setting can seem "barn-like", and service "slow" or "over-familiar".
/ **Details:** *Midnight, Sun 11 pm; closed Mon L; no Amex.*

The Duke's Head SW15   £33   Ⓐ
8 Lower Richmond Rd   8788 2552
A "lovely airy dining room" with "amazing river views" is the star turn at this "friendly" (and "child-friendly") Putney landmark, which serves "really good, standard pub fare". / **Details:** *www.dukesheadputney.co.uk; 10.30 pm.*

E&O W11   £43   Ⓐ⭐
14 Blenheim Cr   7229 5454   5–1A
After all these years, Will Ricker's "frenetically buzzing" Notting Hill hang-out is "still happening" – its staff put "bags of energy and enthusiasm" into serving up "innovative" Pan-Asian fusion bites that are "bursting with flavour". / **Details:** *www.rickerrestaurants.com; 11 pm, Sun 10.30 pm; booking: max 6.*

The Eagle EC1   £25   Ⓐ
159 Farringdon Rd   7837 1353
This "funky" gastropub – London's first, 1992 – is, for its many devoted fans, "still the best"; "complacent" service has tested their loyalty over the years, though, and in truth the "gutsy" fare no longer stands out.
/ **Details:** *10.30 pm; closed Sun D; no Amex; no booking.*

Eagle Bar Diner W1   £31   Ⓐ⭐
3-5 Rathbone Pl   7637 1418   3–1A
"Delicious" burgers, "great" cocktails and shakes that "ROCK" keep the "fun" vibe grooving along at this "clubby" diner, just north of Oxford Street; "it can be loud later on". / **Details:** *www.eaglebardiner.com; Mon-Wed 11 pm, Thu-Sat 1 am; closed Sun D; no Amex; need 6+ to book.*

Earl Spencer SW18   £36   Ⓐ⭐
260-262 Merton Rd   8870 9244
"A beacon in a culinary desert"; this large, "lively" and "convivial" Southfields fixture is "just how a gastropub should be", and it offers "big portions" of "the best comfort food" – no wonder it's "always hard to get a table". / **Details:** *www.theearlspencer.co.uk; 10 pm, Sun 9.30 pm; no booking.*

Edokko WC1   £42   ⭐⭐
50 Red Lion St   7242 3490   1–1D
Upstairs (the better option), it's "shoes off, and cross-legged at low tables", at this "authentically rickety" Japanese, off Holborn; it serves "some of the best sushi in town", with "impeccable style and grace", and at "good prices" too – particularly the "bargain set lunch".
/ **Details:** *10 pm; closed Sat L & Sun; no Amex.*

Eight Over Eight SW3 £45 A✪✪
392 King's Rd 7349 9934 4–3B

It may be a "chic" Chelsea "scene", but Will Ricker's "buzzy" hang-out doesn't just trade on its "people-watching" possibilities – service is "friendly", and the fusion fare is "beautiful" and "delicious".
/ **Details:** www.rickerrestaurants.com; 11 pm, Sun 10.30 pm; closed Sun L.

Electric Brasserie W11 £43 A
191 Portobello Rd 7908 9696 5–1A

This "sexy" all-day brasserie has become a "humming" – and at times "unbearably noisy" – epicentre of Notting Hill life; it's no foodie haunt, but its "classic French fare" seems improved of late (and – if you "scramble for a table" – they do a "cool brunch").
/ **Details:** www.the-electric.co.uk; 10.45 pm.

Emile's SW15 £37 A✪
96 Felsham Rd 8789 3323

A recent revamp has done nothing to dim the charms of Emile Fahy's "very entertaining" Putney backstreet bistro, which just "gets better and better with age"; "London's best beef Wellington" is a perennial attraction, as is an "exceptional-value wine list".
/ **Details:** www.emilesrestaurant.co.uk; 11 pm; D only, closed Sun; no Amex.

The Engineer NW1 £43
65 Gloucester Ave 7722 0950

This "bubbly" Primrose Hill gastropub has long been a fashionable hang-out, and "on a summer day, there are few nicer places than the garden"; the food is "not as good as used to be", though, and the setting is starting to look a little "tired". / **Details:** www.the-engineer.com; 11 pm, Sun 10.30 pm; no Amex.

Enoteca Turi SW15 £49 ✪
28 Putney High St 8785 4449

It's not just the "phenomenal" all-Italian wine list that makes it "worth the trip to Putney", to visit the Turi family's "cosy" and "obliging" fixture – it also serves up "some of the best Italian cooking in town". / **Value tip:** set weekday L £32 (FP). **Details:** www.enotecaturi.com; 11 pm; closed Sun.

Eriki NW3 £35 ✪✪
4-6 Northways Pde, Finchley Rd 7722 0606

"Superb" regional cooking – with "subtle spicing and rich flavours" – wins applause for this Swiss Cottage Indian, and the service is "charming" too; a St John's Wood branch (RIP) never really got off the ground. / **Value tip:** set weekday L £21 (FP). **Details:** www.eriki.co.uk; 10.30 pm.

Esarn Kheaw W12 £24 ⭐⭐

314 Uxbridge Rd 8743 8930 6–1B
The "amazing Northern Thai grub" at this low-key Shepherd's Bush café
is some of the best in town; the place never seems to attract nearly the
following it deserves. / **Details:** www.esarnkheaw.co.uk; 11 pm; closed Sat L &
Sun L; no Amex.

L'Escargot W1 £50 Ⓐ⭐

48 Greek St 7437 2679 3–2A
This "classic" Soho "gem" remains an "impressive all-rounder",
with "fine" décor, "very professional" service and notably "solid" Gallic
cuisine; it's "perfect for a business lunch", and "tremendous value pre-
theatre". / **Value tip:** set weekday L £33
(FP). **Details:** www.whitestarline.org.uk; 11.30 pm; closed Sat L & Sun.

Eyre Brothers EC2 £50 ⭐

70 Leonard St 7613 5346
"Hearty" dishes and "keen" service win consistent praise for this
"relaxed" Shoreditch Hispanic, especially as a "discreet" and "spacious"
business venue; its "hip" styling, though, can sometimes seem a touch
"clinical". / **Details:** www.eyrebrothers.co.uk; 10.45 pm; closed Sat L & Sun.

El Faro E14 £43 ⭐⭐

3 Turnberry Quay 7987 5511
A "hidden gem" near Crossharbour DLR; it serves some "wonderful"
and "authentic" Spanish dishes – including "outstanding tapas" –
and has nice waterside tables too. / **Details:** www.el-faro.co.uk; 11 pm;
closed Sun D.

Ffiona's W8 £45 Ⓐ

51 Kensington Church St 7937 4152 4–1A
"If you get Ffiona onside", this "old-fashioned" Kensington fixture can
offer a "unique and brilliant" experience; the "no-nonsense" bistro fare,
though, plays second fiddle to the joys of la patronne "buzzing around
the room". / **Details:** www.ffionas.com; 11 pm, Sun 10 pm; D only, closed Mon;
no Amex.

Fifteen Restaurant N1 £70

15 Westland Pl 0871 330 1515
Is Jamie finally getting his Hoxton project sorted? – a high proportion
of reports still dismiss it as "pretentious" and "over-priced", but those
who find the service "knowledgeable" and the Italian food "enjoyable"
were rather more in evidence this year. / **Details:** www.fifteenrestaurant.net;
9.30 pm; booking: max 6.

Fifteen Trattoria N1 £54

15 Westland Pl 0871 330 1515
"The most reliable part of the Fifteen operation" – the cheaper ground
floor of Jamie's Hoxton Italian has "enthusiastic" staff, and offers
"robust" and "flavoursome" fare (including "brilliant" breakfasts) that
generally lives up to the prices. / **Details:** www.fifteen.net; 10 pm; booking:
max 12.

54 Farringdon Road EC1 £34 ⭐

54 Farringdon Rd 7336 0603
The style may be "very odd" – "mixing Malaysian dishes with Gallic
classics" – but the really extraordinary thing about this "interesting"
Farringdon newcomer is... "it works!" / **Details:** 11 pm; closed Sat L & Sun.

Fig N1 £41 Ⓐ⭐
169 Hemingford Rd   7609 3009
*"Terrific and adventurous" cooking – and "superlative service" too –
are making quite a name for this "wonderful little hide-away", "tucked
away in elegant Barnsbury". / Details: www.fig-restaurant.co.uk; 10.15 pm,
Sun 9 pm; D only, closed Sun-Tue.*

La Figa E14 £38 Ⓐ⭐
45 Narrow St   7790 0077
*"Amazing pizza", "huge portions" and "very friendly staff" are among
the highlights which – by common consent – make this Docklands spot
"an absolutely stunning local Italian". / Details: 11 pm, Sun 10.30 pm.*

Fino W1 £52 Ⓐ⭐
33 Charlotte St   7813 8010   1–1C
*"Outstanding tapas" (plus "an interesting wine and sherry selection")
maintain a formidable reputation – and following – for the Hart
brothers' "buzzy" Spanish restaurant, in a Fitzrovia basement.
/ Details: www.finorestaurant.com; 10.30 pm; closed Sat L & Sun; booking:
max 12.*

First Floor W11 £42 Ⓐ
186 Portobello Rd   7243 0072   5–1A
*An "endearing" Portobello Market outfit, long liked for its "gorgeous"
and "eccentric" décor, rather than the "very up-and-down" realisation
of its "quirky" menu. / Details: www.firstfloorportobello.co.uk; 11 pm; closed
Mon & Sun D.*

Fish Club SW11 £31 ⭐⭐
189 St John's Hill   7978 7115
*"A simple thing done very, very well"; this "unassuming but fantastic"
Battersea chippy offers "a really interesting selection of fish" encrusted
in "lovely, golden, crispy batter", and served with "seriously chunky
home-made chips". / Details: www.thefishclub.com; 10 pm, Sun 9 pm;
closed Mon.*

Fish Hook W4 £46 ⭐
6-8 Elliott Rd   8742 0766   6–2A
*Who cares if it's "a tight squeeze"? – fish dishes "of a very high and
consistent standard" (as well as some "first-class wines") draw a big
crowd to Michael Nadra's "plain" Chiswick spot; a "great-value" lunch
is a highlight. / Value tip: set weekday L £27 (FP). Details: www.fishhook.co.uk;
10.30 pm, Sun 10 pm.*

5 Cavendish Square W1 £65 ✖
5 Cavendish Sq   7079 5000   2–1C
*This vast, OTT Marylebone townhouse – a bar/club/restaurant – is an
ideal venue for those who suffer from delusions of oligarchical grandeur;
the food, though, is often a "waste of time". / Value tip: set dinner £44
(FP). Details: www.no5ltd.com; 10.30 pm; closed Sat L & Sun D; no trainers.*

Five Hot Chillies HA0 £23 ⭐
875 Harrow Rd   8908 5900
*"Authentic, and worth the trip" – this grungy BYO Indian cafeteria, on a
busy Sudbury highway, is a "very friendly" place, where the "spicy" and
"excellent" scoff offers "great value". / Details: 11.30 pm.*

The Flask N6 £29 **Ⓐ**
77 Highgate West Hill 8348 7346
It's the "fabulous olde worlde building" that makes this famous Highgate coaching inn of note, and it's especially nice on days you can sit outside – the "simple" fare is very much a secondary attraction. / Details: 10pm; no Amex.

Flat White W1 £ 9 **Ⓐ ✪ ✪**
17 Berwick St 7734 0370 2–2D
"The best-ever coffee" – "like crack cocaine with froth" – has reporters addicted to this "cramped" Kiwi-run Soho spot; there are also (arguably rather pricey) biscuits and cakes. / Details: www.flat-white.co.uk; L only; no credit cards.

Foliage
Mandarin Oriental SW1 £82
66 Knightsbridge 7201 3723 4–1D
"Get a window table", if you can, at this "elegant" (if arguably rather dull) Knightsbridge dining room, as there are some "lovely park views"; Chris Staines's "innovative" cuisine continues to win high acclaim, but his "culinary high jinks" have, of late, sometimes fallen a little flat. / Value tip: set weekday L £38 (FP). Details: www.mandarinoriental.com; 10.30 pm; booking: max 6.

Four O Nine SW9 £44 **Ⓐ**
409 Clapham Rd 7737 0722
Behind a "speakeasy-style entrance", this "cosy" and "romantic" Clapham "gem" (over a pub) offers food that's usually "good", and occasionally "sublime"; it's beginning to build "quite a local following". / Details: www.fouronine.co.uk; 10.30 pm; D only.

Four Regions TW9 £36
102-104 Kew Rd 8940 9044
A Richmond "old favourite" which maintains its popularity in spite of its rather "standard" Chinese food, and a "bright" re-fit that some regulars find "disastrous". / Details: 11.30 pm.

The Four Seasons W2 £27 **✪**
84 Queensway 7229 4320 5–1C
"One of the most authentic Chinese restaurants in London", this "crammed" Bayswater veteran is especially known as "THE place for duck"; service, though, is "even less charming than at the neighbouring establishments", and the queue is "perpetual". / Details: 11 pm; no Amex.

The Fox & Hounds SW11 £38 **Ⓐ ✪**
66 Latchmere Rd 7924 5483
It's "a proper boozer" (with "a top selection of beers"), but this "crammed" Battersea pub also "does everything right" on the food front, offering "unfussy" Mediterranean fare that's "bursting with flavour". / Details: www.thefoxandhoundspub.co.uk; 10.30 pm, Sun 10 pm; Mon-Thu D only, Fri-Sun open L & D.

The Fox and Anchor EC1   **£35**   **A**
115 Charterhouse St   7250 1300
*Once celebrated as a "dusty old boozer", this Smithfield spot has been
"gloriously restored" by new owners; "rare beers" and "an incomparable
selection of whiskies" now accompany some "straight-down-the-line"
British fare – not least "legendary" breakfasts, complete with a pint
of Guinness. / Details: www.foxandanchor.co.uk; 10 pm; closed Sat & Sun.*

The Fox Reformed N16   **£34**   **A**
176 Stoke Newington Church St   7254 5975
*"There are better places to eat in N16", but this offbeat wine bar
veteran benefits from a particularly quirky charm, and a cute small
garden. / Details: www.fox-reformed.co.uk; 10.30 pm; closed weekday L.*

Franco Manca SW9   **£12**   ⭐⭐
Unit 4 Market Row   7738 3021
*"A new wood-burning stove, imported from Naples" advertises the
seriousness of intent of this recent newcomer, in the atmospheric Brixton
Market site that was formerly Eco (RIP); fans already claim it offers
"the best pizza outside Italy". / Details: www.francomanca.com; L only,
closed Sun; no Amex.*

Frantoio SW10   **£42**   **A**
397 King's Rd   7352 4146   4–3B
*Transcending its location in a "dreary '60s shopping strip",
this "buzzing" and "friendly" World's Ender is almost invariably hailed
as a "reliable local Italian". / Value tip: set weekday L £27
(FP). Details: 11.15 pm.*

Fresco W2   **£15**   ⭐
25 Westbourne Grove   7221 2355   5–1C
*A Bayswater pit stop "gem", notable for its "wonderful juices", "superb
salads" and "fresh falafels". / Details: www.frescojuices.co.uk; 11 pm.*

La Fromagerie Café W1   **£28**   **A**⭐⭐
2-4 Moxon St   7935 0341   2–1A
*"Inventive" breakfasts and "great, freshly-prepared salads" – plus,
of course, a "fantastic array of cheeses" – draw a dedicated following
to this "cramped" but "special" Marylebone deli/café.
/ Details: www.lafromagerie.co.uk; 7.30 pm, Sat 7 pm, Sun 6 pm; L only;
no booking.*

The Frontline Club W2   **£42**   **A**
13 Norfolk Pl   7479 8960   5–1D
*"Fascinating photos" line the walls of this "atmospheric" journos'
rendezvous in Paddington; it's not the "variable" food that whets the
palate here, however, but rather Malcolm Gluck's "scarily extensive"
("fixed mark-up") wine list. / Details: www.frontlineclub.com; 10.30 pm,
Sun 10 pm.*

Fuzzy's Grub   **£12**   ⊗⊗

6 Crown Pas, SW1   7925 2791   2–4D
96 Tooley St, SE1   7089 7590
15 Basinghall St, Unit 1 Mason's Ave, EC2   7726 6771
56-57 Cornhill, EC3   7621 0444
58 Houndsditch, EC3   7929 1400
10 Well Ct, EC4   7236 8400
22 Carter Ln, EC4   7248 9795
62 Fleet St, EC4   7583 6060

A *"very English"* and impeccably *"friendly"* chain of upmarket caffs,
applauded for their *"outrageously good sandwiches"* (*"a full Sunday
roast squeezed into a bap"*) and *"heavenly hangover-cure breakfasts"*.
/ **Details:** www.fuzzysgrub.com; 3 pm-4 pm; closed Sat & Sun except SE1 &
EC4; no credit cards; no booking.

Galvin at Windows
Park Lane London Hilton Hotel W1   **£81**   Ⓐ

22 Park Ln, 28th Floor   7208 4021   2–4A

"You can't fail to be impressed" by the *"unforgettable views"* from this
28th-floor Mayfair eyrie, which makes it a 'natural' for business
or romance; the Galvin brothers' two-year-old régime is rather losing its
lustre, though – prices can now seem *"astronomical"*, and the food
is *"disappointing at times"*. / **Value tip:** set weekday L £48
(FP). **Details:** www.galvinatwindows.com; 10.45 pm; closed Sat L & Sun D;
no trainers.

Galvin Bistrot de Luxe W1   **£44**   Ⓐ⊗⊗

66 Baker St   7935 4007   1–1A

With its *"crisp"* service of *"gutsy"* Gallic fare in an *"elegant"* setting,
the Galvin brothers' *"humming"* two-year-old, near Baker Street tube,
is *"a class act"*; *"a very safe bet for most occasions"*, it has become
a true benchmark, and has an enormous following. / **Value tip:** set dinner
£32 (FP). **Details:** www.galvinuk.com; 11 pm, Sun 9. 30 pm.

Ganapati SE15   **£29**   Ⓐ⊗

38 Holly Grove   7277 2928

"A hidden treasure in deepest Peckham" – this *"funky south Indian
diner"* offers *"excellent"* food, *"mostly at communal tables"*.
/ **Details:** www.ganapatirestaurant.com; 10.45 pm; closed Mon; no Amex.

Garrison SE1   **£40**   Ⓐ

99-101 Bermondsey St   7089 9355

"It's worth living in SE1 for", say fans of this *"quirky"* and *"fabulously
atmospheric"* Bermondsey boozer; the cooking is *"consistently good"*
too. / **Details:** www.thegarrison.co.uk; 10 pm, Sun 9.30 pm.

Gastro SW4   **£45**   Ⓐ
67 Venn St   7627 0222
The atmosphere is certainly "très français", and the scrambled eggs are
undoubtedly "great", but otherwise reports on this "romantic" bistro,
near the Clapham Picture House, are rather mixed. / Value tip: set
weekday L £22 (FP). Details: midnight; no Amex.

The Gate W6   **£39**   ★★
51 Queen Caroline St   8748 6932   6–2C
"Unerringly good" veggie fare – "the best and most imaginative" of its
type in London – again wins accolades for this "pleasant" venue, in an
airy former church hall, near Hammersmith Broadway; "lovely outdoor
seating in summer". / Details: www.thegate.tv; 10.45 pm; closed Sat L & Sun.

Le Gavroche W1   **£136** Ⓐ★
43 Upper Brook St   7408 0881   2–2A
"Still a winner, after all these years" – Michel Roux Jr's "terrific" Mayfair
veteran offers "the ultimate old-school dining experience", with "perfect,
classic haute cuisine", "astonishingly competent" staff, and "a wine
list second to none"; but "ouch, the bill…". / Value tip: set weekday L £61
(FP). Details: www.le-gavroche.co.uk; 10.45 pm; closed Sat L & Sun; jacket
required.

Geeta NW6   **£18**   ★
57-59 Willesden Ln   7624 1713
"Smiley, ever-present family members" add life to the "distinctly low-
brow" interior of this Kilburn veteran, still extolled by its small fan club
for its "excellent", "home-cooked" Indian scoff at "unbelievable" prices;
you can BYO too. / Details: 10.30 pm, Fri & Sat 11.30 pm; no Amex.

Gem N1   **£22**   Ⓐ★
265 Upper St   7359 0405
"It really is a gem!" – this "welcoming" Kurdish outfit, in Islington, offers
"always-good" food ("wonderful, fresh bread", especially) at "amazing"
prices; service is "excellent" too. / Details: midnight.

The Giaconda Dining Room WC2   **£30**   ★
9 Denmark St   7240 3334   3–1A
First solo UK venture of Aussie chef Paul Merrony, this small and basic
newcomer (right by Centrepoint) is one of those rare places which –
in an entirely un-precious way – is really all about the food, offering
notably satisfying bistro cooking (and very decent wines) at bargain-
basement prices. / Details: www.giacondadining.com; 9.30 pm; closed
Sat & Sun.

Giusto W1   **£35**
43 Blandford St   7486 7340   1–1A
"Don't be put off by the café-like exterior" – or the basement location –
of this Marylebone newcomer, on the site of La Spighetta (RIP); the food
– including pizza – is usually at least "decent", and our experience
coincides with those who found it "really excellent". /

The Glasshouse TW9 £52 ⭐⭐
14 Station Pde 8940 6777
"Easily the rival of its siblings, such as Chez Bruce"; this "quietly-situated" destination (right by Kew Gardens Tube) not only offers Anthony Boyd's "supremely flavoursome" cooking, but also "super" service and "fabulous" wine; "a bit more space between tables wouldn't harm", though. / **Value tip:** *set weekday L £39 (FP).* **Details:** *www.glasshouserestaurant.co.uk; 10.30 pm.*

Golden Hind W1 £19 ⭐⭐
73 Marylebone Ln 7486 3644 1–1A
For "the best fish 'n' chips in W1", seek out this "basic" but "lovely" Marylebone chippy (which does "proper puds" too); BYO. / **Details:** *10 pm; closed Sat L & Sun.*

Good Earth £44 ⭐
233 Brompton Rd, SW3 7584 3658 4–2C
143-145 The Broadway, NW7 8959 7011
A "smart" Chinese mini-chain with "professional" service, "attractive" décor and notably "consistent" food. / **Details:** *www.goodearthgroup.co.uk; 10.45 pm.*

Gordon Ramsay SW3 £118 Ⓐ⭐⭐
68-69 Royal Hospital Rd 7352 4441 4–3D
"Faultless" cooking (from new head chef Clare Smyth) is part of the "absolutely amazing" dining experience on offer at Gordon Ramsay's "luxurious" (if slightly "muted") Chelsea HQ; it's a shame, though, that prices have "shot up" in the year which has seen the food – for the first time in nine years – clearly beaten by a rival. / **Value tip:** *set weekday L £68 (FP).* **Details:** *www.gordonramsay.com; 11 pm; closed Sat & Sun; no jeans or trainers; booking: max 8.*

Gordon Ramsay at Claridge's
Claridge's Hotel W1 £90
55 Brook St 7499 0099 2–2B
This Art Deco Mayfair chamber is "losing it", year after year; the food is distinctly "pedestrian", service "needs work" and prices are "very inflated" – "you're just paying for the name". / **Value tip:** *set weekday L £45 (FP).* **Details:** *www.gordonramsay.com; 11 pm; no jeans or trainers; booking: max 8.*

Gordon's Wine Bar WC2 £23 Ⓐ❌
47 Villiers St 7930 1408 3–4D
A "murky" and ancient wine bar, near Embankment tube, worth seeking out for its "excellent" wine and its "amazing" setting – "cosy" vaults in winter, or the "great" (and ever more vast) summer terrace; the food is "adequate", but a bit of a side show. / **Details:** *www.gordonswinebar.com; 11 pm, Sun 10 pm; no booking.*

The Goring Hotel SW1 £75 Ⓐ
15 Beeston Pl 7396 9000 1–4B
"For a smart lunch with grandpa", nowhere could beat the "calm" dining room of this "charmingly civilised" and "so very English" family-owned hotel, near Victoria; it is is also particularly popular for business (and for "memorable" breakfasts too). / **Details:** *www.goringhotel.co.uk; 10 pm; closed Sat L; jacket & tie; booking: max 12.*

The Gowlett SE15 £28 **Ⓐ✪**
62 Gowlett Rd 7635 7048
*Peckham folk don't stint in their praise for this "fantastic" local,
and applaud its "excellent" pizza and its "friendly" staff; "plenty of good
beers" too. / Details: www.thegowlett.com; 10.30 pm.*

Great Eastern Dining Room EC2 £40 **Ⓐ✪**
54-56 Great Eastern St 7613 4545
*Who cares if it sometimes seems "too cool for school"? – this "buzzy"
pan-Asian hang-out, in Shoreditch, "always offers a great evening out",
thanks to its "fantastic" fusion fare (and "an extensive list of cocktails"
too). / Details: www.rickerrestaurants.com; 11 pm; closed Sat L & Sun.*

Great Queen Street WC2 £37 **✪**
32 Great Queen St 7242 0622 3–1D
*"Robust", "no-nonsense" British fare helps this "down-to-earth" Covent
Garden yearling win wide acclaim as a "real foodie location"; its style
can be so "unnecessarily basic", though, as to seem "verging
on pretentious". / Details: 10.30 pm; closed Mon L & Sun D; no Amex.*

Green & Red Bar & Cantina E1 £38 **Ⓐ✪**
51 Bethnal Green Rd 7749 9670
*"All the fun of the real Mexico" is to be found at this funky bar/cantina,
near Brick Lane, where the "surprisingly good" dishes (from a "limited"
menu) are some of London's most "authentic"; the occasional reporter,
though, senses a slight drift in standards since the early days.
/ Details: www.greenred.co.uk; 10.30 pm; closed L.*

Green's SW1 £67 **Ⓐ**
36 Duke St 7930 4566 2–3D
*Simon Parker Bowles's "discreet" and "club-like" St James's bastion
"unfailingly" pleases Establishment types with its "civilised" style and its
"simple" and "well-prepared" cooking; fish is the highlight of the
"nursery-fare" menu. / Details: www.greens.org.uk; 11 pm; May-Sep closed
Sun; no jeans or trainers.*

The Greenhouse W1 £90 **Ⓐ**
27a Hays Mews 7499 3331 2–3B
*Marlon Abela's investment has "worked wonders" on the interior of this
Mayfair veteran, "tucked-away" in a mews; "comical" prices, though, still
dent enthusiasm both for the "fabulous" wine list and for Antonin
Bonnet's "complex" cuisine (though London's chefs, we're told, see him
as 'one to watch'). / Value tip: set weekday L £55
(FP). Details: www.greenhouserestaurant.co.uk; 10.30 pm; closed Sat L & Sun;
booking: max 6-10.*

Grenadier SW1 £36 **Ⓐ**
18 Wilton Row 7235 3074 4–1D
*"Quietly tucked-away" in a cuter-than-cute Belgravia mews, this picture-
book pub is "in all the tourist guides"; the food in the dining room,
however, is generally "bland" – stick to a sausage and a Bloody Mary
at the bar. / Details: www.pubexplorer.co.uk; 9.30 pm.*

Ground W4 £25 Ⓐ ⭐
219-221 Chiswick High Rd   8747 9113   6–2A
"It beats GBK anytime!"; even reporters who are *"not really into burgers"* still love a visit to this *"bright"* and *"casual"* Chiswick café, where *"superb meat"* is *"cooked to perfection"*, and *"sides and drinks are excellent"* too. / **Details:** www.groundrestaurants.com; Sun-Mon 10 pm, Tue-Thu 10.30 pm, Fri & Sat 11 pm.

(Ground Floor) Smiths of Smithfield EC1 £23 Ⓐ
67-77 Charterhouse St   7251 7950
"Get there early at the weekend" (you can't book) for an *"awesome brunch"* – complete with a *"NY-style, casual vibe"* – in the bar of this large Smithfield warehouse-conversion.
/ **Details:** www.smithsofsmithfield.co.uk; L only.

The Gun E14 £46 Ⓐ
27 Coldharbour Ln   7515 5222
"A riverside pub with a difference" – this popular Isle of Dogs *"gem"* is *"well worth the walk from Canary Wharf"*, thanks not least to its *"lovely"* views and its sometimes *"excellent"* food; service, though, seems increasingly *"lax"*. / **Details:** www.thegundocklands.com; 10.30 pm.

Gung-Ho NW6 £34 Ⓐ
328-332 West End Ln   7794 1444
"Enjoyable", *"consistent"* and *"popular"*, this Chinese veteran has now re-established itself as *"one of West Hampstead's best places"*; the staff are *"really nice"* too. / **Details:** www.stir-fry.co.uk; 11.30 pm; no Amex.

Haché £30 Ⓐ ⭐
329-331 Fulham Rd, SW10   7823 3515   4–3B
24 Inverness St, NW1   7485 9100
The *"seriously delicious"* burgers at this *"funky"* duo *"knock the spots off all the Gourmet This & That chains"*; as well as the Camden Town original, there's now a Chelsea outlet (formerly the site of a Randall & Aubin). /

Hakkasan W1 £74 Ⓐ ⭐
8 Hanway Pl   7927 7000   3–1A

"It's impossible not to feel cool", at this *"sexy"*, *"NY-style"* basement, hidden-away off Oxford Street; prices may be *"astronomical"*, but the *"vivid"* oriental dishes (including *"exceptional"* dim sum) generally live up to them; this year saw less *"snooty"* service too.
/ **Details:** www.hakkasan.com; 11.30 pm, Fri-Sat 12.30 am; no jeans or trainers.

Haozhan W1 £32
8 Gerrard St 7434 3838 3–3A

This "quality newcomer", in the heart of Chinatown, is "definitely at the upper end of the scale for the area"; the décor may be a bit "bland", but the "unusual" Chinese dishes are usually "skillful", and sometimes "inspired". / *Details:* www.haozhan.co.uk; 11.30 pm, Fri & Sat midnight, Sun 11 pm.

The Havelock Tavern W14 £36
57 Masbro Rd 7603 5374 6–1C

"Mouthwatering" food, "famously disinterested staff" and a "convivial" vibe regularly feature in reports on this famous Olympia backstreet gastroboozer; a slight slip in ratings boosts those who say it's "not as exceptional since it changed hands", but others insist that: "after a wobble, it's back on form". / *Details:* www.thehavelocktavern.co.uk; 10 pm, Sun 9.30 pm; no credit cards; no booking.

Hawksmoor E1 £52
157 Commercial St 7247 7392

This "clubby" and "noisy" Spitalfields steakhouse is getting a bit cocky; fans still say it offers "the best steak and chips in town" (and "magnificent cocktails"), but service is increasingly "disappointing", and critics think prices are "taking the p***". / *Details:* www.thehawksmoor.co.uk; 10.30 pm; closed Sat L & Sun.

Hélène Darroze
The Connaught Hotel W1 £100
Carlos Pl 7499 7070 2–3B

This grand Mayfair dining room, formerly occupied by the Ramsay group's Angela Hartnett, re-opened as this guide was going to press, with a star Parisian chef at the helm; we did try to bring you a first-week review, but arrived for lunch to find that the hotel had managed to lose our booking... / *Details:* www.the-connaught.co.uk; 10.30 pm; closed Sat & Sun; jacket & tie.

Hellenik W1 £34
30 Thayer St 7935 1257 1–1A

A "time-warp classic" where the dishes are "outstanding", or a "grubby" place serving "uninspired" fare? – both schools of thought are well represented in feedback on this Greek taverna, in Marylebone; either way, it's "packed every lunchtime". / *Details:* 10.45 pm; closed Sun; no Amex.

Hereford Road W2 £40

3 Hereford Rd   7727 1144   5–1B

An "interesting" and "uncompromising" menu (à la St John) wins praise – from some quarters – for this Bayswater spot as a "fabulous newcomer"; its décor is "chilly", though, and sceptical reporters think its arrival has generally been "over-hyped". / **Details:** www.herefordroad.org; 10.30 pm.

Hibiscus W1 £83

29 Maddox St   7629 2999   2–2C

"Ludlow's finest arrives in Mayfair"; "after all the hype", though, Claude Bosi's début has proved "not fully convincing" – many reporters do hail his "massively accomplished" cuisine, but others find the food "unfashionably fussy", and the "luxurious" décor seems rather uninspired. / **Value tip:** set weekday L £38

(FP). **Details:** www.hibiscusrestaurant.co.uk; 10.30 pm; closed Sat & Sun.

High Road Brasserie W4 £47

162-166 Chiswick High Rd   8742 7474   6–2A

In classic Nick ('Soho House') Jones style, this "animated" Chiswick brasserie is an "always-bustling" neighbourhood linchpin, usually much-populated with "media folk"; after a fair start, however, the food is now "distinctly average" – "breakfast is what they do best".

/ **Details:** www.highroadhouse.co.uk; 10.45 pm, Fri & Sat 11.45 pm.

Hilliard EC4 £26

26a Tudor St   7353 8150

"It does a roaring take-away trade with the local lawyers", but you can also eat-in, at this "upmarket, 'gastro'-snack bar", by the Temple; it does "really clever and well-produced sarnies, salads and cakes", and decent wines too. / **Details:** 7 pm; closed Sat & Sun.

Hix Oyster & Chop House EC1 £48

35-37 Greenhill Rents, Cowcross St   7017 1930

Ex-Caprice supremo Mark Hix's much-hyped, no-frills Farringdon newcomer – on the former site of Rudland & Stubbs (RIP) – offers sometimes "excellent", plainly-British cooking; "you'd have thought he'd have got some better staff, though" (and not "stand there all evening gassing to his mates"). / **Value tip:** set Sun L £36

(FP). **Details:** www.restaurantsetcltd.com; 11 pm; closed Sat L & Sun D.

Holly Bush NW3 £36

22 Holly Mount   7435 2892

The food is "nothing special" – "pies", "sausages", "excellent cheese", "well-kept ales" – but this "lovely" Hampstead hostelry makes an ideal pit stop for those "who prefer a pub to be a pub".

/ **Details:** www.hollybushpub.com; 10 pm, Sun 9 pm; no Amex.

Holy Cow SW11 £20

166 Battersea Pk Rd   7498 2000

"I'm afraid it's only a delivery service, but this is the BEST", say fans of this "delicious" Indian take-away, in Battersea.

/ **Details:** www.holycowfineindianfood.com; 11 pm, Sun 10.30 pm; D only.

Hot Stuff SW8 £22 🅰️⭐⭐
19 Wilcox Rd   7720 1480
Brave the "dodgy" Vauxhall location – film buffs may recognise the streetscape from 'My Beautiful Launderette' – to truffle out this "tiny" but "awesome" BYO caff; "the guy who runs it is a star", and he serves up some "fabulous" curries at "incredible" prices.
/ Details: www.eathotstuff.com; 10 pm; closed Sun.

Hunan SW1 £54 ⭐⭐
51 Pimlico Rd   7730 5712   4–2D
"Just do as Mr Peng tells you and you will eat very well", at this "very plain and crammed" Pimlico Chinese; as Peng Sr takes over from Peng Jr, though, "touchy" service has occasionally been an issue (especially "if you go off-piste, and actually want to see a menu").
/ Details: www.hunanlondon.com; 11 pm; closed Sun.

Ikeda W1 £70 ⭐⭐
30 Brook St   7629 2730   2–2B
*Little-known but "top-notch", this Japanese Mayfair veteran may have "no atmosphere", but – especially "for sushi" – it's a "pricey-but-worth-it" destination. / **Value tip:** set weekday L £55 (FP). **Details:** 10.30 pm; closed Sat L & Sun.*

Inaho W2 £33 ⭐⭐
4 Hereford Rd   7221 8495   5–1B

*"Flawless" sushi (and other "delicious" Japanese fare) makes this "tiny" and "eccentric" Bayswater shack "one of London's best unsung heros"; "service is very poor – only one person for the whole place – but maybe that's how they keep prices low". / **Value tip:** set weekday L £20 (FP). **Details:** 11 pm; closed Sat L & Sun; no Amex or Maestro.*

Indian Ocean SW17 £26
216 Trinity Rd   8672 7740
*A notably "reliable" and popular Wandsworth curry house; the cooking is "not the most adventurous", but "the friendly service is pitched just right". / **Details:** 11.30 pm.*

Indian Zing W6 £34 🅰️⭐
236 King St   8748 5959   6–2B
*Manog Vasaikar's "zesty" and "creative" subcontinental cooking makes it "really worth a trek" to this "bustling" and very "welcoming" Hammersmith two-year-old. / **Details:** www.indianzing.co.uk; 10.30 pm.*

Inside SE10   £41 ⭐

19 Greenwich South St   8265 5060

"Pity about the cramped conditions", at Guy Awford's *"unpretentious"* dining room – his *"assured"* cooking is *"easily the best in the Greenwich desert"*. / **Details:** www.insiderestaurant.co.uk; 10.30 pm, Fri-Sat 11pm; closed Mon & Sun D.

Isarn N1   £35 ⭐

119 Upper St   7424 5153

"Staff couldn't be more helpful", at this *"small but perfectly-formed"* Islington Thai – a *"clean, modern"* venture serving food that's *"delicate, flavour-packed and fragrant"*. / **Details:** www.isarn.co.uk; 11 pm.

Ishbilia SW1   £38 ⭐

9 William St   7235 7788   4–1D

"A tasteful refurbishment" has improved the all-round appeal of this Knightsbridge oasis, and its mezze and other Lebanese fare are just as *"good"* as ever. / **Details:** www.ishbilia.com; 11.30 pm.

Isola del Sole SW15   £36 ⭐

16 Lacy Rd   8785 9962

"A hidden gem in a Putney sidestreet" – *"a great local"*, with *"very friendly"* service and *"surprising and tasty"* Sardinian fare. / **Details:** www.isoladelsole.co.uk; 10.30 pm; closed Sun; no Amex.

The Ivy WC2   £56 Ⓐ

1 West St   7836 4751   3–3B

"Don't knock it!", say fans of this Theatreland legend, for whom – despite increasingly *"ho-hum"* cooking – it remains an *"always-buzzing"* favourite; nowadays, however, it can seem a bit of *"cliché"* – *"is it really worth paying through the nose just to rubberneck the odd soap star?"* / **Value tip:** set Sun L £44 (FP). **Details:** www.the-ivy.co.uk; midnight; booking: max 6.

Iznik Kaftan SW3   £37

99-103 Fulham Rd   7581 6699   4–2C

Offshoot of a quirky little outfit in Highbury Park, this *"upmarket"* and ornately-furnished Brompton Cross newcomer has impressed early-days reporters with its *"interesting"* Turkish fare. / **Details:** www.iznik.co.uk/kaftan/; midnight.

Jashan HA0   £25 ⭐

1-2 Coronet Pde, Ealing Rd   8900 9800

"A top-notch meal for the money" is to be had at this friendly canteen, which serves a *"varied"* south Indian menu. / **Details:** 10.30 pm; no Amex; need 6+ to book, Sat & Sun.

Jin Kichi NW3   £35 ⭐⭐

73 Heath St   7794 6158

"Nothing changes (thankfully!)" – *"great-value, fresh sushi, sashimi and yakitori"* still pack 'em in at this *"firm-favourite"* Hampstead Japanese veteran; it's a *"welcoming"* place too. / **Details:** www.jinkichi.com; 11 pm, Sun 10 pm; closed Mon, Tue-Fri D only, Sat & Sun open L & D.

Joe Allen WC2 £40 Ⓐ

13 Exeter St 7836 0651 3–3D
A "tremendous" ambience has long made this "fun" American
basement, in Covent Garden, a "favourite post-theatre haunt"; the food
– including the famous off-menu burger – is "patchy" though,
and service sometimes "couldn't care less". / **Value tip:** set weekday L £30
(FP). **Details:** www.joeallen.co.uk; 12.45 am, Sun 11.45 pm; booking: max 10
Fri & Sat.

Julie's W11 £50 Ⓐ

135 Portland Rd 7229 8331 5–2A
An "absolutely charming, subterranean rabbit warren"; this "secret hide-
away", in Holland Park, "hasn't changed in 30 years", and is still
"probably the most romantic venue in all of west London"; the food,
though, is "from the Dark Ages". / **Details:** www.juliesrestaurant.com; 11 pm.

Kai Mayfair W1 £70 ⓿⓿

65 South Audley St 7493 8988 2–3A
"Stunning" and "beautifully-presented" food, backed up by a "premium"
wine list, inspires the highest acclaim for this "top-quality" Mayfair
Chinese; it's equally suited "to business or romance". / **Value tip:** set
weekday L £44 (FP). **Details:** www.kaimayfair.com; 10.45 pm.

Karma W14 £28 ⓿

44 Blythe Rd 7602 9333 6–1D
This "posh" but "welcoming" Olympia Indian offers some "great" and
"different" dishes – the sole problem seems to be that "they never have
enough customers to create a buzzy ambience".
/ **Details:** www.k-a-r-m-a.co.uk; 11.30 pm; no Amex.

Kastoori SW17 £26 ⓿⓿

188 Upper Tooting Rd 8767 7027
"An explosion of tastes" awaits visitors to this "dingy" family-run Tooting
stalwart, which offers "simply stunning" east African/south Indian cuisine
– the survey's best vegetarian fare – at "ridiculously low" prices.
/ **Details:** 10.30 pm; closed Mon L & Tue L; no Amex or Maestro; booking:
max 12.

Kazan £34 ⓿

93-94 Wilton Rd, SW1 7233 7100 1–4B
34-36 Houndsditch, EC3 7626 2222
Pimlico's "local marvel" is building an ever-growing following, thanks
to its "tasty" Turkish dishes, its "very knowledgeable" service and its
"fun" atmosphere; mid-2008 saw the opening of a City offshoot. /

Ken Lo's Memories SW1 £54 ⓿

67-69 Ebury St 7730 7734 1–4B
An "upmarket" and "charming" Belgravia "stalwart" which continues
to offer "traditional" Chinese food that – more consistently that its
Kensington sibling's nowadays – is "always of a high standard".
/ **Details:** www.memories-of-china.co.uk; 11 pm; closed Sun L.

Kiku W1 £52 ⭐

17 Half Moon St   7499 4208   2–4B

"Even the décor is authentic." ("which means that it could
be improved!"), at this "high-quality" Mayfair Japanese; "excellent" sushi
and sashimi are the culinary high points – they do a "bargain set lunch"
too. / **Value tip:** set weekday L £31 (FP). **Details:** www.kikurestaurant.co.uk;
10.15 pm; closed Sun L.

Koba W1 £44

11 Rathbone St   7580 8825   1–1C

"Helpful staff maintain a watchful eye", at this "buzzy" Fitzrovia
Korean, where first-timers enjoy the "novel" experience of a tabletop
BBQ, and regulars praise the "fresh" cooking and "lovely" sauces.
/ **Details:** 11 pm; closed Sun L.

Kolossi Grill EC1 £24 🅐

56-60 Rosebery Ave   7278 5758

"Old-fashioned, dotty and not entirely reliable, but to be supported for
old times' sake" – this "'60s throw-back" taverna maintains a dedicated
Clerkenwell following (not least for its "unbeatable-value" lunches).
/ **Value tip:** set weekday L £15 (FP). **Details:** www.kolossigrill.com; 11 pm; closed
Sat L & Sun.

Konstam at the Prince Albert WC1 £43 ⭐

2 Acton St   7833 5040

Having "all food sourced within the M25" sounds "like a gimmick",
but "it seems to work" at Oliver Rowe's "funky" King's Cross pub-
conversion, which offers "interesting" dishes in a "relaxed", if "rather
odd", setting. / **Details:** www.konstam.co.uk; 10.30 pm; closed Sat L & Sun.

Kovalam NW6 £22 ⭐

12 Willesden Ln   7625 4761

"Very good" and "authentic" south Indian dishes again win praise for
this hidden-away Kilburn-fringe spot.
/ **Details:** www.kovalamrestaurant.co.uk; 11 pm.

Kurumaya EC4 £31 ⭐

76-77 Watling St   7236 0236

"One of the rare, reliable cheap eateries in the City" – this Kaiten-Zushi
outfit near Mansion house is often "first-class".
/ **Details:** www.kurumaya.co.uk; 9.30 pm; closed Sat & Sun.

Kyashii
The Kingly Club WC2 £70

4 Upper St Martin's Ln   7836 5211   3–3B

On the fringe of Covent Garden, a blingy basement newcomer;
unfortunately, we didn't have the chance to check out its mega-pricey
Japanese fare before this guide went off to the printers, but press
reviews have not all been kind. / **Details:** www.kinglyclub.com/sml/kyashii.htm;
10.30 pm, Thu-Sat 11.30 pm; closed Sun; no trainers.

The Ladbroke Arms W11 £38 🅐⭐

54 Ladbroke Rd   7727 6648   5–2B

A "top" Notting Hill boozer with "lots of charm", and offering "simple"
but "scrummy" cooking that "never fails to live up to expectations";
"arrive early", if you want a seat on the sunny terrace.
/ **Details:** www.capitalpubcompany.com; 9.30 pm; no booking after 7.30 pm.

Ladurée £64 ⭐

Harrods, 87-135 Brompton Rd, SW1   7730 1234   4–1D
71-72 Burlington Arc, Piccadilly, W1   7491 9155   2–3C

"Delightful, decadent and oh-so-French" – the famous Parisian tearoom's London offshoots inspire rapturous reports; the 'signature' macarons are of course *"to die for"*, but more substantial dishes (Harrods only) are *"delicious"* – if, naturally, *"pricey"* – too. / *Details:* W1 6 pm, SW1 9 pm, Sun 6 pm.

Lahore Kebab House E1 £22 ⭐⭐

2-4 Umberston St   7488 2551

"Legendary kebabs" and *"brilliant lamb chops"* headline the *"exceptional-value"* Pakistani grub on offer at this *"hectic"*, *"no-frills"* East Ender – *"rough and ready"*, but a *"classic"*; BYO. / *Details:* midnight; need 8+ to book.

Lamberts SW12 £44 Ⓐ⭐⭐

2 Station Pde   8675 2233

"Top local recommendation after Chez Bruce!"; this *"special"* but *"unpretentious"* all-rounder, near Balham tube, makes *"a great find"*, thanks to its *"imaginatively-constructed food"* and *"fantastic"* service – and all at *"brilliant-value-for-money"* prices. / *Value tip:* set dinner £27 (FP). *Details:* www.lambertsrestaurant.com; 10.30 pm, Sun 9 pm; closed weekday L & Sun; no Amex.

The Landau
The Langham W1 £75

1c, Portland Pl, Regent Street   7965 0165   1–1B

"Liveried, super-attentive staff" are but one part of the formula that makes this *"sumptuous"* (*"glitzy"*) new hotel dining room a fine-dining *"beacon"* in the purlieus of Oxford Circus; Andrew Turner's menus are certainly on the *"fiddly"* side, but fans say results are *"divine"*. / *Value tip:* set weekday L £54 (FP). *Details:* www.thelandau.com; 11 pm, Sun 10 pm; no trainers.

Lanes
East India House E1 £52
109-117 Middlesex St   7247 5050

The year which saw a relaunch of this east-City basement inspired wildly varying reports, so we don't think a rating appropriate; let's hope history bears out the reporter who says: "the greatly improved room now matches the consistently excellent and unpretentious food".
/ **Details:** www.lanesrestaurant.co.uk; 10 pm; closed Sat L & Sun.

Latium W1 £44 ★★
21 Berners St   7323 9123   2–1D
"Assured cooking with real flair", "passionate" service and "excellent prices" make Maurizio Morelli's slightly "hard-edged" five-year-old, just north of Oxford Street, "one of the best Italians in town".
/ **Details:** www.latiumrestaurant.com; 10.30 pm, Fri-Sat 11pm; closed Sat L & Sun.

Launceston Place W8 £53 Ⓐ★★
1a Launceston Pl   7937 6912   4–1B

"Tucked-away in Kensington", this discreet townhouse was re-launched by D&D London in early-2008, with ex-Pétrus chef Tristan Welch at the stove; our visit was is in-line with a few adulatory early reports, which hail a "great" and "classy" make-over. / **Value tip:** set weekday L £41 (FP). **Details:** www.danddlondon.com; 11 pm; closed Mon L.

The Ledbury W11 £75 Ⓐ★★
127 Ledbury Rd   7792 9090   5–1B
Brett Graham's "subtly inventive" cuisine is "absolutely top-drawer", and it's served "with ease and efficiency", at this increasingly high-profile Notting Hill destination; the "intimate" room is "beautifully decorated" too. / **Value tip:** set Sun L £54 (FP). **Details:** www.theledbury.com; 10.30 pm.

Lemonia NW1 £34 Ⓐ
89 Regent's Park Rd 7586 7454
Perpetually "jam-packed" with "happy people", this landmark Primrose Hill taverna has an "unbeatable" atmosphere; the food seems ever more "ordinary", though, and "expensive for what it is".
/ **Details:** *11.30 pm; closed Sat L & Sun D; no Amex.*

Levant W1 £48 Ⓐ
Jason Ct, 76 Wigmore St 7224 1111 2–1A
"Still a great night out" – however, the attractions of this nightclubby and romantic Lebanese, in a Marylebone basement, have nothing at all to do with the food. / **Details:** *www.levant.co.uk; 11.30 pm.*

Lindsay House W1 £84
11-15 Swallow St 7439 0450 3–3A
This "lovely old Soho townhouse" is losing the "special" charm that's long made it "perfect for business or romance"; it doesn't help that the food – overseen by Richard Corrigan – seems ever more "underwhelming" and "overpriced". / **Value tip:** *set pre theatre £52 (FP).* **Details:** *www.lindsayhouse.co.uk; 10.30 pm; closed Sat L & Sun.*

Lisboa Pâtisserie W10 £ 6 ⭐⭐
57 Golborne Rd 8968 5242 5–1A
This "unique" North Kensington institution – "a wonderful, authentic Portuguese pâtisserie" – is always mobbed, and for good reason: "my Lisbon friend swears the cakes are almost as good as his mother's". / **Details:** *7.30 pm; L & early evening only; no booking.*

LMNT E8 £30 ⒶⓍ
316 Queensbridge Rd 7249 6727
A Hackney "Aladdin's Cave" of "crazy" décor, where the booths in particular are "great for hiding away"; fans say the food is "tasty" too – others that it's "cheap, but not particularly pleasant". / **Details:** *www.lmnt.co.uk; 10.45 pm; no Amex.*

Locanda Locatelli
Churchill InterCont'l W1 £60 Ⓐ⭐
8 Seymour St 7935 9088 1–2A
"A good whiff of glamour" adds to the allure of Giorgio Locatelli's "de luxe" Marylebone Italian, where most (if not quite all) reporters find "real heart" shines through in the "inspiring" but "unfussy" cooking. / **Details:** *www.locandalocatelli.com; 11 pm, Fri & Sat 11.30 pm; booking: max 8.*

The Lock Dining Bar N17 £41
Heron Hs, Hale Wharf, Ferry Ln 8885 2829
"West End-quality" cooking and a "superb front-of-house team" make it worth truffling out this "off-the-beaten-track" Tottenham two-year-old; "once inside, you forget you're on a main road, in a disused office block". / **Details:** *www.thelock-diningbar.com; 10.30 pm; closed Mon, Sat L & Sun D.*

Lucky Seven
Tom Conran Restaurants W2 £30 Ⓐ⭐
127 Westbourne Park Rd 7727 6771 5–1B
A tiny, "funky-retro" Bayswater diner that's the spitting image of "a Lower East Side burger joint"; "you may have to share your booth with strangers", but it's worth it for the "killer burgers" and "excellent milkshakes". / **Details:** *www.tomconranrestaurants.com; 11 pm; no Amex; no booking.*

Ma Goa SW15 £33
244 Upper Richmond Rd   8780 1767
"Beautiful" Goan dishes "bursting with flavour" are served with
"understated charm and efficiency" at this "homely" family-run Putney
*fixture. / **Details:** www.ma-goa.com; 11 pm, Sun 10 pm; closed Mon,*
Tue–Sat D only, Sun open L & D.

Madhu's UB1 £37
39 South Rd   8574 1897
This "top-notch" Indian is "well worth a trip to Southall"; "the owners'
Kenyan origins show through in the unusual spicing" of the "sublime"
dishes, which are served by "smiling" staff in quite a "smart" setting.
*/ **Details:** www.madhusonline.com; 11.30 pm; closed Tue, Sat L & Sun L.*

Magdalen SE1 £46
152 Tooley St   7403 1342

"The pedigree of the kitchen shines through", in the "superb" and
"gutsy" cooking on offer at this British yearling, not far from Tower
Bridge; the interior is "unatmospheric" or "calming", to taste.
*/ **Details:** www.magdalenrestaurant.co.uk; 10.30 pm; closed Sat L & Sun.*

Maggie Jones's W8 £48
6 Old Court Pl   7937 6462   4–1A
"On a cold day, hole up" at this "cosy" Kensington veteran, where the
"quirky" and "seductive" rustic décor is perfect for a "smoochy" dinner;
the "hearty" comfort food, though, is "very average" nowadays.
*/ **Details:** 11 pm.*

Maison Bertaux W1 £9
28 Greek St   7437 6007   3–2A
A "timeless magic" envelops this "rickety" but "charming" Soho
*"institution" – serving "good pastries" since 1871. / **Details:** 11 pm,*
Sun 7 pm; no credit cards; no booking.

Malabar W8 £32
27 Uxbridge St   7727 8800   5–2B
For a "good-value posh curry", the "skilfully blended" cuisine at this
"friendly" neighbourhood "favourite", near Notting Hill Gate, "always
*hits the spot". / **Details:** www.malabar-restaurant.co.uk; 11.30 pm.*

Malabar Junction WC1 £40
107 Gt Russell St   7580 5230   1–1C
A "spacious" and "uncrowded" spot, with "wonderfully laid-back service"
and "consistently great south Indian food"; only its obscure Bloomsbury
*location discourages a wider following. / **Details:** www.malabarjunction.com;*
11 pm.

Mandarin Kitchen W2 £36 ⭐⭐
14-16 Queensway   7727 9012   5–2C
"An amazing choice" of "absolutely stunning" Chinese seafood
(most famously, "divine lobster noodles") makes it "worth the
aggravation" of a visit to this ultra-"seedy", but always "bustling",
Bayswater institution. / *Details:* 11.30 pm.

Mangal Ocakbasi E8 £20 ⭐⭐
10 Arcola St   7275 8981
"Almost unbelievable value" is to be had at this "simple but sensational"
Turkish grill, in Dalston, where specialities include "the best lamb cutlets
ever"; BYO. / *Details:* www.mangal1.com; midnight; no credit cards.

Mango Tree SE1 £27 ⭐
5-6 Cromwell Buildings, Red Cross Way   7407 0333
"Always busy" (and noisy too), this straight-down-the-line modern Indian
is a very handy stand-by, right by Borough Market.
/ *Details:* www.justmangotree.co.uk; 11 pm.

Marco
Stamford Bridge SW6 £62
Fulham Rd   7915 2929   4–4A

MPW's grand newcomer, bizarrely located adjacent to Stamford Bridge,
is oddly decked-out in '90s-nightclub style; it's praised by some reporters
for its "fantastic", classic Gallic cuisine and its "great" (if "expensive")
wine list, but there have also been some "woeful" meals recorded.
/ *Details:* www.marcorestaurant.co.uk; closed Mon & Sun.

Marcus Wareing at the Berkeley – see Pétrus

Market NW1 £37 ⭐
43 Parkway   7267 9700
"A great addition to Camden Town"; this "informal" (and often "noisy")
newcomer offers "heart-warming" British bistro fare – from a daily-
changing menu – at very "tempting" prices. / *Details:* 10.30 pm; closed
Sun D.

maze W1 £70 ⭐
10-13 Grosvenor Sq   7107 0000   2–2A
Jason Atherton's "meticulous" preparation of "daring" but "dainty"
dishes wins enthusiastic acclaim for this Ramsay-group hot spot
in Mayfair; most reporters find it a "lively" place too, but there's also
a slight feeling it "lacks personality".
/ *Details:* www.gordonramsay.com/maze; 10.30 pm.

maze Grill W1 £72

10-13 Grosvenor Sq 7107 0000 2–2A

"Perfectly-cooked steaks" – with the help of an American broiler that's unique in this country – have helped this bright, new extension to maze make a "very strong start", sometimes "patchy" service notwithstanding. / **Value tip:** set weekday L £46 (FP). **Details:** www.gordonramsay.com; 10 pm; no trainers.

Memsaheb on Thames E14 £24

65/67 Amsterdam Rd 7538 3008
"Views of the Thames add to the experience", at this local Indian "gem", on the Isle of Dogs. / **Details:** www.memsaheb.com; 11.30 pm; closed Sat L.

The Mercer EC2 £50

34 Threadneedle St 7628 0001
"Safe" brasserie fare, "above-average" décor and an "unusually long" wine list ensure this "welcome", "NY-style" City-central newcomer "hits all the right notes for a business lunch".
/ **Details:** www.themercer.co.uk; 9.30 pm; closed Sat & Sun.

Metrogusto N1 £44

13 Theberton St 7226 9400
Fans praise the "authentic" cuisine, the "fantastic range of wines" and the "excellent" service at this Islington Italian; for critics, though, the food simply "tries too hard". / **Details:** www.metrogusto.co.uk; 10.30 pm, Thu-Sat 11-30 pm; Mon-Fri D only; booking: max 8, Sat & Sun.

Michael Moore W1 £52

19 Blandford St 7224 1898 1–1A
Mr Moore's Marylebone dining room may be "cramped", but he is a "passionate" and "inventive" chef, whose dishes can be a "revelation"; his staff are "absolutely charming" too. / **Value tip:** set weekday L £33 (FP). **Details:** www.michaelmoorerestaurant.com; 10.30 pm; closed Sat L & Sun.

Mini Mundus SW17 £36

218 Trinity Rd 8767 5810
"They don't rush you", at this "lovely" family-run local, in Wandsworth, where the "good-value" Gallic cooking "always makes for a good outing"; (they "also now do take-away"). / **Details:** www.mini-mundus.co.uk; 10.30 pm; closed Mon L.

Mirch Masala £26 ⭐⭐

171-173 The Broadway, UB1 8867 9222
3 Hammersmith Rd, W14 6702 4555 6–1D
1416 London Rd, SW16 8679 1828
213 Upper Tooting Rd, SW17 8767 8638
111 Commercial Rd, E1 7247 9992

"Amaze your palate", with a trip to one of these "Formica-table",
BYO Pakistani caffs – they serve "simply amazing" curries at "dirt-
cheap" prices; "there's now one opposite Olympia too".
/ **Details:** midnight.

Miyama W1 £60 ⭐⭐

38 Clarges St 7499 2443 2–4B

What it "lacks in atmosphere" – quite a lot! – this Mayfair Japanese
veteran makes up for, in spades, with its "gracious" service and its
"excellent" (if undoubtedly "expensive") food.
/ **Details:** www.miyama.co.uk; 10.15 pm; closed Sat L & Sun L.

Momo W1 £58 Ⓐ

25 Heddon St 7434 4040 2–2C

Dark and "sexy", it may be, but Mourad Mazouz's "fun" West End
Moroccan is sadly also "a triumph of style over substance" – the food
is "average", and service is sometimes "shocking". / **Value tip:** set
weekday L £34 (FP). **Details:** www.momoresto.com; 11 pm; closed Sun L.

Monmouth Coffee Company £10 Ⓐ⭐⭐

27 Monmouth St, WC2 7379 3516 3–2B
2 Park St, SE1 7645 3585

"A simple formula that works to perfection"; it comprises "quite simply,
the best coffee" and a small selection of "superb" baked goods, served
in characterful premises near Borough Market; (the Covent Garden
original branch is drinks-only). / **Details:** www.monmouthcoffee.co.uk; L &
afternoon tea only; closed Sun; no Amex; no booking.

Morgan M N7 £53 ⭐⭐

489 Liverpool Rd 7609 3560

Morgan Meunier's "brilliant" restaurant showcases his "theatrical" Gallic
cuisine that's amongst London's very best – it doesn't really matter that
the décor of this pub-conversion is somewhat "plain", or its Holloway
location rather "dodgy". / **Value tip:** set weekday L £39
(FP). **Details:** www.morganm.com; 9.30 pm; closed Mon, Tue L, Sat L & Sun D;
no Amex; booking: max 6.

Moro EC1   **£46** ⭐⭐
34-36 Exmouth Mkt   7833 8336

A dozen years on, there's still "a real buzz" about Sam and Samantha Clarke's Exmouth Market "gem", where "punchy" Spanish/Moorish cuisine and "brilliant" wines are served up by "lovely" staff in a "relaxed" (if sometimes "deafening") setting. / **Details:** *www.moro.co.uk; 10.30 pm; closed Sun.*

Mosaica
The Chocolate Factory N22   **£40** Ⓐ⭐
Unit C005, Clarendon Rd   8889 2400
A "very quirky" Wood Green dining room, located "behind a factory"; it's a "fun" and "atmospheric" setting in which to enjoy some "interesting" and "seasonal" cooking.
/ **Details:** *www.mosaicarestaurants.com; 9.30 pm; closed Mon, Sat L & Sun D.*

Mosaico W1   **£64**
13 Albemarle St   7409 1011   2–3C
This "stylish" Mayfair basement Italian wins praise as a "reliable" choice, especially on business; even those who think the food "very good", though, may conclude that "it doesn't justify the bill".
/ **Value tip:** *set weekday L £47 (FP).* **Details:** *www.mosaicorestaurant.co.uk; 10.30 pm; closed Sat L & Sun.*

Mr Chow SW1   **£73**
151 Knightsbridge   7589 7347   4–1D
It was madly fashionable back in the '60s, and this Knightsbridge Chinese is still, for fans, "one of the best"; sceptics, though, are more inclined to notice its "extortionate" prices. / **Details:** *www.mrchow.com; midnight.*

Mr Wing SW5   **£40** Ⓐ
242-244 Old Brompton Rd   7370 4450   4–2A
"After a bit of a dip, Mr Wing is back on form"; this Earl's Court veteran – with its "jazz, fish tanks and great Chinese food" – is a "spot-on" all-rounder (especially for a party, or romance). / **Details:** *www.mrwing.com; midnight.*

Nahm
Halkin Hotel SW1   **£80**
5 Halkin St   7333 1234   1–3A
David Thompson's Belgravia Thai is revered by foodies for its "passionate and challenging" cuisine – even they generally concede, however, that it comes at "outrageous" prices, and that the "stark" chamber in which it is served has all the atmosphere "of the moon". / **Value tip:** *set weekday L £49 (FP).* **Details:** *www.nahm.como.bz; 10.30 pm; closed Sat L & Sun L.*

Namo E9 £29 Ⓐ⭐
178 Victoria Park Rd 8533 0639
*"Owner Lynne really does know what she's doing", at this "friendly"
Vietnamese near Victoria Park, which serves "excellent dishes
at reasonable prices". / Details: www.namo.co.uk; 11 pm; closed Mon, Tue L,
Wed L & Thu L; no Amex.*

Nanglo SW12 £27 Ⓐ⭐
88 Balham High Rd 8673 4160
*"As good a local Indian as you'll find"; this "bastion" of Balham (recently
refurbished) is a "friendly" place, with a reputation for "first-class"
Nepalese food. / Details: 11.30 pm; D only.*

The Narrow E14 £37
44 Narrow St 7592 7950
*Thanks to the "Ramsay effect", it's "hard to get a table" at his
Limehouse boozer; apart from the "beautiful Thames views", however,
this is a fairly standard gastropub – indeed, not a few reporters leave
disappointed at finding everything "so very average".
/ Details: www.gordonramsay.com; 10 pm.*

Nautilus NW6 £30 ⭐
27-29 Fortune Green Rd 7435 2532
*"For a fish 'n' chips fix" – especially a kosher one, using matzo meal
batter – it's hard to beat this "brightly-lit" and "old-fashioned"
West Hampstead caff. / Details: 10 pm; closed Sun; no Amex.*

New Tayyabs E1 £23 ⭐⭐
83 Fieldgate St 7247 9543
*"Bloody brilliant curries and lamb chops to die for" – at "how-do-they-
do-it" prices – ensure this "basic" BYO East End Pakistani is always
"insanely busy"; "book, or risk standing in a mile-long queue".
/ Details: www.tayyabs.co.uk; 11.30 pm.*

1901
Andaz Hotel EC2 £62
40 Liverpool St 7618 7000
*This large and "beautiful" (if slightly "soulless") City dining room –
formerly called Aurora – is much more "impressive" in its new
incarnation; with its "top-notch" cuisine, and its "knowledgeable and
friendly service", it's "perfect for a formal business lunch". / Value tip: set
weekday L £44 (FP). Details: www.andaz.com; 10 pm; closed Sat & Sun;
booking: max 8.*

Nobu
Metropolitan Hotel W1 £82 ⭐
Old Park Ln 7447 4747 2–4A
*"Orgasmic" Japanese-fusion dishes still win acclaim for this Mayfair
legend, but it's far from being London's No.1 oriental nowadays – service
can be "horrendous", and even fans can feel the prices "leave a bitter
taste in the mouth". / Details: www.noburestaurants.com; 10.15 pm; booking:
max 12*

Nobu Berkeley W1 £80

15-16 Berkeley St   7290 9222   2–3C

Entered via a "loud" and "clubby" bar, the younger and brasher of the Mayfair Nobus can seem "way more fun" than Park Lane; just like the original, though, its cuisine seems ever more "over-rated", not helped by "rip-off" prices and staff who "seem to be on work experience". / **Details:** www.noburestaurants.com; 1.30 am; closed Sat L & Sun L.

Noor Jahan   £35   ✪

2a Bina Gdns, SW5   7373 6522   4–2B
26 Sussex Pl, W2   7402 2332   5–1D
It looks "very average", but this "stalwart" South Kensington Indian is a "classic" of its kind; "very well-prepared" curries at "inexpensive" prices ensure that both it and its Bayswater spin-off are "always buzzing". / **Details:** 11.30 pm.

The Normanby SW15   £32   Ⓐ✪

231 Putney Bridge Rd   8874 1555
Early reports are few, but all hail this "high-class" gastropub as a "magic addition to the Putney scene", thanks to its "original" cooking – it "beats the pants off most of the competition". / **Details:** www.thenormanby.co.uk; 10 pm.

North China W3   £27   ✪

305 Uxbridge Rd   8992 9183   6–1A
"You battle with the locals" to get into this "ordinary-looking" neighbourhood Chinese, in a "grotty" bit of Acton – an "unlikely" find, with "delightful" staff and "mouth-watering" food. / **Details:** www.northchina.co.uk; 11 pm.

North Sea Fish WC1   £28   ✪

7-8 Leigh St   7387 5892
It may look "faded", but this "traditional" Bloomsbury chippy is one of the best-known near the centre of town, thanks to its "amazing fresh fish". / **Details:** 10.30 pm; closed Sun.

Notting Hill Brasserie W11   £59   Ⓐ✪

92 Kensington Park Rd   7229 4481   5–2B
A "delightful" townhouse-restaurant offering a "pretty much faultless" mix of "spectacular" food, "excellent" service and a "lovely vibe (often enhanced by a jazz trio)"; "it's far from cheap, but worth every penny". / **Value tip:** set Sun L £45 (FP). **Details:** www.nottinghillbrasserie.co.uk; 11 pm; closed Sun D.

Number Twelve WC1 — £45
12 Upper Woburn Pl 7693 5425
Santino Busciglio's cooking has created a ripple of interest in this new, but "rather '90s", hotel dining room, near Euston; sceptical reporters feel his food is "fine, but far from impressive", but others like his "combination of Italian heritage, seasonal British ingredients and superb wine". / **Details:** www.numbertwelverestaurant.co.uk; 10.15 pm; closed Sat L & Sun D.

Numero Uno SW11 — £40   🄰
139 Northcote Rd 7978 5837
"Real Italians serve up real Italian food", at this "always-full" and "wonderfully buzzing local" — a "trusty" Battersea favourite. / **Details:** 11.30 pm; no Amex.

O'Zon TW1 — £26
33-35 London Rd 8891 3611
An "efficient" operation, offering "good oriental food in the heart of Twickenham", and "good value" too; "don't try it on a match day". / **Details:** 11 pm.

The Oak W2 — £40   🄰🟊
137 Westbourne Park Rd 7221 3355 5–1B
A "gorgeous" and "laid-back" ambience with tons of "buzz" makes this former boozer — recently re-launched, after a fire — the "perfect local" for Notting Hillbillies; "outstanding" thin-crust pizzas are the house speciality. / **Details:** www.theoaklondon.com; 10.30 pm, Sun 9 pm; Mon-Thu closed L; no booking.

Odette's NW1 — £70
130 Regent's Park Rd 7586 8569
Last year's lavish (and slightly "weird") refurb of this famously "romantic" Primrose Hill veteran divides reporters — supporters find it "delightful", but to critics it's plain "off-putting", and even fans of Bryn Williams's "top-class" cuisine caution that it's "very, very expensive". / **Details:** www.odettesprimrosehill.com; 10.30 pm; closed Mon & Sun D.

Odin's W1 — £52   🄰
27 Devonshire St 7935 7296 1–1A
This "elegant" and "civilised" Marylebone dining room is "one of the few that still do the starched-linen thing properly"; even some fans fear its "old-school" cooking risks becoming "tired", but when on form it's still "first-rate". / **Details:** www.langansrestaurants.co.uk; 11 pm; closed Sat L & Sun; booking: max 10.

Ye Olde Cheshire Cheese EC4 — £35   🄰🅧
145 Fleet St 7353 6170
Just off the Strand, this perfect Dickensian relic — complete with "roaring fire" — is in all the tourist guides; its "typical pub fare", however, could usefully be brought a little more up-to-date. / **Details:** 9.30 pm; closed Sun D; no booking, Sat & Sun.

Oliveto SW1 — £44   🟊
49 Elizabeth St 7730 0074 1–4A
"The best, thinnest pizza in London", say fans, is to be had at this "cramped" and "noisy" Belgravia Sardinian. / **Details:** www.olivorestaurants.com; 11 pm; booking: max 7 at D.

Olivo SW1 £47 Ⓐ⭐

21 Eccleston St 7730 2505 1–4B
*"Lots of regulars" frequent this "attractive" and "tightly-packed"
Belgravia favourite, noted for its "friendly" service and its "genuine
Sardinian home-cooking".* / **Details:** www.olivorestaurants.com; 11 pm; closed
Sat L & Sun L.

Olivomare SW1 £51 ⭐

10 Lower Belgrave St 7730 9022 1–4B
*"Perfectly cooked" Sardinian dishes – not least "really interesting fish" –
is helping to carve out quite a reputation for this "über-chic" ("sterile")
Belgravia yearling.* / **Details:** www.olivorestaurants.com; 11 pm; closed Sun.

Olley's SE24 £32 ⭐

65-67 Norwood Rd 8671 8259
*Offering "probably the best fish 'n' chips in South London", this "cross
between a chippy and a bistro", in Brockwell Park, makes "a pleasant
surprise in a culinary desert".* / **Details:** www.olleys.info; 10.30 pm;
closed Mon.

1 Lombard Street EC3 £80

1 Lombard St 7929 6611
*A "great location for business entertaining", opposite Bank, has helped
make this former banking hall a top City rendezvous, if one priced firmly
for "expense-accounters"; this year, however, saw a bizarre dive
in standards across the board (and in both the brasserie and the
restaurant).* / **Details:** www.1lombardstreet.com; 9.45 pm; closed Sat & Sun.

One-O-One
Sheraton Park Tower SW1 £70 ⭐⭐

101 Knightsbridge 7290 7101 4–1D
*Pascal Proyart's "blissful" seafood cooking – now served "tapas"-style –
remains "unrivalled" in London; it's a shame, then, that – although
a recent revamp has somewhat improved this previously dire
Knightsbridge chamber – it still feels rather "cold".* / **Value tip:** set
weekday L £36 (FP). **Details:** www.oneoonerestaurant.com; 10 pm.

L'Oranger SW1 £85

5 St James's St 7839 3774 2–4D
*"Luxurious" and classically Gallic, this St James's restaurant has long
been viewed as a "class act" (for either business or romance); as at
most other members of the London Fine Dining Group, however,
standards have been notably unsettled after the recent change
of ownership.* / **Value tip:** set weekday L £60 (FP). **Details:** www.loranger.co.uk;
11 pm; closed Sat L & Sun; booking: max 8.

Origin Asia TW9 £35 ⭐

100 Kew Rd 8948 0509
*"Not your standard curry house"; this "accommodating" Richmond
venture wins praise for its "delicious" and "imaginative" Indian fare.*
/ **Details:** www.originasia.co.uk; 11 pm.

Orrery W1   **£72**
55 Marylebone High St   7616 8000   1–1A
*This "gracious" dining room – overlooking a churchyard, and serving
up some "classy" Gallic cuisine – has long been acclaimed as the D&D
group's "crown jewel"; standards drifted this year, though, but prices
remain "astronomical".* / **Value tip:** set weekday L £45
(FP). **Details:** www.orreryrestaurant.co.uk; 10.30 pm, Thu-Sat 11 pm; booking:
max 12.

Oslo Court NW8   **£52**   Ⓐ⭐
Charlbert St, off Prince Albert Rd   7722 8795
*This "restaurant time forgot", near Regent's Park, attracts
an appropriately mature clientele – "we were the only table under 80!";
its "always-friendly" staff serve up "gigantic" dishes that are
"surprisingly good… if you like '70s-Italian food" (save space for
a pudding from the groaning trolley).* / **Value tip:** set weekday L £39
(FP). **Details:** 11 pm; closed Sun.

Osteria Basilico W11   **£43**   Ⓐ⭐
29 Kensington Park Rd   7727 9957   5–1A
*"Always loud and busy", this Italian "favourite" in the heart of Notting
Hill is still cranking out "great pizza" and "excellent pastas" in a "fun"
and "cosy" setting; service, however, seems entirely random – by turns,
"über-friendly", "surly", "slow" and "attentive".*
/ **Details:** www.osteriabasilico.co.uk; 11.30 pm, Sun 10.30 pm; no booking, Sat L.

Osteria Emilia NW3   **£38**
85b, Fleet Rd   7433 3317
*"A welcome addition to the generally grim Hampstead restaurant
scene"; the former Zamoyski (RIP) premises were re-launched all'italiana
in early-2008, by the owners of the "excellent" deli opposite; early
reports are all encouraging.* / **Details:** www.osteriaemilia.com; 10 pm; closed
Mon L, Sat L & Sun.

Osteria Stecca NW8   **£46**
1 Bleinham Ter   7328 5014
*"Finally they put some vibe into one of London's best-looking Italians" –
this St John's Wood newcomer (formerly called Rosmarino, RIP) has won
instant praise for its "fresh" cooking and "great mix of wines"; iffy press
reviews, however, suggest success may be going to their heads.*
/ **Details:** www.osteriastecca.com; 10.30 pm, Sat 11 pm, Sun 10 pm.

Ottolenghi   **£37**   🔵🔵
13 Motcomb St, SW1   7823 2707   4–1D
63 Ledbury Rd, W11   7727 1121   5–1B
1 Holland St, W8   7937 0003   4–1A
287 Upper St, N1   7288 1454
*"Amazingly, the food is just as scrumptious as it looks", at these
"seriously posy" café/delis (whose communal tables are "besieged" for
weekend brunch); they charge "a small fortune" for "couture" tapas,
"phenomenal" salads and "sublime" cakes.* / **Value tip:** set always available
£25 (FP). **Details:** www.ottolenghi.co.uk; 10.15 pm; W11 8pm, Sun 6 pm;
N1 closed Sun D, Holland St takeaway only; W11 & SW1 no booking, N1 booking
for D only.

(Restaurant)
Oxo Tower SE1   **£72**   ❌

Barge House St   7803 3888
*The "marvellous" views "may make you forget the food, but not the bill",
at this "somewhat embarrassing" 8th-floor South Bank landmark, which
continues to trade shamelessly on its location, and offers "dire" cooking
and "dismal" service at "crazy" prices.* / **Value tip:** *set weekday L £50
(FP).* **Details:** *www.harveynichols.com; 11 pm, Sun 10 pm; booking: max 14.*

The Painted Heron SW10   **£45**   ⭐⭐

112 Cheyne Walk   7351 5232   4–3B
*"So original" – the "exquisite" cooking at this "upmarket but
unpretentious" Indian is bettered by few others in the capital; it's "a bit
hard to find", though, just off Chelsea Embankment.*
/ **Details:** *www.thepaintedheron.com; 11 pm; closed Sat L & Sun.*

The Palmerston SE22   **£37**   ⭐

91 Lordship Ln   8693 1629
*"One of the very few seriously good gastropubs in south London",
this "friendly" East Dulwich boozer is "still going strong", offering food
that's "good, simple and well-executed".* / **Value tip:** *set weekday L £22
(FP).* **Details:** *www.thepalmerston.net; 10 pm, Sun 9.30 pm; no Amex.*

Pantechnicon Rooms SW1   **£51**   Ⓐ

10 Motcomb St   7730 6074   4–1D
*From the Thos. Cubitt team, an even smarter new Belgravia gastropub,
with an upstairs dining room whose restrained grandeur wouldn't look
out of place in a gentleman's club; it offers a wide-ranging menu,
well realised, at prices which – assuming you steer clear of the caviar
and so on – needn't break the bank.* / **Details:** *www.thepantechnicon.com;
11 pm, Sun 10.30 pm.*

Paolina Café WC1   **£18**   ⭐

181 Kings Cross Rd   7278 8176
*For "very good value" around King's Cross, you won't do much better
than this "tasty" Thai café; "BYO is a bonus" too.* / **Details:** *10 pm; closed
Sun; no credit cards.*

Pappa Ciccia   **£28**   Ⓐ⭐

105-107 Munster Rd, SW6   7384 1884
41 Fulham High St, SW6   7736 0900
90 Lower Richmond Rd, SW15   8789 9040
*With their "great thin-crust pizza" and "fresh" pasta, these "squashed"
and "fun" Italian locals win much praise; prices are "very reasonable",
and you can BYO too (modest corkage).* / **Details:** *www.pappaciccia.com;
11 pm, Sat & Sun 11.30 pm; SW6 no credit cards.*

Paradise by Way of Kensal Green W10 £43 Ⓐ⭐
19 Kilburn Ln   8969 0098

This big, "buzzing", "beautiful" and vaguely Gothic favourite has long
been a "real find" in a still-unlikely area, thanks not least to its
"imaginative" cuisine; other attractions include a bar, dance-floor,
garden, roof terrace... / **Details:** www.theparadise.co.uk; 10.30 pm,
Sun 8 pm; closed weekday L.

The Parsee N19 £36 ⭐
34 Highgate Hill   7272 9091
"Unusual" and "lovely" Parsee food never seems to win this Highgate
Indian the following it deserves – thanks, we suspect, to its atmosphere-
free interior, it can be surprisingly "empty". / **Details:** www.the-parsee.com;
10.45 pm; D only, closed Sun.

Pasha SW7 £48 Ⓐ
1 Gloucester Rd   7589 7969   4–1B
"Rose petals sprinkled on the stairs" and belly dancing help set the
ultra-"romantic" scene at this South Kensington townhouse-Moroccan;
the food, though, "leaves much to be desired", and sometimes
just seems a "rip-off". / **Details:** www.pasha-restaurant.co.uk; midnight,
Thu-Sat 1 am; booking: max 10 at weekends.

Patara £45 ⭐
15 Greek St, W1   7437 1071   3–2A
3-7 Maddox St, W1   7499 6008   2–2C
181 Fulham Rd, SW3   7351 5692   4–2C
9 Beauchamp Pl, SW3   7581 8820   4–1C
This "smart" Thai group remains an utter paragon of consistency –
"courteous" and "lovely" staff dish up "flawless" and "delicate" dishes
in each of its "extremely pleasant" branches.
/ **Details:** www.pataralondon.com; 10.30 pm.

Patterson's W1 £61 ⭐
4 Mill St   7499 1308   2–2C
"Inventive" dishes are pulled off with "flair", if "sometimes unevenly",
at this family-run Mayfair establishment – it makes an "enjoyable all-
rounder", despite its "understated" going-on "bland" interior; "bargain"
prix-fixe lunch. / **Value tip:** set weekday L £39
(FP). **Details:** www.pattersonsrestaurant.com; 11 pm; closed Sat L & Sun.

Pearl WC1 £71
252 High Holborn   7829 7000   1–1D
"The room is spectacular or sterile, depending on your point of view",
but – thanks to Jun Tanaka's "complex" and "unexpectedly good"
cuisine – this former Holborn banking hall often impresses; in a different
way, the "insane" wine mark-ups do too. / **Value tip:** set weekday L £48
(FP). **Details:** www.pearl-restaurant.com; 10 pm; closed Sat L & Sun.

Pearl Liang W2 £34

8 Sheldon Sq   7289 7000   5–1C

This "stylish" and "eclectic" Chinese yearling – "tucked-away" in an "obscure" Paddington Basin basement – is widely tipped as well "worth searching out" for its "excellent dim sum" (and other "interesting" dishes). / *Details: www.pearlliang.co.uk; 11 pm.*

E Pellicci E2 £14

332 Bethnal Green Rd   7739 4873

"An amazing experience in an unexpected situation" – "one of the last proper East End caffs", serving up "the best breakfast in London", in (listed) Art Deco splendour. / *Details: 5pm; L only, closed Sun; no credit cards.*

Petek N4 £28

96 Stroud Green Rd   7619 3933

An extremely "cheerful" and "upmarket" Finsbury Park "kebab house", which offers "an interesting take on the usual Turkish dishes", and is unsurprisingly "very popular". / *Details: 11 pm; Mon-Thu D only, Fri-Sun open L & D.*

Petersham Hotel TW10 £52

Nightingale Ln   8940 7471   2–3B

"Beautiful views over the Thames" help make this conventional hotel dining room in Richmond "a perfect choice for a swanky Sunday lunch", or for any other "celebratory" meal. / *Details: www.petershamhotel.co.uk; 9.45 pm, 8.45 pm Sun; –.*

Petersham Nurseries TW10 £61

Off Petersham Rd   8605 3627

"Sitting amidst roses, pots and plants" ("all for sale") – that's the "unusual" but "fantastic" setting for this glasshouse-café, "in the middle of a garden centre"; Skye Gingall creates some "stunning" dishes from "exceptionally fine produce", but even fans find the prices "horrendous". / *Details: www.petershamnurseries.com; L only, closed Mon.*

La Petite Maison W1 £63

54 Brooks Mews   7495 4774   2–2B

This "sophisticated", if "outrageously expensive", Mayfair yearling – a take-off of a fashionable Nice establishment – is always "packed" with a "chichi" crowd, drawn by its "skillful" dishes (for sharing) and its "classy" vibe. / *Details: www.lpmlondon.co.uk; 10.30 pm; closed Sun D.*

Pétrus SW1
(now renamed Marcus Wareing at The Berkeley) **£101** Ⓐ⭐⭐
Wilton Pl 7235 1200 4–1D
*"Better now than Gordon Ramsay!"; Marcus Wareing's "incomparable"
Knightsbridge dining room – with its "sublime" cuisine, its "immaculate"
service and its "stupendous" wine list – out-scored his ex-boss's across
the board this year; the only real caveat is that ambience loses
something if you don't sit in the main room; NB: by the time you read
this, the restaurant's name may have changed. / **Value tip:** set weekday L
£56 (FP). **Details:** www.the-berkeley.co.uk; 10.45 pm; closed Sat L & Sun;
no jeans or trainers; booking: max 10.*

Pham Sushi EC1 **£25** ⭐⭐
159 Whitecross St 7251 6336
*"You can't fault the food" – some of "the best sushi in London" – at this
"excellent", if low-key, destination, near the Barbican.
/ **Details:** www.phamsushi.co.uk; 10 pm; closed Sat L & Sun.*

Philpotts Mezzaluna NW2 **£41** Ⓐ⭐
424 Finchley Rd 7794 0455
*"A north London spot that always hits the mark" – David Philpott's
"intimate" and "reliable" Childs Hill fixture has "very friendly" staff,
and it serves "great-value" Italian cooking too.
/ **Details:** www.philpotts-mezzaluna.com; 11 pm; closed Mon & Sat L; no Amex.*

Pho **£22** Ⓐ⭐
3 Great Titchfield St, W1 7436 0111 2–1C
56 Goodge St, W1 1–1B
126 King's Cross Rd, WC1 7833 9088
86 St John St, EC1 7253 7624
*"You just wish there were more places like 'em" – "busy", "Formica-
table" noodle shops, where "sweet" staff serve up "consistently delicious
Vietnamese street food". /*

Phoenix Bar & Grill SW15 **£43** Ⓐ⭐
162-164 Lower Richmond Rd 8780 3131
*This "buzzy" neighbourhood spot in Putney has "steadily improved",
to the extent it outperforms its sibling Sonny's nowadays; its all-round
formula includes often-"excellent" food and "welcoming" service, and a
"pleasant terrace" too. / **Value tip:** set dinner £29
(FP). **Details:** www.sonnys.co.uk; 10.30 pm, 11 pm.*

Pied à Terre W1 **£91** ⭐
34 Charlotte St 7636 1178 1–1C
*"An exemplar of quality fine dining"; David Moore's "discreet" Fitzrovian
fully shows off Shane Osborn's talent for "foodie fireworks" (without
"anything daft or over-wrought"), and the service is "consummately
professional" too; most reporters like its "cosy" and "narrow" dining
room (but to a few, it's "ambience-free"). / **Value tip:** set weekday L £51
(FP). **Details:** www.pied-a-terre.co.uk; 11 pm; closed Sat L & Sun; booking: max 6.*

Pigalle Club W1 **£64** Ⓐ
215-217 Piccadilly 7734 8142 2–3D
*The food's "incidental", but this supper club right by Piccadilly Circus
is "great for a late-night boogie, and has some fun acts too".
/ **Details:** www.thepigalleclub.com; 11.30 pm; D only, closed Sun.*

Pinchito EC1 £28
32 Featherstone St   7490 0121
"Tasty, authentic and nicely-sized tapas in a buzzy bar setting" win
*a warm reception for this "really Catalan" newcomer, near Old Street
tube. / **Details:** www.pintxopeople.co.uk; midnight; closed Sat L & Sun.*

Pizza Metro SW11 £35
64 Battersea Rise   7228 3812
*"Great metre-long slabs of traditionally-topped pizzas" –
"the best in London" ("and I'm Italian!") – make this "exuberant",
"crowded" and "noisy" Neapolitan a Battersea hang-out that's well
"worth a detour". / **Details:** 11 pm; closed Mon, Tue-Thu D only,Fri-Sun open
L & D; no Amex.*

Plateau E14 £70
Canada Pl   7715 7100
*The interior may be "functional", but this fourth-floor Canary Wharf
business favourite has a vista of a "fabulous cityscape, especially
at night"; "as at other D&D operations", though, the food
is "not exciting" and "very pricey for what you get"; NB: "the bistro
is better than the restaurant". / **Value tip:** set dinner £45
(FP). **Details:** www.plateaurestaurant.co.uk; 10.30 pm; closed Sat L & Sun D.*

Poissonnerie de l'Avenue SW3 £58
82 Sloane Ave   7589 2457   4–2C
*"Excellent" fish and seafood dishes are often reported at this Brompton
Cross veteran; it's infamously associated with a "purple-rinse" crowd...
but then "old people often know best". / **Value tip:** set weekday L £43
(FP). **Details:** www.poissonneriedelavenue.co.uk; 11.15 pm; closed Sun.*

La Porte des Indes W1 £56
32 Bryanston St   7224 0055   1–2A
*"A spectacular, two-floor setting, complete with indoor waterfall" helps
make a visit to this "Tardis-like" basement, near Marble Arch,
a "special" experience; the "pricey" Indian cuisine is "unusual" (in that
it's Frenchified) and it's "good" too – "especially for those who don't like
fiery food". / **Details:** www.pilondon.net; 11.30 pm, Sun 10.30 pm; closed Sat L.*

Il Portico W8 £40
277 Kensington High St   7602 6262   6–1D
*An "old-fashioned" Italian (handily located by Kensington's cinema),
that's long been a local "favourite"; the food is "reliable,
not spectacular", but the approach is "very friendly" and "honest".
/ **Details:** www.ilportico.co.uk; 11.15 pm; closed Sun, & Bank Holidays.*

La Poule au Pot SW1 £50
231 Ebury St   7730 7763   4–2D
*This "quirky" Pimlico "perennial" is – as usual – the survey's No.
1 romantic tip, thanks to its "so French" mix of "candlelight",
"dark corners", "rustic" décor and "cuisine bourgeoise"; service is a little
"unpredictable", though, and the cooking can seem "somewhat heavy
handed". / **Value tip:** set weekday L £33 (FP). **Details:** 11 pm, Sun 10 pm.*

The Prince Of Wales SW15 £36
138 Upper Richmond Rd   8788 1552
*"A fabulous new Putney gastropub", universally hailed by early reporters
as a "friendly" place, offering "good food at reasonable prices".
/ **Details:** www.princeofwalesputney.co.uk; 10 pm, Sun 9.30 pm.*

Princess Garden W1 £50 ⭐⭐
8 North Audley St 7493 3223 2–2A
This "upmarket" Chinese is in "a different class" from most of its traditional competitors thanks to its "smart" (if "stark") décor and "smooth" service; the food is "superior" too, and "not too pricey, for Mayfair". / Details: www.princessgardenofmayfair.com; 11.15 pm.

Princess Victoria W12 £37 Ⓐ⭐
217 Uxbridge Rd 8749 5886 6–1B
A magnificent, newly-revamped Victorian pub, on a lonely bit of Shepherd's Bush highway; an early visit found brilliantly-realised, if straightforward, fare served rather sluggishly, but with charm. / Details: www.princessvictoria.co.uk; 10.30 pm, Sun 9.30 pm.

Prism EC3 £74
147 Leadenhall St 7256 3875
"Spacious" and "convenient for City clients" – Harvey Nics's converted banking hall, near Leadenhall Market, has obvious advantages for a business rendezvous; the "beautiful" interior is rather dead, however, and the cuisine, though "fine", is "overpriced". / Details: www.harveynichols.com; 10 pm; closed Sat & Sun.

The Providores W1 £61
109 Marylebone High St 7935 6175 1–1A
"It'll dazzle your taste buds", say fans of Peter Gordon's "unique" Pacific Rim cuisine (and there is a "fabulous list of NZ wines" to go with it); doubters find dishes "over-complicated", though, and this first-floor Marylebone dining-room is rather "pokey". / Details: www.theprovidores.co.uk; 10.30 pm; booking: max 12.

(Tapa Room)
The Providores W1 £40
109 Marylebone High St 7935 6175 1–1A
An "interesting selection" of light dishes helps make this "funky" and "noisy" Marylebone bar/diner very popular (especially for the "really different, but fabulous" brunch); prices, though, are "on the high side". / Details: www.theprovidores.co.uk; 10.30 pm.

Quadrato
Four Seasons Hotel E14 £75
Westferry Circus 7510 1857
"In the desert that is Canary Wharf dining", this swish (but "morgue-like") chamber is seen by some reporters as "the best choice for a business lunch", offering "generally good" Italian cuisine; it also does an "amazing" Sunday brunch. / Details: www.fourseasons.com; 10.30 pm.

Queen's Head W6 £30 Ⓐ
13 Brook Grn 7603 3174 6–1C
A potentially "fantastic" Brook Green tavern, with a "cosy and romantic" beamed interior and a vast and lovely garden; shame about the food, though, which is somewhere between "reliable" and "disappointing". / Details: www.thespiritgroup.com; 10 pm, Sun 9 pm; no booking.

Le Querce SE23　　　　　　　　　**£31**　　　⭐⭐
66-68 Brockley Rise　8690 3761
This Brockley "hidden gem" certainly "doesn't look much from the outside", but it's of note for its "simple and very genuine Italian food", which includes "wonderful home-made pasta", and "amazing gelati in adventurous flavours" too. / **Details:** *10.30 pm; closed Mon; no Amex.*

Quilon SW1　　　　　　　　　**£57**　　　⭐⭐
41 Buckingham Gate　7821 1899　1–4B
The interior may be "slightly depressing" and "hotel-esque" – no wonder Michelin recently gave this place a star! – but this "posh" Indian, near Buckingham Palace, offers "sophisticated" cuisine which seems to have blossomed even further under the attention directed to it by the tyre men. / **Value tip:** *set weekday L £37 (FP).* **Details:** *www.thequilonrestaurant.com; 11 pm, Sun 10.30 pm; closed Sat L.*

Quirinale SW1　　　　　　　　　**£57**　　　⭐
North Ct, 1 Gt Peter St　7222 7080　1–4C
"A beacon in the Westminster desert" – this "light", "quiet" and "airy" basement offers "imaginative" and "varied" Italian cooking, sometimes of an "exceptional" standard. / **Details:** *www.quirinale.co.uk; 10.30 pm; closed Sat & Sun.*

Quo Vadis W1　　　　　　　　　**£70**
26-29 Dean St　7437 9585　3–2A

British hotel grill rooms of times past provide the Hart brothers' inspirations for the relaunch of this '20s Soho classic; that may explain its ultra-straightforward food, and low-key interior design – it all adds up to a quality experience, if one that arguably lacks pizzazz. / **Details:** *www.quovadissoho.co.uk; 11 pm; closed Sun.*

Racine SW3　　　　　　　　　**£50**　　　🅐⭐
239 Brompton Rd　7584 4477　4–2C
"A class act"; this "delightful corner of France, in Knightsbridge" – notable both for its "meticulous" service and for its "honest-to-goodness" fare – mercifully suffered no discernible ill effects from last year's departure of co-founder Henry Harris... but as this guide goes to press, we hear he's decided to go back anyway! / **Value tip:** *set always available £33 (FP).* **Details:** *10.30 pm.*

Ragam W1　　　　　　　　　**£28**　　　⭐⭐
57 Cleveland St　7636 9098　1–1B
"A dive, but the food is always fantastic"; this "tiny" stalwart, near the Telecom Tower, may be "tatty", but its south Indian (mostly veggie) food is "absolutely the best", and "served with a genuine smile"; BYO. / **Details:** *www.mcdosa.co.uk; 11 pm, Fri & Sat 11.30 pm, Sun 10.30 pm.*

Randall & Aubin W1 £44 Ⓐ
16 Brewer St 7287 4447 2–2D
"It's fun to watch and be watched", perching on a stool at this "bustling" heart-of-sleazy-Soho seafood and champagne bar, which serves up some "lovely", simple fare. / Details: www.randallandaubin.co.uk; 11 pm; no booking.

Rasa £33 ✪✪
5 Charlotte St, W1 7637 0222 1–1C
6 Dering St, W1 7629 1346 2–2B
Holiday Inn Hotel, 1 Kings Cross, WC1 7833 9787
56 Stoke Newington Church St, N16 7249 1340
This Indian chain "knocks all others into the shade", thanks to its "phenomenal" Keralan food and its "helpful" staff; it's primarily veggie, but Dering St and N16 (Travancore) also serve meat, while Charlotte St (Samudra) majors in "vivid" fish and seafood; see also Rasa N16. / Details: www.rasarestaurants.com; 10.45 pm; Dering St W1 closed Sun, N16 D only Mon-Sat, N1 L only Mon-Fri, Charlotte St W1 closed Sun L, NW1 Mon - Fri L only, Rathbone St W1 Mon - Fri L only, WC1 closed Sun.

Rasa N16 £26 ✪✪
55 Stoke Newington Church St 7249 0344
"The original Stokie Rasa" is "always busy... mainly with people coming back"; its "incomparable" veggie Keralan fare "throws all sorts of exotic and wonderful flavours at you", and at "shockingly low prices" too. / Details: www.rasarestaurants.com; 10.45 pm, Fri & Sat 11.30 pm; closed weekday L.

Rasoi Vineet Bhatia SW3 £80 ✪
10 Lincoln St 7225 1881 4–2D
"Sublime and zingy" spicing creates "1001 intoxicating flavours" for visitors to Vineet Bhatia's "tucked-away" Chelsea townhouse – a "bizarre" home for such a pre-eminent "nouvelle-Indian"; prices are "sky high", though, and – perhaps with the distraction of the Urban Turban launch? – ratings overall slipped this year. / Value tip: set weekday L £46 (FP). Details: www.rasoirestaurant.co.uk; 11 pm; closed Sat L & Sun.

Rebato's SW8 £32 Ⓐ
169 South Lambeth Rd 7735 6388
Thanks to its "wonderful", "it-could-be-Spain" ambience and "supremely nice" staff, "people just love" this "unchanging" Vauxhall "stalwart" – eat "cheap" tapas in the "crowded" bar, or visit the restaurant and take a "Tardis ride to the '70s". / Details: www.rebatos.com; 10.45 pm; closed Sat L & Sun.

Red Fort W1 £60 ✪
77 Dean St 7437 2525 3–2A
For a "very central" Indian, it's hard to beat this "quiet" and "gracious" veteran (which underwent a "fresh and modern" revamp a few years ago) – its "excellent" cuisine is up there with the Tamarinds and Cinnamon Clubs of the world. / Value tip: set pre theatre £40 (FP). Details: www.redfort.co.uk; 11.30 pm; closed Sat L & Sun.

Le Relais de Venise L'Entrecôte W1   £35   A ⭐

120 Marylebone Ln   7486 0878   1–1A

"Regular queues" attest to the (growing) popularity of this "crowded" Parisian import, where "the only choice you need make is the wine" – otherwise it's "steak, steak, steak", plus "proper" thin cut fries and an "intriguing" secret sauce (and seconds if you want 'em).
/ **Details:** www.relaisdevenise.com; 10.45 pm, Sun 10.30 pm.

Retsina NW3   £36

48-50 Belsize Ln   7431 5855

"Mama's in the kitchen and son's serving", at this Belsize Park yearling – fans say it's "everything a family-run Greek should be", but not all reporters are convinced its standards are being maintained.
/ **Details:** 11 pm; no Amex.

Rhodes 24 EC2   £68   A

25 Old Broad St   7877 7703

"Amazing views" ("to impress any client") help create "a professional environment for business", at Gary Rhodes's 24th-floor City dining room, where the British grub is "totally consistent", if "eye-wateringly-priced"; NB: "allow extra time for lifts and officious security measures".
/ **Details:** www.rhodes24.co.uk; 9 pm; closed Sat & Sun; no shorts; booking essential.

Rhodes W1 Restaurant
Cumberland Hotel W1   £87

Gt Cumberland Pl   7616 5930   1–2A

"Brilliant and inventive", or "underwhelming in its over-complication"? – both schools of thought are strongly represented in feedback on Gary R's "luxurious" and "rather self-conscious" yearling, near Marble Arch.
/ **Value tip:** set weekday L £56 (FP). **Details:** www.rhodesw1.com; 10.30 pm; closed Mon, Sat L & Sun; no trainers.

Rib Room
Jumeirah Carlton Tower Hotel SW1   £85

2 Cadogan Pl   7858 7250   4–1D

"What must those poor Yanks think, getting charged a hundred bucks for a grill?" – the roast beef (and steak) may arguably be "the best in town", but this Knightsbridge dining room is a "staid" place that critics find "obscenely expensive". / **Value tip:** set weekday L £63 (FP). **Details:** www.jumeirah.com; 10.45 pm, Sun 10.15 pm.

El Rincón Latino SW4   £28   A

148 Clapham Manor St   7622 0599

"The liveliest and friendliest tapas bar ever"; this little-known "family-run affair", in Clapham, serves up "traditional" dishes at "amazingly low prices". / **Details:** 11.30 pm; closed Mon, Tue L, Wed L, Thu L, Fri L & Sun D.

Ristorante Semplice W1 £46

10 Blenheim St 7495 1509 2–2B

WINNER 2009

🏇 RÉMY MARTIN
FINE CHAMPAGNE COGNAC

"You'd never know you were just off Oxford Street", at this "hidden-away" Mayfair yearling – a "caring" (if "somewhat cramped") kind of place, offering some "terrific" modern Italian cuisine.
/ ***Details:*** *www.ristorantesemplice.com; 10.30 pm; closed Sat L & Sun.*

The Ritz Restaurant
The Ritz W1 £100 Ⓐ

150 Piccadilly 7493 8181 2–4C
To visit this "divine" Louis XVI-style chamber, overlooking Green Park, is to enter "a cosseted world of butter-poached lobster and champagne" – "not for modernists", clearly, but a wow for old-fashioned romantics; the food is "much-improved" on a few years ago… but then it had an awfully long way to go. / ***Value tip:*** *set weekday L £68 (FP).* ***Details:*** *www.theritzlondon.com; 10.30 pm; jacket & tie required.*

Riva SW13 £50 ⭐

169 Church Rd 8748 0434
"Superb, simple, seasonal cooking" and "skilled" service have – despite occasional protests that the place is "over-hyped" – long won approval for Andreas Riva's "smooth" Barnes Venetian; prepare, though, to "make your own atmosphere". / ***Details:*** *10.30 pm; closed Sat L.*

The River Café W6 £64 Ⓐ⭐

Thames Wharf, Rainville Rd 7386 4200 6–2C
"Outside, on a warm summer evening" – that's the time to visit Rose Gray and Ruth Rogers' world-famous (but "casual") Hammersmith Italian; the "simple" rustic cooking "continues to be memorable"… but "OMG, the prices are insane". / ***Details:*** *www.rivercafe.co.uk; 9 pm, Sat 9.15 pm; closed Sun D.*

Roast
The Floral Hall SE1 £55

Stoney St 7940 1300
Only for "gorgeous" breakfasts and brunches can this "fantastic" first-floor space, above Borough Market, be safely recommended – otherwise, its British fare is too often "a waste of ingredients", and the service can be a "nightmare" too. / ***Value tip:*** *set Sun L £41 (FP).* ***Details:*** *www.roast-restaurant.com; 10.45 pm; closed Sun D.*

Roka W1 £53

37 Charlotte St 7580 6464 1–1C

For "Zuma minus the attitude", seek out its "more relaxed" Fitzrovia sibling – the latter "oozes cool" and serves up an "absolutely amazing" mix of "obliging" service and "sublime" Japanese fare (including "brilliant robata grill dishes"); the basement Shochu bar also offers "a really hip night out". / **Details:** www.rokarestaurant.com; 11.15 pm; booking: max 8.

Ronnie Scott's W1 £44

47 Frith St 7439 0747 3–2A

The legendary Soho jazz club may offer a "wonderful" night out, but it's mainly down to "the atmosphere and the music" – "let's be honest, you don't come here for the food". / **Details:** www.ronniescotts.co.uk; 3 am, Sun midnight; D only.

Rosemary Lane E1 £44

61 Royal Mint St 7481 2602

This "hidden gem", in a former boozer, lurks in the no-man's-land just east of Tower Hill; it's a "homely" – some say "romantic" – place, where the cooking is "seasonal" and "precise". / **Value tip:** set weekday L £29 (FP). **Details:** www.rosemarylane.btinternet.co.uk; 10 pm; closed Sat L & Sun.

Roussillon SW1 £73

16 St Barnabas St 7730 5550 4–2D

"A great unsung hero of London gastronomy"; Gerard Virolle's "exceptional" tasting menus – with "beautifully matched" wines – are the star attraction at this "classy" but perhaps slightly "sombre" Pimlico fixture, which never quite achieves the profile it deserves. / **Value tip:** set weekday L £50 (FP). **Details:** www.roussillon.co.uk; 11 pm; closed Sat L & Sun; booking: max 11.

Royal China Club £57

40-42 Baker St, W1 7486 3898 1–1A
68 Queen's Grove, NW8 7586 4280

"Clattering deep-sea horrors in the aquarium" set the scene at the fine dining flagship of the well-known Chinese chain, in Marylebone; it serves "superb dim sum" and other "first-rate" fare ("with a strong bias to fish"), but even fans can't help noting it's "very, very expensive"; a St John's Wood twin recently opened.
/ **Details:** www.royalchinagroup.co.uk.

Rules WC2   **£60**   Ⓐ

35 Maiden Ln   7836 5314   3–3D

"Popular with US tourists, but who cares?" – why shouldn't they like this beautiful Covent Garden veteran (1798), with its "quirky" character and its "honest, traditional fare" (with "great game in season" a highlight); NB: the splendid upstairs rooms are no longer used for private hire.
/ **Details:** www.rules.co.uk; 11.30 pm, Sun 10.30 pm; no shorts.

Sagar   **£22**   ✪✪

17a, Percy St, W1   7631 3319   2–2B
157 King St, W6   8741 8563   6–2C
27 York St, TW1   8744 3868

Now with a branch in central London, this growing South Indian veggie chain combines "courteous" and "smiley" service with "superb" and "subtle" cooking, and all at "incredibly reasonable" prices. / **Value tip:** set weekday L £12 (FP). **Details:** www.gosagar.com; Sun-Thu 10.45 pm, Fri & Sat 11.30 pm.

St Alban SW1   **£52**

4-12 Lower Regent St, Rex Hs   7499 8558   2–3D

Corbin & King's efforts to perfect their "calm" Theatreland yearling are bearing fruit – the "Med-inspired" cooking is now very "decent" (if not yet inspired), and the service well up to their trademark "effortlessly slick" level; perhaps one day everyone will love the "somewhat weird", "'70s airport lounge" interior too. / **Details:** www.stalban.net; midnight, Sun 11 pm.

St John EC1   **£48**   ✪✪

26 St John St   7251 0848

"Take your courage in both teeth, and eat the unthinkable"; Fergus Henderson's "passionate", "functional"-looking Smithfield shrine to "nose-to-tail eating" (with much emphasis on the offally bits) has now achieved international acclaim as a "uniquely British" institution.
/ **Details:** www.stjohnrestaurant.com; 11 pm; closed Sat L & Sun.

St John Bread & Wine E1   **£40**   ✪✪

94-96 Commercial St   7251 0848

"Awesome" (determinedly "unfussy") British dishes and "eclectic" wine – all at very "affordable" prices – make for a "cool" overall experience at this "noisy and very plain" Spitalfields Market canteen; "where else can you just walk in and order brains on toast?"
/ **Details:** www.stjohnbreadandwine.com; 10.30 pm; closed Sun D.

St Johns N19 £39

91 Junction Rd   7272 1587

A "lovely, high-ceilinged dining room" (built as a music hall) helps create a "vibey" ambience at this "so popular" Archway gastropub; as ever, its "delicious", "seasonal" cooking wins high praise, but there were also a fair few "blips" this year. / **Details:** 11 pm, Sun 9.30 pm; Mon-Thu D only, Fri-Sun open L & D; booking: max 12.

Sake No Hana SW1 £111

23 St James's St   0871 7925 8988   2–4C

"Oh my God, I can't believe how bad it was!"; Alan Yau's "surprisingly weak" Japanese newcomer (on the former St James's site of Shumi, RIP) is an out-and-out turkey – it inspires far too many reports of "clueless" staff, serving up "bland and disappointing" food at "ridiculous" prices. / **Details:** 11 pm, Sat 11.30 pm; closed Sun; no trainers.

Saki Bar & Food Emporium EC1 £44

4 West Smithfield   7489 7033

"A basement Japanese, with a proper sushi bar", and which offers "amazing oriental cocktails" too; in fact, this "ambitious" Smithfield operation lacks only one thing – "atmosphere". / **Details:** www.saki-food.com; 10.30 pm; closed Sat L & Sun.

Sale e Pepe SW1 £46

9-15 Pavilion Rd   7235 0098   4–1D

"Crazy Italian staff" dish out "a lot of banter" – as well as "ample" and "reliable" classic dishes – at this "fun", "cramped" and "noisy" trattoria, near Harrods. / **Details:** www.saleepepe.co.uk; 11.30 pm; closed Sun; no shorts.

Salt Yard W1 £37

54 Goodge St   7637 0657   1–1B

"Stunning" tapas – "novel combos" of "well-sourced Spanish and Italian ingredients" – and a "dangerously drinkable" wine list underpin the "mad popularity" of this "casual" and "friendly" Fitzrovian; (beware the "pokey" basement, though). / **Details:** www.saltyard.co.uk; 11 pm; closed Sat L & Sun.

Santa Maria del Sur SW8 £38

129 Queenstown Rd   7622 2088

"Is there better steak in London?" than at this "brilliant", if "very basic", Battersea meat-eaters' "haven"; "as we say in Argentina, que barbaro!" / **Details:** www.buenayre.co.uk; 10.30 pm; closed weekday L.

Santini SW1 £66

29 Ebury St   7730 4094   1–4B

"Well-spaced tables" help this once-glamorous Belgravia Italian retain something of a business following among reporters; it's "eye-wateringly expensive for what it is", though, given the "disappointingly ordinary" food, and sometimes "appalling" service. / **Details:** www.santini-restaurant.com; 11 pm; closed Sat L & Sun L.

Sargasso Sea N21 £55

10 Station Rd   8360 0990

It's "a little pricey for Winchmore Hill", but this first-rate local offers "very good" fish cooking, and a "special" all-round experience. / **Value tip:** set weekday L £31 (FP). **Details:** www.sargassosea.co.uk; 10.30 pm; closed Mon, Tue L, Wed L, Sat L & Sun D.

Sarracino NW6 £38 ⭐

186 Broadhurst Gdns 7372 5889

"Baked in a roaring fire in full view" – the pizza (sold "al metro")
is "excellent", and "great-value" too, at this "relaxed, friendly and tightly-
packed" West Hampstead Italian. / **Details:** www.sarracinorestaurant.com/;
11 pm; closed weekday L.

Scalini SW3 £58 🅰⭐

1-3 Walton St 7225 2301 4–2C

"Not cheap but great fun" – this "tightly-packed" and "noisy" Italian
is "perpetually mobbed" with a well-heeled Knightsbridge crowd.
/ **Details:** midnight.

Scarpetta TW11 £35 🅰⭐

78 High St 8977 8177

"A great local Italian", in downtown Teddington, praised for both its
"authentic" wood-fired pizza and its "delicious fresh pasta";
unsurprisingly, it's "always very busy". / **Details:** www.scarpetta.co.uk;
11 pm; no shorts.

The Scarsdale W8 £33 🅰

23a Edwardes Sq 7937 1811 6–1D

A "fabulous" Kensington hostelry on one of London's prettiest squares;
it retains the feel of "a real pub", and the menu hasn't 'gone gastro'
either – you get "good Sunday roasts", "succulent" burgers and so on.
/ **Details:** 10 pm.

Scott's W1 £68 🅰⭐

20 Mount St 7495 7309 2–3A

"A great revival of a wonderful institution"; just like its sibling J Sheekey,
this "beautifully refurbished" Mayfair veteran offers "sublime" seafood
cooking and "super-slick" service; the more spacious interior here
affords more chances to "see-and-be-seen", however – perhaps why it's
fast becoming the 'new Ivy'. / **Details:** www.scotts-restaurant.com; 10.30 pm.

Seven Stars WC2 £28 🅰

53 Carey St 7242 8521 1–2D

A "quirky" boozer behind the Royal Courts of Justice that's "full of
character", thanks to landlady Roxy Beaujolais's "eccentric,
and sometimes rude" service; the food is "variable, but often good".
/ **Details:** 11 pm.

Shanghai Blues WC1 £53 ⭐

193-197 High Holborn 7404 1668 3–1D

"Spot-on cocktails" and "chic" décor set the tone of this "pricey"
Holborn yearling, where "great dim sum" is the high point of some
"very good" Chinese cuisine. / **Details:** www.shanghaiblues.co.uk; 11.30 pm.

J Sheekey WC2 £63 🅰⭐⭐

28-32 St Martin's Ct 7240 2565 3–3B

For the sixth year, the survey's most-mentioned destination –
this "very special" Theatreland "classic" offers a "polished" formula
of "simple" but "superlative" fishy fare, served up by "brisk" but
"courteous" staff, in a "gorgeous" "warren" of panelled rooms.
/ **Details:** www.j-sheekey.co.uk; midnight.

Shikara SW3   **£29** ☆

87 Sloane Ave   7581 6555   4–2C

*Beware, 'hot' means 'HOT', at this "well-priced" but "under-rated" curry house, whose straightforward approach is rather at odds with its chichi Brompton Cross location. / **Details:** www.shikara.com; 11.30 pm.*

Shogun W1   **£61** ☆

Adam's Row   7493 1255   2–3A

*An "easily-missed" Japanese basement, in Mayfair, where the décor is "poor and tired-looking", but the "wonderful" food and "excellent" service more than make up for it. / **Details:** 11 pm; D only, closed Mon.*

Simpson's Tavern EC3   **£28** Ⓐ

38 1/2 Ball Ct, Cornhill   7626 9985

Most (if not quite all) reporters love this "jolly good-value" ancient chophouse, in a City back-alley, where "perfect" waitresses ("all 70+") serve up "traditional British food" in "proper portions".
*/ **Details:** www.simpsonstavern.co.uk; L only, closed Sat & Sun.*

Simpsons-in-the-Strand WC2   **£60** ✖

100 Strand   7836 9112   3–3D

It retains a good degree of "old worlde" charm (and breakfast is a highlight), but this Covent Garden temple to roast beef can seem a "disappointing" sort of place, with "badly-trained" staff and "leaden" fare; (rather worryingly, the management here are also in charge of re-launching the neighbouring Savoy in 2009).
*/ **Details:** www.fairmont.com/simpsons; 10.45 pm, Sun 9 pm; no jeans or trainers.*

Singapore Garden NW6   **£36** ☆

83a Fairfax Rd   7624 8233

A "tucked-away" Swiss Cottage favourite; "amusing" staff and "very reliable" pan-oriental dishes ensure it's "always packed".
*/ **Details:** www.singaporegarden.co.uk; 11 pm, Fri-Sat 11.30 pm.*

Sitaaray WC2   **£33** Ⓐ☆

167 Drury Ln   7269 6422   3–1C

*A "very kitsch" Bollywood-themed Covent Garden Indian, that can be "immense fun"; menus are all 'set', making it especially well-suited to a party. / **Details:** www.sitaaray.com; 1 am.*

(Lecture Room)
Sketch W1   **£101** ✖

9 Conduit St   0870 777 4488   2–2C

*"Full of people with more money than sense"; a "super-value" set lunch aside, few reporters have much nice to say about this "pretentious" and "blindingly expensive" Mayfair dining room, associated with Parisian über-chef Pierre Gagnaire. / **Value tip:** set weekday L £39 (FP). **Details:** www.sketch.uk.com; 10.30 pm; closed Mon, Sat L & Sun; booking: max 8.*

(Gallery)
Sketch W1 £66
9 Conduit St 0870 777 4488 2–2C
"Unless you feel the need 'to be seen'", this "shockingly overpriced"
Mayfair fashionista hot spot is "just not worth it" – "rude" service and
"crummy" food figure in far too many reports, and even the "quirky"
*décor is inspiring ever less excitement. / **Details:** www.sketch.uk.com; 1 am;*
D only, closed Sun; booking: max 12.

Skylon
South Bank Centre SE1 £56
Southbank Centre, Belvedere Rd 7654 7800 1–3D
"The RFH deserves better" than the year-old D&D-group régime at this
vast Thames-side chamber, where "off-hand" staff serve up food that's
"average at best" – as so often with the group, the "stunning view"
*is presumably supposed to compensate for everything else. / **Value***
***tip:** set weekday L £43 (FP). **Details:** www.danddlondon.com; 10.45 pm.*

Ⓐ⭐
Snazz Sichuan NW1 £32
37 Chalton St 7388 0808
"Scarily fiery" Sichuan cuisine, "as authentic as it gets", is the draw
to this "off-the-beaten-track" yearling, near Euston, where "genuine"
staff add to the ambience (and "recent improvements to the décor"
*have helped too). / **Details:** www.newchinaclub.co.uk; 10.30 pm.*

Ⓐ⭐
Sotheby's Café W1 £46
34 New Bond St 7293 5077 2–2C
You may eat "cheek by jowl", at this "buzzy" café, off the foyer of the
famous Mayfair auction house, but it offers a "very classy" experience
*overall, and the food is "always delicious". / **Details:** www.sothebys.com;*
L only, closed Sat & Sun.

Ⓐ
Souk Medina WC2 £32
1A Short Gdns 7240 1796 3–2B
"A good place, if you're in a big group who really don't care about the
food" – this Moroccan 'riad'-style joint, on the fringe of Covent Garden,
is tailor-made for parties, thanks to its "fab service and lovely vibe".
*/ **Details:** www.soukrestaurant.co.uk; midnight.*

Ⓐ⭐
Spacca Napoli W1 £29
101 Dean St 7437 9440 2–1D
This "fun" trattoria, just off Oxford Street, is especially worth knowing
about for its "perfect" pizza-by-the-metre; no wonder it's "always
*packed with Italians". / **Details:** www.spaccanapoli.co.uk; 11 pm.*

⭐
The Square W1 £88
6-10 Bruton St 7495 7100 2–2C
"You're sure to impress your client", at this "very professional" and
"formal" Mayfair venue, thanks to Philip Howard's "fantastically crafted"
dishes and a "stupendous selection of wine"; despite all this excellence,
*though, the overall effect can seem a little "dull". / **Value tip:** set*
*weekday L £48 (FP). **Details:** www.squarerestaurant.org; 10.45 pm; closed*
Sat L & Sun L.

Sree Krishna SW17 £24

192-194 Tooting High St   8672 4250

You get "loads of flavour for amazing prices", at this "reliable" and "authentic" south Indian veteran, in Tooting. / **Details:** www.sreekrishna.co.uk; 10.45 pm, Fri & Sat midnight.

Story Deli
The Old Truman Brewery E1 £27

3 Dray Walk   7247 3137

"Scrumptious", "paper-thin" pizzas help fuel the "mad popularity" of this "original" and "very organic" hang-out, in a "converted retail unit off Brick Lane" – "an intimate space with a large communal table and mismatched fixtures and fittings". / **Details:** 9 pm during summer.

Suka
Sanderson W1 £70

50 Berners St   7300 1444   2–1D

Few – and mostly negative – reports on this oh-so-trendy design-hotel dining room, just north of Oxford Street; it can seem "frighteningly expensive", especially for Malaysian food, which "doesn't lend itself well to such a chichi environment". / **Details:** www.sandersonlondon.com; 12.30 am, Sun 10.30 pm.

Sukho Thai Cuisine SW6 £39

855 Fulham Rd   7371 7600

"Sparkling" cuisine – "the best Thai food in London", say some reporters – makes this "cramped", but "charming" and "colourful" Fulham gem "very, very popular, so book". / **Details:** 11 pm.

Sumosan W1 £75

26b Albemarle St   7495 5999   2–3C

Re-establishing itself as a "good alternative to Nobu"; this "trendy" Mayfair Japanese has "a newly-acquired buzz", and serves some "superb" dishes (including "very good sushi"); prices are "extreme", of course, so remember the "incredible-value" lunch deal. / **Value tip:** set weekday L £37 (FP). **Details:** www.sumosan.com; 11.30 pm; closed Sat L & Sun L.

Le Suquet SW3 £53

104 Draycott Ave   7581 1785   4–2C

"You still get the best plâteau de fruits-de-mer in town", at this "très français" veteran, near Brompton Cross – it "never changes" ("which, in this case, is a good thing"). / **Value tip:** set weekday L £36 (FP). **Details:** 11.30 pm.

Sushi-Hiro W5 £39

1 Station Pde   8896 3175

"An authentic experience that can be a bit overwhelming for westerners"; "phenomenally fresh" sushi and sashimi that's "a work of genius" come at "incredibly low prices" at this ultra-"utilitarian" diner, near Ealing Common Tube – it's "well worth the trek". / **Details:** 9 pm; closed Mon; no credit cards.

Sushi-Say NW2 £40 ⭐⭐
33b Walm Ln 8459 7512
"Forget the West End, and head here for the best sushi in town";
this "family-owned" café is an "amazing find in Willesden Green" –
the food is "outstanding", and the service is "so polite" too.
/ **Details:** 10 pm, Sat & Sun 10.30 pm; closed Mon; no Amex.

The Swan W4 £37 Ⓐ
119 Acton Ln 8994 8262 6–1A
"With all the gastropubs there are in Chiswick, to stand out is quite
something" – a feat this hidden-away local pulls off, thanks to its
"seasonal" food, "smiling" staff and "the bonus of a great garden".
/ **Details:** 10.30 pm; closed weekday L; no booking.

The Swan At The Globe SE1 £41 Ⓐ
New Globe Walk 7928 9444
"Make sure you book a table with a river-view", if you visit the elegant
first-floor brasserie of the South Bank tavern by Shakespeare's Globe;
the "simple" food is no great shakes, but generally gets a thumbs-up.
/ **Details:** www.swanattheglobe.co.uk; 10.30 pm.

The Table SE1 £32 ⭐
83 Southwark St 7401 2760
Part of the Southwark offices of a prominent firm of architects,
this "stylish" canteen can make an "outstanding" destination for
breakfast or a "healthy" lunch. / **Details:** www.thetablecafe.com; 9 pm;
Mon-Thu & Sat L only, Fri open L & D, closed Sun.

Taiwan Village SW6 £27 ⭐
85 Lillie Rd 7381 2900 4–3A
"Choose 'leave it to the chef', and let them entertain you" – that's the
way to get the best from this "out-of-the-way" Fulham Chinese, where
the food is usually "amazing". / **Details:** www.taiwanvillage.com; 11.30 pm;
closed Mon L.

Tajima Tei EC1 £31 ⭐
9-11 Leather Ln 7404 9665
"There's a high percentage of Japanese diners", at this "slightly tatty"
and "off-the-beaten-track" oriental, near Hatton Gardens – must have
something to do with "authentic" food at "excellent" prices.
/ **Details:** www.tajima-tei.co.uk; 10 pm; closed Sat L & Sun.

Taman Gang W1 £77 Ⓐ
141 Park Ln 7518 3160 1–2A
A lavish Mayfair basement hang-out for "oligarchs and Eurotrash";
the oriental food is "very acceptable", but can also – surprise, surprise –
seem "overpriced". / **Details:** www.tamangang.com; 11.30 pm; D only, closed
Sun; booking: max 6.

Tamarind W1 £58 ⭐
20 Queen St 7629 3561 2–3B
Alfred Prasad's "mouthwatering" and "delicate" cuisine maintains this
"sophisticated" Mayfair venture in the vanguard of the 'nouvelle Indian'
movement; for a basement, "it feels quite airy and spacious" too. / **Value
tip:** set weekday L £42 (FP). **Details:** www.tamarindrestaurant.com; 11.15 pm;
closed Sat L.

Tandoori Lane SW6 £26

131a Munster Rd 7371 0440

"Behind blacked-out windows", in deepest Fulham, this superior Indian veteran has long been of note for its "friendly" service and its "good, non-greasy curries". / Details: 11.15 pm; no Amex.

Tandoori Nights SE22 £31

73 Lordship Ln 8299 4077

"Light and fresh-tasting dishes" have made this "absolutely excellent" curry house "the default choice in the area" for many East Dulwich types; unsurprisingly, it gets "very crowded and noisy". / Details: 11.30 pm; closed weekday L & Sat L.

Tatsuso EC2 £80

32 Broadgate Circle 7638 5863

The décor is "naff" (especially in the basement restaurant, less so in the ground-floor teppan-yaki), but this veteran Broadgate Japanese remains a "great business lunch venue", thanks to its "very authentic" cuisine; prices, though, are "breathtaking". / Details: 10.15 pm; closed Sat & Sun.

Tawana W2 £33

3 Westbourne Grove 7229 3785 5–1C

"Where are all the people?" – despite its "consistently good Thai food", this unpretentious establishment, by the Queensway junction, is "often inexplicably empty". / Details: www.tawana.co.uk; 11 pm.

Ten Ten Tei W1 £35

56 Brewer St 7287 1738 2–2D

A "grotty"-looking Soho dive that's "always filled with Japanese customers", thanks to its "tasty", "quick" and "authentic" scoff that "doesn't cost the earth". / Details: 10 pm; closed Sun; no Amex.

Tendido Cuatro SW6 £38

108-110 New King's Rd 7371 5147

Despite the 'Cuatro', this is actually the third venture from the Cambio de Tercio team; a new Parson's Green tapas bar, it's a congenial, colourful, spacious sort of place, with food that, on our early-days visit, was very good indeed. / Details: 11 pm.

Tentazioni SE1 £53

2 Mill St 7394 5248

An "eager-to-please" chef/patron cooks up some "rich and luxurious" Italian dishes at this "intimate" and "un-rushed" Bermondsey spot; doubters find the food a touch "fussy", though. / Value tip: set weekday L £20 (FP). Details: www.tentazioni.co.uk; 10.45 pm; closed Mon L, Sat L & Sun.

Terranostra EC4 £43

27 Old Bailey 3201 0077

A "decent" new Italian, near the Old Bailey, that's "better than it looks from the outside"; "lovely" staff present Sardinian cooking that's a "cut above" the norm, and "reasonably priced" too. / Details: www.terranostrafood.co.uk; 10 pm; closed Sat L & Sun.

Texture W1   **£70**
34 Portman Sq   7224 0028   1–2A

WINNER 2009

RÉMY MARTIN
FINE CHAMPAGNE COGNAC

An "innovative" Marylebone newcomer, offering "spectacular"
contemporary cooking (albeit in a style ridiculed by critics for its "smears
and foams"); the dining room makes the most elegant possible use
of the difficult space that was formerly Deya (RIP).
/ **Details:** www.texture-restaurant.co.uk; 11 pm; closed Mon & Sun.

Theo Randall
InterContinental Hotel W1   **£78**
1 Hamilton Pl   7318 8747   2–4A
"OK, the room is dull and windowless", but the "sparkling" Italian food
"makes up for it", say fans of this "gloomy" Mayfair yearling (named
after its chef, who was formerly top toque at the River Café); critics who
find it "over-hyped and over-priced", though, are gaining ground. / **Value
tip:** set weekday L £52 (FP). **Details:** www.theorandall.com; 11.15 pm; closed
Sat L & Sun.

Thomas Cubitt SW1   **£54**
44 Elizabeth St   7730 6060   1–4A
In surprisingly "under-served" Belgravia, this "posh" but "lively"
gastropub remains "streets ahead" of other local hang-outs; upstairs
(price given), the "tranquil and relaxing" dining room serves up some
quite "interesting" dishes too. / **Value tip:** set weekday L £39
(FP). **Details:** www.thethomascubitt.co.uk; 10 pm.

The Three Bridges SW8   **£37**
153 Battersea Park Rd   7720 0204
"Don't be deceived by the modest looks" or the "unpromising" location
of this Italian newcomer, near Battersea Dogs Home; "exuberant"
service and "un-flashy" food in "generous" portions make it "the perfect
local". / **Details:** www.thethreebridges.com; 11 pm; closed Sun.

Toff's N10   **£31**
38 Muswell Hill Broadway   8883 8656
Fans say it's "worth a ticket" – "parking is a nightmare" – to enjoy the
"fantastic" fish 'n' chips served in "vast" portions at this "friendly"
Muswell Hill stalwart. / **Details:** www.toffsfish.co.uk; 10 pm; closed Sun;
no booking, Sat.

Tom Aikens SW3 £91

43 Elystan St   7584 2003   4–2C

*Tom Aikens's "Zen-like" ("cold") Chelsea HQ serves up "elaborate" –
and sometimes "astonishing" – dishes, which critics have always
dismissed as "trying too hard"; as his empire grows, though, results are
becoming ever more "hit-and-miss", and yet prices remain
as "unbelievable" as ever. / **Value tip:** set weekday L £45
(FP). **Details:** www.tomaikens.co.uk; 11 pm; closed Sat & Sun; jacket and/or tie;
booking: max 8.*

Tom Ilic SW8 £38   ●●

123 Queenstown Rd   7622 0555

*"Tom Illic is trying very hard", at this Battersea newcomer (on the
former site of the Food Room, RIP), and many reporters already
attest to the "unbelievable value" offered by his "hearty" and
"innovative" cuisine; sometimes "chaotic" service needs work, though,
as does the "dreary" décor. / **Details:** www.tomilic.com; 10.30 pm; closed
Mon, Tue L, Sat L & Sun D.*

Toto's SW1 £66   Ⓐ

Lennox Gardens Mews   7589 0075   4–2C

*"Hidden-away", near Harrods, a "lovely", "professional" and "old-
fashioned" Italian that's always been regarded as quite a "gem";
doubters, though, are beginning to find the approach rather "dated".
/ **Value tip:** set weekday L £50 (FP). **Details:** 11 pm, Sun 10.30 pm.*

Trader Vics
Hilton Hotel W1 £70   ✖

22 Park Ln   7208 4113   2–4A

*"Past the sell-by"; this Park Lane basement tikki-bar may still
do "very good cocktails", but service is "uninterested", food "disgraceful"
and prices "astonishing". / **Details:** www.tradervics.com; 12.30 am; closed
Sat L & Sun L.*

Trinity SW4 £51   ✪

4 The Polygon   7622 1199

*Adam Byatt's "seriously accomplished" cooking makes for some
"extraordinary" dining experiences at this "quiet" Clapham yearling;
shame that its opening was "over-hyped", though, which led some
reporters to visit with unduly lofty expectations. / **Value tip:** set weekday L
£36 (FP). **Details:** www.trinityrestaurant.co.uk; 10.30 pm; closed Mon L.*

Les Trois Garçons E1 £73   Ⓐ

1 Club Row   7613 1924

*It's the "OTT" décor – "stuffed animals in tiaras", and so on – which
can make this East End pub-conversion an "absolutely fabulous"
destination (especially "for a first date"); its "bistro fare", however,
comes at "haute-cuisine prices". / **Value tip:** set always available £47
(FP). **Details:** www.lestroisgarcons.com; 9.30 pm; D only, closed Sun.*

La Trompette W4 £55   Ⓐ✪✪

5-7 Devonshire Rd   8747 1836   6–2A

*"Sophisticated" yet "very understated" – this Chiswick sidestreet jewel
is "well worth the journey", thanks to James Bennington's "dazzling"
cuisine ("especially at the price"), the "exceptional" service and a wine
list that's "one of the best thought-through and best-value in the capital".
/ **Value tip:** set weekday L £39 (FP). **Details:** www.latrompette.co.uk; 10.30 pm,
Sun 10 pm; booking: max 6.*

Troubadour SW5 £32 Ⓐⓧ
263-267 Old Brompton Rd   7370 1434   4–3A
"The bohemian atmosphere of the '60s" lives on at this "chilled" Earl's
Court coffee house (and it has a nice "sun trap" garden too); service
is "patchy", though, and the food "below par".
/ **Details:** www.troubadour.co.uk; 11.30 pm; no Amex.

La Trouvaille W1 £50 Ⓐ⭐
12a Newburgh St   7287 8488   2–2C
"An excellent bolt hole, off Carnaby Street", which certainly is a 'find',
thanks to its "superior" Gallic fare, "fantastic" wines, "friendly" staff and
"elegant and cosy" setting; "downstairs is the more casual wine bar –
upstairs the more formal dining room". / **Value tip:** set weekday L £33
(FP). **Details:** www.latrouvaille.co.uk; 11 pm; closed Sun.

Tsunami SW4 £37 ⭐
5-7 Voltaire Rd   7978 1610
What's up, at this "really quite amazing" Clapham Japanese?;
its "Zuma-quality sushi at local prices" is (mostly) "still up to scratch",
but service has often seemed "inattentive" of late, and the "dated and
tacky" décor now "needs refreshing".
/ **Details:** www.tsunamirestaurant.co.uk; 10.30 pm, Fri & Sat 11 pm,
Sun 9.30 pm; closed weekday L.

Two Brothers N3 £30 ⭐
297-303 Regent's Park Rd   8346 0469
"We've been dining here monthly for nearly 20 years, and it never
disappoints!" – this Finchley institution is hailed by its large fan club
as "the best chippy in London"; (the brothers departed this year,
but feedback suggests that standards have been maintained, and maybe
even improved). / **Details:** www.twobrothers.co.uk; 10.15 pm; closed Mon &
Sun; no booking at D.

2 Veneti W1 £54
10 Wigmore St   7637 0789   2–1B
"Impeccable" and "friendly" service is the stand-out feature of this
"authentic" Venetian yearling, near the Wigmore Hall; a "fabulous wine
list" rounds off a "classy" formula that's especially popular for business.
/ **Details:** www.2veneti.com; 10.30 pm; closed Sat L & Sun.

Ubon E14 £80
34 Westferry Circus   7719 7800
Nobu's "relaxed" Canary Wharf cousin is often preferred to the Mayfair
branches – it's "easier to book", has a "much more impressive view"
and comes "without all the nonsense"; unfortunately, however, bills here
are just as "outrageous". / **Details:** www.noburestaurants.com; 10 pm; closed
Sat L & Sun.

Uli W11 £30 ⭐
16 All Saints Rd   7727 7511   5–1B
This "charming" North Kensington neighbourhood spot has got the lot –
"service with a big smile", a menu offering an "eclectic mix" of "Thai-
influenced, Chinese" dishes, and a "lovely garden"; "let Michael choose
for you, and you won't go far wrong". / **Details:** www.uli-oriental.co.uk;
11 pm; D only, closed Sun; no Amex.

Umu W1 £120

14-16 Bruton Pl 7499 8881 2–2C

"This is simply IT", say fans of Marlon Abela's "chic" Japanese, in the heart of Mayfair, who extol its "divine" and "beautiful" Kyoto-style cuisine; prices are "quite extortionate", though, and service more "variable" than you might hope. / Details: www.umurestaurant.com; 10.30 pm; closed Sat L & Sun; no trainers; booking: max 14.

Uno SW1 £45

1 Denbigh St 7834 1001 1–4B

Having outgrown its pizzeria origins, this Pimlico corner spot is nowadays a cool-looking but "friendly", full-service Italian, offering a "very good" overall experience; it deserves to be more widely known. / Details: www.uno1.co.uk; 11pm, Sun & Mon 10.30 pm.

Upstairs Bar SW2 £38

89b Acre Ln (door on Branksome Rd) 7733 8855

"A very French and charming little eyrie above a main Brixton thoroughfare" – its "delicious" food, "attentive service" and "cosy" ambience make it "exceptional in every way". / Details: www.upstairslondon.com; 9.30 pm, Sat 10.30 pm; D only, closed Mon & Sun.

Le Vacherin W4 £42

76-77 South Pde 8742 2121 6–1A

Malcolm John's "little sliver of France in Chiswick" was "much improved by a revamp this year"; other aspects of this "great, great local" are unchanged, though – not least its "simple fare", offering "real Gallic flavours". / Details: www.levacherin.co.uk; 10.30 pm, Fri & Sat 11 pm, Sun 10 pm; closed Mon L.

Vanilla W1 £55

131 Great Titchfield St 3008 7763 2–1C

A "cool" and "funky" new basement operation "tucked-away" in Fitzrovia; newspaper critics lined up to slag it off, but we're with the numerous thirtysomethings who say it's a "hidden treasure", with a "great bar", an "inventive menu", and staff "who can't do enough for you". / Value tip: set weekday L £31 (FP). Details: www.vanillalondon.com; 10 pm; closed Mon, Sat L & Sun; no trainers.

Veeraswamy W1 £52

Victory Hs, 99-101 Regent St 7734 1401 2–3D

With its "sophisticated" cuisine and "sensual" décor, "London's oldest Indian, near Piccadilly Circus, still beats most of the opposition hands-down"; it manages to be both "traditional and fun", all at the same time. / Details: www.realindianfood.com; 10.30 pm, Sun 10 pm; booking: max 12.

El Vergel SE1 £18 ⒶⒶ

8 Lant St 7357 0057

"Is this the best cheap food in London?"; "zesty" Latino dishes at "ludicrously low prices" make it well "worth seeking out" this "cantina-style" joint, "hidden down a backstreet in Borough"; hurry... "you won't get a seat after 1 pm". / Details: www.elvergel.co.uk; breakfast & L only, closed Sat D & Sun; no credit cards.

Vijay NW6 £28 Ⓐ

49 Willesden Ln 7328 1087

"The décor's stuck in the '60s, but that's part of the quirky charm" of this "friendly" Kilburn veteran, to which fans return "time after time" for "great curries at low prices". / Details: www.vijayindia.com; 10.45 pm, Fri-Sat 11.30 pm.

Vino Rosso W4 £49 Ⓐ

9 Devonshire Rd 8994 5225 6–2A

This "deceptively modest-looking local Italian", in Chiswick, is a significant "cut above" the norm, and offers "surprisingly high-quality cooking" and super service. / Value tip: set weekday L £29 (FP). Details: www.vino-rosso.co.uk; 10.30 pm, Fri & Sat 11 pm, Sun 9.30 pm.

Vinoteca EC1 £35 Ⓐ

7 St John St 7253 8786

A "fabulous" and "reasonably-priced" wine selection is "enthusiastically" served at this "always-busy" Clerkenwell two-year-old; the "sturdy" bistro-fare is "lovely" too – no wonder it's "a bugger to get a table"! / Details: www.vinoteca.co.uk; 10 pm; closed Sun; no Amex.

Vrisaki N22 £30 Ⓐ

73 Myddleton Rd 8889 8760

"I dare you to try and finish the mezze!"; the food "just keeps coming", at this "consistently good" Greek taverna – an "institution", in an "unlikely" location, in a Bounds Green sidestreet. / Details: midnight, Sun 9 pm.

The Wallace
The Wallace Collection W1 £46 Ⓐ

Hertford Hs, Manchester Sq 7563 9505 2–1A

The "lovely" covered courtyard of this Marylebone palazzo is a setting to "lift the spirits" (and at night, you can even "see the stars"); the food – though "enjoyable" – can seem "overpriced", however, and service is sometimes "non-existent". / Details: www.thewallacerestaurant.com; Fri & Sat 9.30 pm; Sun-Thu closed D.

Wapping Food E1 £47 Ⓐ

Wapping Power Station, Wapping Wall 7680 2080

"You'll be surprised and impressed", by this "cavernous", "derelict-chic" East End power station – "a bizarre but wonderful" venue that's also surprisingly "romantic"; the food is "reliably imaginative", but is eclipsed by the "superb" Aussie wine list. / Details: www.thewappingproject.com; 10.30 pm; closed Sun D.

The Well EC1 £38 Ⓐ ✪

180 St John St 7251 9363
"A long-standing Clerkenwell gastropub, with an ever-growing clientele drawn from the apartment blocks sprouting all around"; no complacency, though – the food is now "very good" indeed.
/ **Details:** www.downthewell.com; 10.30 pm, Sun 10 pm.

The Wet Fish Cafe NW6 £39 Ⓐ

242 West End Ln 7443 9222
An "unusual and interesting" interior – an old fish shop – provides the "terrific" setting for this West Hampstead local, whose "well thought-out" menu is not in fact particularly fishy.
/ **Details:** www.thewetfishcafe.co.uk; 11 pm; closed Mon; no Amex.

Whits W8 £47 ✪

21 Abingdon Rd 7938 1122 4–1A
"A great find"; this "small but perfectly-formed" Kensington sidestreet "gem" offers "skillful" food, plus notably "charming" and "attentive" service. / **Details:** www.whits.co.uk; 10.30 pm; closed Mon, Tue–Sat D only, closed Sun D.

Wild Honey W1 £48 ✪

12 St George St 7758 9160 2–2C
"Another hit from the Arbutus team", say fans of this wildly popular Mayfair yearling, which similarly offers "gutsy" cuisine and "brilliant wines by the carafe"; doubters sniff a touch of "hype" though, and find the "crowded" setting rather "boring". / **Value tip:** set pre theatre £32 (FP). **Details:** www.wildhoneyrestaurant.co.uk; 10.30 pm, Sun 9.30 pm.

William IV NW10 £31 Ⓐ ✪

786 Harrow Rd 8969 5944
"You feel a million miles from the Harrow Road" – especially in the "beautiful" garden – at this "airy" (but "noisy") Kensal Green pub; it makes a "great local", where the fare includes "interesting tapas" and "gorgeous Sunday roasts". / **Details:** www.williamivlondon.com; 10.30 pm, Fri & Sat 11 pm, Sun 9.30 pm.

Wiltons SW1 £86 Ⓐ

55 Jermyn St 7629 9955 2–3C
"More gentleman's club than restaurant", this "classic" St James's fish specialist is a bastion of the sort of "stuffy" and "old-fashioned" values rarely seen nowadays – perhaps why riffraff may just find the place an "utter rip-off". / **Details:** www.wiltons.co.uk; 10.30 pm; closed Sat & Sun; jacket required.

The Windsor Castle W8 £29 Ⓐ

114 Campden Hill Rd 7243 8797 5–2B
With its wonderful "Olde English setting" and a "fantastic beer garden" ("if the sun shines"), it's no surprise that this ancient pub, near Notting Hill Gate, is always busy; in recent times, however, its fairly traditional grub has seemed ever more "average".
/ **Details:** www.windsorcastlepub.co.uk; 10 pm; no booking.

The Wine Library EC3   **£26**   A X

43 Trinity Sq   7481 0415

"The best range of wines at the most affordable prices" (retail,
plus modest corkage) draws City oenophiles to this merchant's cellar
(where nobody cares that the accompanying pâté and cheese buffet is a
bit *"pedestrian"*); thankfully, *"BlackBerries don't work down here..."*
/ **Details:** www.winelibrary.co.uk; 8 pm, except Mon 6 pm; L & early evening only,
closed Sat & Sun.

(Winter Garden)
The Landmark NW1   **£75**   A

222 Marylebone Rd   7631 8000

An *"impressive"* atrium provides the *"stunning"* setting for dining at this
Marylebone hotel; prices can seem *"outrageous"*, but the place is still
nominated for *"peaceful"* business meals, or for the *"memorable Sunday
champagne brunch"*. / **Value tip:** set weekday L £58
(FP). **Details:** www.landmarklondon.co.uk; 10.30 pm; no trainers; booking:
max 12.

The Wolseley W1   **£54**   A

160 Piccadilly   7499 6996   2–3C

"For sheer buzz" – Corbin & King's *"gloriously civilised"* grand café,
by the Ritz, is an all-hours *"people-watching heaven"* (and a *"power
scene"* too); utterly *"fabulous"* breakfasts aside, though, realisation of its
long and varied menu teeters on the brink of *"average"*.
/ **Details:** www.thewolseley.com; midnight, Sun 11 pm.

Wright Brothers SE1   **£40**   A ✩ ✩

11 Stoney St   7403 9554

"The freshest oysters in London" head up the array of *"beautiful, simple
seafood"* on offer at this *"cramped"* – but *"unique"*, *"fun"* and
"brilliantly buzzy" – Borough Market spot.
/ **Details:** www.wrightbros.eu.com; 10.30 pm; closed Sun.

Yauatcha W1 £50
Broadwick Hs, 15-17 Broadwick St   7494 8888   2–2D

"The best dim sum this side of Hong Kong" (plus "amazing" cocktails)
draw huge crowds to Alan Yau's "moody" Soho basement… which may
be why service is sometimes "surly"; on the ground floor, they also serve
"the most beautiful cakes". / *Details:* 11.30 pm.

Yi-Ban £31
Imperial Wharf, Imperial Rd, SW6   7731 6606   4–4B
Regatta Centre, Dockside Rd, E16   7473 6699
A "super, first-floor waterside location" – "with great views over
to London City Airport" – adds to the appeal of this "huge" Chinese
venture, which serves "excellent" food, including "a wide range of dim
sum"; (it also has an "expensive but worth-it" Fulham sibling, which
is rather under-patronised by virtue of its obscure position).
/ *Details:* www.yi-ban.co.uk; 10.45 pm; SW6 closed Sun; minimum £10.

Yming W1 £33
35-36 Greek St   7734 2721   3–2A
"Far better than Chinatown" – just on the other side of Shaftesbury
Avenue, Christine Lau's "civilised" Soho "secret" offers dishes ranging
from "flavoursome" to "exciting", as well as "efficient" service that's full
of "friendly charm". / *Details:* www.yminglondon.com; 11.45 pm; closed Sun.

Yoshino W1 £38
3 Piccadilly Pl   7287 6622   2–3D
"Like a little slice of Tokyo, tucked-away just off Piccadilly" –
this Japanese "secret" has "charming" staff, who dish up "super fresh
and zesty" sushi and sashimi, in a "peaceful" contemporary setting.
/ *Details:* www.yoshino.net; 9 pm; closed Sun.

Yum Yum N16 £29
187 Stoke Newington High St   7254 6751
"Yum yum indeed!"; this "always-reliable-and-popular Stokie Thai"
is now – after its move a couple of years ago – a "huge" place, but it
maintains "a brilliant atmosphere", and the food is "consistently
delicious" too. / *Details:* www.yumyum.co.uk; 11 pm, Fri & Sat midnight.

Zafferano SW1 £63 Ⓐ

15 Lowndes St   7235 5800   4–1D

"Classy, but not uptight", this Belgravia fixture has long been renowned as a *"cracking"* Italian; it remains a good all-rounder, but – like some other members of the London Fine Dining Group – has suffered a notable decline in ratings since the acquisition by John De Stefano in 2007. / **Details:** www.zafferanorestaurant.com; 11 pm, Sun 10.30 pm.

Zaika W8 £52 ✪✪

1 Kensington High St   7795 6533   4–1A

"A wonderful, under-rated Indian restaurant"; Sanjay Dwivedi's *"astonishing"* and *"innovative"* cuisine makes this *"upscale"* (if slightly *"cavernous"*) former Kensington banking hall a *"truly gourmet"* destination. / **Value tip:** set pre theatre £35 (FP). **Details:** www.zaika-restaurant.co.uk; 10.45 pm, Sun 9.45 pm.

Zuma SW7 £65 Ⓐ✪✪

5 Raphael St   7584 1010   4–1C

With its *"mind-blowingly good"* Japanese-fusion fare and its maniacally *"buzzing"* bar, this *"flashy"* Knightsbridge hang-out still *"has the edge over Nobu"* as London's No. 1 oriental; be warned, though: *"you have to climb over the Lamborghinis to get in"*.
/ **Details:** www.zumarestaurant.com; 10.45 pm, Sun 9.45 pm; booking: max 8.

LONDON AREA
OVERVIEWS

CENTRAL

Soho, Covent Garden & Bloomsbury
(Parts of W1, all WC2 and WC1)

£80+	Lindsay House	British, Modern	
	L'Atelier de Joel Robuchon	French	Ⓐ ✕
	Asia de Cuba	Fusion	Ⓐ
£70+	Quo Vadis	British, Traditional	
	Pearl	French	
	Kyashii	Japanese	
£60+	Simpsons-in-the-Strand	British, Traditional	✕
	Rules	"	Ⓐ
	J Sheekey	Fish & seafood	Ⓐ ✪ ✪
	Red Fort	Indian	✪
	Buddha Bar	Pan-Asian	
£50+	The Ivy	British, Modern	Ⓐ
	Clos Maggiore	French	Ⓐ ✪
	L'Escargot	"	Ⓐ ✪
	La Trouvaille	"	Ⓐ ✪
	Yauatcha	Chinese	Ⓐ ✪ ✪
	Shanghai Blues	"	✪
£40+	Joe Allen	American	Ⓐ
	Arbutus	British, Modern	✪
	Konstam	"	✪
	Randall & Aubin	French	Ⓐ
	Ronnie Scott's	International	Ⓐ ✕
	Dehesa	Italian	Ⓐ ✪
	Number Twelve	"	
	Barrafina	Spanish	Ⓐ ✪ ✪
	Malabar Junction	Indian	Ⓐ ✪
	Edokko	Japanese	✪ ✪
	Benja	Thai	✪
	Patara	"	✪
£35+	Andrew Edmunds	British, Modern	Ⓐ
	Aurora	"	Ⓐ
	Great Queen Street	British, Traditional	✪
	Cork & Bottle	International	Ⓐ
	Ten Ten Tei	Japanese	✪
£30+	The Giaconda	British, Modern	✪
	Ciao Bella	Italian	Ⓐ
	Souk Medina	Moroccan	Ⓐ
	Yming	Chinese	✪
	Sitaaray	Indian	Ⓐ ✪
	Rasa Maricham	Indian, Southern	✪ ✪
	Bincho Yakitori	Japanese	Ⓐ ✪
	Haozhan	Pan-Asian	✪
£25+	Seven Stars	International	Ⓐ
	Spacca Napoli	Italian	Ⓐ ✪
	North Sea Fish	Fish & chips	✪
	Busaba Eathai	Thai	Ⓐ ✪
£20+	Gordon's Wine Bar	International	Ⓐ ✕
	Centrepoint Sushi	Japanese	Ⓐ ✪
	Pho	Vietnamese	Ⓐ ✪

£15+	Paolina Café	Italian	✪
	Bar Italia	Sandwiches, cakes, etc	Ⓐ
	Cha Cha Moon	Chinese, Dim sum	Ⓐ✪

| £10+ | Monmouth Coffee Company | Sandwiches, cakes, etc | Ⓐ✪✪ |
| | Apostrophe | " | Ⓐ✪ |

£5+	Caffé Vergnano	Italian	Ⓐ✪
	Flat White	Sandwiches, cakes, etc	Ⓐ✪✪
	Maison Bertaux	"	Ⓐ

Mayfair & St James's (Parts of W1 and SW1)

| £130+ | Le Gavroche | French | Ⓐ✪ |

| £120+ | Umu | Japanese | ✪ |

| £110+ | Sake No Hana | " | |

£100+	Sketch (Lecture Rm)	French	✪
	The Ritz Restaurant	"	Ⓐ
	Alain Ducasse	"	

| £90+ | The Greenhouse | " | Ⓐ |
| | G Ramsay at Claridges | " | |

£80+	Dorchester Grill	British, Modern	
	Wiltons	British, Traditional	Ⓐ
	The Square	French	✪
	Galvin at Windows	"	Ⓐ
	Hibiscus	"	
	L'Oranger	"	
	Nobu	Japanese	✪
	Nobu Berkeley	"	

£70+	maze Grill	British, Modern	✪
	maze	French	✪
	Hélène Darroze	"	
	Cipriani	Italian	✪
	Theo Randall	"	
	Kai Mayfair	Chinese	✪✪
	Hakkasan	"	Ⓐ✪
	Taman Gang	"	Ⓐ
	China Tang	"	
	Trader Vics	Indonesian	✪
	Ikeda	Japanese	✪✪
	Sumosan	"	✪

£60+	Patterson's	British, Modern	✪
	Pigalle Club	"	Ⓐ
	Bellamy's	"	
	Green's	British, Traditional	Ⓐ
	The Albemarle	"	
	Scott's	Fish & seafood	Ⓐ✪
	Bentley's	"	✪
	La Petite Maison	French	Ⓐ✪
	Sketch (Gallery)	"	
	Mosaico	Italian	
	Ladurée	Afternoon tea	✪
	Benares	Indian	✪
	Miyama	Japanese	✪✪
	Shogun	"	✪

£50+	Le Caprice	British, Modern	Ⓐ✪
	The Wolseley	"	Ⓐ
	Boudin Blanc	French	Ⓐ✪
	Bord'Eaux	"	
	Alloro	Italian	✪
	Cecconi's	"	Ⓐ
	St Alban	Mediterranean	
	Momo	Moroccan	Ⓐ
	Princess Garden	Chinese	✪✪
	Veeraswamy	Indian	Ⓐ✪
	Tamarind	"	✪
	Quilon	Indian, Southern	✪✪
	Kiku	Japanese	✪

£40+	Sotheby's Café	British, Modern	Ⓐ✪
	Wild Honey	"	✪
	Ristorante Semplice	Italian	✪
	Levant	Lebanese	Ⓐ
	Chor Bizarre	Indian	Ⓐ✪
	Chisou	Japanese	✪
	Patara	Thai	✪

| £35+ | Al Sultan | Lebanese | ✪ |
| | Yoshino | Japanese | ✪ |

| £30+ | Rasa | Indian, Southern | ✪✪ |

| £25+ | Busaba Eathai | Thai | Ⓐ✪ |

| £10+ | Fuzzy's Grub | Sandwiches, cakes, etc | ✪✪ |
| | Apostrophe | " | Ⓐ✪ |

Fitzrovia & Marylebone (Part of W1)

| £90+ | Pied à Terre | French | ✪ |

| £80+ | Rhodes W1 Restaurant | " | |

£70+	The Landau	British, Modern	
	Texture	French	✪
	Orrery	"	
	Suka	Malaysian	

£60+	The Providores	Fusion	
	Locanda Locatelli	Italian	Ⓐ✪
	5 Cavendish Square	"	✪
	Defune	Japanese	✪✪

£50+	Vanilla	British, Modern	Ⓐ✪
	Odin's	British, Traditional	Ⓐ
	L'Autre Pied	French	✪
	Michael Moore	International	✪
	2 Veneti	Italian	
	Fino	Spanish	Ⓐ✪
	Royal China Club	Chinese	✪
	La Porte des Indes	Indian	Ⓐ
	Roka	Japanese	Ⓐ✪✪
	Aaya	"	Ⓐ✪
	Crazy Bear	Thai	Ⓐ✪

| £40+ | Back to Basics | Fish & seafood | ✪✪ |
| | Galvin Bistrot de Luxe | French | Ⓐ✪✪ |

	The Wallace	"	Ⓐ
	Archipelago	Fusion	Ⓐ✪
	Providores (Tapa Room)	"	
	Latium	Italian	✪✪
	Koba	Korean	
	Bam-Bou	Vietnamese	Ⓐ
£35+	Le Relais de Venise	French	Ⓐ✪
	Giusto	Italian	
	Salt Yard	Mediterranean	✪
£30+	Hellenik	Greek	
	The Beehive	Italian	✪
	Eagle Bar Diner	Burgers, etc	Ⓐ✪
	Rasa Samudra	Indian, Southern	✪✪
	Dinings	Japanese	Ⓐ✪✪
£25+	La Fromagerie Café	Sandwiches, cakes, etc	Ⓐ✪✪
	Ragam	Indian	✪✪
£20+	Sagar	"	✪✪
	Pho	Vietnamese	Ⓐ✪
£15+	Golden Hind	Fish & chips	✪✪
£10+	Apostrophe	Sandwiches, cakes, etc	Ⓐ✪

Belgravia, Pimlico, Victoria & Westminster (SW1, except St James's)

£100+	Marcus Wareing at the Berkeley	French	Ⓐ✪✪
£80+	Rib Room	British, Traditional	
	Foliage	French	
	Nahm	Thai	
£70+	The Goring Hotel	British, Traditional	Ⓐ
	One-O-One	Fish & seafood	✪✪
	Roussillon	French	✪✪
	Apsleys	Italian	
	Mr Chow	Chinese	
£60+	Toto's	Italian	Ⓐ
	Zafferano	"	Ⓐ
	Santini		
	Boisdale	Scottish	Ⓐ
	Ladurée	Afternoon tea	✪
	The Cinnamon Club	Indian	Ⓐ✪
£50+	Pantechnicon Rooms	British, Modern	Ⓐ
	Thomas Cubitt	"	Ⓐ
	Olivomare	Fish & seafood	✪
	La Poule au Pot	French	Ⓐ
	Quirinale	Italian	✪
	Hunan	Chinese	✪✪
	Ken Lo's Memories	"	✪✪
	Amaya	Indian	Ⓐ✪✪
£40+	Daylesford Organics	British, Modern	Ⓐ
	Le Cercle	French	Ⓐ✪✪
	Olivo	Italian	Ⓐ✪
	Uno	"	Ⓐ✪

	Caraffini	"	Ⓐ
	Sale e Pepe	"	Ⓐ
	Oliveto	*Pizza*	✪
£35+	Grenadier	*British, Traditional*	Ⓐ
	Ottolenghi	*Italian*	✪✪
	Ishbilia	*Lebanese*	✪
£30+	Kazan	*Turkish*	✪
	Blue Jade	*Thai*	
£25+	Cyprus Mangal	*Turkish*	✪
£10+	Apostrophe	*Sandwiches, cakes, etc*	Ⓐ✪

WEST

Chelsea, South Kensington, Kensington, Earl's Court & Fulham (SW3, SW5, SW6, SW7, SW10 & W8)

£110+	Gordon Ramsay	French	Ⓐ✪✪
£100+	Blakes	International	Ⓐ✪
£90+	Ambassade de l'Ile	French	
	Aubergine	"	
	Tom Aikens	"	
£80+	The Capital Restaurant	"	✪
	Rasoi Vineet Bhatia	Indian	✪
£70+	Brunello	Italian	
£60+	Clarke's	British, Modern	✪
	Babylon	"	Ⓐ
	Marco	"	
	Bibendum	French	Ⓐ
	Zuma	Japanese	Ⓐ✪✪
£50+	Launceston Place	British, Modern	Ⓐ✪✪
	Poissonnerie de l'Av.	Fish & seafood	Ⓐ✪
	Le Suquet	"	✪
	Racine	French	Ⓐ✪
	Belvedere	"	Ⓐ
	Scalini	Italian	Ⓐ✪
	Zaika	Indian	✪✪
	Chutney Mary	"	Ⓐ✪
	Bombay Brasserie	"	
	Awana	Malaysian	✪
	Blue Elephant	Thai	Ⓐ
£40+	Whits	British, Modern	✪
	Bumpkin	British, Traditional	Ⓐ✪
	Ffiona's	"	Ⓐ
	Maggie Jones's	"	Ⓐ
	Le Colombier	French	Ⓐ
	Daphne's	Italian	Ⓐ✪
	Frantoio	"	Ⓐ
	Il Portico	"	Ⓐ
	Cambio de Tercio	Spanish	Ⓐ✪✪
	Pasha	Moroccan	Ⓐ
	Good Earth	Chinese	✪
	Mr Wing	"	Ⓐ
	The Painted Heron	Indian	✪✪
	Eight Over Eight	Pan-Asian	Ⓐ✪✪
	Patara	Thai	✪
£35+	Ottolenghi	Italian	✪✪
	Tendido Cuatro	Spanish	✪
	La Bodeguita del Medio	Cuban	Ⓐ
	Beirut Express	Lebanese	✪
	Iznik Kaftan	Turkish	
	Noor Jahan	Indian	✪
	Sukho Thai Cuisine	Thai	Ⓐ✪✪
£30+	The Scarsdale	International	Ⓐ
	The Atlas	Mediterranean	Ⓐ✪

	Haché	*Steaks & grills*	Ⓐ✪
	Basilico	*Pizza*	✪
	Troubadour	*Sandwiches, cakes, etc*	Ⓐ⊗
	Yi-Ban	*Chinese*	Ⓐ✪
	Malabar	*Indian*	Ⓐ✪
£25+	The Windsor Castle	*International*	Ⓐ
	Chelsea Bun Diner	*"*	
	Pappa Ciccia	*Italian*	Ⓐ✪
	Byron	*Burgers, etc*	Ⓐ
	Taiwan Village	*Chinese*	✪
	Shikara	*Indian*	✪
	Tandoori Lane	*"*	✪
	Addie's Thai Café	*Thai*	Ⓐ✪
£20+	Costa's Fish	*Fish & chips*	✪
	Churchill Arms	*Thai*	Ⓐ✪
	Café 209	*"*	Ⓐ

Notting Hill, Holland Park, Bayswater, North Kensington & Maida Vale (W2, W9, W10, W11)

£70+	The Ledbury	*French*	Ⓐ✪✪
£60+	Beach Blanket Babylon	*British, Modern*	Ⓐ⊗
	Angelus	*French*	
£50+	Notting Hill Brasserie	*British, Modern*	Ⓐ✪
	Julie's	*"*	Ⓐ
	Assaggi	*Italian*	✪✪
£40+	Paradise, Kensal Green	*British, Modern*	Ⓐ✪
	First Floor	*"*	Ⓐ
	The Frontline Club	*"*	Ⓐ
	Bumpkin	*British, Traditional*	Ⓐ✪
	Hereford Road	*"*	
	Le Café Anglais	*French*	
	Electric Brasserie	*International*	Ⓐ
	The Oak	*Italian*	Ⓐ✪
	Osteria Basilico	*"*	Ⓐ✪
	Bombay Palace	*Indian*	✪✪
	E&O	*Pan-Asian*	Ⓐ✪
£35+	The Ladbroke Arms	*British, Modern*	Ⓐ✪
	Ottolenghi	*Italian*	✪✪
	Crazy Homies	*Mexican/TexMex*	Ⓐ✪
	Beirut Express	*Lebanese*	✪
	Mandarin Kitchen	*Chinese*	✪✪
	Bombay Bicycle Club	*Indian*	✪
	Noor Jahan	*"*	✪
£30+	Lucky Seven	*American*	Ⓐ✪
	Al-Waha	*Lebanese*	✪
	Pearl Liang	*Chinese*	Ⓐ✪
	Inaho	*Japanese*	✪✪
	Uli	*Pan-Asian*	✪
	Tawana	*Thai*	✪
£25+	The Four Seasons	*Chinese*	✪
£15+	Fresco	*Lebanese*	✪

| £5+ | Lisboa Pâtisserie | *Sandwiches, cakes, etc* | ✪✪ |

Hammersmith, Shepherd's Bush, Olympia, Chiswick, Acton & Ealing (W4, W3, W5, W6, W12, W14)

Price	Restaurant	Cuisine	
£60+	The River Café	*Italian*	Ⓐ✪
£50+	La Trompette	*French*	Ⓐ✪✪
£40+	High Road Brasserie	*British, Modern*	
	Fish Hook	*Fish & seafood*	✪
	Le Vacherin	*French*	✪
	Cibo	*Italian*	✪
	Vino Rosso	*"*	✪
£35+	The Anglesea Arms	*British, Modern*	Ⓐ✪✪
	The Havelock Tavern	*"*	✪
	The Carpenter's Arms	*"*	
	Duke Of Sussex	*"*	
	Princess Victoria	*British, Traditional*	Ⓐ✪
	Annie's	*International*	Ⓐ
	The Swan	*Mediterranean*	Ⓐ
	The Gate	*Vegetarian*	✪✪
	Madhu's	*Indian*	Ⓐ✪✪
	Sushi-Hiro	*Japanese*	✪✪
£30+	Queen's Head	*British, Modern*	Ⓐ
	Indian Zing	*Indian*	Ⓐ✪
£25+	Ground	*Burgers, etc*	Ⓐ✪
	Adams Café	*Moroccan*	
	Chez Marcelle	*Lebanese*	✪✪
	North China	*Chinese*	✪
	Mirch Masala	*Indian*	✪✪
	Agni	*"*	✪
	Anarkali	*"*	✪
	Karma	*"*	✪
£20+	Best Mangal	*Turkish*	Ⓐ✪
	Sagar	*Indian*	✪✪
	Esarn Kheaw	*Thai*	✪✪

NORTH

Hampstead, West Hampstead, St John's Wood, Regent's Park, Kilburn & Camden Town (NW postcodes)

£70+	Landmark (Winter Gdn)	*British, Modern*	Ⓐ
	Odette's	*"*	
£50+	L'Aventure	*French*	Ⓐ✪
	Oslo Court	*"*	Ⓐ✪
	Royal China Club	*Chinese*	✪
£40+	The Engineer	*British, Modern*	
	Philpotts Mezzaluna	*Italian*	Ⓐ✪
	Osteria Stecca	*"*	
	Good Earth	*Chinese*	✪
	Atma	*Indian*	✪
	Sushi-Say	*Japanese*	✪✪
£35+	Market	*British, Modern*	✪
	The Wet Fish Cafe	*"*	Ⓐ
	Holly Bush	*British, Traditional*	Ⓐ
	L'Absinthe	*French*	Ⓐ
	Retsina	*Greek*	
	Sarracino	*Italian*	✪
	Osteria Emilia	*"*	
	Eriki	*Indian*	✪✪
	Bombay Bicycle Club	*"*	✪✪
	Jin Kichi	*Japanese*	✪✪
	Singapore Garden	*Malaysian*	✪
£30+	Daphne	*Greek*	Ⓐ
	Lemonia	*"*	Ⓐ
	William IV	*Mediterranean*	Ⓐ✪
	Haché	*Steaks & grills*	Ⓐ✪
	Nautilus	*Fish & chips*	✪
	Basilico	*Pizza*	✪
	Snazz Sichuan	*Chinese*	Ⓐ✪
	Gung-Ho	*"*	Ⓐ
£25+	Alisan	*"*	✪✪
	Jashan	*Indian*	✪
	Vijay	*"*	✪
	Café Japan	*Japanese*	✪✪
£20+	Five Hot Chillies	*Indian*	✪
	Kovalam	*"*	✪
£15+	Geeta	*"*	✪

Hoxton, Islington, Highgate, Crouch End, Stoke Newington, Finsbury Park, Muswell Hill & Finchley (N postcodes)

£80+	Bacchus	*British, Modern*	✪
£70+	Fifteen Restaurant	*Italian*	
£50+	Sargasso Sea	*Fish & seafood*	Ⓐ✪
	Morgan M	*French*	✪✪
	Fifteen Trattoria	*Italian*	

£40+	Mosaica	*British, Modern*	Ⓐ✪
	The Lock Dining Bar	*"*	
	Fig	*French*	Ⓐ✪
	Metrogusto	*Italian*	Ⓐ
£35+	The Clissold Arms	*British, Modern*	
	St Johns	*British, Traditional*	Ⓐ
	Ottolenghi	*Italian*	✪✪
	The Parsee	*Indian*	✪
	Isarn	*Thai*	✪
£30+	Vrisaki	*Greek*	✪
	Banners	*International*	Ⓐ
	The Fox Reformed	*"*	Ⓐ
	Toff's	*Fish & chips*	✪
	Two Brothers	*"*	✪
	Basilico	*Pizza*	✪
	Rasa Travancore	*Indian, Southern*	✪✪
£25+	The Flask	*British, Traditional*	Ⓐ
	Petek	*Turkish*	Ⓐ
	Rasa	*Indian, Southern*	✪✪
	Yum Yum	*Thai*	Ⓐ✪
£20+	Gem	*Turkish*	Ⓐ✪
	Anglo Asian Tandoori	*Indian*	✪

SOUTH

South Bank (SE1)

£70+	Oxo Tower (Rest')	British, Modern	✪
£50+	Skylon	"	
	Roast	British, Traditional	
	Tentazioni	Italian	✪
£40+	Garrison	British, Modern	✪
	The Swan At The Globe	"	✪
	Wright Brothers	Fish & seafood	✪✪✪
	Magdalen	French	✪
	Brew Wharf	"	✪
	Champor-Champor	Fusion	✪✪
	Delfina Studio Café	International	✪
£35+	The Anchor & Hope	British, Traditional	✪✪
£30+	The Table	British, Modern	✪
	Bincho Yakitori	Japanese	✪✪
£25+	Mango Tree	Indian	✪
£15+	El Vergel	South American	✪✪✪
£10+	Monmouth Coffee Company	Sandwiches, cakes, etc	✪✪✪
	Fuzzy's Grub	"	✪✪
£5+	Caffé Vergnano	"	✪✪

Greenwich, Lewisham & Blackheath (All SE postcodes, except SE1)

£40+	Chapter Two	British, Modern	✪
	Inside	"	✪
£35+	The Palmerston	"	✪
£30+	Le Querce	Italian	✪✪
	Arancia	"	✪✪
	Olley's	Fish & chips	✪
	Babur Brasserie	Indian	✪✪✪
	Tandoori Nights	"	✪✪
£25+	The Gowlett	Pizza	✪✪
	Ganapati	Indian	✪✪

Battersea, Brixton, Clapham, Wandsworth Barnes, Putney & Wimbledon (All SW postcodes south of the river)

£50+	Chez Bruce	British, Modern	✪✪✪
	Trinity	"	✪
	Riva	Italian	✪
£40+	Lamberts	British, Modern	✪✪✪
	Phoenix	"	✪✪
	Four O Nine	"	✪
	Gastro	French	✪

	Donna Margherita	*Italian*	Ⓐ✪✪
	Enoteca Turi	"	✪
	Numero Uno	"	Ⓐ
£35+	Tom Ilic	*British, Modern*	✪✪
	Earl Spencer	"	Ⓐ✪
	Emile's	"	Ⓐ✪
	The Prince Of Wales	"	✪
	Upstairs Bar	*French*	Ⓐ✪✪
	Brasserie James	"	✪
	Mini Mundus	"	Ⓐ
	Annie's	*International*	Ⓐ
	Isola del Sole	*Italian*	✪
	Pizza Metro	"	✪
	The Three Bridges	"	
	The Fox & Hounds	*Mediterranean*	Ⓐ✪
	Santa Maria del Sur	*Argentinian*	✪
	Bombay Bicycle Club	*Indian*	✪
	Tsunami	*Japanese*	✪
£30+	The Normanby	*British, Modern*	Ⓐ✪
	The Duke's Head	"	Ⓐ
	Fish Club	*Fish & seafood*	✪✪
	Rebato's	*Spanish*	Ⓐ
	Basilico	*Pizza*	✪
	Dalchini	*Chinese*	Ⓐ✪
	Bayee Village	"	
	Ma Goa	*Indian*	Ⓐ✪
	The Banana Leaf Canteen	*Pan-Asian*	Ⓐ✪
£25+	Pappa Ciccia	*Italian*	Ⓐ✪
	Il Cantuccio di Pulcinella	"	
	El Rincón Latino	*Spanish*	Ⓐ
	Kastoori	*Indian*	✪✪
	Mirch Masala SW17	"	✪✪
	Nanglo	"	Ⓐ✪
	Chutney	"	✪
	Indian Ocean	"	
	Amaranth	*Thai*	✪
£20+	Hot Stuff	*Indian*	Ⓐ✪✪
	Holy Cow	"	✪
	Sree Krishna	"	✪
£10+	Franco Manca	*Pizza*	✪✪

Outer western suburbs
Kew, Richmond, Twickenham, Teddington

£60+	Petersham Nurseries	*British, Modern*	Ⓐ✪
£50+	The Glasshouse	"	✪✪
	Petersham Hotel	"	Ⓐ

£40+	Brula	French	Ⓐ
	A Cena	*Italian*	Ⓐ✪
£35+	Scarpetta	*"*	Ⓐ✪
	Four Regions	*Chinese*	
	Origin Asia	*Indian*	✪
£25+	O'Zon	*Chinese*	
£20+	Sagar	*Indian*	✪✪

EAST

Smithfield & Farringdon (EC1)

£60+	Club Gascon	*French*	★
£40+	St John	*British, Traditional*	★★
	Hix	*"*	★
	Comptoir Gascon	*French*	Ⓐ★★
	Bleeding Heart	*"*	Ⓐ★
	Café du Marché	*"*	Ⓐ★
	Moro	*Spanish*	★★
	Saki Bar & Food Emporium	*Japanese*	★
£35+	The Well	*British, Modern*	Ⓐ★
	Vinoteca	*"*	Ⓐ
	The Fox and Anchor	*British, Traditional*	Ⓐ
	Cellar Gascon	*French*	
£30+	Tajima Tei	*Japanese*	★
	54 Farringdon Road	*Malaysian*	★
	Cây Tre	*Vietnamese*	★
£25+	The Eagle	*Mediterranean*	Ⓐ
	Pinchito	*Spanish*	★
	Pham Sushi	*Japanese*	★★
£20+	Smiths (Ground Floor)	*British, Modern*	Ⓐ
	Kolossi Grill	*Greek*	Ⓐ
	Pho	*Vietnamese*	Ⓐ★

The City (EC2, EC3, EC4)

£80+	1 Lombard Street	*British, Modern*	
	Tatsuso	*Japanese*	
£70+	Prism	*British, Modern*	
£60+	Rhodes 24	*"*	Ⓐ
	1901	*French*	
£50+	The Mercer	*British, Modern*	
	Coq d'Argent	*French*	
	L'Anima	*Italian*	Ⓐ★
	Eyre Brothers	*Spanish*	★
£40+	The Don	*British, Modern*	Ⓐ★
	Terranostra	*Italian*	
	Gt Eastern Dining Room	*Pan-Asian*	Ⓐ★
	D Sum 2	*"*	
£35+	Ye Olde Cheshire Cheese	*British, Traditional*	Ⓐ✗
£30+	Kazan	*Turkish*	★
	Kurumaya	*Japanese*	★
£25+	Hilliard	*British, Modern*	Ⓐ★★
	The Wine Library	*British, Traditional*	Ⓐ✗
	Simpson's Tavern	*"*	Ⓐ
£10+	Fuzzy's Grub	*Sandwiches, cakes, etc*	★★
	Apostrophe	*"*	Ⓐ★

East End & Docklands (All E postcodes)

Price	Restaurant	Cuisine	Ratings
£80+	Ubon	*Japanese*	
£70+	Les Trois Garçons	*French*	Ⓐ
	Plateau	*"*	
	Quadrato	*Italian*	
£60+	Beach Blanket Babylon	*British, Modern*	Ⓐ ✖
£50+	Lanes	*"*	
	Hawksmoor	*Steaks & grills*	✪
£40+	The Gun	*British, Modern*	Ⓐ
	Wapping Food	*"*	Ⓐ
	St John Bread & Wine	*British, Traditional*	✪ ✪
	Rosemary Lane	*French*	✪
	Il Bordello	*Italian*	Ⓐ ✪
	El Faro	*Spanish*	✪ ✪
	Café Spice Namaste	*Indian*	✪ ✪
£35+	The Narrow	*British, Traditional*	
	La Figa	*Italian*	Ⓐ ✪
	Ark Fish	*Fish & chips*	✪
	Buen Ayre	*Argentinian*	Ⓐ ✪
	Green & Red Bar & Cantina	*Mexican/TexMex*	Ⓐ ✪
£30+	LMNT	*British, Modern*	Ⓐ ✖
	Yi-Ban	*Chinese*	Ⓐ ✪
£25+	Story Deli	*Organic*	Ⓐ ✪
	Mirch Masala	*Indian*	✪ ✪
	Namo	*Vietnamese*	Ⓐ ✪
£20+	Mangal Ocakbasi	*Turkish*	✪ ✪
	Clifton	*Indian*	✪
	Memsaheb on Thames	*"*	✪
	Lahore Kebab House	*Pakistani*	✪ ✪
	New Tayyabs	*"*	✪ ✪
£10+	E Pellicci	*Italian*	Ⓐ

LONDON
INDEXES

INDEXES

BREAKFAST
(with opening times)

Central
The Albemarle *(7)*
Apostrophe: *Barrett St W1, Tott' Ct Rd W1, WC2 (7)*
Apsleys *(7)*
Asia de Cuba *(6)*
Bar Italia *(7)*
Bord'Eaux *(7)*
Caffè Vergnano: *WC2 (8, Sun 11)*
Cecconi's *(7)*
The Cinnamon Club *(Mon-Fri 7.30)*
Daylesford Organics *(8, Sun 11)*
Dorchester Grill *(7, Sat & Sun 8)*
Eagle Bar Diner *(Sat 10, Sun 11)*
5 Cavendish Square *(8)*
Flat White *(8, Sat & Sun 9)*
La Fromagerie Café *(Mon 10.30, Tue-Fri 8, Sat 9, Sun 10)*
Fuzzy's Grub: *SW1 (7)*
Galvin at Windows *(7)*
Gordon's Wine Bar *(Mon-Fri 8)*
The Goring Hotel *(7, Sun 7.30)*
Joe Allen *(8)*
Ladurée: *W1 (9); SW1 (9, Sun noon)*
The Landau *(7)*
Maison Bertaux *(8.30, Sun 9)*
Monmouth Coffee Company: *WC2 (8)*
Number Twelve *(7)*
Ottolenghi: *SW1 (8, Sun 9)*
The Providores *(9, Sat & Sun 10)*
Providores (Tapa Room) *(9, Sat & Sun 10)*
Rib Room *(7, Sun 8)*
The Ritz Restaurant *(7, Sun 8)*
Simpsons-in-the-Strand *(Mon-Fri 7.30)*
Sotheby's Café *(9.30)*
The Wallace *(10)*
The Wolseley *(7, Sat & Sun 8)*

West
Adams Café *(7.30, Sat 8.30)*
Annie's: *W4 (Tue - Thu 10, Fri & Sat 10.30, Sun 10)*
Beirut Express: *W2 (7)*
Blakes *(7.30)*
Brunello *(6.45)*
Bumpkin: *W11 (Sat noon)*
The Carpenter's Arms *(9)*
Chelsea Bun Diner *(7, Sun 9)*
Electric Brasserie *(8)*
Fresco *(8)*
The Frontline Club *(8)*
High Road Brasserie *(7, Sat & Sun 8)*
Julie's *(9)*
Lisboa Pâtisserie *(7)*
Lucky Seven *(Tue - Sun 10)*
Ottolenghi: *W11 (8, Sun 9)*
Pappa Ciccia: *Fulham High St SW6 (7.30)*
Troubadour *(9)*

North
Banners *(9, Sat & Sun 10)*
The Engineer *(9)*
Fifteen Trattoria *(7.30, Sun 8)*
Landmark (Winter Gdn) *(7)*
Ottolenghi: *N1 (8, Sun 9)*
The Wet Fish Cafe *(9)*

South
Annie's: *SW13 (Tue-Sun 10)*
The Duke's Head *(10, Sun noon)*
Garrison *(8, Sat & Sun 9)*
Gastro *(8)*
Monmouth Coffee Company: *SE1 (7.30)*
Petersham Hotel *(7, Sat & Sun 8)*
El Rincón Latino *(Sat & Sun 11)*
Roast *(7, Sat 8)*
The Table *(7.30, Sat 9)*
El Vergel *(8.30, Sat 10.30)*

East
L'Anima *(7)*
Apostrophe: *all east branches (7)*
Bleeding Heart *(7)*
Comptoir Gascon *(9, Sat 10.30)*
Coq d'Argent *(Mon-Fri 7.30)*
The Fox and Anchor *(7)*
Fuzzy's Grub: *EC2, Cornhill EC3, Fleet St EC4, Well Ct EC4 (7)*
The Gun *(Sat & Sun 11.30)*
Hilliard *(8)*
The Mercer *(7.30)*
1901 *(7)*
E Pellicci *(7)*
Pinchito *(10)*
Prism *(8)*
Quadrato *(6.30, Sun 8)*
St John Bread & Wine *(9, Sat & Sun 10)*
Smiths (Ground Floor) *(7, Sat 10, Sun 9.30)*
Wapping Food *(Sat & Sun 10)*
The Well *(Sat & Sun 10.30)*

BRUNCH MENUS

Central
Aurora
Boisdale
Le Caprice
Cecconi's
Daylesford Organics
Eagle Bar Diner
La Fromagerie Café
Galvin at Windows
The Ivy
Joe Allen
Ladurée: *SW1*
Ottolenghi: *all branches*
The Providores
Providores (Tapa Room)
The Wolseley

West
Annie's: *all branches*

INDEXES

INDEXES

ENTERTAINMENT
(Check times before you go)

Central

Boisdale
(jazz, Mon-Sat)
Le Caprice
(pianist, nightly)
Ciao Bella
(pianist, nightly)
Eagle Bar Diner
(DJ, Wed-Sat)
Hakkasan
(DJ, nightly)
Ishbilia
(live music, Thu-Sat, regular belly dancing)
Joe Allen
(pianist, Mon-Sat)
Kai Mayfair
(harpist, Thu and various other days)
Levant
(belly dancer, nightly)
Momo
(live world music, Tue & Wed)
Pearl
(pianist)
Pigalle Club
(live music, nightly)
La Porte des Indes
(jazz, Sun brunch)
Red Fort
(DJ, Thu-Sat)
Rib Room
(pianist, Mon-Sun)
The Ritz Restaurant
(string quartet, Mon-Thu; live music, Fri & Sat)
Roka
(DJ, Thu-Sat)
Ronnie Scott's
(jazz, nightly)
Simpsons-in-the-Strand
(pianist, nightly)
Sketch (Gallery)
(DJ, Thu-Sat)
Souk Medina
(belly dancer, Thu-Sat)
Taman Gang
(DJ, Thu-Sat)
Trader Vics
(guitarist, nightly)

West

Babylon
(live music, Thu D; magician Sun)
Beach Blanket Babylon: all branches
(DJ, Fri & Sat)
Belvedere
(pianist, nightly, Sat & Sun all day)
La Bodeguita del Medio
(occasional live music)
Le Café Anglais
(magician Sun lunch)
Chutney Mary
(jazz, Sun L)
Mr Wing
(jazz, Fri & Sat)
Notting Hill Brasserie
(jazz, nightly)

Pasha
(belly dancer, nightly)
Troubadour
(live music, most nights)
William IV
(DJ, Fri-Sat)

North

Landmark (Winter Gdn)
(pianist & musicians, daily)
Yum Yum
(DJ, Fri)

South

Bayee Village
(pianist, Mon-Wed)
Donna Margherita
(live music, weekly)
The Gowlett
(DJ, Sun)
Santa Maria del Sur
(live music, Mon)
The Three Bridges
(Italian singer, Sat)

East

Beach Blanket Babylon: all branches
(DJ, Fri & Sat)
Café du Marché
(pianist & bass, nightly)
Coq d'Argent
(jazz, Sun L)
D Sum 2
(some scheduled live music)
Great Eastern Dining Room
(DJs, Fri & Sat)
Green & Red Bar & Cantina
(DJ, Thu-Sat)
LMNT
(opera, Sun)
1901
(pianist, nightly)
1 Lombard Street
(jazz, Fri D)
Smiths (Ground Floor)
(DJ, Wed-Sat)
Yi-Ban: E16
(live music, Fri & Sat)

LATE
(open till midnight or later as shown; may be earlier Sunday)

Central

Al Sultan
Asia de Cuba *(midnight, Thu-Sat 12.30 am)*
Bar Italia *(open 24 hours, Sun 3 am)*
Bentley's
Le Caprice
Cecconi's
China Tang
Cyprus Mangal *(Sun-Thu midnight, Fri & Sat 1 am)*
Eagle Bar Diner *(Thu-Sat)*
Hakkasan *(midnight, ex Mon & Sun)*

INDEXES

PRIVATE ROOMS

(for the most comprehensive
listing of venues for functions –
from palaces to pubs – visit
www.hardens.com/party, or buy
*Harden's London Party, Event &
Conference Guide*, available in all
good bookshops)
* particularly recommended

Daphne's (40)
E&O (20)
Eight Over Eight (14)
First Floor (28,44)
Five Hot Chillies (25)
The Frontline Club (50)
Ground (45)
High Road Brasserie (12)
Iznik Kaftan (75)
Julie's (12,16,16,24,32,45)
Karma (30,40)
Launceston Place (12)
Lucky Seven (45)
Madhu's (35)
Malabar (30)
Mr Wing (6,6,20)
Noor Jahan: W2 (16)
North China (30)
Notting Hill Brasserie (44)
The Oak (16)
Paradise by Way of Kensal
    Green (20,50)
Pasha (20)
Pearl Liang (45)
Poissonnerie de l'Avenue (20)
Princess Victoria (60)
Rasoi Vineet Bhatia (8,18)
Le Suquet (16,25)
Taiwan Village (17)
Tandoori Lane (16)
Tawana (50)
Tom Aikens (10)
Troubadour (70,120)
Le Vacherin (30)
William IV (100)
Zuma (14,10)

North

Alisan (12)
Anglo Asian Tandoori (30)
Bombay Bicycle Club: NW3 (30)
Daphne (50)
The Engineer (20,32)
Geeta (45)
Gem (100)
Good Earth: NW7 (30)
Gung-Ho (24)
Holly Bush (40)
Lemonia (40)
Market (12)
Metrogusto (30)
Morgan M (14)
Osteria Emilia (30)
The Parsee (18)
Rasa Travancore: N16 (25)
Rasa (30)
Retsina (50)
Royal China Club: NW8 (12,12)
Sarracino (40,50)
Snazz Sichuan (10)
Sushi-Say (8)
Toff's (24)
Vrisaki (15)
Yum Yum (100)

South

Amaranth (25)
Annie's: SW13 (35)
Arancia (8)
Bayee Village (30)
Bombay Bicycle Club: SW12 (25)
Brew Wharf (80)
Brula (24,10,10)
Champor-Champor (8)
Chapter Two (60)
Chez Bruce (14)
Dalchini (40)
The Duke's Head (50)
Earl Spencer (70)
Emile's (50)
Enoteca Turi (22)
The Fox & Hounds (25)
Garrison (25)
The Palmerston (32)
Petersham Hotel (26)
Scarpetta (25)
Sree Krishna (50,60)
The Swan At The
    Globe (14,70,200)
Tentazioni (25)
Trinity (12)

East

L'Anima (14,6)
Bleeding Heart (20,35,45)
Café du Marché (30,60)
Café Spice Namaste (40)
Cellar Gascon (20)
Clifton (160)
The Don (24,12)
El Faro (60)
The Gun (14,22)
Hawksmoor (10)
Lanes (28)
The Mercer (6,40)
Moro (14)
The Narrow (14)
New Tayyabs (40)
Ye Olde Cheshire Cheese (15,50)
1 Lombard Street (50)
Plateau (24)
Prism (20,40)
St John (18)
Saki Bar & Food Emporium (10)
Smiths (Ground Floor) (24,12,10)
Tajima Tei (16,6,5)
Tatsuso (8)
Les Trois Garçons (10)
Vinoteca (30)
The Well (70)
Yi-Ban: E16 (30)

ROMANTIC

Central

Andrew Edmunds
Archipelago
Aurora
Bam-Bou
Boudin Blanc
Buddha Bar

ROOMS WITH A VIEW

NOTABLE WINE LISTS

LONDON
MAPS

MAP1 - WEST END OVERVIEW

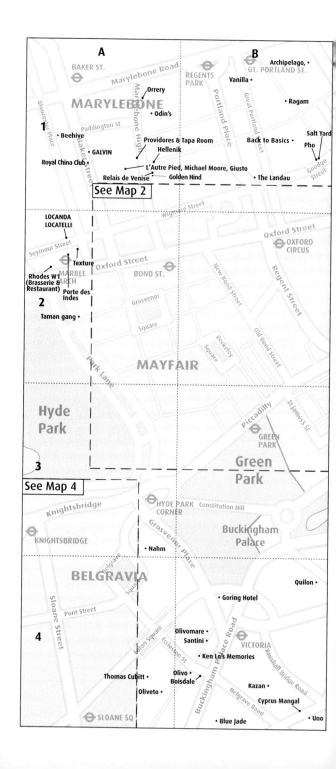

MAP1 - WEST END OVERVIEW

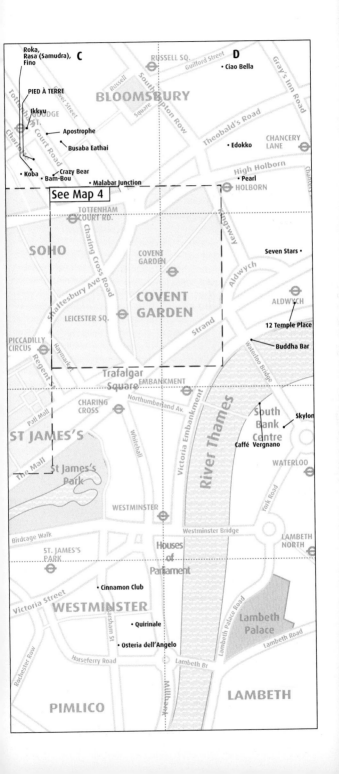

Roka,
Rasa (Samudra), **C**
Fino

RUSSELL SQ.
Guilford Street

• Ciao Bella

Gray's Inn Road

Russell Square

BLOOMSBURY

Southampton Row

D

PIED À TERRE

Theobald's Road

CHANCERY
LANE

Ikkyu

GOODGE
ST.

• Apostrophe

• Edokko

• Busaba Eathai

High Holborn

• Koba • Crazy Bear
Bam-Bou

• Pearl

• Malabar Junction

HOLBORN

Tottenham Court Road

Charing

Gower Street

Court Road

Kingsway

Chancery

See Map 4

TOTTENHAM
COURT RD.

SOHO

Charing Cross Road

COVENT
GARDEN

Seven Stars •

Aldwych

**COVENT
GARDEN**

ALDWYCH

LEICESTER SQ.

Strand

12 Temple Place

**PICCADILLY
CIRCUS**

Shaftesbury Ave

• Buddha Bar

Haymarket

Regent St.

Waterloo Bridge

Trafalgar
Square EMBANKMENT

CHARING
CROSS

Northumberland Ave.

South
Bank

Skylon •

Pall Mall

ST JAMES'S

Whitehall

Victoria Embankment

River Thames

Centre
Caffè Vergnano

WATERLOO

The Mall

St James's
Park

York Road

WESTMINSTER

Westminster Bridge

LAMBETH
NORTH

Birdcage Walk

ST. JAMES'S
PARK

Houses
of
Parliament

Lambeth Palace Road

• Cinnamon Club

Victoria Street

WESTMINSTER

Gastham St.

**Lambeth
Palace**

• Quirinale

Lambeth Road

• Osteria dell'Angelo

Rochester Row

Horseferry Road

Lambeth Br.

Millbank

PIMLICO

LAMBETH

MAP 2 - MAYFAIR, ST JAMES'S & WEST SOHO

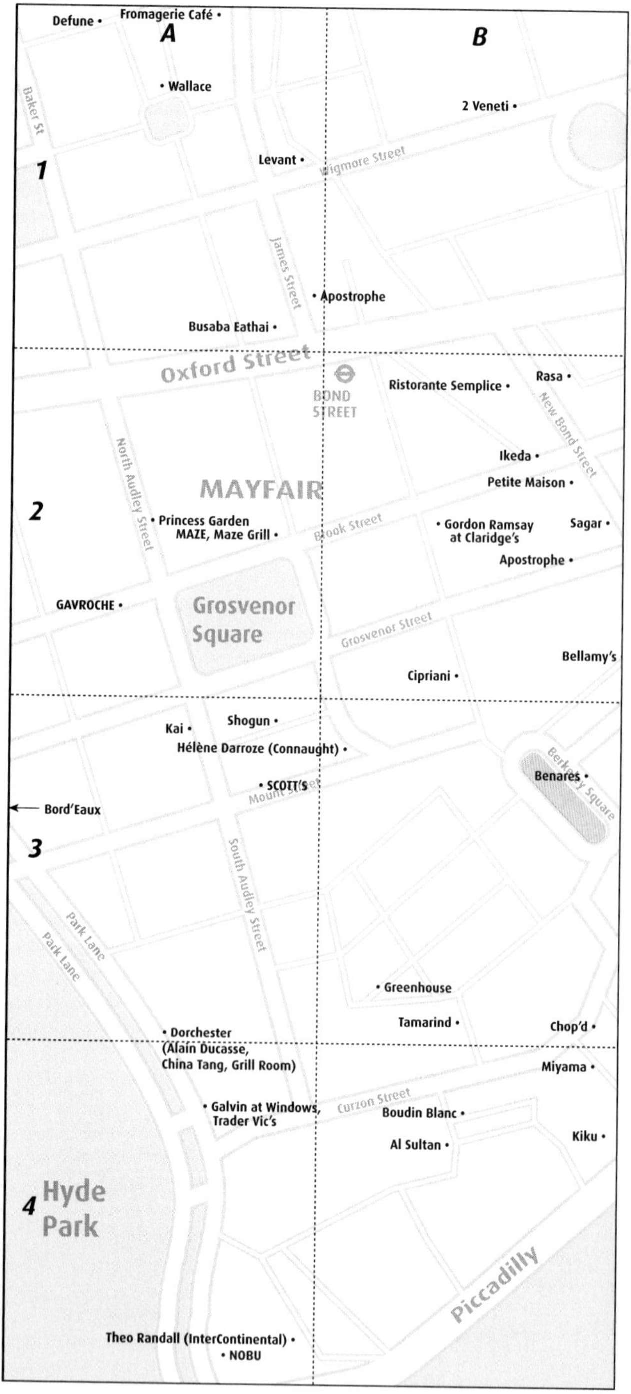

Defune •   Fromagerie Café •

A

B

• Wallace

2 Veneti •

Levant •

Wigmore Street

1

Baker St

James Street

• Apostrophe

Busaba Eathai •

Oxford Street

BOND STREET

Ristorante Semplice •

Rasa •

New Bond Street

Ikeda •

Petite Maison •

North Audley Street

MAYFAIR

• Princess Garden
MAZE, Maze Grill •

Brook Street

• Gordon Ramsay
at Claridge's

Sagar •

Apostrophe •

2

GAVROCHE •

**Grosvenor
Square**

Grosvenor Street

Bellamy's

Cipriani •

Kai •

Shogun •

Hélène Darroze (Connaught) •

Berkeley Square

• SCOTT'S

Mount Street

Benares •

◄— Bord'Eaux

3

South Audley Street

Park Lane

Park Lane

• Greenhouse

Tamarind •

Chop'd •

• Dorchester
(Alain Ducasse,
China Tang, Grill Room)

Miyama •

• Galvin at Windows,
Trader Vic's

Curzon Street

Boudin Blanc •

Al Sultan •

Kiku •

4 **Hyde
Park**

Piccadilly

Theo Randall (InterContinental) •
• NOBU

MAP 2 - MAYFAIR, ST JAMES'S & WEST SOHO

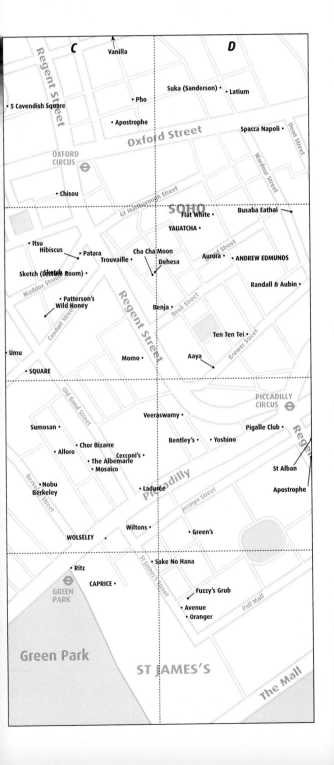

MAP 3 - EAST SOHO, CHINATOWN & COVENT GARDEN

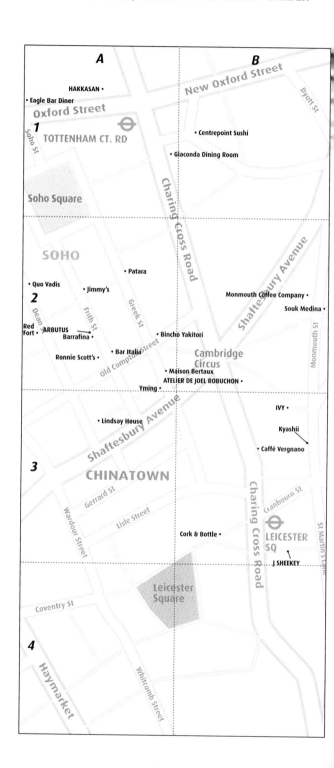

A

B

New Oxford Street

HAKKASAN •

• Eagle Bar Diner

Oxford Street

Dyott St

1

TOTTENHAM CT. RD

• Centrepoint Sushi

• Giaconda Dining Room

Soho St

Soho Square

Charing Cross Road

SOHO

Shaftesbury Avenue

• Patara

• Quo Vadis   • Jimmy's

Monmouth Coffee Company •

2

Souk Medina •

Frith St

Greek St

Monmouth St

Dean St

Red
Fort • ARBUTUS

Barrafina •

• Bincho Yakitori

• Bar Italia

Ronnie Scott's •

Old Compton Street

Cambridge
Circus

• Maison Bertaux

ATELIER DE JOEL ROBUCHON •

Yming •

IVY •

• Lindsay House

Kyashii

Shaftesbury Avenue

• Caffé Vergnano

3

CHINATOWN

Gerrard St

Cranbourn St

Charing Cross Road

Wardour Street

Lisle Street

Cork & Bottle •

LEICESTER
SQ

St Martin's Lane

J. SHEEKEY

Leicester
Square

Coventry St

Whitcomb Street

4

Haymarket

MAP 3 - EAST SOHO, CHINATOWN & COVENT GARDEN

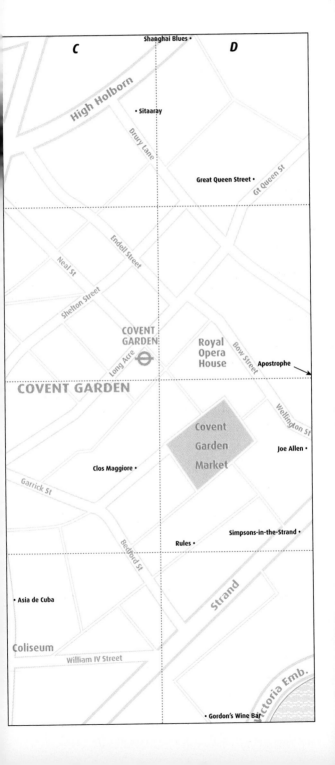

MAP 4 - KNIGHTSBRIDGE, CHELSEA & SOUTH KENSINGTON

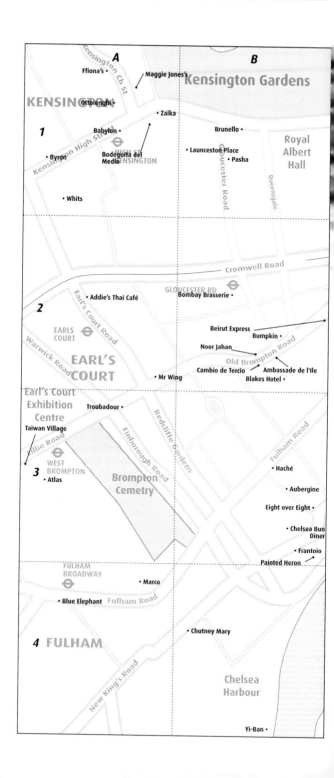

A

Ffiona's •

Maggie Jones's •

Kensington Gardens

KENSINGTON

Ottolenghi •

• Zaika

B

1

Babylon •

Brunello •

Royal
Albert
Hall

• Byron

• Launceston Place

Bodeguita del
Medio KENSINGTON

• Pasha

Gloucester Road

Queensgate

• Whits

Cromwell Road

2

• Addie's Thai Café

GLOUCESTER RD

Bombay Brasserie •

EARLS
COURT

Earl's Court Road

Beirut Express

Bumpkin •

Warwick Road

EARL'S
COURT

Noor Jahan

Old Brompton Road

Cambio de Tercio

Ambassade de l'Ile

• Mr Wing

Blakes Hotel •

Earl's Court
Exhibition
Centre

Troubadour •

Redcliffe Gardens

Taiwan Village

Lillie Road

Finborough Road

Fulham Road

WEST
BROMPTON

3

• Atlas

Brompton
Cemetery

• Haché

• Aubergine

Eight over Eight •

• Chelsea Bun
Diner

• Frantoio

Painted Heron

FULHAM
BROADWAY

• Marco

• Blue Elephant   Fulham Road

4 FULHAM

• Chutney Mary

New King's Road

Chelsea
Harbour

Yi-Ban •

MAP 4 - KNIGHTSBRIDGE, CHELSEA & SOUTH KENSINGTON

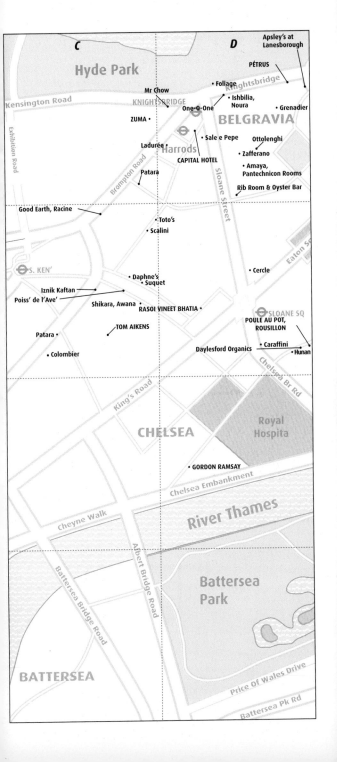

C

D

Apsley's at Lanesborough

Hyde Park

PÉTRUS

Foliage

Knightsbridge

Kensington Road

Mr Chow

KNIGHTSBRIDGE

Ishbilia, Noura

One-O-One

Grenadier

ZUMA

BELGRAVIA

Exhibition Road

Ladurée

Sale e Pepe

Ottolenghi

Harrods

CAPITAL HOTEL

Zafferano

Patara

Amaya, Pantechnicon Rooms

Brompton Road

Sloane Street

Rib Room & Oyster Bar

Good Earth, Racine

Toto's

Scalini

Eaton Sq

S. KEN'

Cercle

Daphne's
Suquet

Iznik Kaftan

Poiss' de l'Ave'

SLOANE SQ

Shikara, Awana

RASOI VINEET BHATIA

POULE AU POT, ROUSILLON

TOM AIKENS

Patara

Daylesford Organics

Caraffini

Colombier

Hunan

King's Road

Chelsea Br Rd

CHELSEA

Royal Hospita

GORDON RAMSAY

Chelsea Embankment

Cheyne Walk

River Thames

Albert Bridge Road

Battersea Bridge Road

Battersea Park

BATTERSEA

Price Of Wales Drive

Battersea Pk Rd

MAP 5 - NOTTING HILL & BAYSWATER

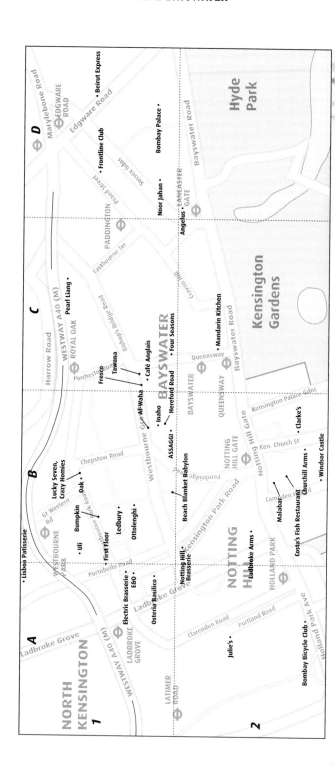

MAP 6 - HAMMERSMITH & CHISWICK

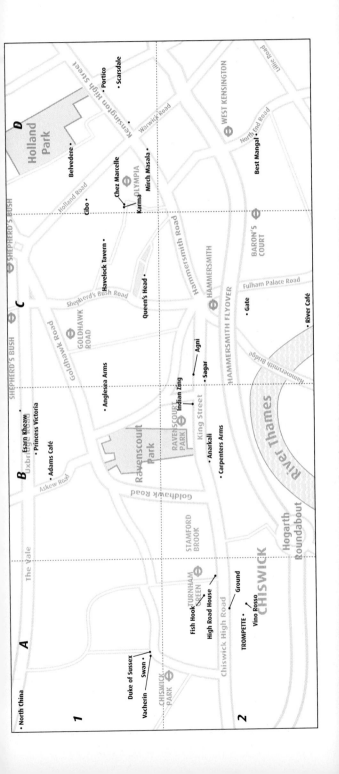

UK SURVEY RESULTS & TOP SCORERS

PLACES PEOPLE TALK ABOUT

These are the restaurants outside London that were mentioned most frequently by reporters (last year's position is shown in brackets). For the list of London's most mentioned restaurants, see page 34.

Yang Sing

1   Fat Duck (1)
    Bray, Berks
2   Manoir aux Quat' Saisons (2)
    Great Milton, Oxon
3   Waterside Inn (3)
    Bray, Berks
4   Hind's Head (4)
    Bray, Berks
5   Yang Sing (6)
    Manchester

Magpie

6= Chapter One (13)
    Locksbottom, Kent
6= Seafood Restaurant (5)
    Padstow, Cornwall
8= Anthony's (9)
    Leeds
8= Vineyard/Stockcross (10)
    Stockcross, Berkshire
10 Magpie (8)
    Whitby, N Yorks

Croma

11 Hand & Flowers (17)
    Marlow, Bucks
12 Croma (15)
    Manchester
13= Champignon Sauvage (19=)
    Cheltenham, Gloucs
13= Star Inn (12)
    Harome, N Yorks
13= Terre à Terre (11)
    Brighton

Rick Stein's Café

16 Hambleton Hall (-)
    Hambleton, Rutland
17 Olive Branch (14)
    Clipsham, Rutland
18 Rick Stein's Café (16)
    Padstow, Cornwall
19= Northcote (–)
    Langho, Lancs
19= Bordeaux Quay (–)
    Bristol

TOP SCORERS

All restaurants whose food rating is ✪✪; plus restaurants whose price is £50+ with a food rating of ✪.

£120+	Waterside Inn *(Bray)*	✪✪Ⓐ
	Le Manoir aux Quat' Saisons *(Great Milton)*	✪✪Ⓐ
£110+	The Fat Duck *(Bray)*	✪
£100+	Gidleigh Park *(Chagford)*	✪✪Ⓐ
£90+	Vineyard at Stockcross *(Stockcross)*	✪Ⓐ
£80+	Andrew Fairlie *(Auchterarder)*	✪✪Ⓐ
	Hambleton Hall *(Hambleton)*	✪✪Ⓐ
	Lucknam Park *(Colerne)*	✪✪Ⓐ
	Inverlochy Castle *(Fort William)*	✪Ⓐ
	L'Ortolan *(Shinfield)*	✪Ⓐ
	The French Horn *(Sonning-on-Thames)*	✪Ⓐ
	The Oak Room *(Marlow)*	✪Ⓐ
	Midsummer House *(Cambridge)*	✪
	Number One *(Edinburgh)*	✪
£70+	Bath Priory Hotel *(Bath)*	✪✪Ⓐ
	Bohemia *(Jersey)*	✪✪
	Harry's Place *(Great Gonerby)*	✪✪
	La Bécasse *(Ludlow)*	✪✪
	Le Poussin at Whitley Ridge *(Brockenhurst)*	✪✪
	The Kitchin *(Edinburgh)*	✪✪
	Champany Inn *(Linlithgow)*	✪Ⓐ
	Gravetye Manor *(East Grinstead)*	✪Ⓐ
	Holbeck Ghyll *(Windermere)*	✪Ⓐ
	Kinnaird House *(Dunkeld)*	✪Ⓐ
	Lords of the Manor *(Upper Slaughter)*	✪Ⓐ
	Seafood Restaurant *(Padstow)*	✪Ⓐ
	Sharrow Bay *(Ullswater)*	✪Ⓐ
	Simpsons *(Birmingham)*	✪Ⓐ
	Summer Lodge *(Evershot)*	✪Ⓐ
	Charlton House *(Shepton Mallet)*	✪
	Juliana's *(Chipping Campden)*	✪
	Longueville Manor *(Jersey)*	✪
	Restaurant Martin Wishart *(Edinburgh)*	✪
	Restaurant Sat Bains *(Nottingham)*	✪
£60+	Mr Underhill's *(Ludlow)*	✪✪Ⓐ
	Northcote *(Langho)*	✪✪Ⓐ
	Plas Bodegroes *(Pwllheli)*	✪✪Ⓐ
	Summer Isles Hotel *(Achiltibuie)*	✪✪Ⓐ
	The Three Chimneys *(Dunvegan)*	✪✪Ⓐ
	Artichoke *(Amersham)*	✪✪
	Champignon Sauvage *(Cheltenham)*	✪✪

TOP SCORERS

	No 6 Café *(Padstow)*	✪✪
	The Abbey Restaurant *(Penzance)*	✪✪
	The Crown at Whitebrook *(Whitebrook)*	✪✪
	The Harrow at Little Bedwyn *(Marlborough)*	✪✪
	Airds Hotel *(Port Appin)*	✪Ⓐ
	Gilpin Lodge *(Windermere)*	✪Ⓐ
	Hotel Tresanton *(St Mawes)*	✪Ⓐ
	Kinloch Lodge *(Sleat)*	✪Ⓐ
	Linthwaite House *(Windermere)*	✪Ⓐ
	Mallory Court *(Bishops Tachbrook)*	✪Ⓐ
	Read's *(Faversham)*	✪Ⓐ
	Rhubarb *(Edinburgh)*	✪Ⓐ
	Seafood Restaurant *(St Andrews)*	✪Ⓐ
	The Castle Hotel *(Taunton)*	✪Ⓐ
	Yorke Arms *(Ramsgill-in-Nidderdale)*	✪Ⓐ
	Abstract *(Edinburgh)*	✪
	Avenue *(Winchester)*	✪
	Horn of Plenty *(Gulworthy)*	✪
	L'Enclume *(Cartmel)*	✪
	The Moody Goose *(Midsomer Norton)*	✪
	Underscar Manor *(Applethwaite)*	✪
£50+	Hipping Hall *(Kirkby Lonsdale)*	✪✪Ⓐ
	Monachyle Mhor *(Balquhidder)*	✪✪Ⓐ
	Thackeray's *(Tunbridge Wells)*	✪✪Ⓐ
	The Cellar *(Anstruther)*	✪✪Ⓐ
	The Peat Inn *(Cupar)*	✪✪Ⓐ
	The Vanilla Pod *(Marlow)*	✪✪Ⓐ
	Tyddyn Llan *(Llandrillo)*	✪✪Ⓐ
	Bosquet *(Kenilworth)*	✪✪
	Drakes *(Ripley)*	✪✪
	Fraiche *(Oxton)*	✪✪
	Gamba *(Glasgow)*	✪✪
	Goodfellows *(Wells)*	✪✪
	Ostlers Close *(Cupar)*	✪✪
	Purnells *(Birmingham)*	✪✪
	Walnut Tree *(Abergavenny)*	✪✪
	West Stoke House *(Chichester)*	✪✪
	Babington House *(Babington)*	✪Ⓐ
	Black Bull *(Moulton)*	✪Ⓐ
	Brockencote Hall *(Chaddesley Corbett)*	✪Ⓐ
	Cavendish *(Baslow)*	✪Ⓐ
	Combe House Hotel & Restaurant *(Honiton)*	✪Ⓐ
	Darroch Learg *(Ballater)*	✪Ⓐ
	Gaucho Grill *(Manchester)*	✪Ⓐ
	Hartwell House *(Aylesbury)*	✪Ⓐ
	Lavender House *(Brundall)*	✪Ⓐ
	Llangoed Hall *(Llyswen)*	✪Ⓐ
	Newick Park *(Newick)*	✪Ⓐ
	Percy's *(Virginstow)*	✪Ⓐ
	Samuel's *(Masham)*	✪Ⓐ
	St Helena's *(Elstow)*	✪Ⓐ

TOP SCORERS

The Albannach *(Lochinver)*	✪Ⓐ
The Cross *(Kingussie)*	✪Ⓐ
The Loft Restaurant *(Beaumaris)*	✪Ⓐ
Vintners Rooms *(Edinburgh)*	✪Ⓐ
Wesley House *(Winchcombe)*	✪Ⓐ
22 Mill Street *(Chagford)*	✪
Abstract *(Inverness)*	✪
Allium *(Fairford)*	✪
Anthony's *(Leeds)*	✪
Dining Room *(Ashbourne)*	✪
Fairyhill *(Reynoldston)*	✪
Fishes Cafe & Seafood Bar *(Burnham Market)*	✪
JSW *(Petersfield)*	✪
La Potinière *(Gullane)*	✪
Little Barwick House *(Barwick)*	✪
Lumière *(Cheltenham)*	✪
Restaurant Nathan Outlaw *(Fowey)*	✪
Rookery Hall Hotel & Spa *(Nantwich)*	✪
Royal Oak *(White Waltham)*	✪
Seafood Restaurant *(St Monans)*	✪
Sienna *(Dorchester)*	✪
Smiths Brasserie *(Ongar)*	✪
The Olive Tree *(Bath)*	✪
The Weavers Shed *(Golcar)*	✪
Three Lions *(Stuckton)*	✪
Tony Tobin @ The Dining Room *(Reigate)*	✪

£40+	Chapter One *(Locksbottom)*	✪✪Ⓐ
	Ee-Usk (Seafood Restaurant) *(Oban)*	✪✪Ⓐ
	Great House *(Lavenham)*	✪✪Ⓐ
	Jeremy's at Borde Hill *(Haywards Heath)*	✪✪Ⓐ
	Nutter's *(Norden)*	✪✪Ⓐ
	Riverside *(Bridport)*	✪✪Ⓐ
	The Olive Branch *(Clipsham)*	✪✪Ⓐ
	The Star Inn *(Harome)*	✪✪Ⓐ
	Trawlers *(East Looe)*	✪✪Ⓐ
	5 North Street *(Winchcombe)*	✪✪
	Alimentum *(Cambridge)*	✪✪
	Apicius *(Cranbrook)*	✪✪
	Braidwoods *(Dalry)*	✪✪
	Gingerman *(Brighton)*	✪✪
	J Baker's Bistro Moderne *(York)*	✪✪
	Riddle & Finns *(Brighton)*	✪✪
	Terre à Terre *(Brighton)*	✪✪
	The Hind's Head *(Bray)*	✪✪
	Vine Leaf *(St Andrews)*	✪✪
	West House *(Biddenden)*	✪✪

£30+	22 Chesterton Road *(Cambridge)*	✪✪Ⓐ
	Kinara *(Westerham)*	✪✪Ⓐ
	Michael's *(Southport)*	✪✪Ⓐ
	Quince & Medlar *(Cockermouth)*	✪✪Ⓐ

165

TOP SCORERS

	Sportsman *(Whitstable)*	✪✪Ⓐ
	Wheeler's Oyster Bar *(Whitstable)*	✪✪Ⓐ
	Cafe Maitreya *(Bristol)*	✪✪
	Culinaria *(Bristol)*	✪✪
	David Bann *(Edinburgh)*	✪✪
	Dilli *(Altrincham)*	✪✪
	Les Mirabelles *(Nomansland)*	✪✪
	Maliks *(Cookham)*	✪✪
	Mother India *(Glasgow)*	✪✪
	Ramsons *(Ramsbottom)*	✪✪
	The Highwayman *(Kirkby Lonsdale)*	✪✪
	Yang Sing *(Manchester)*	✪✪
£25+	Aagrah *(Shipley)*	✪✪
	Golden Palace *(Harrow)*	✪✪
	Hansa's *(Leeds)*	✪✪
	Magpie Café *(Whitby)*	✪✪
	Xian *(Orpington)*	✪✪
£20+	Akbar's Balti *(Bradford)*	✪✪Ⓐ
	Anstruther Fish Bar *(Anstruther)*	✪✪
	Mumtaz Paan House *(Bradford)*	✪✪
	Punjab Tandoori *(Manchester)*	✪✪
	Stein's Fish & Chips *(Padstow)*	✪✪
£15+	Superfish *(Tolworth)*	✪✪
	The Company Shed *(West Mersea)*	✪✪
£10+	Aldeburgh Fish And Chips *(Aldeburgh)*	✪✪

UK DIRECTORY

Harbourmaster £ 42 🅐⭐
Quay Pde SA46 0BA (01545) 570755
"A large picture-window overlooking the harbour" is a recent improvement to this "lovely hide-away", by the quayside; its "locally-sourced" food – "especially the seafood" – "always delivers clean and simple flavours". / **Sample dishes:** *crunchy vegetable & herb salad, cider vinegar dressing; Welsh black fillet, dauphinoise, red wine sauce; crème brûlée.* **Details:** *www.harbour-master.com; 9 pm; closed Mon L; no Amex.* **Accommodation:** *13 rooms, from £100.*

Bistro Verde £ 35 🆃
Units 1-2 The Grn AB11 6NY (01224) 586180
"A lovely restaurant tucked-away in a quiet corner of Aberdeen city", tipped for its "very good seafood". / **Details:** *9 pm.*

Cafe 52 £ 37 ⭐
52 The Green AB11 6PE (01224) 590094
"A lovely restaurant in a quiet corner of the city"; the cooking is often "creative", but – presumably reflecting local sourcing – the "best burger in the UK" is a particular highlight. / **Sample dishes:** *Greek salad tartlet with Feta, basil, tomato and caramelized red onion; fillet steak with sauté aubergines and Dolcelatte mash served with beetroot and shallot jus.* **Details:** *www.cafe52.net; 9.30 pm; no Amex.*

Cafe Boheme £ 38 🆃
23 Windmill Brae AB11 6HU (01224) 210677
"Being small is the secret of its success", say fans of this "friendly" spot, tipped especially for its "excellent-value early-evening menu". / **Sample dishes:** *puff pastry tart with onion purée, sautéed mushrooms, shaved Parmesan & pesto dressing; pan fried duck breast, beetroot gratin, red wine & olive jus; orange, date & cardamon tart, mascarpone sorbet.* **Details:** *www.cafebohemerestaurant.co.uk; 9 pm; closed Mon & Sun; no Amex.*

Cinnamon £ 29 🆃
476 Union St AB10 1TS (01224) 633328
A trendy Indian, tipped for its wide-ranging menu; (in the absence of much competition, however, it is occasionally suggested that it is "a bit over-hyped" locally). / **Sample dishes:** *tandoori roast Scottish king scallops; chicken cafarel; kulfi.* **Details:** *www.cinnamon-aberdeen.com; midnight.*

Silver Darling £ 62 🅐
Pocra Quay, North Pier AB11 5DQ (01224) 576229
"You get to watch the boats go by as you eat", at this former lighthouse, long regarded as "Aberdeen's finest" place to eat; to fans it's "an all-round gem", where fish and seafood are realised with "finesse", but it also inspired a couple of duff reports this year. / **Sample dishes:** *mosaic of scallops & salmon marinated in lime, vanilla & hazelnut oil, with shredded carrot & celeriac; roast fillet of monkfish, chickpea & aubergine, cumin purée, grilled courgette & asparagus, chorizo & chive dressing; chocolate & Earl Grey tea mousse, Bailey's ice cream & Earl Grey syrup.* **Details:** *www.silverdarlingrestaurant.co.uk; beside harbour master's tower; 9 pm; closed Sat L & Sun; children: +16 after 8 pm.*

Penhelig Arms   £ 38
LL35 0LT   (01654) 767215
*"Hope it's just teething troubles" – there are some unhappy reports
on the recent take-over (by Brains Brewery) of this popular, formerly
family-owned, Cardigan Bay inn, especially as to the dumbing down
of the wine list; we've deferred a rating till next year.
/ Details: www.penheligarms.com; 9 pm; no Amex. Accommodation: 15
rooms, from £90.*

Swan Hotel   £ 29
Great North Rd LS25 3AA   (0113) 281 3205
*A 16th-century inn, particulary tipped for its "very good-value
weekday carvery". / Sample dishes: seafood parcel; fillet steak; home-made
Bailey's & coffee roulade. Details: 10 pm, Sun 9.30 pm; D only, ex Sun open L &
D; no Amex; book only for restaurant.*

Angel Hotel   £ 43
15 Cross St NP7 5EN   (01873) 857121
*This "historic" hotel is being upgraded to "a high standard" under its
current ownership (which it shares with the re-launched Walnut Tree);
it is universally hailed by reporters for its "very good food" and its
"wonderful" ("mainly French") staff. / Sample dishes: creamed Portobello
mushroom on toasted beer bread; guinea-fowl pot roast with Savoy cabbage and
pearl barley broth; blueberry custard tart and vanilla ice cream.
Details: www.angelhotelabergavenny.com; 10 pm. Accommodation: 30 rooms,
from £85.*

Clytha Arms   £ 36
NP7 9BW   (01873) 840206
*Its interior strikes the odd reporter as rather "shabby", but this
boozer-cum-restaurant, near the Brecon Beacons, wins consistent
praise for its "beautiful" food. / Sample dishes: oysters in Thai dipping
sauce; herbed loin of lamb with bubble & squeak; chocolate cake with Seville
orange ice cream. Details: www.clytha-arms.com; on Old Abergavenny to Raglan
Rd; 9.30 pm; closed Mon L & Sun D. Accommodation: 4 rooms, from £80.*

The Hardwick   £ 44
Old Raglan Rd NP7 9AA   (01873) 854220
*"Adventurous dishes, exploiting local ingredients" excited many
enthusiastic reports from reporters on this "enjoyable" venture, which
is "among the best gastropubs in Wales"; (they have big plans too,
having just secured planning for a major expansion).
/ Sample dishes: pan fried smoked haddock & curry risotto cake with soft boiled
egg and pea shoots; roast loin of rare breed middle white pork, with haricot beans,
purple sprouting broccoli, dandelion, pancetta & rocket salad; panettone crème
brûlée. Details: www.thehardwick.co.uk; 10 pm; closed Mon & Sun D; no Amex.*

Walnut Tree £ 55

Llandewi Skirrid NP7 8AW   (01873) 852797

WINNER 2009

RÉMY MARTIN

"Back on excellent form!" – it would be "good to see Shaun Hill back in the kitchen" anywhere, but even more so when he's taken over the best-known restaurant in Wales, and "returned it to its former glory"; "the friendliest staff" present his "wonderful, perfectly balanced food from local ingredients"... and it's "brilliant value" too.
/ *Sample dishes:* calf's sweetbreads with potato & olive cake; roast squab pigeon breast with pastilla of legs; Hungarian trifle. *Details:* www.thewalnuttreeinn.com; 3m NE of Abergavenny on B4521; 10 pm; closed Mon & Sun.

ACHILTIBUIE, HIGHLAND 9–1B

Summer Isles Hotel £ 67

IV26 2YQ   (01854) 622282
"Beautiful surroundings, fantastic seafood" – that's not far from the whole story on this remote and "stunning located" haven, where the cooking is almost invariably hailed as "outstanding".
/ *Sample dishes:* filo parcel of monkfish tails with a tamarind sauce & warm oatmeal loaf; roast rib of Aberdeen angus beef, with wild mushrooms & red onions in red wine. *Details:* www.summerisleshotel.co.uk; 25m N of Ullapool on A835; 8 pm; no Amex; children: 8+. *Accommodation:* 13 rooms, from £140.

ACTON TRUSSELL, STAFFORDSHIRE 5–3B

Moat House £ 45

Lower Penkridge Rd ST17 0RJ   (01785) 712217
"A good find off the M6", this canal-side hotel dining room is tipped for food that's "really good" by local standards – perhaps why it can be "horrendously busy". / *Sample dishes:* French quail, potato hash brown, lentils, black pudding, fried quail's egg, quail jus; sirloin steak served with thick chips cooked in duck fat, field mushroom, plum tomato and bearnaise sauce; rhubarb and apple brûlée, custard ice cream, crumble and rhubarb syrup. *Details:* www.moathouse.co.uk; Junction 13 off the M6, follow signs for A449; 9.30 pm; no jeans. *Accommodation:* 41 rooms, from £135.

ADDINGHAM, WEST YORKSHIRE 5–1C

Fleece £ 32

152-4 Main St LS29 0LY   (01943) 830491
Getting a table can be "a chore", at this "traditional" country inn (no booking), which offers "carefully cooked local and seasonal food" in a "friendly and efficient" manner. / *Sample dishes:* tapas selection; meat & potato pie; sticky toffee pudding. *Details:* 9.15 pm, Sun 8pm.

Clenaghans   **£ 36**   🌀
48 Soldierstown Rd BT67 0ES   (02892) 652952
A "wonderful old pub"; reports this year were thin on detail, but in
former surveys features that have rated mention include a fiddler,
the open fires, and some decent accommodation.
/ **Sample dishes:** ravioli of confit duckling, lobster aroma, chilli gremolata and
crème fraîche; Irish beef fillet, potato croquette, port wine beurre rouge, pâté of
Irish brie. **Details:** www.clenaghans.com; on B105; 9.30 pm; D only, closed
Mon & Sun; children: +12 Fri & Sat. **Accommodation:** 5 rooms, from £85.

Aldeburgh Fish And Chips   **£ 13**   ⭐⭐
226 High St IP16 4BZ   (01728) 454685
"Somewhere the hype is all true!" – "the freshest fish and chips,
eaten on the sea wall" make this famous chippy a simply "wonderful"
destination. / **Details:** 8 pm; serving times vary seasonally; no credit cards.

The Lighthouse   **£ 35**
77 High St IP15 5AU   (01728) 453377
The Big Cheese locally – this "recently made-over" fish bistro is,
say fans, an "imaginative", "stylish" and "welcoming" destination,
and one that's "still packing 'em in"; there's a slight feeling, though,
that it has "slipped a bit". / **Sample dishes:** pan fried scallop and bacon
salad and citrus crème fraîche; fillet of sea bass and roast red peppers, spinach
and new potatoes; boozy banana pancakes with toffee crunch ice cream.
Details: www.thelighthouserestaurant.co.uk; 10 pm; closed one week in Jan and
one week in Oct.

152   **£ 38**   ⭐
152 High St IP15 5AX   (01728) 454594
Thanks, it seems, to its new chef – and his "simple" but "delicious"
and "imaginative" cuisine – this "fun, efficient and modern"
restaurant is re-establishing itself in reporters' good books.
/ **Sample dishes:** gravalax of salmon with potato and chive salad; pan fried skate
in black batter saffron potatotes and Savoy cabbage; sharp lemon tart with red
berry compote. **Details:** www.152aldeburgh.co.uk; 10; closed Tue (& Mon
in winter).

Regatta   **£ 33**
171-173 High St IP15 5AN   (01728) 452011
In "highly competitive Aldeburgh", this "casual" ("large and noisy")
fish restaurant is the well-established No. 2, offering food that's
"nothing fancy" but "always reliable".
/ **Details:** www.regattaaldeburgh.com; 9.30 pm; closed Sun D Nov-Feb.

The Wentworth Hotel   **£ 32**
Wentworth Rd IP15 5BD   (01728) 452312
Just "what you'd expect from an old-fashioned, seaside hotel" –
a "civilised" and "comfortable" dining room that's "well run",
and offers food that's "good without having any pretensions
to gastronomy". / **Sample dishes:** crispy lardon, quail egg salad, blue cheese
dressing; roast rump of Suffolk lamb, rosemary mash, wild mushroom and
peppercorn sauce; white chocolate bread and butter pudding with custard.
Details: www.wentworth-aldeburgh.com; 9 pm. **Accommodation:** 35 rooms,
from £140.

ALDFORD, CHESHIRE   5–3A

The Grosvenor Arms   £ 32   Ⓐ
Chester Rd CH3 6HJ   (01244) 620228
A "posh" pub with a "fantastic garden", in a "lovely" ducal village;
it's a "pleasant", "informal" hang-out that's consistently very popular,
and offers a "varied" menu, plus good wines and real ales.
/ *Sample dishes:* goats cheese crottin rolled in toasted fennel seeds with oven
dried tomatoes; slow roast belly pork with a tarragon cream sauce and apple
dauphinoise; sticky toffee pudding with butterscotch sauce and vanilla ice cream.
Details: www.brunningandprice.co.uk; 6m S of Chester on B5130; 10 pm,
Sun 9 pm; children: 14+ at D.

ALNWICK, NORTHUMBERLAND   8–1B

Blackmore's   £ 35   Ⓣ
Bondgate Without NE66 1PN   (01665) 602395
A new boutique-hotel, whose chef used to be top toque at Newcastle
United; it's tipped as a "promising" venture, which makes good use
of "locally-sourced food". / **Details:** www.blackmoresofalnwick.com; 9.30 pm.

ALTRINCHAM, CHESHIRE   5–2B

Note: See also Juniper, under Manchester

Dilli   £ 34   ✪✪
60 Stamford New Rd WA14 1EE   (0161) 929 7484
"An outstanding Indian restaurant practising Ayurvedic cooking
methods to produce a fabulous range of high-quality sub-continental
dishes"; the setting may be "crowded" and sometimes "rowdy",
but this suburban "hidden gem" is a "triumph" nonetheless.
/ *Sample dishes:* tiger prawns creamed yoghurt with saffron, chargrilled;
lamb curry with ginger, fennel and saffron. **Details:** www.dilli.co.uk; on A538;
11pm, 10 sun.

Man-Zen   £ 34   Ⓣ
169 Ashley Rd WA15 9SD   (0161) 9281222
A top Altrincham tip – a "lively" Chinese where the food is "always
good", and the service "usually is too". / **Details:** www.manzenhale.co.uk;
11 pm; D only, ex Sun open L & D.

ALVERSTON, WARWICKSHIRE   21–C

Baraset Barn   £ 40   Ⓐ
Pimlico Ln CV37 7RF   (01789) 295510
"Now under new management, almost back to the very high standard
it had in its early days" – this impressively-converted barn appears –
on the basis of somewhat limited feedback – to be a "fantastic"
informal eatery. / *Sample dishes:* eggs florentine, toasted muffin, buttered
spinach and hollandaise; pan fried fillets of seabass with rosemary sauté potatoes,
piedmont peppers and beurre blanc; coffee and pecan pudding, caramel sauce
and vanilla mascarpone. **Details:** www.barasetbarn.co.uk; 9.30 pm; closed Sun D;
no Amex.

Amberley Castle   **£ 72**   **Ⓐ**
BN18 9LT   (01798) 831992
*It's early days, but it rather seems that new owners Von Essen are 'dumbing down' the cuisine at this fairy-tale castle; for romance, though, you still can't beat the "perfect" setting, which comes complete with portcullis and ramparts. / **Sample dishes:** scallops served with kohlrabe and pansy purée, crisp pork belly, shoots and wild herbs; 59 degrees Lancashire pork loin, smith apples, creamed shallots and braised crubeen; spiced peanut and caramel parfait, hot fried chocolate and praline creame.*
Details: www.amberleycastle.co.uk; N of Arundel on B2139; 9 pm; jacket or tie required; booking: max 8; children: 12+. **Accommodation:** 19 rooms, from £175.

Britannia Inn   **£ 31**   **★**
Elterwater LA22 9HP   (01539) 437210
*A "warm", "sociable" and "very busy" pub, in a "delightful village", where the cuisine – featuring "excellent local meat and fish" – is "hearty yet sophisticated". / **Sample dishes:** king scallop; venison steak; blueberry brûlée.* **Details:** www.britinn.co.uk; 9.30 pm; no Amex; booking: max 6; children: before 9 pm only. **Accommodation:** 9 rooms, from £76.

Drunken Duck   **£ 47**   **Ⓐ**
Barngates LA22 0NG   (01539) 436347
*"Isolated, yet known to many" – this "wonderfully-located" inn-cum-microbrewery remains a key Lakeland destination; its "London prices" are an unwelcome surprise, though, especially as its food can seem somewhat "unadventurous". / **Sample dishes:** seared mackerel, beetroot risotto; loin eye and rack of venison, braised puy lentils,mashed potatoes,venison and juniper sausage; praline soufflé with pistachio ice cream.*
Details: www.drunkenduckinn.co.uk; 3m from Ambleside, towards Hawkshead; 9 pm; booking: max 6. **Accommodation:** 17 rooms, from £120.

The Glass House   **£ 36**   **Ⓐ**
Rydal Rd LA22 9AN   (01539) 432137
*This former mill is potentially a "stylish", "pleasant" and "affordable" sort of place, but the cooking standards are quite up-and-down – "they need another visit from Gordon Ramsay". / **Sample dishes:** mushroom risotto with white truffle oil & Parmesan crisp; poached darn of salmon with Jersey new potatoes, green bean & leaf salad, chive butter sauce; summer pudding with marscapone & fresh berry coulis.*
Details: www.theglasshouserestaurant.co.uk; behind Little Bridge House; 9.30 pm, Sat 10 pm; no Amex; children: 5+ at D.

Lucy's on a Plate   **£ 34**
Church St LA22 0BU   (01539) 431191
*Lucy has expanded her empire of late: food is now served in new premises (formerly The Porthole, RIP) near the original deli – fans love its "energetic" style and "eccentric tapas/mezze" menu, but critics say it's "over-stretching itself by cramming too many people in". / **Sample dishes:** marinated pork fillet with stir fry vegetables, served in a tortilla basket with a sour cream and honey dressing; medallions of lamb on a bed of sweet potato and a root vegetable confit; sticky banana pudding with custard.*
Details: www.lucysofambleside.co.uk; centre of Ambleside; 9 pm.

Rothay Manor £ 51 ⓣ
Rothay Bridge LA22 0EH (01539) 433605
A "cosy" country house hotel tipped by some reports for a "vaut-le-voyage" afternoon tea, and "good" dinners too.
/ **Details:** www.rothaymanor.co.uk; 9 pm; no jeans or trainers; no booking, Sat D; children: 7+ at D. **Accommodation:** 19 rooms, from £150.

Zeffirelli's £ 28
Compston Rd LA22 9AD (01539) 433845
A "big and bustling" but "classy" vegetarian restaurant, attached to a cinema, where "very good pizzas" are a speciality; the daytime fare is "always good" – by night, the place can seem a bit of a "production line". / **Sample dishes:** goat's cheese and fresh chive soufflé, on a bed of rocket with a walnut and pear dressing; penne tossed in fresh basil and pine nut pesto topped with rocket and roast cherry tomatoes; double chocolate mousse cake with raspberry coulis. **Details:** www.zeffirellis.com; 10 pm; no Amex.

AMERSHAM, BUCKINGHAMSHIRE 3–2A

Artichoke £ 60 ⭐⭐
9 Market Sq HP7 0DF (01494) 726611
Laurie Gear's "cosy" venture offered some "innovative" and "brilliant" food, but it was closed by a fire in mid-2008; he hopes to be up-and-running again by 2009. / **Sample dishes:** Dorset crab, dill gnocchi, cucumber tagliatelle, warm fennel soup; fillet of Aberdeen angus beef, kohl rabi, spinach, black truffle, foie gras, pomme purée, pickled walnuts, blue cheese foam; hazelnut dacquoise, banana mousse, frangelico chocolate granache, hazelnut chantilly, chocolate sorbet. **Details:** www.theartichokerestaurant.co.uk; 10 pm; closed Mon & Sun; no Amex.

Famous Fish £ 38
11 Market Sq HP7 0DF (01494) 728665
This South African fish-specialist offers a wide-ranging menu, and its "great food and atmosphere" are consistently well-rated by numerous reporters. / **Sample dishes:** mussels poached in tomato sauce, olive oil, & white wine, served with a touch of cream; piri-piri prawn & chicken pot; malva punch pudding. **Details:** in Old Amersham; 10 pm; closed Sun; no Amex.

Gilbey's £ 44
1 Market Sq HP7 0DF (01494) 727242
This "attractive" bolt-hole may only offer a "fairly standard bistro-type menu", but its notably "excellent" wine list helps maintain it as a "perennial favourite" locally. / **Sample dishes:** wild mushroom & madeira millefeuille with mizuna; braised pork belly with pickled pink cabbage and celeriac mash; apricot tarte Tatin with amaretto & almond ice cream.
Details: www.gilbeygroup.com; in Old Amersham; 9.30 pm, Sat 9.45 pm.

ANSTRUTHER, FIFE 9–4D

Anstruther Fish Bar £ 21 ⭐⭐
42-44 Shore St KY10 3AQ (01333) 310518
"Spanking fresh fish" ("just off the boats") in "great batter", and served with "delicious chips" – no wonder "there's always a queue" for this famous chippy. / **Sample dishes:** prawn cocktail; haddock and chips; ice cream. **Details:** www.anstrutherfishbar.co.uk; 10 pm; no Amex.

The Cellar £ 52 A ✪ ✪

24 East Grn KY10 3AA (01333) 310378

"For superlative cooking of fish straight from the sea, nowhere else comes close…" to the Jukes's "unique" venture of a quarter of a century's standing, and it also offers a "very good wine list"; the setting – a "cave-like" room near the harbour – is "very unusual" too. / *Sample dishes:* tart of lobster and smoked salmon; grilled halibut with greens, pinenuts, smoked bacon and basil mash; individual pavlova with lemon curd ice cream and rhubarb. *Details:* in the harbour area; 9.30 pm; closed Mon L & Sun.

APPLECROSS, WESTER ROSS   9–2B

Applecross Inn £ 31 ✪

Shore St IV54 8LT (01520) 744262

A "real pub", of note for its "simple but wonderful fish" and the "freshest seafood"; it has a "remote and lovely setting" too. / *Sample dishes:* fresh local oysters; prawns in hot lemon and garlic butter, salad and crispy bread; apple and plum crumble with custard. *Details:* www.applecross.uk.com; off A896, S of Shieldaig; 9 pm; no Amex; need 4+ to book. *Accommodation:* 7 rooms, from £100.

APPLETHWAITE, CUMBRIA   7–3C

Underscar Manor £ 65 ✪

CA12 4PH (01768) 775000

"People may say it's a bit chintzy and old-fashioned" – or "amusingly formal", if you prefer – but reports still usually express affection for this "fantastically-located" country house hotel, where the food can be "outstanding"; the DB&B package is particularly recommended. / *Sample dishes:* roast quail breast with spring roll of quail leg, leek mushroom & pine kernel cannelloni; local loin of venison with venison ragu, wild mushrooms, carrots & cumin, spring cabbage & juniper, & potato cake; summer fruit pudding with crème fraîche ice cream. *Details:* www.underscarmanor.co.uk; on A66, 17m W of M6, J40; 8.30 pm; jacket required at D; children: 12+. *Accommodation:* 11 rooms, from £180.

ARLINGHAM, GLOUCESTERSHIRE   2–2B

The Old Passage Inn £ 47

Passage Rd GL2 7JR (01452) 740547

A "delightfully-situated" spot, "way off the beaten track"; it's made a name for "superb" fish and seafood, but changed hands quite recently – given conflicting reports of the new régime, we don't think a rating appropriate this year. / *Details:* www.fishattheoldpassageinn.co.uk; 9 pm; closed Mon & Sun D; no Amex. *Accommodation:* 3 rooms, from £95.

ARUNDEL, WEST SUSSEX   3–4A

Arundel House £ 45 A ✪

11 High St BN18 9AD (01903) 882136

"The best place locally, by miles"; this restaurant-with-rooms, in the shadow of the castle, seems to have raised its game significantly in the past year; it's often hailed for its "fantastic" food, "friendly" service and "pleasant" atmosphere. / *Sample dishes:* Cornish crab & ginger twice-baked with sweet red pepper coulis; saddle of local venison, fondant potato, wilted spinach and red wine; local rhubarb cheesecake rhubarb & custard ice cream. *Details:* www.arundelhouseonline.co.uk; 9 pm; closed Sun; children: 14+ D. *Accommodation:* 5 rooms, from £100.

ASCOT, BERKSHIRE 3–3A

Ascot Oriental £ 37 ⭐
London Rd SL5 0PU   (01344) 621877
Thanks to its "yummy", "fresh-tasting" food, Konrad Liu's "upmarket"
and "welcoming" Chinese/Thai establishment "never fails to please".
/ *Sample dishes:* sautéed chicken; side of beef with chilli and black beans;
banana fritter and ice cream. *Details:* www.ascotoriental.com; 2m E of Ascot
on A329; 10.30 pm.

The Thatched Tavern £ 41 Ⓣ
Cheapside Rd SL5 7QG   (01344) 620874
An "olde-worlde" gastropub, tipped for its "consistent presentation
and quality". / *Sample dishes:* smoked ham, chorizo & chicken terrine
wrapped in bacon with sweet pepper relish; pan-fried pork medalllions with
a parsnip purée and ginger roast baby carrots; sticky toffee pudding with toffee
sauce. *Details:* www.thethatchedtavern.co.uk; 2m from Ascot, signed
to Cheapside village; 9.30 pm, Sat 10 pm.

ASENBY, NORTH YORKSHIRE 8–4C

Crab & Lobster £ 48 Ⓐ ⭐
Dishforth Rd YO7 3QL   (01845) 577286
"A quirky gastropub with equally quirky rooms" – renowned for its
"great seafood" and "very good fish", and for its "fantastic" interior
packed with atmospheric "clutter"; "shame you always have to fight
for a table". / *Sample dishes:* Shetland mussels with cabbage, smoked bacon,
crème fraîche, chives & parsley; honey spiced breast of duck, confit brown onion
mash, buttered greens, port wine gravy; sticky date pudding, butterscotch sauce,
double vanilla ice cream. *Details:* www.crabandlobster.co.uk; at junction of Asenby
Rd & Topcliffe Rd; 9 pm, 9.30 pm Sat. *Accommodation:* 14 rooms, from £150.

ASHBOURNE, DERBYSHIRE 5–3C

Dining Room £ 50 ⭐
33 St. John's St DE6 1GP   (01335) 300666
An ambitious small restaurant, with "innovative" cuisine, using
"excellent local produce"; "don't know why it isn't Michelin-starred",
muses one reporter. / *Sample dishes:* salmon, Cornish mackerel soldier,
horseradish, cucumber, lemon oil, lime jelly, wild rice krispies; beef, thornham
oyster, vegetables, fried mock onion Guinness gravy, beetroot thyme jelly,
horseradish potato soldier; wakefield rhubarb & custard.
Details: www.thediningroomashbourne.co.uk; closed Mon & Sun; no Amex;
children: 12+.

ASHBURTON, DEVON 1–3D

Agaric £ 45
30 North St TQ13 7QD   (01364) 654478
A restaurant-with-room – and a cookery school too – which is highly
rated by all reporters for its "consistently good food".
/ *Sample dishes:* warm salad of pigeon breast and smoked bacon with beechroot
finished with raspberry vinegar; grilled brill steak with grilled fennel sorrel
hollandaise; lemon polenta cake with clotted cream ice cream and raspberry and
honey sorbet. *Details:* www.agaricrestaurant.co.uk; 9.30 pm; closed Mon & Tue,
Sat L & Sun D; no Amex. *Accommodation:* 5 rooms, from £70.

Sweet Olive   **£ 42** ⭐

Baker St OX11 9DD   (01235) 851272

*"A couple of guys from Alsace" serve up "superb French bistro fare"
that's "well worth a detour", at this "excellent restaurant within
a village pub"; the wine list is "impressive" too.* / **Sample dishes:** *tiger
prawns in tempura, roquette salad & spicy soy dressing; escalope of venison with
creamed cabbage, port wine sauce & chips; home-made treacle sponge, custard &
vanilla ice cream.* **Details:** *www.sweet-olive.com; Half a mile off the A417
between Streatley & Wantage; 9 pm; closed Feb.*

Ⓐ⭐⭐

Andrew Fairlie

Gleneagles Hotel   **£ 87**

PH3 1NF   (01764) 694267

*In the bowels (no windows!) of this famous hotel, a "dark, modern-
chic" setting for a "truly great all-round experience" – Andrew Fairlie's
"exquisite" food is "probably the equal of any in Scotland".*
/ **Sample dishes:** *home smoked Scottish lobster with lime and herb butter;
roast fillet of lamb; hot Valrhona chocolate biscuit.*
Details: *www.andrewfairlie.com; 10 pm; L only, closed Sun; children: 12+.*
Accommodation: *273 rooms, from £320.*

River Cottage Canteen   **£ 44**

Trinity Sq EX13 5AN   (01297) 631862

*Hugh Fearnley-Whittingstall's first foray into restaurants – next to his
food store – is, as you might hope, hailed for its "simple" but "value-
for-money" fare, with a "heavy emphasis on local produce".*
/ **Sample dishes:** *Cornish asparagus, poached duck egg and summer truffle
dressing; slow roast shoulder and roast saddle of lamb, organic potatoes & greens;
rhubarb upside-down cake, ice cream.* **Details:** *www.rivercottage.net; 9.30 pm;
closed Mon D & Sun D.*

Hartwell House   £ 59   Ⓐ ⭐
Oxford Rd HP17 8NR   (01296) 747444
*For "a delightful gastronomic experience in a beautiful location",
this very grand Jacobean country house is consistently well-rated (if by
a relatively small fan club). / **Sample dishes:** confit of Cornish mackerel with
a pressed tomato terrine; loin of lamb with braised lef, rosti potato, pea purée &
sauté morel mushrooms; orange soufflé with orange tiramisu & amaretto ice
cream. **Details:** www.hartwell-house.com; 2m W of Aylesbury on A418; 9.45 pm;
no jeans or trainers; children: 6+. **Accommodation:** 49 rooms, from £280.*

Mela   £ 26   Ⓣ
103 London Rd HP22 5LD   (01296) 630110
*If you're looking for curry, this town-centre spot is tipped
as "a fabulous friendly place with the loveliest staff in the area".
/ **Details:** 11 pm; D only.*

Babington House   £ 53   Ⓐ ⭐
BA11 3RW   (01373) 812266
*The "fantastically-located" rural outpost of the Soho House empire
is open for dining only to guests and members; the fare "doesn't try
too hard, but is great for what it is". / **Details:** www.babingtonhouse.co.uk;
11 pm; open to residents & members only for L & D all week.
Accommodation: 28 rooms, from £225.*

Hassop Hall   £ 46   Ⓐ
DE45 1NS   (01629) 640488
*"The family are on hand to make you feel very welcome", at the
Chapmans' "tasteful" and "wonderful" country house hotel, to which
a visit always inspires "a real sense of occasion"; "the menu hasn't
changed for decades" – for most reporters, that's a good thing!
/ **Sample dishes:** pine kernel, walnut & goats' cheese salad with fruited melba
toast; oven-roast cajun salmon with tomato & cucumber salad; summer pudding.
Details: www.hassophall.co.uk; on the B6001 Bakewell - Hathersage Road,
Junction 29 of M1; 9 pm; closed Mon L, Sat L & Sun D. **Accommodation:** 13
rooms, from £95.*

The Monsal Head Hotel   £ 29   Ⓐ
DE45 1NL   (01629) 640250
*If you "sit outside in the sun, drinking real ales on tap",
this "beautifully-located" hikers' pub is undoubtedly a fab destination;
it offers a "hearty" menu of "traditional pub fare and rather old-
fashioned dinner-party dishes". / **Sample dishes:** crispy pork spring rolls
made with shredded spiced slow roast pork belly, vegetables and hoisin sauce;
roast bacon joint with honey roast root vegetables, topped with toasted sesame
seeds and a mustard jus; chocolate nemesis. **Details:** www.monsalhead.com;
Just up from Ashford in the Water on the B6465; 9.30 pm, Sat & Sun 9 pm;
no Amex. **Accommodation:** 7 rooms, from £90.*

Darroch Learg £ 58

Braemar Rd AB35 5UX   (01339) 755443

Thanks not least to its "rather remote" location, the Franks family's country house hotel is a "special-occasion destination par excellence", and offers food that's "very enjoyable". / **Sample dishes:** *Scottish wood pigeon, foie gras & shallot pie with fig jam; venison loin with creamed summer greens, chick pea croquette and goats cheese gnocchi; warm white and milk chocolate cake with crème fraîche.* **Details:** *www.darrochlearg.co.uk; on A93 W of Ballater; 9 pm; D only, ex Sun open L & D; no Amex.* **Accommodation:** *17 rooms, from £130.*

Monachyle Mhor £ 50

FK19 8PQ   (01877) 384622

"A total delight"; Tom Lewis's "trendy, but still cosy" small hotel – remotely and "beautifully" located "up a long dirt road" – offers "original and brilliantly-prepared" dishes, "personable" service and "glorious" loch-views. / **Sample dishes:** *monkfish tail with artichokes, blush vine tomatoes, garden cress and cider and red onion butter sauce; guinea fowl breast, herbed pistachio farci, leeks fondue, dauphines potato, asparagus spears and mustard seed sauce; raspberry clafoutis served with vanilla ice cream.* **Details:** *www.mhor.net; Take the Kings House turning off the A84; 8.45 pm; no Amex; children: 12+ at D.* **Accommodation:** *14 rooms, from £105.*

Thai Orchid £ 29

56 Northbar St OX16 0TL   (01295) 270833

An Aladdin's cave of an Thai restaurant, tipped for its "good-value lunchtime buffet". / **Sample dishes:** *fresh mussels steamed in Thai spices & herbs; strips of beef marinated in soya bean sauce stir fried with pepper, onion, tomato & brandy sauce.* **Details:** *www.thaiorchidbanbury.co.uk; 10.30 pm.*

The Milton £ 38

AB31 5QH   (01330) 844566

We received little (but all-favourable) feedback on this restaurant near Crathes Castle, but – in default of much else – we've continued to list it as a top tip hereabouts. / **Sample dishes:** *pan fried free range chicken livers in madeira, with garlic and cream, served with warm brioche; pedigree rare breed pork sausages with grain mustard mash and red onion confit; warm chocolate ganache tart with cardamom anglaise and whisky and oatmeal ice cream.* **Details:** *www.themilton.co.uk; On the North Deeside road, opposite the Crathes castle junction; 9.30 pm, 6.30 pm Sun; closed Sun D.*

The Yew Tree   **£ 30**
CT15 7JH   (01304) 831000
*"A welcome and exciting addition to the Kent dining scene"; with its
"subtle" and "exceptional" cuisine and its "absolutely extraordinary"
wine list, this is most definitely "not just another gastropub"; it's the
fruits of a partnership between two Bens: Bevan a local wine
merchant (the "ebullient host") and Williams, an ex-Square chef.*
/ **Details:** *www.yewtree.info; 9 pm; closed Sun D; no Amex.*

Emchai   **£ 24**   ⭐
78 High St   EN5 5SN   (020) 8364 9993
*A "Spartan but stylish" spot, serving "Malaysian and other oriental
cuisines", and invariably well rated for its "delicious food at very
reasonable prices".* / **Sample dishes:** *buttermilk prawns; sanbei chicken;
tapioca pudding.* **Details:** *11 pm.*

Barnsley House   **£ 62**
GL7 5EE   (01285) 740000
*Fans vaunt the dining room of this trendy country house hotel as a
"very special, lovely and airy place" with "excellent" food;
not everyone is impressed, though, and there's a continuing feeling
that prices are "excessive".* / **Sample dishes:** *bresaola with goats cheese,
walnuts and black pepper; rack of lamb with fritedda (peas, beans and
artichokes); semifreddo of white chocolate and almonds.*
Details: *www.barnsleyhouse.com; 9.30 pm, Sat & Sun 10 pm; no Amex.*
Accommodation: *18 rooms, from £295.*

Elio's   **£ 38**   🅣
11 Market Pl   DN18 5DA   (01652) 635147
*A marketplace Italian that's often "busy", tipped for a "fresh fish
selection of excellent quality".* / **Sample dishes:** *home-made fishcakes;
sautéed lamb; panna cotta with berries.* **Details:** *A15 towards Humber Bridge,
first exit into Barton upon Humber; 10 pm; closed Sat L & Sun.*
Accommodation: *5 rooms, from £85*

Pebble Beach **£ 45**

Marine Drive BH25 7DZ (01425) 627777

*"Excellent seafood is complemented by a spectacular cliff-top location" ("with wonderful views of the Isle of Wight") at this "surprisingly sophisticated" venture, unanimously hailed by reporters as "a real treat". / **Sample dishes:** aubergine & rosemary goat cheese; monkfish tail with a saffrom mussel rice & romesco sauce; hot chocolate fondant with pistachio ice cream & raspberry sauce. **Details:** www.pebblebeach-uk.com; 9.30 pm, Fri & Sat 10 pm.*

Pebble Beach **£ 44**

Marine Drive BH25 7DZ (01425) 627777

*"Great fish and setting" – that's the gist of all commentary of Pierre Chevillard's cliff-top restaurant; arrive early if you want a table on the "fantastic" terrace. / **Details:** www.pebblebeach-uk.com; 9.30 pm; booking essential. **Accommodation:** 3 rooms, from £89.95.*

Little Barwick House **£ 50**

BA22 9TD (01935) 423902

*A "delightful country house hotel dining room", where the food is often "surprisingly good"; it has a "beautiful setting" too, and most reporters find it "admirable in all respects". / **Sample dishes:** pan-fried scallops, pea purée, crispy bacon and white truffle oil; medallions beef, dauphinoise potatoes, red onion confit and red wine sauce; raspberries and strawberries in a brandy snap basket with peach ice cream. **Details:** www.littlebarwick.co.uk; Take the A37 Yeovil to Dorchester road, turn left at the brown sign for Little Barwick House; 9 Tue-Fri, 9.30 Sat; closed Mon, Tue L & Sun D; no Amex; children: 5+. **Accommodation:** 6 rooms, from £100.*

Cavendish **£ 51**

Church Ln DE45 1SP (01246) 582311

*"On the edge of the Chatsworth Estate", this "very comfy" hotel is "worth a detour" for its (usually) "splendid" food; the "good-value", no-bookings conservatory is particularly recommended. / **Sample dishes:** pan roast breast of wood pigeonwith artichoke purée, wild mushrooms, red wine butter; seared king scallopswith a warm spiced potato and black onion seed salad, guacamole and roast red pepper butter; iced white chocolate, pistachio and nougat parfaitwith orange and pistachio tuilles. **Details:** www.cavendish-hotel.net; 10 pm. **Accommodation:** 24 rooms, from £155.*

Fischers at Baslow Hall   **£ 80**
Calver Rd DE45 IRR   (01246) 583259
*This "lovely country house" has long had the reputation for dishing
up "the best food in Derbyshire"; most reporters still agree, but some
complained this year of "exorbitant" costs and "pretentious" service –
standards at Sunday lunch, in particular, seem in need of attention.
/ **Sample dishes:** terrine of foie gras with Yorkshire forced rhubarb & toasted
brioche; roast best end & braised shoulder of Derbyshire lamb with pommes
boulangère & rosemary jus; raspberry soufflé with raspberry sorbet.*
Details: *www.fischers-baslowhall.co.uk; on the A623 ; 9 pm; closed Mon L &
Sun D; no jeans or trainers; children: 12+ at D.* **Accommodation:** *11 rooms,
from £140.*

Rowley's   **£ 41**
Church Ln DE45 IRY   (01246) 583880

*A spin off from nearby Baslow Hall, this "bright" and "airy"
(and rather "bare") pub-conversion is consistently praised for its
"robust" cuisine and its "attentive" service.
/ **Details:** www.rowleysrestaurant.co.uk; 9 pm, Fri & Sat 10 pm; closed Sun D;
no Amex.*

BASSENTHWAITE LAKE, CUMBRIA   7–3C

Pheasant Hotel   **£ 43**
CA13 9YE   (01768) 776234
*An ancient coaching inn, where a "really super old-fashioned cooked
breakfast" gets star billing; other meals too, however, are generally
"above-average". / **Details:** www.the-pheasant.co.uk; 8.30 pm; no Amex;
no jeans or trainers; children: 12+ at D.* **Accommodation:** *15 rooms,
from £130.*

BATH, BATH & NE SOMERSET   2–2B

The mismatch between Bath's evident wealth and beauty
on the one hand, and its indifferent-quality restaurant scene
on the other, remains striking. This should be a city
of destination-dining, but the only establishment that could
really said to attain any such status is the grand hotel, *Bath
Priory*. The only independent restaurant of any real note
in the city-centre proper is the *Olive Tree*.

Bath Priory Hotel £ 78 Ⓐ✪✪

Weston Rd BA1 2XT (01225) 331922

"Poetical, surprising, audacious…" – Chris Horridge's *"wonderful"* cuisine inspires lyrical feedback from reporters; what's more – with its *"beautiful"* room, and its *"well-informed"* service – this luxurious hotel offers a *"gorgeous"* dining experience across the board.
/ **Sample dishes:** paillette of rabbit, forgotten hedge herbs and flowers of the moment; slow poached beef, banana shallot with comfreyexilir vegetal flavours; collage of fruit, some as nature intended, with rhubarb essence.
Details: www.thebathpriory.co.uk; 1m W of city centre, past Victoria Park; 9.30 pm; no jeans or trainers; children: 8+ D. **Accommodation:** 27 rooms, from £250.

Boojon £ 15 ✪

28 Charles St BA1 1HU (01225) 429429

"Without a doubt the most reasonable, delicious and attentive Indian restaurant in Bath, made all the better by its BYO policy"; it's something of a *"hidden secret"*, but – according to its small fan club – *"a stunning find"*. / **Details:** 11 pm; no Amex.

Demuths £ 40 ✪

2 North Parade Pas BA1 1NX (01225) 446059

A *"vegetarian heaven"*, in the very *"heart of Bath"* – a *"quirky"* sort of place, under the same management for over two decades, and offering an *"interesting"* and *"different"* menu; *"even for Bath"*, though, it can seem *"a bit pricey"*. / **Sample dishes:** smoked cheese polenta; sweet potato cauliflower gratin; apricot calvados tart.
Details: www.demuths.co.uk; 10 pm; no Amex; booking: max 4 at D, Fri & Sat; children: 6+ at D.

The Eastern Eye £ 32 Ⓣ

8a Quiet St BA1 2JS (01225) 422323

Tipped for its *"particularly grand"* Georgian setting, this Thai establishment is *"full of character"*; it can be *"noisy"*, though, and the food is sometimes *"indifferent"*. / **Sample dishes:** dhaka chicken roll; chicken tikka nowabdar; gulab jamon. **Details:** www.easterneye.co.uk; 11.30 pm.

Firehouse Rotisserie £ 35 Ⓣ

2 John St BA1 2JL (01225) 482070

A *"popular and crowded"* pizzeria, offering pizzas and meaty fare from a spit; by local standards – an important qualification – it is tipped for its *"reasonable prices"*. / **Sample dishes:** barbecue duck quesadilla with tomato chile jam; Pacific crab & salmon cakes with pico de gallo salsa & coriander lime crème fraîche; warm double chocolate brownie with coconut ice cream. **Details:** www.firehouserotisserie.co.uk; 11 pm; closed Sun.

FishWorks £ 45 ✪

6 Green St BA1 2JY (01225) 448707

You certainly *"don't go for the setting"* (it's *"rather cramped"*), but the original branch of what is now a national fishmonger-cum-bistro chain still wins a thumbs-up from reporters, thanks to its *"brilliant fresh fish, simply cooked"*. / **Sample dishes:** mussels steamed with wine garlic & parsley; yellowtail kingfish yakatori; baked chocolate pudding.
Details: www.fishworks.co.uk; 10.30 pm.

Hole in the Wall £ 36
16 George St BA1 2EH (01225) 425242
*The cellar location is "lovely and cosy, or dark and gloomy, depending on how you look at it", but this is a "reasonably reliable" destination (and "really good-value for lunch"); you'd still never guess, though, that – in a former guise – it was one of the England's seminal post-war restaurants. / **Sample dishes:** pork fillet, black pudding & apricot terrine; braised lamb shank with garlic, rosemary & red wine & creamed parsnip purée; strawberry shortbread cheesecake. **Details:** www.theholeinthewall.co.uk; 10 pm, Sun 9.30 pm; closed Sun L.*

The Hop Pole £ 38
7 Albion Buildings, Upper Bristol Rd BA1 3AR (01225) 446327
*"A little gem of a place on the outskirts of Bath, with a charming garden for al fresco dining in the summer", and tipped for its "good food" too. / **Sample dishes:** grilled tiger prawns; grilled Barbary duck breast; chocolate junkyard. **Details:** www.bathales.com; opp Victoria Park; 9 pm, Sat 9.30 pm; closed Sun D.*

The Hudson Bar & Grill £ 48
14 London St BA1 5BU (01225) 332323
*"A solid operation, in a culinary desert" – this "friendly" and "helpful" pub-conversion is of particular note for its "fantastic steaks" (and "great grills" generally); "good wine" too. / **Details:** www.hudsonbars.co.uk; 10.30 pm; D only, closed Sun.*

King William £ 37
36 London Rd BA1 5NN (01225) 428096
*You get "fabulous" food from a "really strong British menu", at this popular gastropub, which "still has the feel of an old local boozer"; it's a "real and authentic Bath treat" (and there are few enough of those!); "book ahead on Sundays". / **Sample dishes:** salt beef and horseradish cream, green bean and radish salad; rump of lamb and slow roast fennel, green beans and garlic and tarragon dressing; summer pudding. **Details:** www.kingwilliampub.com; 11 pm, midnight weekends.*

Loch Fyne £ 42
24 Milsom St BA1 1DG (01225) 750120
*This "reliable" and "predictable" – "boring", if you prefer – outpost of the national fish and seafood chain is hailed by fans as "a cut above the usual"; it certainly generates an impressive volume of feedback. / **Sample dishes:** haddock chowder; king scallops with garlic butter and new potatoes; chocolate and orange tart. **Details:** www.lochfyne.com; 9.45 pm, Fri & Sat 10.45 . **Accommodation:** 9 rooms, from £85.*

Mai Thai £ 29
6 Pierrepont St BA2 4AA (01225) 445557
*One of the city's better orientals, tipped for its "consistently good Thai food", and its "always-efficient service". / **Sample dishes:** hot and sour sweet prawns; green curried chicken; banana fritter with ice cream. **Details:** www.maithai.co.uk; 10.30 pm, Fri & Sat 10.45 pm.*

The Olive Tree
Queensberry Hotel   **£ 51**
Russell St BA1 2QF   (01225) 447928
*A "favourite" destination for some reporters – this popular cellar-restaurant feels a bit basement-y, but is again winning positive reports for its "highly-skilled" cuisine. / **Sample dishes:** pan seared monkfish cheeks with broad beans, fine beans, spinach & lemon butter; roast rump of lamb with roast peppers, grilled courgette & aubergine; mango cocktail with chocolate brioche. **Details:** www.thequeensberry.co.uk; 9.45 pm; closed Mon L.*
***Accommodation:** 29 rooms, from £110.*

Pump Rooms   **£ 39**
The Pump Room, Stall St BA1 1LZ   (01225) 444477
*This gracious Georgian room is "a joy", and every visitor to Bath should experience it at least once – ideally for tea or coffee; the food is incidental. / **Details:** www.searcys.co.uk; by the Abbey; L only, open until 10 pm in July & Aug; no booking, Sat & Sun.*

Raphael   **£ 37**
Gascoyne Hs, Upper Borough Walls BA1 1RN
(01225) 480042
*"A lively and well-organised brasserie, ideal for pre-theatre in the centre of Bath"; it's an "intimate" sort of place, commended by all who comment on it. / **Details:** www.raphaelrestaurant.co.uk; 10.15 pm.*

BAUGHURST, HAMPSHIRE   2–3D

The Wellington Arms   **£ 42**
Baughurst Rd RG26 5LP   (0118) 9820110
*A "real gem" of a pub-conversion, consistently praised for its "seriously good" cooking (using eggs from their own chickens, honey from their own beehives, and – coming soon – pigs!); main gripes? – "tightly packed" and "too popular". / **Sample dishes:** line-caught trout, potted with lemon zest, dill, white wine and shallots; slow roast belly pork with crackling on sticky red cabbage with damson plums; steamed apple and syrup sponge with proper custard. **Details:** www.thewellingtonarms.com; 9.30 pm; closed Mon, Tue L & Sun D; no Amex.*

BAWTRY, SOUTH YORKSHIRE   5–2D

China Rose   **£ 32**
16 South Pde DN10 6JH   (01302) 710461
*"Perhaps better in a group than à deux" – this "unattractive" but "good" Chinese café is a top cheap 'n' cheerful local tip. / **Sample dishes:** scallops with cashew nuts; fillet steak Cantonese style; banana fritter. **Details:** www.chinarose-bawtry.co.uk; 10 pm, Fri & Sat 10.30 pm; D only.*

BEACONSFIELD, BUCKINGHAMSHIRE   3–3A

The Royal Standard Of England   **£ 26**
Brindle Ln HP9 1XT   (01494) 673382
"An absolutely fantastic pub, that's supposedly the oldest freehouse in the country"; its "good, honest pub grub" includes some "great daily specials".

The Spice Merchant   **£ 43** ⭐

33 London End HP9 2HW (01494) 675474

"As far as you can get from a sloppy korma!" – this *"posh Indian"*
is roundly praised as an *"expensive-but-worth-it"* treat, offering
"original" and *"succulent"* cuisine; *"go in summer – the garden
is gorgeous"*. / **Sample dishes:** *chicken cooked with green chilli sauce, mixed
peppers & flavoured with dill leaves; tandoori baked lamb chops cooked with
typical punjabi style lamb mince & green peas.*
Details: *www.spicemerchantgroup.net; 11 pm, Sun 9.30 pm.*

BEARSTED, KENT   3–3C

Soufflé   **£ 42** ⭐

31 The Green ME14 4DN (01622) 737065

Oft-*"memorable"* cooking distinguishes this *"unpretentious"* and
somewhat *"cramped"* restaurant, which overlooks the green of a
village near Leeds Castle; service, though, can be *"slow"*.
/ **Sample dishes:** *salad of roast quail with creamed celeriac & Spanish pancetta;
rib eye steak with button mushrooms, bearnaise sauce, galette potatoes &
spinach; pear tarte Tatin with amaretto ice cream.*
Details: *www.soufflerestaurant.net; off M20; 9.30 pm; closed Mon, Sat L &
Sun D.*

BEAUMARIS, ISLE OF ANGLESEY   4–1C

Ⓐ⭐

The Loft Restaurant
Ye Olde Bull's Head   **£ 50**

Castle St LL58 8AP (01248) 810329

"An oasis in these parts"; the *"comfortable"* modern brasserie
attached to this ancient inn offers *"very decent food with
exceptionally friendly service, and at very attractive prices"*; upstairs,
there's a *"small but rather chic restaurant"* which *"really would cut
the mustard in London"*. / **Sample dishes:** *breast of quail, truffled pea
velouté, pancetta and a fried quail's egg; saddle of wild venison, tomato farci,
celeriac lasagne, roast garlic and chocolate sauce; melting ginger parkin, clotted
cream, caramel anglaise and gingerbread tuille.* **Details:** *www.bullsheadinn.co.uk;
On the High Street, opposite the Spar shop; 9.30 pm; D only, closed Sun; no jeans;
children: 8+ at D.* **Accommodation:** *13 rooms, from £105.*

BECKENHAM, KENT   3–3B

Mello   **£ 42**

2 Southend Rd BR3 1SD (020) 8663 0994

Fans say you get *"good"* food and *"very friendly"* service at this
upmarket suburban venue; of late, however, reports have become
rather mixed. / **Sample dishes:** *tian of Cornish crab, shrimps and sweet
pepper purée, crushed avocado and toasted rye bread; assiette of pork and
creamed cabbage, apple purée and prune and calvados jus; hot chocolate fondant
with pistachio ice cream.* **Details:** *www.mello.uk.com; Opposite Beckenham
Junction Station; 10 pm; closed Sun D.*

BELFAST, COUNTY ANTRIM   10–1D

We hear that Belfast is on the up, but the number of places
in town that reporters identify as of any particular
interest remains limited. The best all-rounder is arguably the
Bo Tree – as the same proprietors used to run Oxford's
best all-rounder that's perhaps not such a surprise! For the
best non-ethnic cooking, we'd suggest not falling for the local
'celebrity' angle, and seeking out the lesser-known delights
of *Alden's* and *Ginger*.

Aldens £ 38

229 Upper Newtownards Rd BT4 3JF (028) 9065 0079

"Never fails to impress": that's the gist of all commentary on Jonathan Davis's "reliable" destination, which we suspect – albeit on the basis of relatively low feedback – again to be offering the best food in the Province. / Sample dishes: steamed mussels with white wine, parsley and garlic; fillet of seabass, asparagus, peas and prawn sauce; baked tamarillos with raspberry coulis and vanilla ice cream. Details: www.aldensrestaurant.com; 2m from Stormont Buildings; 10 PM, Sat & Sun 11PM; closed Sat L & Sun.

Bo Tree £ 35

31 University Rd BT7 1NA (028) 9024 7722

From the founders of the (mega-popular) Chiang Mai Kitchen in Oxford – a restaurant fans nominate for "the best Thai food in Belfast", and in an "elegant" and "spacious" setting too. / Sample dishes: beef satay; green chicken curry; crispy fried banana. Details: www.botreethai.com; 10.30 pm; closed Sun.

Cayenne £ 47

7 Ascot Hs, Shaftesbury Sq BT2 7DB (028) 9033 1532

"Rankin's best in Belfast", says a fan of the TV-chef city-centre bistro; it attracts relatively few reports, though, and those there are tend to confirm that standards can be rather "hit-and-miss". / Sample dishes: pork pot stickers with Asian salad; breast of duck & seared scallops with sesame rice & orange miso; buttermilk panna cotta with rhubarb compote & pistachio shortbread. Details: www.rankingroup.co.uk; near Botanic Railway Station; 10.15 pm, Fri & Sat 11pm, Sun 8.45 pm; closed Mon L, Sat L & Sun L.

Deanes £ 56

34-40 Howard St BT1 6PF (028) 9056 0000

Michael Deane is a Grand Fromage in the Province, and his various gaffs attract a fair degree of conflicting commentary (ranging from "best in Belfast" to "poor value for money") – currently, the best would appear to be the city-centre one listed (which now offers bistro dining throughout). / Sample dishes: artichoke velouté with smoked ricotta and chervil dumplings; duck breast, hammed leg with parsnip & sage tart, chestnut honey and vanilla; warm chocolate fondant, stout ice cream & macadamia tuille. Details: www.michaeldeane.co.uk; near Grand Opera House; 10 pm, 10.30 pm Thu-Sat; closed Sun.

Ginger £ 40

7-8 Hope St BT12 5EE (0871) 426 7885

"Belfast's best place for a casual meal" – Simon McCance's "cramped" bistro is "always busy", thanks to its "well-executed" cuisine and its "friendly" service; "lunch is particularly good value". / Sample dishes: fried squid with sweet chilli dip & piquant onion salsa; salad of hake with baby potatoes, green beans, and coconut curry; crème brûlée with raspberry compote. Details: www.gingerbistro.com; 10 pm Tue-Sat, 9 pm Mon; closed Mon L & Sun; no Amex.

James Street South £ 48

21 James Street South BT2 7GA (028) 9043 4310

"High-quality food" and "excellent, friendly service" make Niall McKenna's city-centre establishment popular with almost all who comment on it, a "somewhat austere" interior notwithstanding. / Sample dishes: sautéed foie gras and macerated apple and rhubarb; loin of lamb with a lamb pithivier, asparagus, mint jus; apple tarte Tatin and vanilla bean ice cream. Details: www.jamesstreetsouth.co.uk; behind the City Hall, off Bedford Street ; 10.30 pm; closed Sun L.

Nick's Warehouse   **£ 42**
35 Hill St BT1 2LB (028) 9043 9690
*One of the earliest trendy eateries in the city-centre, whose
"innovative and reasonably-priced lunch menu" helps maintain
popularity as a business rendezvous; critics, though, find it a rather
pricey place that's "not as good as it thinks it is".*
/ **Sample dishes:** tomato, fontina cheese and basil pesto puff pastry tranche with
onion marmalade; grilled hake with papaya and crayfish salad with herb oil; pecan
and raisin chocolate brownie. **Details:** www.nickswarehouse.co.uk; behind
St Anne's Cathedral; 9.30 pm; closed Mon D, Sat L & Sun; children: 18+ at 9 pm.

Roscoff Brasserie   **£ 46**
7-11 Linenhall St BT2 8AA (028) 9031 1150
*Paul Rankin's "buzzy" city-centre operation is never less than
"reliable", and some reporters say it's "great"; shame the prices can
sometimes seem a bit "Dick Turpin-like".*
/ **Details:** www.rankingroup.co.uk; 10.15 pm, Fri & Sat 11.15 pm; closed Sat L &
Sun D.

Tedfords Restaurant   **£ 46**   **ⓣ**
5 Donegall Quay BT1 3EF (028) 9043 4000
*Again tipped for its "delicious" cuisine, this cosy restaurant is situated
in an old chandlery; more comments next year please...*
/ **Sample dishes:** smoked salmon, crab mayonnaise, warm potato bread & soft
quail egg; pan roast turbot & scallops, crab, crushed new potatoes, buttered
asparagus, hollandaise; white chocolate & Baileys crème brûlée with shortbread.
Details: www.tedfordsrestaurant.com; 9.30 pm; closed Mon, Tue L, Sat L & Sun;
children: "not a family restaurant".

Zen   **£ 33**   **ⓣ**
55-59 Adelaide St BT2 8FE (028) 9023 2244
*A "noisy" joint, tipped for its "well-cooked and presented dishes from
across the Orient", and "interesting cocktails" too.* / **Sample dishes:** salt
and chilli soft shell crab with shaven curry leaf; diced fillet of duck breast with fresh
mint and red pickle ginger. **Details:** www.eatbelfast.com; 11.30 pm,
Sun 10.30 pm; closed Sat L.

BEMBRIDGE, ISLE OF WIGHT   2–4D

The Crab And Lobster Inn   **£ 37**   **Ⓐ★**
32 Forelands Field Rd PO35 5TR (01983) 872244
*"A super place for seafood lovers" – this seaside inn remains
"very popular", thanks in particular to the fish platters, which are
"predictably good".* / **Sample dishes:** crab & lobster soup; seafood tagliatelli;
treacle sponge & custard. **Details:** www.crabandlobsterinn.co.uk; 9 pm, Fri & Sat
9.30 pm ; no Amex. **Accommodation:** 5 rooms, from £80.

BENDEROLCH, ARGYLL & BUTE   9–3B

Isle of Eriska   **£ 48**   **Ⓐ★**
Ledaig PA37 1SD (01631) 720371
*Fortunately it's "worth the drive"; reporters leave "never
disappointed" from this luxurious but "isolated" hotel – a "romantic"
destination, where the food invariably satisfies.* / **Sample dishes:** seared
monkfish salad; loin of pork; banana soufflé and sorbet.
Details: www.eriska-hotel.co.uk; 9 pm; no jeans or trainers; children: 6pm;
high tea for resident's chldren. **Accommodation:** 25 rooms, from £300.

BERKHAMSTED, HERTFORDSHIRE 3–2A

Eat Fish ★ **£ 40**
163-165 High St HP4 3HB (01442) 879988
"The menu is mostly fish, as you'd expect", at this well-regarded local eatery (which now has a Bedford sibling); notwithstanding the odd quibble, reporters generally laud its "utterly delightful" staff and its "beautifully fresh" dishes. | Sample dishes: grilled sardines with chilli, garlic & coriander dressed leaves; fillet of salmon with saffron potatoes, creamy leeks & capers; lemon posset and orange short bread. Details: www.eatfish.co.uk; 10 pm, Sun 9pm.

BEVERLEY, EAST YORKSHIRE 6–2A

The Pipe & Glass Inn Ⓐ★ **£ 40**
West End HU17 7PN (01430) 810246
"Probably the top local rival to the Star at Harome"; it's perhaps no coincidence that James Mackenzie – chef/patron of this "beautifully-located" pub-cum-restaurant – used to cook at said local hero, and his "thoughtful" cooking is "interesting" and "well-presented". | Details: www.pipeandglass.co.uk; 9.30 pm; closed Mon & Sun D; no Amex.

BIDDENDEN, KENT 3–4C

West House ★★ **£ 47**
28 High St TN27 8AH (01580) 291341
"A jewel in the Kent countryside", offering the "outstanding" cuisine of a "perfectionist" chef (Graham Garrett), and "relaxed" service too, in a setting some reporters find "romantic"; "this is the best value you'll ever find in a Michelin-starred restaurant". | Details: www.thewesthouserestaurant.co.uk; 9.30 pm; closed Mon, Sat L & Sun D; no Amex.

BIGBURY-ON-SEA, DEVON 1–4C

Burgh Island Hotel Ⓐ **£ 73**
TQ7 4BG (01548) 810514
"A fantastic trip back to the '30s, with service to match" – this "wacky", "retro" Art Deco hotel feels like an "Agatha Christie novel" (yes, she did stay here); the food is "fine, if a tad pricey", but "not really why you go". | Sample dishes: poached lobster, tuna, sushi rice, seaweed, avocado, sesame seed; pan fried John Dory, crushed ratte potato, shaved fennel, chilli, brown shrimp, rapeseed dressing; Godminster cheddar, Exmoor blue, Pavé d'Affinois, quince, lavosh. Details: www.burghisland.com; 9.30 pm; no Amex; jacket & tie at D; children: 12+ at D. Accommodation: 24 rooms, from £355.

Oyster Shack Ⓐ★ **£ 36**
Millburn Orchard Farm, Stakes Hills TQ7 4BE (01548) 810876
"On a sunny day, it feels like the South of France", at this "buzzy", if "basic", stalwart, which is reached via a tidal road; "marvellous seafood at reasonable prices" makes this a place "well worth finding". | Details: www.oystershack.co.uk; 9 pm; L only, closed Mon.

⭐

The Bildeston Crown
The Crown Hotel   **£ 40**
High St IP7 7EB   (01449) 740510
*"One to watch!"; Chris Lee's lavishly updated inn is often hailed
by reporters for its "highly unusual and imaginative" – if arguably
rather "showy" – cuisine; service, though, "is in need of significant
improvement".* / **Sample dishes:** *ham hock terrine foie gras, rabbit, beetroot;
fillet of turbot, braised oxtail, flageolet beans,pancetta & tomato confit;
dark chocolate fondant, mocha ice cream, zabaglione.*
Details: *www.thebildestoncrown.com; 10 pm, 9.30 pm Sun.*
Accommodation: *12 rooms, from £120.*

Ⓣ

Magic Mushroom   **£ 37**
Barleyland Rd CM11 2UD   (01268) 289963
*Sometimes tipped as "the best modern establishment in the area",
this Med-inspired spot, in an age-old building, is also dismissed
as "veering between pleasant and overpriced".* / **Sample dishes:** *sautéed
chicken livers with pancetta and sweet chilli vinaigrette; fillet of beef on Stilton
creamed baby spinach with veal jus; hot chocolate fondant with maple walnut ice
cream.* **Details:** *www.magicmushroomrestaurant.co.uk; next to "Barleylands
Farm"; midnight; closed Mon L, Sat L & Sun D; no Amex; no shorts.*

Perhaps, just perhaps, the hype about Birmingham is finally
beginning to become true. The number of dining out
destinations that might be of interest to a visitor remains
small compared to, say, Manchester, but some of them are
really of very good quality nowadays (in a way that tends
to elude the north western city).

The city has a bright new star, *Purnell's*, to add to the already-
established local top dog *Simpson's*. At a less ambitious level,
Lasan and *Opus* are of some note, and *Café Ikon* has remained
a remarkably resilient good-quality stand-by over many years.

Bank   **£ 45**
4 Brindleyplace B1 2JB   (0121) 633 4466
*It's handy for breakfast, a quick lunch, pre-theatre, and also for
business… but this large and "noisy" brasserie can still seem "bland",
"expensive" and "mediocre".* / **Sample dishes:** *fresh asparagus with
a lightly poached free-range egg & hollandaise sauce; crispy duck with Chinese
greens, sesame & honey dressing; chocolate fudge pudding with vanilla ice cream.*
Details: *www.bankrestaurants.co.uk; 10.30 pm, Fri & Sat 11 pm.*

Bar Estilo   **£ 30**   Ⓣ
110-114 Wharfside St B1 1RF   (0121) 643 3443
*In the Mailbox, a lavishly-furnished and "busy" outpost of a national
bar chain, tipped for its "large and varied menu, smiley service,
and tasty and well-presented food".* / **Sample dishes:** *mini chorizo &
morcilla cooked in white wine; chicken thighs in a creamy almond & saffron sauce
served with aromatic rice; triple chocolate sundae.* **Details:** *www.barestilo.co.uk;
11 pm.*

The Bucklemaker   £ 42
30 Mary Ann St, St Paul's Sq B3 1RL   (0121) 200 2515
An "intimate", "traditional-style" Jewellery Quarter veteran, tipped for
the always-"consistent" quality of its food (using "the best seasonal
ingredients"), and its service. / **Sample dishes:** pan seared pigeon
breast with lentils; roast cannon of lamb on confit belly with minted greens and
rosemary jus; apple pie with cinnamon with crème anglaise and vanilla ice cream.
Details: www.thebucklemaker.co.uk; 10.30 pm; closed Sat L & Sun.

Café Ikon
Ikon Gallery   £ 28
Oozells Sq, Brindleyplace B1 2HS   (0121) 248 3226
For "the best Spanish food in Birmingham", this tapas bar veteran,
attached to an art gallery, is the place to go – it's a "great lunchtime
café", and is very popular "pre-Symphony Hall" too.
/ **Sample dishes:** grilled red peppers with anchovies; seared tuna steak with basil,
lime and chilli; organic lemon sorbet with cava. **Details:** www.ikon-gallery.co.uk;
10 pm; closed Sun D; no Amex; children: 18+ after 9 pm.

Chez Jules   £ 29
5a Ethel St, off New St B2 4BG   (0121) 633 4664
Notwithstanding the odd "off" experience this year, this Gallic bistro
is still usually tipped as a good "cheap and cheerful" option.
/ **Sample dishes:** poached pears & chilli syrup served   with thyme infused pecan
nuts; mussels, prawns & salmon stew with aioli mayonnaise & croutons.
Details: www.chezjules.co.uk; 11 pm; closed Sun D; no Amex.

Chung Ying Garden   £ 31
17 Thorp St B5 4AT   (0121) 666 6622
Consistent reports confirm this Chinatown landmark – which offers
a "highly-varied range of dishes, including dim sum" – "lives up to
to its reputation for good food and service"; it has a rather similar
twin at 16-18 Wrottesley Street (tel 622 5669). / **Sample dishes:** pork
yuk shung; sliced lamb in satay sauce with ho fun; yeung chow fried rice.
Details: www.chungying.co.uk; 11 pm.

Cielo   £ 45
6 Oozells Sq B1 2JB   (0121) 6326882
The style is "a bit WAG-y" for some tastes, but this Brindleyplace
Italian offers "good" cooking (with the "bargain early dinner"
particularly recommended), and "friendly" service too.
/ **Sample dishes:** fresh mussels in saffron cream infused with garlic tomato and
parsley; roast belly of pork with roast apples, served in a creamed calvados and
sultana jus; poached pear in white wine with william pear sorbet and cantuccini
biscuits. **Details:** www.cielobirmingham.com; 11 pm, 10 pm Sun.

Hotel du Vin et Bistro   £ 45
25 Church St B3 2NR   (0121) 200 0600
One of the better dining rooms in the boutique-hotel group,
this "lively" place is, for some reporters, the city's
"best hotel/bar/restaurant"; it's an "efficient" all-rounder, but it is of
course the "amazing wine list" which really stands out.
/ **Sample dishes:** lamb's kidneys and wild mushrooms on toast, mustard crème;
calf's liver, pomme purée, crispy pancetta, sauce diable; lemon parfait.
Details: www.hotelduvin.co.uk; 10 pm, Fri & Sat 10.30 pm; booking: max 10.
Accommodation: 66 rooms, from £140.

Itihaas   £ 38
18 Fleet St B3 1JL   (0121) 212 3383
Near the Science Museum, an Indian restaurant that inspires hugely
positive ratings, albeit from a tiny fan club. / **Sample dishes:** chicken
tikka; lamb curry; carrot cake and kulfi ice cream. **Details:** www.itihaas.co.uk;
11, 10.30 Sun; closed Sat L & Sun L.

Jyoti £ 17

569-571 Stratford Rd B11 4LS   (0121) 766 7199

*Tipped as "a nice change from all the balti houses", this "consistently good" Sparkbrook Gujarati is a "welcoming" place, offering "very good" food; BYO. / **Details:** www.jyotisvegetarian.co.uk; 9.15 pm; closed Mon, Tue-Thu D only; no Amex.*

Kinnaree Thai Restaurant
The Mailbox, Holiday Wharf Building £ 29

22 Water Front Walk B1 1SN   (0121) 6656568

*"Very romantic at night", this canal-side Thai restaurant is also tipped as an "enjoyable" destination at any time (including "for a business lunch"). / **Sample dishes:** chicken satay; panang curry; sticky rice with mango. **Details:** www.kinnaree.co.uk; 11 pm, 10.30 pm Sun.*

Lasan £ 40

3-4 Dakota Buildings, James St B3 1SD   (0121) 2123664

*"Lovely, fresh-tasting and interesting food" – and "with a difference" too – makes this contemporary-style operation in the Jewellery Quarter very popular with reporters; "the new branch, in Hall Green, is just as good". / **Sample dishes:** Goan lemon sole kafrial, marinated in yoghurt and mint, tandoori roast and tomato cucumber salad and mint coriander dressing; seared breast of duck and onion and tomato curry flavoured and roast coconut, poppy and melon seeds; mango and almond crumble with iced apple custard. **Details:** www.lasan.co.uk; 11 pm, 10 pm Sun; closed Sat L.*

Malmaison £ 44

B1 1RD   (0121) 246 5000

*A city-centre brasserie hailed by reporters as a surprisingly good all-rounder, even if it can get rather "noisy"; "good to see an hotel chain offering a home-grown, local menu". / **Sample dishes:** sautéed chicken liver on brioche with a bourguignonne vinaigrette; pan fried monkfish with braised lettuce, pickled baby carrots and watercress purée; caramelised peach tarte fine with smoked almond and honey ice cream. **Details:** www.malmaison.com; 10.30 pm. **Accommodation:** 189 rooms, from £160.*

MUST £ 35

11-13 Newhall St B3 3NY   (0121) 212 2266

*Impressive ratings from reporters – but nothing in the way of words! – on this new dim sum bar and restaurant in the Business Quarter. / **Sample dishes:** lettuce wraps with minced pork and bamboo shoots; king prawn and vermicelli hot pot with onoki, ginger and spring onion; red bean mashed pancake with vanilla ice cream. **Details:** www.mustgroup.co.uk; 10.30 pm; closed Sun.*

Opus Restaurant £ 42

54 Cornwall St B3 2DE   (0121) 200 2323

*"Solid" brasserie food of consistent "good quality" – with a "bargain wine list" too – helps make this "well-spaced" city-centre venue "one of Birmingham's top restaurants". / **Sample dishes:** roast quail & black pudding salad; lime based scallops with free range belly of pork; apple upside down cake. **Details:** www.opusrestaurant.co.uk; 10.30 pm, Sat 11.30 pm; closed Sat L & Sun.*

Pascal's £ 45

1 Montague Rd B16 9HN   (0121) 455 0999

*Jessica's (RIP) was "a hard act to follow", and its successor on this Edgbaston site seems, by comparison, a rather "safe" sort of destination, but a "professional and friendly" one nonetheless. / **Details:** www.pascalsrestaurant.co.uk; 10 pm; closed Mon, Sat L & Sun; no Amex.*

Purnells £ 58

55 Cornwall St B3 2BH (0121) 212 9799

"Not for the unadventurous", "challenging", "ever-changing"… – ex-Jessica's (RIP) chef Glynn Purnell's "sensational" cooking looks set to put this city-centre newcomer very firmly on the map.

/ **Sample dishes:** *poached egg yolk, smoked haddock milk foam, cornflakes, curry oil; rump tail of beef, warm pea salad, peach cooked in szechuan pepper; lemon & honey parfait, griottines, lemon sorbet & ginger biscuit.*

Details: *www.purnellsrestaurant.com; 9.30 pm; closed Mon, Sat L & Sun; children: 12+.*

San Carlo £ 40

4 Temple St B2 5BN (0121) 633 0251

"Very busy" as always, this long-established city-centre Italian is currently "improving" again (though the odd service "hassle" still features in the occasional report); fish is a highlight of the "good-basic" cuisine. / **Details:** *www.sancarlo.co.uk; near St Philips Cathedral; 11 pm.*

Simpsons £ 70

20 Highfield Rd B15 3DU (0121) 454 3434

"Still the classiest destination in Birmingham"; Andreas Antona's "smart", "civilised" and quite "formal" restaurant, in a "sensitively restored" Georgian house, in Edgbaston, attracts impressively consistent praise for its "outstanding" cooking and "caring" service; NB: look out for a spin-off brasserie, Simply Simpson's, expected to open somewhere in town during the currency of this guide.

/ **Sample dishes:** *fillet of albacore tuna a la plancha, summer fruits, basil, verjus syrup; duo of Cornish lamb, roast loin, slow cooked shoulder, radish, chick peas, green beans, lovage & Feta cheese; apple & blackberry crumble soufflé, vanilla ice cream.* **Details:** *www.simpsonsrestaurant.co.uk; 9 pm; closed Sun D.*

Accommodation: *4 rooms, from £160.*

BISHOP'S STORTFORD, HERTFORDSHIRE   3–2B

The Lemon Tree £ 35

14-16 Water Ln CM23 2LB (01279) 757788

An intimate and tightly-packed town-centre bistro, tipped for "good food and polite service"; many alcoves make it quite "romantic" too. / **Sample dishes:** *potted kipper pâté and melba toast and tomato relish; confit of lamb and dauphinoise potatoes; traditional queen of puddings and cream.*

Details: *www.lemontree.co.uk; past 'Coopers', then 1st left; 9.30 pm; closed Sun D.*

Mallory Court   **£ 65**   ⒶⓊ

Harbury Ln CV33 9QB   (01926) 330214

*This "elegant and comfortable" country house hotel (designed
by Lutyens) offers a "memorable" combination of "personal" service
and "serious" cooking; (there's also a cheaper conservatory brasserie,
which inspires more mixed reviews). / **Sample dishes:** dressed crab, fennel,
cider and wasabi bavarois with potato tuile; pan fried escalope of cod fillet, lobster
tortellini and bisque style sauce; baked lemon cream, spiced poached figs and
bergamot ice cream. **Details:** www.mallory.co.uk; 2m S of Leamington Spa,
off B4087; 8.30 pm. **Accommodation:** 30 rooms, from £135.*

Eagle & Child   **£ 33**   Ⓣ

Maltkiln Ln L40 3SG   (01257) 462297

*Slightly mixed views on this "popular" boozer, but it is tipped for its
"traditional" fare, plus some "excellent real ale".
/ **Sample dishes:** smoked fish; local pigeon, mushroom & brandy sauce; sticky
toffee pudding. **Details:** www.ainscoughs.co.uk; M6, J27; 8.30 pm; no Amex.*

Kwizeen   **£ 34**   Ⓣ

47-49 King St FY1 3EJ   (01253) 290045

*In a gastronomic desert, a restaurant where the chef is surprisingly
"highly-skilled"; locally-sourced lunchtime menus find particular favour.
/ **Sample dishes:** Lancashire cheese soufflé pancake; suckling pig and bacon
roulade; hot chocolate pudding with hot chocolate and chocolate ice cream.
Details: www.kwizeenrestaurant.co.uk; 100 yards inland from the Winter
Gardens; 9 pm; closed Sat L & Sun; no Amex; no shorts.*

The White Horse Hotel   **£ 36**   Ⓣ

4 High St NR25 7AL   (01263) 740574

*A seaside inn, tipped for "good, well-presented food" and a "friendly"
bar. / **Sample dishes:** seared scallops, saffron ginger purée, crisp Parma ham;
pork tenderloin, herb creamed butter beans, spinach and white wine sauce; quince
and frangipan tart with crème anglaise. **Details:** www.blakeneywhitehorse.co.uk;
Off the A149; 9 pm; no Amex. **Accommodation:** 9 rooms, from £70.*

The Plough At Bolnhurst   **£ 45**   ⒶⓊ

MK44 2EX   (01234) 376274

*"What a cracker!"; this "small country pub" is "consistently packed",
thanks not least to Martin Lee's "good-quality" cuisine –
"the best in the area by some considerable margin".
/ **Details:** www.bolnhurst.com; 9.30 pm; closed Mon & Sun D; no Amex.*

The Devonshire Arms   **£ 76**
BD23 6AJ   (01756) 710441
*"Whether you want fine-dining in The Burlington, or go more casual
in the brasserie" fans of this ducally-owned inn say it offers "all one
could expect" (especially its "encyclopaedic wine list"); the dining
room can seem too "rarified", though, and "way, way overpriced" –
perhaps a new chef will buck things up. / Sample dishes: white salmon,
crab salad, passionfruit, avocado sorbet & caviar; lamb textures, broccoli purée,
tomato, olive, anchovy and goat's cheese; caramelised apple pie mousse, apple
sorbet, blackberry jelly, crisp filo. Details: www.devonshirehotels.co.uk; on A59,
5m NE of Skipton; 9.30 pm; closed Mon, Tue-Sat D only, Sun open L &
D; no jeans or trainers. Accommodation: 40 rooms, from £235.*

Pond Café   **£ 42**   Ⓣ
Pond Church Village Rd   PO38 IRG   (01983) 855666
*Overlooking the eponymous stretch of water, a restaurant tipped for
its "lovely setting", and offering a "crisply-realised" menu and
"seamless" service. / Details: www.thepondcafe.com; 9.30 pm; closed Tue &
Wed L; no Amex.*

Millstream Hotel   **£ 46**   Ⓣ
PO18 8HL   (01243) 573234
*It can seem "rather pricey" for what it is, but this "pretty", "old-style"
hotel – near the "picturesque" harbour – is still tipped for its
"decent" food. / Sample dishes: smoked chicken risotto with baby gems,
Parmesan crisp and Caesar dressing; Chateaubriand, vegetables bouquet,
dauphinoise potatoes, bearnaise sauce and red wine jus. Details:
Details: www.millstream-hotel.co.uk; A259 from Chichister; 9.15 pm; no jeans
or trainers. Accommodation: 35 rooms, from £142.*

The Manor Restaurant   Ⓐ
Eastwell Manor   **£ 59**
Eastwell Pk   TN25 4HR   (01233) 213000
*The setting is "second to none" at this Elizabethan country house
hotel; feedback on the cuisine, however, is limited and once again
rather mixed. / Sample dishes: London cured smoked salmon with traditional
accompaniments; grilled lobster with herb and garlic butter, bearnaise sauce, salad
leaves and nicola potatoes; nougatine parfait with red fruit sorbet.
Details: www.eastwellmanor.co.uk; 3m N of Ashford on A251; 9.30 pm; no jeans
or shorts; booking: max 8. Accommodation: 23 rooms, from £140.*

Bistro on the Beach   **£ 31**   Ⓣ
Solent Promenade, Southbourne Coast Rd   BH6 4BE
(01202) 431473
*Tipped for a "beach-front location that cannot be bettered",
this tucked-away Southborne operation offers "fabulous" fish ("but at
fabulous prices to go with it!"). / Sample dishes: avocado and prawn salad;
seared tuna steak on stir fried vegetables. Details: www.bistroonthebeach.com;
2m E of town centre in Southbourne; 9.30 pm; D only, closed Sun-Tue (open every
day, all day in Summer); no Amex.*

Chez Fred £ 17

10 Seamoor Rd BH4 9AN (01202) 761023

"The best fish 'n' chips you can get" in these parts; *"you may have to wait for it"*, though, at this renowned Westbourne institution.
/ **Sample dishes:** haddock and chips; sticky toffee pudding.
Details: www.chezfred.co.uk; 1m W of town centre; 9.45 pm, 9 Sun; closed Sun L; no Amex; no booking.

Mandarin £ 29

194-198 Old Christchurch Rd BH1 1PD (01202) 290681

"The best Chinese food locally" – this veteran establishment is tipped as *"always very good"*. / **Sample dishes:** grilled pork dumplings 'Peking style'; sizzling king prawns with black bean and garlic sauce.
Details: www.themandarin.net; 11 pm, Fri & Sat 11.30 pm.

Ocean Palace £ 32

8 Priory Rd BH2 5DG (01202) 559127

Other aspects of the operation may not excite (and the acoustics are *"terrible"*), but the *"tasty"* fare at this Chinese fixture is *"still going strong"*. / **Sample dishes:** crispy pancake roll; chicken with bamboo shoots & Chinese mushrooms; toffee banana. **Details:** www.oceanpalace.co.uk; 11 pm.

West Beach £ 43

Pier Approach BH2 5AA (01202) 587785

With its *"stunning views over the beach"*, this large fish restaurant certainly has *"location, location and location"* on its side; *"perhaps it's too popular for its own good"*, though – service is *"slow"* and it gets very *"crowded"* and *"noisy"*; the food, though, is generally *"OK"*.
/ **Sample dishes:** asparagus wrapped with Parma ham, smoked cheddar; pan-fried fillets of bream, garlic infused wild mushrooms, spinach; warm treacle tart with lemon zest clotted cream. **Details:** www.west-beach.co.uk; 10 pm.

BOWNESS, CUMBRIA 7–3D

Miller Howe £ 55

Rayrigg Rd LA23 1EY (01539) 442536

No one doubts the *"fabulous view from the restaurant"*, at this once-famous country house hotel; numerous reporters, though, feel its *"over-fussy"* cuisine is nowadays *"living on its past reputation"*.
/ **Sample dishes:** trio of Scottish salmon; seared, rillette and smoked; mutton with shallot purée, fondant potatoes, braised root vegetables and poultry reduction; twice baked gingerbread soufflé with ginger ice cream and toffee sauce.
Details: www.millerhowe.com; on A592 between Windermere & Bowness; 8.45 pm; children: 8+. **Accommodation:** 15 rooms, from £105.

BRADFORD, WEST YORKSHIRE 5–1C

Akbar's Balti £ 22

1276 Leeds Rd BD3 3LF (01274) 773311

"The best curry ever!" – this *"buzzing"* Indian is heartily applauded for its *"marvellous"* food and its *"fantastic value"*.
/ **Sample dishes:** lightly spiced minced lamb, onions & sweetcorn wrapped in a thin crispy pastry; chicken cooked with fresh ginger, onions, tomatoes, capsicums & chillies; soft, juicy sponge balls served with hot creamy sauce or ice cream.
Details: www.akbars.co.uk; midnight; D only; no Amex.

Karachi £ 11

15-17 Neal St BD5 0BX (01274) 732015

"Great and authentic curries from Bradford's oldest curry house"; who cares if *"the food quality is inversely proportional to that of the décor"*? – *"as bargains go, this must be the best in the country"*.
/ **Sample dishes:** beef samosa; chicken masala; gulab jamon. **Details:** 1 am, 2 am Fri & Sat; no credit cards.

Kashmir £ 12

27 Morley St BD7 1AG (01274) 726513

*"I've been going for 40 years, and still enjoy it!" – this curry veteran
has a name as a "cheap and cheerful" Bradford tradition;
some cognoscenti, however, say "Why? It's no better than many
others".* / **Details:** *3 am.*

Love Apple Cafe £ 26 ⓣ

34 Great Horton Rd BD7 1AL (01274) 744075

*For when you don't feel like curry – a "cheap and cheerful" sort
of place, that's "great for a quick meal alone or with friends";
the menu is rather miscellaneous, but quality is "reliable".*
/ **Sample dishes:** *vine leaves on green leaves with Feta cheese; chicken burritos;
home-made strawberry cheesecake.* **Details:** *www.loveapplecafe.co.uk;
near Bradford University, alongside the Alhambra theatre; 9 pm.*

Mumtaz Paan House £ 24 ⭐⭐

Great Horton Rd BD7 3HS (01274) 571861

*"One of the best curry houses in the UK"; this famous destination –
"a palace of glass and marble in a less-than-salubrious area" – offers
"fantastic" Kashmiri dishes at "consistently good-value" prices;
the setting is "busy but uplifting" too.* / **Sample dishes:** *chicken boti;
karahi gosht; chocolate gâteau.* **Details:** *www.mumtaz.com; midnight.*

BRAMPTON, CUMBRIA 7–2D

Farlam Hall £ 52 Ⓐ

CA8 2NG (01697) 746234

*"A time warp with steady standards" – this "comfy" country house
hotel is "full of old-world charm and courtesy", and offers an "un-
flash" formula which includes "consistently good" food.*
/ **Sample dishes:** *confit of pressing duckling leg on salad with raspberry & walnut
oil dressing; loin of local lamb marinated in rosemary & corn oil carved onto herb
mashed potato, cheery tomatoes, & lamb jus; orange marmalade jelly with orange
segments and orange & Grand Marnier.* **Details:** *www.farlamhall.co.uk; 2.5m S.E
of Brampton on A689, not in Farlam Village; 8.30 pm; D only; no shorts; children:
5+.* **Accommodation:** *12 rooms, from £280.*

BRANCASTER STAITHE, NORFOLK 6–3B

White Horse £ 35 Ⓐ

Main Rd PE31 8BY (01485) 210262

*"You get the finest sunset in Britain", claim fans of this estuary-side
inn (with "fabulous views over the saltings to the sea");
on most (if not quite all) accounts, its "fresh, lovely and
unpretentious" fish and seafood provide another reason to make the
trip.* / **Sample dishes:** *locally-smoked salmon with black pepper, lemon and herb
oil; roast rump of English spring lamb with rosti potato, buttered spinach and
thyme jus; chocolate marquise with clotted cream and black cherries.*
Details: *www.whitehorsebrancaster.co.uk; 9 pm; no Amex.*
Accommodation: *15 rooms, from £120.*

BRAY, WINDSOR & MAIDENHEAD 3–3A

Caldesi In Campagna £ 55

Old Mill Ln SL6 2BG (01628) 788500

*"What a find!", say supporters of this "attractive" new rustic-Tuscan,
which seems at its best as a lunch destination; it strikes some
reporters as "very expensive", though – as at the Marylebone parent,
not all reporters are quite convinced that it's worth it.*
/ **Sample dishes:** *corzetti; Tuscan stew; amaretto panna cotta.*
Details: *www.campagna.caldesi.com; 11 pm; closed Mon & Sun D.*

The Fat Duck   £115
1 High St SL6 2AQ   (01628) 580333

Heston Blumenthal's "incomparable" pub-conversion is – according to a recent worldwide poll of foodie journos – second only to Spain's El Bulli in international fame, and most reporters are indeed blown away by the "theatrical" experience it offers; non-converts can find his 'molecular gastronomy' to be "absurdly expensive", though, and there is the occasional reporter who "around course 17, lost the will to live". / **Sample dishes:** cauliflower risotto, carpaccio of cauliflower and chocolate jelly; saddle of venison, celeriac, marron glacé and sauce poivrade; civet of venison with pearl barley and red wine venison and frankincense tea; galette of rhubarb, neroli scented yoghurt, crystallised coconut and rhubarb sorbet. **Details:** www.fatduck.co.uk; 9 pm; closed Mon & Sun D; closed 2 weeks at New Year.

The Hind's Head   £ 43
High St SL6 2AB   (01628) 626151

"You can sample Heston's genius simply", at his "buzzing" pub. just over the road from The Fat Duck; service can be "inflexible", but the take on "old-fashioned" British dishes is "unbelievably brilliant" – not least, of course, his "historic" triple-cooked chips. / **Sample dishes:** rabbit & bacon terrine with cucumber pickles; skate wing with capers, lemon & parsley; poached pear in red wine & spices. **Details:** www.hindsheadhotel.co.uk; From the M4 take exit to Maidenhead Central, then go to Bray village; 9.30 pm; closed Sun D.

Riverside Brasserie   £ 46
Monkey Island Ln, Bray Marina SL6 2EB   (01628) 780553

With its hard-to-find Bray Marina location, it's no surprise that this "relaxed" brasserie – open only in summer – is of most note for its "very pleasant" ambience; even though the menu is "restricted", however, it is consistently well executed. / **Details:** www.riversidebrasserie.co.uk; follow signs for Bray Marina off A308; 9.30 pm.

Waterside Inn   £127
Ferry Rd SL6 2AT   (01628) 620691

"Out of town, and out-of-this-world"; its appeal "might be considered a tad old-fashioned", but – for reporters of all ages – Michel Roux's Thames-side veteran is a "romantic" destination that's simply "stunning in every way" (and currently on a 'high'); summer tables on the "beautiful" terrace are especially prized. / **Sample dishes:** foie gras with fig chutney; grilled rabbit fillets with glazed chestnuts & armagnac sauce; warm caramelized Brittany style pastry with plum sorbet. **Details:** www.waterside-inn.co.uk; off A308 between Windsor & Maidenhead; 10 pm; closed Mon & Tue (open Tue D Jun-Aug); no jeans or trainers; booking: max 10. **Accommodation:** 11 rooms, from £200.

BREARTON, NORTH YORKSHIRE 8–4B

The Malt Shovel £ 36
HG3 3BX (01423) 862929
This "friendly", "family-run" former pub is unanimously acclaimed,
under its new ownership, for offering "lovely food" (including
"an excellent selection of fish") in a "pleasant setting". / **Details:** off
A61, 6m N of Harrogate; 10 pm; closed Mon, Tue & Sun D; no Amex; need 8+
to book.

BRECON, POWYS 2–1A

Felin Fach Griffin £ 40
Felin Fach LD3 0UB (01874) 620111
"Gastropub extraordinaire!"; "the food's a match for any restaurant
in the metropolis", say fans of the "very rustic-feeling dining room"
of this "beautiful country pub", in the Brecon Beacons.
/ **Sample dishes:** local smoked salmon tartare, crème fraîche & black pepper
tuile; local Welsh rib-eye, red onion confit, chips & béarnaise; vanilla crème brûlée
with piña colada. **Details:** www.eatdrinksleep.ltd.uk; 20 mins NW of Abergavenny
on A470; 9.30 pm; closed Mon L; no Amex. **Accommodation:** 7 rooms,
from £97.50.

BRIDGE OF ALLAN, STIRLINGSHIRE 9–4C

Clive Ramsay £ 32
Henderson St FK9 4HR (01786) 831616
"Café by day, bistro by night" – this "simple" operation serves
a "short" menu tipped for its "good value"; popularity is such that
it can get "hectic". / **Sample dishes:** mussels; chicken with broccoli and mash
with mustard sauce; crème brûlée. **Details:** www.cliveramsay.com; 8.45 pm;
no Amex.

BRIDPORT, DORSET 2–4B

The Bull Hotel £ 37
34 East St DT6 3LF (01308) 422878
It may be "slightly overcrowded and noisy", but the dining room of this
boutique hotel is a top tip for those in search of "simple, tasty food".
/ **Details:** www.thebullhotel.co.uk; 9.30 pm. **Accommodation:** 15 rooms,
from £85.

Hive Beach Cafe £ 38
Beach Rd DT6 4RF (01308) 897070
"Fabulous fresh fish and seafood, served on the beach" – that's the
formula that's made this "brilliantly-situated" café extremely popular.
/ **Sample dishes:** whole grilled bream with asparagus, rosemary hollandaise &
new potatoes; locally made cakes. **Details:** www.hivebeachcafe.co.uk; L only,
varies seasonally; no Amex.

Riverside £ 44
West Bay DT6 4EZ (01308) 422011
"My wife would have quite happily died after her langoustines here!";
this "stunningly-located" seaside café, "on a little island in the river",
has long been "one of the best-known restaurants on the south
coast", and with good reason – "fish doesn't come any better" than
the "huge range" on offer here.
/ **Details:** www.thefishrestaurant-westbay.co.uk; 9 pm; closed Mon & Sun D
(closed end of Nov until mid February); no Amex.

Brook's   £ 38
6 Bradford Rd HD6 1RW   (01484) 715284
*Celebrating two decades in business this year, Darrell Brooks's "busy" but "intimate" candlelit venture continues to offer food that's "imaginative" and "well-presented". / **Sample dishes:** crab and sweetcorn fritter with ratatouille salsa; braised shoulder of lamb with smoked bacon, rosemary and puy lentils; ginger and chocolate sponge served with whipped cream. **Details:** www.brooks-restaurant.co.uk; 11 pm; D only, closed Sun; no Amex.*

Although in a much smaller way – obviously – the dining scene of 'London by the Sea' has a diversity emulating that of the capital. Only the two *Gingerman* restaurants stand out as 'plain vanilla' modern British dining rooms, but there are specialists in seafood (*Riddle & Finns*) and veggie fare (*Terre à Terre*), as well as in each of the major oriental cuisines (*Aumthong Thai*, *China Garden* and *Murasaki*).

When it comes to brunching, Brighton arguably trumps the metropolis. *Bills* and the *Real Eating Co* are two names leading a strong field.

Aumthong Thai   £ 25
60 Western Rd BN3 1JD   (01273) 773922
*"No frills, just smiling faces and fantastic Thai food" – that's the deal that inspires rapturous reports on this "value-for-money" destination, where the food is "beautifully cooked and presented". / **Sample dishes:** baked pork spare ribs, marinated with honey sauce and spices; pad prik chicken; ice cream. **Details:** www.aumthong.com; 11 pm, 10 pm Sun; closed Mon L.*

Bill's   £ 27
100 North Rd, The Depot BN1 1YE   (01273) 692894
*"The best café in the country!" (well, almost) – this "crowded" favourite cooks up "local" food "consistently well", and it makes a "fabulous place for breakfast or lunch"; it can be "noisy" and "hectic", though, and you may have to queue. / **Sample dishes:** home-made lasagne; baked orange and gingerbread cheesecake with mascarpone, blood oranges and chocolate sauce. **Details:** www.billsproducestore.co.uk; 8 pm; closed Sun D; no Amex.*

Casa Don Carlos   £ 23
5 Union St BN1 1HA   (01273) 327177
*"A long-time good tapas place", in the Lanes; a "really friendly and buzzy" establishment, it offers "above-average" fare. / **Sample dishes:** meatballs; chickpeas and spinach; chocolate mousse. **Details:** 11 pm.*

China Garden   £ 34
88-91 Preston St BN1 2HG   (01273) 325124
*"Excellent dim sum", on Sundays, is a much-lauded highlight of this "fast and friendly" Chinese; it has a "good location", too, near the sea-front. / **Sample dishes:** deep fried crab's claw stuffed with mashed prawns served with a sweet and hot dip; sliced chicken with Chinese mushrooms; lemon ice cream with a soft lemon liquor centre coated with crushed lemon meringue. **Details:** www.chinagarden.name; opp West Pier; 11.30 pm.*

Donatello   **£ 29**
1-3 Brighton Pl BN1 1HJ   (01273) 775477
In the Lanes, a "good basic Italian", with an "easy-going atmosphere";
its "cheap and cheerful" attractions ensure it's "always busy".
/ **Sample dishes:** aubergines baked with tomato, mozzarella, bechamel &
Parmesan cheese; escalopes of veal cooked with garlic, tomato, white wine,
oregano, capers and parsley; chocolate truffle gâteaux.
Details: www.donatello.co.uk; 11.30 pm.

Due South   **£ 43**
139 King's Arches BN1 2FN   (01273) 821218

"For a casual outing, with a great location and atmosphere",
this "fantastically-situated" beatified hang-out has a lot going for it,
including sometimes "very tasty" food; standards generally, though,
have seemed rather "lazy" of late (and "tables away from the
windows feel like eating in a coal hole"). / **Sample dishes:** home-made
black pudding & sweetbreads with crème fraîche; stuffed saddle of rabbit with
local mushrooms, braised puy lentils, & a mustard tuile; baked alaska with lemon
liquor. **Details:** www.duesouth.co.uk; Brighton Beach, below the Odeon cinema;
9.30 pm.

English's   **£ 50**
29-31 East St BN1 1HL   (01273) 327980
Feedback on this ancient parlour, in the Lanes, is totally polarised –
fans say that, on a warm evening, its terrace is "the best place
in England for fish", but there are as many critics who just find
standards "very poor" all-round. / **Sample dishes:** mussels with white wine
and cream; pan-fried scallops with sesame seeds and mild chillies; baked lemon
torte with orange and Grand Marnier syrup. **Details:** www.englishs.co.uk; 10 pm.

Food for Friends   **£ 37**
17-18 Prince Albert St BN1 1HF   (01273) 202310
"A long-established vegetarian", in the Lanes, that's "kept up a good
standard after a change of ownership", and offers food that's "fresh,
well prepared, and to-the-point". / **Sample dishes:** beetroot gnocchi with
roast cherry tomatoes, baby beetroot and toasted pinenuts in a crushed basil and
Parmesan pesto; baked ricotta and pecorino gallette topped with cardamon
scented honey roast Mediterranean vegetables; cardamom and saffron crème
caramel served with fresh blackberries. **Details:** www.foodforfriends.com; 10 pm,
Fri & Sat 10.30 pm.

La Fourchette   **£ 40**
105 Western Rd BN1 2AA   (01273) 722556
This "high-class" modern French bistro "has its ups and downs,
but when it's good it's very good indeed"; last year it also spawned
a "nice offshoot" in Kemptown (at 120 St George's Road,
tel 682200). / **Sample dishes:** sauté king prawns with garlic & parsley sauce;
free range guinea fowl with pommes purées & wild mushrooms; crème catalane
with anis & cinnamon flavour. **Details:** www.lafourchette.co.uk; 10.30 pm.

The Ginger Pig £ 33

3 Hove St BN3 2TR (01273) 736123

"The only drawback is that you can't book", at this "very busy" and "upmarket" Hove gastropub yearling – an "unpretentious"-looking hang-out, offering "good, locally-sourced British food".

/ **Sample dishes:** *gin soused salmon gravalax with pickled cucumber & spring herbs; seared calves liver with champ potatoes, pancetta & pickled shallots; sticky toffee pudding with salt caramel, brown bread & armagnac ice cream.*
Details: *www.gingermanrestaurant.com; 10 pm.* **Accommodation:** *11 rooms, from £100.*

⭐

The Gingerman
Drakes Hotel £ 49

44 Marine Pde BN2 1PE (01273) 696934

Very much on a par with the original – this Gingerman offshoot in a Kemp Town design-hotel is widely rated as "a gem", with "subtle" cuisine, and "relaxed but professional" service. / **Sample dishes:** *tea smoked duck breast with pickled red cabbage and cress salad; fillet of local red mullet with vanilla carrot purée, saffron potatoes and tapenade dressing; chocolate tart with orange custard and root ginger ice cream.*
Details: *www.gingermanrestaurants.com; 10 pm; closed weekday L.* **Accommodation:** *20 rooms, from £100.*

⭐⭐

Gingerman £ 40

21a Norfolk Sq BN1 2PD (01273) 326688

"The original, and still the best part of the Gingerman empire" – "a very intimate bistro-like" set-up in the Lanes, offering food that's almost invariably hailed as "wonderful". / **Sample dishes:** *seared wood pigeon with roast balsamic baby beets, rocket and Parmesan; braised rabbit pie with honey and thyme glazed Chantenay carrots and pomme purée; poached marsala peaches with amaretto ice cream.*
Details: *www.gingermanrestaurants.com; off Norfolk Square; 9.15 pm; closed Mon.*

Graze £ 41

42 Western Rd BN3 1JD (01273) 823707

At its best, this "trendy" ("black walls with green lighting!") Hove grazing "concept" still offers "fantastic" and "interesting" dishes; of late, however, execution has sometimes fallen short.
/ **Sample dishes:** *roast onion tart with goat's cheese; venison pie; chocolate orange mousse with orange ice cream.* **Details:** *www.graze-restaurant.co.uk; 10 pm; closed Mon & Sun D.*

Ⓣ

Havana £ 52

32 Duke St BN1 1AG (01273) 773388

Given its scale, and location, in the Lanes, this large and stylish venue – where the décor is somewhat Caribbean (but the food isn't) – attracts little feedback; some reporters, though, still tip it for its "great, chilled ambience". / **Sample dishes:** *roast scallops with mushroom & chive dressing; roast fillet of seabass with Japanese aubergine caviar & oyster sauce; dark chocolate tart on coffee biscuit.* **Details:** *www.havana.uk.com; 10.30 pm, Fri & Sat 11 pm, Sun 10 pm; no jeans or trainers; children: 6+ at D.*

Ⓐ

Hotel du Vin et Bistro £ 45

Ship St BN1 1AD (01273) 718588

"It's the wine list and the ambience that does it", say fans of this popular branch of the boutique-hotel chain, housed in a "fascinating" old building in the Lanes; as usual, the food is "reliable, rather than stunning", and totally outgunned by the wine list.
/ **Sample dishes:** *smoked salmon with a blini; roast pork belly, creamed Savoy cabbage & madeira sauce; crème brûlée.* **Details:** *www.hotelduvin.com; 9.45 pm, Fri & Sat 10.15 pm; booking: max 10.* **Accommodation:** *37 rooms, from £160.*

Indian Summer   **£ 28** ⭐

69 East St BN1 1HQ   (01273) 711001

"Authentic cuisine with a twist" – offering "fantastic fresh flavours" –
makes this small Indian venture, near the Lanes, very popular with
almost all who comment on it; there's also a branch in Hove
*(5 Victoria Terrace, tel 773090). / **Sample dishes:** masala dosa; peshawari*
lamb; ginger pudding with ginger brandy sauce.
Details: *www.indian-summer.org.uk; 10.30 pm, Sun & Mon 10 pm; closed*
Mon L.

Murasaki   **£ 33** ⭐

115 Dyke Rd BN1 3JE   (01273) 326231

"Very fresh sushi"" is just one of the attractions that makes this
"buzzy" Japanese cafe, in Seven Dials, "a great local stand-by".
*/ **Sample dishes:** sushi; aubergine miso yuki. **Details:** 11 pm; closed Mon;*
no Amex.

Pintxo People   **£ 36**

95-99 Western Rd BN1 2LB   (01273) 732323

What a shame! – after all the "hype", this "buzzy" tapas two-year-
old has "nothing much to make it stand out from the crowd
nowadays", and its Spanish cuisine is too often "very average".
*/ **Details:** www.pintxopeople.co.uk; 11.30 pm; closed Sun.*

Real Eating Company   **£ 40** ⭐

86-87 Western Rd BN3 1JB   (01273) 221444

"It has much more competition than when it started, but the Real
Eating Company is still the queen of Brighton's breakfasts", says one
of the many fans of this "top-notch" organic deli/restaurant.
*/ **Details:** www.real-eating.co.uk; 9.30 pm; closed Mon D & Sun D.*

Regency   **£ 23**

131 Kings Rd BN1 2HH   (01273) 325014

This "cut-above" chippy, "overlooking the beach", is hard to beat
if you're looking for a "traditional" feast for all the family; "fantastic
seafood platters" are the top tip.
*/ **Details:** www.theregencyrestaurant.co.uk; opp West Pier; 11 pm.*
Accommodation: *30 rooms, from £65.*

Riddle & Finns   **£ 46** ⭐⭐

12b, Meeting House Ln BN1 1HB   (01273) 323008

"A tantalising display of seafood tempts you in" to this "indulgent"
fish and seafood bar in the Lanes, where the food is "fresh" and
"fantastic", and service is "charming" – "what more could you want?"
*/ **Details:** www.riddleandfinns.co.uk; 10 pm.*

Seven Dials   **£ 44**

1-3 Buckingham Pl BN1 3TD   (01273) 885555

This "popular" and "relaxing" venue inhabits slightly "echo-y"
premises that were once a bank; the "friendly" service can be a bit
"dizzy", but the "unfussy modern cuisine" is usually "enjoyable".
*/ **Details:** www.sevendialsrestaurant.co.uk; 10.30 pm; closed Sun D.*

Tallula's Tea Rooms   **£ 23** Ⓣ

9 Hampton Pl BN1 3DA   (01273) 710529

"All the things you might want to eat for breakfast, served quickly and
with quality ingredients" – a tip for those seeking inspiration among
*Brighton's many breakfast and brunch spots. / **Details:** 6 pm; L only.*

Terre à Terre   **£ 43**   ✪✪

71 East St BN1 1HQ   (01273) 729051

*"Unbeatable for veggies and non-veggies alike"; "every dish provides an incredible array of flavours", at "Britain's best no-meat restaurant", in the Lanes; presentation is "inventive" too. / **Sample dishes:** twice baked soufflé with asparagus & Parmesan, with wild garlic velouté, spring chive bulbs, parsley root packed potato & asparagus tips, finished with chantery carrot blitz; tandoori spiced tikka halloumi kebab with charred onion & cherry tomatoes, served with hot fry spice curry leaf potatoes & chilli spinach, yoghurt cumin salt cooler, lime & aubergine pickle & indi web shred; treacle & crumb tart, served with poached rhubarb compote & hibiscus ripple clotted ice.*
Details: *www.terreaterre.co.uk; 10.30 pm; closed Mon; booking: max 8 at weekends.*

BRINKWORTH, WILTSHIRE   2–2C

The Three Crowns   **£ 36**

The Street SN15 5AF   (01666) 510366

*"A pleasant gastropub, in an area where good options for eating out are sparse" – reporters differ, though, as to whether the long menu in its dining conservatory is "interesting" or "over-ambitious". / **Sample dishes:** marinated kangaroo, venison & ostrich, with a sauce of sun dried tomatoes, wild mushrooms, button onions, flamed with brandy and finished with cream; home-made strawberry & champagne ice cream.*
Details: *www.threecrowns.co.uk; 9.30 pm, Sun 9 pm.*

BRISTOL, CITY OF BRISTOL   2–2B

Perhaps it's partly accounted for by the large number of student customers, but Bristol is emerging as a city with an impressive ethnic restaurant scene, and offers an enticing variety of good-quality Indian restaurant at different price-levels. Otherwise, *Bell's Diner* and *Culinaria* are the names of real note, and, for veggies, *Cafe Maitreya*.

The Albion   **£ 43**   🅐

Boyces Ave BS8 4AA   (0117) 9733522

*"Delicious food in a classic pub environment" – that's the deal that making this Clifton boozer very popular with all who comment on it. / **Sample dishes:** three ways with pigs heads and fried eggs; wild halibut, mushrooms and whelk butter sauce; Valrhona chocolate fondant with milk sorbet.*
Details: *www.thealbionclifton.co.uk; 9.30; closed Mon & Sun.*

Bell's Diner   **£ 43**   🅐✪

1 York Rd BS6 5QB   (0117) 924 0357

*"A top-notch gourmet experience"; Chris Wicks's "small and intimate" fixture may be "relaxed and informal" and in a "gritty part of town" (Montpelier), but his "superb" and "imaginative" cuisine continues to make it one of the city's restaurant-institutions. / **Sample dishes:** canneloni truffle toney, goats cheese, melon, merlot vinegar; lamb onion soubise, hot pot lamb offal, oyster, lavender jus; banana soufflé with toffee ice-cream. **Details:** www.bellsdiner.co.uk; 10 pm; closed Mon L, Sat L & Sun.*

Bocacina   **£ 24**   🆃

184c, Wells Rd, Lower Knowle BS4 2AL   (0117) 9713377

*Sibling to Bocanova – a "good-value" Brazilian-influenced pizza parlour, that's usually "packed". / **Sample dishes:** tangy mango salads; selection of pizzas; sticky ginger, orange & cinnamon cake.*
Details: *www.acappellas.co.uk; 10:30pm Mon-Sun; no Amex.*

Bocanova £ 42

90 Colston St BS1 5BB   (0117) 929 1538

A "huge loft-like venue", tipped as offering "something for everyone"
– sometimes including "live music, or wondrous art exhibitions" –
and consequently being "very popular"; the menu is notionally
Brazilian (but "they are amenable to adapting it for you").
/ *Sample dishes:* casquinha de siri; chargrilled mature Brazilian sirloin steak with
a red wine, plum tomato, basil provencal sauce, served with rocket and balsamic
vinaigrette. *Details:* www.bocanova.co.uk; 10.30 pm, Fri & Sat 11 pm; closed
Mon, Tue & Sun; no Amex.

Bordeaux Quay £ 44

Canons Rd BS1 5UH   (0117) 943 1200

"Right on the docks" (and with "super views"), this "buzzing", post-
industrial conversion – comprising deli, brasserie and restaurant –
has become the best-known place in town; everyone loves its "ethical"
and "locally-sourcing" policies, but those who find standards
"variable" may also find the place "over-hyped" (or "overpriced").
/ *Sample dishes:* smoked eel, horseradish crème fraîche; chicken breast,
chanterelles, leeks, carrots & chive mash; rhubarb crumble, crème anglaise.
Details: www.bordeaux-quay.co.uk; 10 pm; closed Sun.

Boston Tea Party £ 18

75 Park St BS1 5PF   (0117) 929 8601

"It's great to see a thriving coffee chain not owned by a faceless
multinational"; this particular outlet – all "comfy sofas and huge
paintings" – is a "friendly" and "amenable" destination, offering
"the best tea and coffee in Bristol"; nice garden too.
/ *Sample dishes:* falafel; carrot cake. *Details:* www.bostonteaparty.co.uk; 8 pm;
no Amex; no booking.

Budokan £ 27

31 Colston St BS1 5AP   (0117) 914 1488

Part of a "small local chain" that's consistently hailed for its "great,
reasonably-priced pan-Asian dishes"; the "rapid REfuel" (pre-7.30pm)
menu comes particularly recommended. / *Sample dishes:* Thai fish cakes
with sweet chilli sauce; pad Thai with shrimp and chicken; lychee sorbet.
Details: www.budokan.co.uk; 11 pm; closed Sun.

Cafe Maitreya £ 32

89 St Marks Rd, Easton BS5 6HY   (0117) 951 0100

"By far the best veggie in the South West"; the "excellent and
creative" cooking at this "surprisingly-located" establishment
(near Stapleton Road BR) wins rave reviews – "even from dyed-in-the-
wool carnivores". / *Sample dishes:* crisp beet green lava bread; asparagus,
pied bleu mushroom and smoked ricotta blanket; baked lemon and macadamia
cheesecake. *Details:* www.cafemaitreya.co.uk; 9.45; D only, closed Mon & Sun;
no Amex.

Culinaria £ 39

1 Chandos Rd BS6 6PG   (0117) 973 7999

"Still the best food in Bristol, albeit not in the most comfortable
setting" – Stephen Markwick's "bland"-looking Redland bistro offers
"simple" but "expertly-prepared" dishes that are "consistently first-
class"; "you have to book weeks ahead". / *Sample dishes:* ham hock
terrine, celeriac remoulade; poached fillet of brill, prawns, asparagus & cream;
blueberry sherry trifle. *Details:* www.culinariabristol.co.uk; 9.30 pm; closed
Sun-Tue, Wed L & Thu L; no Amex.

Dynasty   **£ 40** ⭐

16a St. Thomas St BS1 6JJ (0117) 925 0888

"The best Chinese ever!" – this barn-like oriental has quite a local fan club, not least on Sundays, as a place "for dim sum and people-watching"; it recently opened a large spin-off, Zen Harbour-side – one to watch, we suspect. / **Details:** www.dynasty-bristol.co.uk; 11.30 pm.

Fishers   **£ 34**

35 Princess Victoria St BS8 4BX (0117) 974 7044

"A pleasant seafood restaurant in Clifton, that's uncomplicated and fairly priced"; it's an "unpretentious", and perhaps "unsophisticated" place... "but it works". / **Sample dishes:** pan fried king scallops; fillet of seabass with crab risotto cake; sticky toffee pudding.
Details: www.fishers-restaurant.com; 10.30 pm, Sun & Mon 10 pm.

FishWorks   **£ 44** 🅣

128 Whiteladies Rd BS8 2RS (0117) 974 4433

One of the first branches of the fishmonger-cum-café chain, still often tipped for serving up "the freshest fish"; it takes much flak, though, for its "extortionate" pricing. / **Sample dishes:** mussels steamed with wine garlic & parsley; yellowtail kingfish yakatori; baked chocolate pudding.
Details: www.fishworks.co.uk; 10.30 pm.

The Glass Boat   **£ 43** 🅐

Welsh Back BS1 4SB (0117) 929 0704

"It's the location that keeps it afloat"; this permanently-moored barge has a "perfect romantic setting", but views on its cooking range all the way from "enjoyable" to "sloppy and overpriced".
/ **Sample dishes:** breast of chicken stuffed with braised oxtail served with baby fennel, creamed Savoy cabbage and monkfish velouté; monkfish baked in Prosciutto on a bed of creamy Savoy cabbage; rhubarb and stem ginger brûlée with chocolate dipped vanilla shortbread. **Details:** www.glassboat.co.uk; below Bristol Bridge; 10.30 pm; closed Sat L & Sun D.

Goldbrick House   **£ 46** 🅐

69 Park St BS1 5PB (0117) 945 1950

Food that's generally "spot-on" (and "very good wines" too) ensure this year-old restaurant and champagne bar "live up to the hype" – "there are quite a few places broadly like this in town, but this is one of the few that actually delivers". / **Sample dishes:** salmon gravadlax with dill & vodka; fillet of beef Wellington, celeriac purée, & wild mushrooms; blueberry crème brûlée with amaretti biscuits. **Details:** www.goldbrickhouse.co.uk; 11 pm, Sun 6 pm; closed Sun D.

Hotel du Vin et Bistro   £ 45   Ⓐ

Sugar Hs, Narrow Lewins Mead BS1 2NU   (0117) 925 5577
"A lovely night out" is to be had at this *"most atmospheric"*
warehouse-conversion, which remains one of the top destinations
in town; food may be *"somewhat unoriginal"*, but it's the *"endless
wine list"* which draws the punters in. / **Sample dishes:** *squid, chorizo &
crayfish salad; honey-glazed loin of pork with mustard mash; sticky toffee pudding
with clotted cream.* **Details:** *www.hotelduvin.com; 9.45 pm, Fri-Sun 10.15 pm;
booking: max 10.* **Accommodation:** *40 rooms, from £135.*

Kathmandu   £ 26   ✪

Colston Tower, Colston St BS1 5AQ   (0117) 9294455
"Still consistently excellent"; this Indian favourite *"hits the spot"* for all
who comment on it, particularly its *"oustanding"* Nepalese
specialities. / **Details:** *www.kathmandu-curry.com; 11 pm, Sat 11.30 pm.*

Krishna Inn   £ 23   Ⓣ

4 Byron Pl, Triangle South BS8 1JT   (0117) 9276864
*An inexpensive, modern south-Indian; feedback is scarce,
but continues to affirm its continuing high standard of cooking.*
/ **Sample dishes:** *mixed platter; Kerala fish curry; payasam.*
Details: *www.keralagroup.co.uk; 11 pm Fri & Sat midnight.*

Mud Dock Café
CycleWorks   £ 39   Ⓐ

40 The Grove BS1 4RB   (0117) 934 9734
*Service can be "flaky", but the "simple" fare at this first-floor café
(over a bike shop) is generally "well cooked" – especially "the best Full
English"; and anyway, "who cares about the food, with a view like
this?"* / **Sample dishes:** *fish cakes; burger; bread & butter pudding.*
Details: *www.mud-dock.com; close to the Industrial Museum & Arnolfini Gallery;
10 pm; closed Mon D & Sun D.*

Old India
Stock Exchange Buildings   £ 29   ✪

34 St Nicholas St BS1 1TL   (0117) 9221136
"Interesting" Indian food that's *"well-cooked and spiced"* is but one
of the attractions of this city-centre spot, which is also noted for its
"fascinating" setting (which makes *"good use"* of its location in an
ancient building). / **Sample dishes:** *chicken malai grill; crab masala; mango
kulfi.* **Details:** *www.oldindia.co.uk; midnight; closed Sun.*

Olive Shed   £ 37

Floating Harbour, Princes Whf BS1 4RN   (0117) 929 1960
*A "rather out-of-the-way" waterside spot, with a "surprisingly
ambitious" menu, and offering some "unusual" and "hearty" fare
("mostly organic").* / **Details:** *www.theoliveshed.com; 10 pm; closed Mon &
Sun D; no Amex.*

One Stop Thali Café   £ 22   Ⓐ✪

12 York Rd BS6 5QE   (0117) 942 6687
"A top cheap and cheerful option in Bristol"; this *"wildly-decorated"*
and *"Bohemian"* Montpelier Indian delivers up *"so much good food
on a big tray, for so little money"*; also in Easton and Totterdown.
/ **Details:** *www.onestopthali.co.uk; 10 pm; D only, closed Mon; no Amex.*

Primrose Café   **£ 34**

1 Boyces Ave BS8 4AA   (0117) 946 6577

A "sweet" back-street hang-out in a "village-y" Clifton location, which
is a top spot for brunch or a daytime snack, but which also
"transforms well into an evening bistro" (especially downstairs);
"organic and seasonal ingredients predominate", and "they use them
very well". / **Details:** 9.30 pm; Sun D; no Amex; no booking at L.

Quartier Vert   **£ 40**

85 Whiteladies Rd BS8 2NT   (0117) 973 4482

A veteran Clifton bar, under the same ownership as the more recent
Bordeaux Quay, offering a "quietly stylish", and rather "expensive",
formula which mixes some "modern Anglo-French fare" with classic
tapas dishes. / **Details:** www.quartiervert.co.uk; 10 pm; Sun D only in summer;
no Amex.

Rajpoot   **£ 38**

52 Upper Belgrave Rd BS8 2XP   (0117) 973 3515

A "very smart" Indian of long standing, where the food is usually
"truly excellent". / **Details:** www.rajpootrestaurant.co.uk; 11 pm; D only,
closed Sun.

riverstation   **£ 43**

The Grove BS1 4RB   (0117) 914 4434

"The setting on the dockside is just wonderful", and this "unusual"
spot ("a converted harbour police station") is a "lovely venue";
it's "style-over-substance" though, and the restaurant can seem
"bland" and "sterile" – "stay downstairs in the bar by the water".
/ **Details:** www.riverstation.co.uk; 10.30 pm, Fri & Sat 11 pm; closed Sat L &
Sun D; no Amex.

Sands   **£ 33**

95 Queens Rd BS8 1LW   (0117) 973 9734

A subterranean Lebanese establishment, tipped as "great for a slightly
'different' night out"; "good veggie choices" too.
/ **Details:** www.sandsrestaurant.co.uk; 11 pm.

Severnshed   **£ 40**

The Grove, Harbourside BS1 4RB   (0117) 925 1212

A "fun" and "noisy" bar/brasserie occupying "a great building on the
harbour-side"; the food's "not memorable" – and service is sometimes
"woeful" – but "they are always busy, so must be doing something
right". / **Details:** www.severnshed.co.uk; 10.30 pm.

Teohs   **£ 24**

26-34 Lower Ashley Rd BS2 9NP   (0117) 907 1191

Tipped for its "brilliant-value food" – a pan-Asian refectory that's
"always crowded with locals". / **Sample dishes:** crispy mini spring rolls;
Singapore curry laksa; caramelised banana. **Details:** www.teohs.net; 100 yds from
M32, J3; 10.30 pm; closed Sun; no Amex.

The Goose £ 49
OX49 5LG   (01491) 612304
*Supporters say you get a "luxurious and sophisticated experience",
at this restaurant in a 17th-century building, but even fans can find
it an "atmosphere-free" location (perhaps unsurprising, as it has
a Michelin star!); NB: the chef changed post-survey, so we don't think
a rating is appropriate. / **Sample dishes:** terrine of white chicken with
shitake mushrooms, Parma ham & confit chicken 'bon bon'; roast rump of lamb,
braised shoulder, fondant potato; warm pistachio sponge cake, condensed milk ice
cream, poached rhubarb & rhubarb purée.*
Details: *www.thegooserestaurant.co.uk; M40, J6 near Watlington; 9.30 pm;
closed Mon & Sun D.*

Druidstone Hotel £ 36
SA62 3NE   (01437) 781221
*Under the same ownership since the early-'70s, this "higgledy-
piggledy house" has a dining room (and terrace) with "one of Britain's
most breathtakingly beautiful views"; standards of food and service
have arguably "lacked consistency" of late ("but, in a strange way,
that's also one of its charms"). / **Sample dishes:** beetroot chutney & goat's
cheese puff pastry tarts; lamb stuffed with apricot and rosemary on black pudding
mash; hot chocolate fudge cake. **Details:** www.druidstone.co.uk; from B4341
at Broad Haven turn right, then left after 1.5m; 9.30 pm.*
Accommodation: *11 & 7 holiday cottages rooms, from £68.*

Buckland Manor £ 72
WR12 7LY   (01386) 852626

*An "idyllically-situated" country house hotel, part of the Von Essen
group, that's especially tipped as a destination for a "relaxing" lunch.
/ **Sample dishes:** steamed wild mushroom and chicken timbale with a Parmesan
tuile and calvados cream; ballotine of cornfed chicken filled with a tarragon and
pistachio mousse morel cream sauce; hot passion fruit soufflé with honey ice-cream
and fine tuile biscuit. **Details:** www.bucklandmanor.co.uk; 2m SW of Broadway
on B4632; 9 pm; jacket & tie at D; booking: max 8; children: 12+.*
Accommodation: *13 rooms, from £265.*

Lygon Arms   **£ 60**   ✖

High St WR12 7DU   (01386) 852255

Despite some lingering fame and a magnificent barrel-vaulted setting, it's becoming ever-more difficult to justify the inclusion in the guide of this "overpriced" and "disappointing" dining room.
/ **Sample dishes:** chicken liver parfait, toasted brochet and apple chutney; pan seared sea bass with crushed potatoes, asparagus and warm tomato and caper dressing; peach melba, peach sorbet and raspberry dressing. **Details:** www.barcelo-hotels.co.uk; just off A44; 9 pm; D only, from end June to end Sept, ex Sun open L & D; no jeans. **Accommodation:** 77 rooms, from £133.

Russell's   **£ 48**

20 High St WR12 7DT   (01386) 853555

"A stylish brasserie, in a lovely Cotswold village" – a good all-rounder that particularly stands out by virtue of its "non-traditional" ambience.
/ **Details:** www.russellsofbroadway.com; 9.30 pm; closed Sun D.
Accommodation: 7 rooms, from £120.

BROCKENHURST, HAMPSHIRE   2–4C

Le Poussin at Whitley Ridge   **£ 71**   ⭐⭐

Beaulieu Rd SO42 7QL   (0238) 028 2944

"Classic food is well-sourced, superbly cooked and served with charm", say fans of the Aitken family's small country house hotel, "beautifully located in the heart of the New Forest"; for a few dissenters, though, its approach is too "hushed", and "not as good as it thinks it is". / **Details:** www.lepoussin.co.uk; 9.30 pm; no Amex; children: 8+ at D. **Accommodation:** 18 rooms, from £190.

Rhinefield House   Ⓐ
Hand Picked Hotels   **£ 55**

Rhinefield Rd SO42 7QB   (01590) 622922

In an "enchanting" New Forest setting, a luxurious Victorian country house hotel where the "well-presented" food invariably impresses – feedback is too modest in volume, though, to justify awarding a 'star'.
/ **Details:** www.handpicked.co.uk; 9.30 pm; D only, ex Sun open L & D; no jeans or trainers. **Accommodation:** 50 rooms, from £230.

Simply Poussin   **£ 36**

The Courtyard, Brookley Rd SO42 7RB   (01590) 623063

In a "quiet corner of a New Forest village", a restaurant that spawned the Aitken family's local mini-empire; it's really for the "ridiculously good-value lunch" that it's most worth seeking out nowadays – otherwise, it can appear "lacklustre". / **Sample dishes:** twice baked cheese soufflé; fillet of beef with chunky chips, watercress salad, confit shallot & red wine sauce; hot chocolate fondant. **Details:** www.simplypoussin.co.uk; behind Bestsellers Bookshop; 9 pm; closed Mon & Sun; no Amex; children: 8+ at D.

BRODICK, ISLE OF ARRAN   7–1A

Creelers Seafood Restaurant   **£ 43**   ⭐

Home Farm KA27 8DD   (01770) 302810

If you're lucky, you may be able to enjoy "fish caught by the owner", when you visit this good-all-round fish bistro (which has an outpost in Edinburgh too). / **Details:** www.creelers.co.uk; 9.30 pm; closed Thu; no Amex.

Tamasha £ 41

131 Widmore Rd BR1 3AX   (020) 8460 3240

"Not a curry house, but a true Indian!" – this colonial-style subcontinental is "always a very good experience". / **Sample dishes:** Norwegian salmon marinated in cream cheese, crushed peppercorns & garlic; lamb marinated with dark rum, red wine, garlic, ginger, cumin & mustard seeds, with onions, coriander and almonds; dark chocolate sauce surrounded by mint covered in dark chocolate. **Details:** www.tamasha.co.uk; 10.30 pm; no shorts. **Accommodation:** 7 rooms, from £65.

Lavender House £ 50

39 The St NR13 5AA   (01603) 712215

Richard Hughes' "lovely, romantic thatched-house" inspires extremely flattering reviews, thanks to its "elegant but relaxed" style and its "wonderful" food. / **Sample dishes:** tureen of local duck with orange and liquorice dressing; fillet and shin of beef, smoked potato purée, roast baby onions and port wine; iced peanut butter parfait with banana coconut marshmallow and cinnamon doughnuts. **Details:** www.thelavenderhouse.co.uk; 9.30 pm; D only, closed Sun & Mon; no Amex.

The Stapleton Arms £ 34

Church Hill SP8 5HS   (01963) 370396

"A very high standard of country restaurant, in an area short of such places"; it's a "welcoming, friendly and relaxed" joint that attracts consistent praise; Sunday lunch is a highlight. / **Sample dishes:** smoked chicken & grape terrine; roast chicken breast with chorizo & broad bean cream; pedro ximenez cheesecake with seasonal berries. **Details:** www.thestapletonarms.com; 10 pm, 9.30 pm Sun. **Accommodation:** 4 rooms, from £110.

The Dysart Arms £ 36

Bowes Gate Rd CW6 9PH   (01829) 260183

A "characterful" country pub with a dining room serving a "varied menu" and "well-kept beers"; service, though, can be "hit-and-miss". / **Sample dishes:** wild mushroom and cream cheese pâté on toasted granary bread; walnut crusted cod with cauliflower purée, purple broccoli and a herb cream; chocolate and orange cheesecake. **Details:** www.dysartarms-bunbury.co.uk; 9.30 pm, 9 pm Sun; no Amex; children: 10 + after 6 pm.

The Lamb £ 47

Sheep St OX18 4LR   (01993) 823155

It's not quite back to the glory days of the ancien régime, but this "delightful restaurant" – part of an inn in this equally "delightful town" – is still tipped for its "simple but tasty" fare. / **Sample dishes:** goat's cheese raviolis with caramelized red onion jam; roast chicken breast with sweet potato purée, herb roast vegetables and crispy pancetta; trio of vanilla - steamed vanilla pudding, crème brûlée and vanilla ice cream. **Details:** www.cotswold-inns-hotels.co.uk/lamb; A40 from Oxford toward Cheltenham; 9.30 pm, Sun 9 pm; no jeans or trainers. **Accommodation:** 17 rooms, from £145.

Fishes Cafe & Seafood Bar £ 54
Market Pl PE31 8HE (01328) 738588

"It's simply perfect, from the fresh fish to the service… and you can even stay now!", say fans of the Owsley-Browns' *"outstanding"* fish-restaurant in *"a lovely market town"*, near the coast; this all comes *"at a price"*, though, and the approach is a bit *"Islington"* for some tastes. / **Sample dishes:** *shrimp cocktail with local samphire; grilled hake with garlic butter; sticky toffee pudding with vanilla ice cream.*
Details: *www.fishesrestaurant.co.uk; on the B1355, near King's Lynn; 8 pm; closed Mon & Sun L; no Amex; children: 8+ after 8.30 pm.* **Accommodation:** *2 rooms, from £130.*

Hoste Arms £ 43
The Green PE31 8HD (01328) 738777

This *"buzzing"*, *"quirky"* and *"stylish"* former coaching inn inspires a host of contradictory views – on a good night it can be *"lovely"*, but too often it *"fails to deliver what it has promised"*, and ends up seeming *"pretentious"*. / **Sample dishes:** *seared scallops, parsnip purée, baby leeks, lobster froth; roast rosette of English lamb, minted celert, spinach & parmentier potatoes; orange flower panna cotta, citrus segments, lime sorbet.*
Details: *www.hostearms.co.uk; 6m W of Wells; 9 pm; no Amex.*
Accommodation: *36 rooms, from £122.*

Maison Bleue £ 38
30-31 Churchgate St IP33 1RG (01284) 760623

"A great taste of France"; the Crépy family's (recently modernised) bistro remains *"universally popular"* with reporters, thanks to its *"expertly-prepared"* cooking, its *"supreme"* service and its *"always-happy"* atmosphere. / **Sample dishes:** *asparagus velouté served with seared hand-dive king scallops; roast fillet of white sea bass with a leek and carrot julienne, white wine sauce; nougat parfait with cruchy almonds and nuts and a red foot curry.* **Details:** *www.maisonbleue.co.uk; near the Cathedral; 9.30 pm; closed Mon & Sun; no Amex.*

St James £ 41
30 High St WD23 3HL (020) 8950 2480

"A reliable life-saver in a severely lacking culinary desert" – this *"smart, modern venue"* on an *"historic high street"* offers a modern British menu that fans say is *"excellent value"*; critics, though, feel it's over-rated locally, and only *"OK"*.
/ **Sample dishes:** *smoked chicken & caramelised onion millefeuille; roast loin of lamb en croute with parmentier potatoes, leeks, baby carrots, rosemary & plum sauce; chocolate tart with pistachio ice cream.*
Details: *www.stjamesrestaurant.co.uk; opp St James Church; 9 pm; closed Sun D; booking essential.*

Mhor Fish £ 33
75-77 Main St FK17 8DX (01877) 330213

Offshoot of Monachyle Mhor in Balquhidder – an *"amazing"* conversion of a former chippy, that offers *"beautifully fresh fish, cooked to perfection"*, and *"fantastic oysters"* too.
/ **Sample dishes:** *grilled langoustines with garlic butter; roast monkfish on a bed of steamed puy lentils, fine beans & roast butternut squash; home-made brandy & chocolate fondant.* **Details:** *www.benledicafe.co.uk; 8.45 pm; no Amex.*

The Place   £ 38
New Lydd Rd TN31 7RB   (01797) 225057
Ignore the "awful" external appearance of this motel-like building –
it's "clean" and "modern" dining room is "right on the beach",
and offers some "surprisingly good" cooking (including "excellent
seafood"). / **Details:** www.theplacecambersands.co.uk; 9 pm, Fri & Sat
9.30 pm. **Accommodation:** 18 rooms, from £80.

Cambridge, like Oxford, has always been an infamously poor
place to eat, and this – very broadly – remains true. Unlike
Oxford, however, the city does have some decent
restaurants… if you venture a short way from the centre –
Midsummer House, Alimentum and 22 Chesterton Road.

Alimentum   £ 42
152-154 Hills Rd CB2 8PB   (01223) 413000
His style may be "pared-down" – certainly compared to his previous
stint at Midsummer House! – but David Williams produces dishes
"on a par with some of London's best", at this much-lauded Franco-
Spanish newcomer; be warned, though – the restaurants location,
near the Cineworld complex, is "dreadful". / **Sample dishes:** mosaic
of duck, Tobermoray cheese; four hour roast pork belly, home-made black pudding;
tiramisu, espresso jelly. **Details:** www.restaurantalimentum.co.uk; 9.30 pm, Fri &
Sat 10 pm; closed Sun; booking essential.

Backstreet Bistro   £ 37
2 Sturton St CB1 2QA   (01223) 306306
Hidden-away on a "quiet street", this "buzzy" bistro has a small but
diverse fan club; the food "if not exciting, is plentiful and well done".
/ **Sample dishes:** timbale of smoked salmon and mackeral horseradish and
crème fraîche dressing; rouge veal with braised fennel and Pernod and cream
sauce; pear and chocolate brownie. **Details:** www.back-street.co.uk; 9.30 pm,
10 Fri, Sat 9.30 Sun; children: 4+.

The Black Cat Cafe   £ 14
2 The Broadway CB1 3AH   (01223) 248972
A top tip for "great cakes, coffees and sandwiches"; service, though,
can be "painfully bad". / **Details:** www.blackcatcafeonline.com; 6 pm;
no booking.

The Cambridge Chop House   £ 36
1 Kings Pde CB2 1SJ   (01223) 359506
"A useful addition to city-centre dining" – this recent arrival offers
sometimes "excellent" British food (including a "top steak and kidney
pudding"); for the best ambience, "sit downstairs").
/ **Sample dishes:** baked duck parcel with sweet & sour cucumber; mutton
Barnsley chop, garlic mashed potato, winter greens & gravy.
Details: www.cambscuisine.com/chophouse; 10.30 pm, Sat 11 pm, Sun 9.30 pm.

Charlie Chan   £ 24
14 Regent St CB2 1DB   (01223) 359336
"Still the best Chinese restaurant in Cambridge, or in fact one of the
best restaurant of any type" – all reporters find this stalwart's
standards "surprisingly good", and its prices are "reasonable" too;
"live music at weekends". / **Sample dishes:** sweet and sour pork; crispy
duck. **Details:** 11 pm.

Cotto £ 38
183 East Rd CB1 1BG (01223) 302010
This popular produce-led restaurant was sold in mid-2008, and is being re-launched by Hans Schweitzer, formerly executive chef at the celebrated Sandy Lane Hotel in Barbados – should be 'one to watch'. / **Sample dishes:** *beef fillet carpaccio; sea bream in tomato, saffron, shallot, and white wine broth; vanilla and vin santo panna cotta, blood orange and crushed cantuccini salad.* **Details:** *www.cottocambridge.co.uk; 9.30 pm Fri, 9 pm Sat; opening times based on seasons; no Amex.*

Dojo £ 22 🇹
1-2 Millers Yd, Mill Ln CB2 1RQ (01223) 363471
This "very lively" student "favourite" – "tucked-away" near the river – is again tipped as "the best speedy noodle joint in town". / **Sample dishes:** *chilli sichuan king prawn min.* **Details:** *www.dojonoodlebar.co.uk; off Trumpington St; 11 pm; no Amex; no booking.*

Fitzbillies £ 37 🇹
52 Trumpington St CB2 1RG (01223) 352500
Some accuse it of being "hyped", but this offshoot of the famous local bakery is tipped by fans as a "favourite lunch and tea spot" (with "delicious mezze platters" something of a speciality). / **Sample dishes:** *goat's cheese & sweet shallot tart with mixed leaves & balsamic glaze; sea bass served with a salad of new potatoes, tomato concasse, olives & capers; Chelsea bun ice cream.* **Details:** *www.fitzbillies.com; 8pm, Sat & Sun 9.45 pm ; closed Sun D.*

Graffiti
Hotel Felix £ 48
Whitehouse Ln CB3 0LX (01223) 277977
This design-hotel dining room inspires muted feedback; to fans it's "reasonable" and "enjoyable" – to sceptics "quite boring and often bland". / **Sample dishes:** *cripsy goat's cheese, baby beetroot and asparagus, sultana purée; seared red mullet, brown shrimp risotto, buttered baby leeks; vanilla panna cotta, apricot compote, local honey.* **Details:** *www.hotelfelix.co.uk; 10 pm, Fri & Sat 10.30 pm, Sun 9.30 pm.* **Accommodation:** *52 rooms, from £180.*

Hotel Du Vin £ 45
15-19 Trumpington St CB2 1QA (01223) 227330
"Sticking to the tried-and-tested H du V formula, but it works" – all reporters agree this new boutique-hotel bistro has been "a welcome addition to central Cambridge"; as always, though, it's the "wide and excellent choice of wines" which steals the show. / **Sample dishes:** *warm duck confit with puy lentils; seared haunch of venison with polenta, plum tomato and woodland mushroom; Cambridge burnt cream.* **Details:** *www.hotelduvin.com; 10 pm, Sat & Sun 10.30 pm.*

Loch Fyne £ 42
37 Trumpington St CB2 1QY (01223) 362433
OK, "it's a chain", but this city-centre spot (the original branch) can still make a "useful port in a storm", and it inspires a surprisingly high volume of reports; portions can seem "small", but the seafood is "always good". / **Details:** *www.lochfyne.com; opp Fitzwilliam Museum; 10 pm.*

Midsummer House £ 85

Midsummer Common CB4 IHA (01223) 369299

Daniel Clifford's "astonishing" food and a "wonderful" setting undoubtedly make this riverside spot a "simply fantastic" destination; while fans feel the final bill is "worth it", however, critics find the place "overpriced", especially as service can be "impersonal".
/ **Sample dishes:** seared hand dived scallops, celeriac, truffle, Granny Smiths and caramel; braised turbot with peanuts and pistachios, sea scallops, cos lettuce, asparagus and vanilla; vanilla roast pineapple, coconut gâteaux, pineapple sorbet and fresh lime. **Details:** www.midsummerhouse.co.uk; On the river Cam, near Mitchams Corner and the boat sheds; 9.30 pm; closed Mon, Tue L & Sun.

Rainbow Café £ 33

9a King's Pde CB2 ISJ (01223) 321551
"A crowded and buzzing veggie cafe, with a devoted regular following"; it offers some "first-rate" dishes, and even has a convenient location ("in a cellar, opposite King's").
/ **Details:** www.rainbowcafe.co.uk; 9 pm; no Amex.

Savino's £ 15

3 Emmanuel St CBI INE (01223) 566186
"A solid Italian café", tipped for "top paninis, soup and cakes", and "still the best coffee in Cambridge". / **Details:** 8 pm, Sun 6 pm; no Amex.

22 Chesterton Road £ 37

22 Chesterton Rd CB4 3AX (01223) 351880
A "tiny" Edwardian terrace near the Cam is the home to David Carter's very personal establishment; it continues to inspire rave reviews for his "well-conceived and very well-executed" cuisine, at "fantastic" prices. / **Sample dishes:** roulade of smoked salmon with radish, dandelion, spring onion and horseradish; braised collar of pork with new season vegetables, sage and mustard; dark chocolate delice, coffee granite and ginger brêton sablé. **Details:** www.restaurant22.co.uk; 9.45 pm; D only, closed Mon & Sun; children: 12+.

CANTERBURY, KENT 3–3D

ABode Canterbury
County Hotel £ 47

High St CTI 2RX (01227) 766266
"At last, one can eat in Canterbury!", says a fan of this "trendy" new boutique-hotel dining room, which comes ready-branded with the name of celebrity chef Michael Caines; in the early days, however, it too often "promised much, but failed to deliver".
/ **Details:** www.ABodehotels.co.uk.

Augustines £ 45
1-2 Longport CT1 1PE (01227) 453063
With its "London-style approach", this Georgian townhouse is accorded "top marks for food and service" by some reporters; not everyone likes the ambience, though. / **Sample dishes:** home cured salmon grab lax with blinis and dill mustard; roast breast Gressingham duck with gin and juniper sauce, honey parsnips and fondant potatoes; white chocolate and pistachio parfait with dark chocolate sauce and almond nougatine.
Details: www.augustinesrestaurant.co.uk; near the Cathedral; 9 pm; closed Mon & Sun; booking: max 7.

Café des Amis £ 29 Ⓐ
95 St Dunstan's St CT2 8AD (01227) 464390
"Well-established, well-run, well-loved" – this "cheap", "cheerful" and "buzzy" Mexican, by Westgate Towers, has long been an extremely "popular" stand-by. / **Sample dishes:** spiced duck rolled in crispy corn tortillas, with a shredded yucatansalad and mango salsa; roast vegetables, black beans, salad, Feta, sour creamchilpotle salsa on a grilled wheat tortilla; rich chocolate fondue with fresh fruitscream & biscuits.
Details: www.cafedez.com; by Westgate Towers; 10 pm; booking: max 6 at D, Fri & Sat.

Cafe Mauresque £ 30
8 Butchery Ln CT1 2JR (01227) 464300
One of the more "sensual" and "exotic" Canterbury destinations: this Moorish/North African joint is a notably "reliable" option, whether for tapas or for something more substantial. / **Sample dishes:** grilled home-made merguez sausages; grilled halloumi and olive brochette; chocolate ganache and cinnamon hazelnut cake. **Details:** www.cafemauresque.com; 10 pm.

Goods Shed £ 39 ★
Station Road West CT2 8AN (01227) 459153
Located in the same "former railway goods shed", and above a (permanent) Farmer's Market, this "interesting" venture sources all its "local and seasonal" produce from down below; it's "a brilliant concept", say fans, offering "tantalising" fare that's as "perfectly fresh" as you might hope. / **Sample dishes:** seared king scallops with bean salad & chorizo; fillet of hake with brown shrimps and aioli; lemon posset with yogurt cake. **Details:** www.thegoodsshed.net; 9.30 pm; closed Mon & Sun D.

CARDIFF, CARDIFF 2–2A

Cardiff is such a charming city, architecturally speaking, that one can't help thinking it should have more good restaurants than it does. In terms of cuisine, however, it remains quite remarkably backwards. In the city-centre, the only operation of any note at all is the long-established Le Monde.

Ana Bela Bistro £ 37 Ⓣ
5 Pontcanna St CF11 9HQ (029) 2023 9393
Tipped as "better than many more 'prestigious' ventures" – not hugely difficult in this particular city – this Pontcanna establishment is vaunted as a "great little place". / **Details:** www.ana-bela.co.uk; 9.30 pm, 10 pm Sat & Sun; closed Mon & Sun.

Armless Dragon £ 39

97 Wyeverne Rd CF2 4BG (029) 2038 2357

This stalwart bistro in the depths of Cathays is currently on a 'high', and its cuisine is hailed as "creative" and "interesting".
/ ***Sample dishes:*** *home cured Welsh organic salmon with lemon and dill sorbet; sirloin Welsh black beef with fava beans, carrot purée & rosemary mash; barra brith with Celtic whisky crème anglaise.* ***Details:*** *www.thearmlessdragon.co.uk; 10 min outside city-centre; 9 pm, Fri & Sat 9.30 pm; closed Mon, Sat L & Sun.*

Champers £ 35

61 St Mary St CF10 1FE (029) 2037 3363

A "consistently reliable" city-centre stand-by (the posh bit of the La Brasserie complex), tipped for its "outstanding fish and steak" – you choose at the counter, and your food is then cooked to order.
/ ***Details:*** *www.le-monde.co.uk; near Castle; 10.30 pm.*

The Cinnamon Tree £ 29

173 Kings Rd CF11 9DE (029) 2037 4433

Tipped for its "very good and freshly-cooked food", this contemporary-style Indian inspires only positive commentary. / ***Sample dishes:*** *chicken chat; tandoori maharaja massala.* ***Details:*** *www.thecinnamontree.co.uk; 11 pm; closed Fri L.*

Le Gallois Y Cymro £ 43

6-10 Romilly Cr CF11 9NR (029) 2034 1264

"Sophisticated" food and a stylish modern setting make this Canton brasserie "the best" – and arguably "the only decent" – place in Cardiff; performance has still been rather "variable" of late, but – after a kitchen shake-up in early-2008 – one early-days report says it's "back to its old form". / ***Sample dishes:*** *Roquefort soufflé, rocket salad, balsamic dressing; grilled fillet of wild sea bass with samphire, horseradish pomme purée, langoustine sauce; caramelised lemon tart, caramel ice cream.*
Details: *www.legallois-ycymro.com; 1.5m W of Cardiff Castle; 9.30 pm, Fri & Sat 10 pm; closed Mon & Sun D; no Amex.*

Gilbys £ 45

Old Port Rd CF5 6ND (029) 2067 0800

A large out-of-town venue, tipped for its "innovative" and "well-executed" cuisine. / ***Sample dishes:*** *tomato & mozzarella salad with crisp basil leaves, aged balsamic reduction and olive oil; peppered honey-glazed Gressingham duck breast with bubble & squeak, poached chestnuts & wild mushroom and redcurrant sauce; poached red and white wine pears with a sweet ginger parfait, vanilla syrup and aromatic red wine syrup.*
Details: *www.gilbysrestaurant.co.uk; 5 miles from coverhill cross; 10 pm; closed Sun D; children: 7+.*

Happy Gathering £ 28

233 Cowbridge Road East CF11 9AL (029) 2039 7531

"A good-quality place in a part of the world where good Chinese food is hard to find"; it's a "great family restaurant" too, where "a top treat is Sunday dim sum". / ***Sample dishes:*** *roast king prawns with salt & chilli; sizzling steak in black pepper sauce.* ***Details:*** *10.30 pm.*

Le Monde £ 37

62 St Mary St CF10 1FE (029) 2038 7376

The serve-yourself formula can seem a bit downmarket (or "interesting", as one reporter put it), but this more upmarket sibling to La Brasserie generally pleases reporters; "the fish of the day is usually very good". / ***Sample dishes:*** *scallops grilled with lemon butter sauce; fillet steak with jacket potato and vegetables; chocolate brownie with vanilla ice cream.* ***Details:*** *www.le-monde.co.uk; 11 pm; closed Sun; need 10+ to book.*

Thai House £ 32 ⭐

3-5 Guiford Cr CF10 2HJ (029) 2038 7404

*An authentic oriental establishment that's "always excellent" –
and there are not many other places round here you can say that
about! / **Sample dishes:** fresh prawns marinated in lime, coriander & chilli;
grilled fillet of Welsh lamb marinated in light soy, honey & mint, served with
a lime, honey & chilli dressing; Thai style coconut crème caramel in a
honey & amaretto sauce.* **Details:** www.thaihouse.biz; 10.30 pm; closed Sun.

Tides Bar And Grill
St David's Hotel & Spa £ 60 ❌

Havannah St CF10 5SD (029) 2045 4045

*"Very disappointing and extortionately priced" – the "very ordinary"
dining room of this landmark hotel in the Bay really should be better
than this; much better. / **Details:** www.principal-hotels.com; in Cardiff Bay;
10.15 pm.* **Accommodation:** 120 rooms, from £120.

CARTHORPE, NORTH YORKSHIRE 8–4B

The Fox and Hounds Inn £ 35 ⭐

DL8 2LG (01845) 567433

*"Appetising" food in "generous" portions makes the Taylors'
freehouse – in the family since 1983, but "now run by the younger
generation" – a destination that's "always good". / **Sample dishes:** duck
filled filo parcels with a plum sauce; roast rack of English lamb on a blackcurrant
crouton with redcurrant gravy; sticky ginger pudding with home-made orange
sorbet and crunchy sugared nuts.* **Details:** www.foxandhoundscarthorpe.co.uk;
9.30 pm; closed Mon.

CARTMEL, CUMBRIA 7–4D

Aynsome Manor £ 38 Ⓣ

LA11 6HH (015395) 36653

*Looking for a tip for a "comfy country house retreat" with "home-
cooked" food? – this "genteel" establishment, in "beautiful
surroundings", is tipped as just such. / **Sample dishes:** deep fried blue
Stilton and chive beignettes served with apple, sultana, and gem lettuce salad;
pan fried breast of local salmon served on fresh asparagus spears edged with
caviar and saffron cream sauce.* **Details:** www.aynsomemanorhotel.co.uk;
off A590, 0.5m N of village; 8.30 pm; D only, ex Sun open L only; children: 5+ in
restaurant at D.* **Accommodation:** 12 rooms, from £168.

L'Enclume £ 66 ⭐

Cavendish St LA11 6PZ (01539) 536362

*"It's food Jim, but not as we know it!" – Simon Rogan's "brilliant"
molecular gastronomy can be "pretentious to the point of funny",
but it's also "extremely memorable", and helps set up a "theatrical"
overall experience at his "stunningly-situated" restaurant-with-rooms,
which took on a more "spacious and bare" look this year.
/ **Sample dishes:** foie gras, figscorn, sweet bracken; eel-veal ragout; menthol
frappé.* **Details:** www.lenclume.co.uk; just off the ; 9.15 pm; closed Mon,
Tue-Fri D only; children: 10+ at D.* **Accommodation:** 12 rooms, from £98.

Rogan & Co £ 40

The Sq LA11 6QD (015395) 35917

*In mid-2008, Simon Rogan opened a more casual bar and restaurant
in a 16th-century building not far from L'Enclume; inviting inevitable
comparison with Heston Blumenthal's Hind's Head, it should be one
to watch. / **Details:** www.roganandcompany.co.uk; 9 pm.*

Creel Inn £ 34 Ⓐ⭐
AB39 2UL (01569) 750254
For "super" food in a "stunning" location, it's hard to beat this cliff-top operation; as you would hope, "very good fish" is the highlight.
/ **Sample dishes:** crab soup; home-made venison pie; sticky apple and carrot pudding. **Details:** www.thecreelinn.co.uk; 4m S of Stonehaven on A92; 9.30 pm, 9 pm Sun.

Caunton Beck £ 36
Main St NG23 6AB (01636) 636793
"A home from home at any time of day", just off the A1 – this "comfortable" gastropub excites steady praise for its "unfailingly reliable" food and its "consistent" overall standards.
/ **Sample dishes:** grilled red mullet with creamed leeks, peas and orange rinde sauce; salt roast hake with herb mash, slow-dried tomatoes and black olive vinaigrette; warm gingerbread with blueberry ice-cream.
Details: www.wigandmitre.com; 6m NW of Newark past British Sugar factory on A616; 10 pm.

Brockencote Hall £ 50 Ⓐ⭐
DY10 4PY (01562) 777876
A very English-looking country house hotel – perhaps a little "staid" for some tastes – where the dining room is "French through and through", and which fans insist is "the Midlands' most amazing restaurant". / **Details:** www.brockencotehall.com; on A448, just outside village; 9.30 pm; closed Sat L. **Accommodation:** 17 rooms, from £120.

Gidleigh Park £105 Ⓐ⭐⭐
TQ13 8HH (01647) 432367
A "magical Dartmoor setting" sets the scene at this "relaxed" Tudorbethan mansion; combine it with Michael Caines's "truly memorable", "classic" cuisine and "outstanding" service, and you have an overall experience which is "nigh on perfect".
/ **Sample dishes:** ravioli of Brixham crab with a lemongrass and ginger sauce; pan-fried sea bream with Thai purée, sautéed mushrooms, mangetout and fresh noodles with a lemongrass foam; banana parfait with lime foam.
Details: www.gidleigh.com; from village, right at Lloyds TSB, take right fork to end of lane; 9 pm; children: 7+ at D. **Accommodation:** 24 rooms, from £310.

22 Mill Street £ 54 ⭐
22 Mill St TQ13 8AW (01647) 432244
Not yet a huge amount of feedback on the new régime at this small restaurant; an early-days reporter was "very impressed", though, so it's is quite possible that we may – again – be able to pronounce this place quite a 'destination' in next year's guide.
/ **Details:** www.22millstreetrestaurant.co.uk; 9.30 pm; closed Mon, Tue L & Sun; children: 14+. **Accommodation:** 2 rooms, from £75.

Colette's
The Grove   **£ 73**
WD3 4TG   (01923) 296015
"Top-quality food… but take your gold card" – it only has
a modest fan club among reporters, but the fine-dining room at this
contemporary-style luxury hotel is generally rated a pretty *"special"*
destination. / **Sample dishes:** *salad of native lobster with white asparagus and
a lavender honey dressing; slow roast aylesbury duck, peas and carrots, pastilla
of morteau sausage; cold bitter chocolate moelleux, raspberries and milk ice
cream.* **Details:** *www.thegrove.co.uk; J19 or 20 on M25; 9.30 pm; D only, closed
Mon & Sun; jacket.* **Accommodation:** *227 rooms, from £295.*

The Glasshouse
The Grove   **£ 55**
WD3 4TG   (01923) 296015
*Fans say the "something-for-everyone" buffet-restaurant of this
'groovy-grand' country house hotel is "a fun place to visit once in a
while"; critics, though, complain of "no atmosphere", and say that:
"for the prices, you can expect more than this".*
/ **Sample dishes:** *roast salmon with beetroot & orange salad, orange & dill crème
fraîche; whole roast wood pigeon, rosemary farce anglaise; chocolate & passionfruit
savarin.* **Details:** *www.thegrove.co.uk; 9.30 pm, Sat 10.30 pm, Sun 9.30 pm.*
Accommodation: *227 rooms, from £295.*

Seven Tuns   **£ 35**   🅣
Queen St GL54 4AE   (01285) 720242
*An old inn, whose good-all-round gastropub formula makes it a top tip
in a surprisingly thin area.* / **Details:** *9.30 pm, 9 pm Sun; no Amex.*

The Punch Bowl   **£ 55**   🅣
The Street CM1 4QW   (01245) 231222
*David Kelsey's "inimitable personal touch" has added life to a meal
at this Tudor inn for more than 30 years now; it offers a wine
list that's "well worth tucking in to" too.*
/ **Details:** *www.thepunchbowl.co.uk; 9.30 pm; closed Mon, Tue, Wed, Thu, Fri L,
Sat L & Sun D.*

Brasserie Blanc
The Queen's Hotel   **£ 41**
The Promenade GL50 1NN   (01242) 266800
*Very uneven feedback on this "squashed" celeb-chef-branded
brasserie; fans – especially those eating off its "unbeatable-value
lunch and early-evening menus" – say it's "very enjoyable", but critics
just find it "disappointing, especially given its pedigree".*
/ **Sample dishes:** *Roquefort soufflé, pear & walnut salad; Dutch calves liver,
dauphinoise potatoes, caper & sherry vinegar sauce; baked alaska.*
Details: *www.brasserieblanc.com; 10.30 pm, Sat 11 pm, Sun 10 pm.*

Café Paradiso
Hotel Kandinsky

£ 39

Bayshill Rd GL50 3AS (01242) 527788

The buzzy brasserie of a design-hotel, tipped in particular for the quality of its pizzas, but also as a good all-rounder.
/ **Sample dishes:** *chargrilled artichoke with goats cheese and walnut salad; Gloucestershire pork osso buco served with spinach risotto; apple rhubarb millefeuille.* **Details:** *www.aliashotels.com; 10 pm.* **Accommodation:** *48 rooms, from £120.*

Champignon Sauvage

£ 64

24-28 Suffolk Rd GL50 2AQ (01242) 573449

"One of the UK's gastronomic gems!" – David Everitt-Mathiass's offers some "marvellous", "intelligent" and "imaginative" cuisine at this celebrated city-centre fixture, and it is underpinned by "incomparable" service (from wife Helen), plus a "superb" and "ungrabbily-priced" wine list; the setting is "unstuffy" too, if on the "bright" side. / **Sample dishes:** *seared dived Shetland scallops, wood sorrel, raw cauliflower, cauliflower purée, cumin froth; chump of Cotswold lamb, Jerusalem artichoke cream, globe arichokes with liquorice and almonds; hot fig tart with browned butter ice cream.* **Details:** *www.lechampignonsauvage.co.uk; near Cheltenham Boys College; 9 pm; closed Mon & Sun.*

Daffodil

£ 40

18-20 Suffolk Pde GL50 2AE (01242) 700055

The "wonderful Art Deco setting" of this former cinema has now been given a "glamorous" make-over courtesy of Laurence Llewelyn-Bowen; the food is perhaps a bit of an incidental attraction, but "jazz and themed nights" are worth seeking out, and the set-price lunches offer particularly "good value". / **Sample dishes:** *garden pea and mint soup; Thai monkfish & prawn currywith long grain jasmine rice; glazed lemon tartwith rhubarb compote & crème fraîche.*
Details: *www.thedaffodil.co.uk; just off Suffolk Square; 9.45 pm; closed Sun.*

Lumière

£ 51

Clarence Pde GL50 3PA (01242) 222200

"A lovely and intimate restaurant you would hardly notice from the street" – it's worth seeking out, though, for the Chapmans' "creative" and "individual" cooking. / **Sample dishes:** *seared diver scallops with sweetcorn succotash and green pea purée; chargrilled springbok fillet, wild mushroom mash, red wine and shallot sauce; white chocolate espresso torte with a bitter chocolate sorbet.* **Details:** *www.lumiere.cc; off the promenade on the inner ring; 8.30 pm; D only, closed Mon & Sun; no Amex; booking: max 10; children: 6+.*

Mayflower   **£ 36**   Ⓣ
32-34 Clarence St GL50 3NX   (01242) 522426
"Very consistent throughout its 26 year history" – this *"reliable"*
Chinese remains a top tip locally. / **Sample dishes:** chicken pastry;
king prawns with spicy red pepper sauce; toffee bananas with sesame seeds.
Details: www.themayflowerrestaurant.co.uk; 10.30 pm.

Ruby   **£ 26**   Ⓣ
52 Suffolk Rd GL50 2AQ   (01242) 250909
*Tipped for "consistently reliable" standards, a Chinese establishment
of long standing, where the set lunch is praised for its particularly
good value.* / **Details:** near Cheltenham Boys College; 11.15 pm.

Storyteller   **£ 34**   Ⓐ
11 North Pl GL50 4DW   (01242) 250343
"One of the quirkier places you'll find", this *"very friendly"* and
consistent restaurant makes a particular feature of its pick-your-own
"walk-in wine cellar". / **Sample dishes:** smoked trout on chick pea hummus
with dill & sour cream dressing, corn crisps & red pepper relish; marinated duck,
onions, peppers & beans with flour tortillas, sour cream, grated cheese
guacamole & tomato salsa; vanilla blueberry cheesecake.
Details: www.storyteller.co.uk; near the cinema; 10 pm; no Amex.

CHESTER, CHESHIRE   5–2A

Albion Inn   **£ 21**   Ⓣ
Park St CH1 1RN   (01244) 340345
*Non-parents love the child-free policy ("a real bonus these days"),
and this ultra-traditional boozer, near the Newgate, generally offers
"good food" too.* / **Sample dishes:** lambs liver and onions in a cider gravy;
curry of the day; farmhouse Cheshire cheese with a rich fruit cake.
Details: www.albioninnchester.co.uk; 8 pm; closed Sun D; no credit cards;
need 6+ to book; children: 18+. **Accommodation:** 2 rooms, from £75.

Aqua-Vitus   **£ 33**   Ⓣ
58 Watergate St CH1 2LA   (01244) 313721
*A Swedish/French destination with "a definite style of its own";
it's almost invariably tipped as a "really nice place", thanks not
least to the "excellent-value lunch menu".* / **Sample dishes:** Atlantic
prawns on dill marinated cucumber, diced tomato finished with Parmesan crisp;
grilled Welsh rib-eye steak glazed with Feta cheese and pepper and red wine jus;
red wine poached pear with chantilly cream. **Details:** www.aquavitus.co.uk;
10.30 pm; closed Sun.

Simon Radley at
The Chester Grosvenor   **£ 85**
Eastgate CH1 1LT   (01244) 324024
*In autumn 2008, the well-known 'Arkle' restaurant at this grand city-
centre hotel is being re-launched under the name of the chef who's
won it a Michelin star for 18 consecutive years – so long as you're
after a "no-expense-spared" destination, this 'newcomer' should
remain one of the North West's leading lights.*
/ **Sample dishes:** battenburg cold press of bresse chicken and squab with
pistachio brittle; duck poached and seared with langoustine bouillon, herb farfalle
and a crispy salad; warm vanilla and lime risotto with iced buternut and chocolate
Parmesan. **Details:** www.chestergrosvenor.com; 9 pm; D only, closed Mon & Sun;
no jeans or trainers; children: 12+. **Accommodation:** 80 rooms, from £229.

Moules A Go Go £ 37
39 Watergate Row CH1 2LE (01244) 348818

"A fun place to eat in the (first-floor) 'rows'"; moules/frites are "well-prepared", and there's a range of other dishes too.
/ **Sample dishes:** house salad with crispy Peking duck; pan fried sea bass with asparagus and lemon risotto; caramel waffles with caramel ice cream.
Details: www.moulesagogo.co.uk; 10 pm, Sun 9 pm.

CHETTLE, DORSET   2–3C

Castleman Hotel £ 34
DT11 8DB (01258) 830096

"Piles of 'Country Life', 'The Field' and Christie's catalogues" set the tone at this "pleasant and ancient hotel", which enjoys a "quiet rural setting"; on the food front, they put in a lot of effort, and results are often "excellent". / **Sample dishes:** smoked haddock, spinach and prawn gratin glazed with Gruyère cheese; roast rack of lamb with rosemary, garlic and red wine with potato rosti; strawberries with meringues and cream.
Details: www.castlemanhotel.co.uk; 9 pm; D only, ex Wed & Sun open L & D; no Amex. **Accommodation:** 8 rooms, from £80.

CHICHESTER, WEST SUSSEX   3–4A

Comme Ça £ 47
67 Broyle Rd PO19 6BD (01243) 788724

"Very Gallic, friendly and efficient" service is a hallmark of this "attractive" French restaurant; its "traditional" cooking is "consistently enjoyable", and its "terrific-value deals" make it "an excellent complement to the Festival Theatre". / **Sample dishes:** Stilton soufflé with pickled walnuts, chive, and apple dressing; roast salmon fillet topped with anchovy butter, garnished with pepper caramel quail's eggs, Parmesan shavings and grillled asparagus; rhubarb tart. **Details:** www.commeca.co.uk; 0.5m N of city-centre; 10.30 pm; closed Mon, Tue L & Sun D; no Amex.

Dining Room £ 46
31 North St PO19 1LY (01243) 537352

A "pleasant wine bar/restaurant", housed in a "delightful Georgian house", tipped for its "beautiful" dining room and "sound" cuisine.
/ **Sample dishes:** Dolcelatte, pine nuts & spinach filo parcel; pan seared wood pigeon breast, watercress risotto; blueberry crème brûlée.
Details: www.thediningroom.biz; 8.45 pm, Fri & Sat 9.30 pm; closed Sun; children: 14+.

West Stoke House £ 55
PO18 9BN (01243) 575226

"An utterly fabulous gastronomic experience"; the food at this "lovely country house" is "second to none" hereabouts, and service – "friendly, and with no pretensions" – is "great" too.
/ **Details:** www.weststokehouse.co.uk; 9 pm; closed Mon, Tue & Sun D.

CHIGWELL, ESSEX   3–2B

The Bluebell £ 50
117 High Rd IG7 6QQ (020) 8500 6282

"A favourite of the Chigwell ladies-who-lunch", this popular local restaurant is especially recommended for "Essex's best-value Sunday lunch". / **Sample dishes:** pressed cured ham hock with mustard pickle and dressed rocket; roast rump of English lamb with a celeriac and potato gratin, fine beans, roast shallotsand a rich rosemary sauce; apricot and frangipane pithivier with peach schnapps anglaise. **Details:** www.thebluebellrestaurant.co.uk; 10 pm, Sat 12.30 am; closed Mon, Sat L & Sun D.

The Froize Free House Restaurant   £ 36   ⭐
The St IP12 3PU   (01394) 450282
A much-above-average buffet is the draw to this country inn; all the food is good, but the "great range of desserts" attracts particular compliments. / Sample dishes: creamy crayfish risotto with basil & tomato; marsh lamb with sweet cherry tomatoes; pavlova. Details: www.froize.co.uk; 8.30 pm but varies seasonally; closed Mon, Tue D, Wed D & Sun D.

The Sir Charles Napier   £ 47   🅐
Spriggs Alley OX39 4BX   (01494) 483011
"Lovely in both summer and winter", Julie Griffiths's "slightly Bohemian" Chilterns "village inn-cum-restaurant" has long been widely known as a "cosy home-from-home", with a "beautiful garden"; the food "can be excellent" too. / Sample dishes: seared loin of rabbit, confit leg, broad beans & summer truffle glaze; whole roast Cornish lobster with Jersey royals & summer vegetables; gooseberry fool with citrus madeleine. Details: www.sircharlesnapier.co.uk; M40, J6 into Chinnor, turn right at roundabout, carry on straight up hill for 2 miles; 10 pm; closed Mon & Sun D; children: 6+ at D.

Bybrook Restaurant   🆃
Manor House Hotel   £ 77
Castle Combe SN14 7HR   (01249) 782206
Particularly tipped for its romantic possibilities – an impressive manor house which continues to inspire all-round satisfaction; more reports please! / Sample dishes: organic salmon with beetroot carpaccio, pickled vegetables & honey mustard dressing; slow cooked cannon of lamb, crushed peas, onion soubis & minted pea emulsion; iced nutmeg parfait, blackberry & apple pudding, blackberry sorbet. Details: www.exclusivehotels.co.uk; 9.30 pm, Fri & Sat 10 pm; closed Tue D, Wed D, Thu D & Sat L; no trainers. Accommodation: 48 rooms, from £235.

Juliana's   ⭐
Cotswold House Hotel   £ 70
High Street GL55 6AN   (01386) 840330
"Immensely cosmopolitan, sophisticated and clever food" is the hallmark of the new chef at this "beautifully located" hotel on the square of a "tourist trap" Cotswold village; feedback is limited, but all of it positive. / Sample dishes: coddled egg and wild mushrooms, duck leg pancetta and cep sauce; fillet of brill, braised lettuce,chestnuts and pork belly lardons; marinated poached pineapple, coconut porridge and sesame seed crisp. Details: www.cotswoldhouse.com; 9.45 pm; D only, closed Mon & Sun. Accommodation: 29 rooms, from £150.

CHIPPING, LANCASHIRE 5–1B

Gibbon Bridge £ 38 A ⭐
Green Ln PR3 2TQ (01995) 61456
"A fabulous country retreat"; the dining room of this attractive hotel,
amidst the *"spectacular scenery"* of the Forest of Bowland, offers
"good no-nonsense food in wonderful surroundings";
the accommodation is *"top-rate"* too. / **Sample dishes:** *ravioli of crab &
lobster on a shellfish broth; loin of lamb topped with a spinach & mint mousse,
served pink on a bed of Mediterranean vegetables with a redcurrant jus;
hazelnut & raspberry meringue with chocolate sauce.*
Details: *www.gibbon-bridge.co.uk; 9.00pm.* **Accommodation:** *30 rooms,
from £130.*

CHOLMONDELEY, CHESHIRE 5–3A

⭐
Cholmondeley Arms £ 31
SY14 8HN (01829) 720300
In a former schoolhouse, by the gates to the Cholomondeley Estate,
a *"busy"* but *"friendly"* boozer unanimously acclaimed for its
"good food" (and an *"excellent range of wines"* too).
/ **Sample dishes:** *smoked haddock tartlet grilled with Gruyère; chicken
breast with a mushroom, Dijon mustard & cream sauce; black cherry pavlova.*
Details: *www.cholmondeleyarms.co.uk; on A49, 6m N of Whitchurch; 10.30 pm;
no Amex.* **Accommodation:** *6 rooms, from £80.*

CIRENCESTER, GLOUCESTERSHIRE 2–2C

T
Tatyan's £ 30
27 Castle St GL7 1QD (01285) 653529
Over two decades in business, a Chinese restaurant which continues
to be tipped for its good all-round standards. / **Sample dishes:** *sweet &
sour crispy wan ton; stir fried chicken with Chinese mushrooms.*
Details: *www.tatyans.com; near junction of A417 & A345; 10.30 pm; closed
Sun L.*

CLACHAN, CAIRNDOW 9–3B

A ⭐
Loch Fyne Oyster Bar £ 42
PA26 8BL (01499) 600236
"You can't argue with the freshness and quality of the seafood" –
or the *"fantastic"* loch-side location – at the original LFOB (owned
separately from the chain), even it has become *"a bit pricey of late"*;
"the on-site shop is well worth a visit" too. / **Sample dishes:** *oysters;
grilled whole lemon sole with baby capers & parsley butter.*
Details: *www.loch-fyne.com; 10m E of Inveraray on A83; 8.30 pm, after Oct
7.30 pm.*

CLAVERING, ESSEX 3–2B

The Cricketers £ 39
Wicken Rd CB11 4QT (01799) 550442
"Jamie Oliver's dad is still on top form", says a fan of his family's *"old-
fashioned, low-ceilinged"* pub, on the village green, which offers
"consistently good" food in *"hearty"* portions.
/ **Sample dishes:** *pappardelle with black pudding, bacon and marjoram in a fresh
globe artichoke pesto; loin of pork, sliced on to an apricot and sage sauce,
with crackling and a sausage meat stuffing; crème brûlée with fruit coulis.*
Details: *www.thecricketers.co.uk; on B1038 between Newport & Buntingford;
9.30 pm.* **Accommodation:** *14 rooms, from £110.*

The Bell And Cross £ 36

Holy Cross DY9 9QL (01562) 730319

Tipped as a "really nice place for a family lunch" – a "chilled" sort of country pub, where the food is "great", and the service is "friendly to kids". / **Sample dishes:** *glazed spinach, mushroom & Gruyère tart with roast beet salad; roast chicken with tomato piazzola sauce & basil potato gnocchi; warm Belgian waffle, banana & butterscotch, toffe ripple ice cream.* **Details:** *www.bellandcrossclent.co.uk; 9 pm, 9.30 pm Fri & Sat; no Amex.*

Four Stones £ 36

Adams Hill DY9 9PS (01562) 883260

"A very popular Italian, serving top-quality dishes", and tipped for its "excellent fish". / **Sample dishes:** *freshly sliced Parma ham accompanied with fans of Galia melon; roast duck coated with a mixed citrus & Cointreau sauce; pinenut semifreddo.* **Details:** *www.thefourstones.co.uk; 10 pm; closed Mon & Sun D.*

The Olive Branch £ 43

Main St LE15 7SH (01780) 410355

"One of Middle England's best gastropubs"; Sean Hope & Ben Jones's "excellently-run operation", in a "delightful Rutland village", is much more than "a pit stop for A1 travellers" – the style may be "unpretentious", but the food is often "phenomenal". / **Sample dishes:** *shallot tatin with glazed colston bassett Stilton & rocket leaves; sea bream with pesto tagliatelle; queen of puddings, raspberry ripple ice cream.* **Details:** *www.theolivebranchpub.com; 2m E from A1 on B664; 9.30 pm; no Amex.* **Accommodation:** *6 rooms, from £90.*

Inn at Whitewell £ 48

Forest of Bowland BD7 3AT (01200) 448222

"One of the most spectacular settings in Britain" helps create many "special" experiences at this "posh pub", "deep in the Trough of Bowland"; although it's "not quite as good since the extension a couple of years ago", it still offers food that's "way above average for a country inn". / **Sample dishes:** *seared king scallops with a warm salad of soft noodles; roast loin of venison with pears poached in port; home-made puddings.* **Details:** *www.innatwhitewell.com; 9.30 pm; D only (bar meals only at L); no Amex.* **Accommodation:** *23 rooms, from £93.*

Kirkstile Inn £ 30
Loweswater CA13 0RU (01900) 85219
"A great and unchanged Cumbrian pub, serving hearty fare"
(and with its "own brewery" too); "it can get very busy, so it's at its
best in the evenings and out-of-season". / **Sample dishes:** *black pudding,*
pan-fried in beer batter and rich red wine sauce; home-made chicken, leek and
mustard pudding and mushroom and white wine sauce; apple and summer fruit
crumble and cream. **Details:** *www.kirkstile.com; 9 pm; no Amex.*
Accommodation: *8 rooms, from £43.50.*

Quince & Medlar £ 36 Ⓐ✪✪
13 Castlegate CA13 9EU (01900) 823579
"Who need meat when vegetarian food can be this good?" –
this townhouse-restaurant charms all reporters with its "imaginative"
cuisine, its "relaxed" surroundings and its "discreet" service.
/ **Details:** *www.quinceandmedlar.co.uk; next to Cockermouth Castle; 9.30 pm;*
D only, closed Mon & Sun; no Amex; children: 5+.

Lucknam Park £ 83 Ⓐ✪✪
SN14 8AZ (01225) 742777

One of the diminishing band of grand country house hotels
in independent ownership, this is an impressive destination that's
simply "very hard to fault" on any front; star billing, of course, goes to
Hywel Jones's "truly exceptional" cuisine. / **Sample dishes:** *caramelised*
veal sweetbreads, lasagne of ceps, langoustines, sautérnes and rosemary foam;
pot roast red leg partridge, parsnip fondant, creamed Savoy cabbage, autumn veg
purée and spiced pear; hot Valrhona chocolate fondant, toasted almond ice cream,
pumpkin confit and orange ganache. **Details:** *www.lucknampark.co.uk; 6m NE*
of Bath; 9.30 pm; no jeans or trainers; children: 5+ at D. **Accommodation:** *41*
rooms, from £265.

The Ostrich Inn £ 36 Ⓣ
High St SL3 0JZ (01753) 682628
"One of the oldest pubs in the UK", recently refurbished; it generally
offers "good food and service", and is tipped as "a perfect detour,
en route to Windsor Great Park". / **Sample dishes:** *salt & pepper squid*
with sweet chilli & coriander mayonnaise; ostrich Wellington with buttered garden
peas; melting chocolate fondant. **Details:** *www.theostrichcolnbrook.co.uk;*
9.15 pm, 5.30 pm Sun.

The Withies Inn   £ 42   Ⓐ
Withies Ln GU3 1JA   (01483) 421158
"Not much has changed in 30 years", at this "destination" boozer
in the Surrey Hills – a "lovely" place, which is "very old-fashioned"
(and, for what it is, "quite expensive"). / **Sample dishes:** Arbroath
Smokies wth lemon mayonnaise; suckling pig; bread and butter pudding.
Details: www.thewithiesinn.com; off A3 near Guildford, signposted on B3000;
9.30 pm, Sun 4 pm; closed Sun D.

Pecks   £ 45   ★
Newcastle Rd CW12 4SB   (01260) 275161
The Peck family's "consistently reliable" venture pleases all who report
on it with its "excellent standards and its distinctive, nay unique style";
dinner menus change seasonally, and are a five or seven-course, no-
choice affair, served at a single sitting nightly.
/ **Details:** www.pecksrest.co.uk; off A34; 8 pm; closed Mon & Sun D; booking
essential.

Trengilly Wartha Inn   £ 34
Nancenoy TR11 5RP   (01326) 340332
A quite remote rural inn; most reporters like its "interesting" food,
"well-sourced" wines and large whisky selection, but the odd sceptic
finds it "average, and not worth the trip down windy Cornish roads".
/ **Sample dishes:** pan-fried scallops with crème fraîche, spring onion & saki
pickled ginger sauce; line-caught sea bass fillet, with rosemary beurre blanc,
dauphinoise potatoes & steamed vegetables; trio of crèmes brûlées.
Details: www.trengilly.com; 1m outside village; 9.30; no Amex.
Accommodation: 8 rooms, from £80.

Bel & The Dragon   £ 39
High St SL6 9SQ   (01628) 521263
"A lovely olde worlde beamed building" – complete with a "roaring
open fire" – houses this "stylish" branch of a small gastropub chain –
a "friendly" and "consistent" sort of place, offering decent "bistro-
style food". / **Sample dishes:** tian of crab with guacamole, tomato broth &
herb salad served with melba toast; half a roast free range corn fed chicken with
hand cut chips, sage and onion stuffing, bread sauce and roasting jus; chocolate
nut browie with mint chocolate chip ice cream and chocolate sauce.
Details: www.belandthedragon-cookham.co.uk; opp Stanley Spencer Gallery;
10 pm.

Ferry   £ 35   Ⓣ
Sutton Rd SL6 9SN   (01628) 525123
This former Harverster enjoys "fantastic views of Cookham Bridge",
and is well-supported as a "great riverside pub" – the food may
be "fine", but it's the location which gets people really excited.
/ **Sample dishes:** chicken liver coarse pâté with onion marmalade and toast; fillet
steak with whole king prawn, watercress & frites; warm chocolate brownie.
Details: www.theferry.co.uk; 10 pm.

Maliks £ 39

High St SL6 9SF (01628) 520085

The setting may be "very unusual for an Indian restaurant" – "in olde worlde beamed style, with two roaring fires" – but there's nothing archaic about the "vibrant" spicing of the cuisine here; it's "worth a trip". / Sample dishes: chicken with peanut sauce; green chicken curry; hot rice pudding. Details: www.maliks.co.uk; from the M4, Junction 7 for A4 for Maidenhead; 11.30 pm, Sun 10.30 pm.

CORBRIDGE, NORTHUMBERLAND 8–2B

The Angel of Corbridge £ 36

Main St NE45 5LA (01434) 632119

A former coaching inn in a rather thin area, with a contemporary menu that's generally tipped as "reliable". / Sample dishes: twice baked cheese and chive soufflé with Parmesan crème; chargrilled tuna steak with salad; warm apple and cranberry cake with hazelnut ice cream. Details: www.theangelofcorbridge.co.uk; 8.45 pm; closed Sun D; no Amex. Accommodation: 5 rooms, from £85.

CORSE LAWN, GLOUCESTERSHIRE 2–1B

Corse Lawn Hotel £ 44

GL19 4LZ (01452) 780771

The Hine family's elegant (Queen Anne) village house hotel is a "cheerful" and "reliable" sort of place, offering "interesting and well-cooked food". / Sample dishes: chargrilled squid with white bean and chorizo stew; glazed leg of duckling, celeriac purée and baby onions; warm pecan pie with maple ice cream. Details: www.corselawn.com; 5m SW of Tewkesbury on B4211; 9 pm, Sun 9.30 pm; no jeans or trainers. Accommodation: 19 rooms, from £150.

CORTON DENHAM, SOMERSET 2–3B

The Queen's Arms £ 33

DT9 4LR (01963) 220317

"In the heart of south Somerset", "a great country pub with good food and friendly staff"; summertime visitors also benefit from its "lovely sunny courtyard and garden". / Sample dishes: snout-tail terrine with apple dressing; sage marinated pork tenderloin with roast rhubarb; maple grilled figs with home-made honeycomb ice cream. Details: www.thequeensarms.com; 11 pm, Sat 10 pm, Sun 9.30 pm.

COVENTRY, WEST MIDLANDS 5–4C

Thai Dusit £ 30

39 London Rd CV1 2JP (024) 7622 7788

"Authentic" fare is the draw to this "friendly" Thai spot; well, it can't be the location… / Sample dishes: chicken marinated with coriander root, cracked black pepper & oyster sauce wrapped in pandan leaves & deep fried; stir fried beef with red wine sauce, carrot, onion, spring onion, mangetout, on top of golden cashew nuts; coconut pancake roll. Details: 11 pm.

COWBRIDGE, VALE OF GLAMORGAN 1–1D

Farthings £ 35

54 High St CF71 7AH (01446) 772990

"A good atmosphere, and food to match"; this market-town restaurant is never going to set the world on fire, but it's tipped as a "reliable" sort of place, with a "nice courtyard for a summer lunch". / Sample dishes: cockle, leek, & lava bread risotto; fillet steak with smoky onions, home-made chips, tomatoes & spinach; raspberry & hazelnut meringue. Details: www.farthingsofcowbridge.co.uk; 9.30 pm, 10 pm Fri & Sat; no Amex.

COWLEY, GLOUCESTERSHIRE 2–1C

Cowley Manor £ 51 ✖
GL53 9NL (01242) 870900
*Must try harder!; this contemporary country house hotel – which gets
a lot of press for its spa – attracts very few reports, too many
of which suggest "disappointing food and no atmosphere".
/ **Sample dishes:** honey and sesame coated goat's cheese with grilled vegetables
and balsamic vinegar; stuffed saddle of wild rabbit with sautéed potatoes,
forest mushrooms, button onions, tarragon cream sauce; molten chocolate pudding
with pistachio ice cream. **Details:** www.cowleymanor.com; 10 pm, Fri & Sat
11 pm. **Accommodation:** 30 rooms, from £245.*

CRAGG VALE, WEST YORKSHIRE 5–1B

The Hinchliffe £ 31 Ⓣ
Mytholm Rd HX7 5TA (01422) 883256
*A "very pleasant" rural pub, tipped for its "very good food", and its
"exceptional personal service". / **Details:** www.thehinchliffe.com; 8.30 pm;
closed Mon & Tue; no Amex.*

CRANBROOK, KENT 3–4C

Apicius £ 42 ✪✪
23 Stone St TN17 3HF (01580) 714666
*Tim Johnson's "really delicious" food is "getting recognised" (but, even
so, more ardent fans say that "one Michelin star is not enough!");
the "plain" and "calm" space is well-liked too, although it is
"very small". / **Sample dishes:** roast scallop and bacon brochettes, linguini and
vanilla sauce; slow roast shoulder of pork, cream potatoes, cabbage and
caramelized apples; pear and frangipane tarts, sauce anglais and crushed
macaroons. **Details:** www.restaurant-apicius.co.uk; 9 pm; closed Mon, Tue L,
Sat L & Sun D; no Amex; children: 8+.*

CRASTER, NORTHUMBERLAND 8–1B

Jolly Fisherman £ 18
NE66 3TR (01665) 576461
*"Fabulous lobster soup, crab sandwiches, great beer and fabulous sea
views to boot" – all attractions of this popular coastal boozer;
the décor is "nondescript" at best, though, and service has its ups and
downs. / **Sample dishes:** crab soup; kipper pâté; apple crumble.
Details: www.thejollyfisherman.org.uk; near Dunstanburgh Castle; 8 pm; L only;
no credit cards; no booking.*

CREIGIAU, CARDIFF 2–2A

Caesars Arms £ 38
Cardiff Rd CF15 9NN (029) 2089 0486
*A popular rural destination, where you choose your food from the
chiller – a "wonderful selection of fresh fish, superb black beef and
lamb" – and it's cooked to your order; it can get "frantic" at busy
times. / **Sample dishes:** asparagus & shaved Parmesan; lamb with leek;
raspberry & hazelnut pavlova. **Details:** beyond Creigiau, past golf club; 10 pm;
closed Sun D.*

The Bear   **£ 36**   ❌

High St NP8 1BW   (01873) 810408

"Oh dear, oh dear, oh dear"; this well-known coaching inn still wins praise as a "cosy" place with "solid" cooking, but there's a growing feeling among reporters that what "used to be a haven" can be a "disappointing" (even "grim") experience nowadays.

*/ **Sample dishes:** warm salad of black pudding, chorizo, smoked bacon & rocket, with a tomato tapenade; Welsh lamb shank, served with colcannon potato, red current & mint jus. **Details:** www.bearhotel.co.uk; 9.30 pm; D only, ex Sun open L only, closed Mon; children: 7+. **Accommodation:** 34 rooms, from £86.*

Nantyffin Cider Mill   **£ 41**

Brecon Rd NP8 1SG   (01873) 810775

This early-wave gastropub in the "lovely surroundings" of a former drovers' inn has been popular since the early '90s; in recent years, though, standards have sometimes seemed rather "variable" – perhaps newly installed owners (and chef) will pep things up.

*/ **Sample dishes:** grilled Welsh goat's cheese on a toast crouton; confit of home-reared Welsh lamb on a bed of creamed mashed potatoes with a rosemary and garlic sauce; chocolate truffle torte with whipped cream. **Details:** www.cidermill.co.uk; on A40 between Brecon & Crickhowell; 9.30 pm; closed Mon (& Sun D in winter); no Amex.*

Crinan Hotel   **£ 58**   ⓣ

PA31 8SR   (01546) 830261

*An elegant hotel, tipped as a "cheerful" all-round dining destination, and benefiting from "impressive" views; there's also a school of thought, however, that prices are set "with rich American tourists in mind". / **Sample dishes:** risotto of Shetland crab, roast shellfish sauce & a salad of fennel & chervil; roast saddle of venison, slow cooked haunchSavoy cabbage & confit potatoes; millefeuille of English rhubarb & almonds, crème chantilly. **Details:** www.crinanhotel.com; 8.30 pm; no Amex. **Accommodation:** 20 rooms, from £95/person.*

The Bath Arms   **£ 35**   ⭐

Clay St BA12 8AJ   (01985) 212262

On the Longleat estate: a "quaint old pub, serving imaginative food"; on the downside, it can get "crowded and rushed".

*/ **Sample dishes:** fillet of rabbit with foie gras and lentil dressing; roast breast of chicken with blue cheese fritters & rocket pesto; chocolate brownie with honeycomb ice cream. **Details:** www.batharmscrockerton.co.uk; 9.30 pm; no Amex. **Accommodation:** 2 rooms, from £75.*

The Punch Bowl   **£ 45**   Ⓐ

LA8 8HR   (01539) 568237

*A "smart" but "relaxed" inn, whose enormous following belies its "hard-to-find" (but "beautiful") location; there's the occasional sentiment that it's "trying too hard", but most reporters think the food is "terrific". / **Details:** www.the-punchbowl.co.uk; off A5074 towards Bowness, turn right after Lyth Hotel; 9.30 pm. **Accommodation:** 9 rooms, from £110.*

CROYDON, SURREY 3–3B

Banana Leaf £ 28 ⭐

7 Lower Addiscombe Rd CR0 6PQ   (020) 8688 0297

The place may "look like a bog standard curry house", but the "fresh" and "authentic" food on offer at this "inexpensive" South Indian "gem" really is very good indeed. / **Sample dishes:** potato bhaji; Malabar fish curry. **Details:** www.a222.co.uk/bananaleaf; near East Croydon station; 11 pm.

CRUDWELL, WILTSHIRE 2–2C

The Potting Shed £ 32 🅐⭐

The St SN16 9EW   (01666) 577833

A "terrific, newly-refurbished pub", already being hailed by reporters for its "great" food "based on seasonal, local produce"; "good beer" too. / **Sample dishes:** ham hock terrine, onion & balsamic chutney & toast; whole pan roast gilt head bream, pea & herb risotto; chocolate mousse with cherries soaked in kirsch. **Details:** www.thepottingshedpub.com; 9.30 pm; closed Sun D; no Amex. **Accommodation:** 12 rooms, from £105.

CUCKFIELD, WEST SUSSEX 3–4B

Ockenden Manor £ 70 🆃

Ockenden Ln RH17 5LD   (01444) 416111

An "intimate" country house hotel, tipped for its "traditional atmosphere and service", and its "innovative" cuisine. / **Sample dishes:** braised cheek & confit belly of pork; scallop & turbot with purple sprouting brocoli; caramelised lemon tart with blackcurrant sorbet. **Details:** www.hshotels.co.uk; 9 pm; no jeans. **Accommodation:** 22 rooms, from £160.

CUPAR, FIFE 9–3D

Ostlers Close £ 52 ⭐⭐

25 Bonnygate KY15 4BU   (01334) 655574

"Continuing its amazing standards, deserving of a Michelin star" – Jimmy and Amanda Graham's long-established town-centre venture continues to impress with its locally-sourced cuisine. / **Details:** www.ostlersclose.co.uk; centrally situated in the Howe of Fife; 9.30 pm; closed Sun & Mon, Tue-Fri D only, Sat L & D; children: 6+ at D.

The Peat Inn £ 50 🅐⭐⭐

KY15 5LH   (01334) 840206

Chef/patron "Geoff Smeddle really has made a great start", at this celebrated country inn, and all reports on his tenure to-date are a hymn of praise to its "gorgeous" Scottish cuisine and "lovely" atmosphere. / **Details:** www.thepeatinn.co.uk; at junction of B940 & B941, SW of St Andrews; 9 pm; closed Mon & Sun. **Accommodation:** 8 rooms, from £190.

DALRY, AYRSHIRE 9–4B

Braidwoods £ 47 ⭐⭐

Drumastle Mill Cottage KA24 4LN   (01294) 833544

"Always a warm welcome from Nicola and excellent food from Keith" – that's the straightforward but top quality formula that makes the Braidwoods' "very impressive" cottage-restaurant a "delight" for all who comment on it. / **Details:** www.braidwoods.co.uk; 9 pm; closed Mon, Tue L & Sun D; closed 2 weeks in Jan & Sep; children: 12+ at D.

Coach And Horses   £ 34   Ⓐ
School Ln RH17 7JF   (01825) 740369
A "small" and "cosy" country pub, serving "consistently high-quality food and excellent beer"; the restaurant occupies "converted oak-beamed stables", and has a "pretty garden, with idyllic views". / *Sample dishes:* game offal brochette on split pea and white truffle oil purée in red wine jus; grilled Toulouse sausages on braised butterbeans, blushed tomatoes, bacon and basil; white chocolate panna cotta with mixed berry compote. *Details:* www.coachandhorses.danehill.biz; off A275; 9 pm, Fri & Sat 9.30 pm.

New Angel   £ 58
2 South Embankment TQ6 9BH   (01803) 839425
That John Burton-Race's "hyped" and "over-priced" harbour-side restaurant (once The Carved Angel) was ever given a Michelin star was a joke, and last year's behind-the-scenes turmoil – during which it shut with no notice, then re-opened – has done nothing to put it on a more even keel... / *Sample dishes:* carpaccio of Dexter beef with horseradish cream, rocket and Parmesan; saddle of lamb and garlic, creamed potatoes and tomatoes, smoked bacon and basil minestrone; glazed orange tart with lemon sorbet. *Details:* www.thenewangel.co.uk; opp passenger ferry pontoon; 9.30 pm; closed Mon, Tue L & Sun D; no Amex. *Accommodation:* 6 rooms, from £130.

Fawsley Hall   £ 56   Ⓐ
NN11 3BA   (01327) 892000
"Reliably good" – if "pricey for what it is" – this plush country house hotel has a modest following among reporters, both as a "romantic hide-away" and as a "good place for entertaining". / *Sample dishes:* pigeon & its own tea & parfaitpickled pear/celeriac/hazelnuts; sautéed turbot & oxtailsmoked marrowbone/salsify/daikon/Jersey royals; bitter chocolate soufflé/avocado ice cream/sea salt caramel. *Details:* www.fawsleyhall.com; on A361 between Daventry & Banbury; 9.30 pm, Sun 9 pm. *Accommodation:* 52 rooms, from £159.

Dunkerley's   £ 42
19 Beach St CT14 7AH   (01304) 375016
This "old-fashioned" seafood parlour "retains its reputation for good, local fish"; there are some gripes, however, at efforts to pack 'em in (or, rather, out, on the terrace), and, at times, "demand exceeds the kitchen's capacity". / *Sample dishes:* shellfish broth, poached oyster; pan-fried duck breastbraised red cabbage, fondant potato, turnip sauce poivradé; toffee brûléecox's apple purée and almond tuille. *Details:* www.dunkerleys.co.uk; 9.30 pm; closed Mon L. *Accommodation:* 16 rooms, from £100.

Boathouse   £ 36
Mill Ln CO7 6DH   (01206) 323153
Generally a "reliable" destination – this "pleasant" former boathouse, in Constable Country, offers an "excellent range of dishes", in a "lovely setting". / *Sample dishes:* stirred tomato & roast butternut squash risotto, canola oil; marinated roast garlic & lemon chicken, horseradish & chive cream, sauté potatoes; white chocolate & mango cheesecake, chantilly cream. *Details:* www.dedhamboathouse.com; 9.30 pm; closed Mon & Sun D; no Amex.

Milsoms　　　　　　　　　　　　　**£ 40**
Stratford Rd CO7 6HW (01206) 322795
*This all-day, no-booking sibling to the famous Talbooth can be a
"useful" destination – and it's certainly a "popular" one –
even though the food is "not always up to scratch", and service can
be "arrogant". / Sample dishes: shredded duck tacos with hoi sin sauce;
pork belly with black pudding mash, sauerkraut and rich jus; triple chocolate
brownie with honeycomb ice cream. Details: www.milsomhotels.com; Just off the
A12, the Stratford St Mary turning; 9.30 pm; no booking. Accommodation: 15
rooms, from £80.*

The Sun Inn　　　　　　　　　　　**£ 35**
High St CO7 6DF (01206) 323351
*In Constable Country, this "high-class gastropub serves seasonal food
and a good range of ales"; some reports, however, suggest it's starting
to live down to its "tourist trap location". / Sample dishes: fresh pasta
stuffed with veal, pigeon, pancetta with juniper & nutmeg butter & Parmesan;
old spot pork loin braised in milk, sage & lemon, with celeriac, thyme, chestnuts &
pancetta; hazelnut & espresso cake, vin santo ice cream.
Details: www.thesuninndedham.com; 11 pm, Sun 9.30 pm; no Amex.
Accommodation: 5 rooms, from £90.*

Le Talbooth　　　　　　　　　　　**£ 56**
Gun Hill CO7 6HP (01206) 323150
*It has a "riverside setting to die for", but this famous Constable
Country veteran (est. 1952) again attracts very mixed reports –
fans insist it's "a good old-favourite", but for too many reporters it's
"well past its sell-by". / Sample dishes: smoked Scottish salmon, shallot &
capers, granary bread; roast tenderloin of veal, mushroom tortelloni,
baby vegetables, cep butter sauce; coconut & mango Bakewell tart, pineapple
sorbet, Barbadian rum syrup. Details: www.milsomhotels.com; 5m N
of Colchester on A12, take B1029; 9.30 pm; closed Sun D; no jeans or trainers.*

DENHAM, BUCKINGHAMSHIRE　　　　3–3A

Swan Inn　　　　　　　　　　　　**£ 36**　Ⓐ
Village Rd UB9 5BH (01895) 832085
*Is a location in a "picturesque village" and easy accessibility (from J1
of the M4) allowing this "fine gastropub", in an "olde worlde"
building, to become "complacent"? – the food is still "above-average",
but some reporters fear it's "not as good as it used to be".
/ Sample dishes: oak smoked bacon on bubble & squeak with hollandaise
sauce & poached egg; pan-roast organic Scottish salmon on olive, confit tomato &
caper berry linguini with dressed rocket; iced banana parfait with toffee biscuit
crumb. Details: www.swaninndenham.co.uk; 9.30 pm, Fri & Sat 10 pm .*

DERBY, DERBYSHIRE　　　　　　5–3C

Anoki　　　　　　　　　　　　　**£ 38**
First Floor, 129 London Rd DE1 2QN (01332) 292888
*An "interesting" Indian in an old cinema, that inspires much feedback;
fans say its "excellent" food makes it "Derby's premier Indian",
but there's also a school of thought that it is "over-rated".
/ Sample dishes: chicken tikka; chicken makhani. Details: www.anoki.co.uk;
11.30 pm; D only.*

Darleys **£ 50**
Darley Abbey Mill DE22 IDZ (01332) 364987
*This former mill has a "lovely location" by the water, and is arguably
"the only place with decent cooking for miles around"; even ardent
fans acknowledge there are negatives, though – these include
"cheesy" décor, "Muzac", "Mayfair prices" and "countless foams and
accoutrements". / **Sample dishes**: peppered duck breast, spinach and herb
salad, cherry dressing; fillet of beef, oxtail compote, Swiss chard, Bordeaux sauce;
peppermint truffle, chocolate tuille, dark chocolate sauce.
Details: www.darleys.com; 2m N of city centre by River Derwent; 9.30 pm; closed
Sun D; no Amex.*

Masala Art **£ 35**
6 Midland Rd DE1 2SN (01332) 292629
*"In an unremittingly awful town for restaurants", this "solid" and
"classy" curry house "shines like a beacon", say fans; its ratings are
undercut, though, by those who find it "pricey", or "over-designed".
/ **Sample dishes**: lamb marinated in fresh mint & cracked black pepper with
mint and yoghurt dressing; shoulder of lamb braised with whole spices, tomatoes,
ginger and garam masala; pistachio kulfi. **Details**: www.masala-art.co.uk; 11 pm;
D only, closed Sun; children: 10+.*

Restaurant Zest **£ 41**
16d, George St, Friar Gate DE1 1EH (01332) 381101
*"Interesting food, reasonably-priced food in the centre of Derby –
is this a miracle?"; the only gripe about this "solid" bistro is that:
"the lighting's a bit bright". / **Details**: www.restaurantzest.co.uk; 10 pm;
closed Sun.*

DINTON, BUCKINGHAMSHIRE 2–3C

La Chouette **£ 49** ⭐
Westlington Grn HP17 8UW (01296) 747422
*Le patron relishes his rôle as a "belligerent Belgian", but he "never
fails to deliver in terms of first-class full-on cooking, and sheer
entertainment"; extras include a "great wine list, with fantastic
vintages of the classics", plus "Freddie's thoughts on the issues of the
day". / **Sample dishes**: smoked salmon with red wine and stawberries; veal liver
lyonnaise with bacon and vinegar; chocolate soufflé. **Details**: off A418 between
Aylesbury & Thame; 9 pm; closed Sat L & Sun; no Amex.*

DODDISCOMBSLEIGH, DEVON 1–3D

Nobody Inn **£ 32**
EX6 7PS (01647) 252394
*A "quaint, out-of-the-way" rural inn, long acclaimed for its "fantastic
cheese selection", "world-encircling wine list" and "astounding whisky
range"; an early report of its new owners suggest its traditionally
"unexciting" menu is due for a shake up – "at last, new owners with
an interest in food!" / **Sample dishes**: fresh Brixham crab and avocado salad;
grilled whole lemon sole topped nut brown butter and lemon juice with fresh herb
mash; bread and butter pudding made with Devonshire toasted teacakes.
Details: www.nobodyinn.co.uk; off A38 at Haldon Hill (signed Dunchidrock);
9 pm; D only; no Amex. **Accommodation**: 4 rooms, from £60.*

DORCHESTER, DORSET 2–4B

Sienna **£ 50** ⭐
36 High West St DT1 1UP (01305) 250022
*"The best food in Dorset" ("well, the best my pocket will stand,
anyway!") – this small restaurant inspires a necessarily
modest volume of commentary, but all of it very positive.
/ **Details**: www.siennarestaurant.co.uk; 9.30 pm; closed Mon & Sun; no Amex;
children: 10+.*

DORE, SHEFFIELD 5–2C

Moran's £ 42 Ⓣ
289 Abbeydale Road South S17 3LB (01142) 350101
A small wine bar, tipped as "a gem in an otherwise disappointing city". / Sample dishes: tempura of soft shell crab on a sesame dressed Asian salad and a sweet chili dipping sauce; roast honey and peppercorn glazed duck breast with sardalaise potatoes, roast shallots and cassis sauce; warm chocolate and pecan nut brownie with a chocolate and honey sauce and pistachio ice cream. Details: www.moranssheffield.co.uk; 9.30 pm; closed Mon, Tue L & Sun D; no Amex.

DORKING, SURREY 3–3A

Stephan Langton £ 40 Ⓣ
Friday St, Abinger Common RH5 6JR (01306) 730775
It may be "difficult to find", but this "remote" rural pub has the most "beautiful location", and it's tipped as "worth the journey". / Details: www.stephan-langton.co.uk; off A25 at Wotton; 9 pm, Fri & Sat 9.30 pm; closed Mon & Sun D.

DOUGLAS, ISLE OF MAN 7–4B

Ciappelli's £ 63
Admiral Hs, 12 Loch Promenade IM1 2LX (01624) 677442
A "trendy and modern" destination, which is sometimes reckoned to offer "the best food on the island"; it's "painfully expensive", though, notes a reporter from… Chelsea! / Sample dishes: lentil, spinach, and smoked bacon soup; hare cooked in Barolo, with roast root vegetables, Parmesan & olive oil mash; lemon & almond cake, amaretto ice cream, lemon syrup. Details: www.ciappellis.com; 9.30 pm; closed Sat L & Sun; no jeans or trainers.

DUMFRIES, DUMFRIES AND GALLOWAY 7–2C

Linen Room £ 43 ★
53 St Michaels St DG1 2QB (01387) 255689
"High-quality Scottish produce" is used to "extremely imaginative" effect, says a fan of this small, town-centre restaurant; its style can seem "pretentious", though, to the extent harsh critics see it as "a bit of an '80s throw-back" - perhaps a new chef will silence such thoughts. / Sample dishes: plum tomato consomme, balsamic caviar and basil tortellini; monkfish cheek and fennel gnocchi and a squid ink emulsion; passion fruit soufflé and coconut cannelloni and passion fruit leather. Details: www.linenroom.com; straight across from St. Michael's Kirk; 9.30 pm; closed Mon & Tue.

DUNKELD, PERTH & KINROSS 9–3C

Kinnaird House £ 74 Ⓐ★
Kinnaird Estate PH8 0LB (01796) 482440
"A wonderful country retreat, with lovely staff"; this "top-notch" (Relais & Châteaux) country house hotel, in 9,000 acres, is almost invariably judged to be an "exceptional" all-rounder. / Sample dishes: scallop and white asparagus, sweet potato purée and truffle dressing; stuffed breast of guinea fowl and spiced aubergine cannellini, spinacha and madeira sauce; hot orange and Grand Marnier soufflé, vanilla nougat and honeycomb. Details: www.kinnairdestate.com; 8m NW of Dunkeld, off A9 onto B898; 9.30 pm; jacket; children: 10+. Accommodation: 9 rooms, from £275.

The Three Chimneys   **£ 64**   A ✿ ✿
Colbost IV55 8ZT   (01470) 511258
*"A stunning restaurant in a stunning setting"; almost all reports
on Eddie and Shirley Spear's isolated cottage are a hymn of praise
to its "cosy" style, "assured" service and "exquisite local produce,
unfussily cooked to perfection"; there's no denying, though, that –
for the occasional visitor – the "hype" surpasses the reality.*
/ **Sample dishes:** *seared breast of wood pigeon with celeriac remoulade, bacon,
fancy kale & redcurrant game gravy; citrus-steamed wild sea bass & lobster with
rosti; hot marmalade pudding with Drambuie custard.*
Details: *www.threechimneys.co.uk; 5m from Dunvegan Castle on B884
to Glendale; 9.30 pm; closed Sun L; children: 8+.* **Accommodation:** *6 rooms,
from £265.*

Bistro 21   **£ 42**
Aykley Heads Hs DH1 5TS   (0191) 384 4354
*"Our favourite 'local restaurant', and the only one in Durham with
any real distinction" – in default of much competition hereabouts,
this well-established spot in a "charming" former farmhouse certainly
ought to shine!* / **Sample dishes:** *cheddar and spinach soufflé;
pan-roast halibut with asparagus, tomao confit and sage; custard tart with nutmeg
ice cream.* **Details:** *www.bistrotwentyone.co.uk; near Durham Trinity School;
10.30 pm; closed Sun; booking: max 10.*

Gourmet Spot   **£ 49**   ✿
The Ave DH1 4DX   (0191) 384 6655
*Sean Wilkinson is already being crowned by fans as the "Heston
Blumenthal of the North", and most reporters are wowed by the
"amazing, laboratory-style" cuisine on offer at this Nevilles Cross
yearling; in the nature of the thing, however, not everyone
is convinced.* / **Sample dishes:** *king prawn tempura, pickled ginger, fennel &
grapefruit foam; guinea fowl wild mushroom risotto with Parmesan froth; tea &
toast with jam and biscuits.* **Details:** *www.gourmet-spot.co.uk; 9.30 pm; D only,
closed Mon & Sun.*

Pump House   **£ 50**   ✘
Farm Rd DH1 3PJ   (0191) 386 9189
*A courtyard table at this converted Victorian pumping station on a
summer's evening is "to die for"; otherwise reports can be extremely
critical, saying the place is "overpriced", and "wouldn't survive
elsewhere".* / **Details:** *www.thepumphouserestaurant.co.uk; 9.30 pm.*

Jolly Sportsman   **£ 40**   ✿
Chapel Ln BN7 3BA   (01273) 890400
*In "sylvan surroundings", on the South Downs, a "hidden-gem" of a
gastropub that's in truth been well and truly discovered for many
years; it maintains "high standards", though, and offers "hearty" food,
plus a "vast selection of beers, and good-value wine".*
/ **Sample dishes:** *chilled spiced cucumber soup and tea smoked salmon; rump of
local lamb, boulangere potatoes, summer veg; apricot, walnut, ginger and toffee
pudding and cream.* **Details:** *www.thejollysportsman.com; NW of Lewes;
midnight; closed Mon & Sun D; no Amex.*

Gravetye Manor   £ 75   Ⓐ★

Vowels Ln RH19 4LJ   (01342) 810567

A "stunning" location – an Elizabethan country house in "beautiful" grounds – sets the scene at this Relais et Châteaux property, where the approach is "formal but friendly"; "truly excellent" food helps create a "superb" all-round experience. / **Sample dishes:** ballotine of salmon; chargrilled loin of veal with capsicum dressing; tiramisu with white coffee ice cream. **Details:** www.gravetyemanor.co.uk; 2m outside Turner's Hill; 9.30 pm; jacket & tie; children: 7+. **Accommodation:** 18 rooms, from £170.

Trawlers   £ 42   Ⓐ★★

On The Quay PL13 1AH   (01503) 263593

"Great food, great view, great service" – if you're looking for "ultra-fresh fish, simply cooked", you're unlikely to do much better than this "magical" harbour-side spot. / **Sample dishes:** spicy louisiana style seafood gumbo; crispy skin sea bass with a lobster thermidor sauce; trio of pots: lemon posset, crème brûlée & a white chocolate panacotta.
Details: www.trawlersrestaurant.co.uk; 9.30 pm; D only, closed Mon & Sun.

Blue Lion   £ 42   Ⓐ

DL8 4SN   (01969) 624273

Fans "return time and time again" to this "relaxed and friendly" hostelry, set amidst "lovely countryside" in the Dales; its "always-reliable" food is consistently praised, but it's "perhaps not such good value as it once was". / **Sample dishes:** salad of black pudding, smoked bacon and shallots topped with a poached egg; chargrilled fillet of beef with a Shiraz sauce, shallots, lardons and mushrooms; a tatin of pineapple with home-made pineapple sorbet. **Details:** www.thebluelion.co.uk; between Masham & Leyburn on A6108; 9.15 pm; D only, ex Sun open L & D; no Amex. **Accommodation:** 15 rooms, from £89.

The Mirabelle
The Grand Hotel   £ 55   Ⓐ

King Edwards Pde BN21 4EQ   (01323) 412345

"Travel back a century or so", when you visit the "beautiful", high-ceilinged dining room of this grand Edwardian hotel; not everyone is quite convinced, but most reporters say the food is "seldom less than very good". / **Sample dishes:** duck egg benedictine; herb crusted lamb cutlet, boulangere potatoes; caramelised croissant and chocolate pudding. **Details:** www.grandeastbourne.com; 9.45 pm; closed Mon & Sun; jacket or tie required at D; children: 12+ at D. **Accommodation:** 152 rooms, from £190.

Haxted Mill   £ 45

Haxted Rd TN8 6PU   (01732) 862914

"Idyllic inside and out" – a "quirkily-run" former mill, where "wonderful fish" is a highlight. / **Sample dishes:** squid, chorizo sausage, tomato concasse; Louisiana blackened red fish with lime mash; hazelnut parfait. **Details:** www.haxtedmill.co.uk; between Edenbridge & Lingfield; 9 pm; closed Mon & Sun D; no Amex.

Until a few years ago, Edinburgh had few restaurants which might be said to be causing culinary excitement. Now it has two: the longer-established *Restaurant Martin Wishart*, and pretender *The Kitchin* (which, of the two, is currently creating more buzz).

There are also some mid-range restaurants of real culinary interest – *David Bann* (a veggie good enough for carnivores) and *Roti* (an unusually good Indian restaurant). Also a couple of places which stand out for the remarkable charm of their setting – the *Witchery by the Castle* (the best-known place in town) and the *Vintners' Rooms*.

Beyond these top names, there's an impressive supporting cast of mid-range restaurants worthy of one of our 'star' awards. For casual dining, Leith, and its waterside, remains the best place to go for a range of fun and relatively inexpensive options.

Abstract   £ 62   ⭐

33-35 Castle St EH1 2EL   (0131) 229 1222
"Décor just the right side of kitsch", "fabulous cocktails" and a "piano bar" set a "relaxed" tone at this ambitious venture, praised by most reporters for its "very good" and "inventive" cuisine (albeit in the "foams and twiddles" style). / **Sample dishes:** *pressed terrine of sardine escabeche, parsley and carrot; pig trotter wrapped in Parma ham, with black pudding and veal sweetbread; apple soufflé, manzana shooter, caramel ice cream.* **Details:** *www.abstractedinburgh.com; 10 pm; closed Mon & Sun.*

The Atrium   £ 50

10 Cambridge St EH1 2ED   (0131) 228 8882
"Benefiting from a much-needed make-over", the city's original trendy restaurant has received notably more favourable reports of late; it can still seem "complacent", though, and the atmosphere can still fail to thrill. / **Sample dishes:** *seared scallops, confit chicken wings, organic lemon chutney; roast leg of organic chicke, ratte potatoes with spinach, fresh morel and shallot cream sauce; dark and white chocolate pave griottines, vanilla ice cream and sweet wine syrup.* **Details:** *www.atriumrestaurant.co.uk; by the Usher Hall; 10 pm; closed Sat L & Sun (except during Festival).*

Bell's Diner   £ 26   ⓣ

7 St Stephen St EH3 5EN   (0131) 225 8116
A long-established Stockbridge diner, tipped for "the best burgers in town"; it's a "relaxed" sort of place too, where prices are "reasonable". / **Details:** *10 pm; closed weekday L & Sun L; no Amex.*

blue bar café   £ 43

10 Cambridge St EH1 2ED   (0131) 221 1222
The Atrium's "casual" brasserie sibling, on the floor above, is "a simple but good spot, with well-made bistro fare, served by helpful staff". / **Sample dishes:** *haricot bean & mushroom ragout, rocket, Parmesan; ballotine of corn-fed chicken, wild mushroom stuffing, mash; dark chocolate mousse, crème fraîche ice cream.*
Details: *www.bluescotland.co.uk; by the Usher Hall; 10.30 pm, Fri & Sat 11 pm; closed Sun (except during Festival).*

Cafe Marlayne   £ 28   Ⓐ⭐

7 Old Fishmarket Close EH1 1RW   (0131) 2253838
"An atmospheric French café in the heart of Edinburgh", consistently recommended for offering "impressively substantial" fare at "modest" prices. / **Details:** *10 pm; no Amex.*

Le Café St-Honoré £ 43 Ⓐ

34 NW Thistle Street Ln EH2 1EA (0131) 226 2211

This "authentically French" stalwart, tucked away in the New Town, is a "dependable" favourite, with a "great" and – to some – "romantic" atmosphere; there's a slight feeling, though, that it's been "resting on its laurels" of late – perhaps new management (from March 2008) will pep things up. / **Sample dishes:** braised squid and mussels; sirloin steak au poivre mixed salad and potatoes; crème brûlée biscotti and apricot compot. **Details:** www.cafesthonore.com; 10 pm.

Calistoga £ 33 ✪

93 St Leonards St EH8 9QY (0131) 668 4207

A "good wine selection at reasonable prices" ("just a £5 mark-up per bottle") is a highlight at this "original", "café-style" Californian-inspired venture; the "interesting" food usually gets the thumbs-up too. / **Sample dishes:** spiced cucumber & Galia melon gazpacho; seared lamb gigot chop with tempura cauliflower and broccoli and a sweet chilli mint sauce; spiced banana loaf with chocolate fondant. **Details:** www.calistoga.co.uk; 10 pm; closed Tue L & Wed L; no Amex.

Centotre £ 46

103 George St EH2 3ES (0131) 225 1550

A "glamorous" and "lively" all-day New Town Italian, which aims to be to Auld Reekie what The Wolseley is to London; "standards have slipped", though, and the food is "under-whelming", and "expensive for what it is". / **Sample dishes:** speck di prosciuto with a light canellini bean, garlic, parsley and extra virgin olive oil salad; veal pan-fried Milanese style in egg and breadcrumbs served with sauté potatoes and fresh rocket; Valrhona chocolate truffle cake. **Details:** www.centotre.com; Mon - Fri 10 pm, Fri & Sat 11 pm, Sun 8 pm; closed Sun D.

Creelers £ 46

3 Hunter Sq EH1 1QW (0131) 220 4447

This "bustling" seafood restaurant has a handy location, just off the Royal Mile; its straightforward fish and seafood is generally well received too. / **Sample dishes:** tuna carpaccio with wasabi mayo & herb salad; spiced mixed seafood laksa with a timbale of jasmine rice; hazelnut & chocolate torte with coffee ice cream. **Details:** www.creelers.co.uk; 10.30 pm.

Daniel's £ 34 Ⓣ

88 Commercial St EH6 6LX (0131) 553 5933

Tipped as "the place for an inexpensive lunch with friends" – a "very friendly" Leith bistro serving "rustic/hearty" Gallic fare and "some interesting Alsace wines". / **Sample dishes:** provençale fish soup; cassoulet; spicy ice cream terrine. **Details:** www.daniels-bistro.co.uk; 10 pm.

David Bann £ 31 ✪✪

56-58 St Marys St EH1 1SX (0131) 556 5888

David Bann's "remarkable" and "imaginative" cuisine is "so good, you don't actually notice it's vegetarian", say fans of this "buzzing" venture in the Old Town, which is decorated in a "stylishly modernist" fashion. / **Sample dishes:** tartlet of goats cheese and slow dried tomato; harissa roast aubergine, aduki, sweet pepper; malt whisky panna cotta. **Details:** www.davidbann.com; 10 pm, Fri & Sat 10.30 pm.

Dusit **£ 37**

49a Thistle St EH2 1DY   (0131) 220 6846

"Aromatic" Thai food – "of consistently high quality, and beautifully-presented" – wins continued acclaim for this "noisy" New Town spot. / **Sample dishes:** *chicken marinated in Scotch whisky and sesame dressing, wrapped in pandan leaf; steak stir-fry with baby aubergine, fresh peppercorns, fresh chilli, grachi and holy basil; steamed ivory rice pudding with coconut cream, served with fresh fruits.* **Details:** *www.dusit.co.uk; 11 pm.*

First Coast **£ 31**

99-101 Dalry Rd EH11 2AB   (0131) 3134404

"Away from the tourist hordes", this "reliable" bistro, near Haymarket Station, is "the sort of neighbourhood spot of which every medium-sized town should have at least one" – it offers "simple" and "seasonal" fare, at "good-value" prices. / **Sample dishes:** *hot smoked salmon salad, home-made salad cream; confit pork belly, mash, honey and ginger gravy; steamed apricot pudding, amaretto custard.* **Details:** *www.first-coast.co.uk; 10.30 pm; closed Sun.*

Fishers Bistro **£ 38**

1 The Shore EH6 6QW   (0131) 554 5666

You get "great fish and seafood", and a "fun night out" too, at this "friendly" and "always-reliable" operation, near the Leith waterfront; (they just bought The Shore next door, so some change may be afoot). / **Sample dishes:** *pan-fried baby squid with a horseradish gremolata & parsley aioli; whole lemon sole grilled with basil, fennel, & pinenut butter; sticky toffee pudding with vanilla ice cream.* **Details:** *www.fishersbistros.co.uk; 10.30 pm.*

Fishers in the City **£ 36**

58 Thistle St EH2 1EN   (0131) 225 5109

This New Town warehouse-conversion lost out to its Leith sibling in the survey this year, thanks to the odd gripe that's its "resting on its laurels"; for "businessmen, tourists and locals", however, it remains a "reliable stand-by", with "fish the obvious attraction". / **Sample dishes:** *pan-fried monkfish served in curried mussel broth with onion paratha; pan-fried fillet of stone bass with gazpacho & cucumber, mint & chilli salad; caramelized peaches with glass biscuits & peach sorbet.* **Details:** *www.fishersbistros.co.uk; 10.30 pm.*

Forth Floor
Harvey Nichols **£ 55**

30-34 St Andrew Sq EH2 2AD   (0131) 524 8350

"Marvellous" views of the city "always impress", at this "buzzy" department store venue; the same can't necessarily be said of the "pricey" food, but the place does have its fans, who insist it's a "superb" all-rounder. / **Sample dishes:** *white bean and quail egg ravioli with wilted sorrel, mint and roast pistachio; roast loin and smoked belly of rabbit with watercress purée and herb gnocchi; tea panacotta with toast and jam ice cream.* **Details:** *www.harveynichols.com; 10 pm; closed Mon D & Sun D; booking: max 8.*

Le Garrigue £ 39

31 Jeffrey St EH1 1DH (0131) 557 3032

"Everything is beautifully cooked, with a genuine flavour of France", at this "tiny" restaurant, in the Old Town, whose chef, Jean-Michelle Gauffre, hails from Languedoc; the only complaint? – "shame it isn't bigger". / **Sample dishes:** warm lamb pies with spices and mint, on a bed of leeks salad; cassoulet with pork, lamb, duck confit, Toulouse sausage and lingot beans served with a crispy walnut salad; tangy lemon tart with orange flower ice cream. **Details:** www.lagarrigue.co.uk; 9.30 pm; closed Sun.

Glass & Thompson £ 24

2 Dundas St EH3 6HZ (0131) 557 0909

Tipped for its "unvarying quality", a New Town café/deli that makes "a great place for a quick soup and a sandwich, or a longer Sunday brunch"; on a nice day, you can sit outside too. / **Sample dishes:** Brie de Meaux salad; vegetarian pâté platter; fig, walnut & apricot torte. **Details:** L only.

Grain Store £ 48

30 Victoria St EH1 2JW (0131) 225 7635

"A pleasant surprise tucked away in the Grassmarket" – this "secluded" two-year-old is "a real treat", combining "well-judged" cooking, "engaging" service and a "homely and rustic" atmosphere. / **Sample dishes:** home-smoked salmon with petite herb salad and sauce gribiche; saddle of roe deer, braised roe deer shoulder and pancetta with red wine & risotto; strawberry tarte Tatin with home-made vanilla bean ice cream. **Details:** www.grainstore-restaurant.co.uk; 10 pm.

Henderson's £ 29

94 Hanover St EH2 1DR (0131) 225 2131

If you're looking for a "hearty" but "healthy" meal, this veggie old-timer, in a "no-frills" New Town basement, combines "a good salad bar, with a separate bistro-style restaurant" – both are "reliable". / **Sample dishes:** goats cheese tart; Moroccan stew; sour cream with sliced fruits & ginger. **Details:** www.hendersonsofedinburgh.co.uk; 10 pm; closed Sun; no Amex.

Iglu £ 37

2b, Jamaica St EH3 6HH (0131) 476 5333

"Enough to give 'ethical eateries' a good name!"; this largely organic New Town spot offers a "simple menu" which pleases most, if not quite all, who report on it. / **Sample dishes:** Scottish smoked rainbow trout salad; roast rump of local organic lamb; summer berry charlotte. **Details:** www.theiglu.com; 10 pm; children: 14+ for D.

Indian Cavalry Club £ 44

22 Coates Cr EH3 7AF (0131) 220 0138

This locally-celebrated Indian of 21 years standing doesn't yet seem to be quite up-to-speed in its new New Town location (just across the road from the old one); fans say it's "pricey, but worth if for the quality", but not everyone agrees, and service can "take forever". / **Details:** www.indiancavalryclub.co.uk; between Caledonian Hotel & Haymarket Station; 10.45 pm.

Kalpna £ 28

2-3 St Patrick Sq EH8 9EZ (0131) 667 9890

Near the University, this "simple", "family-run and long-established" Gujarati canteen has long prospered as a "great-value" proposition – be it the "eat-all-you-can buffet lunch or more structured evening menu". / **Sample dishes:** pakoras; dam aloo kashmiri; metka. **Details:** www.kalpnarestaurant.com; 10.30 pm; closed Sun; no Amex; no booking at L.

The Kitchin £ 71 ⭐⭐

78 Commercial Quay EH6 6LX (0131) 555 1755

"It's getting harder and harder to get a table", at Tom Kitchin's "stylish" warehouse-conversion yearling – already the hottest place in town by far; it's not the slightly "low-key" atmosphere that packs 'em in, but his "amazingly good", "seasonal" fare (and "excellent" service too). / *Sample dishes:* roast langoustine tails and boned and rolled pig's head and a crispy ear salad; whole monkfish tail seasoned with olives, lemon zest and herbs, wrapped in pancetta; millefeuille of summer fruits and almonds and light citrus cottage cheese cream and elderflower syrup. *Details:* www.thekitchin.com; 10 pm; closed Mon & Sun.

Maison Bleue £ 40 Ⓣ

36-38 Victoria St EH1 2GW (0131) 226 1900

A romantically rustic Old Town spot which inspires surprisingly few reports, but such as there are tip its "imaginative" food from "excellent ingredients that are well cooked and presented". / *Sample dishes:* haggis balls fried in beer batter with clapshot potatoes and whisky sauce; medallions of venison with a sweet red chili, black pepper and brandy sauce and pommes lyonnaise; sticky toffee pudding with toffee sauce and vanilla ice cream. *Details:* www.maison-bleue.co.uk; 11 pm.

Mussel Inn £ 32

61-65 Rose St EH2 2NH (0131) 225 5979

"Cheap, and reasonably cheerful" – the "no-frills" charms of this "busy", "basic" and "crowded" seafood bistro, just off Princess Street, have won it a healthy following among reporters. / *Sample dishes:* grilled queen scallops with crispy Serrano ham, rocket, Parmesan and a yellow pepper dressing; mussels served in white wine, garlic, shallots and cream with crusty bread; chocolate and almond torte served with honey and crème fraîche. *Details:* www.mussel-inn.com; 10 pm.

Number One ⭐
Balmoral Hotel £ 82

1 Princes St EH2 2EQ (0131) 557 6727

"The standard is always the same: excellent!" – thus says one fan of the very "professional" basement dining room of Edinburgh's grandest hotel; especially if you go for one of Jeff Bland's wine-matched tasting menus, the experience can be "nigh on perfect". / *Sample dishes:* Anjou pigeon, spiced cous cous, filo roll & macadamia nut pesto; beef fillet, celeriac purée, confit potato & smoked tomato chutney; banana parfait, salted caramel, peanuts & a sherry & maple reduction. *Details:* www.roccofortehotels.com; 10.30 pm; D only; no jeans or trainers. *Accommodation:* 188 rooms, from £290.

Oloroso £ 57 Ⓐ

33 Castle St EH2 3DN (0131) 226 7614

"Be optimistic about the weather, and book a place on the terrace", if you make a summer visit to this "see-and-be-seen" rooftop perch – a "great setting", with "fab views" and a "brilliant bar"; the food is "enjoyable" too, but "so overpriced" for what it is. / *Sample dishes:* rabbit with carrot, fennel & a thyme glaze; pan fried monkfish with curried chickpeas, pickled cauliflower & spinach; white chocolate & praline semifreddo. *Details:* www.oloroso.co.uk; 10.15 pm; no Amex.

Original Khushi's £ 24 Ⓐ ⭐

26-30 Potterow EH1 2HE (0131) 220 0057

"Freshly-cooked" Indian food ("with liberal use of spices") – plus "kind and inviting" service – wins an enthusiastic following for this BYO operation in the Old Town; it moved location in recent times, and the only gripe is that some people preferred its old, more basic style! / **Sample dishes:** tandoori chicken; lamb curry; toffee fudge sundae. **Details:** www.khushis.com; 11 pm, Sun 10 pm.

Outsider £ 33 Ⓐ

15-16 George IV Bridge EH1 1EE (0131) 226 3131

"A brilliant view of the castle and an airy interior" help maintain this "lively" and "buzzing" venue as one of the groovier hang-outs in town; the "interesting" menu revolves around "platters to share, featuring kebabs". / **Sample dishes:** Thai chicken; rib eye steak; chocolate brownie. **Details:** 11 pm; no Amex; booking: max 10.

Le Petit Paris £ 33

38-40 Grassmarket EH1 2JU (0131) 226 2442

"A small, cramped and very French restaurant", in the Grassmarket; "run by a group of young Frenchmen, it seems to have been transported somehow direct from France" – "if you're looking for classics at low prices, it never fails". / **Details:** www.petitparis-restaurant.co.uk; near the Castle; 10.30.

Restaurant Martin Wishart £ 71 ⭐

54 The Shore EH6 6RA (0131) 553 3557

"The best restaurant in Scotland", according to its many fans – the Wisharts' "classy" (if quite "plain") Leith dining room offers "brilliant" and "unfaltering" cuisine, and the service is "excellent" too – "they're striving so hard for two Michelin stars, there seem to be more waiters every time I go!" / **Details:** www.martin-wishart.co.uk; near Royal Yacht Britannia; 9 pm; closed Mon & Sun; booking: max 10.

Rhubarb Ⓐ⭐
Prestonfield Hotel £ 65

Priestfield Rd EH16 5UT (0131) 225 1333

"Stylish, slightly OTT, but very comfy" – the Witchery's "luxurious" country house outpost is an obvious option for a romantic get-away; most reporters think the food lives up too, but doubters find it "overpriced". / **Details:** www.rhubarb-restaurant.com; 10 pm, Fri & Sat 11 pm; children: 12+ at D, none after 7pm. **Accommodation:** 23 rooms, from £225.

Roti £ 38 ⭐

70 Rose St North Ln EH3 8BU (0131) 221 9998

"Now in bigger premises" – and "at last away from the dismal back-street it used to inhabit" – this modern Indian remains "an all-time favourite" for some locals reporters thanks to its "imaginative" dishes. / **Details:** www.roti.uk.com; 10.30 pm; closed Mon, Sat L & Sun.

Skippers £ 41 Ⓐ

1a Dock Pl EH6 6LU (0131) 554 1018

"Set on the docks of Leith", this "rustic, old-fashioned restaurant" is "very good at what it does" – "lovely, tasty fish" served in a "warm and friendly" (if "cramped") setting. / **Sample dishes:** marlin & swordfish carpaccio with a prawn, capsicum pickle & wasabi paste; whole grilled Dover sole with a smoked tomato butter & sautéed samphire grass; blueberry cheesecake. **Details:** 10 pm.

The Stockbridge £ 44
54 St Stephen's St EH3 5AL (0131) 2266766
Still surprisingly thin commentary on this "pleasant, relaxing and comfortable basement restaurant", again tipped for its menu of "beef, game and fish", "well cooked and prepared".
/ **Sample dishes:** *sautéed Scottish rabbit loin with wild mushrooms, truffles & crispy Parma ham; poached rainbow trout fillet with brandade, vine tomatoes, dill, cider vinegar syrup & sevruga caviar; trio of chocolate.*
Details: *www.thestockbridgerestaurant.com; 9.30 pm; closed Mon, Tue-Fri D only, Sat & Sun open L & D.*

Sweet Melindas £ 37
11 Roseneath St EH9 1JH (0131) 229 7953
"In the heart of student flat-land" (Marchmont), a "busy local" that impresses almost all reporters with its "excellent fish".
/ **Sample dishes:** *sweet Thai fishcakes with cabbage salad & sweet dipping sauce; chargrilled tuna steak, crab, basil mayonnaise & red chard salad; Valrhona chocolate torte.* **Details:** *www.sweetmelindas.co.uk; 10 pm; closed Mon L & Sun.*

The Tower
Museum of Scotland £ 49
Chambers St EH1 1JF (0131) 225 3003
A venue that's become well-known, not least for its "fantastic views across Edinburgh"; for an establishment that's "otherwise so ordinary", however, it can seem "grossly overpriced".
/ **Sample dishes:** *seared foie gras with prawn & lentil salad; roast lamb with broad beans & minted mash; chocolate & praline fondant with caramelized oranges.* **Details:** *www.tower-restaurant.com; 11 pm.*

Urban Angel £ 26
121 Hanover St EH2 1DJ (0131) 2256215
A New Town café/deli – ideal for brunch or lunch – where the "fresh and interesting organic food never lets you down"; service, though, can be "slow" and "off-hand". / **Sample dishes:** *braised squid with red wine, madeira, chorizo & broad beans; lamb shoulder noisette with haricots vert & red wine jus; pineapple meringue pie with coconut sorbet.*
Details: *www.urban-angel.co.uk; 10 pm; closed Sun D.*

Valvona & Crolla £ 44
19 Elm Row EH7 4AA (0131) 556 6066
For fans, "there's nowhere better for a light, Italianate lunch" than this famous deli-café (where "you'll probably have to queue"); it's hard to avoid the impression that it "trades on its reputation", though – far too many reporters find it "hyped", "unexciting" and "expensive", and with "appalling service" too. / **Sample dishes:** *salmon bruschetta; crespelle with wild mushrooms & pancetta; panna cotta with Drambuie.*
Details: *www.valvonacrolla.com; at top of Leith Walk, near Playhouse Theatre; L only.*

VinCaffe £ 44
11 Multrees Walk EH1 3DQ (0131) 557 0088
"Disappointing given the Valvona pedigree"; this busy Italian may be applauded by fans for its "simple and genuine" dishes, but it draws too many reports of "incompetent" cooking and "unresponsive" service. / **Sample dishes:** *salmon bruschetta; crespelle with wild mushrooms & pancetta; panna cotta with Drambuie.* **Details:** *www.valvonacrolla.com; 9.30 pm, Fri & Sat 10 pm; closed Sun D.*

Vintners Rooms £ 52 Ⓐ ⭐

87a Giles St EH6 6BZ   (0131) 554 6767

*"A great place to impress your date"; few venues feel as "special"
as this "romantic, candlelit dining room in an old wine warehouse",
a short walk from Leith's waterfront; service is "impeccable" too,
and the "traditional" Franco-Scottish food is reliably of "high quality".
/ Sample dishes: foie gras & langoustine terrine with fig chutney; roast Aberdeen
angus fillet, Perigord truffle sauce; panna cotta with Scottish raspberries.*
Details: *www.thevintnersrooms.com; 10 pm; closed Mon & Sun.*

The Witchery by the Castle £ 58 Ⓐ

Castlehill, The Royal Mile EH1 2NF   (0131) 225 5613

*A "wonderfully romantic" setting – mad Gothic dungeon-meets-
opulent Secret Garden – creates a "terrific atmosphere" at this Old
Town veteran; perhaps predictably the food is "pricey for what it is",
but the bible of a wine list is "unbelievable". / Sample dishes: terrine
of wild rabbit and Toulouse sausage with beetroot remoulade and herb salad;
grilled fillet of beef with savoury bread and butter pudding, celeriac purée and
smoked garlic; chocolate and griottine cherry clafoutis.*
Details: *www.thewitchery.com; 11.30 pm.* **Accommodation:** *7 rooms,
from £295.*

EGLWYSFACH, POWYS 4–3D

Ynyshir Hall £ 84 Ⓣ

SY20 8TA   (01654) 781209

*A tiny volume of reports on this grand and "old-fashioned" country
house hotel (Von Essen), but it is tipped as "a great treat for a special
occasion". / Sample dishes: cheese soufflé; Welsh lamb, garlic and rosemary
potatoes, courgette, tomato fondue, white wine jus; treacle tart.*
Details: *www.ynyshirhall.co.uk; signposted from A487; 8.45 pm; no jeans
or trainers; children: 9+.* **Accommodation:** *9 rooms, from £180.*

ELIE, FIFE 9–4D

Sangster's £ 45 ⭐

51 High St KY9 1BZ   (01333) 331001

*Bruce Sangster is an "enthusiastic" chef, and the cuisine at his
"intimate" (and sometimes "quiet") restaurant offers "nothing over-
elaborate" – "just great ingredients, perfectly combined".
/ Sample dishes: twice baked soufflé; slow cooked fillet blade of Scottish beef,
roast fillet, broad beans, wild mushrooms, asparagus; trio of desserts: milk
chocolate mousse, lemon raspberry cream, vanilla crème brûlée.*
Details: *www.sangsters.co.uk; 8.30 pm; no Amex; no jeans or shorts; children:
12+ at D.*

ELLAND, WEST YORKSHIRE 5–1C

La Cachette £ 27 ⭐

31 Huddersfield Rd HX5 9AW   (01422) 378833

*"Lots of booths and alcoves" add to the charm of this popular
brasserie, where "excellent service" contributes to an all-round
impression of "high standards". / Sample dishes: warm duck confit salad,
hoi sin, rocket & spring onion; mini oxtail pie, slow braised pigs cheek, crushed
roast roots, red wine jus; vanilla crème brûlée with raspberry compote.*
Details: *www.lacachette-elland.com; 9.30 pm, Fri & Sat 10pm; closed Sun;
no Amex.*

ELLESMERE PORT, CHESHIRE 5–2A

Jabula Restaurant £ 32 Ⓣ
1 South Pier Rd CH65 4FW (0151) 3551163
"A fantastic African restaurant", overlooking the Ship Canal;
its "amazing décor" helps make it a top tip in a town without many
competing culinary attractions. / **Sample dishes:** crocodile on garlic bread;
game Africa; chocolate fudge cake. **Details:** www.jabula-restaurant.co.uk; off the
M53; 9.30 pm; closed Mon L; no Amex.

ELSTEAD, SURREY 3–3A

The Golden Fleece £ 26 Ⓣ
Farnham Rd GU8 6DB (01252) 702349
"Excellent" and "authentic" Thai cuisine makes this "homely village
pub" a top tip in these parts. / **Sample dishes:** spring rolls, prawn toast,
chicken satay; cashew nut with chicken; apple pie. **Details:** 11 pm; no Amex;
children: 14+ after 6 pm.

ELSTOW, BEDFORDSHIRE 3–1A

St Helena's £ 50 Ⓐ★
High St MK42 9XP (01234) 344848
In a Tudor building, a "classic" restaurant, offering a "quality" menu
that "attracts custom from far and wide"; a "brilliant wine list" and
"efficient service" are major supporting attractions. / **Details:** off A6,
S of Bedford; 9 pm; closed Mon, Sat L & Sun; children: 12+.

ELY, CAMBRIDGESHIRE 3–1B

Old Fire Engine House £ 39
25 St Mary's St CB7 4ER (01353) 662582
You get proper "home cooking" – "they even offer second helpings!"
– at the Jarman family's "unashamedly traditional" and "homely"
fixture; located near the Cathedral, it's an "incredibly friendly" local
landmark of 40 years' standing. / **Sample dishes:** herrings pickled in dill
with cucumber & yoghurt; breast of duck with orange onion & brandy sauce;
apple & blackberry crumble. **Details:** www.theoldfireenginehouse.co.uk; 9 pm;
closed Sun D; no Amex.

EMSWORTH, HAMPSHIRE 2–4D

Ⓐ★

Fat Olives £ 41
30 South St PO10 7EH (01243) 377914
A former cottage near the water houses this "fantastic local";
"book well ahead" to enjoy its "unfailing" cooking, which is "prepared
with care and attention". / **Sample dishes:** pigeon, puy lentils, balsamic &
garlic sauce; monkfish, mushroom & salsify, caramelised onions, verjus cream
sauce; cinnamon & clove roast pear, honey panna cotta.
Details: www.fatolives.co.uk; 10 pm; closed Mon & Sun; no Amex; children: 8+.

36 on the Quay £ 62
47 South St PO10 7EG (01243) 375592
With its "wonderful location" by the harbour, and food that can
be "outstanding", Ramon Farthing's well-established restaurant has
an awful lot going for it; it's "expensive", though, and continually gives
rise to the occasional report of "appalling" service.
/ **Details:** www.36onthequay.co.uk; off A27 between Portsmouth & Chichester;
9.45 pm; closed Mon & Sun. **Accommodation:** 4 (plus cottage) rooms,
from £95.

Edwinns   **£ 36**

Wick Rd TW20 0HN   (01784) 477877

Tucked-away in an "delightful setting", on the fringe of Windsor Great Park – an attractive outlet of a small chain, tipped for its "useful brasserie cooking in an area badly served by restaurants".

/ ***Sample dishes:*** *grilled green-lipped mussels with a Stilton crust; braised crispy Gressingham duck with olive oil mash, basalmic onions, sautéed cabbage; sunken chocolate pudding, Bailey's cream.* ***Details:*** *www.edwinns.co.uk; 10 pm, Sun 9.30 pm.*

Le Raj   **£ 25**

211 Fir Tree Rd KT17 3LB   (01737) 371371

*"Far-removed from a run-of-the-mill 'Indian'" – this "innovative" subcontinental offers "vibrant" food that "isn't cheap, but does offer value-for-money". / **Details:** www.lerajrestaurant.co.uk; next to Derby race course; 11 pm; no jeans or trainers.*

Sangthai   **£ 30**

Church Cottage YO19 6EX   (01904) 728462

"Fantastic Thai food in a bizarre converted bungalow location" – that's the deal at this "tightly-packed" oriental.

/ ***Details:*** *www.sangthai.co.uk; flexible; closed Mon, Tue-Thu & Sat D only.*

Good Earth   **£ 43**

14-18 High St KT10 9RT   (01372) 462489

*Even fans concede it's "rather expensive", but this "mock-palatial" oriental (part of a small chain) is a "very smooth" all-rounder, with "better-than-average" cooking. / **Sample dishes:** rainbow scallops on skewers steamed with prawns & vegetables; sizzling lamb in iron pot with spring onions & ginger; toffee apple. **Details:** www.goodearthgroup.co.uk; 11.15 pm, Sun 10.45 pm; booking: max 12, Fri & Sat.*

Layla   **£ 30**

110 High St KT10 9QL   (01372) 462333

A "terrific newcomer" offering "very tasty Lebanese food", and already attracting "ladies who lunch", and – by night – a well-heeled Middle Eastern clientèle; "great bar too" ("for Esher").

/ ***Details:*** *www.laylarestaurant.co.uk; 10.30 pm.*

Sherpa   **£ 31**

132 High St KT10 9QJ   (01372) 470777

*"A pleasant and flavoursome variation on your standard 'Indian'" – this "spacious" and "friendly" Nepalese is a "good-value" spot with "a big local following". / **Details:** www.sherpakitchen.co.uk; 11 pm.*

Siam Food Gallery   **£ 40**

95-97 High St KT10 9QE   (01372) 477139

*A suburban Thai with a fair following among reporters, and tipped for its "dependable" standards. / **Details:** 11 pm.*

ESKMILLS, EAST LOTHIAN　　　　　　　　9–4C

Ⓐ

The Glasshouse At Eskmills　　　**£ 35**
Station Hs, Station Rd EH21 7PQ　(0131) 2735240
*This strikingly-designed yearling has inspired fewer reports than
we would have expected; some do indeed speak of "top-notch
surroundings and reliable cuisine", but there is also a school
of thought that the food is "rather ordinary for the price".*
/ ***Sample dishes:*** *grilled asparagus,enoki mushroom salad, poached egg yolk &
truffle oil; John Dory fillet,mussel,clam & garden pea risotto; banoffee cheesecake,
chocolate orange & almond crisps.* ***Details:*** *www.theglasshouseateskmills.com;
10 pm.*

ETON, WINDSOR & MAIDENHEAD　　　3–3A

Ⓣ

Gilbey's　　　**£ 39**
82-83 High St SL4 6AF　(01753) 854921
*Near the College, a convivial wine bar with a "very pleasant"
(if "cramped") adjoining conservatory restaurant; it's tipped for the
"good value" of its lunch and early-evening menus (and its superior
wine list).* / ***Sample dishes:*** *carpaccio of pigeon breast, aubergine chutney,
parmsean biscuit; roast pork belly with mushrooms & sage, celeriac mash &
madeira sauce; blood orange cheesecake with light ginger syrup.*
Details: *www.gilbeygroup.com; 10 min walk from Windsor Castle; 9.30 pm.*

EVERSHOT, DORSET　　　　　　　　　　2–4B

ⒶⒼ

Summer Lodge
Country House Hotel & Restaurant　**£ 78**
Summer Lodge DT2 0JR　(01935) 482000
*"Hidden-away in the lovely Dorset countryside", this "peaceful" small
country house hotel (Relais & Châteaux) makes "a brilliant place
to impress a date"; the staff "really know how to look after you",
the food is "excellent", and the wine "amazing".* / ***Sample dishes:*** *duo
of local beef 'croquette' & marinated, with rocket mayonnaise; seared local sea
bass with wild garlic linguini, shallot & herb 'vierge'; a trio of caramel desserts:
parfait, banoffee pie & sticky toffee.* ***Details:*** *www.summerlodgehotel.co.uk;
12m NW of Dorchester on A37; 9.30 pm; no shorts.* ***Accommodation:*** *24
rooms, from £340.*

EVESHAM, WORCESTERSHIRE　　　　　2–1C

Ⓐ

Evesham Hotel　　　**£ 42**
Coopers Ln WR11 1DA　(01386) 765566
*"An incredible range of wines from all over the world… excluding
France" is a highlight at "the best family-friendly hotel ever", which
is run, "with much humour", by the "eccentric" John Jenkinson;
the food is not the main point.* / ***Sample dishes:*** *slices of honeydew melon,
served with chilled blackberry & orange compote; coconut salmon & prawns;
plum soup with cinnamon cream filled profiteroles.*
Details: *www.eveshamhotel.com; 9.30 pm; booking: max 12.*
Accommodation: *40 rooms, from £117.*

EXETER, DEVON　　　　　　　　　　　1–3D

Ⓖ

Effings　　　**£ 33**
50 Fore St TQ9 5RP　(01803) 863435
*"Half a dozen tables at the back of a deli", offering some "lovely"
dishes, based in part on the shop's offering.* / ***Sample dishes:*** *Spanish
tasting plate; breton rabbit casserole; gratin of fresh-picked local fruits with
home-made ice cream.* ***Details:*** *www.effings.co.uk; 4.30 pm; closed Sun; no credit
cards.*

Café Paradiso
Hotel Barcelona **£ 42** Ⓐ
Magdalen St EX2 4HY (01392) 281000
*In a funky design-hotel, an "agreeable" dining room, with a pleasant
outdoor seating area; the food is "not bad, and sometimes very
good". / **Sample dishes:** risotto, field mushroom, wild garlic & pecorino; crisp
silver mullet fillet, wilted spinach, herb gnocchi & red wine sauce; treacle tart,
Devonshire clotted cream. **Details:** www.aliasbarcelona.com; 10 pm, Sun 9 pm;
booking: max 8. **Accommodation:** 46 rooms, from £125.*

Michael Caines
ABode **£ 63**
Cathedral Yd EX1 1HD (01392) 223 638
*This "spacious" and "elegant" ("slightly cold") dining room,
"overlooking the Cathedral", is generally praised as a "good but
pricey" venue; reports are mixed, though, and some reporters find
bills disproportionate. / **Sample dishes:** pan fried Brixham scallops with
crispy belly pork, pea purée, shallots & bacon velouté; roast loin of lamb with
potato boulangere, fennel purée & tapenade jus; lime leaf panna cotta with
coconut sorbet & exotic fruit salad. **Details:** www.abodehotels.co.uk; 9.30 pm;
closed Sun; booking essential. **Accommodation:** 53 rooms, from £125.*

FAIRFORD, GLOUCESTERSHIRE 2–2C

Allium **£ 52** ✪
1 London St GL7 4AH (01285) 712200
*Having survived the floods, Erica and James Graham's "charming and
relaxed restaurant in a pretty Cotswold village" has re-emerged as a
"welcoming" destination where "the food is sometimes amazing".
/ **Sample dishes:** poached wood pigeon with mushrooms and pan fried foie gras;
assiette of hogget; iced rhubarb and lavender parfait with clotted cream ice cream.
Details: www.allium.uk.net; 9pm; closed Mon, Tue, Wed L, Thu L, Fri L, Sat L &
Sun D; no Amex; booking: max 10.*

FALMOUTH, CORNWALL 1–4B

Bistro de la Mer **£ 39** Ⓣ
28 Arwenack St TR11 3JB (01326) 316509
*A French restaurant (run by an English family), which is "mainly
focussed on fish"; it attracts only a few reports, but all tipping it as
"quite exceptional". / **Sample dishes:** Cornish crab soup; roast rump
of marinated lamb, niçoise vegetables, black olives, beaujolais and thyme
reduction; valrhona dark chocolate and Grand Marnier chantilly, carrot and blood
orange syrup. **Details:** www.bistrodelamer.com; 9:30pm, 10pm weekend;
no Amex.*

The Flying Fish Restaurant Ⓣ
St Michael's Hotel & Spa **£ 36**
Gyllyngvase Beach TR11 4NB (01326) 312707
*A "smart"-ish restaurant, plus jollier bistro, in an agreeable, modern
family hotel. / **Sample dishes:** grilled gevrik goat's cheese with sweet & sour
beetroot, Granny Smith & pine nuts; duo of Cornish pork, confit belly, roast loin,
with lentils, bacon & a port jus; warm financier spiced poached pear with
home-made vanilla ice cream. **Details:** www.stmichaelshotel.co.uk; 9 pm,
9.30 pm Sat & Sun. **Accommodation:** 62 rooms, from £82.*

The Sticky Prawn **£ 46** ⭐

Flushing Quay TR11 5TY (01326) 373734

*"Fish as fresh as you've ever tasted, served right on the quay" – that's
the deal at this simple shed, which has fantastic harbour-views.*
/ Sample dishes: *duck & chicken liver parfait; Cornish shellfish linguini with chilli,
garlic & parsley; home-made strawberry shortbread with Cornish clotted cream.*
Details: *www.thestickyprawn.co.uk; late; closed Sun D.*

FARNHAM NR BLANDFORD, DORSET 2–3C

Museum Inn **£ 42** 🅰️⭐

DT11 8DE (01725) 516261
*"A special pub, deep in darkest Dorset" – a "smart but informal"
place that can seem "a surprising find, in the middle
of almost nowhere"; its high-quality "British food with a twist"
is "worth the drive". / Sample dishes:* *pastry case of sautéed chicken livers,
new forest mushrooms with tarragon and sherry vinegar; whole grilled lemon sole
and glazed salsify. saffron cocotte potatoes, tomatoes and chives; citrus lemon tart,
berry compote, mascarpone cream. Details:* *www.museuminn.co.uk; Off the
A354, signposted to Farnham; 9.30pm, 9pm Sun; no Amex. Accommodation:* *8
rooms, from £110.*

FAVERSHAM, KENT 3–3C

The Railway Hotel **£ 37** ⭐

Preston St ME13 8PE (01795) 538322
*"An attractive restoration of a formerly grotty Victorian pub", the rear
room of which is making quite a name for its "imaginative" and
"fairly-priced" cuisine (much of it "ethically-sourced and foraged");
the bar still makes a "decent" boozer too!*
/ Details: *www.railwayhotelfaversham.co.uk.*

Read's **£ 69** 🅰️⭐

Macknade Manor, Canterbury Rd ME13 8XE (01795) 535344

*"A very good place, and not just by Kent standards" – this "lovely
relaxed country house restaurant-with-rooms" remains widely praised
by reporters for its "very professional" standards across the board.
/ Details:* *www.reads.com; 9.30 pm; closed Mon & Sun. Accommodation:* *6
rooms, from £250.*

General Tarleton £ 41
Boroughbridge Rd HG5 0PZ (01423) 340284
*Feedback is a little up-and-down, but this "friendly" and "stylish" roadside gastropub generally impresses reporters with its "quality" cuisine. / **Sample dishes:** seafood in a crisp pastry bag with lobster sauce; crisped slow braised shoulder of lamb with creamed potatoes, spinach, thyme, confit garlic & tomato concasse jus; sticky toffee pudding with butterscotch sauce and vanilla pod ice cream. **Details:** www.generaltarleton.co.uk; 2m from A1, J48 towards Knaresborough; 9.15 pm. **Accommodation:** 14 rooms, from £129.*

The Bricklayers Arms £ 41 ✪
Hogpits Bottom HP3 0PH (01442) 833322
*"Wonderful and unpretentious cooking" – "just what pub food is all about" – makes this rural inn an "amazing" destination for most reporters; one or two sceptics, though, found "high hopes unfulfilled, after all this County Dining Pub of the year hype". / **Sample dishes:** home smoked duck breast with foie grasmi-cuit shavings served in a pastry basket with a leaf salad, grilled almonds and a honey dressing; chicken breast with melted mozzarella and pancettaserved with a tomato comfit and a basil cream*; bourbon vanilla crème brulée. **Details:** www.bricklayersarms.com; 9.30 pm, Sun 8.30 pm.*

The Griffin Inn £ 45 🅐✪
TN22 3SS (01825) 722890
*An "archetypal country gastropub", set "in a sleepy village", and with "commanding views" from its "fabulous" garden; as such, it's "an absolute tourist Mecca", and "not cheap", but the "reliable" cooking is "top-notch"; "when he's in full flow" – owner James adds "eccentric charm" too. / **Sample dishes:** fresh Portland crab, grilled courgette & fennel salad, aioli & crostini; rack of lamb, puy lentils, pancetta & rosemary, anchovy dressing; pear tart tatin. **Details:** www.thegriffininn.co.uk; off A272; 9.30 pm; closed Sun D (in winter). **Accommodation:** 13 rooms, from £85.*

Crannog £ 41 🅣
at the Waterfront, The Underwater Centre PH33 6DB
(01397) 705589
*"Back on the pier" (after a brief absence following a flood), this rather "romantic" establishment offers "reliable seafood in a great setting, overlooking Loch Linnhe". / **Sample dishes:** herb crusted haddock goujons; monkfish; cranachan panacotta (Drambuie, toasted oats, and honey panna cotta with raspberries). **Details:** www.crannog.net; 9 pm; no Amex.*

Inverlochy Castle £ 89 🅐✪
Torlundy PH33 6SN (01397) 702177
*You get "wonderful food and fantastic service", at this baronial pile, which has a "terrific setting" at the foot of Ben Nevis; if there is a 'catch', it's that – predictably – the food can seem "expensive" for what it is. / **Details:** www.inverlochycastlehotel.com; off A82, 4 m N of Ft. William; 10 pm; jacket & tie required at D; children: 8+ at D. **Accommodation:** 17 & gate lodge rooms, from £300.*

The Other Place   £ 40
41 Fore St PL23 1AH   (01726) 833636
"Excellent fish" and *"good views from the window tables"* –
two unbeatable attractions of this popular seaside spot (which is no
longer under the same ownership as Sam's).
/ ***Details:*** *www.samsfowey.co.uk; 9.30 pm; no Amex.*

The Q Restaurant
The Old Quay House   £ 50
28 Fore St PL23 1AQ   (01726) 833302
*On a sunny day, it's worth "fighting for a table on the terrace" –
which has "stunning" views – of this waterside boutique hotel;
the cuisine is "solid", but something of a supporting attraction.*
/ ***Sample dishes:*** *foie gras parfait, with sauternes jelly & sourdough; lemon sole
à la grénobloise; tarte Tatin with calvados crème fraîche.*
Details: *www.theoldquayhouse.com; 9 pm; children: 8+ at
D.* ***Accommodation:*** *12 rooms, from £160.*

Restaurant Nathan Outlaw
Marina Villa Hotel   £ 58
17 Esplanade PL23 1HY   (01726) 833315
*"Polished" cooking, using "excellent local ingredients", and at
"superb" prices, is already winning many accolades for this year-old
venture (from a chef who, on his travels, has left a small galaxy
of Michelin stars in his wake); the "spacious" dining room "overlooks
the beach", but it's ambience can seem rather "cold".*
/ ***Details:*** *www.themarinahotel.co.uk; 9 pm; closed Mon L, Tue L, Wed L, Thu L &
Sun; no jeans or trainers; children: 12+.* ***Accommodation:*** *37 rooms,
from £160.*

Sam's   £ 25
20 Fore St PL23 1AQ   (01726) 832273
*"Possibly the perfect holiday restaurant", this "fantastically popular
bistro" serves up "fresh and simple fish dishes" in a "great
atmosphere"; for some tastes it can get just a bit too "manic"
at night.* / ***Details:*** *www.samsfowey.co.uk; 10 pm.*

Chequers   £ 42
SG8 7SR   (01763) 208369
*Fans of this "lovely old place" say its "good and well-presented" fare
makes it "an object-lesson for upmarket pubs"; there's also a school
of though, which says it's "lost its edge".* / ***Sample dishes:*** *pan fried
scallop with a curly endive and mange tout salad with a ginger dressing served with
French bread; oven roast free range chicken breast stuffed with basil and
mozzarella wrapped in Parma ham served with champ potatoes and roast tomato
sauce; apple strudel with cream or ice cream.*
Details: *www.thechequersfowlmere.co.uk; on B1368 between Royston &
Cambridge; 9.30 pm; children: 14+.*

Off The Square   £ 35
3 Church St IP13 9BE   (01728) 621232
*"Very good, for the area, and with the stated intention of getting still
better" – Suffolk foodies are very keen to support this "professional
but informal" all-rounder; it has a "great location", and "should
be more popular".* / ***Details:*** *www.otsframltd.co.uk; 9.15 pm; closed Mon &
Sun D.*

The Fox & Goose £ 37 🅐 ⭐
IP21 5PB (01379) 586247
"Adventurous" cooking is served in a "gorgeous" setting, at Paul Yaxley and Sarah Farrar's village inn; it's a "really friendly and helpful" place too. / *Sample dishes:* open ravioli with crab, prawns & smoked salmon with fresh herbs, tomato confit & lemon; loin of pork with fondant potatoes, with apple & parsley crumble, mushroom boudin, spinach & pork jus; passion fruit parfait with strawberries & black pepper & sesame seed meringue biscuit. *Details:* www.foxandgoose.net; off A140; 8.45 pm, Fri & Sat 9 pm, Sun 8.15 pm; closed Mon; no Amex; children: 9+ for D.

Alford Arms £ 37
HP1 3DD (01442) 864480
"If you don't know the local lanes, then finding the place can be a bit of an adventure", but this "friendly rural pub" – in an "exquisite village" – is "always full, even on weekdays" thanks to its "hearty" and "above-average" fare. / *Sample dishes:* oak smoked bacon on bubble and squeak with holandaise sauce; crispy Oxfordshire pork belly and onion roly poly with sticky roast parsnips; crème brûlée.
Details: www.alfordarmsfrithsden.co.uk; near Ashridge College and vineyard; 10 pm; booking: max 12.

Headlam Hall £ 43 🅐
DL2 3HA (01325) 730238
A "friendly" and "cheerful" country house hotel; its cuisine has no great aspirations, but almost invariably seems to 'hit the spot'. / *Details:* www.headlamhall.co.uk; 9.15 pm; no shorts. **Accommodation:** 40 rooms, from £110.

Elephant Royale £ 40 🅣
579-581 Cranbrook Rd IG2 6JZ (020) 8551 7015
A superior 'local' restaurant (which has a better-known sibling on the Isle of Dogs), tipped for its "well-prepared and cooked Thai fare"; be warned, though – the pianist can be "loud". / *Sample dishes:* Thai spare ribs; grilled duck on a bed of fried spinach & tamarind sauce; Thai pancakes. *Details:* www.elephantroyale.com; 11.30 pm.

Eslington Villa Hotel £ 35
8 Station Rd NE9 6DR (0191) 487 6017
It's located "in the middle of the town", but this old-fashioned establishment has the feel of a "country house hotel"; most (if not quite all) reports praise its "very traditional" and "consistent" cooking. / *Sample dishes:* smoked salmon & seafood rillette with marinated peppers, rocket & aged balsamic; roast chicken breast with goat's cheese polenta, grilled vegetables & rocket pesto; chocolate truffle with black cherries & vanilla mascarpone. *Details:* www.eslingtonvilla.co.uk; A1 exit for Team Valley Trading Estate, then left off Eastern Avenue; 9.30 pm; closed Sat L & Sun D. **Accommodation:** 18 rooms, from £89.50.

Perhaps it's the inspiration of *Rogano* – the famously Art Deco seafood restaurant – which has led to a certain fish-and-seafood bias among Glasgow's leading restaurants. Such dishes are the speciality at *Gamba* (food-wise, probably the best place in town) as well as at the popular *Two Fat Ladies*. The latter operation now has a splendid new outpost in the attractive Victorian 'Buttery' building. The city also has a vibrant Indian restaurant scene, with *Mother India* long the top tip in town.

Otherwise, it's difficult to avoid the feeling that the Glasgow restaurant scene is a bit cosy and complacent. It's wonderful, in some ways, that the city keeps alive such institutions as *Rogano* and the very '70s *Ubiquitous Chip*, but these establishments do give the impression that they are resting on their laurels nowadays.

Babbity Bowster £ 33
16-18 Blackfriar's St G1 1PE   (0141) 552 5055
This Merchant City "stalwart" in a Robert Adam-designed building is one of the city's best-known hostelries; if "not exciting", the food is "OK", in both the bar and the dining room upstairs.
/ **Sample dishes:** steamed west coast mussels in a creamy white wine sauce; herb and Dijon mustard rack of lamb with a thyme and red wine jus; white chocolate and raspberry terrine. **Details:** www.babbity.com; 10.30 pm; D only, closed Mon & Sun. **Accommodation:** 6 rooms, from £60.

Brian Maule at Chardon D'Or £ 56
176 West Regent St G2 4RL   (0141) 248 3801
A "handsome room" and "first-class" service have helped make Brian Maule's "understated" venture something of "an expense-accounter's favourite"; the cooking is "uneven", though, and can seem "overpriced". / **Sample dishes:** fried ox tongue salad with capers, gherkins, shallots, sherry vinegar jus; canon of lamb fillet with crushed peas, hint of mint, deep fried parsnip crisp; citrus tart with a rhubarb sorbet.
Details: www.brianmaule.com; 9.30 pm; closed Sat L & Sun.

(Two Fat Ladies at) The Buttery £ 41
652 Argyle St G3 8UF   (0141) 221 8188

WINNER 2009

RÉMY MARTIN
FINE CHAMPAGNE COGNAC

With its "lovely old-style glamour" and "very good fish and seafood", this local fish franchise has finally put some much-needed va-va-voom into these impressive old Victorian premises, near the SECC.
/ **Sample dishes:** roast free range chicken Caesar salad; fillet of wild brown trout, prawns, asparagus, orange and almond butter; biscuit and banana pavlova.
Details: www.twofatladiesrestaurant.com; 10 pm.

Café Gandolfi　　　　　　　　　**£ 37**　　　Ⓐ

64 Albion St G1 1NY   (0141) 552 6813

"There's a great buzz" at this Merchant City favourite, known for its *"lovely"* décor and *"super"* staff, not its *"limited"* menu; there's also a *"superb selection of wines"* (available both in the café, and the upstairs bar, which is a *"good-value"* dining destination in its own right). / **Sample dishes:** *cullen skink; smoked venison with gratin dauphinose; rhubarb tart.* **Details:** www.cafegandolfi.com; near Tron Theatre; 11.30 pm; no booking, Sat.

Café India　　　　　　　　　**£ 35**　　　Ⓣ

171 North St G1 1LH   (0141) 248 4074

Re-located, after a fire, within the Merchant City, this local institution is tipped for offering some *"unusual"* dishes; it is again sometimes nominated as offering *"the best curry in Glasgow"*. / **Sample dishes:** *onion bhaji; chicken tikka.* **Details:** www.cafeindiaglasgow.com; midnight.

The Dhabba　　　　　　　　　**£ 34**　　　✪

44 Candleriggs G1 1LE   (0141) 5531249

An *"innovative"* menu makes it worth seeking out this *"buzzy"* Merchant City Indian, which is also of note for its *"excellent"* and *"extremely friendly"* service. **Sample dishes:** *lamb soup with peppercorn; spicy panfried monkfish; milk dumplings fried and soaked in sugar syrup.* **Details:** www.thedhabba.com; 11 pm.

La Fiorentina　　　　　　　　　**£ 40**　　　Ⓣ

2 Paisley Rd, West G51 1LE   (0141) 4201585

A *"top-class Italian"*, on the outskirts of the city, that's tipped as *"worth seeking out"*, thanks not least to its *"unusually good and varied"* menu and wine list. / **Sample dishes:** *bruschetta margherita; pizza topped with mozzarella, Dolcelatte cheese, apple and crushed hazelnuts; zuppa italia.* **Details:** www.la-fiorentina.com; 10.30 pm; closed Sun.

Gamba　　　　　　　　　**£ 52**　　　✪✪

225a West George St G2 2ND   (0141) 572 0899

"Exquisite" and *"flavourful"* dishes – *"a wide range of fish and seafood, but also catering well for non-fish-eaters"* – contribute to the *"very enjoyable"* experience on offer at this city-centre basement; it's also tipped as *"a great venue for a business lunch"*. / **Sample dishes:** *fish soup with crabmeat, stem ginger and prawn dumplings; pan-fried hake with capers, shrimps, whole almonds and parsley; five spice panna cotta with poached pears.* **Details:** www.gamba.co.uk; 10.30 pm; closed Sun; children: 14+.

Gandolfi Fish　　　　　　　　　**£ 40**

64 Albion St G1 1NY   (0141) 552 9475

An *"urban-chic"* offshoot of Cafe Gandolfi, mostly praised as a *"welcome addition just a few doors up from the original"*, with *"very good-quality fish dishes"*; misfires, however, are not unknown. / **Details:** www.cafegandolfi.com; 10.30 pm, Sun 9 pm.

Ichiban　　　　　　　　　**£ 23**　　　Ⓣ

50 Queen St G1 3DS   (0141) 204 4200

A city-centre oriental tipped for *"sushi and other delights"*, at *"great-value"* prices; there's another branch at 184 Dumbarton Road (tel 334 9222). / **Sample dishes:** *beef chilli ramen; kaisen rice.* **Details:** www.ichiban.co.uk; 10 pm, Fri & Sat 11 pm; need 10+ to book.

The Italian Kitchen   **£ 33** Ⓣ
64 Ingram St G1 1EX   (0141) 5721472
A "very busy" Merchant City pizzeria; it's sometimes criticised for
being a bit complacent, but still tipped for "good pizza and pasta".
/ **Sample dishes:** mussels in white wine and cream; daube of beef in red wine
sauce; caramelised apple tart and caramel sauce and ice cream.
Details: www.italian-kitchen.co.uk; in the heart of the Merchant City, to the
east of the city centre; 10 pm, 10.30 pm Fri & Sat.

Kember & Jones   **£ 26** Ⓣ
134 Byres Rd G12 8TD   (0141) 337 3851
Tipped for its "wonderful soups, cakes and coffee", this West End
café has quite a reputation; indeed, they can get "too busy… and
sometimes it shows". / **Details:** www.kemberandjones.co.uk; 10 pm,
Sun 6 pm; no booking.

Mother India   **£ 30** ⭐⭐
28 Westminster Ter G3 7RU   (0141) 221 1663
"Glasgow's best Indian", for some reporters – a "great-value"
institution, south of Kelvingrove Park, serving up "tapas"-style dishes,
which deliver some "terrific flavours". / **Details:** www.motherindia.co.uk;
beside Kelvingrove Hotel; 10.30 pm; closed Mon L & Tue L.

Number 16   **£ 32** Ⓣ
16 Byres Rd G11 5JY   (0141) 339 2544
A "tiny bistro-style restaurant", near Dumbarton Road, invariably
tipped for "good food and value". / **Sample dishes:** hot smoked salmon &
watercress salad with alioli; braised belly of pork with spiced green lentils,
pak choi & baby corn; walnut & honey tart with banana parfait.
Details: www.number16.co.uk; 10 pm, 9 pm Sun.

Paperinos   **£ 31** Ⓣ
283 Sauchiehall St G2 3HQ   (0141) 332 3800
Tipped as usual for its "good standards", this popular pizza house
remains as reliable as ever; there's also a West End branch (at 227
Bryres Road, tel 0141 334 3811). / **Sample dishes:** smoked salmon
roulade; pappardelle monteprandone; New York cheesecake with chocolate chip
ice-cream. **Details:** www.paperinos.com; 10.50 pm.

Rogano Seafood Bar & Restaurant **£ 62** Ⓐ
11 Exchange Pl G1 3AN   (0141) 248 4055
A "superb Art Deco space" makes this "long-in-the-tooth" city-centre
legend "a memorable destination"; it's a shame, though, that the food
is so resolutely "average", and "pricey" too.
/ **Details:** www.roganoglasgow.com; 10.30 pm.

Sarti's   **£ 30** Ⓐ
121 Bath St G2 2SZ   (0141) 204 0440
A "genuine family-Italian", in the city-centre, famed for its "excellent"
pizzas and its "lively" atmosphere; nowadays, however,
some reporters find the place rather "uninspiring".
/ **Details:** www.sarti.co.uk; 10.30 pm; no booking at L.

78 St Vincent £ 42 Ⓣ

78 St Vincent's St G2 5UB   (0141) 248 7878

A city-centre brasserie in an impressive former banking hall; it's a handy sort of place, of most note for its "great atmosphere".
/ ***Sample dishes:*** *langoustines with rocket and sesame chili and ginger dressing; breast of Mallard duck with confit black on re wine mulled pear with a star anise scented sauce; chocolate, honey, and rosemary tart served with fresh berries.*
Details: *www.78stvincent.com; 2 mins from George Sq; 10 pm, Fri & Sat 10.30.*

Stravaigin £ 45 ✪

28 Gibson St G12 8NX   (0141) 334 2665

Recently re-launched, Colin Clydesdale's "busy", "Scottish-fusion" bar/restaurant has maintained its position as a Glaswegian "favourite", known for "exotic" creations prepared "with a very sure touch". / ***Details:*** *www.stravaigin.com; 11 pm; Mon-Thu D only, Fri-Sun open L & D.*

The Butterfly & The Pig £ 26 Ⓣ

153 Bath St G2 4SQ   (0141) 221 7711

An informal bar/restaurant, tipped for its use of "fresh supplies straight from farmers around Scotland".
/ ***Details:*** *www.thebutterflyandthepig.com; 9 pm, Sun 6 pm; no Amex.*

Two Fat Ladies £ 37 ✪

88 Dumbarton Rd G11 6NX   (0141) 339 1944

"A long-standing Glasgow institution", this "nice little restaurant" has quite a name for "glorious seafood"; there's a branch in the city-centre too (at 118a Blythswood Street, tel 847 0088), and also at the Buttery (see also). / ***Sample dishes:*** *roast pepper and pesto tart, glazed goats' cheese; fillet of sea bass, mustard and syboe mash; strawberry pavlova.*
Details: *www.twofatladiesrestaurant.com; 10.30 pm.*

Ubiquitous Chip £ 58 Ⓐ

12 Ashton Ln G12 8SJ   (0141) 334 5007

This "once-excellent" Glasgow "institution" risks "trading on past glories" nowadays; with its "lively" atmosphere and "attractive" décor, it's "still fun", but the "seasonal Scottish fare" is too often "mediocre" and "too expensive". / ***Sample dishes:*** *pan fried scallops with potato rosti, stewed garlic & a Chambéry coral sauce; pork fillet stuffed with prunes, with garlic crushed potatoes, lemon & vermouth carrots; strawberry brioche with basil ice cream.* ***Details:*** *www.ubiquitouschip.co.uk; behind Hillhead station; 11 pm.*

GODALMING, SURREY 3–3A

Bel & The Dragon £ 42 Ⓐ

Bridge St GU7 3DU   (01483) 527333

It's the setting in a "fantastic converted church" that makes this "lively" branch of a small gastropub chain of particular note; even if the food does come in "massive" portions, though, it's often "not as special as you'd hope". / ***Sample dishes:*** *tian of crab with guacamole, tomato broth & herb salad served with melba toast; half a roast free range corn fed chicken with hand cut chips, sage and onion stuffing, bread sauce and roasting jus; chocolate nut browie with mint chocolate chip ice cream and chocolate sauce.*
Details: *www.belandthedragon-godalming.co.uk; 10 pm, Sat 10.30, Sun 9 pm; no Amex.*

La Luna   **£ 47**   ⭐

10-14 Wharf St   GU7 INN   (01483) 414155

Often reported to be "worth a detour" – or "the best Italian for miles around" – this town-centre operation is a "classy" place, where the "superb" wine list is of particular note; the cooking, though, can sometimes be "inconsistent". / **Sample dishes:** *tempura courgette flower stuffed with mozzarella and served in a chilled tomato guazzetto; pan fried guinea fowl breast and leg confit in its own jus and sweet and sour aubergine; Tahitian vanilla panna cotta served with fresh strawberries.*
Details: *www.lalunarestaurant.co.uk; Between the High Street and Flambard Way; 10 pm; closed Mon & Sun.*

GODSTONE, SURREY   3–3B

The Bell   **£ 35**   Ⓣ

128 High St   RH9 8DX   (01883) 741877

A simple gastropub, which continues to be tipped for its decent across-the-board standards. / **Sample dishes:** *caramelised onion tart, goats cheese, rocket; venison, wild mushroom, baby onion, pancetta hot pot; apple and blackberry crumble with custard.* **Details:** *www.thebellgodstone.co.uk; 11.*

GOLCAR, WEST YORKSHIRE   5–1C

The Weavers Shed   **£ 55**   ⭐

Knowl Rd   HD7 4AN   (01484) 654284

"Fine local ingredients" (often "home-grown") are presented in "interesting combinations", at the Jackson family's "homely" but "first-class" dining room, in a former mill; NB: lunch – when a "very simple" menu is offered – is noted as much less of an attraction than dinner. / **Details:** *www.weaversshed.co.uk; 9 pm; closed Mon, Sat L & Sun.*
Accommodation: *5 rooms, from £90.*

GOLDSBOROUGH, NORTH YORKSHIRE   8–3D

The Fox And Hounds Inn   **£ 38**   Ⓐ⭐

YO21 3RX   (01947) 893372

"Really good simple food, beautifully cooked and presented", and "incredible views" too – the only thing wrong with ex-Ivy chef Jason Davies's cliff-top inn is that it's "rather difficult to find". / **Details:** *8.30 pm; closed Mon, Tue & Sun D; no Amex.*

GORING, BERKSHIRE   2–2D

Leatherne Bottel   **£ 63**   Ⓐ

Bridleway   RG8 0HS   (01491) 872667

"A great spot for watching the sunset", this long-established riverside spot is presided over by a "charming chef/directrice"; a few critics say "it's lost its X factor" of late, but most accounts still say this is "a real out-of-town treat". / **Sample dishes:** *hand picked Portland crab, crab croquette and lemon aioli; roast saddle of venison and lemon, thyme fondant potatoes, creamed leeks, ratatouille, jumiper and red wine sauce; brandy snap basket and selection of home-made ice creams and sorbets.*
Details: *www.leathernebottel.co.uk; 0.5m outside Goring on B4009; 9 pm; closed Mon & Sun D; children: 10+ for D.*

GRANGE-OVER-SANDS, CUMBRIA   7–4D

Hazelmere   **£ 31**
1-2 Yewbarrow Ter LA11 6ED   (01539) 532972
"Mouth-watering cakes", "excellent home-style cooking", and an
"impressive range" of both tea and coffee – that's the deal at this
"beautiful" Victorian café, in a notoriously "sedate" town.
/ **Sample dishes:** *potato pancakes with smoked salmon & lime crème fraîche*
sauce; Cambrian lamb tattiepot with home-made pickled red cabbage;
Cumberland rum nicky with locally made ice cream.
Details: *www.hazelmerecafe.co.uk; Nr Grange-over-Sands; L only.*

GRASMERE, CUMBRIA   7–3D

The Jumble Room   **£ 41**   **Ⓐ ✪**
Langdale Rd LA22 9SU   (01539) 435188
This small restaurant in a pretty village is "a delightful find" –
a "consistently friendly and enjoyable" place, serving "great fresh
food". / **Sample dishes:** *Hyderabad chicken marinated in cardomom, garlic, chili*
and yoghurt and fresh mango and soused carrots; roast organic lamb and new
potatoes, rosemary, garlic, ratatouille and baked fennel; ginger biscuit crunch and
lemon posset and cherries. **Details:** *www.thejumbleroom.co.uk; Halfway along the*
Langdale road, between two hotels; midnight; closed Mon & Tue; no Amex.

GREAT BARROW, CHESHIRE   5–2A

The Foxcote   **£ 34**   **Ⓣ**
Station Ln CH3 7JN   (01244) 301343
A "friendly" restaurant in a former pub, where the food is tipped for
its "high standards"; fish is the house speciality. / **Sample dishes:** *tower*
of avocado and brown shrimps; pan-fried sea bass with crab & banana crumble;
dark chocolate nemesis with poached pear and mandarin sorbet.
Details: *www.thefoxcote.com; 9.30; closed Sun D.*

GREAT DUNMOW, ESSEX   3–2C

Starr   **£ 69**   **Ⓐ**
Market Pl CM6 1AX   (01371) 874321
"It just gets better and better", says one of the many fans of this
quarter-centenarian market square "gem", which is "run by people
who are passionate about food, and focussed on serving their
customers"; overall perceptions, however, are undercut by the
vociferous minority who find prices "way OTT". / **Sample dishes:** *Devon*
crab with brown shrimp, avocado purée, crème fraîche; John Dory roast in ras
al hanout, spiced cauliflower, crisp onions, golden sultanas; vanilla parfait &
toasted bread praline, raspberries, peach sorbet. **Details:** *www.the-starr.co.uk;*
8m E of M11, J8 on A120; 9.30 pm; closed Sun D; no jeans or trainers.
Accommodation: *8 rooms, from £130.*

GREAT GONERBY, LINCOLNSHIRE   5–3D

Harry's Place   **£ 75**   **✪ ✪**
17 High St NG31 8JS   (01476) 561780
"You know you're experiencing something special", when you visit the
Hallams family's "hidden gem"; it's not just the "lovingly-prepared"
food (by Harry) or the "quite exceptional" service (by Caroline),
but also the fact that "there are only three tables, at which
a maximum of ten people in total can be served...".
/ **Sample dishes:** *tureen of Orkney scallops, red pepper, and leeks set in a*
sauternes and herb jelly; loin of black pork with foie gras de canard and Bramley
apple, served with a sauce of Vouvray, sage and tarragon; cherry brandy jelly
served with yogurt and black pepper. **Details:** *on B1174 1m N of Grantham;*
9.30 pm; closed Mon & Sun; no Amex; booking essential; children: 5+.

Anupam Restaurant   **£ 30**
85 Church St WR14 2AE (01684) 573814
"Very popular, and deservedly so"; Mr Khayser's colourfully-decorated
Indian, near the theatre, is a magnet for *"curry addicts"*.
/ **Sample dishes:** *poppadoms and chutneys; dalloshi chicken.*
Details: *www.anupam.co.uk; midnight.*

Le Manoir aux Quat' Saisons   **£125**
Church Rd OX44 7PD (01844) 278881

"Superb in every respect"; Raymond Blanc *"puts all 'ees lurve"* into
this *"breathtakingly beautiful"* manor house, *"and it shows through"* –
both in the *"exquisite"* food, and in service that *"goes the extra mile"*;
the bill may be *"as mind-blowing as the wine list"*, but most reporters
find a visit here *"worth every penny"*. / **Sample dishes:** *smoked haddock
soup, seabass tartare and oscietra caviar; assiette of suckling pig in its own
roasting juices; finest home-made croustade pastry with caramelised braeburn
apples, honey and ginger ice cream.* **Details:** *www.manoir.com; from M40, J7 take
A329 towards Wallingford; 10 pm.* **Accommodation:** *32 rooms, from £395.*

The Nags Head   **£ 40**
London Rd HP16 0DG (01494) 862200
*Early days for the new régime at this Chilterns boozer, but it's already
tipped for its "fabulous food and ambience".* / **Sample dishes:** *brochette
of tiger prawns on a rosemary stick with a seasonal vegetable stir fry & a light
curry cream; pan fried fillets of sea bream served with a saffron, white wine &
cream sauce with vegetable crisps; crepe filled with a Cointreau mascarpone
cream & citrus fruits.* **Details:** *www.nagsheadbucks.com; Off the A413; 9.30 pm;
closed Sun D.* **Accommodation:** *7 rooms, from £90.*

Falkland Arms   **£ 34**
The Green OX7 4DB (01608) 683653
*A "fabulous" pub, say fans, who tip its "good home-cooking" and
"one of the best selections of whisky and unusual wines".*
/ **Sample dishes:** *baked fig stuffed with goat's cheese, Parma ham, and quince
jelly; pan fried sea bass, spring vegetables and new potatoes; sticky toffee pudding.*
Details: *www.falklandarms.org.uk; A361 between Banbury & Chipping Norton;
8 pm; closed Sun D; children: 16+.* **Accommodation:** *5 rooms, from £80.*

The Inn At Grinshill   £ 44   Ⓣ
The High St SY4 3BL   (01939) 220410
*In a part of the world without too many such places, a country pub tipped for its "imaginative menus", and "lovely staff" too.
/ **Sample dishes:** tiger prawns & king scallops kebab; pan fried duck breast, warm onion & orange marmalade, fondant potato & red berry jus; baked vanilla cheesecake, red berries & red wine syrup. **Details:** www.theinnatgrinshill.co.uk; 9.30 pm; no Amex. **Accommodation:** 6 rooms, from £120.*

Auberge   £ 44   Ⓐ
Jerbourg Rd, St Martin's GY4 6BH   (01481) 238485
*As well as "brilliant views" (towards St Peter Port), this contemporary cliff-top venture offers food of "consistently good quality" (with "interesting" fish dishes a highlight). / **Sample dishes:** Gorgonzola panna cotta with tomato and pepper chutney and roast cashew nuts; beef fillet Wellington with roast cèpes fine green beans and roast garlic jus; soft centered chocolate and banana bread pudding with milk chocolate ice cream. **Details:** www.theauberge.gg; 9 pm.*

Christophe   £ 48   Ⓐ⭐
Fermain Ln GY1 1ZZ   (01481) 230725
*"Divine" – Christophe Vincent's "fantastic" and "so friendly" spot inspires rave reviews from all (but one) of the reporters who comment on it, with the crab lasagne, in particular, a top tip; the hillside location, "with a great view out to sea" is "hard to beat" too. / **Sample dishes:** langostine in ginger broth; saddle of venison, chestnut purée, chocolate oil; prune and armagnac iced nougat. **Details:** www.christophe-restaurant.co.uk; 10 pm; closed Mon & Sun D.*

Da Nello   £ 35
46 Lower Pollet St, St Peter Port GY1 1WF   (01481) 721552
*In the heart of St Peter Port, a "busy" and "friendly" Italian veteran, housed in surprisingly impressive premises; reporters universally hail it as a "reliable" and "good-value" choice. / **Sample dishes:** roast sweet balsamic onions; fillet of John Dory with scalloped potatoes and saffron oil; marscapone and ginger cheesecake. **Details:** 10 pm.*

Le Petit Bistro   £ 40   Ⓣ
56 Le Pollet GY1 1WF   (01481) 725055
*A "very cosy" St Peter Port establishment, tipped for its "good romantic setting", and its "very French" approach. / **Details:** www.lepetitbistro.co.uk; 10 pm, 10.30 pm Fri & Sat; closed Sun.*

Café de Paris   £ 40
35 Castle St GU1 3UQ   (01483) 534896
*It may look "worryingly like a Café Rouge", but this "old-fashioned" town-centre fixture has something of a following for its "solid" cuisine; critics, though, dismiss the food as "much of a muchness". / **Sample dishes:** roast goat cheese served with mixed lettuce and citrus dressing; casserole of rabbit with mustard sauce, baby spinach and sauté potatoes; rhubarb crumble. **Details:** www.cafedeparisguildford.co.uk; 9.30 mon-thu, 10.30 fri&sat.*

Dolce Vita   **£ 43**   **T**

Trinity Gate, 14 Epsom Rd GU1 3JQ   (01483) 511544

An "attractive" modern Italian, tipped for its good-all-round standards; there's also a ground-floor Spanish tapas bar, but it attracted less feedback this year. / Sample dishes: smoked haddock and salmon pâté with melba toast and sour cream and dill dip; grilled calf liver and baconserved with chive mash, roast garlic and shallots; claire fontaineorange charlotte on Grand Marnier sponge. Details: www.dolcevitarestaurant.co.uk; 10.30pm; closed Sun D.

Rumwong   **£ 34**   **A**

18-20 London Rd GU1 2AF   (01483) 536092

"Even Thais eat here", observes a fan of this long-established, family-run spot; the food is often "excellent", but the place is particularly known for its "special and different" atmosphere.
/ Details: www.rumwong.com; 10.30 pm; closed Mon; no Amex.

The Thai Terrace   **£ 35**   **A ✪**

Castle Car Pk, Sydenham Rd GU1 3RT   (01483) 503350

"The location – the top of a car park – is unpromising", but "Guildford is lucky" to have this "classy" Thai "oasis", with its "exotic" décor, "super views" and "enjoyable" food; the place can, however, get "very noisy and busy". / Details: opposite Guildford Castle in town centre; 11 pm; closed Sun.

GULLANE, EAST LOTHIAN   9–4D

La Potinière   **£ 52**   **✪**

Main St EH31 2AA   (01620) 843214

"Like dining in someone's house… but with better food!"; this "intimate" and "self-effacing" destination offers "lovingly-crafted", and "locally-sourced" cuisine, and – thanks to the efforts of co-owners Keith Marley and Mary Runciman – is "always a very enjoyable experience". / Details: www.la-potiniere.co.uk; 20m E of Edinburgh, off A198; 8.30 pm; closed Mon & Tue; Oct-Apr closed Sun D; no Amex; booking essential.

GULWORTHY, DEVON   1–3C

Horn of Plenty   **£ 65**   **✪**

PL19 8JD   (01822) 832528

"A lovely setting overlooking the Tamar Valley" has long been a high-point at this celebrated restaurant-with-rooms; on the food front, it has attracted mixed feedback in recent times, but recent reports have tended more to praise its "beautifully-presented" cuisine.
/ Sample dishes: pan fried scallops wrapped in smoked salmon on a pea pancake with light white wine & truffle velouté; loin of Devonshire lamb with red wine shallots & cassis flavoured sauce; delice of chocolate with hazelnut sauce & orange confit. Details: www.thehornofplenty.co.uk; 3m W of Tavistock on A390; 9 pm; no jeans or trainers; children: 10+ at D. Accommodation: 10 rooms, from £160.

GUNTHORPE, NOTTINGHAMSHIRE   5–3D

Tom Browns Brasserie   **£ 37**   **T**

The Old School Hs NG14 7FB   (0115) 9663642

A romantic river-sider that's "worth a journey" for its "great food" (and, in particular, its "great-value early-bird menu").
/ Sample dishes: home smoked Gressingham duck breast, with mouli, spring onion & diakon & sekora cress salad; spiced rump of lamb with squash purée, parsnip rosti & lamb jus; rich chocolate fondant with orange peel ice cream. Details: www.tombrowns.co.uk; 10 pm.

Amba £ 33

106-108 Ashley Rd WA14 2UN (0161) 928 2343

Among the many restaurants in this affluent suburb, this "attractive" contemporary outfit is "extremely popular", and particularly tipped for its lunch and early-evening menus. / *Sample dishes:* oven baked field mushrooms with grilled Cornish brie, roast tomato with balsamic syrup; Mexican chargrilled chicken with green salad, guacamole, red pepper relish and sour cream and crispy potato skins; warm treacle tart with lemongrass crepe. *Details:* www.amba.uk.com; 0.5m SE of Altrincham; 10.30 pm.

Design House £ 40

Dean Clough HX3 5AX (01422) 383242

"The epitome of cool" – the dining facilities of this former mill, now housing an arts and media centre, are tipped for their "excellent" standards all-round, with meat dishes a highlight. / *Sample dishes:* chilled trio of melon, cinnamon syrup and melon soup; spiced Moroccan lamb shank, almond, cinnamon and chick pea beignet, harisa dressing; glazed coffee brûlée tart, iced cappuccino. *Details:* www.designhouserestaurant.co.uk; from Halifax follow signs to Dean Clough Mills; 9.30 pm; closed Sat L & Sun.

1885 The Restaurant £ 33

Recreation Ground HX4 9AJ (01422) 373030

An "unpretentious family-run restaurant", in converted Victorian cottages overlooking the Pennines; it is distinguished – say most reports – by its "warm" and "personal" service and its "consistently fabulous food". / *Sample dishes:* quail poached in honey, pickled beetroot,caramelised pistachios, fennel shoots; roast Goosnargh duck, glazed poached pear,chorizo tappenade; vanilla cream with champagne poached strawberries. *Details:* www.1885therestaurant.co.uk; 9.30 pm; closed Mon, Tue–Sat D only, closed Sun D; no Amex.

Shibden Mill Inn £ 39

Shibden Mill Fold HX3 7UL (01422) 365840

This ancient inn – which has a "formal" upstairs dining room – is uniformly praised as an "outstanding all-round experience". / *Details:* www.shibdenmillinn.com; off the A58, Leeds/Bradford road; 9.15 pm, Sun 7.30 pm. *Accommodation:* 11 rooms, from £95.

Finch's Arms £ 31

Oakham Rd LE15 8TL (01572) 756575

"Expansive views across Rutland Water" give this "gastropub-with-rooms" a "great setting"; service can be a touch "hit-and-miss", but it's an "engaging" spot offering food that's "competent, and not overpriced". / *Sample dishes:* scallops; Gressingham duck breast; cherry trifle. *Details:* www.finchsarms.co.uk; 9.30 pm, Sun 8 pm. *Accommodation:* 6 rooms, from £75.

Hambleton Hall   **£ 85**   Ⓐ⭐⭐

LE15 8TH   (01572) 756991

Set in "lovely" grounds, and with "outstanding views" over Rutland Water, Tim Hart's "serene" and "welcoming" country house hotel offers a "perfect" setting in which to enjoy Aaron Patterson's "exquisite" cuisine; prices, of course, are "eye-watering".
/ **Sample dishes:** *mosaic of chicken, foie gras & veal sweetbreads, with hazelnuts & orange; braised troncon of turbot witth morels & English asparagus; passion fruit soufflé with passion fruit & banana sorbet.*
Details: *www.hambletonhall.com; near Rutland Water; 9.30 pm.*
Accommodation: *17 rooms, from £205.*

Caffe La Fiamma   **£ 35**   Ⓐ

Hampton Court Rd   KT8 9BY   (020) 8943 2050

A "friendly" Italian, with "great views over Bushey Park"; "for a tourist area, the food is surprisingly good too". / **Sample dishes:** *cup mushrooms filled with herbs, garlic and Parmesan cheese in a white wine baked in the oven in bechamel sauce; long pasta with lobster meat, sping onions and cherry tomatoes in a white wine sauce; panna cotta.*
Details: *www.lafiamma.co.uk; 11 pm.*

Castle Cottage   **£ 46**   Ⓣ

Pen Llech   LL46 2YL   (01766) 780479

Overlooking Harlech Castle, a restaurant-with-rooms tipped for the quality of both its seafood and its steak. / **Sample dishes:** *goats cheese grilled on a red onion marmalade croute with a carpaccio of beetroot; rack of local lamb roast with a herb crust, served with rosemary & garlic mashed potatoes, red wine jus; home-made ice creams or sorbets.*
Details: *www.castlecottageharlech.co.uk; nr the castle, just off the high street; 9 pm; D only; no Amex.* **Accommodation:** *7 rooms, from £106.*

Maes y Neuadd   **£ 47**   Ⓐ⭐

Talsarnau   LL47 6YA   (01766) 780200

"Old-fashioned and charming" — this country house hotel, with views of Snowdon, pleases all round, not least with "wonderful food, from their own estate". / **Sample dishes:** *pressed tureen of ham hock, potato and spring onion with beetroot salad; pressed braised belly and loin of pork and lentil casserole, with creamy spring cabbage; pear and anise tarte Tatin with orange cream.* **Details:** *www.neuadd.com; 3m N of Harlech off B4573; 8.45 pm; no Amex; no shorts; children: 8+.* **Accommodation:** *15 rooms, from £99.*

The Star Inn £ 49
YO62 5JE (01439) 770397

"Probably Britain's best gastropub" – Andrew & Jacquie Pern's "rustic" legend "excels on every level"; the "cosy" interior is "gorgeously romantic", staff are "always welcoming" and the "locally-sourced" food, served in hearty portions, is "fabulous" too.
/ **Sample dishes:** dressed white crab meat with plum tomato & basil salad, green herb mayonnaise, bloody mary dressing; pan roast haunch of roe deer with a little venison 'cottage pie', Scottish girolle mushroom & tarragon juices; baked ginger parkin with rhubarb ripple ice cream, spiced syrup.
Details: www.thestaratharome.co.uk; 3m SE of Helmsley off A170; 9.30 pm, Sun 6 pm; closed Mon L & Sun D; no Amex. **Accommodation:** 14 rooms, from £130.

Bean Tree £ 42
20a Leyton Rd AL5 2HU (01582) 460901
"Standards are well up to those in London", say supporters of this ambitious local; there's also quite a lot of feedback, however, to the effect that it's been "resting on its laurels" of late. / **Sample dishes:** field mushroom soup with black truffle oil; pot roast guinea fowl with mustard puy lentils and game jus; poached ear with chocolate brownie and fruit coulis.
Details: www.thebeantree.com; 9.30 pm; closed Mon, Sat L & Sun D.

Chef Peking £ 33
5-6 Church Grn AL5 2TP (01582) 769358
"A notch above the typical Chinese restaurant", this long-established spot is tipped for its "consistent" standards. / **Details:** just off the High Rd; 10.45 pm.

The Fox £ 39
469 Luton Rd AL5 3QE (01582) 713817
"The best that Harpenden has to offer" – this "lively" pub "seems to maintain a good standard" on the food front; "the main problem is that the portions are sometimes too large". / **Sample dishes:** onion & goats cheese tart with roast cherry tomatoes; sea bass fillets with creamed potato, crayfish & tomato hollandaise; apple & strawberry crumble with fresh custard.
Details: www.thefoxharpenden.co.uk; 10 pm.

The White Horse £ 48
Hatching Grn AL5 2JP (01582) 469290
"Novelli never fails", say fans of this celeb-chef-branded boozer; unfortunately, however, there are almost as many strident critics, who report a "really disappointing" experience, made worse by "sloppy service", "big bills" and a "cold" atmosphere.
/ **Sample dishes:** pan seared scallops, chilled summer pea mousse, pancetta; lavender honey roast breast of duck, slow cooked leg cannelloni, pickled wild mushrooms; baked chocolate fondant, white chocolate curd, cherry ripple ice cream. **Details:** www.atouchofnovelli.com; Along the high street towards St Albans, turn right to Redbourn, situated off Redbourn Lane; 9.30 pm; closed Mon & Sun D.

Bettys £ 35
1 Parliament St HG1 2QU (01423) 877300
"A wonderful tea-room from a bygone era"; this "quintessentially
English" institution combines all the key aspects of our native cuisine
– "you queue for a table", "there's a superb choice of teas", and it
does "the best breakfast outside a five-star hotel".
/ **Sample dishes:** crab, prawn & avocado salad; smoked chicken & asparagus
rösti; lemon meringue pancakes. **Details:** www.bettysandtaylors.co.uk; 9 pm;
no Amex; no booking.

The Boar's Head £ 45
Ripley Castle Estate HG3 3AY (01423) 771888
A "lovely" inn, "sat on the edge of the castle" in a village just outside
the town; it's a "lovely" and "relaxed" place, where the food is often
"inventive". / **Sample dishes:** sweetcorn mousselobster vinaigrette, crisp
pancetta; roast breast of free range chickencreamed leeks ,fondant potato, cooking
juices; trio of English appleapple sponge, tart fine, Granny Smith sorbet.
Details: www.boarsheadripley.co.uk; off A61 between Ripon & Harrogate; 9 pm.
Accommodation: 25 rooms, from £125.

Brio £ 33
Hornbeam Pk, The Lenz HG2 8RE (01423) 870005
Tipped "for a quick lunch, rather than an extended meal", this Italian
restaurant, on a business park, has all the "reasonably-priced" charm
that has made its Leeds parent very popular. / **Sample dishes:** Prosciutto
di Parma & melone; chicken and mushroom maccheroni; chocolate panna cotta.
Details: www.brios.co.uk; 10 pm; closed Sun; no Amex.

Drum & Monkey £ 37
5 Montpellier Gdns HG1 2TF (01423) 502650
A reputation for "classic seafood" at "reasonable prices" ensures this
place is "always packed to the brim"; compared to the ancien régime,
however, there's a lingering feeling that it has "lost its finesse".
/ **Sample dishes:** prawn and spinach delice; monkfish aux crevettes; sherry triffle.
Details: www.drumandmonkey.co.uk; 10 pm, 6.45 pm; no Amex; booking:
max 10.

Hotel du Vin et Bistro £ 45
Prospect Pl HG1 1LB (01423) 856800
Fuelled by the "extensive" wine list, there's "always a good vibe"
at this "lively" branch of the boutique-hotel chain; service can
be "amateurish" though, and the food "mediocre to say the least".
/ **Sample dishes:** seared swordfish, roast peppers & balsamic; roast rabbit loin,
tagliatelle, broad beans, girolles; Madagascan vanilla panna cotta, autumn berry
compote. **Details:** www.hotelduvin.com; 9.45 pm, Fri & Sat 10.15 pm.
Accommodation: 43 rooms, from £95.

Loch Fyne £ 42
Cheltenham Pde HG1 1DD (01423) 533070
"Very good fresh seafood" makes this outlet of the national chain
a consistently popular destination, somewhat "erratic" service
notwithstanding. / **Sample dishes:** oysters; grilled whole lemon sole with baby
capers & parsley butter. **Details:** www.loch-fyne.com; 10 pm, Sat 10.30 pm.

Orchid **£ 42** ⭐

28 Swan Rd HG1 2SE (01423) 560425

So varied are the styles of cooking that it's tempting to assume that the "Pacific Rim cuisine" on offer at this "stylish" restaurant will somehow suffer; not a bit of it, though – "the chefs are up to it", and popularity is such that "booking is essential".
/ **Sample dishes:** *prawn toast; pork tonkatsu; steamed banana cake.*
Details: *www.orchidrestaurant.co.uk; 10 pm; closed Sat L.* **Accommodation:** *36 rooms, from £99.*

Quantro **£ 35**

3 Royal Pde HG1 2SZ (01423) 503034

A "light and modern" spot in the city-centre that's mainly praised for its "consistently good", "upmarket formula" and its "very professional" standards; there were, however, a couple of 'off' reports this year. / **Details:** *www.quantro.co.uk; 10 pm, Sat 10.30 pm; closed Sun.*

Rajput **£ 34** ⭐

11 Cheltenham Pde HG1 1DD (01423) 562113

"Fresh and zingy curries" ("beware, they're addictive!") – plus some "unusual" other dishes – win adulatory reviews for this (generally) "friendly" Indian. / **Details:** *www.rajput.co.uk; midnight; D only; no Amex.*

HARROW, MIDDLESEX 3–3A

Golden Palace **£ 29** ⭐⭐

146-150 Station Rd HA1 2RH (020) 8863 2333

"Why go into central London?"; this "traditional" Cantonese may be "ugly" but it serves "the best dim sum" – "I lived for many years in the East, and this is undoubtedly the most authentic Chinese restaurant in the capital". / **Sample dishes:** *dim sum platter; Szechuan chicken; cream custard bun.* **Details:** *11.30 pm.*

Incanto **£ 43**

41 High St, Harrow On The Hill HA1 3HT (0208) 426 6767

"You could impress anyone here", say regular patrons of this "excellent" suburban Italian, who extol its "professional" service and "interesting and well-presented food"; feedback, however, is not quite consistent. / **Sample dishes:** *home-made caramelle pasta filled with wild mushrooms & mixed Italian cheeses; oven baked halibut wrapped in a potato crust with a garden pea purée; rhubarb & mango panna cotta.*
Details: *www.incanto.co.uk; 10.30 pm; closed Mon & Sun D.*

Skipjacks **£ 15** ⓣ

268-270 Streatfield Rd HA3 9BY (020) 8204 7554

Looking for some "excellent fish and chips"? – this locally-renowned destination is tipped as the place. / **Details:** *10.30 pm; closed Sun.*

HARWICH, ESSEX 3–2D

The Pier at Harwich **£ 55**

The Quay CO12 3HH (01255) 241212

"Good" fish dishes (albeit "from a slightly old-fashioned menu") win quite a few fans for the Milsom ('Tolbooth') family's waterside operation; there seems scant reason, however, to opt for the upstairs restaurant over the cheaper room below (recently refurbished).
/ **Details:** *www.milsomhotels.com; 9.30 pm; no jeans.* **Accommodation:** *14 rooms, from £105.*

HASLEMERE, SURREY 3–4A

The Inn On The Hill £ 41

Lower St GU27 2PD   (01428) 642006

Tipped especially for its "sumptuous steaks" and its "excellent-value-for-money lunch deals" – a trendified pub, near the railway station.
/ **Sample dishes:** boerworst - south African sausage; Barbary duck breast pan fried with honey & soy with dauphinoise potatoes & French beans; home-made English rhubarb cheesecake. **Details:** www.tailormadepub.co.uk; 10 pm, Sun 9 pm; booking essential. **Accommodation:** 8 rooms, from £80.

HASTINGS, EAST SUSSEX 3–4C

The Mermaid Café £ 25

2 Rock-a-Nore Rd TN34 3DW   (01424) 438100

*New owners appear to have wrecked this famous seaside destination – "it's no better than any other chippy nowadays, and worse than many". / **Details:** 7.30 pm; closed Mon D, Tue D, Wed D & Thu D; no credit cards; no booking.*

HATCH END, GREATER LONDON 3–2A

Sea Pebbles £ 24

348-352 Uxbridge Rd HA5 4HR   (020) 8428 0203

"The best fish 'n' chips for miles", at "really good-value" prices, attracts rave local write-ups for this North London chippy; "you don't go for the décor", though, and "service could be better" too.
/ **Details:** 10 pm; closed Sun; debit cards only; need 10+ to book.

HATFIELD PEVEREL, ESSEX 3–2C

Blue Strawberry £ 37

The Street CM3 2DW   (01245) 381333

*"A fabulous local restaurant, where you always receive a warm welcome"; "booking is essential at weekends". / **Sample dishes:** fresh asparagus in smoked salmon glazed with cheesy hollandaise sauce; fresh seafood bound in tomato & saffron based sauce; baked chocolate tart orange syrup & mascarpone. **Details:** www.bluestrawberrybistro.co.uk; 3m E of Chelmsford; 10 pm; closed Sat L & Sun D.*

HATFIELD, HERTFORDSHIRE 3–2B

Nolita £ 53

Great North Rd AL9 6NA   (01707) 644858

"A hidden Herts gem"; this "London-style modern Italian" – twinned with Soho's Little Italy – may seem "slightly flashy", but it "has a high standard of cooking" (and is "great for parties" too).
/ **Details:** www.nolitarestaurant.co.uk; midnight, Thu-Sat 2 am; no shorts.

HATHERSAGE, DERBYSHIRE 5–2C

The Walnut Club £ 46

Unit 6, The Sq, Main Rd S32 1BB   (01433) 651155

*This "environmentally conscious", "all-organic" venture inspires very varied feedback; for fans it's "always good, and sometimes outstanding" – to foes it's "nothing special", and "has a long way to go to meet its aspirations". / **Sample dishes:** seared Scottish scallops; stuffed globe artichoke with mushroom & leek duxelle; summer berry pavlova. **Details:** www.thewalnutclub.com; 10 pm, Sun 4 pm; closed Mon & Sun D; no Amex.*

Weaver's £ 33 ⭐

15 West Ln BD22 8DU (01535) 643822

"A Yorkshire gem" – this "bustling and friendly" Bronteland
restaurant-with-rooms, now run by the second generation
of Rushworths, again wins praise for its "very good and tasty food".
/ **Details:** www.weaversmallhotel.co.uk; 1.5m W on B6142 from A629,
near Parsonage; 9 pm; closed Mon, Tue L, Sat L & Sun D; children: 5+ on Sat.
Accommodation: 3 rooms, from £99.

The Half Moon £ 28 🅐⭐

The St RH17 5TR (01444) 461227

"A buzzing country pub", praised for "good, simple and hearty food
in large quantities". / **Sample dishes:** ciabatta with basil pesto, houmos and
tomato olive tapenade; oak smoked chicken, asparagus and Parmesan risotto,
leaf salad. **Details:** www.thehalfmoonwarninglid.co.uk; 9.30 pm; closed Sun D;
no Amex; no booking; children: 14+.

Jeremy's at Borde Hill £ 49 🅐⭐⭐

Balcombe Rd RH16 1XP (01444) 441102

Thanks to his "well-executed and innovative cooking", Jeremy
Ashpool's "charming and unpretentious" country restaurant
is "knocking on the door of a Michelin star"; "if weather permits,
the outside terrace overlooking the lovely gardens is an added bonus".
/ **Sample dishes:** salad of poached skate; roast breast and confit duck leg; white
and dark chocolate mousse and blackberry sauce and tuile.
Details: www.jeremysrestaurant.com; Exit 10A from the A23; 10 pm; closed
Mon & Sun D.

Sky Apple Cafe £ 21 ⭐

182 Heaton Rd NE6 5HP (01912) 092571

"A casual, part-time BYO veggie whose freshly-prepared original
concoctions can't fail to please even committed carnivores"; "booking
is essential in the evenings". / **Sample dishes:** ricotta cheese, Parmesan,
black olive, sun dried tomatoes & pesto poached into a light dumpling; balls
of deep-fried goat's cheese, roast red pepper & chives, dipped in Japanese panko
breadcrumbs & sesame seeds; banana spring rolls with chocolate sauce,
ice cream & sesame seed praline. **Details:** www.skyapple.co.uk; 9 pm; closed
Mon, Tue D & Sun D; no credit cards.

The Feathers Inn £ 33 ⭐

Hedley-on-the-Hill NE43 7SW (01661) 843607

"Fantastic local produce, cooked to an excellent standard" has made
quite a name for this "wonderful" boozer; "it's a bit hard to find,
but worth the hunt". / **Sample dishes:** home-made black pudding, poached
free range egg and devilled gravy; wild salmon with new potatoes and broad beans;
burnt Northumbrian cream. **Details:** www.thefeathers.net; 8.30 pm; closed Mon.

Feversham Arms Hotel & Verbana Spa £ 54
YO62 5AG (01439) 770766
*A chic, "cosy and comfortable" country inn that continues to impress most reporters with its "good menu choice" and its "first-class traditional cuisine"; even fans, however, can find the style "a bit too fancy!" / **Sample dishes:** crab & langoustine linguini, herb salad; poached loin of wild rabbit, asparagus & morel, champagne velouté; praline mousse, mascarpone sorbet. **Details:** www.fevershamarmshotel.com; 9.30 pm; no trainers; children: 12+ after 8 pm. **Accommodation:** 27 rooms, from £140.*

Halzephron Inn £ 34
TR12 7QB (01326) 240406
*"Good wholesome local produce" is used to excellent (and "substantial") effect at this "friendly" inn – highlights include "fresh fish" and "fabulous puddings" (plus "a good range of beers and wines"). / **Sample dishes:** crab, chilli, prawn, & saffron risotto with Parmesan & herbs; pork tenderloin filled with mushroom & herb duxelle served on a bed of spinach with a filo basket of wild mushrooms; baked American cheesecake. **Details:** www.halzephron-inn.co.uk; 9 pm. **Accommodation:** 2 rooms, from £90.*

Cochin £ 28 ✪
61 High St HP1 3AF (01442) 233777
*"Unique in Hemel, perhaps in Herts too" – this "friendly" south Indian (specialising in seafood) provides "very good and unusual" cooking, and also "fantastic value". / **Sample dishes:** mussel molly; kozhi biriyani; banana dosa. **Details:** www.thecochincuisine.com; 10.45 pm, Fri & Sat 11.30 pm .*

Cock £ 38 Ⓐ✪
High St PE28 9BJ (01480) 463609
*"A convivial pub/restaurant, in a delightful village", with "delicious food" and particularly "pleasant" service. / **Sample dishes:** duck parcel with sweet and sour cucumber; roast chump of lamb with black pepper polenta & roast pear; strawberry pavlova. **Details:** www.cambscuisine.com; 9 pm, Fri & Sat 9.30 pm, Sun 8.30 pm; no Amex.*

Cherry Tree Inn £ 36 Ⓣ
RG9 5QA (01491) 680430
*An old pub, recently updated, which is tipped for offering some "very good food" (as well as "superb beer"). / **Sample dishes:** crispy duck salad with bean shoots, watercress & served with a honey soy & sesame dressing; slow roast belly of Gloucester old spot pork served with creamed mash, smoked black pudding & a cider jus; treacle tart served with vanilla ice cream. **Details:** www.thecherrytreeinn.com; 10; closed Sun D; no Amex. **Accommodation:** 4 rooms, from £95.*

Hotel du Vin et Bistro £ 48
New St RG9 2BP (01491) 848400
A "great" location (in the old Brakspear's brewery, near the river)
"is a key attraction", at this newish branch of the boutique-hotel
chain; critics feel that "the food lacks the polish of Bristol
or Winchester", but the wine, as ever, saves the day.
*/ **Sample dishes:** gazpacho with crab tian & lobster oil; lamb cutlets with ham*
*and cheese dauphinoise & Reform sauce. **Details:** www.hotelduvin.com;*
*10.30 pm. **Accommodation:** 43 rooms, from £135.*

Spice Merchant £ 48 ⭐
Thameside RG9 2LJ (01491) 636118
"The Indian restaurant of choice for miles around", thanks to its
"excellent" food; "something is missing on the atmosphere front,
though" – "the modern décor can make it feel like a dentist's waiting
*room". / **Sample dishes:** lamb osso bucco in masala with pineapple; monkfish*
in traditional Goan style sauce with coconut & curry leaves.
***Details:** www.spicemerchantgroup.net; 11 pm.*

HEREFORD, HEREFORDSHIRE 2–1B

Café at All Saints £ 22 ⭐
All Saints Church, High St HR4 9AA (01432) 370415
"Just a café, but sometimes spectacular" – this bustling self-service
eatery in a "stunningly-restored" setting pleases all reporters with its
*"adventurous and tasty food". / **Sample dishes:** casserole*
of roast peppers & chick peas in roast paprika sauce; pan-fried mackerel fillet with
melted onions & black olives; stout cake in chocolate sauce.
***Details:** www.cafeatallsaints.co.uk; near Cathedral; L only; closed Sun; no Amex;*
no booking; children: 6+ upstairs.

Castle House Restaurant
Castle House Hotel £ 48
Castle St HR1 2NW (01432) 356321
On the plus side this "calm oasis" in a Georgian townhouse has
a good riverside location, and no-one dislikes its "superior" cooking;
it provoked some criticism this year, however, for being "too safe",
*or "fine but overpriced". / **Sample dishes:** Asian spiced pressing of duck,*
gooseberry & chilli jam, bean sprout salad; seared tuna loin, tomato salsa, braised
little gem, roast aubergine purée; white chocolate & lemon mousse, compote
*of raspberries, hazelnut praline. **Details:** www.castlehse.co.uk; 10 pm, Sun 9 pm.*
***Accommodation:** 15 rooms, from £175.*

HERSHAM, SURREY 3–3A

The Dining Room £ 38 🅰⭐
10 Queens Rd KT12 5LS (01932) 231686
"An eclectic mix of traditional English comfort food and some
Mediterranean-influenced dishes" wins praise at this "interesting"
destination – a "cottage"-style building, where "the dining room
*is divided into several smaller area". / **Sample dishes:** black pudding,*
poached duck egg, crispy bacon & toasted soda bread; steak & kidney pudding;
spotted dick sponge pudding topped with raisins & sultanas in sugar syrup &
*custard. **Details:** www.thediningroom.co.uk; 10.30 pm; closed Sat L & Sun D.*

Luciano's £ 38
2 Ferriby Rd HU13 0PG (01482) 641109
An unpretentious Italian, tipped for its "good, home-cooked food".
/ **Sample dishes:** *antipasti; linguine à la marinara; seafood and pasta in a white wine sauce; fresh fruit cheesecake.* **Details:** *www.lucianosrestaurant.co.uk; on the weir in Hessle, they are the bright orange building on the corner; 10 pm ; no Amex.*

The Angel £ 42
BD23 6LT (01756) 730263

"Bliss!"; the all-round charms of this "snug" and "busy" inn – with its "definitely superior pub grub", including "great fish dishes", plus "well-selected wines" – have made this a leading destination for a quarter of a century; "if you want to eat in the bar, get there early".
/ **Sample dishes:** *black pudding and apple croquette with mustard sauce and spring cabbage; locally shot wood pigeon with buttered Savoy cabbage mushroom and artichoke timbale and truffled red wine sauce; cinnamon brioche perdue with deep fried ice cream.* **Details:** *www.angelhetton.co.uk; 5m N of Skipton off B6265 at Rylstone; 9 pm; D only, ex Sun open L only.* **Accommodation:** *5 rooms, from £130.*

Bouchon Bistrot £ 34
4-6 Gilesgate NE46 3NJ (01434) 609943
"A welcome addition to the culinary desert that is the Tyne Valley" – a Gallic run bistro already being tipped for its "authentic" charms.
/ **Details:** *www.bouchonbistrot.co.uk; 9.30 pm; closed Mon & Sun D.*

Barnacles £ 39
Watling St LE10 3JA (01455) 633220
*"This simply IS the seafood restaurant in this part of the world"; with its "superb ingredients and imaginative dishes",
this establishment overlooking a lake is all the more worth knowing about in a "culinary desert".* / **Sample dishes:** *salmon and coriander fishcakes with spicy tomato ketchup; fillet of wild seabass on creamed mash with a cider & clam sauce; black cherry & frangipane tart with vanilla anglaise.* **Details:** *www.barnaclesrestaurant.co.uk; 9.30 pm; closed Sat L & Sun; no Amex.*

The Lamb Inn £ 35

High St SP3 6DP (01747) 820573

Just off the A303, a very handy stop-off (an outpost of London's Boisdale), tipped for its "wide range" of food that's somewhere between "above-average" and "OK". / **Sample dishes:** *local steamed asparagus spears, free range poached egg and tarragon butter; braised oxtail and spring cabbage on a bed of crushed Jersey royals; sticky toffee pudding and vanilla ice cream.* **Details:** *www.lambathindon.co.uk; 2 minutes from the A350, 5 minutes from the A303; 9.30 pm. 9 pm Sun.* **Accommodation:** *14 rooms, from £75.*

Lord Poulett Arms £ 34 🅰⭐

TA17 8SE (01460) 73149

"An unexpected treat, just off the gastronomic desert that is the A303" – *"an ultra-traditional country pub", offering "good, honest food, prepared with flair, not pretence"; "a nice place to over-night" too.* / **Sample dishes:** *British beef carpaccio, lemon and white truffle dressing and shaved Parmesan; nroast chicken on smoked bacon and spring onion crushed potatoes; elderflower snowconw, macerated strawberries, puff pastry crisp.* **Details:** *www.lordpoulettarms.com; 9 pm; no Amex.* **Accommodation:** *4 rooms, from £88.*

The Dartmoor Union £ 34 🅣

Fore St PL8 1NE (01752) 830288

A modern and stylish pub/restaurant; top tip is to look out for its "excellent special offers". / **Sample dishes:** *gravadlax of salmon with a sweet mustard mayonnaise; marinated loin of pork with slow cooked belly, pan fried hogs pudding and black pudding and wilted baby spinach; chocolate pots with a pistachio crunch.* **Details:** *www.dartmoorunion.co.uk; 9 pm, Sun 8.30 pm; no Amex.*

Victoria Hotel £ 47

Park Rd NR23 1RG (01328) 711008

A "good location", on the beach, has made this "laid-back" beach-facing pub a big hit with the Chelsea set; it stands accused by some sceptics, though, of "trading on its location". / **Sample dishes:** *tea cured salmon, warm potato blinis with vanilla dressing; seared Gressingham duck breast with beetroot purée & a redcurrant jus; milk chocolate fondant with roast pistachio ice cream.* **Details:** *www.victoriaatholkham.co.uk; 9 pm; no Amex; booking essential.* **Accommodation:** *10 rooms, from £120.*

Combe House Hotel & Restaurant   **£ 58**   Ⓐ ⭐
EX14 3AD   (01404) 540400
"A beautiful building" (an Elizabethan house) in *"idyllic surroundings"*
makes this *"deepest-Devon"* operation a *"memorable"* destination;
given the setting, the fare is surprisingly *"contemporary"*, and –
like the wine list – *"top-class"*. / **Sample dishes:** scallops with spiced
cauliflower purée and ginger velouté; roast chicken breast with truffle gnocchi,
wild mushrooms and asparagus; muscat poached pear with iced nougat parfait.
Details: www.thishotel.com; off A30, 20 minutes from Exeter; 9.30 pm; no Amex.
Accommodation: 16 rooms, from £170.

Ⓣ

Oak Room Restaurant
Tylney Hall   **£ 60**
Rotherwick   RG27 9AZ   (01256) 764881
"Pricey" and *"rather old-fashioned"*, this country house hotel inspires
only modest survey feedback, but its *"good and interesting"* wine
list features in all of it. / **Sample dishes:** duck liver & foie gras terrine with
confit grapes; pan fried fillet of pollack with pea purée, capers, olives & shrimps;
tiramisu with amaretto milkshake. **Details:** www.tylneyhall.com; 10 pm, 9.30 pm;
jacket and/or tie. **Accommodation:** 112 rooms, from £195.

Ⓐ

The Bell Inn   **£ 37**
High Rd   SS17 8LD   (01375) 642463
"A high standard of cooking and a good-value wine list" make this
ancient and *"attractive"* inn popular with many local reporters.
/ **Sample dishes:** wild rabbit and confit foie gras with grape chutney and
toast brioche; garlic roast rack of lamb on parsnip fondant, duxelle and sweet
potato crème; Bramley apple and toffee crème brûlée with apple sorbet.
Details: www.bell-inn.co.uk; signposted off B1007, off A13; 9.45 pm; booking:
max 12. **Accommodation:** 15 rooms, from £50.

⭐

Lino's   **£ 37**
122 Market St   CH47 3BH   (0151) 632 1408
"Established on the Wirral for over 20 years" – the Galantini family's
"comfortable" Italian is a *"favourite"* destination for many reporters,
who like not just its *"reliable"* food, but also service *"which is so very
memorable"*. / **Sample dishes:** mozzarella wrapped in Serrano ham, baked,
served on a mixed salad and sun dried tomato dressing and chopped basil;
breast of guinea fowl, pan fried, served in a tomato. spinach, garlic and cream
sauce; panettone and brioche hot chocolate pudding and crème anglaise and ice
cream. **Details:** www.linosrestaurant.co.uk; 3m from M53, J2; 10 pm; closed Sun,
Mon and Sat L; no Amex.

⭐

Bradley's   **£ 34**
84 Fitzwilliam St   HD1 5BB   (01484) 516773
"Always reliable and good value" – that's the gist of all feedback
on Andrew Bradley's *"busy"* town-centre bistro. / **Sample dishes:** warm
salad of Toulouse sausage, mushroom & chats; confit of duck leg with braised red
cabbage, black pudding & apple sauce; ginger sponge and custard.
Details: www.bradleys-restaurant.co.uk; 10 pm; closed Sat L & Sun; no Amex.

Nawaab **£ 26** ⓣ
35 Westgate HD1 1NY   (01484) 422775
*A town-centre tip for "tasty food", served in a "pleasant atmosphere";
they do "good offers" too. / **Sample dishes:** fish masala; chicken badami;
makta kulfi. **Details:** www.nawaabs.net; between bus & railway stations; 11 pm;
D only.*

HULL, KINGSTON UPON HULL 6–2A

Cerutti's **£ 42**
10 Nelson St HU1 1XE   (01482) 328501
*An "old-established riverside seafood restaurant", in a Georgian house
– the food "may not always be inspired", but it is generally "reliable".
/ **Sample dishes:** fish cakes served with herb sauce; plaice Véronique poached
fillets of plaice with green grapes, glazed with a white wine sauce; white chocolate
and coconut cheesecakes served with apricots. **Details:** www.ceruttis.co.uk; follow
signs to fruit market; 9.30 pm; closed Sat L & Sun.*

HUNSDON, HERTFORDSHIRE 3–2B

The Fox And Hounds **£ 38** Ⓐ ★
2 High St SG12 8NH   (01279) 843999
*With its "old-fashioned atmosphere (in the best sense)", this "great
local pub" (with "good beers") continues to offer "top-drawer food"
from an "ever-changing" menu. / **Sample dishes:** mussels, shallots,
leeks, & cider; saddle of lamb, gratin dauphinoise & green beans; blood orange &
mint jelly. **Details:** www.foxandhounds-hunsdon.co.uk; situated just off the A414,
10 min from Hertford; 10 pm; closed Mon & Sun D; no Amex.*

HUNTINGDON, CAMBRIDGESHIRE 3–1B

Old Bridge Hotel **£ 43** Ⓐ
1 High St PE29 3TQ   (01480) 424300
*Many "delightful" evenings are spent – especially on the terrace –
at this "friendly" dining room, which is run by John Hoskins ("the only
Master of Wine in the hotel industry"); this year, though, there were
also a couple of middling reports. / **Sample dishes:** carpaccio of smoked
duck with hazelnut dressing, pear fondant & frisee lettuce; pan fried fillet of sea
bream with sauteed rainbow chard, new potatoes & cherry tomato sauce; sticky
toffee pudding with sticky toffee sauce & vanilla ice cream.
Details: www.huntsbridge.com; off A1, off A14; 10 pm. **Accommodation:** 24
rooms, from £125.*

HURLEY, BERKSHIRE 3–3A

Black Boys Inn **£ 43**
Henley Rd SL6 5NQ   (01628) 824212
*This 17th-century inn is praised by fans for its "intimate" style and for
Simon Bonwick's "masterly" cooking; it also inspired a few
'off' reports this year, however, from those who encountered "average
food served by disinterested staff". / **Sample dishes:** chaud froid
of oysters & scallops with oyster vinaigrette; slow cooked roast Devon lamb
"bourgeoisie"; banana bavarois, caramelised banana & treacle syrup.
Details: www.blackboysinn.co.uk; 9 pm; closed Mon & Sun; no Amex; children:
12+. **Accommodation:** 8 rooms, from £75.*

11 The Quay   £ 49

11 The Quay EX34 9EQ (01271) 868090

*Surprisingly few reports on Damien Hirst's harbour-side venture
(which is adorned with examples of his oeuvre); it's sometimes tipped
as a "delight", but feedback is not consistent. / **Sample dishes:** seafood
platters.* **Details:** *www.11thequay.co.uk ; 9.30 pm.*

Bettys   £ 35

32-34 The Grove LS29 9EE (01943) 608029

*"For some reason a far more enjoyable experience than the
Harrogate version"; this "family-friendly but still civilised" teashop is,
of course, most notable for its "brilliant cakes and tea", but other
dishes are "delicious" too; "long waits for tables" are all part of the
fun. / **Sample dishes:** crab, prawn & avocado salad; smoked chicken &
asparagus rösti; lemon meringue pancakes.* **Details:** *www.bettysandtaylors.com;
5.30 pm; no Amex; no booking.*

The Box Tree   £ 58

35-37 Church St LS29 9DR (01943) 608484

*"Simon Gueller is an excellent chef", and fans of this "ultra-traditional
old-timer" say it just gets "better and better"; critics, though,
say "the pricing really holds it back" – "it could be outstanding,
but verges on being a rip-off". / **Sample dishes:** galantine of free-range
chicken, spiced pear chutney, toasted rye bread; wild Cornish line-caught seabass
puy lentils, port reduction & crispy pancetta; pyramid nougatine glace, with fresh
raspberries.* **Details:** *www.theboxtree.co.uk; on A65 near town centre; 9.30 pm;
closed Mon & Sun D; no Amex; children: 10+ at D.*

Far Syde   £ 34

1-3 New Brook St LS29 8DQ (01943) 602030

*"Great value for lunch, but good at any time of day" – if you're
looking for an all-day stand-by, this rather slick-looking establishment
is a top tip locally. / **Sample dishes:** chicken & mozzarella fritters served on a
waterchestnut & lychee salad with tomato & chilli jam; duck breast served
on aubergine purée and olive mash with goat's cheese & mushroom wontons;
chocolate soufflé garnished with bananas in rum syrup & caramel ice cream.*
Details: *www.thefarsyde.co.uk; 10 pm; closed Mon & Sun; no Amex.*

Ilkley Moor Vaults   £ 34

Stockeld Rd LS29 9HD (01943) 607012

*Joe McDermott's relaxed gastropub is tipped by a local as a
"provincial", "cheap and cheerful" version of Smithfield's celebrated
St John restaurant. / **Sample dishes:** potted crab & toast; lamb stew; steamed
marmalade pudding & custard.* **Details:** *www.ilkleymoorvaults.co.uk; 9 pm,
9.30 pm Fri & Sat; closed Sun D.*

The Howard Arms   £ 37   Ⓐ⭐

Lower Grn CV36 4LT   (01608) 682226

A "superb village-green location" and "beautiful Cotswolds countryside" set the scene at this "lovely country pub"; numerous reports imply that "standards are being maintained under its new owners" (who took over in 2007), not least of the "imaginative" cuisine. / **Sample dishes:** spicy lamb costas with tsatsiki; panfried calf's liver, buttered onions, crisp bacon and balsamic dressing; Cointreau cheesecake and caramelised oranges. **Details:** www.howardarms.com; 8m SW of Stratford-upon-Avon off A4300; 9.30 pm, Fri & Sat 10 pm, Sun 9 pm; no Amex. **Accommodation:** 3 rooms, from £105.

Abstract   ⭐
Glenmoriston Townhouse Hotel   £ 59

Ness Bank IV2 4SF   (01463) 223777

"A real treat" – this riverside hotel dining room achieves "impressive" results from "top-notch" ingredients; service is "attentive" too (if perhaps a little "lacking in confidence"); the brasserie offers a cheaper option. / **Sample dishes:** pan seared with braised pork and pineapple; local rump of lamb, spiced aubergine purée, Israeli couscous, confit tomato and black olives, lamb jus; pineapple 'rum baba', clear caramel tube with pineapple mousse, pineapple sorbet. **Details:** www.abstractrestaurant.com; 10 pm; D only, closed Mon & Sun. **Accommodation:** 30 rooms, from £130.

Mustard Seed   £ 37

16 Fraser St IV1 1DW   (01463) 220220

A two-tier operation benefiting from a "lovely" setting, overlooking the river; reports on the food are generally a touch up-and-down, but the lunchtime menu is tipped for its "exceptional value". / **Sample dishes:** home-made salmon mousse with salad garnish and sour cream; chargrilled swordfish loin with a beetroot and apple salsa. **Details:** www.themustardseedrestaurant.co.uk; On the bank of the Ness river; 9.45 pm.

Rocpool   £ 48

1 Ness Walk IV3 5NE   (01463) 717274

Mainly notable for rarity value (and its "lovely terrace, overlooking the Ness"), this ambitious Italian outfit does what it does "competently, ma senza brio". / **Details:** www.rocpoolrestaurant.com; 10 pm; closed Sun L; no Amex.

Baipo   £ 31   ⭐

63 Upper Orwell St IP4 1HP   (01473) 218402

The setting may be "very ordinary", but this "consistent" Thai veteran is still of note for its "really top-class food". / **Sample dishes:** golden pastry cups filled with a mixture of minced chicken, sweetcorn, onions and green-red pepper; dry aromatic ground peanut curry with coconut milk and lime leaves; ice cream. **Details:** www.baipo.co.uk; 10.45 pm; closed Mon L & Sun; no Amex.

Hintlesham Hall £ 66 ⊗

Dodge St IP8 3NS (01473) 652334
*A famous and "beautiful" country house hotel which remains
a "missed opportunity"; the food "fails to match the setting",
and harsher critics say the place is just "trading on its name".*
/ **Details:** www.hintleshamhall.com; 4m W of Ipswich on A1071; 9.30 pm; closed
Sat L; jacket at D; children: not welcome at dinner. **Accommodation:** 33 rooms,
from £150.

Il Punto £ 36 Ⓐ

Neptune Quay IP4 1AX (01473) 289748
*"Lovely" Gallic food and a "lovely" setting too – on a moored boat –
still make this Crépy-family restaurant a hit with most reporters;
standards are "slipping", though, and it's "nothing like as good as the
family's other establishments".* / **Details:** www.ilpunto.co.uk; 9.30 pm; closed
Mon & Sun; no Amex.

The Ship Inn £ 35 Ⓣ

Church Ln IP10 0LQ (01473) 659573
*Tipped as an "excellent lunch destination", a cramped and ancient
inn offering "standard fare" of consistently "good quality".*
/ **Details:** 9.30 pm, 9 pm Sun; no Amex; children: 14+.

Trongs £ 31 ✪

23 St Nicholas St IP1 1TW (01473) 256833
*"A fabulous family-run restaurant"; this "top-notch" Chinese veteran
is "still the best for miles around", and attracts (almost) unanimous
raves from those who comment on it.* / **Sample dishes:** steamed scallops
with garlic; chicken with lemongrass & garlic; toffee lychee with steamed ginger.
Details: 10.30 pm; closed Sun; booking essential.

IRELAND, BEDFORDSHIRE 3–1A

Black Horse £ 42 Ⓐ✪

SG17 5QL (01462) 811398
*"There's nothing too fancy or pretentious" about this "consistently
good gastropub", located in an "isolated hamlet" in "a sleepy part
of the county"; it's a "stylish" place, though, where the food
is delivered "with pride and passion".* / **Sample dishes:** wild rabbit smoked
bacon roulade with organic rosemary jelly and toasted croute; medallions
of Cornish lamb with spinach and white pudding stuffing served with parisienne
potatoes, creamed celerac and a rosemary and tomato jus; raspberry soufflé
served with caramel and chocolate sauce. **Details:** www.blackhorseireland.com;
10 pm; closed Sun D. **Accommodation:** 2 rooms, from £55.

ITTERINGHAM, NORFOLK 6–4C

Walpole Arms £ 36 Ⓐ✪

The Common, Itteringham NR11 7AR (01263) 587258
*"Off the beaten track, but worth the effort" – this old oak-beamed
pub-cum-dining room offers a "robust" and "interesting" menu
of "fresh"-tasting dishes.* / **Sample dishes:** terrine of pigeon, prune & pork;
roast cod with chorizo & lemon risotto; baked white chocolate cheese cake.
Details: www.thewalpolearms.co.uk; 9 pm, Sun 7 pm; closed Sun D; no Amex.

Bohemia
The Club Hotel & Spa £ 70
Green St, St Helier JE2 4UH (01534) 880588
"Beyond compare!" – fans of Shaun Rankin's cooking don't mince
words in their rave-reviews of his *"unique"* cuisine, which combines
"classical and modern influences"; the revamped dining room has
"improved the ambience" too. / **Sample dishes:** foie gras parfait with
betroot jelly, blood orange slad, toasted salad; pot braised maize fed chicken
in sauternes, new season peas and herb gnocchi; delice of Valhrona's chocolate
with cherry sorbet and griottines. **Details:** www.bohemiajersey.com; 10 pm; closed
Sun. **Accommodation:** 46 rooms, from £195.

Green Island Restaurant £ 42
St Clement JE2 6LS (01534) 857787
*There still aren't as many reports as we'd like, but this seafood-
restaurant is once again tipped as a "charming place with superb
food"; book ahead if you want a table on the seaside terrace.*
/ **Sample dishes:** fresh picked crab & courgette salad with avocado and lime
segments; roast tail of monkfish wrapped in Parma ham with a red onion &
parsley potato cake with wilted spinach, sorrel & garlic leaves with Feta oil
dressing; chocolate mousse with a red berry compote, clotted cream, & crushed
honeycomb & vanilla crème fraîche. **Details:** www.greenislandrestaurant.com;
9.30 pm; closed Mon & Sun D; no Amex.

Longueville Manor £ 75
Longueville Rd, St Saviour JE2 7WF (01534) 725501
*"A place to impress"; this "sophisticated" country house hotel has
a "beautiful panelled dining room", where the food and service are
often "faultless"* – the ambience, though, can be rather *"quiet"* for
some tastes. / **Sample dishes:** sesame coated seared tuna and rocket salad,
horseradish cream and caviar sauce; supreme of halibut and new season peas à la
francaise; pineapple soufflé and chocolate, ginger sauce and banana ice cream.
Details: www.longuevillemanor.com; Head from St. Helier on the A3 towards
Gorey; less than 1 mile from St. Helier; 10 pm; no jeans or trainers.
Accommodation: 35 rooms, from £200.

Bridge Street Restaurant £ 29
1 Bridge St LA9 7DD (01539) 738 855
*A "relaxed" townhouse-restaurant, tipped for its "delicious
& imaginative food, beautifully cooked", and served in a "gracious"
atmosphere.* / **Sample dishes:** salmon & monkfish roulade, smoked salmon,
roast honey beetroot, caper & shallot vinaigrette; pan fried gilt head bream,
pan fried king scallops, basil risotto, mango orange dressing; milk chocolate &
honeycombe torte, dark chocolate ganache, snap biscuit, mango ice cream.
Details: www.bridgestreetkendal.co.uk; Just off the A6; 9 pm; closed Mon & Sun;
no Amex.

Bosquet £ 50
97a, Warwick Rd CV8 1HP (01926) 852463
*Bernard and Jane Lignier's "little piece of France, in the heart
of Warwickshire" has long been known for its "wonderful" cuisine;
the décor, though, is rather "overpowering" for some tastes.*
/ **Sample dishes:** light spicy crab salad served with cucumber, avocado and
tomato salsa; wild venison served on a purée of parsnips with honey and pepper
served with a black current and game sauce; blueberry and almond tart served
with home-made vanilla ice cream. **Details:** www.restaurantbosquet.co.uk;
9; closed Mon, Sat L & Sun; closed Aug.

The Pheasant £ 41
Loop Rd PE28 0RE (01832) 710241
Tipped as a "romantic" destination, this pub-cum-restaurant is still associated in the minds of locals with the former Huntsbridge group; it maintains good all-round standards.
/ **Details:** *www.thepheasant-keyston.co.uk; 1m S of A14 between Huntingdon & Kettering, J15; 9.30 pm.*

Firenze £ 42 ⭐
9 Station St LE8 0LN (0116) 279 6260

"A small island of culinary excellence in the cold sea of East Midlands 'cuisine'" – the Poli family's *"award-winning"* Italian has won local renown for its *"first-class"* food and *"intimate"* style; there's a minority view, though, that it's *"pleasant, but somehow promises more than it delivers".* / **Sample dishes:** *spinach, egg and ricotta tart; veal escalope and sweetbread, pan-fried with Parma ham and sage; semifreddo allo zabaglione.*
Details: *www.firenze.co.uk; 10 pm; closed Sun; no Amex.*

Ardeonaig Hotel & Restaurant £ 45
South Loch Tay Side FK21 8SU (01567) 820400
"The best South African wine list ever" (reflecting the owners' nationality) and "a remote location on beautiful Loch Tay" are constants at this ambitious hotel; it's a "firm favourite" for numerous reporters, but we've left it unrated as – following a £1.6m expansion – it was re-launched just after the conclusion of our survey.
/ **Sample dishes:** *smoked salmon, roast homegrown beetroot and rooibos balsamic reduction; twice cooked shoulder of black faced lamb and shallots; chocolate mielie meal pudding with Madagascar vanilla ice cream.*
Details: *www.ardeonaighotel.co.uk; 10.30 pm; no Amex; children: 12+.*
Accommodation: *27 rooms, from £90.*

Ballathie House £ 57
PH1 4QN (01250) 883268
A country house hotel "in a beautiful part of Perthshire", where "a new chef has improved what was already a high standard of food"; service, however, can "lack professionalism". / **Sample dishes:** *chicken liver parfait with brioche; fillet of sea green with wilted greens and sauce vièrge; sticky toffee pudding with butterscotch sauce.*
Details: *www.ballathiehousehotel.com; off B9099, take right from 1m N of Stanley; 8.45 pm; jacket at D; children: 10+ at D.* **Accommodation:** *42 rooms, from £150.*

Bradley's £ 39 Ⓣ
10 South Quay PE30 5DT (01553) 819888
*Tipped for its "excellent wine list", this "pleasantly-situated" quayside establishment is also praised for its "beautiful" food and its "very friendly" service. / **Sample dishes:** medley of melon and pineapple with winter berry compote; honey-glazed Gressingham duck breastcabbage with blackcurrant sauce; dark chocolate tart with amaretto cream.*
Details: *www.bradleysbytheriver.co.uk; 9.30 pm; closed Sun.*

The Kingham Plough £ 42 ★
OX7 6YD (01608) 658327
*A chef arrived from the Fat Duck has ensured a fair amount of "hype" for this "brilliant country pub"; it inspired many reports – mostly describing "serious, high-quality pub food" – but there's still a little work to do on the service front. / **Sample dishes:** goat's cheese soufflée; loin of veal; chocolate fondant with vanilla ice cream.*
Details: *www.thekinghamplough.co.uk; 8.45 pm, Sun 8.30 pm; no Amex.*

Ayudhya £ 33 Ⓣ
14 Kingston Hill KT2 7NH (020) 8549 5984
*"Authentic", "good", "reliable" – the sort of terms which keep popping up in reports on this "old-favourite" Thai. / **Sample dishes:** chicken lemon grass; banana in coconut milk.*
Details: *www.eatdrink.co.uk/ayudhya-kingston; 11 pm, Mon & Sun 10.30 pm; closed Mon L; no Amex.*

Canbury Arms £ 38 ★
49 Canbury Park Rd KT2 6LQ (020) 8255 9129
*This "cheerful and energetic" gastropub – all "pale and muted" décor and "laid-back" style – has become a "firm favourite in the area", serving "traditional" and "tasty" British food "with a difference", in "large portions". / **Sample dishes:** sun dried tomato & goats cheese risotto; grilled whole bream with garlic butter prawns, chips and salad; orange treacle tart, crème fraîche. **Details:** www.thecanburyarms.com; 10 pm, Sun 9 pm.*

fish!kitchen £ 29
58 Coombe Rd KT2 7AF (020) 8546 2886
*Near Norbiton BR, a bistro offering "excellent, if pricey, fish and chips"; it has quite an impressive following among reporters. / **Sample dishes:** smoked haddock rarebit with tomato and basil salad; haddock with chips and mushy peas; vanilla ice cream. **Details:** www.fishkitchen.com; 10 pm; closed Mon & Sun.*

Frère Jacques £ 40 Ⓐ
10-12 Riverside Walk KT1 1QN (020) 8546 1332
*"A stunning riverside location", by Kingston Bridge, and an owner "who treats you like his best friend" are the hallmarks of this "no-nonsense" outfit, which is "good for steak/frites, and other classic bistro fare". / **Sample dishes:** red & yellow endive salad with caramelised apple, goat's cheese and crushed walnut dressing; slow-braised shank of lamb served with fondant potatoes and root vegetables; warm almond & pear tart served with amaretto syrupkumquat sorbet. **Details:** www.frerejacques.co.uk; next to Kingston Bridge and market place; 11 pm; no Amex.*

Riverside Vegetaria   **£ 35**

64 High St   KT1 1HN   (020) 8546 7992

"For veggies and their greedy friends", this "tiny" and "homely" spot dishes up "enjoyable" dishes "spanning many styles of cuisines"; "good setting" too, by the Thames. / **Details:** *www.rsveg.plus.com; 10 mins walk from Kingston BR; 11 pm; no Amex; children: 18+ ex L.*

KINGUSSIE, HIGHLAND   9–2C

The Cross   **£ 56**   Ⓐ⭐

Tweed Mill Brae, Ardbroilach Rd   PH21 1LB   (01540) 661166

"The perfect weekend break!"; "fantastic local produce" is used to very good effect at this "idyllically-located" restaurant-with-rooms, and the wine list is "extensive and great value" too; for those who stay over, "a hearty Scottish breakfast awaits". / **Sample dishes:** *seared scallops, golden raisin purée, caper dressing; breast of Gressingham duck, creamed Savoy cabbage, chicory tarte Tatin; crème caramel, crème brûlée ice-cream.* **Details:** *www.thecross.co.uk; 8.30 pm; D only, closed Mon & Sun; children: 9+.* **Accommodation:** *8 rooms, from £100.*

KIRK DEIGHTON, WEST YORKSHIRE   5–1C

Bay Horse   **£ 36**   ⭐

Main St   LS22 4DZ   (01937) 580058

"Reliably good and interesting food" is served in "huge portions", at this "cosy" and "friendly" gastropub, handily located for the A1. / **Sample dishes:** *fresh Whitby crab soup; East Coast fish pie; traditional bread and butter pudding.* **Details:** *9 pm; closed Mon L & Sun D; no Amex.*

KIRKBY LONSDALE, CUMBRIA   7–4D

Avanti   **£ 36**   Ⓣ

57 Main St   LA6 2AH   (01524) 273500

A 'restaurant, bar, crêperie, garden, and art and coffee shop' – tipped as a "real oasis" in this "charming small market town". / **Sample dishes:** *hand dived scallops with chilli & garlic butter; assiette of lamb with lavender jus; raspberry crème brûlée.* **Details:** *www.baravanti.com; 10 pm, Sun 9.30 pm; no Amex.*

The Highwayman   **£ 34**

LA6 2RJ   (01524) 273338

WINNER 2009

From the Northcote people, a "tastefully-converted" coaching inn that's been instantly acclaimed for "great pub food", which – true to its backers' reputation – makes "imaginative use of local produce". / **Sample dishes:** smoked haddock salad; wild Cumbrian rabbit pie; chocolate & orange pudding. **Details:** www.highwaymaninn.co.uk; 9 pm, 8.30 pm.

Hipping Hall   **£ 58**

Cowan Bridge   LA6 2JJ   (01524) 271187

Chef Jason (Bruno) Birkbeck is "pulling out all the stops", say fans of this "comfortable and cosy" country house hotel, where his "memorable" cuisine – showing "real flair" and with "fantastic attention to detail" – underpins a "first-class" overall experience. / **Sample dishes:** pan fried scallops, cauliflower purée, smoked bacon jus; roast pig's head, crushed ratte potatoes, apple purée, ginger; warm Valhrona chocolate fondant, ivory sorbet, hazelnut crumb. **Details:** www.hippinghall.com; 9.30 pm; D only, ex Sun open L & D; no Amex; children: 10+.
Accommodation: 6 rooms, 3 cottages rooms, from £165.

KNIGHTWICK, WORCESTERSHIRE   2–1B

The Talbot   **£ 43**

WR6 5PH   (01886) 821235

"Honest", "fresh" and "local" cooking pleases (almost) all reporters on this pretty riverside inn, and its "home-brewed beer" seems to slip down very nicely too. / **Sample dishes:** fresh pickled lobster in warm mace butter with avocado ice cream & poached pear salad; saddle of venison with a home-made venison sausage, braised red cabbage & crisp fried forcemeat balls; meringue roulade filled with home-made lemon curd.
Details: www.the-talbot.co.uk; 9m from Worcester on A44; 9 pm; no Amex.
Accommodation: 11 rooms, from £90.

KNUTSFORD, CHESHIRE   5–2B

Belle Époque   **£ 45**

King St   WA16 6DT   (01565) 633060

"Even worse than before" – this long-established venture, in a rare and "stunning" Belle Époque building, does still have a few fans; for too many reporters, however, it is "resting on past laurels" to a quite "awful" extent. / **Sample dishes:** potted Berkshire ham; rack of mutton.
Details: www.thebelleepoque.com; 1.5m from M6, J19; 9.30 pm; closed Sat L & Sun D; booking: max 6, Sat. **Accommodation:** 6 rooms, from £115.

At the Sign of the Angel £ 39

6 Church St SN15 2LB (01249) 730230

It's the location which justifies the tip for this ancient inn – at the heart of a "delightful village", entirely owned by the National Trust. / **Sample dishes:** *Stilton and walnut pâté with apple and sage jelly; roast rack of English lamb servied with rosemary mash and onion gravy; home-made meringue with fruit compote and clotted crème.* **Details:** *www.lacock.co.uk; close to M4, J17; 9 pm; closed Mon L.* **Accommodation:** *11 rooms, from £120.*

The Hare £ 50

Ermin St RG17 7SD (01488) 71386

A "very classy" village inn, which changed hands in the course of our surveying year – one report of the new régime, tips the food as "excellent". / **Details:** *www.theharerestaurant.co.uk; 9.30 pm; closed Mon & Sun D.*

Bay Horse £ 37

Bay Horse Ln LA2 0HR (01524) 791204

"Imaginative", "locally-sourced" food has made quite a name for Craig Wilkinson's high-quality gastropub; "note, however, that it's 100% gastro and 0% pub" nowadays, and has arguably "lost a bit of charm" along the way. / **Sample dishes:** *smoked Goosnargh duck Caesar salad; baked salmon fillet, confit fennel, new potatoes & lemon butter; panna cotta with orange.* **Details:** *www.bayhorseinn.com; 0.75m S of A6, J33 M6; 9 pm; closed Mon & Sun D.* **Accommodation:** *3 rooms, from £89.*

Pizza Margherita £ 29

2 Moor Ln LA1 1QD (01524) 36333

"Still good, after nearly 30 years"; this "welcome oasis", owned by the sister of PizzaExpress's founder, still specialises in "top-rate pizza". / **Details:** *www.pizza-margherita.co.uk; 10.30 pm.*

Langar Hall £ 48

Church Ln NG13 9HG (01949) 860559

"A warm welcome" from patronne Imogen Skirving adds to the "charming" style of this "eccentric" and "romantic" county house hotel (which she converted from her family's home 25 years ago); "very professional" staff and "delicious, locally-sourced food" complete the formula. / **Sample dishes:** *creamed goat's cheese and dried tomatoes, tomato jelly and basil oil; pan fried calves' liver, red onion tart tatin and Parmesan polenta; knickerbocker glory.* **Details:** *www.langarhall.com; off A52 between Nottingham & Grantham; 9 pm; no Amex; no trainers.* **Accommodation:** *12 rooms, from £95.*

LANGHO, LANCASHIRE 5–1B

Northcote £ 65 A ✪ ✪

Northcote Rd BB6 8BE (01254) 240555

*Nigel Haworth & Craig Bancroft are dropping 'Manor' from the name as they spend £3m on refurbishing this "simply outstanding" restaurant-with-rooms; reports remain a hymn of praise to its "wonderful twists on British regional dishes", and its "professional and genuine desire to please". / **Sample dishes:** organic salad, forager's bacon, soft hen's egg, cheese and summer truffle; lamb, girolles, samphire and new potato soufflé; melting ginger pudding, simpson's iced double cream and caramel custard. **Details:** www.northcote.com; M6, J31 then A59; 9.30 pm. **Accommodation:** 14 rooms, from £180.*

LANGSHOTT, SURREY 3–3B

Langshott Manor £ 59 ⓣ

Ladbroke Rd RH6 9LN (01293) 786680

*A top tip for those wanting a quality rendezvous near Gatwick – a "pricey" country house hotel, close by, with "solid" standards. / **Sample dishes:** ballotine of red mullet, marinated squid and saffron jelly; poached, confit and roast poussin with polenta and oregano; dark chocolate and rosewater fondant with orange ice cream. **Details:** www.langshottmanor.com; Just off the A23, in Horley; 9.30 pm; no trainers. **Accommodation:** 22 rooms, from £190.*

LANGTON GREEN, KENT 3–4B

The Hare £ 31

Langton Rd TN3 0JA (01892) 862419

*A "proper" pub that's a "perennial local favourite"; it's a "good all-rounder", whose "hearty food and good value" rarely disappoint. / **Sample dishes:** twice baked Roquefort & tarragon soufflé; chicken breast with asparagus and wild mushrooms; lemon posset with ginger snap biscuits. **Details:** www.hare-tunbridgewells.co.uk; on A264 to East Grinstead; 9.30 pm, Fri & Sat 10 pm, Sun 9 pm; no Amex; children: 18+ at D.*

LAPWORTH, WARWICKSHIRE 5–4C

The Boot Inn £ 38 A

Old Warwick Rd B94 6JU (01564) 782464

*"A lovely canal-side pub-restaurant, which does above-average food at reasonable prices in a fabulous location"; "nice garden" too. / **Sample dishes:** warm tart of pumpkin, goats cheese and thyme; slow braised blade of beef bourgignonne on creamed mash. **Details:** www.bootinnlapworth.co.uk; off A34; 10 pm.*

LAVENHAM, SUFFOLK 3–1C

Angel £ 34

Market Pl CO10 9QZ (01787) 247388

*It is always difficult to discern exactly what's going on during a year in which an establishment changes hands (so we've left this one unrated); there's a hint, though, that group ownership has left this ancient inn "dependable, but not quite as good" as it was before. / **Sample dishes:** smoked salmon and marinated crawfish tails in lime chilli and coriander; honey-glazed duck breast with spring cabbage with red wine and cranberry sauce; crème brûlée. **Details:** www.maypolehotels.com; on A1141 6m NE of Sudbury; 9.15 pm; no Amex. **Accommodation:** 8 rooms, from £85.*

Great House   **£ 41**   A ★★

Market Pl CO10 9QZ   (01787) 247431

*It's hard to beat the Crépy family's "charming and brilliant" venture,
housed in a "fine ancient building", "overlooking a square in one
of England's most attractive villages"; a "fresh and sophisticated"
revamp has revitalised its looks, and it continues to serve "first-class"
Gallic cuisine.* / **Sample dishes:** grilled marinated fillet of red mullet served
on braised chicory with a caramel and lime jus; grilled marinated saddle of venison
served with a poached pear in red wine and a rich cranberry and red wine sauce;
raspberry tartlet on a pistachio custard cream served with a pistachio crème
anglaise. **Details:** www.greathouse.co.uk; follow directions to Guildhall; 9.30 pm;
closed Mon & Sun D; closed Jan; no Amex. **Accommodation:** 5 rooms,
from £96.

LEEDS, WEST YORKSHIRE   5–1C

As a dining destination, Leeds seems slightly to have lost its
way of late. Its eminent Chinese restaurant was
lost to redevelopment, and *Anthony's* – which at one point
looked set to be notable at a national level – seems to drifting
somewhat.

The city does have a good range of ethnic restaurants,
though, and a famously big and brassy big-night-out
destination (*Bibi's*).

Aagrah   **£ 27**   A ★

Aberford Rd LS25 2HF   (0113) 287 6606

*This "lively" city-centre Indian is "to the same superb standard as the
rest of this local chain" – it's "reliable and friendly, and the food
is always tasty and well-cooked".* / **Sample dishes:** seekh kebab; chicken
mangalore; ras malai. **Details:** www.aagrah.com; from A1 take A642 Aberford
Rd to Garforth; 11.30 pm, 11 pm Sun; closed Sat L & Sun L.

Akbar's   **£ 30**   ★

16 Greek St LS1 5RU   (0113) 242 5426

*You may get "rammed-in like sardines", at this city-centre Indian,
but its food is "hard to fault".* / **Sample dishes:** onion bhaji; chicken balti;
ras malai. **Details:** www.akbars.co.uk; midnight; D only.

Anthony's   **£ 58**   ★

19 Boar Ln LS1 6EA   (0113) 245 5922

*If the Fat Duck really deserves three Michelin stars, it is hard
to understand the tyre men's continuing refusal in any way
to recognise the "outstanding" quality of Anthony Flynn's cuisine;
most reports, as ever, extol the "fantastic delights" offered by a meal
here, but some feedback suggests that – in the absence of the long-
overdue accolade from the Guide Rouge – the place is rather losing
heart.* / **Sample dishes:** white onion risotto; roast duck with chocolate and soya;
caramelized pear with goats cheese. **Details:** www.anthonysrestaurant.co.uk;
9.30 pm; closed Mon & Sun; no Amex.

Anthony's at Flannels   **£ 28**   ★

68-78 Vicar Ln LS1 7JH   (0113) 242 8732

*"Accomplished" cooking (overseen by local hero Anthony Flynn)
is served in a "large, bright and airy room", at this first-floor spin-off,
above a clothes shop – "a lovely place for lunch".* / **Sample dishes:** oak
smoked salmon & prawn fishcakesred pepper & tomato salsa,caviar vinaigrette;
thyme & garlic roast lamb rump,dauphinoise potatoes, caponata; strawberry
Bakewell tart served with vanilla& balsamic ice cream.
Details: www.anthonysatflannels.co.uk; 6 pm, Fri-Sat 11 pm Sun 5 pm; closed
Mon; no Amex.

Art's £ 35 Ⓐ

42 Call Ln LS1 6DT (0113) 243 8243

A "stalwart", but a perennially "youthful" one; this popular institution "in the youthful heart of Leeds" is a "very relaxed" sort of place, where food can be "a little bland" but is generally "reliable". / **Sample dishes:** potato & vegetable samosas with babaganoush & a carrot, mint & coriander salad; braised lamb shank with a root vegetable casserole; sticky toffee pudding with butterscotch sauce with vanilla ice cream. **Details:** www.artscafebar.co.uk; near Corn Exchange; 10 pm, 2 am Sat; no booking, Sat & Sun L.

Bibis £ 40 Ⓐ

Criterion Pl, Swinegate LS1 4AG (0113) 243 0905

"If you don't mind WAGs", then a "stunning" Art-Deco interior and "fantastic" cocktails justify the trip to this "fun" and "glitzy" Italian legend; the food's "only average", though, and rather "overpriced". / **Sample dishes:** lightly fried goat's cheese; stuffed with garlic butter and breadcrumbed, gently fried served with steamed rice; golden caramel crème brûlée served with a light spiced tuile biscuit. **Details:** www.bibisrestaurant.com; 11.30 pm; no booking, Sat.

Brasserie Forty 4 £ 40 Ⓣ

44 The Calls LS2 7EW (0113) 234 3232

"What they do is done well, but they've been doing it a long time now"; this canal-side brasserie may not raise the pulse nowadays, but it's still tipped as "a reliable stand-by". / **Sample dishes:** English asparagus with a crispy egg; chicken satay cardamom rice and coconut curry sauce; traditional Spanish almond cake. **Details:** www.brasserie44.com; 10pm mon-fri, 10.30 sat; closed Sun.

Brio £ 37 ✪

40 Great George St LS1 3DL (0113) 246 5225

A "very good" and "authentic" city-centre Italian which is particularly popular at lunchtime (and also does a "good-value early-evening menu"); it has an offshoot at The Light (tel 243 5533), which majors in pizza. / **Sample dishes:** Prosciutto di Parma & melone; chicken and mushroom maccheroni; chocolate panna cotta. **Details:** www.brios.co.uk; 10.30 pm; closed Sun.

Bryan's £ 26

9 Weetwood Ln LS16 5LT (0113) 278 5679

It can seem "pricey", but this "renowned" Headingley chippy is consistently well-rated for offering fish 'n' chips "streets ahead of the competition". / **Sample dishes:** queen scallops with cheese and garlic butter; haddock fillet; home-made three core sponge and custard. **Details:** off Otterley Rd; 9.30 pm, Sun 7 pm; no Amex; need 8+ to book.

Casa Mia Grande £ 36

33-35 Harrogate Rd LS7 3PD (0870) 444 5154

"Still a favourite, especially for excellent pasta and seafood" – this "busy" Italian offers "a wide-ranging" menu which pleases most reporters most of the time; there are also outposts at 10-12 Steinbeck Lane and Millennium Square (same tel throughout). / **Sample dishes:** pan-fried forest mushrooms with white wine, garlic and olive oil, served on Italian toasted ciabatta; medallion of veal topped with Parma ham and cooked with white wine, fresh sage and a demi-glace sauce; cherry cheesecake. **Details:** www.casamiaonline.co.uk; 10.30 Fri & Sat 11 pm, Sun 9:30 pm.

Chaophraya £ 30
20a, First Floor, Blayds Ct LS2 4AG   (0113) 244 9339
"Getting better every year"; the *"really flavoursome"* fare on offer at this *"authentic"* establishment, near the railway station, is *"definitely the best Thai food in Leeds"*. / **Sample dishes:** chicken marinated in Thai herbs and honey on bamboo skewerscharcoal served with peanut sauce; grilled sirloin beef fillet with Thai salad and mint sauce with sliced grape; tiramisu. **Details:** www.chaophraya.co.uk; in Swinegate; 10.30 pm.

Flying Pizza £ 32
60 Street Ln LS8 2DQ   (0113) 266 6501
"The food takes second place to the people-watching", at this famously swanky but otherwise *"average"* Roundhay pizzeria; and *"you can always admire the flash cars parked outside…"* / **Sample dishes:** wild mushrooms sautéed in white wine, garlic & tomato on bruschetta; pizza topped with mozzarella, wild mushroom and Parmesan; tiramisu brûlée. **Details:** www.theflyingpizza.co.uk; just off A61, 3m N of city centre; 11 pm, Sun 10 pm .

Fourth Floor Café
Harvey Nichols £ 37
107-111 Briggate LS1 6AZ   (0113) 204 8000
Perhaps Harvey Nics's best dining operation, this *"lively"* venue is often praised for its *"high standards"*; even fans can find it *"overpriced"*, however, but you can always fall back on the *"great people-watching"* (or the *"stunning"* wine — *"be sure to ask for the 'big' list"*). / **Sample dishes:** goat's cheese, poached pear, roast hazelnuts, watercress and rocket salad; pan-fried duck breast, buttered noodles, black olive dressing; raspberry and peach melba trifle. **Details:** www.harveynichols.com; 10 pm; L only, except Thu-Sat when L & D; no booking, Sat L.

Fuji Hiro £ 23
45 Wade Ln LS2 8NJ   (0113) 243 9184
"A simple and unpretentious noodle bar in the city-centre", universally hailed for its *"tasty"* and *"enjoyable"* fare. / **Sample dishes:** chicken dumplings; soba noodles. **Details:** 10 pm, Fri & Sat 11 pm; need 5+ to book.

La Grillade £ 42
Wellington St LS1 4HJ   (0113) 245 9707
After 25 years in the same ownership, this *"very, very French"* outfit is still *"a good place to eat"*; *"it's much nicer inside than the exterior would lead you to believe"*. / **Sample dishes:** toasted goat's cheese on a bed of green salad; grilled salmon with white butter and spinach sauce; chocolate mousse. **Details:** www.lagrillade.co.uk; 10 pm; closed Sat L & Sun.

Hansa's £ 26
72-74 North St LS2 7PN   (0113) 244 4408
"Sublime" Gujarati cuisine, served *"with flair"*, continues to make Mrs Hansa-Dabhi's city-centre veteran a smash hit with all who report on it — *"it's the only place I'm happy to go veggie!"* / **Sample dishes:** colocasta leaves pasted with a curried batter, rolled, steamed, and then stir-fried with mustard and sesame seeds; Indian runner beans and aubergine curry; semolina cooked in vegetable ghee with sultanas, almond and cardomon. **Details:** www.hansasrestaurant.com; 10.30 mon-sat 11; D only, ex Sun L only; no Amex.

Little Tokyo £ 28
24 Central Rd LS1 6DE   (0113) 2439090
"Reliable, well-priced and right in the city-centre" — this *"genuine-feeling"* little Japanese (behind Debenhams) offers *"a good choice of soups, noodles, sushi and bento boxes"*; look out for the *"interesting Saturday night entertainment"*! / **Details:** www.littletokyo.co.uk; 10 pm, Fri & Sat 11 pm; need 8+ to book.

Livebait £ 39

The Calls LS2 7EY (0113) 2444144

Admittedly only a chain outlet – and one that "could be better" – but, in a city with few competing seafood specialists, this mill-conversion is sometimes tipped for its "great fish".

/ **Sample dishes:** *crab cakes with a cajun potato salad and remoulade dressing; masala spice sea bass fillet, cardamom roast sweet potatoes and green mango salsa; sticky toffee pudding with banana, served with vanilla ice cream.*
Details: *www.livebaitrestaurant.co.uk; 10.30 pm; closed Sun.*

No 3 York Place £ 45

3 York Pl LS1 2DR (0113) 245 9922

A well-reputed, city-centre site, still credited by most reporters with turning out "good food at reasonable prices"; "attentive" staff, however, don't entirely succeed in dispelling a somewhat "cold" aura.

/ **Sample dishes:** *risotto of prawns, coriander and chili oil; belly pork in honey, a spaghetti of vegetables and soya dressing; cold caramel soufflé with sablé biscuits.* **Details:** *www.no3yorkplace.co.uk; 9.30 pm; closed Sat L & Sun.*

The Piazza by Anthony

42 Call Ln LS1 6DT

A late 2008 venture from Anthony Flinn on the ground floor of the Corn Exchange including a brasserie and café amongst many foody attractions – should be an interesting addition to the city.

The Reliance £ 25

76-78 North St LS2 7PN (0113) 295 6060

A "slightly boho" bar restaurant, tipped as "just the place for a low-key weekday supper"; it's "great for breakfast with the papers too".

/ **Details:** *www.the-reliance.co.uk; 10 pm; no booking.*

The Restaurant Bar & Grill £ 40

3 City Sq LS1 2AN (0113) 244 9625

"A good location in the centre of town" – the old central post office – provides a "relaxed" (if "rather crowded") setting for an outpost of this buzzy mini-group; "the menu is ordinary, but well-cooked". / **Details:** *www.therestaurantbarandgrill.co.uk; 11 pm, 10.30 pm Sun.*

Rico £ 35

450 Roundhay Rd LS8 2HU (0113) 2959697

A "very popular" Lady Wood Italian, tipped as "still beating its near neighbour, the Flying Pizza, particularly in the value-for-money stakes". / **Details:** *10.30 pm, 11 pm Fri & Sat.*

Sala Thai £ 26

13-17 Shaw Ln LS6 4DH (0113) 278 8400

"Outstanding food, beautifully presented" (and with "plenty of choice for veggies") wins praise for this "recently renovated" Thai.

/ **Details:** *www.salathaileeds.co.uk; just off Otley Rd, near Arndale Centre; 11 pm; closed Sat L & Sun.* **Accommodation:** *rooms, from £-.*

Salvo's   £ 38 ⭐

115 Otley Rd LS6 3PX (0113) 275 5017
*"If only you didn't have to queue" for this "eternally cramped" but "true" Italian, in Headingley; it's "hard to beat", though, for "fantastic" pizza and other "delicious" dishes at "reasonable" prices. / **Details:** www.salvos.co.uk; 2m N of University on A660; 10.30 pm, Sun 9 pm; no booking at D.*

The Olive Press   £ 40 ⓣ

Canal Whf, Water Ln LS11 5PS (0113) 244 6611
*A tip for "excellent food served quickly for a lunchtime business meeting" – (Lancastrian) chef Paul Heathcote's canal-side restaurant inspires very little commentary, but all of it suggesting consistent high standards. / **Sample dishes:** hand carved Prosciutto di San Daniele with melon; whole grilled sea bream stuffed with lemon, fennel & watercress salad, salsa verde; chocolate amarone with strawberries. **Details:** www.heathcotes.co.uk; off M621, J3, behind Granary Wharf; 10pm, 11pm sat, 9pm sun.*

Sous le Nez en Ville   £ 38

Quebec Hs, Quebec St LS1 2HA (0113) 244 0108
*"A good and reliable French menu", an "exceptional wine list", and "wildly idiosyncratic" service contributes to the all-round charm of this city-centre basement (where the early-bird menu is a top local attraction). / **Sample dishes:** deep fried brie with mango & pepper chutney; chargrilled venison stack served pink, parsnip rosti, wild mushrooms & redcurrant jus, crispy sweet potatoes; trio of chocolate. **Details:** www.souslenez.com; 10 pm, Sat 11 pm; closed Sun; no Amex.*

Sukhothai   £ 27 ⭐

8 Regent St LS7 4PE (0113) 237 0141
*"A bustling Thai in Chapel Allerton", with "reasonable prices and friendly service"; recent expansion seems, if anything, to have improved an overall "excellent dining experience". / **Sample dishes:** fried chicken wing with minced chicken & bean thread noodle, with sweet chilli sauce; mixed seafood cooked in a clay pot with galangal, lemongrass, sweet basil & chilli; steamed mango rolls & ice cream. **Details:** www.thaifood4u.co.uk; 11 pm; closed Mon L; no Amex.*

Tampopo   £ 26 ⓣ

15 South Pde LS1 5QS (0113) 245 1816
*A "pleasant and inexpensive choice" – a branch of a Wagamama-esque SE Asian chain, often tipped as being "very good for a quick lunch, or pre-theatre dinner". / **Sample dishes:** three skewers of grilled marinated king prawns topped with toasted sesame seeds & served with fresh lime; yellow noodles, chicken breast and prawns in a fiery coconut broth with mint, cucumber, red onion, tofu & lime; ginger crème brûlée. **Details:** www.tampopo.co.uk; 11 pm, Sun 10 pm; need 7+ to book.*

Whitelocks Luncheon Bar   £ 26

Turk's Head Yd, off Briggate LS1 6HB (0113) 245 3950
*Essentially an "old-fashioned" Victorian boozer, this "odd and unique place" – in the very heart of the city – offers "hearty and traditional English fare" in "huge portions"; it is sometimes said to be "past its best", but – stop press – this may change, as a new management team is arriving in September 2008. / **Sample dishes:** shallow fried whitebait in garlic and lemon butter; home-made steak and ale pie, potatoes, seasonal vegetables & onion gravy; sweet Yorkshire pudding, vanilla ice cream and maple syrup. **Details:** www.whitelocks.co.uk; 9 pm, Sun 5pm; no Amex.*

Bobby's £ 23 ⭐
154-156 Belgrave Rd LE4 5AT   (0116) 266 0106
A shabby Golden Mile veteran, with quite a name for its "great and genuine Indian food, with plenty of flavour, texture and taste"; the "wide range of sweetmeats" and veggie options are the star turns. / **Details:** www.eatatbobbys.com; 10 pm; no Amex.

Case £ 40 🅐
4-6 Hotel St LE1 5AW   (0116) 251 7675
"The best Leicester local for anything other than a curry"; this trendy-looking survivor (housed in a converted factory) suffers from "occasional blips with the food", but generally pleases. / **Sample dishes:** seared king scallops with fried prawn and leeks; chargrilled fillet of beef and mushroom cream; raspberry and Bailey's crème brûlée with shortbread. **Details:** www.thecase.co.uk; near the Cathedral; 10.30 pm; closed Sun.

Saffron Spice £ 27
41-43 Belgrave Rd LE4 6AR   (0116) 266 8809
As the Friends Tandoori, this Golden Mile landmark always "came up trumps", thanks to its "very tasty but lighter-than-average Indian cooking"; it recently changed owners and name – hence we've removed its rating – but according to management "nothing else has changed... including the staff and chef". / **Details:** 11.30 pm, 10.30 pm Sun; closed Sun L.

Boat Yard £ 40 ❌
8-13 High St SS9 2EN   (01702) 475588
An "extensive sea-view" and a "beautiful setting" help make this "cheerful and buzzy" waterside spot very popular; prices are "well up to London standards", though, and there's a pretty clear view from reporters that the food and service are not. / **Sample dishes:** tender slices of beef cooked in orange blossom honey and sesame seeds with blueberry dressing and finely sliced fresh plum; crispy confit of duck leg with carmelized plum and spiced orange sauce; Grand Marnier and orange parfait served with orange marmalade sauce. **Details:** www.theboatyardrestaurant.co.uk; near railway station; 10 pm; closed Mon, Tue L & Sun D; no Amex.

The Sand Bar £ 33
71 Broadway SS9 1PE   (01702) 480067
"Candles, seafood and a view of the water makes for a lovely evening", says a fan of this "local bar and restaurant"; one former fan though, found it somewhat "overpriced" this year. / **Details:** www.sandbarandseafood.co.uk; midnight, Sun 6 pm.

The Kings Head £ 45
Ivinghoe LU7 9EB   (01296) 668388
The experience can seem a bit like "stepping back to the '70s", but this grand and "proper" village inn wins praise for its "rich" and "complex" dishes (with duck the speciality); the lunchtime menu is "amazing value". / **Details:** www.kingsheadivinghoe.co.uk; 3m N of Tring on B489 to Dunstable; 9.30 pm; closed Sun D; jacket & tie required at D.

Ⓐ

Auberge du Lac
Brocket Hall   **£ 78**
AL8 7XG   (01707) 368888
"The setting overlooking the lake" – with a large terrace – makes this "real hide-away" a "perfect spot", especially on a sunny day; the food "has gone up a notch since the Novelli days", and is now "very acceptable". / **Sample dishes:** caramelised hand dived scallops, prune rolled confit pork belly, white onion purée, lime and five spice jus; orange marinated breast of magret duck, braised leg rolled inpain d'epice, kohlrabi and sweet potato; thyme roast pineapple, banana mousse and pineapple sorbet.
Details: www.brocket-hall.co.uk; on B653 towards Harpenden; 9.30 pm; closed Mon & Sun D; no jeans or trainers. **Accommodation:** 16 rooms, from £260.

Ⓣ

Lewtrenchard Manor   **£ 58**
EX20 4PN   (01566) 783256
An Elizabethan country house hotel (Von Essen), in a truly "magnificent" setting, and tipped in particular for its "excellent-value" set lunch. / **Sample dishes:** warm black pudding tureen and piccalilli vegetables and roast shallot purée; pan fried dory, lightly curried apple, broad beans and coriander; hot chocolate tart and gooseberry ice cream.
Details: www.lewtrenchard.co.uk; off A30 between Okehampton & Launceston; 9 pm; closed Mon L; no jeans or trainers; children: 8+ at D. **Accommodation:** 14 rooms, from £150.

★

Bill's   **£ 27**
56 Cliffe High St   BN7 2AN   (01273) 476918
This "hugely busy" but "relaxed" cafe has become a local institution, especially popular for "affable breakfasting"; it's often "noisy", though, and critics find it a touch "hyped". / **Sample dishes:** home-made lasagne; baked orange and gingerbread cheesecake with mascarpone, blood oranges and chocolate sauce. **Details:** www.billsproducestore.co.uk; 5 pm; closed Sun; no Amex.

Ⓐ

Star Inn   **£ 42**
The Street   CB8 9PP   (01638) 500275
"Hearty Spanish dishes at a beautiful country pub" – that's the "interesting" formula that wins general approval for this "fine" racing-country hostelry. / **Sample dishes:** mussels; wild boar; home-made pavlova.
Details: on B1063 6m SE of Newmarket; 10 pm; closed Sun D.

Arundell Arms   **£ 54**
Fore St   PL16 0AA   (01566) 784666
"A hidden gem of a restaurant in a traditional hotel in a small village", offering "classic dishes lavishly-executed from fresh ingredients"; it's been under the same ownership for over four decades, and "standards are maintained". / **Sample dishes:** goats cheese with Bath Olivers; casserole of John Dory, sea trout quenelles, scallops and sole with girolle mushrooms; gratin of strawberries and raspberries with a champagne sabayon.
Details: www.arundellarms.com; 0.5m off A30, Lifton Down exit; 9.30 pm; no jeans or shorts. **Accommodation:** 21 rooms, from £170.

Alexanders at Limpsfield
The Old Lodge   £ 48
High St RH8 0DR   (01883) 714365

Despite food that's "always wonderful", this "friendly" and "relaxed" restaurant has only built up a small fan club among reporters – something to do with the "London prices", presumably (so the "good-value Wednesday tasting menus" are especially worth seeking out). / **Sample dishes:** ravioli filled with prawn mousse, roast prawn and crab served on a bed of crushed peas, with lemon veloute; fillet of Scotch beef served on a bed of spinach and creamed mushroom served with tomato relish, roast fig and a mushroom velouté; puff pastry wrapped poached pear stuffed with almonds, served with pear sorbet and amaretto anglais.
Details: www.alexanders-limpsfield.co.uk; 9.30 pm; closed Mon, Tue & Sun D.

Browns Pie Shop   £ 30
33 Steep Hill LN2 1LU   (01522) 527330

"Uncomfortable" and "hectic" but an institution – this stalwart housed in "old vaults" is still tipped for its "good pies, good value and friendly service"; even supporters, though, may feel it's "not what it was". / **Sample dishes:** Lincolnshire haslet served with 'house' Bramley apple jelly; steak & kidney pie; sticky toffee pudding. **Details:** www.brownspieshop.co.uk; near the Cathedral; 10 pm; no Amex.

Fourteen   £ 32
14 Bailgate LN1 3AE   (01522) 576556

"A little haven of delight, in a city with too many chain restaurants and cafés"; it's generally tipped as a pretty "slick"-looking operation, and has a "handy" central location too. / **Sample dishes:** pan-fried red mullet with beetroot, white bean, and orange salad; rump of lamb, Jersey potatoes, apricot braised shallots; Bailey's crème brûlée. **Details:** 10 pm.

The Old Bakery   £ 44
26-28 Burton Rd LN1 3LB   (01522) 576057

In the shadow of the castle walls, "a surprisingly decent find", where the food and service – more consistently of late – are of a "high standard"; "local ingredients" are "imaginatively" used too... by a chef who hails from southern Italy. / **Sample dishes:** carpaccio of ostrich with horseradish cream; baby pig roast with fennel & fresh herbs, garlic potatoes & smoked pancetta; mascarpone mousse, cantucci biscuits soaked in vin santo. **Details:** www.theold-bakery.co.uk; 9 pm; closed Mon; no jeans.
Accommodation: 4 rooms, from £63.

The Wig & Mitre   £ 38
30-32 Steep Hill LN2 1TL   (01522) 535190

A "traditional favourite", near the Cathedral; it doesn't have nearly the following it once did, but is still sometimes tipped as a nice place for a "relaxed" meal at the bar. / **Sample dishes:** salmon, monkfish and herb terrine with celeriac horseradish remoulade; sesame and soy marinated duck breast with slow cooked duck leg and vegetable spring roll on a bed of Chinese leaves and hoisin; baked lime cheesecake with home-made ginger nuts and passion fruit sorbet. **Details:** www.wigandmitre.com; between Cathedral & Castle; 11 pm.

Champany Inn £ 73 🅐⭐
EH49 7LU (01506) 834532

If you're looking for a "classic red-meat" experience, this celebrated inn (also famous for its wine list) is hard to beat; prices are "eye-watering", though, and non-meat dishes can be "clumsy"; NB: "it's probably worth the queue for the slightly cheaper adjacent chop house". / **Sample dishes:** *hot smoked salmon; sirloin steak; home-made cheesecake.* **Details:** *www.champany.com; 2m NE of Linlithgow on junction of A904 & A803; 10 pm; closed Sat L & Sun; no jeans or trainers; children: 8+.* **Accommodation:** *16 rooms, from £135.*

The Castle £ 28 🆃
SA62 3UG (01437) 781445

"A pub overlooking a pretty harbour", tipped for its "all home-made" food and its "comprehensive" selection of fresh local fish and seafood. / **Sample dishes:** *tomatoes served with a grilled goats cheese; fillet steak wrapped in bacon served with tomatoes, mushroom and onion rings with new potatoes or chips; Alabama fudgecake with cream or ice cream.* **Details:** *www.castlelittlehaven.co.uk; 9.* **Accommodation:** *2 rooms, from £80.*

East Beach Cafe £ 35
BN17 5GB (01903) 731903

This "architecturally surprising" new-build café looks "fantastic" ("literally") or "weird", to taste, and has an interior that works best by day (thanks not least to some "great views"); "great seafood" is the highlight of the "short and simple menu", of which realisation is somewhat "variable". / **Sample dishes:** *potted shrimp; seafood pasta; treacle tart.* **Details:** *www.eastbeachcafe.co.uk; 8.30 pm, Sat & Sun 9 pm.*

The year in which Liverpool has been a capital of culture has hardly caused a sea change when it comes to the city's traditionally dire restaurants. Its erstwhile culinary champions seem to have lost their way. It must say something that one of the city's most eminent all-rounders – *Everyman Bistro* – is a self-service canteen that's been in business for more than 30 years!

Perhaps *Panoramic* is what we've all been waiting for? It's early days, and it certainly has location, location and location to recommend it.

Alma De Cuba 🆃
St Peter's Church £ 42
Seel St L1 4AZ (0151) 7027394

"Feeling more like a bar at night" (and with "good cocktails too"), this Cuban (and more) establishment in a former church is tipped for its "outstanding" atmosphere. / **Sample dishes:** *pata negro ham (black footed pig) premium cured Spanish iberico ham; chicken breast, chorizo crushed potatoes, balsamic and sunblush tomato dressing; sticky toffee pudding with honeycombe ice cream and chocolate candy.* **Details:** *www.alma-de-cuba.com; 11 pm, midnight Fri & Sat; no shorts.*

Delifonseca £ 30 ⭐

12 Stanley St L1 6AF (0151) 255 0808

A "busy and pleasant bistro" which inhabits a "simply-furnished dining room over a super deli" – a "quality foodie venture" with "good-value" Latino/Italian dishes, "many of which are brilliant".
/ **Details:** www.delifonseca.co.uk; 9 pm, Fri & Sat 9.30 pm; closed Sun; no Amex.

Ego £ 33 ⓣ

Federation Hs, Hope St L1 9BW (0151) 706 0707

Tipped for "great pre-theatre deals", this Mediterranean bistro/wine bar, near the Philharmonic Hall, attracts consistently positive reports.
/ **Sample dishes:** grilled goat's cheese on toasted brioche with carmelized red onions and a fig and blueberry jam; pork fillet wrapped in Serrano ham served with a sherry, apricot, and spinach sauce; passion fruit crème brûlée.
Details: www.egorestaurants.com; 10.30 pm.

Everyman Bistro £ 23 Ⓐ⭐

5-9 Hope St L1 9BH (0151) 708 9545

"It may be called a bistro, but it's really a big pub-like rendezvous where you see everyone in Liverpool, eventually" – David Scott's "atmospheric" canteen-style veteran (est. 1970) remains a key local destination, thanks not least to its "amazingly good and slightly 'different' food". / **Sample dishes:** sweet potato and watercress soup; Greek lamb, organic beans, and marinated Feta with rice; apple and ground almond Eve's pudding. **Details:** www.everyman.co.uk; midnight, Fri & Sat 2 am; closed Sun.

Gulshan £ 29 ⓣ

544-548 Aigburth Rd L19 3QG (0151) 427 2273

"Still the best Liverpool has to offer" – in a city with little of interest on the curry front, this "flock-free" Aigburth fixture is one of the few places tipped for a spice-fix. / **Sample dishes:** gently spiced salmon rolled into filo pastry & deep fried; special masala with king prawn, chicken tikka, lamb tikka, tomatoes & mushrooms in a cream & wine sauce topped with scrambled egg soufflé & cheese; Indian ice cream with mangoes.
Details: www.gulshan-liverpool.com; 11 pm, Sun 11.30 pm; D only; no shorts.

Keith's Wine Bar £ 26 ⓣ

107 Lark Ln L17 8UR (0151) 728 7688

A Sefton Park wine bar whose Bohemian charms have long made it a popular local destination, and tipped for its "amazing value" wines.
/ **Sample dishes:** Mediterranean platter; char-grilled swordfish and lemon butter,potatoes and vegetables; Bakewell tart and ice cream.
Details: www.larklane.co.uk; 10.30 pm, Fri & Sat 12.30; need 6+ to book.

The London Carriage Works
Hope Street Hotel £ 60

40 Hope St L1 9DA (0151) 705 2222

This trendy brasserie in a boutique-hotel got rather mixed reports this year; fans still see it as "Liverpool's best", but even some of them concede "that's not saying much" – critics just say it's now "overpriced", and has "lost what made it special".
/ **Sample dishes:** pressed potato and Manchego terrine and Parma ham, tomato fondue and chorizo; pan seared calves liver and pancetta and caramelized onions with Parmesan mash; Cheshire duck egg custard tart and clotted cream ice cream.
Details: www.tlcw.co.uk; Opposite the Philharmonic Hall; 10 pm; no shorts.
Accommodation: 48 rooms, from £140.

Malmaison   £ 44

William Jessop Way, Princes Dock L3 1QW   (0151) 229 5000

*This year-old branch of the "trendy" design-hotel chain is tipped for its "generous portions"; food-wise, though, it can seem to be "trying to punch above its weight". / **Sample dishes:** ballotine of Goosenargh chicken leg stuffed with tarragon mousse and a rocket salad; port of Lancaster smoked haddock 'shepherd's pie'; mille feuille of rhubarb and honey syrup.* **Details:** www.malmaison-liverpool.com; 10.30 pm. **Accommodation:** 130 rooms, from £99.

Mei Mei   £ 32

9-13 Berry St L1 9DF   (0151) 7072888

*A "consistently good Chinese restaurant", on the fringe of the city-centre. / **Details:** 11.30 pm, Fri & Sat midnight, Sun 10 pm; no Amex.*

Olive Press   £ 37

25-27 Castle St L2 4TA   (0151) 2272242

"A cut above ordinary pizza places", or "never quite delivering what the price and pedigree require"? – that's the area of dispute on this "buzzy" city-centre Mediterranean, which is part of the empire of leading North Western chef Paul Heathcote. / **Sample dishes:** chargrilled asparagus, crab & watercress, peas & mint, chilli oil; chargrilled swordfish steak, arecchiette zucchini, chilli, garlic & Parmesan; affogato, vanilla ice cream with espresso & frangelico. **Details:** www.heathcotes.co.uk; 10 pm, Fri & Sat 11 pm, Sun 9 pm.

Panoramic
Beetham West Tower   £ 50

Brook St L3 9PJ   (0151) 236 5534

*"Be there at sunset for truly outstanding views" – from the 34th floor! – at this elevated newcomer, which "claims to be the highest restaurant in the UK" (and where "they've spent a fortune on the décor"); there's the odd bit of the "you-can't-eat-the-view" sniping you might expect, but the food is generally found surprisingly OK. / **Details:** www.panoramicliverpool.com/.*

Puschka   £ 36

16 Rodney St L1 2TE   (0151) 708 8698

*"Consistently good food and friendly staff" have won a more-than-local fan club for this small and funky outfit, which is a match for its grander neighbours; popularity is so great, though, that it can be "better mid-week". / **Details:** www.puschka.co.uk; 10 pm; closed Mon, Tue-Thu D only, Sun L only; no Amex; no trainers.*

Sapporo Teppanyaki   £ 42

134 Duke St L1 5AG   (0151) 705 3005

*A Japanese establishment near Chinatown, where "very entertaining" chefs perform "amazing displays of culinary technique"… "and the food's pretty good too". / **Details:** www.sapporo.co.uk; 11 pm, Sun 10.30 pm; no shorts.*

Simply Heathcote's   £ 38

Beetham Plaza 25, The Strand L2 0XL   (0151) 236 3536

*Not far from the Liver Building, an "interesting glass-walled venue", often tipped as a group or function venue; the food, though, inspires every shade of report from "excellent" to "very disappointing". / **Sample dishes:** black puding with ham hock & rhubarb chutney; seared fillet of sea bream with red peppers, garlic, borlotti beans & spinach; bread & butter pudding, apricot compote & clotted cream. **Details:** www.heathcotes.co.uk; 10 pm.*

60 Hope Street £ 46

60 Hope St L1 9BZ (0151) 707 6060

*The city's original contemporary-style restaurant is now once again "probably the best overall", offering "good food, well prepared, and at reasonable prices"; some reporters prefer the basement bistro to the pricier ground-floor restaurant. / **Sample dishes:** seared scallops with sautéed chicken livers, raisin purée & pistachio cream; roast loin of Cumbrian venison with roast beetroot, parsnip purée & juniper jus; rhubarb & custard trifle with popping candyrhubarb & custard trifle with popping candy. **Details:** www.60hopestreet.com; 10.30 pm; closed Sat L & Sun.*

Tai Pan £ 26

WH Lung Bdg., Great Howard St L5 9TZ (0151) 207 3888

*A "warehouse-like" dining room – above a supermarket – that's "always very busy with the local Chinese/Asian community, especially for dim sum on Sundays". / **Sample dishes:** chicken satay; fillet steak of beef with black pepper; ice cream. **Details:** 11.30 pm, Sun 9.30 pm.*

Yuet Ben £ 24

1 Upper Duke St L1 9DU (0151) 709 5772

*"Went back after 20 years, still excellent" – this "consistently good" and "friendly" Chinese veteran is "an MSG-free haven", and "good for veggies too". / **Details:** www.yuetben.co.uk; 11 pm; D only, closed Mon.*

LLANDEGLA, WREXHAM 5–3A

Bodidris Hall Hotel £ 34

LL11 3AL (01978) 790434

*Tipped for its "beautiful setting" (on an estate of 6,500 acres), this medieval country house hotel offers food that's "very good value at lunch, but quite pricey in the evening". / **Sample dishes:** tian of smoked chickenWaldorf salad, frisee endive, pomace oil; paupiette of local pheasantchive scented polenta, rosemary and redcurrant jus; honeycomb parfaitmango sauce. **Details:** www.bodidrishall.com; on A5104 from Wrexham; 8.45 pm; children: 14+ at D. **Accommodation:** 9 rooms, from £99.*

LLANDRILLO, DENBIGHSHIRE 4–2D

Tyddyn Llan £ 57

LL21 0ST (01490) 440264

*"A real Welsh treat that's definitely worth the detour" – Bryan & Susan Webb's "wonderfully-situated" restaurant-with-rooms makes "meticulous" use of "local" produce to create "melting" dishes; there's also a "stunning" wine list (largely available in halves or by the glass). / **Sample dishes:** griddled scallops, vegetable relish & rocket; roast pigeon with braised butter beans, Savoy cabbage & morels; prune & almond tart with mascarpone ice cream. **Details:** www.tyddynllan.co.uk; on B4401 between Corwen and Bala; 9 pm; closed Mon (Tue-Thu L by prior arrangement only); no Amex; booking essential Tue L-Thu L. **Accommodation:** 13 rooms, from £110.*

Bodysgallen Hall £ 56
LL30 1RS (01492) 584466

*A grand and potentially "lovely" country house hotel, set in 200 acres, just outside the resort; it seems to have "gone downhill" of late, though, with numerous reports of the "didn't-quite-work" "expensive", and "doesn't-live-up" variety. / **Sample dishes:** tian of goats cheese with red pepper, smoked pimento and saffron cream; fillet of Welsh beef wih braised oxtail, creamed celeriac and horseradish; rhubarb créme brûlée with a ginger and rhubarb sorbet. **Details:** www.bodysgallen.com; 2m off A55 on A470; 9.15 Sun-Thu, 9.30 Fri; no jeans or trainers; booking: max 10; children: 8+. **Accommodation:** 31 rooms, from £175.*

St Tudno Hotel & Terrace Restaurant £ 48
Promenade LL30 2LP (01492) 874411

*This dining room of this Victorian hotel, near the pier, has long had a very high reputation, but of late the feeling has developed that it's "living on past glories"; in compensation – "a massive wine list, to suit all tastes and pockets". / **Sample dishes:** tarragon & scallop tortellini with pea shoots & langoustine dressing; fillet steak Wellington with braised baby gem & smoked brandade; tiramisu with chocolate, hazelnut, coffee sorbet, & toasted biscotti biscuit. **Details:** www.st-tudno.co.uk; 9.30 pm; no shorts; children: 6+. **Accommodation:** 19 rooms, from £130.*

T

Waterdine £ 47
Llanfair Waterdine LD7 1TU (01547) 528214

*A tip for those in search of a restaurant-with-rooms in these parts, praised for its "excellent" Gallic cooking, and its "friendly" style. / **Sample dishes:** terrine of Gloucester old spot pork with black fig & rasberry chutney; Barbary duck breast with braised lettuce; iced apricot parfait. **Details:** www.waterdine.com; 9 pm; closed Mon & Sun D; no Amex; booking essential; children: 12+ at D. **Accommodation:** 3 rooms, from £80.*

T

Lake Country House £ 59
LD4 4BS (01591) 620202

*"A classic country house hotel, now boasting a new annexe", tipped for its "great service" and its "excellent choice of dishes" (all veggie). / **Sample dishes:** tureen of Cornish fish and pickled carrot, coriander and lime dressing; breast of free-range chicken, Herefordshire asparagus, spinach, new potatoes and wild mushrooms; dark chocolate panna cotta and basil ice cream and strawberry salad. **Details:** www.lakecountryhouse.co.uk; off A483 at Garth, follow signs; 9.15 pm; jacket & tie required; children: 8+ at D. **Accommodation:** 30 rooms, from £170.*

A

Corn Mill £ 32
Dee Ln LL20 8PN (01978) 869555

*A gastropub in an attractively converted mill tipped for its "truly wonderful setting" (with "a large deck projecting over the fast-running River Dee"); the food, though, "ranges from great to dire". / **Sample dishes:** grilled black pudding on bubble & squeak with onion gravy a poached egg; slow roast belly pork with apple dauphinoise vegetables and wholegrain mustard sauce; Baileys pancetta. **Details:** www.brunningandprice.co.uk; 9.30 pm, Sun 9 pm .*

Lake Vyrnwy Hotel   £ 46   Ⓐ✪
Lake Vyrnwy SY10 0LY   (01691) 870692
*"A real destination"; this Baronial-style hotel was originally built
to house the engineers who built the lake it now overlooks; its style
can seem "a little dated" nowadays, but most reports are
of "superbly-prepared food" (albeit from a "limited menu"),
and "incredible" views too. / **Sample dishes:** chargrilled fillet of trout and
niçoise salad and parsley; honeyed breast of duck and buttered greensa and risotto
fritters; sable biscuits layered with passion fruit curd and raspberries and toffee
sauce. **Details:** www.lakevyrnwyhotel.co.uk; on B4393 at SE end of Lake Vyrnwy;
9.15 pm; no shorts. **Accommodation:** 52 rooms, from £120.*

Carlton Riverside   £ 48   Ⓣ
Dolecoed Rd LD5 4RA   (01591) 610248
*The former Carlton House hotel moved in recent times to new
premises overlooking the River Irfon; consistently high ratings from
reporters make it a top tip if you should find yourself in this part
of the world. / **Sample dishes:** air dried ham with a pea mousse and peashoot
salad; hand seared fillet of beef, purple sprouting broccoli organic asparagus,
crushed new potatoes, blazed baby carrots and red wine and wild mushroom
sauce; chocolat au St Emilion slice with crème presse and almond praline.
Details: www.carltonrestaurant.co.uk; 8.30 pm; D only; no Amex; booking:
max 10. **Accommodation:** 5 rooms, from £65.*

Llangoed Hall   £ 58   Ⓐ✪
LD3 0YP   (01874) 754525
*Bernard Ashley's grand country house hotel has a "lovely setting and
views", and impresses pretty much everyone who reports on it with its
"faultless" food and service. / **Sample dishes:** assiette of continental meats,
baby leaf and sunblush tomato salad; supreme free range chicken and fondant
potatoes and asparagus velouté; coffee and Bailey's crème brûlée and pecan nut
cookies. **Details:** www.llangoedhall.com; 11m NW of Brecon on A470; 10 pm;
closed weekday L; jacket required at D; children: 8+. **Accommodation:** 23
rooms, from £210.*

The Albannach   £ 59   Ⓐ✪
IV27 4LP   (01571) 844407
*"A stunning location, exceptionally-crafted menus and 'individual'
accommodation" – that's the deal that again wins acclamation for
Colin Craig and Lesley Crosfield's small and remote hotel.
/ **Sample dishes:** mousseline of halibut, sauce vierge, and lobster; roast saddle
of wild roe deer, heritage root vegetables and game chocolate sauce; brioche and
butter pudding and pepper ice cream, vanilla poached pears.
Details: www.thealbannach.co.uk; 8 pm; D only, closed Mon; no Amex; children:
12+. **Accommodation:** 5 rooms, from £250.*

LOCKSBOTTOM, KENT   3–3B

Chapter One   £ 45
Farnborough Common BR6 8NF (01689) 854848
*"Everything a good restaurant should be" – this "classy" operation
is all the more worth knowing about in "a part of Kent which lacks
good places"; Andrew McLeish's cuisine would be a "special treat"
anywhere, though, and it has a huge following. / Sample dishes: jugged
hare with pancetta & potato espuma; roast chicken, with smoked pork belly, spring
peas & sauce chasseur; hot chocolate fondant with tahitian vanilla ice cream.
Details: www.chaptersrestaurants.com; just before Princess Royal Hospital;
10.30 pm; booking: max 12.*

LONG CRENDON, BUCKINGHAMSHIRE   2–2D

Angel   £ 46
47 Bicester Rd HP18 9EE   (01844) 208268
*A bistro often hailed for offering the "most reliable food in the
neighbourhood" (with fish a particular "treat"); there was also some
feeling this year, however, that it's "not up to its old standard".
/ Sample dishes: twice baked cheese soufflé glazed with garlic and parsley
sauce; poached smoked hadddock on leek and mustard mash with poached egg
and cheese sauce; tree of orange chocolate marquees with white and dark
chocolate mousse and a rich chocolate brownie with chocolate sauce.
Details: www.angelrestaurant.co.uk; 2m NW of Thames, off B4011; 9.30 pm;
closed Sun D; no Amex; booking: max 12, Fri & Sat. Accommodation: 4 rooms,
from £95.*

LONG MELFORD, SUFFOLK   3–1C

Scutchers   £ 44
Westgate St CO10 9DP   (01787) 310200
*A "reliable" family-bistro that gets a fair degree of feedback, and is
pretty consistently tipped as "very good for the area".
/ Details: www.scutchers.com; 9.30 pm; closed Mon & Sun.*

LONGFRAMLINGTON, NORTHUMBERLAND 8–2B

Anglers Arms   £ 35
Weldon Bridge NE65 8AX   (01665) 570271
*"Dine in the railway carriage for maximum ambience", if you visit this
"great value-for-money" dining destination; wherever you sit, though,
it's tipped for its "interesting food combinations that work well".
/ Sample dishes: garlic king prawns; honey roast of Barbary duck; Baileys
cheesecake. Details: www.anglersarms.com; 9.30 pm; no Amex.
Accommodation: 7 rooms, from £75.*

LONGRIDGE, LANCASHIRE   5–1B

The Longridge Restaurant   £ 51
104-106 Higher Rd PR3 3SY   (01772) 784969
*The original restaurant of big-name North Western chef Paul
Heathcote, this converted cottage still impresses some reporters with
its "very good" dishes (using "local produce"), but the style can also
seem "fussy" and "unmemorable". / Sample dishes: hand carved
Cumbrian air dried ham and tracklements; pan fried fillets of John Dory, braised
English lettuce, peas, broad beans and new potatoes; bread and butter pudding,
clotted cream and apricot compote. Details: www.heathcotes.co.uk; follow signs
for Jeffrey Hill; 9.30 pm, 8.30 pm Sun; closed Mon & Sat L.*

Peat Spade Inn   **£ 42**   Ⓐ
SO20 6DR   (01264) 810612
"A charming village on the Test" is the location for this "smart and
cosy" inn, which is "a clear favourite with locals and passers-by";
"the menu is clever for a pub", and "well cooked".
/ **Details:** www.peatspadeinn.co.uk; 1.25m from Stockbridge; 9 pm; closed Sun D;
no Amex. **Accommodation:** 6 rooms, from £110.

Ⓣ

The South Lodge
South Lodge Hotel   **£ 49**
Brighton Rd RH13 6PS   (01403) 891711
"An excellent all-rounder" – this grand country house hotel
is particularly tipped for its "breathtaking views over the Sussex
countryside"; (it recently doubled in size, and opened a new eatery:
'The Path'). / **Sample dishes:** scallop, truffle panacotta, pink grapefruit; saddle
of lamb, potato fondant, red onion marmalade, lamb jus; organic chocolate delice,
spearmint ice cream. **Details:** www.exclusivehotels.co.uk; opposite the Crabtree
pub 1 mile up road from Leonards Lee gardens; 9.30 pm; jacket & tie; children:
12+. **Accommodation:** 89 rooms, from £230.

The Fox Inn   **£ 36**   Ⓐ★
GL56 0UR   (01451) 870555
"Slightly away from the tourist honey-pots", this "very busy" but
"reliable" inn makes "a fabulous place to spend an evening"; the food
is "really good", and the atmosphere is "buzzy" too.
/ **Sample dishes:** roast squash risotto; slow-cooked lamb shank with red wine,
rosemary & roast garlic; crème brûlée. **Details:** www.foxinn.net; on A436 near
Stow-on-the-Wold; 10 pm, Sun 9.30 pm; no Amex. **Accommodation:** 3 rooms,
from £68.

★★

La Bécasse   **£ 70**   ★★
17 Corve St SY8 1DA   (01584) 872325
Chef Will Holland's "amazing" and "distinctive" cuisine "deserves
more recognition", say the many fans of this year-old foodie temple
(on the former site of Hibiscus, and now run by the team from
Shinfield's L'Ortolan); the word doesn't seem to be fully out yet,
however, and the place can be "quiet". / **Sample dishes:** Scottish
langoustine carpaccio, "water dressing" and claw beignet; chargrilled guinea fowl
breast, leg ballotine with pickled pink peppercorns, asparagus, strawberry and
tarragon jus; pineapple carpaccio, fresh mango, cardamom sugar and creamy rice.
Details: www.labecasse.co.uk; 9pm; closed Mon, Tue L & Sun; no Amex.

Koo   **£ 31**
127 Old St SY8 1NU   (01584) 878462
"Refreshingly different in a town better known for its expensive
eateries" – this "friendly" café offers "good and homely Japanese
cooking". / **Sample dishes:** sushi; breaded prawns and wasabi mayonnaise and
stir-fried beef in a fruity garlic soy sauce; Japanese desert platter.
Details: www.koo-ook.co.uk; Off the A49; 9 pm; D only, closed Mon & Sun.

Mr Underhill's　　　　　　　　**£ 63**　　Ⓐ✪✪

Dinham Wier SY8 1EH (01584) 874431

"Exquisite" food (and a "fascinating range of wines") is all part of an "unfussy and friendly" formula that makes the Bradleys' restaurant-with-rooms a "simply top-drawer" experience (and attracting some of the very highest ratings in the survey); it's "excellent value" too.
/ *Sample dishes: crispy sea bream with spiced couscous, chorizo and horseradish vinaigrette; venison with red wine and thyme, and pea purée; hot fondant apricot tart with four kinds of apricots.* **Details:** *www.mr-underhills.co.uk; 8.15 pm; D only, closed Mon & Tue; no Amex; children: 8+.* **Accommodation:** *8 rooms, from £140.*

LUXBOROUGH, SOMERSET　　　　　　　1–2D

The Royal Oak Inn　　　　　　　**£ 37**　　Ⓣ

TA23 0SH (01984) 640319

Tipped as "charming", "lovely", "friendly" and "comfortable", a dining pub also complimented for its "good range of food".
/ **Details:** *www.theroyaloakinnluxborough.co.uk; 9 pm; no Amex.* **Accommodation:** *11 rooms, from £65.*

LYDFORD, DEVON　　　　　　　　　　1–3C

The Dartmoor Inn　　　　　　　**£ 41**

Moorside EX20 4AY (01822) 820221

"The food, using mainly local produce, continues to excel", at the Burgesses' former coaching inn; the place can suffer, though, from being "under-staffed". / **Sample dishes:** *autumn squash salad with courgette flowers and Parmesan shavings; roast new season English partridge with Savoy cabbage, bacon and a port wine sauce; vanilla panna cotta with red berry sauce.* **Details:** *www.dartmoorinn.com; near Dartmoor National Park; 9.30 pm; closed Mon L & Sun D; children: 5+ at weekends.* **Accommodation:** *3 rooms, from £100.*

LYDGATE, GREATER MANCHESTER　　　5–2B

The White Hart　　　　　　　　**£ 45**　　✪

51 Stockport Rd OL4 4JJ (01457) 872566

"Consistent over many years" – this "local pub/restaurant/bistro", on the edge of the Pennines, continues to please all who report on it.
/ **Sample dishes:** *ham hock and Lancashire black pudding terrine with home-made piccalilli and toasted granary bread; roast Goosnargh duck breast with sautéed spring greens and orange roast baby carrots; chocolate mousse pot with milk sorbet and shortbread biscuit.* **Details:** *www.thewhitehart.co.uk; 2m E of Oldham on A669, then A6050; 9.30 pm.* **Accommodation:** *12 rooms, from £120.*

LYME REGIS, DORSET　　　　　　　　2–4A

Harbour Inn　　　　　　　　　**£ 35**　　Ⓣ

The Cobb, Marine Pde DT7 3JF (01297) 442299

"A safe haven, where you are always sure of good food and good value for money" – this "enthusiastic" beach-side boozer offers food in both bar and restaurant, but the former is tipped as the one with the better view! / **Sample dishes:** *smoked salmon & shellfish cocktail with citrus dressing; fillet of halibut with smoked salmon butter with vegetables & roast new potatoes; treacle tart served with custard cream.* **Details:** *9 pm.*

Hix Oyster and Fish House £ 50
Cobb Hs DT7 3JP (01297) 446910
C'leb chef Mark Hix, returns to his Dorset roots, with this small venue with sea views from its bright conservatory area; it opened too late for any survey commentary, but initial press reviews are (as they tend to be for Hix-backed joints) a total rave.
/ **Details:** www.restaurantsetcltd.co.uk; 10 pm; closed Mon.

LYMINGTON, HAMPSHIRE   2–4C

Egan's £ 40
Gosport St SO41 9BE (01590) 676165
A "friendly", "family-run" bistro universally acclaimed by reporters for its "good food and buzzy atmosphere", and for offering "sensational value at lunchtimes"; it was on the market as this guide went to press (but no early sale was expected!). / **Sample dishes:** warm salad of asparagus with poached egg hollandaise; veal kidneys with red wine sauce, bacon lardons, & mushrooms; lemon tart with lemon posset. **Details:** 10 pm; closed Mon & Sun; no Amex; booking: max 6, Sat.

Westover Hall Hotel £ 55   Ⓣ
Park Ln SO41 0PT (01590) 643044
We wish we had more reports on this Victorian country house hotel; it's under new management, but fans say it "still offers stunning levels of food and service". / **Sample dishes:** cherry tomato tatin of crottin goat's cheese; magret of Barbary duck, orange sauce, crushed potato, spinach and spiced bread carrot; dark cherry iced parfait, verbena granite, cherry marmalade. **Details:** www.westoverhallhotel.com; 9 pm; children: 5+ after 5 pm. **Accommodation:** 12 rooms, from £210.

LYNDHURST, HAMPSHIRE   2–4C

Le Poussin at Parkhill £ 63
Beaulieu Rd SO43 7FZ (023) 8028 2944
Still not open again as this guide goes to press! – the Aitkens family first team is still at their Whitley Ridge property, and the Parkhill re-opening has now been put back until spring 2009.
/ **Details:** www.lepoussin.co.uk.

LYTHAM, LANCASHIRE   5–1A

Chicory Restaurant £ 42
5-7 Henry St FY8 5LE (01253) 737111
Reports of this bright modern restaurant have remained very unsettled this year; an optimist insists, however, that the place "has come back to life" since a recent refurbishment (and the resolution of certain ownership issues). / **Sample dishes:** asparagus and mushroom risotto basket, basil and tomato coulis, Parmesan flake; roast fillet of monkfish wrapped in pancetta on basil, sun dried tomatoes and asparagus gnocchi; chocolate crusted hazelnut marquis, chocolate and frangelico syrup. **Details:** www.chicorygroup.co.uk; 9.30 pm.

MADINGLEY, CAMBRIDGESHIRE   3–1B

Three Horseshoes £ 44
CB23 8AB (01954) 210221
This "picturesque thatched gastropub" remains a well-known destination, popular with "Cambridge business folk" (and the odd undergraduate too); it still pleases most people most of the time, even if its new all-Italian menu can give rise to the occasional "nothing-y" result. / **Sample dishes:** heirloom tomatoes with deep-fried buffalo mozzarella, basil & anchovy 'sandwich'; sirloin steak with porcini mushroom bruschetta, gremolata, balsamic roast red onion, watercress & horseradish parsley salsa; summer pudding with valpolicella & clotted cream. **Details:** www.threehorseshoesmadingley.co.uk; 2m W of Cambridge, off A14 or M11; 9 pm, Fri & Sat 9.30 pm, Sun 8.30 pm; no Amex.

Wildings   **£ 32** ⭐
Harbour Rd KA26 9NR (01655) 331401
*"An out-of-the-way location to eat well and talk privately, while
enjoying lovely sea views"; despite the large scale of the operation,
the cooking makes good use of a "great standard of produce"
("especially fish"). / **Sample dishes:** lightly smoked haddock & bacon risotto;
halibut, salmon, monkfish, cod & silverbream panfried with a tomato & basil
vinaigrette; meringue vacherin with fresh berries & a liqueur syrup.
Details: www.wildingsrestaurant.co.uk; Follow the A77 to Turnberry and turn on to
the A719 signposted Maidens.; 9 pm; no Amex. **Accommodation:** 10 rooms,
from £45/person.*

Five Horseshoes   **£ 35** Ⓐ
RG9 6EX (01491) 641282
*"A wonderful place to discover, in the middle of nowhere";
this "relaxed" boozer doesn't just offer "excellent traditional pub
food", but also "fantastic views of rolling hills". / **Sample dishes:** rillettes
of Barbary duck, cornichons, toasted multigrain; loin of pork, trotter ragout, Savoy
cabbage & olive oil mash; yoghurt cheesecake, blueberry compote, cinnamon
yoghurt sorbet. **Details:** www.thefivehorseshoes.co.uk; on B481 between
Nettlebed & Watlington; 9.30 pm, Sun 8.30 pm.*

The Old Bell Hotel   **£ 53**
Abbey Row SN16 0BW (01666) 822344
*"A perfect ancient coaching inn"; with its "superb setting, near a
lovely garden", it comes especially recommended as a "great Sunday
lunch destination". / **Sample dishes:** Cornish scallops, bacon, new potatoes &
fresh peas; line-caught sea bass & langoustine, courgette flower, broad beans &
vierge dressing; Valrhona chocolate fondant with mango & caramel.
Details: www.oldbellhotel.com; next to Abbey; 9 pm, 9.30 Fri & Sat.
Accommodation: 33 rooms, from £125.*

A lot of money has been poured into Manchester restaurants
of late, but the city is still looking for that elusive culinary
heavy hitter. *Vermillion* has had the sort of budget that would
make it a major opening in London, but it's difficult to have
too much confidence that its backers are going to make any
return out of the place. There have been some other
respectable openings of late, such as *The Modern*,
and particularly *Grado*, but none of these are the stuff
of headlines. Leading local chef Paul Heathcote had been
planning to open a headline-catcher, but pulled the scheme
in the summer of 2008 in the light of economic uncertainty.

If you're looking for quality non-ethnic dining and paying your
own way the safest option is still to head off to the 'burbs,
most obviously to West Didsbury's consistently satisfying
Lime Tree.

Let's stay in the city-centre, though, and look at the mid-price options. This is the only city in England where one of the most obvious cuisines to eat is English! *Sam's Chop House* and *Mr Thomas's Chop House*, and the *Market* (assuming the new régime does not make too many changes) really are 'English' restaurants! If you are not in the mood for something quite so traditional, it might be worth going Italian, and checking out the mid-level *San Carlo*, or the pizzeria-level (but very fashionable) *Croma*.

The best city-centre option, however is to eat Chinese, in which cuisine Manchester is pre-eminent outside London. The most notable name is the legendary *Yang Sing* – the city's only nationally-known restaurant – which is ably understudied by such establishments as *Little Yang Sing* and *Pacific*.

At the fun and affordable level, Western Europe's largest student population – bolstered nowadays by a growing army of young professionals resident in the city-centre – helps to support an increasing number of places, such as Kro. There are lots of Indian restaurants too, mainly in the famed curry quarter of Rusholme. Some of them are very good, but they largely remain stuck in a surprisingly downmarket mould.

Akbar's   **£ 27**   ⭐
73-83 Liverpool Rd M3 4NQ   (0161) 8348444
"Expect to queue most nights", at this large and *"really lively"* Castlefield yearling; *"no wonder it's always very busy, as it offers such excellent Indian food at great-value prices"* – *"the family naan has to be seen to be believed"*. / **Details:** www.akbars.co.uk; 11 pm, Fri & Sat 11.30 pm; D only; need 10+ to book.

Armenian Taverna   **£ 31**
3-5 Princess St M2 4DF   (0161) 834 9025
"A long-established basement that has delivered reliably excellent food for more years than I care to remember…" – this city-centre Greek/Armenian continues to inspire many, and almost invariably positive, reports. / **Sample dishes:** stuffed cabbage leaves; Aremnian goulash; baklava. **Details:** www.armeniantaverna.co.uk; 11.30 pm; closed Mon, Sat L & Sun L; children: 3+.

Brasserie Blanc   **£ 41**
55 King St M2 4LQ   (0161) 832 1000
"Well thought-out, for a chain"; this *"consistently pleasing"* brasserie wins particular praise for its *"incredibly cheap"* set menus – and right round the corner from many of the city's most expensive shops too! / **Sample dishes:** Loch Duart salmon, dill gravadlax; rack of Cornish lamb, butter potatoes, green beans; chocolate and hazelnut delice. **Details:** www.brasserieblanc.com; 10.30 pm.

The Bridgewater Hall   **£ 34**   ⓣ
Lower Mosley St M2 3WS   (0161) 950 0000
The Stalls Café/Bar at the home of the Hallé is tipped as *"always a pleasure"* – and of how many other cultural centre dining facilities can the same be said? / **Sample dishes:** pork rillette; millefeuille of salmon & crayfish mousselline; apricot, amaretto & almond sponge. **Details:** www.bridgewater-hall.co.uk; 7.30 pm; openings affected by concert times.

Chaophraya Thai Restaurant & Bar £ 36 Ⓐ ★

Chapel Walks M2 1HN (0161) 832 8342

*"A class Thai act in the city-centre": this "opulent" newcomer –
a restaurant offering "an oasis of calm" above a "bustling" bar –
offers "spot-on" food, "charming" service, and "very good-value set
lunch menus" too; one black mark, though – "the restaurant floor
is totally inaccessible for most disabled people".*
/ **Sample dishes:** *babecue king prawns on bamboo skewers; stir fried lobster with
black pepper sauce; tiramisu.* **Details:** *www.chaophraya.co.uk; 10.30 pm.*

Choice £ 32 Ⓐ ★

Castle Quay M15 4NT (0161) 833 3400

*"Always a safe bet"; this canal-side bar/restaurant boasts
a surprisingly strong silver-haired following among reporters,
considering it's in trendy Castlefield – must have something to do with
"great food, with a local flavour", and "good wines by the glass".*
/ **Sample dishes:** *bubble & squeak cake; belly of pork; sticky peanut toffee
pudding.* **Details:** *www.choicebarandrestaurant.co.uk; 9.45 pm.*

Croma £ 24

1 Clarence St M2 4DE (0161) 237 9799

*"Slick, sophisticated and professional", this "consistent" city-centre
spot may be 'just' a pizzeria, but it's a "vibrant" venue with a huge
following – once again second only to the Yang Sing in the volume
of reports it inspires.* / **Sample dishes:** *baked mushrooms with garlic butter
and worcester sauce; Garstang blue and goat's cheese pizza; chocolate fudge cake.*
Details: *www.croma.biz; off Albert Square; 11 pm, Sun10.30.*

Dimitri's £ 34 Ⓐ

Campfield Arc M3 4FN (0161) 839 3319

*"Especially great in summer, when you can sit 'outside', in the
Victorian arcade" – this "buzzy", "tapas-style" Greek establishment,
just off Deansgate, makes a very handy rendezvous (especially "in a
group").* / **Sample dishes:** *salad; Greek roast lamb; baklava.*
Details: *www.dimitris.co.uk; near Museum of Science & Industry; 11.30 pm.*

East Z East £ 28 ★

Princess St M1 7DL (0161) 244 5353

*"Why go to Wilmslow Road?", when you can get such
"accomplished" and "varied" (and "reasonably priced") Punjabi
cooking at this "lively" spot, on the edge of the city-centre; there's
another branch too – 'Riverside' – but it can seem "a bit soulless".*
/ **Sample dishes:** *chicken samosa; chicken tikka masala; ras malai.*
Details: *www.eastzeast.com; midnight; D only.*

Evuna £ 34 Ⓣ

277 Deansgate M3 4EW (0161) 819 2752

A "traditional" Deansgate tapas bar tipped for its good wine list.
/ **Sample dishes:** *seabass with garlic and chilli; paella; Spanish cheesecake.*
Details: *www.evuna.com; 11 pm, Sun 9 pm.*

French Restaurant
Midland Hotel   £ 55
Peter St M60 2DS   (0161) 236 3333 Ⓐ

*The dining room of this famous Edwardian hotel is known for its
"regal" and "opulent" style; "despite the grandeur", though – think
London's Ritz, albeit on a smaller scale, and with no natural light –
the "poor wine list and only-tolerable cooking don't justify the prices".*
/ **Sample dishes:** *tortellini of woodland mushrooms, corn-fed chicken, black
truffles; guinea fowl, spiced puy lentils, bitter orange; custard tart, nutmeg ice
cream, eccles cake.* **Details:** *www.themidland.co.uk; 10.30 pm, Fri & Sat 11 pm;
D only, closed Mon & Sun; no jeans or trainers.* **Accommodation:** *311 rooms,
from £145.*

Gaucho Grill   £ 50   Ⓐ⭐
2a St Mary's St M3 2LB   (0161) 833 4333

*This "stylish conversion" – a "lively" outpost of the Argentinean
steakhouse chain in an old church by 'House of Fraser' (Kendals) –
"rises above 'chain' quality"; "not cheap, but worth it".*
/ **Sample dishes:** *scallop ceviche; fillet steak; pancakes with vanilla ice cream &
dulce de leche.* **Details:** *www.gauchorestaurants.co.uk; 10.30 pm, Fri & Sat
11 pm.*

Grado   £ 44   Ⓐ⭐
New York St M1 4BD   (0161) 238 9790

*"Slap-bang in the centre of town" (just off Piccadilly Gardens),
this "sleek", "ambitious" and "fiercely Spanish" bar/restaurant has
been a "much-better-than-usual" addition to the Heathcote stable;
the occasional sceptic, though, says: "the jury is still out".*
/ **Sample dishes:** *sardines on toast; duck with fig and honey; Spanish trifle.*
Details: *www.heathcotes.co.uk; 11 pm.*

Great Kathmandu   £ 21   ⭐
140 Burton Rd M20 1JQ   (0161) 434 6413

*"As good as you'll find in the Curry Mile, and still cheap" –
this West Didsbury stalwart is "not the most stylish" place, but its
repertoire of Nepalese dishes is "consistently really good"; possible
expansion is planned.* / **Sample dishes:** *chicken or lamb cooked with
Nepalese herbs & spices; Nepalese mixed masala; kulfi.*
Details: *www.greatkathmandu.com; near Withington hospital; midnight.*

Green's   £ 33
43 Lapwing Ln M20 2NT   (0161) 434 4259

*This "informal" West Didsbury veggie is a "brilliant" place, say fans,
offering a "varied" menu that's "always enjoyable, even for meat-
eaters"; sceptics complain of too much "hype" (but they've
just bought the shop next door to double in size, so they
must be doing something right).* / **Sample dishes:** *deep fried oyster
mushrooms, Chinese pancakes, plum sauce; griddled aubergine and pumpkin curry
with jasmine coconut rice; passion fruit pudding.*
Details: *www.greensrestaurant.net; 4m S of city centre; 10.30 pm; closed
Mon L & Sat L; no Amex.*

Grinch   £ 29   Ⓣ
5-7 Chapel Walks, off Cross St M2 1HN   (0161) 907 3210

*Just off St Anne's Square, this somewhat Bohemian bar/café makes
a "consistently good" stand-by for a quick bite.* / **Sample dishes:** *fried
tempura prawns with garlic mayonnaise; special fried chicken with fries and
barbecue dip; banoffee pancakes, banana, toffee sauce.*
Details: *www.grinch.co.uk; 10 pm.*

Jam Street Cafe £ 23

209 Upper Chorlton Rd M16 0BH (0161) 8819944

A top tip for an "upmarket fry-up" (and for the veggie equivalent too) – this Whalley Range café/bar offers a "limited menu of consistently good food". / **Sample dishes:** *goat's cheese fondue; chicken and chorizo stew; Belgian waffles and ice cream.* **Details:** *just outside Chorlton, towards the centre of town; 9 pm.*

Jem and I £ 37

1c School Ln M20 6RD (0161) 445 3996

"If you can't get a table at the Lime Tree, this is your next option", say fans of this Didsbury spot, who praise its "fantastic, high-quality cooking" and its "convivial" approach; "they need to improve their service", though. / **Sample dishes:** *warm potato cake and smoked salmon, poached egg and hollandaise; roast rack and loin of lamb and rosti potato, butternut squash gratin, confit leeks, French beans and rosemary jus; chocolate truffle cake and crème chantilly.* **Details:** *www.jemandirestaurant.co.uk; 10 pm, Fri-Sat10.30 pm Sun 10 pm; closed Mon L.*

Juniper £ 57

21 The Downs WA14 2QD (0161) 929 4008

Having built up this Altrincham destination over many years, maverick chef Paul Kitching sold out in summer 2008; the new owner is Michael Riemenschneider, who has a Michelin Star for his Abbey Restaurant in Penzance, so the scene is set for this to remain a continuing foodie hotspot. / **Details:** *www.juniper-restaurant.co.uk; 9.30 pm; closed Mon, Tue L, Wed L, Thu L & Sun.*

Koh Samui £ 34

16 Princess St M1 4NB (0161) 237 9511

"Still a really good Thai"; on the fringe of Chinatown, this well worn-in basement operation retains a loyal fan club. / **Details:** *www.kohsamuirestaurant.co.uk; opp City Art Gallery; 11.30 pm; closed Sat L & Sun L.*

Kro Bar £ 22

325 Oxford Rd M13 9PG (0161) 274 3100

Part of a Danish run bar/café empire that any visitor to Manchester ought to know about; as well as being "a really good place for breakfast", it's also tipped for its "great coffee". / **Sample dishes:** *nachos with melted cheese, sour cream and guacamole; hash roast beef, potatoes and onions and a fried egg and beetroot.* **Details:** *www.kro.co.uk/bar; 9 pm; no Amex; children: 18+ .*

The Lime Tree £ 40

8 Lapwing Ln M20 2WS (0161) 445 1217

"For many years, Manchester's best" (of the non-ethnic variety) – this "stylish" and "completely reliable" West Didsbury institution, est. 1988, offers the city's "nearest thing to eating out in London" (says a Hampstead-based reporter); it has a huge fan club. / **Sample dishes:** *sea of hand-dived scallops and sweet chili dressing and crème fraîche; calves liver with champ, onion rings, onion marmalade and red wine jus; warm velvet chocolate torte and pistachio ice cream.* **Details:** *www.thelimetreerestaurant.co.uk; 10 pm; closed Mon L & Sat L.*

Little Yang Sing £ 35

17 George St M1 4HE (0161) 228 7722

This "lively" restaurant (on the site of the original Yang Sing) is one of "Chinatown's best"; there are a few reporters, though, who – while finding it "normally reliable" – are "not sure if it's as good as it was". / **Sample dishes:** *sui mai dim sum; fried beef with green pepper and black bean sauce; caramel dream.* **Details:** *www.littleyangsing.co.uk; 11.30 pm.*

Livebait £ 39

22 Lloyd St M2 5WA (0161) 817 4110

Even fans say it's "lacking in atmosphere", but this brightly-tiled, city-centre branch of the national seafood chain is "still a favourite" for many – "not necessarily cutting-edge, but satisfying"; the feeling is growing, however, that "it has been, and should be better".
/ **Sample dishes:** grilled tiger prawns and rocket and Feta chese salad and a light lemon and olive oil dressing; roast cod fillet and a couscous crust on chick peas and merguez sausage casserole; rum soaked brioche filled and chantilly cream and topped with fresh raspberries, crushed pistachios.
Details: www.livebaitrestaurant.co.uk; 10.15 pm, 10.45 pm Sat, 8.45 pm Sun.

Lounge 10 £ 49 Ⓐ

10 Tib Ln M2 4JB (0161) 834 1331

The "moody" and "sensual" vibe of this boudoir-style joint make it "an awesome place to take your partner" ("or even better your illicit lover"); sadly, though, the food tends to "second-rate" nowadays.
/ **Sample dishes:** king scallops with a brunoise of carrot and courgette and garlic butter; chargrilled sea bass fillet, braised red cabbage, parisian potatoes and sauce orntal; white chocolate bavarois with raspberry coulis.
Details: www.lounge10manchester.co.uk; 10.30 pm, Fri & Sat 11 pm, Sun 9 pm; closed Sat L & Sun.

Love Saves The Day £ 23 ✪

345 Deansgate M3 4LG (0161) 834 2266

"More than just a deli", this local institution has a particular name for its "well-chosen" breakfast menus (including "a proper full English, using high-quality ingredients"). / **Sample dishes:** sweet lime marinated chicken and peach and toasted cashew nut salad; summer sweet vegetable pie with a creamy thyme and majoram bechamel sauce and an Emmental cheese topping with a beetroot, carraway and honey salad; home-made pecan pie and Cheshire ice cream. **Details:** www.lovesavestheday.com; 7 pm, 9 pm Thurs, 6 pm Sat, 4 pm Sun .

The River Restaurant
Lowry Hotel £ 58

Chapel Whf M3 5LH (0161) 827 4041

It seems to be especially for a business lunch – especially if you nab a window table – that this modern hotel dining room, by the (canalised) River Irwell, is worth knowing about; the cooking may be "precise and well-judged", but its prices seem severely to limit its following. / **Details:** www.thelowryhotel.com; 10.30 pm; booking: max 8.
Accommodation: 165 rooms, from £230.

Luso £ 42

63 Bridge St M3 3BQ (0161) 839 5550

"Gutsy", "Portuguese-plus" cuisine and "keen" service (from a husband and wife team) helps win popularity for this "neat" and "minimalist" city-centre yearling; the phrase "hit-and-miss", however, does seem to crop up too often for comfort. / **Sample dishes:** piri-piri chicken livers; home saled cod with crushed new potatoes, black olives, spring onions and a poached egg; egg custard tart with a mini espresso milkshake.
Details: www.lusorestaurant.co.uk ; 10.30 pm, 10 pm Sun.

The Market £ 42

104 High St M4 1HQ (0161) 834 3743

This "quirky", "front-room style" spot – "in a once-quiet corner of Manchester", which is today the trendy Northern Quarter – is one of the city's most dependable culinary institutions; however, its owners of 28 years' standing sold out this year, so a rating is inappropriate.
/ **Sample dishes:** smoked duck with rasberry and walnut salad; pan fried salmon, oven roast tomatoes, courgette ribbons and balsamic syrup; cinnamon and apricot pavlova. **Details:** www.market-restaurant.com; 10 pm, Sun 5 pm; closed Mon & Sun D.

Metropolitan £ 35

2 Lapwing Ln M20 2WS   (0161) 438 2332

*"Full to the brim at weekends" – this big and "buzzing"
West Didsbury pub has "slowly moved upmarket to gastropub status"
over the years; it has quite a name for its "reliable" cuisine, and its
"good value for money".* / *Sample dishes: grilled halloumi and wild
mushrooms on garlic scented granary toast and a rocket, cherry tomato and
asparagus salad; seared duck breast and fondant potatoes, wilted spinach and
redcurrant jus; treacle tart.* **Details:** *www.the-metropolitan.co.uk; near Withington
hospital; 9.30 pm, Fri & Sat 10 pm, Sun 9 pm .*

**Michael Caines At ABode
Abode Hotel** £ 50

107 Piccadilly M1 2DB   (0161) 200 5678

*On balance, this celeb-chef-branded dining room at this new boutique-
hotel, by Piccadilly Station, has been "a welcome addition
to Manchester"; there is, however, still "plenty of scope for
improvement".* / **Details:** *www.michaelcaines.com; 11.30 pm, Fri & Sat late.*

The Modern £ 38

Urbis, Cathedral Gdns M4 3BG   (0161) 605 8282

*"Great food, great location, great views", say fans of this "stylish"
newcomer, on the top floor of a contemporary landmark building
in the city-centre; despite its outlook, though, reporters don't
especially rate the feel of the place, and sceptics find its performance
middling.* / **Details:** *www.themodernmcr.co.uk; 10 pm.*

Moss Nook £ 59

Ringway Rd M22 5NA   (0161) 437 4778

*This "quiet" and "olde-worlde" establishment divides opinion; fans say
its "traditional" cuisine may be "pricey" but is "always of high quality"
– sceptics say the place is now "living on its reputation".*
/ *Sample dishes: pan seared scallops with turbot mousse, tomato and red
pepper sauce; local loin of venison on chive potato purée with a peppercorn sauce;
peach crème brûlée with blueberry sorbet.*
Details: *www.mossnookrestaurant.co.uk; on B5166, 1m from Manchester airport;
9.30 pm; closed Mon, Sat L & Sun; children: 12+.* **Accommodation:** *1 room,
at about £120.*

Mr Thomas's Chop House £ 38

52 Cross St M2 7AR   (0161) 832 2245

*A "marvellous" Victorian interior helps make this "busy" and "cheery"
city-centre tavern something of a "Manchester institution", serving
"proper, hearty Lancashire fare" in "portions to diet for".*
/ *Sample dishes: brown onion soup with a large mature cheddar crouton;
pan seared rump of lamb served on crushed potatoes, black pudding, roast cherry
tomatoes, wilted spinach and balsamic sauce; sticky toffee pudding with toffee ice
cream.* **Details:** *www.tomschophouse.com; 9.30 pm, Sun 8 pm.*

Oca £ 31

Waterside Plaza M33 7BS   (0161) 962 6666

*"No great aspirations, but never fails" – this "ultra-modern" Sale
Italian is tipped for its "good-value pizza and pasta" (and its fabulous
canal-side location too).* / **Details:** *www.ocarestaurant.co.uk; 11 pm,
9.30 Sun; no Amex.*

Olive Press £ 37

4 Lloyds St M2 5AB   (0161) 8329090

*An offshoot of the Paul Heathcote empire, tipped as "yet another
perfectly decent mid-range central Manchester pizza/pasta
restaurant".* / *Sample dishes: chilli & honey seared tuna, rocket & fennel
salad; pan fried potato gnocchi with porcini mushrooms, balsamic onions &
oregano; passion fruit and white peach cheesecake.*
Details: *www.heathcotes.co.uk; 10 pm, Fri & Sat 11 pm, Sun 9 pm.*

Pacific **£ 31** ⭐
58-60 George St M1 4HF (0161) 228 6668
*This unusual Chinatown oriental combines Chinese and Thai floors –
on the ground and first floor, respectively; both win wide-scale
approval (not least for the "best-value business lunch
in Manchester"), but of the two, fans plump for the "more ambitious"
Thai bit. / **Sample dishes:** deep fried stuffed crab claws; king prawns with
sweet & sour chilli sauce. **Details:** www.pacificrestaurant.co.uk; 11.30 pm.*

Palmiro **£ 35** ⭐
197 Upper Chorlton Rd M16 OBH (0161) 860 7330
*The cooking – "proper slow food" – can sometimes be "exciting",
so it's a shame this "quirky" Whalley Range Italian is so inconsistent;
the set-up is "basic" too, and service can be "shoddy".
/ **Details:** www.palmiro.net; 10.30 pm; D only, ex Sun open L & D; no Amex.*

Piccolino **£ 36** Ⓐ
8 Clarence St M2 4DW (0161) 835 9860
*"Nothing flash, but always reliable" – this original branch of what's
nowadays a national pizza/Italian chain is an "absolutely buzzing"
(and sometimes "noisy") central rendezvous, offering fare
of consistent "good quality".
/ **Details:** www.individualrestaurantcompanyplc.co.uk; 11 pm, Sun 10 pm.*

Punjab Tandoori **£ 22** ⭐⭐
177 Wilmslow Rd M14 5AP (0161) 225 2960
*"Fantastic dosas and other southern Indian dishes" – and at
"good prices" too – one again make this well-established spot
"the best in Rusholme", for a number of reporters; service, though,
can be rather too "laid-back". / **Details:** midnight.*

Red Chilli **£ 26** ⭐
70-72 Portland St M1 4GU (0161) 236 2888
*"A real find"; this is a "Sichuan restaurant that tells it how it is",
and its "innovative" and "well-prepared" cuisine has an ardent and
wide-ranging following; "the less familiar the dish is, the better
it seems to be". / **Details:** www.redchillirestaurant.co.uk; 11 pm; need 6+
to book.*

The Restaurant Bar & Grill **£ 43**
14 John Dalton St M2 6JR (0161) 839 1999
*All agree this "popular" city-centre venue is "a good place for people-
spotting"; whereas fans find it a "solid and reliable" hang-out,
however, critics say it's "full of wannabes" and "not worth the
money". / **Details:** www.therestaurantbarandgrill.co.uk; 11 pm, Sun 10.30 pm;
booking: max 8 at weekends.*

Rhubarb **£ 42** ⭐
167 Burton Rd M20 2LN (0161) 448 8887
*"A great local that's always busy and buzzy" – this West Didsbury
spot has "interesting" menus and a "comfortable" interior; it can
occasionally seem a bit "OTT/pretentious", though, and "leg room
is sparse". / **Details:** www.rhubarbrestaurant.co.uk; 10 pm, Mon Tue Wed
9.30pm, Sun 8.30pm ; D only, ex Sun open L & D.*

El Rincon £ 30 **Ⓐ**
Longworth St, off St John's St M3 4BQ (0161) 839 8819
"You really could be in a Valencia back-street", in this "busy"
basement tapas bar "tucked-away off Deansgate"; the food is "tasty"
and "reasonably priced", and there are some "lovely Riojas" to be
had too. / **Details:** off Deansgate; 11 pm.

Sam's Chop House £ 40
Back Pool Fold, Chapel Walks M2 1HN (0161) 834 3210
A "friendly", "old-fashioned" Victorian-style basement in the city-
centre, where "filling" British "classics" are served in a "warm and
cosy" setting; "steak 'n' kidney pud' is a must".
/ **Details:** www.samschophouse.com; 9.30 pm; closed Sun D.

San Carlo £ 40 **Ⓐ**
40 King Street West M3 2WY (0161) 834 6226
This "bright" and "buzzy" Italian, near House of Fraser, improved its
standards across the board this year; it's quite a 'scene' too –
a visiting reporter who wasn't that impressed by the food noted that
he still "wouldn't have missed the performance".
/ **Details:** www.sancarlo.co.uk; 11 pm.

Second Floor Restaurant
Harvey Nichols £ 51
21 New Cathedral St M1 1AD (0161) 828 8898
The food is pure "artistry", say fans of this "bright and modern"
department store dining room (whose chef is notably well-regarded
by her peers in the city); the place still attracts too many detractors,
though, who attack its "inflated" attitude (and prices).
/ **Details:** www.harveynichols.com; 10.30 pm; closed Mon D & Sun D.

Shimla Pinks £ 31
Dolefield, Crown Sq M3 3EN (0161) 831 7099
Having moved last year, this trendy "Indian with a twist" is off again,
in late-2008, to a location in the enormous new Spinningfields
development (so we've left it un-rated); past feedback is rather mixed.
/ **Details:** www.shimlapinksmanchester.com; opp Crown Courts; 11.30 pm, Sat &
Sun 11 pm; closed Sat L & Sun L.

Stock £ 50
4 Norfolk St M2 1DW (0161) 839 6644
Especially for "good-value set lunches", "for functions" or "on opera
nights", this city-centre Italian makes a useful (and improving)
destination; given the glorious setting in the ornate former stock
exchange building, however, there's a lingering feeling it's "still not
what it could and should be". / **Sample dishes:** white crab & hot smoked
salmon cakes set over spaghetti fritto with fresh horseradish crème fraîche; prime
fillet steak set on a potato rosti topped with red onion & black pepper ravioli with
bearnaise sauce; tiramisu. **Details:** www.stockrestaurant.co.uk; 10 pm; closed Sun.

Tai Pan £ 24 **★**
81-97 Upper Brook St M13 9TX (0161) 273 2798
A large Chinese establishment in Longsight, where "excellent value,
and great dim sum" underpin ongoing reporter satisfaction.
/ **Details:** 11 pm, Sun 9 pm.

Tai Wu   £ 26

44 Oxford Rd M1 5EJ   (0161) 2366557

A canteen-style oriental, tipped for its bargain weekday dim sum; whenever you go, it's "better if you take a Chinese-speaker, but the food on the English menu is excellent too". / **Sample dishes:** steak rolls in black pepper sauce; lamb with green pepper & black bean sauce; apple fritter. **Details:** www.tai-wu.co.uk; 2.45 am.

Tampopo   £ 25

16 Albert Sq M2 5PF   (0161) 819 1966

"A viable alternative to the ubiquitous Wagamama!" – this *"city-centre basement"* (which also now has a branch in the Triangle) is *"Manchester's original, cheap and quick noodle bar... and still the best".* / **Sample dishes:** slices of marinated grilled beef served with fiery pickled cabbage; seafood served with chunky udon noodles, leek & red pepper, wok fried with soy & red wine; passion fruit syllabub. **Details:** www.tampopo.co.uk; 11pm, Sun 10 pm; need 7+ to book.

That Café   £ 35

1031-1033 Stockport Rd M19 2TB   (0161) 432 4672

This "friendly" fixture may feel "cosy", but is run with a "steely professionalism", which has helped it survive for over a decade in a dodgy Levenshulme location; the secret? – appealing cooking that "hits the spot every time". / **Details:** www.thatcafe.co.uk; on A6 between Manchester & Stockport; 10.30 pm; closed Mon, Tue-Sat D only, closed Sun D; no Amex.

This & That   £ 9

3 Soap St M4 1EW   (0161) 832 4971

"Outstanding for both veggies and carnivores" – this *"outstanding"* Indian canteen, near the Printworks, has achieved *"local-legend"* status; *"stuff yourself for less than a fiver, nuff said".* / **Details:** 4.30 pm, Fri & Sat 11 pm; no credit cards.

Vermilion   £ 40

Lord North St M40 8AD   (0161) 202 0055

"There seem to be more buddhas than customers", at this *"amazing"* new oriental: *"a multi-million pound opening with all the hype in the world!"; it's "madness"* – and standards are pretty indifferent too – but *"you've still got to applaud the audacity".* / **Details:** www.vermilioncinnabar.com/; 10 pm, Sat 11 pm.

Wing's   £ 40

1 Lincoln Sq M2 5LN   (0161) 834 9000

A good spot for "those who want their Chinese food served in smart Western surroundings" (and ideally with the odd footie celeb thrown in); *it's certainly no bargain, but the food is "very good".* / **Sample dishes:** steamed scallops in shell with garlic and glass vermicelli; roast duck with prawn meat stuffing. **Details:** www.wingsrestaurant.co.uk; midnight, Sun 11 pm; no trainers; children: 11+ after 8 pm Mon-Fri, 21+ at D .

Yang Sing £ 33
34 Princess St M1 4JY (0161) 236 2200

"The best Cantonese in the UK" – Manchester's culinary kingpin
remains a beacon of oriental gastronomy, and serves *"stand-out"*
dishes (not least *"exceptional dim sum"*) in a vast, if *"subdued"*,
setting; *"don't bother with the menu – just tell them how much you
want to spend".* / **Sample dishes:** *spare ribs in orange sauce; crispy chicken
Cantonese style; ice cream and fruit.* **Details:** *www.yang-sing.com; 11.30 pm.*

MARKET HARBOROUGH, LEICESTERSHIRE 5–4D

Han's £ 26
29 St Mary's Rd LE16 7DS (01858) 462288
A *"very busy"* Chinese restaurant of long standing, still tipped for its
"very good food and service". / **Sample dishes:** *spring rolls; beef with green
pepper in black bean sauce; toffee apple.* **Details:** *11 pm; closed Sat L.*

MARLBOROUGH, WILTSHIRE 2–2C

Coles Bar & Restaurant £ 47
27 Kingsbury St SN8 1JA (01672) 515004
This *"warm and friendly"* spot is sometimes tipped
as *"the best in Marlborough"*; its style is *"inventive"* though –
excessively so, for some tastes. / **Sample dishes:** *whole baked Cornish goats
cheese with a walnut crust on a green bean and pesto salad, balsamic reduction;
peppered local venison on a celeriac and potato mash with an orange and
cardamom glaze; honeycomb and vanilla ice cream with hot toffee sauce.*
Details: *www.colesrestaurant.co.uk; 10 pm; closed Sun; no Amex.*

The Harrow at Little Bedwyn £ 68
Little Bedwyn SN8 3JP (01672) 870871
A *"quietly confident"* converted inn, where the food is *"innovative"*
and *"strongly-flavoured"*; the *"extensive wine list"* offers *"a fantastic
selection too, "reaching to the stars, but starting at £20 a bottle"* –
"wine-and-food menus are a good way to sample it".
/ **Sample dishes:** *seared foie gras, scallop & black pudding; fillet of line-caught
turbot, mash, wild mushrooms & truffles; bread & butter pudding, marinated
prunes & rum ice cream.* **Details:** *www.theharrowatlittlebedwyn.co.uk; 9 pm;
closed Mon, Tue & Sun D; no Amex.*

MARLOW, BUCKINGHAMSHIRE 3–3A

The Oak Room
Danesfield House Hotel £ 82
Henley Rd SL7 2EY (01628) 891010
Adam Simmonds's cooking is going *"from strength to strength"*,
say fans of the *"beautiful"* dining room of this elegant country house
hotel. / **Details:** *www.danesfieldhouse.co.uk; 3m outside Marlow on the A4155;
9.30 pm; closed Mon & Tue L; no jeans or trainers.* **Accommodation:** *87 rooms,
from £260.*

Hand & Flowers £ 45
West St SL7 2BP (01628) 482277

"It's hard to get a table" at Tom Kerridge's *"thoroughly enjoyable"* country pub-conversion; a huge fan club says it's *"well worth trying"*, though, thanks to its *"sterling"* cooking – *"far better than the average souped-up boozer"*, at *"only a little above gastropub prices"*.
/ **Sample dishes:** potted Dorset crab with brown bread, cucumber and dill chutney; squab pigeon and foie gras en croûte withgem lettuce, girolles and pomme boulangère; banana soufflé with coconut sorbet and rum anglaise.
Details: www.thehandandflowers.co.uk; 9.30 pm; closed Sun D.
Accommodation: 2 cottages rooms, from £140.

Marlow Bar & Grill £ 41
92-94 High St SL7 1AQ (01628) 488544
"Perfect for a social evening, with one friend or ten" – this *"noisy"* but *"fun"* town-centre linchpin wins over all who report on it; the food, though, is *"safe and tasty"*, rather than anything more.
/ **Sample dishes:** Thai prawn cakes with sweet chili sauce; crispy duck with Chinese greens, sesame and honey dressing; sticky toffee pudding with butterscotch sauce and vanilla ice cream.
Details: www.individualrestaurants.co.uk; Towards the river end of the High Street; 11 pm; booking essential.

The Royal Oak £ 33
Frieth Rd, Bovingdon Grn SL7 2JF (01628) 488611
An old pub, where the cooking displays the odd *"interesting flourish"*, and which is invariably tipped as being *"reliable, sound and good value"*. / **Details:** www.royaloakmarlow.co.uk; half mile up from Marlow High Street; 9.30 pm, Fri & Sat 10 pm.

The Vanilla Pod £ 57
31 West St SL7 2LS (01628) 898101

It was recently *"refurbished in plush tones of brown and cream"*, but Michael Macdonald's *"stylish"* but *"tiny"* venture is of most note for his *"beautiful"* cooking (with vanilla featuring in many dishes), but the service is *"excellent"* too; to a rare extent, pretty much all reports are a hymn of praise. / **Sample dishes:** carpaccio of venison with rosemary & honey vinegar; roast salmon with pancetta, baby pak choi & star anise broth; praline risotto with candied pears. **Details:** www.thevanillapod.co.uk; 10 pm; closed Mon & Sun.

The Appletree Inn £ 40

YO62 6RD (01751) 431457
A "cosy" olde-worlde pub with an "interesting layout", tipped by some reporters for its "good food and attentive service".
/ *Sample dishes:* crab cheesecake with Parmesan crisp and tomato salsa; confit belly pork with black pudding, mustard crème and crispy bacon; marbled chocolate pyramid with chocolate mousse and boozy cherries.
Details: www.appletreeinn.co.uk; 9.30 pm; closed Mon & Tue.

Black Sheep Brewery Bistro £ 34

Wellgarth HG4 4EN (01765) 680101
The food may be "average", but this rustic brewery-annexe is tipped for its "great setting and beer" nonetheless. / *Sample dishes:* chicken Caesar salad; fish & chips; jam roly poly. *Details:* www.blacksheep.co.uk; 9 pm; Sun-Wed L only, Thu-Sat L & D; no Amex.

Samuel's
Swinton Park Hotel & Spa £ 57

HG4 4JH (01765) 680900
A properly "away-from-it-all" country house hotel (set in 200 acres), noted for its "wonderful attention to detail", and for Andy Burton's cooking, which is consistently "very good".
/ *Details:* www.swintonpark.com; 9.30 pm; no jeans or trainers; children: 8+ at D. *Accommodation:* 30 rooms, from £160.

New Yard Restaurant £ 40

Mawgan TR12 6AF (01326) 221595
"In the middle of the impossible-to-find Trelowarren estate", a "delightfully light and airy, modern dining room", tipped for its "local food, sourced, prepared and presented with care".
/ *Sample dishes:* pan fried mackerel fillet with a salad niçoise; medley of fish and crab wrapped in filo pastry and served with summer courgettes and a white wine cream sauce; chilled yogurt and pistachio cake with elderflower crème fraîche.
Details: www.trelowarren.com; 9.30 pm; closed Sun D; no Amex.

Horse & Trumpet £ 50

12 Old Grn LE16 8DX (01858) 565000
A "busy pub/restaurant" (with rooms) in a picturesque village, where the cuisine offers "sometimes surprising combinations of texture and flavour"; the "taster menu, with wine" is a top tip.
/ *Sample dishes:* chicken liver parfait; gilthead sea bream; Valrhona chocolate mousse. *Details:* www.horseandtrumpet; 9.30 pm; closed Mon & Sun D; no Amex; children: 12+ at D. *Accommodation:* 4 rooms, from £75.

Meikleour Hotel £ 31

PH2 6EB (0125) 088 3206

This is really "only a local pub", but its reasonably-priced food – given the number of "very expensive" places round about – is tipped as well worth a detour. / Sample dishes: warm salad of black pudding with bacon lardons and mushrooms; fried haddock in batter of their own ale and spring water, served with chips and peas; sticky toffee pudding with butterscotch sauce and vanilla ice cream. Details: www.meikleourhotel.co.uk; 9 pm; no Amex. Accommodation: 5 rooms, from £120.

Bay Tree £ 48

4 Potter St DE73 8HW (01332) 863358

"As they say in another guide, worth a detour" – Rex Howell's "very popular" former coaching offers "guaranteed good food, and just the right ambience too"; visit at quieter times if you can. / Sample dishes: scallops; breast & confit of guinea fowl; coriander & lychee sorbet. Details: www.baytreerestaurant.co.uk; 10 pm; closed Mon & Sun D.

Cassis

Stanley House Hotel £ 64

Off Preston New Rd BB2 7NP (01254) 769200

The "luxurious" dining room of a newish boutique-hotel; fans say the modern French cuisine is "trying very hard" and can be "wonderful" – sceptics agree that the food's "interesting", but say it often "just misses". / Sample dishes: white asparagus panacotta; shepherds pie with roast rack of lamb; wild strawberry jelly. Details: www.stanleyhouse.co.uk; 9.30 pm, Fri & Sat 9.45 pm; closed Mon, Tue L, Sat L & Sun D; no trainers.

Village Bakery £ 28

CA10 1HE (01768) 881811

"A very busy café" – attached to the famous baker – "where the tea and coffee, the baking and the soups are all first-class"; "wonderful breakfasts" too. / Sample dishes: garlic mushroom & cheese bruschetta; steak & kidney pie; chocolate almond cake. Details: www.village-bakery.com; 10m NE of Penrith on A686; L only; no Amex; need 6+ to book.

The Moody Goose

The Old Priory £ 60

Church Sq BA3 2HX (01761) 416784

A fairly traditional small hotel out in the sticks – run by Stephen & Victoria Shore – that wins praise for its "interesting", high-quality cuisine and its "pleasant" approach generally. / Details: www.moody-goose.com; 9.30 pm; closed Sun D.

Jaipur £ 33
599 Grafton Gate East MK9 1AT (01908) 669796
It's "mesmerising" enough to find a vast, purpose-built palace of a
restaurant in downtown Milton Keynes, but what's perhaps even more
surprising is that it serves "consistently good Indian food".
/ **Sample dishes:** marinated chicken in pandana leaves and sweet sesame sauce;
king prawns in coconut milk and kaffir lime, tamarind and chillies; fresh fruits
of the day. **Details:** www.jaipur.co.uk; near the train station roundabout; they are
the big white building; 11.30 pm; no shorts.

Plough And Flail £ 36 Ⓣ
Paddock Hill Ln WA16 7DB (01565) 873537
A "dependable" gastropub tipped for the steady realisation of its
"extensive and well-prepared menu"; it's even popular with "people
from Wilmslow"! / **Details:** www.thedeckersgroup.com; 9.30 pm, 10 pm Fri &
Sat, 8 pm Sun; closed Sun L.

56 High St. £ 35 Ⓣ
56 High St CH7 1BD (01352) 759225
It's especially tipped for its "fresh fish and seafood", but this small-
scale operation also offers a "pretty good menu all-round".
/ **Details:** www.56highst.com; 9.30 pm, Fri & Sat 10.30 pm; closed Mon & Sun;
no Amex.

The Swan Inn £ 34
The St IP7 7AU (01449) 741391
Nigel and Carol Ramsbottom's well-liked country pub is "excellent",
on most reports; the occasional doubter, though, finds it "over-rated".
/ **Sample dishes:** grilled smoked haddock topped with Welsh rarebit on a warm
tomato salad; roast duck breast on a compote of aubergines, cherry tomato &
basil, with gratin dauphinoise; baked chocolate & amaretto cheesecake.
Details: www.monkseleigh.com; 9 pm; closed Mon & Tue; no Amex.

The Stonemill £ 42
NP25 5SW (01600) 716273
"A 100%-consistent restaurant, with a good atmosphere", located
in an ancient former farmhouse. / **Details:** www.thestonemill.co.uk; 9 pm,
Fri & Sat 9.30; closed Mon & Sun D; no Amex. **Accommodation:** 6 cottages
rooms, from £40.

Morston Hall £ 65
Main Coast Rd NR25 7AA (01263) 741041
"TV success is making it hard to get a table", at Galton Blackiston's
small country house hotel, but feedback was unusually mixed this
year; for many, his "no-choice, seasonal menu" is as "faultless" and
"amazing"-value as ever, but there were also quite a few complaints
about a "conveyor-belt" approach. / **Sample dishes:** petits-pois mousse
with Alsace bacon, shallot rings and pea shoots; slowly roast breast of Gressingham
duck with young carrots, braised turnips, buttery mashed potatoes and red wine
jus; millefeuille of berries with champagne sabayon and garden mint ice cream.
Details: www.morstonhall.com; between Blakeney & Wells on A149; 8 pm;
D only, ex Sun open L & D. **Accommodation:** 13 rooms, from £135.

Beetle & Wedge Boathouse £ 43

Ferry Ln OX10 9JF (01491) 651381

"A gorgeous setting, right by the Thames" creates a "lovely" ambience at this rustic-style rôtisserie (which once traded as 'The Boathouse'); the dishes – mostly from the grill – are "good", but "not particularly interesting". / **Sample dishes:** warm goats cheese salad with beetroot, crouton, lardons & pinenuts; roast supreme of chicken, mushroom duxelle, bacon & red wine jus; steamed treacle sponge with real custard.
Details: www.beetleandwedge.co.uk; on A329 between Streatley & Wallingford, take Ferry Lane at crossroads; 8.45 pm. **Accommodation:** 2 rooms, from £90.

Black Bull £ 55

DL10 6QJ (01325) 377289

A former Pullman railway carriage provides the "romantic" (if "tightly-packed") setting for the dining room of this popular boozer, which – under its new régime – has consolidated a reputation for serving some "excellent" fish. / **Sample dishes:** baked queens scallops in garlic butter with mature cheddar, pine nut thyme crumb topping; roast salmon with tomato, olives, tarragon, pepper & olive oil; hot orange liquor pancakes with vanilla ice cream. **Details:** www.blackbullmoulton.com; 1m S of Scotch Corner; 9.30 pm, Fri & Sat 10 pm; closed Sat L & Sun D; no Amex; children: 7+ .

Cornish Range £ 39

6 Chapel St TR19 6SB (01736) 731488

Set back from the harbour, this attractive restaurant-with-rooms is "quite a find"; it's recommended for its "excellent value-for-money" (especially on the 'early-bird' menu). / **Sample dishes:** crispy belly pork with Cornish hogs pudding, crushed new potatoes & poached egg; roast stuffed monkfish with braised fennel & courgette frittata and a saffron, lemon, tomato & caper dressing; chocolate, ameretti & rum torte with fresh raspberries & clotted cream. **Details:** www.cornishrange.co.uk; on coast road between Penzance & Lands End; 9.30 pm, 9 pm in Winter; no Amex. **Accommodation:** 3 rooms, from £80.

2 Fore Street Restaurant £ 38

2 Fore St TR19 6QU (01736) 731164

WINNER 2009

RÉMY MARTIN
FINE CHAMPAGNE COGNAC

"A wonderful bistro", where "great produce is beautifully served", and at "good-value" prices too; it's only been open for a year or so – "get there before the awards arrive"; (sorry, too late! – Eds). / **Sample dishes:** ham hock terrine with apple, apricot & ginger chutney; whole sea bream with capers, fennel & garden herbs; bitter chocolate tart with caramelized pear. **Details:** www.2forestreet.co.uk; 9.30 pm.

MURCOTT, OXFORDSHIRE

2–1D

Nut Tree Inn £ 45

Main St OX5 2RE (01865) 331253

WINNER 2009

"A pub restaurant that's a cut above the rest" – you get "outstanding food" and "excellent service" at this "charming" thatched inn.
/ **Details:** 9 pm, Sun 8.30 pm; closed Sun D in winter.

MYLOR BRIDGE, CORNWALL

1–4B

The Pandora Inn £ 35

Restronguet Creek TR11 5ST (01326) 372678
It's still tipped for its "amazing" atmosphere and beautiful creek-side location, but – on the food front – this well-known inn has inspired notably mixed reviews of late. / **Sample dishes:** potted chicken liver parfait, basil butter with melba toast; pan fried mackerel fillets with creamy horseradish mash & Mediterranean vegetables; cherry crumble.
Details: www.pandorainn.co.uk; signposted off A390, between Truro & Falmouth; 9 pm, Fri & Sat 9.30 pm.

NANT-Y-DERRY, MONMOUTHSHIRE

2–2A

The Foxhunter £ 46

Abergavenny NP7 9DN (01873) 881101
For a restaurant in a former stationmaster's house "in the middle of nowhere", this family-run establishment inspires an eye-catching volume of reports; on the service front, standards "can vary", so it's fortunate that the food is almost invariably "very good".
/ **Sample dishes:** wild garlic soup, poached egg & grilled bruschetta; smoked haddock, sauté of leeks, spring onions, shellfish & dill; apple & pear elderflower cream. **Details:** www.thefoxhunter.com; 9.30 pm; closed Mon; no Amex.
Accommodation: 2 cottages rooms, from £125.

NANTGAREDIG, CARMARTHENSHIRE

4–4C

Y Polyn Bar & Restaurant £ 40

SA32 7LH (01267) 290000
"No fuss, just great cooking in very pleasant surroundings" – evidently co-patron Simon Wright, who runs this rural gastropub with his wife – really did learn what customers want when he was editor of the AA's restaurant guide! / **Sample dishes:** fish soup, rouille, croutons and Gruyère cheese; roast rack of salt marsh lamb, onion garlic and thyme purée; honey and almond ice cream. **Details:** www.ypolyn.co.uk; 9 pm; closed Mon & Sun D; no Amex.

⭐

Rookery Hall Hotel & Spa
Hand Picked Hotels   **£ 56**
Main Rd CW5 6DQ   (01270) 610016
*"Inventive" cooking that's sometimes "outstanding" is twinned with
an "exceptional" wine list, in the "traditional" and "very comfortable"
dining room of this impressive country house hotel.*
/ **Details:** www.handpicked.co.uk; 9.30 pm; D only, ex Sun open L & D; no jeans
or trainers. **Accommodation:** 70 rooms, from £135.

Ⓣ

White Hart   **£ 36**
High St RG9 5DD   (01491) 641245
*Tipped for "imaginative fish specials, which change with the season
and the catch", this revamped country inn inspires only
complimentary reports. / **Sample dishes:** mussels with white wine, cream
and garlic; sea bass with fennel and olive salad and parsley mash; chocolate
brownie with orange and mascarpone cream.*
Details: www.whitehartnettlebed.com; Between Wallingford & Henley-on-Thames
on the A430; 9.30 pm; closed Sun D. **Accommodation:** 12 rooms, from £95.

The Terrace
Montagu Arms Hotel   **£ 53**
Beaulieu SO42 7ZL   (01590) 612324
*The dining room of a handsome New Forest inn, which is particularly
notable for its friendly service; post-survey a new chef of some note
was appointed, so it may be one to watch.*
/ **Details:** www.montaguarmshotel.co.uk; no jeans or trainers.

Ⓐ

Chewton Glen   **£ 82**
Christchurch Rd BH25 6QS   (01425) 275341

*For "grand eating in the country", few establishments match this
"special" New Forest hotel; you may have to "save up for a while"
to afford it, but all reporters this year said it's "a real treat that's
worth pushing the boat out for". / **Sample dishes:** hand dived Scottish
scallops, Jerusalem artichoke purée, red wine jus; supreme of chicken,;
hot chocolate fondant with pistachio ice cream. **Details:** www.chewtonglen.com;
on A337 between New Milton & Highcliffe; 9.30 pm; children: 5+.*
Accommodation: 58 rooms, from £299.

Café Bleu £ 37 Ⓐ✪
14 Castle Gate NG24 1BG (01636) 610141
"Always a delight" – this "superior" bistro has a notably "pleasant" atmosphere, and quite a reputation locally for infallibly "excellent" modern cuisine; service is "friendly" but can "lack requisite skills".
/ **Sample dishes:** goats cheese with purple potatoes, marinated globe artichokes, capers & toasted pinenuts; seared sea trout with tiger prawn linguini, pak choi & saffron butter; brioche bread & butter pudding with Cornish clotted cream.
Details: www.cafebleu.co.uk; 9.30 pm; closed Sun D; no Amex.

The Crab at Chieveley £ 58
Wantage Rd RG20 8UE (01635) 247550
This "lovely pub in the middle of nowhere" has a huge name for its fish, but was sold as our survey for the year was drawing to a close; the former owner was quite a 'large figure', and it's difficult to believe that the place will not be changed by his absence – in the circumstances, no rating is appropriate. / **Sample dishes:** Cornish crab salad, lemon mayo, red pepper & tomato dressing; oriental infused cod, wilted pak choi, oyster & dill velouté; wild strawberry tart, champagne granite.
Details: www.crabatchieveley.com; M4 J13 to B4494 – 0.5 mile on right; 9 pm, Sat & Sun 9.30 pm. **Accommodation:** 14 rooms, from £160.

Yew Tree Inn £ 48
Hollington Cross, Andover Rd RG20 9SE (01635) 253360
"Marco Pierre White's pet pub" is a "firm favourite" for fans, who extol its "atmospheric" interior and "delicious" ("typical MPW") classic fare; it's something of a "hit-and-miss" experience, though, thanks not least to service that can seem "uncaring".
/ **Sample dishes:** potted shrimps with brown bread and butter; salmon fishcake; Eton mess. **Details:** www.yewtree.tablesir.com; Off the A343, near Highclere Castle; 9:30 pm, 9pm sun. **Accommodation:** 6 rooms, from £100.

Although Newcastle is a famously going-out kind of place – with most of the action centred around the Quayside – it has not traditionally been considered a great quality restaurant destination. It is therefore impressive that it now boasts a number of surprisingly upmarket success-stories such as the *Brasserie Black Door* and *Café 21* (and also '– though we don't award them 'stars'– Jesmond Deen House and Fisherman's Lodge).

On the ethnic front, interest tends to be focussed on subcontinentals, in which context *Rasa* (an import from London) and *Vujon* stand out. Plus, of course, the latest incarnation of the Barn franchise, *Barn Asia*.

Barn Asia £ 38
Waterloo Sq, St James Boulevard NE1 4DN (0191) 2211000

WINNER 2009

RÉMY MARTIN
FINE CHAMPAGNE COGNAC

The locally-celebrated 'Barn' franchise has metamorphosed again, and its latest "typically barmy" incarnation has already gathered a big following for its "interesting mix" of Asian cuisines, offering an intriguing "mix of flavours and textures". / **Sample dishes:** prawn & crab dumplings; Vietnamese shaking beef; peanut, caramel & dark chocolate tart. **Details:** www.barnasia.org; 9.30 pm; closed Mon & Sun.

Blackfriars Restaurant £ 44
Friars St NE1 4XN (0191) 2615945
"Set within an 800 year old monastery and overlooking a medieval courtyard," this city-centre rendezvous certainly boasts an "historic" setting; more generally, its standards are "good(ish)". / **Sample dishes:** seared pigeon breast with crispy leeks & Dijon mustard sauce; Northumbrian sirloin steak, chunky chips, roast herb tomato & red wine sauce; Belgian chocolate tart with pistachio cream. **Details:** www.blackfriarsrestaurant.co.uk; 10 pm; closed Sun D.

Brasserie Black Door £ 45
Biscuit Factory, Stoddard St NE2 1AN (0191) 260 5411
The original Black Door is no more, so this spin-off brasserie is now its backers' main Newcastle operation; it has an "interesting" location – especially if you want to "wander around the adjacent art gallery between courses" – and the cuisine is "delicious" too. / **Sample dishes:** smoked eel, beetroot and watercress salad, horseradish cream; loin of Northumbrian venison, red cabbage, parsnip purée; coconut panna cotta, pineapple sorbet, coconut tuile. **Details:** www.brasserieblackdoor.co.uk; 10 pm; closed Sun D.

Café 21 £ 49
Trinity Gdns NE1 2HH (0191) 222 0755
"Impressive" (if fractionally "soulless") new premises have done little to diminish reporters' affection for Terry Laybourne's re-located Quayside venue, not infrequently hailed as "the best restaurant in Newcastle". / **Sample dishes:** field mushroom fritters with buffalo mozzarella, rocket and basil oil; pan-roast haibut with asparagus, tomato confit and sage; steamed lemon pudding, strawberry jam and crème freiche. **Details:** www.cafetwentyone.co.uk; 10.30 pm, Sun 10 pm.

Café Royal £ 31
8 Nelson St NE1 5AW (0191) 231 3000
"Always crowded" – this "lively" grand café in the city-centre offers "fresh and delicious" savouries, as well as "the best coffee and cakes in town" (and the "best brunch too"); "go at less busy times to try to avoid the crush". / **Sample dishes:** pressed ham and roast red pepper terrine with pea pudding and toast; glazed crab omelette with local dried ham & asparagus; bitter chocolate hazelnut mousse. **Details:** www.sjf.co.uk; 6pm; L only, ex Thu open L & D.

Caffè Vivo   £ 31

29 Broad Chare NE1 3DQ   (0191) 232 1331

A "recently opened, all-day bistro-style Italian"; it is owned by local-hero restaurateur Terry Laybourne (Café 21 et al), which is more than reason enough to tip it! / **Sample dishes:** bucatini with wild mushrooms, pine nuts & herbs; Tuscan style pork roast with fennel, herbs & garlic; panna cotta with braised rhubarb. **Details:** www.caffevivo.co.uk; 10 pm; closed Sun.

Caffe Zonzo   £ 29

87-89 Goldspink Ln NE2 1NQ   (0191) 2304981

"A real Italian restaurant, somewhat unexpected in a residential suburb of Newcastle"; it's tipped as a "brisk and buzzy" place to eat, even if "the menu doesn't vary much". / **Sample dishes:** rosemary Sardinian flat bread with olive oil; rack of lamb on lentils with cherry tomatoes; amaretti-based ricotta cheesecake with a selection of fruit toppings. **Details:** www.caffezonzo.com; 9.15 pm; closed Sun; no Amex.

Fisherman's Lodge   £ 70

Jesmond Dene NE7 7BQ   (0191) 281 3281

"A wonderful setting" – the parkland of Jesmond Dene – helps make a "special occasion" of a trip to this local fixture; on the price front, though, they're "pushing it a bit" nowadays. / **Sample dishes:** goats cheese & herb roulade, beetroot mousse, balsamic foam; pan fried black bream, tempura oyster, caviar cream; caramel torte, butterscotch ice cream, crisp nougatine, caramel mousse. **Details:** www.fishermanslodge.co.uk; 2m from city centre on A1058, follow signposts to Jesmond Dene; 10 pm; closed Mon & Sun.

The Flatbread Cafe   £ 28

69-75 High Bridge NE1 6BX   (0191) 241 5184

"Tapas-type Middle Eastern dishes all come with large flat-breads", at this "friendly" and "different" restaurant; "feasts – featuring dishes from around the globe – are particularly good value". / **Sample dishes:** mixed herbs, Feta cheese and onion salad; chicken, chickpeas & chili; chocolate board. **Details:** www.flatbreadcafe.com; 11 pm; closed Sun.

Francesca's   £ 23

Manor House Rd NE2 2NE   (0191) 281 6586

"The queues say it all" – this "lively" and "convivial" cantina is the place to go if you're looking for "Italian ambiente", and for "cheap and cheerful" scoff too. / **Sample dishes:** king prawns and mussels; chicken Valdostana; tiramisu. **Details:** 9.30 pm; closed Sun; no Amex; no booking.

Jesmond Dene House   £ 63

Jesmond Dene Rd NE2 2EY   (0191) 212 3000

A "beautiful, high-ceilinged room" provides a "lovely" setting for dining at Terry Laybourne's two-year-old venture in a nicely-located Arts & Crafts mansion; cooking that's "fabulous" to fans, however, is "not altogether convincing" to critics, and the overall experience is not helped by service that can be "less than attentive". / **Sample dishes:** Scottish scallops and lemon marmalade and young leeks; Cumbria lamb, celeriac and almond couscous,red onion confit and herb salad; millefeuille of pink pralines, banana butter and yoghurt bitter chocolate sorbet. **Details:** www.jesmonddenehouse.co.uk; out of the city centre, towards Jesmond, which is clearly signposted; 10 pm. **Accommodation:** 40 rooms, from £160.

McCoys Brasserie £ 50

32-34 Mosley Street NE1 1DF (0191) 233 2828

After six years, the McCoys shut up shop at the impressively-located McCoys at the Baltic in June; the same team have now shifted wholesale to this new 50-cover operation.
/ **Details:** www.mccoysbrasserie.com; 10 pm; closed Sun D.

Open Kitchen £ 44   A ⭐

Moor Court Annexe NE3 4YD (0191) 285 2909

"Small but almost perfect" – this bizarrely-located Gosforth "hide-away" – in an Art Deco squash club – "takes pride in producing delicious and well-presented dishes, using much locally-sourced, organic and fair-trade produce". / **Details:** www.theopenkitchen.co.uk; 9.30 pm; D only, ex Sun open L & D.

Pani's £ 27   A

61-65 High Bridge NE1 6BX (0191) 232 4366

"You leave with a smile on your face", from this "crazy", "cheap" Italian, near Grey's Monument; despite the odd gripe about its new layout, the "bustly" ambience was this year rated better than ever.
/ **Sample dishes:** bruschetta; fregola, baby clams, fresh tomato, garlic, parsley & white wine; tiramisu. **Details:** www.paniscafe.co.uk; off Gray Street; 10 pm; closed Sun; no Amex; no booking at L.

Rasa £ 34   ⭐

27 Queen St NE1 3UG (0191) 232 7799

"Outstanding Keralan cooking" helps make this "Northern outpost of a London mini-chain" a "wonderful" and "different" experience, "quietly tucked-away behind the Quayside"; this year, however, also provoked some unexpectedly "average" reports.
/ **Details:** www.rasarestaurants.com; 11 pm; closed Sun.

Sachins £ 28

Forth Banks NE1 3SG (0191) 261 9035

"Unusual and different" dishes with "great flavours" generally commend this Punjabi restaurant on top of Forth Banks to most (if not quite all) reporters. / **Details:** www.sachins.co.uk; behind Central Station; 11.15 pm; closed Sun.

Sale Pepe £ 26

115 St George's Ter NE2 2DN (0191) 281 1431

"Simple, good-quality Italian fare" draws reporters to this "casual" and "busy" spot, which is "ideal for families". / **Details:** 10.30 pm; closed Sun.

Secco Ristorante Salentino £ 42   A

86 Pilgrim St NE1 6SG (0191) 230 0777

"It looks slightly overdone", but fans say this three-floor city-centre Italian "favourite" is a "fantastic" place, with "truly authentic" food; critics, though, find it "cheesy all round". / **Details:** www.seccouk.com; 10 pm; closed Sun.

Vujon £ 35   ⭐

29 Queen St NE1 3UG (0191) 221 0601

"Like stepping into a Delhi restaurant, not the Quayside" – this "authentic" local favourite is widely praised for its "unusual, expertly-made dishes". / **Details:** www.vujon.com; 11.30 pm; closed Sun L.

Three Choirs Vineyards £ 45

(T)

GL18 1LS (01531) 890223

Thanks to its "idyllic setting", the dining room of this leading vineyard is tipped as a "delightful place to visit"; the menu "isn't extensive", and the food is something of a supporting attraction.
/ **Sample dishes:** *seared fillet of tuna loin, lambs leaf & beansprout salad, soy & sesame dressing; seared breast of Gressingham duck with spring onion mash, plum & hoisin sauce; iced peach parfait with a peach shot & coconut tuille.*
Details: *www.threechoirs.com; 9 pm; no Amex.* **Accommodation:** *8 rooms, from £95.*

(A)(★)

Newick Park
Newick Park Hotel £ 58

BN8 4SB (01825) 723633

A "comfortable country house hotel" (privately owned), where Chris Moore's cuisine can be "fabulous"; the "great-value lunch menu" is especially worth seeking out. / **Sample dishes:** *scallop tortellini with vanilla vinegar; roast saddle of lamb, rosemary gnocchi, caramelised smoked garlic and carrot purée; strawberry and guava soup with passionfruit sorbet.*
Details: *www.newickpark.co.uk; off Church Rd; 8.45 pm; booking essential.*
Accommodation: *16 rooms, from £165.*

(A)

The Chandlery £ 39

77-78 Lower Dock St NP20 1EH (01633) 256622

"A clean, smart, modern conversion of the old chandler's store"; the location is "not in the most select part of Newport", but Simon Newcombe's well-rated food can still justify the trip.
/ **Sample dishes:** *lamb and potato torte, cumin infused swede, rosemary jus; lamb and potato torte, cumin infused swede, rosemary jus; vanilla crème brûlée.*
Details: *www.thechandleryrestaurant.com; at the foot of George St bridge on the A48 (hospital side); 10 pm; closed Mon, Sat L & Sun D.*

(A)

Cnapan Country House £ 39

East St SA42 0SY (01239) 820575

The Cooper family's hotel/restaurant near the centre of the town is "very homely and relaxed", and the food it offers is consistently well rated. / **Details:** *www.cnapan.co.uk; on A487 between Fishguard and Cardigan; 9.45 pm; D only, closed Tue; no Amex.* **Accommodation:** *5 rooms, from £80.*

Junction 28 £ 36

Bassaleg NP10 8LD (01633) 891891

A former railway station (complete with replica dining car), in Bassaleg; food-wise "there are some misses, but when it's good it's very good". / **Sample dishes:** *roast pigeon breast and celeriac and potato dauphinoise with a rich wild mushroom sauce; fillet of sea bass on a citrus, baby spinach and fresh basil salad and tempura king prawns; white chocolate and strawberry Cointreau pots.* **Details:** *www.junction28.com; off M4, J28 towards Caerphilly; 9.30 pm; closed Sun D.*

Fistral Blu   £ 35   Ⓐ

Fistral Beach, Headland Rd TR7 1HY (01637) 879444

"Perfect for a summer's day lunch" – this *"brilliantly-located"* spot benefits from a *"spectacular setting"*, and the food is always *"fresh"* and *"interesting"* too. / **Sample dishes:** *chicken piri-piri; Cornish fish pie; Bailey's chocolate torte with kumquat compote and Cornish clotted cream.* **Details:** *www.fistral-blu.co.uk; 10 pm.*

Crooked Billet   £ 43

2 Westbrook End MK17 0DF (01908) 373936

On most accounts, this well-known village pub remains a "beacon" in a thin area, offering "high-quality" food and "a fantastic selection of wines by the glass"; there is the odd critic, though, for whom it's "OK, but doesn't deserve so many accolades". / **Sample dishes:** *goats cheese & caramelised red onion tart, leaves, port dressing; pan fried swordfish, white bean & chorizo crostini, lyonnaise salad, crispy leeks; red wine poached pear & almond tart, vanilla ice cream.* **Details:** *www.thebillet.co.uk; 9.30 pm, 10 pm Fri & Sat; D only, ex Sun open L only.*

Cook & Barker   £ 35

NE65 9JY (01665) 575234

This "pub-with-rooms", just off the A1, serves "reliably good food" that's "good value" too; they're also "very good with children". / **Sample dishes:** *pressed ham terrine with apricot and a home-made chutney; sautéed chicken supreme in garlic and tarragon sauce with king prawns; lemon & lime marscapone cheesecake.* **Details:** *www.cookandbarkerinn.co.uk; 12m N of Morpeth, just off A1; 9 pm.* **Accommodation:** *19 rooms, from £75.*

Les Mirabelles   £ 39   ✪✪

Forest Edge Rd SP5 2BN (01794) 390205

"The only problem is deciding what to eat", at this "gem" of a "family-run" French bistro, "beautifully located" in the New Forest; "divine" cooking and "wonderful" wines come at very reasonable prices. / **Sample dishes:** *fresh scallops & truffles torte with a coral sauce; pan fried fillet of beef with Camembert & calvados sauce; pistachio crème brûlée.* **Details:** *www.lesmirabelles.co.uk; off A36 between Southampton & Salisbury; 9.30 pm; closed Mon & Sun.*

Nutter's   £ 45   Ⓐ✪✪

Edenfield Rd OL12 7TT (01706) 650167

"Junior does his magic in the kitchen, while his father makes a wonderful (and very proud) host" – TV-chef Andrew Nutter's *"unexpected"* restaurant makes a *"superb"* destination for all who comment on it. / **Sample dishes:** *fresh lobster with mango & asparagus salad; medallions of pork with ginger & soy dumplings & tempura spring onions; banana, white chocolate & toffee cheesecake with a custard cream crumb.* **Details:** *www.nuttersrestaurant.com; between Edenfield & Norden on A680; 9.30 pm; closed Mon; closed 2 weeks in Aug.*

Sambucca Cafe And Restaurant **£ 20** Ⓣ
10-11 Union Quay NE30 1HJ (0191) 270 8891
"A neighbourhood pizza and pasta place on the fish quay", tipped for
also *"fabulous fish platters"* and *"amazing value for money"*.
/ *Details: 10.30 pm, Sun 9 pm ; no credit cards.*

Beechwood Hotel **£ 43**
Cromer Rd NR28 0HD (01692) 403231
*This traditionally-styled hotel has "great food" and "wonderfully
attentive service"; if you stay over, you can enjoy a "truly outstanding"
breakfast.* / **Sample dishes:** *seared scallops with pancetta and citrus dressing;
pan-fried breast of chicken on bubble and squeak with thyme jus and and
creamed leeks.* **Details:** *www.beechwood-hotel.co.uk; 9 pm; D only, ex Sun open
L & D; no Amex; children: 10+ at D.* **Accommodation:** *17 rooms, from £120.*

Betty's **£ 35** ★
188 High St DL7 8LF (01609) 775154
"Some people say it's expensive, but you do get what you pay for..."
– *the pros and cons are the same as ever at this latest outlet of the
grand tea-room chain.* / **Sample dishes:** *crab, prawn & avocado salad;
smoked chicken & asparagus rösti; lemon meringue pancakes.*
Details: *www.bettys.co.uk; 5. 30 pm; no Amex.*

McCoys at the Tontine **£ 51**
DL6 3JB (01609) 882 671
*Bang on the A19, a local institution of over three decades' standing,
and still, on most accounts, "a treat", thanks to its "reliable" food and
"confident" service; prices seem "increasingly out of kilter", though,
especially to critics who find the formula "tired".* / **Sample dishes:** *spiced
king prawns with cucumber, radish and bean sprout salad with a coconut and
lemongrass froth; fillet of venison with truffle rosti, buttered Savoy cabbage,
roast beetroot and a port reduction; marinated strawberries and mint, with a
champagne sabayon and elderflower thins.*
Details: *www.mccoysatthetontine.co.uk; junction of A19 & A172; 9.30 pm; bistro
L & D every day, restaurant Sat D only.* **Accommodation:** *6 rooms, from £120.*

Hundred House **£ 40** Ⓣ
Bridgnorth Rd TF11 9EE (01952) 730353
*This "busy" boozer stands out locally (due perhaps in part to a
dearth of local competition); it's generally tipped for offering "good"
food, and even a critic tips its "excellent home-brewed beer".*
/ **Details:** *www.hundredhouse.co.uk; on A442 between Bridgnorth & Telford;
9.30 pm.* **Accommodation:** *10 rooms, from £99.*

Brummells **£ 46** Ⓣ
7 Magdalen St NR3 1LE (01603) 625555
*In the city-centre, a 17th-century building, whose "ambitious" fish and
seafood menus have their fans.* / **Sample dishes:** *seared king scallops with
mint leaf salad and pomegranate chutney; grilled halibut steaks with wild
mushroom and basil compote; iced pear parfait with nutmeg mascarpone and
caramelized pear.* **Details:** *www.brummells.co.uk; 10.30 pm.*

By Appointment   **£ 48**   Ⓐ ✪

25-29 St George's St   NR3 1AB   (01603) 630730

A "many-roomed", "antique-filled" venue, once again praised for its "brilliant" cuisine; "try the special evenings, such as the champagne and canapé river cruise followed by dinner at the restaurant".
/ **Sample dishes:** lobster bisque with croutons and a garlic rouille; sautéed breast of guinea fowl on a field mushroom with a chorizo and basil sauce; rum and raisin steamed sponge pudding with a home-made vanilla ice cream.
Details: www.byappointmentnorwich.co.uk; in a courtyard off Colegate; 9 pm; D only, closed Mon & Sun; no Amex; children: 12+. **Accommodation:** 5 rooms, from £110.

Shiki   **£ 35**   Ⓣ

6 Tombland   NR3 1HE   (01603) 619262

A Tombland spot, tipped for its "technically precise" Japanese cuisine.
/ **Details:** www.shiki.co.uk; 10.30 pm; closed Sun; no Amex.

Waffle House   **£ 21**   Ⓣ

39 St Giles St   NR2 1JN   (01603) 612790

"Used a lot by the locals", this self-explanatory spot is tipped for its "excellent quality and value". / **Sample dishes:** free range oak smoked ham, layered with Lancashire cheddar cheese sauce & mushrooms sautéed with shoyu; hot Dutch apple waffle. **Details:** www.wafflehouse.co.uk; 10 pm; no Amex; need 6+ to book.

NOSS MAYO, DEVON   1–4C

Ship Inn   **£ 40**   Ⓐ

PL8 1EW   (01752) 872387

A "tastefully modernised old fishermen's watering hole", with a "wonderful creek-side setting"; it retains quite a following among reporters, despite food that – under new management – is sometimes no more than "adequate". / **Details:** www.nossmayo.com; 9.30 pm; no Amex.

NOTTINGHAM, CITY OF NOTTINGHAM   5–3D

For a city which is not widely seen as a major dining destination, Nottingham harbours a core of surprisingly impressive, good-quality restaurants in the middle and upper range, including the long-standing *Hart's*, *World Service*, and – at the top end of the market – *Restaurant Sat Bains*. On the ethnic front, *Mem Saab* is of note, and *Chino Latino* also rates mention.

Atlas   **£ 10**   ✪

9 Pelham St   NG1 2EH   (0115) 950 1295

"Every town should have one!" – an "ideal pit stop", of note for its "great sandwiches and coffee". / **Sample dishes:** Prosciutto sweet olive jam, Parmesan and plum tomato sandwich; mozzarella, basil pesto with sundried tomatoes; fresh white chocolate banana cake. **Details:** L only.

Cast   **£ 36**   Ⓣ

The Playhouse, Wellington Circus   NG1 5AN   (0115) 852 3898

The food can be a touch "variable", but the bar/restaurant adjacent to the Playhouse is tipped as a "great, laid-back venue for creative types". / **Sample dishes:** chicken liver pâté, fig jam, melba toast; chicken breast, spring cabbage, Parma ham & sage; chocolate brownie, vanilla ice cream.
Details: www.castrestaurant.co.uk; 10; no Amex.

Chino Latino
Park Plaza Hotel **£ 46**
41 Maid Marian Way NG1 6GD (0115) 947 7444
"Wizard" chefs produce "magic" fusion fare at this would-be "ultra-chic" operation, off the foyer of an hotel; service can be "arrogant", though, and prices strike some reporters as excessive.
*/ **Sample dishes:** rock shrimp tempura; duck and foie gras dumpling; warm layered banana cake and pistachio ice cream.*
Details: *www.chinolatino.co.uk; 10.30 pm; closed Sun.*

Crème **£ 45**
12 Toton Ln NG9 7HA (0115) 939 7422

*"A newish suburban restaurant", tipped for offering "very good value", especially at lunch. / **Sample dishes:** seared king scallops, avocado purée, toasted coconut & foam with apple juice jelly; roast fillet of hare, herb dumpling, wilted leaves, glazed shallots & pickled apple with red wine jus; marinated strawberries, chantilly cream & meringue, apple ice cream with marshmallow & balsamic dust.* ***Details:*** *www.cremerestaurant.co.uk; 9.30 pm; closed Mon, Sat L & Sun D; children: 10+.*

Delilahs **£ 15**
15 Middle Pavement NG1 7DX (0115) 948 4461
"Tiny but great", this "deli/restaurant" is tipped as a "good drop-in" – well, it would be "if you could ever get a seat…"
*/ **Sample dishes:** goat's cheese wrapped in Prosciutto; pan-fried Rocquefort sandwich; brownie with vanilla ice cream.* ***Details:*** *www.delilahfinefoods.co.uk; 7 pm, Sun 5 pm; no Amex.*

French Living **£ 30**
27 King St NG1 2AY (0115) 958 5885
*"It may be a cliché, but this really is a little bit of France in a Nottingham cellar!" – a "useful" and "reliable" sort of place, with an impressively broad fan club. / **Sample dishes:** escargots de Bourgogne; venison with blueberry sauce; crème brûlée with tahiti vanilla.*
Details: *www.frenchliving.co.uk; near Market Square; 10 pm; closed Mon & Sun; no Amex; booking: max 10.*

Georgetown
Colwick Hall Hotel **£ 35**
Racecourse Rd NG2 4BH (0870) 755 7756
A Malaysian (chain) restaurant, near the racecourse, praised for food that's consistently good (if from an "unchanging" menu), and especially tipped for "the best Singapore Sling".
*/ **Sample dishes:** pan fried spicy jumbo prawns; succulent roast chicken with fragrant rice, cucumber and sauces made from blended chillies, soya, ginger, garlic and lime juice served with a clear chicken soup; small bananas with pistachio and coconut ice cream topped with chocolate sauce, almond and coconut flakes.*
Details: *www.colwick-hall.co.uk; 10.30pm.* ***Accommodation:*** *16 rooms, from £140.*

Hart's £ 49
Standard Ct, Park Row NG1 6GN (0115) 911 0666

Standards are "always excellent" (and, if anything, "getting better"), at Tim Hart's "confident" modern brasserie, near the Castle – with its "first-class cuisine" and "smart" service it was once again voted the city's leading eatery. / Sample dishes: pork 'porchetta', vanilla & apple purée, poached rhubarb; pan fried John Dory, haricot beans, iberico chorizo, fennel & vanilla; banana parfait and chocolate tuille, lime froth.
Details: *www.hartsnottingham.co.uk; near Castle; 10.30 pm, Sun 9 pm.*
Accommodation: *32 rooms, from £120.*

Iberico £ 36
The Shire Hall, High Pavement NG1 1HN (01159) 410410
This "trendy" and "slickly-run" bar – "in a crypt underneath a Lace Market museum" – has been a great addition to Nottingham, and offers an "enticing" selection of tapas (both "authentic" and "international"). / Sample dishes: pan fried diver scallop with smoked cured pork belly & cauliflower foam; saddle of rabbit stuffed with morcilla & wild mushroom; lime & ginger parfait with marshmallow & nut sand.
Details: *www.ibericotapas.com; 10 pm; closed Mon & Sun; no Amex; children: 16+ D.*

Laguna Tandoori £ 25
43 Mount St NG1 6HE (0115) 941 1632
A grand and lavishly furnished Indian restaurant particularly recommended as a "wonderful setting for an event", and consistently attracting praise for its high-class cuisine. / Details: nr Nottingham Castle; 11 pm; closed Sat L & Sun L.

The Library Bar Kitchen £ 30
61 Wollaton Rd NG9 2NG (0115) 922 2268
A Swedish tapas bar, in Beeston, tipped as offering "outstanding value for money", especially at lunchtime. / Sample dishes: crispy goat's cheese & filo parcels with an apple & fig compote; aromatic chicken with peanuts, egg fried rice & mint yoghurt; chilled chocolate bread & butter pudding with vanilla ice cream & minted anglaise. Details: www.thelibrarybarkitchen.co.uk; 10 pm; closed Sun; no shorts.

MemSaab £ 38
12-14 Maid Marian Way NG1 6HS (0115) 957 0009
"A class above other Nottingham Indians" – this "friendly" establishment is widely praised for its "refreshing" selection of dishes, which are "spiced with confidence and flair". / Sample dishes: crisp potato cakes infused with cumin and served with garlic and coriander mushrooms; chicken karahi; milk patties served in a saffron infused sauce, garnished with edible rose petals. Details: www.mem-saab.co.uk; near Castle, opposite Park Plaza Hotel; 10.30 pm, Fri & Sat 11 pm, Sun 10 pm; D only; no shorts.

Merchants

Lace Market Hotel £ 46

29-31 High Pavement NG1 1HE (0115) 958 9898

A "smart" boutique-hotel dining room that's a favourite of some
reporters, thanks to its large wine list and "lovely" food; "even in
London, though, it would seem pricey, but in Nottingham…"
/ **Sample dishes:** home smoked chicken, beetroot and micro herb salad and
tapenade vinaigrette; Derbyshire beef sirloin, sweet garlic and potato mash, morel
mushrooms; marshmallow and lime parfait with orange coulis.
Details: www.lacemarkethotel.co.uk; 10.30 pm; closed Mon, Tue–Sat D only,
closed Sun D. **Accommodation:** 42 rooms, from £119.

Petit Paris £ 32

2 Kings Walk NG1 2AE (0115) 947 3767

It's as a "consistently great lunch stop" (or for pre-theatre) that this
"unpretentious" – and often "heaving" – Gallic operation
is most notable; at other times it can seem rather "ordinary".
/ **Details:** www.petitparisrestaurant.co.uk; near Theatre Royal; 10.15 pm;
closed Sun.

Restaurant Sat Bains £ 75 ⭐

Old Lenton Ln NG7 2SA (0115) 986 6566

Sat Bains's "remarkable" and "ingenious" cuisine excites many
"stellar" reports on his tucked-away restaurant-with-rooms (behind
an industrial estate); there are a few caveats, however –
the approach can seem "pretentious", and some reporters find prices
notably "grabby"; stop press – lunch by appointment at a chef's table
is now an option. / **Details:** www.restaurantsatbains.com; 9.30 pm; D only,
closed Mon & Sun; children: 8+. **Accommodation:** 8 rooms, from £90.

Victoria Hotel £ 29

Dovecote Ln NG9 1JG (0115) 925 4049

This "real" pub, by Beeston Station, is "so thriving, it's hard to get
a table"; it doesn't aim to deliver fancy food – just "good, well-priced,
home-cooked" scoff, a "wide range of wines" and some "excellent
real ales". / **Sample dishes:** chicken liver pâté with tequila & cranberry; braised
beef with mushrooms, shallots, smoked bacon & thyme; apple & cinnamon
crumble. **Details:** www.victoriabeeston.co.uk; by Beeston railway station; 8.45 pm,
Wed - Sat 9.30 pm; no Amex; no booking, Sun; children: 18+ after 8 pm.

World Service £ 49 🅰⭐

Newdigate Hs, Castle Gate NG1 6AF (0115) 847 5587

"A splendid all-rounder"; this local legend occupies an "interesting"
space (complete with courtyard, near the Castle) and offers
a "consistent" combination of "the best service", "high-quality"
cooking – "fusion is not a dirty word here" – and a "wine list that's
a buffs' job". / **Sample dishes:** grilled wild sea bass with tomato and basil
bruschetta and mini chorizo sausage; breast of Gressingham duck served pink with
cider fondant potatoes and roast nectarine; dark chocolate morello cherry mousse
pyramid. **Details:** www.worldservicerestaurant.com; 10 pm; children: 12+ at D.

OAKMERE, CHESHIRE 5–2B

Nunsmere Hall £ 61

Tarporley Rd CW8 2ES (01606) 889100

This "attractive" Edwardian country house (with small lake) was re-
emerging as a leading "formal" dining destination in these parts when
it was sold – to the Prima hotel group – in early-2008; in the
circumstances, a proper evaluation of the new régime will sadly have
to wait until next year. / **Sample dishes:** seared scallops, braised pork belly,
apple & vanilla purée; roast Cheshire lamb with garlic & rosemary scented
juices & fondant potato; apple & blackberry crumble with honey ice cream.
Details: www.nunsmere.co.uk; off A49, 4m SW of Northwich; 10 pm; no jeans
or trainers. **Accommodation:** 36 rooms, from £205.

Ee-Usk (Seafood Restaurant) £ 40
North Pier PA35 5QD (01631) 565666

*"The fish couldn't be fresher", as "it's the day's catch landed yards from the restaurant", says a fan of this "efficient" and "stylish" operation, on the pier – a "lovely" setting in which to enjoy a varied menu of "superb" seafood. / **Sample dishes:** 1/2 dozen Lismore oysters; sea bass with creamed leeks and savoury mash; clootie dumpling.* **Details:** *www.eeusk.com; 9.30 pm; no Amex; children: children 10+ at L, not welcome at dinner .*

Bryce's at the Old School House £ 41
RH5 5TH (01306) 627430

*"You don't expect such a marvellous fish restaurant on the edge of the Surrey Hills", but this former pub serves some of "the freshest around". / **Sample dishes:** fish cakes with sweet chilli sauce; chorizo and olive crusted cod fillet potato and shallot rosti, provençale sauce; home-made desserts.* **Details:** *www.bryces.co.uk; 8m S of Dorking on A29; 9 pm; closed Sun D in Nov, Jan & Feb; no Amex.*

The Kings Arms £ 37
Stane St RH5 5TS (01306) 711224

*A pretty old pub-restaurant, which is just the sort of venue for "an absolutely magic Sunday lunch"; the quality of the food "can vary, though, even on the same day". / **Details:** www.thekingsarmsockley.co.uk; A29 S of Dorking; 9 pm, Fri & Sat 10 pm.* **Accommodation:** *6 rooms, from £80.*

The Grapevine £ 42
121 High St RG29 1LA (01256) 701122

*This "pleasant" local bistro changed hands this year; an early report on the new régime suggests its virtues are still essentially unchanged, and it's still tipped as a "friendly" place, serving "decent" food. / **Sample dishes:** basil tartlet, gorgonzola, crème fraîche and herb salad; fillet of salmon, pepper chorizo and minted Jersey royals; rhubarb and ginger pavlova.* **Details:** *www.grapevine-gourmet.com; follow signs from M3, J5; 10 pm; closed Mon & Sun.*

St John £ 49
83 High St RG29 1LB (01256) 702697

*"A real discovery"; this village-restaurant offers an "imaginative" menu, from which results are sometimes "stunningly good". / **Sample dishes:** salad of lobster, anchovy, potato & broad beans; fillet of veal with dauphinoise potato, artichoke purée, truffle & marsala jus; elderflower panna cotta with roast strawberries.* **Details:** *www.stjohn-restaurant.co.uk; Approx 2 miles from the M3, J5; 9 pm; closed Sun.*

Dew Pond £ 46
RG20 9LH (01635) 278408
*"On a summer's evening, the location and the views are fabulous",
at this "consistently good" restaurant (where "wine-themed dinners"
find particular approval); the only criticism? – it's a "little quiet".*
/ **Sample dishes:** *risotto of shrimps, mussels, peas and Parmesan; peppered
saddle of local roe deer, Armagnac sauce, field mushrooms, fondant potato,
crushed root vegetables and French beans; bourbon vanilla crème brûlée with tuile
biscuit, raspberry purée and a seasonal fruit salad.* **Details:** *www.dewpond.co.uk;
6m S of Newbury, off A34; 10 pm; D only, closed Mon & Sun; no Amex;
children: 5+.*

★

Smiths Brasserie £ 50
Fyfield Rd CM5 0AL (01277) 365578
*"A really buzzy" establishment which delivers "friendly" service and
"good food to match"; and "you might even see Rod Stewart".*
/ **Sample dishes:** *fish soup, crouton, saffron mayonnaise & Gruyère cheese;
glazed honey & cinnamon Barbary duck breast on sauté Savoy cabbage;
hot melting chocolate cake with mint choc chip ice cream.*
Details: *www.smithsbrasserie.com; left off A414 towards Fyfield; 10.30 pm;
closed Mon; no Amex; children: 12+.*

★

Butley Orford Oysterage £ 34
Market Hill IP12 2LH (01394) 450277
*The fish is so fresh it "jumps onto your plate", at the Pinney family's
"'50s haven"; "if you want luxury, stay away!", though – service
is "erratic" and the setting is of the "rickety-chairs-and-plastic-top-
tables" variety.* / **Sample dishes:** *smoked salmon pâté; grilled Dover sole;
ice cream bombe.* **Details:** *www.butleyorfordoysterage.co.uk; 9 pm;
Mon-Thu L only, closed Sun D in winter; no Amex.*

The Crown & Castle £ 41
IP12 2LJ (01394) 450205
*"A lovely coastal setting" adds lustre to Ruth & David Watson's
popular hotel; fans vaunt its "superb" and "honest" cooking,
its "very inventive" wine list and its "polite" service – sceptics, though,
say it's "unexceptional" and "just a touch pretentious".*
/ **Sample dishes:** *buffalo mozzarella with pomegranate and rocket; guinea-fowl
with red cabbage and parsnip purée; warm blood orange & ground almond cake
with mascarpone.* **Details:** *www.crownandcastle.co.uk; on main road to Orford;
9.15 pm; closed Sun D in winter; no Amex; booking: max 8; children: 9+ at
D.* **Accommodation:** *18 rooms, from £90.*

★★

Xian £ 29
324 High St BR6 0NG (01689) 871881
*"Low on gloop... high on fresh flavours" – this "buzzing" Chinese has
an "exciting" and "adventurous" menu, and is "always lively and
busy"; book ahead.* / **Sample dishes:** *spicy tao pan beef; roast duck with
sweet plum sauce; toffee apples.* **Details:** *Near the war memorial; 11 pm; closed
Sun L.*

Golden Lion   £ 41

6 West End DL6 3AA   (01609) 883526

*Tipped particularly for its "idyllic village location", this long-established pub-cum-restaurant still offers some pretty good food (even if the menu can seem rather "static"). / **Sample dishes:** smoked haddock & spring onion risotto; salmon fishcake with a spinach & sorrel sauce; warm apple, prune & walnut cake. **Details:** 9 pm; closed Mon L & Tue L; no Amex. **Accommodation:** 3 rooms, from £90.*

Falcon Inn   £ 40

Fotheringay PE8 5HZ   (01832) 226254

*Tipped as "very good for the area", this village inn complete with dining conservatory maintains "high standards" all-round; it has a "beautiful view of the church" too. / **Sample dishes:** chargrilled asparagus with quail's egg vinaigrette & Parmesan; rump of lamb with sautéed potatoes & fine ratatouille; lemon tart with crème fraîche. **Details:** just off A605; 9.15 pm, Sun 8pm.*

The Bush Inn   £ 33

SO24 0RE   (01962) 732764

*A "pretty pub" that's "great in winter with its roaring fires, and wonderful in summer, out by the river"; fans hail its "cracking" cooking, but "popularity with city-based weekenders" can lead to "overwhelmed" service and "boring" food. / **Sample dishes:** black pudding salad with chicory mustard vinaigrette, poached egg, garlic croutons and Parmesan; chargrilled rib-eye steak 8oz served with a garlic and anchovy butter; Valrhona dark chocolate and raspberry crème brûlée. **Details:** www.wadworth.co.uk; just off A31 between Winchester & Alresford; 9pm.*

Some of the restaurants have attractive settings – how could they not in such a beautiful city? – but Oxford remains a spectacularly dreadful place to eat. The only real 'all-rounder' of any note at all is the long-popular Thai, *Chaing Mai*.

Al Shami   £ 24

25 Walton Cr OX1 2JG   (01865) 310066

*"Oxford's best Lebanese" – "tucked away in Jericho" – offers "consistently good" mezze and "a huge list of Château Musar vintages"; fans say it's nothing short of "terrific", and even sceptics concede that it's "a reliable pit stop". / **Sample dishes:** boiled fava beans with lemon juice, olive oil and a touch of garlic; chicken and lamb cubes garnished with onions, mushrooms and tomatoes; Arabic ice cream. **Details:** www.al-shami.co.uk; midnight. **Accommodation:** 12 rooms, from £50.*

Aziz   £ 33

228-230 Cowley Rd OX4 1UH   (01865) 794945

*"Still the definitive Oxford Indian" – this "decent Bangladeshi" is "generally reliable" if you're looking for a "top-class" curry; "service oscillates wildly, however, chiefly dependent on whether or not the charming Aziz himself is present". / **Details:** www.aziz.uk.com; 11.15 pm; closed Fri L.*

336

Bangkok House   **£ 28**

42a High Bridge St OX1 2EP   (01865) 200705

"Consistently good Thai food, served by charming staff" – the theme of most reports on this *"good-value"* oriental, handily located near the station. / **Sample dishes:** chicken & beef satay; chicken & cashew nut; sticky rice & mango. **Details:** 11 pm; closed Sun.

Bar Meze   **£ 32**   Ⓐ

146 London Rd OX3 9ED   (01865) 761106

The food at this Turkish outfit in Headington is *"well presented"*, but it is the *"excellent décor"* that makes the place *"particularly recommended if atmosphere is a crucial factor"*.
/ **Sample dishes:** borek; skewered pieces of marinated chicken cooked over charcoal with onion and peppers; traditional Turkish yogurt with honey and pistachio. **Details:** www.bar-meze.co.uk; 10.30 pm, 11 pm Fri & Sat.

Bombay   **£ 22**   ✪

82 Walton St OX2 6EA   (01865) 511188

"A good BYO Indian", in Jericho, with notably *"friendly and efficient service"* – all reporters agree that it *"never lets you down"*.
/ **Details:** 11 pm; closed Fri L; no Amex.

Branca   **£ 39**   Ⓣ

111 Walton St OX2 6AJ   (01865) 556111

Tipped as *"reliable, quick and lively"*, a Jericho Italian which remains a popular stand-by. / **Sample dishes:** Parma ham, bresaola and salami with sweet balsamic onions; Gloucester old spot pork belly, mash, salsa verde; panna cotta with raspberries. **Details:** www.branca-restaurants.com; 11 pm.

Brasserie Blanc   **£ 41**

71-72 Walton St OX2 6AG   (01865) 510999

Reporters split roughly 50/50 on this Jericho chain-outlet, which bears the name of one of the UK's most famous chefs; fans insist it's *"better now"*, and *"offers a very good deal overall"*, but to doubters it's just *"going through the motions"*. / **Sample dishes:** Loch Duart salmon, dill gravadlax; rack of Cornish lamb, butter potatoes, green beans; chocolate and hazelnut delice. **Details:** www.brasserieblanc.com; 10 pm, 10.30 pm Sat, 9.30 pm Sun.

Browns   **£ 31**   ⊗

5-11 Woodstock Rd OX2 6HA   (01865) 511995

A once-great English bistro, where the food – in defiance of all the laws of physics – is still *"slipping"*, and which can sometimes be *"astonishingly poor"*. / **Sample dishes:** Prosciutto & chorizo with dressed leaves, walnuts and a celeriac coleslaw; Browns steak, mushroom & Guinness pie with French beans and mashed potato; baked vanilla cheesecake with freshly blended strawberries. **Details:** www.browns-restaurants.com; 11 pm, Fri & Sat 11.30 pm, Sun 10.30 pm; need 5+ to book.

Café Coco   **£ 26**   ✪

23 Cowley Rd OX4 1HP   (01865) 200232

"A far better bet than the chains for a casual bite out" – an outfit worth knowing about for its *"interesting pizzas"* and *"delicious burgers"*; *"great cocktails"* too. / **Sample dishes:** garlic bread with houmous; merguez and tzatziki pizza; Belgian waffles. **Details:** 11pm, Sat 12.30am; no booking.

Cherwell Boathouse　　　　　　　£ 37　　Ⓐ

Bardwell Rd OX2 6ST   (01865) 552746

"You can arrive by punt", at this "unique" former boathouse in an "idyllic" waterside location… "but why would you want to?", say critics, who slam its "lazy" food and iffy service; fans, though, claim "standards are on the rise", and vaunt the "interesting" and "decently-priced" wine list. / **Sample dishes:** *wood pigeon breast, pancetta crisp, pomegranate salsa; rump of salt marsh lamb, parsnip salsify, carrot, potato purée; Baileys baked alaska, mint syrup.* **Details:** *www.cherwellboathouse.co.uk; 9.30 pm .*

Chiang Mai　　　　　　　£ 35　　Ⓐ⭐

Kemp Hall Pas, 130a High St OX1 4DH   (01865) 202233

"One of the best eating experiences in Oxford"; "wonderful, fresh Thai food" is served in the "incongruous" setting of this medieval dining room, "down a little alleyway", off the High. / **Sample dishes:** *crispy fried rolls with a sweet and sour plum sauce; stir fried chicken with garlic, pepper, spring onions and coriander; steamed sticky rice with cashew nuts and banana, served with cream.* **Details:** *www.chiangmaikitchen.co.uk; 10.30 pm.*

Chutney's Indian Brasserie　　　£ 27　　Ⓣ

36 St Michael's St OX1 2EB   (01865) 724241

This "buzzy" city-centre spot is still often tipped as "a cut above the average" (although it also induced the odd "terrible" report this year). / **Sample dishes:** *sobzi somosa; tandoori jingha; peshwari chawal.* **Details:** *www.chutneysindianbrasserie.co.uk; 11 pm.*

Cibo!　　　　　　　　　£ 34　　Ⓣ

4 South Pde OX2 7JL   (01865) 292321

An Italian stand-by in Summertown, tipped for its "good food and service, and reasonable prices". / **Sample dishes:** *rocket, tomato, avocado, and treccia di mozzarella salad; risotto with peeled king prawns, courgettes, saffron, garlic, parsley, and a touch of chilli; nougat ice cream topped with hazelnut praline.* **Details:** *www.ilovecibo.co.uk; 10.30 pm, Sun 10 pm; no Amex.*

La Cucina　　　　　　　£ 29

39-40 St Clements OX4 1AB   (01865) 793811

"A fun Italian family-style restaurant", in St Clement's; thanks to its "solid" standards and its "consistently good" value, it enjoys a "rising reputation" (and "can get pretty busy"). / **Sample dishes:** *oven roast pepper with goats cheese, mixed leaves and balsamic reduction; pizza with mozzarella, tomato, fresh chilli, onions, spicy salami, green peppers; vanilla ice cream with espresso.* **Details:** *www.lacucinaoxford.co.uk; 10.30 pm.*

Edamame　　　　　　　£ 17　　Ⓣ

15 Holywell St OX1 3SA   (01865) 246916

You eat "cheek by jowl with other diners", at this "tiny", "cheap and cheerful" café in "a beautiful part of Oxford" (near New College), but it's tipped as a good option for a "quick and healthy" pit stop nonetheless; beware "ever-present queues" though. / **Sample dishes:** *tender pork cutlet, breaded and deep fried, served with a fruity dipping sauce.* **Details:** *www.edamame.co.uk; opp New College; 8.30 pm; L only, ex Fri & Sat open L & D, closed Mon; no Amex; no booking.*

Fishers £ 37

36-37 St Clements OX4 1AJ (01865) 243003

"A dependable Oxford institution, if not a terribly creative one" –
this fish-and-seafood bistro veteran is tipped as *"still worth going to,
if only for its reliability"*. / **Sample dishes:** *crayfish & mixed leaf salad with
lemon dressing; chargrilled swordfish with salad leaves & mango and sweet pepper
salsa; amaretto & espresso poured over vanilla pod ice cream.*
Details: *www.fishers-restaurant.com; by Magdalen Bridge; 10.30 pm; no Amex.*

Gee's £ 40

61 Banbury Rd OX2 6PE (01865) 553540

"The food's good, if not exciting, and the ambience is super", at this
"celebratory" establishment, in a grand conservatory, just north of the
city-centre; it can, however, seem *"overpriced"*. / **Sample dishes:** *goat's
cheese & basil soufflé; grilled John Dory, braised fennel, & blood orange
hollandaise; whisky & marmalade bread & butter pudding.*
Details: *www.gees-restaurant.co.uk; 10.30 pm.*

Grand Café £ 10

84 High St OX1 4BG (01865) 204463

*"Ionic columns, giant mirrors, huge palms and mouthwatering scones
and cakes"* – the attractions one reporter notes at this *"buzzy"*
central café, which also offers an *"enjoyable lunchtime experience"*.
/ **Details:** *L only; no Amex.*

Jamie's Italian £ 38

24-26 George St OX1 2AE (01865) 838383

*The Naked Chef's initial branch of what aims to be a national chain –
with Bath & Kingston coming soon – opened after the survey's close
(hence we've left it un-rated); initial press reviews suggest it's well
pukka, though – get ready to queue.* / **Details:** *www.jamiesitalian.com;
11 pm.*

Malmaison £ 44

3 Oxford Circle OX1 1AY (01865) 268400

A *"converted prison"* is the setting some reporters find *"exciting"* –
others *"odd"* – for this boutique-hotel dining room; it makes
a lacklustre advertisement for the brand – the food's *"nothing to write
home about"*, and service can be *"terrible"*.
/ **Details:** *www.malmaison.com; 10.30 pm.* **Accommodation:** *94 rooms,
from £140.*

The News Café £ 23

1 Ship St OX1 3DA (01865) 242317

Tipped as "a good pit stop all through the day", this central café is of
particular note for its *"delicious viennoiserie and coffee"*.
/ **Sample dishes:** *home-made soup; fish & chips; waffles.* **Details:** *7 pm; L only.*

The Nosebag £ 21

6-8 St Michael's St OX1 2DU (01865) 721033

"Slightly off the tourist track", this long-established veggie café
is worth remembering for its *"lovely fresh salads and quiches,
and always a few good hot dishes too"*. / **Sample dishes:** *beef lasagne;
summer bean stew.* **Details:** *www.nosebagoxford.co.uk; 9.30 pm, Fri & Sat
10 pm, Sun 8.30 pm.*

The Old Parsonage   £ 49

A

1 Banbury Rd OX2 6NN   (01865) 292305

It's still no bargain, but this "fantastic" medieval townhouse-hotel/restaurant (with charming courtyard) seems to be trying harder to live up to its exalted prices; at any rate, it's "excellent for afternoon tea". / **Sample dishes:** *lamb sweetbread, smoked bacon & peas; wild mushroom risotto; chocolate nemesis with crème fraîche.*

Details: *www.oldparsonage-hotel.co.uk; 0.5m N of city centre; 10.30 pm.*
Accommodation: *30 rooms, from £160.*

Pierre Victoire   £ 32

Little Clarendon St OX1 2HP   (01865) 316616

"Does what it says on the tin" – this Gallic bistro dishes up fare that's "neither refined nor adventurous", but at notably "reasonable" prices – lunch, in particular, offers "incredible value".

/ **Details:** *www.pierrevictoire.co.uk; 11 pm, 10 pm Sun; no Amex.*

Quod

X

Old Bank Hotel   £ 37

91-94 High St OX1 4BN   (01865) 799599

A "hustling and bustling" ambience and "a dearth of local alternatives" – these are the features which "keep alive" Jeremy Mogford's "deceptively glitzy" city-centre Italian; service "lacks edge", and the food is "run-of-the-mill". / **Details:** *www.oldbank-hotel.co.uk; opp All Souls College; 11 pm; no booking at D.* **Accommodation:** *42 rooms, from £165.*

Shanghai 30s   £ 35

A

82 St Aldates OX1 1RA   (01865) 242230

An "inventive take on Chinese classics" wins much local acclaim for this "beautifully-furnished" oriental (part of a "lovely 15th-century building"), where lunchtime dim sum is singled out as offering "terrific value"; the place also, however, provokes the occasional "very ordinary" report. / **Details:** *www.shanghai30s.com; 11 pm; closed Mon L.*

Thai Orchid   £ 34

T

58a St Clements St OX4 1AH   (01865) 798044

There's some hot competition locally in this particular cuisine, but this east-city spot is sometimes still tipped as a top choice "if you take surroundings into consideration". / **Details:** *near Headington Park; 10.30 pm; closed Sat L & Sun L.*

OXTON, WIRRAL   5–2A

Fraiche   £ 52

★★

11 Rose Mount CH43 5SG   (0151) 652 2914

Marc Wilkinson's "spectacular" food – "from a tiny kitchen, and with no brigade!" – makes this very personal establishment "a must-visit if you're in the area"; now, if they could just get a bit more buzz...

/ **Sample dishes:** *asparagus pain d'épice egg; rose veal loin slow cooked butternut squash, cep extract; parcel of apple and its own sorbet.*
Details: *www.restaurantfraiche.com; 9 pm; closed Mon, Tue, Wed L & Thu L; no Amex.*

Margot's   £ 37
11 Duke St PL28 8AB   (01841) 533441

Adrian Oliver's "wonderful and unpretentious little restaurant" –
"thankfully not a Stein clone" – is universally hailed by reporters for
its "beautifully-executed" dishes; "book well ahead", though –
*"he needs bigger premises". / **Sample dishes:** Cornish scallops with bacon*
and lemon; breast of chicken, sautéed potatoes, tarragon cream sauce and crispy
*Parma ham; Eton mess. **Details:** www.margots.co.uk; On the back street behind*
the Inner Harbour, on the same road as the Post Office; 9.30 pm.

No 6 Café   £ 62   ⭐⭐
6 Middle St PL28 8AP   (01841) 532093

"An impressive operation with real flair", and one that "strikes a blow
against Rick Stein's local dominance" – Paul Ainsworth's "compact"
three-year-old elicits a hymn of praise for its "always innovative and
beautiful" cooking and its "impeccable" service.
*/ **Sample dishes:** sashimi tuna; monkfish with spring onion, cucumber, Fowey*
mussels and Chinese leaf; cappuccino and doughnuts with crackling candy.
***Details:** www.number6inpadstow.co.uk; Off the main square in Padstow,*
next door to Rick Stein's; 10 pm; D only Fri- Sun, except for residents.

Rick Stein's Café   £ 33   ⭐
10 Middle St PL28 8AP   (01841) 532700

"Like a cramped beach-café" ("but without the views"), Rick Stein's
"fun" operation offers an "earthy" menu, on which "sublime fish 'n'
chips" is the star dish; staff "struggle when the place is full", though –
it's often "best to eat out on the harbour wall".
*/ **Details:** www.rickstein.com; 9.30 pm; no Amex. **Accommodation:** 3 rooms,*
from £90.

St Petroc's Hotel & Bistro   £ 47   ⭐
4 New St PL28 8EA   (01841) 532700
"A casual and friendly" – "noisy" and "rather crowded" –
outpost of the Stein empire, this "reliable" bistro wins praise for its
*"classic" fare. / **Sample dishes:** hot Toulouse sausage with a tomato, caper &*
shallot salad; sea bream with sauce vierge, fennel, spring onions, tomato & mint;
*profiteroles with coffee ice cream. **Details:** www.rickstein.com; 9.30 pm; no Amex.*
***Accommodation:** 10 rooms, from £135.*

Seafood Restaurant £ 75

Riverside PL28 8BY (01841) 532700

"Both Rick Stein and his restaurant are British institutions", and the latter is just "as good as ever after its recent £2.5m re-fit"; a few reporters find prices "hard to digest", but most speak of "orgasmic" fish and "slick" service, leading to a "perfect dining experience" overall. / **Details:** www.rickstein.com; opp harbourmaster's car park; 10 pm; no Amex; booking: max 14; children: 3+. **Accommodation:** 16 rooms, from £135.

Stein's Fish & Chips £ 22

South Quay PL28 8BL (01841) 532700

The setting may be "an unpromising shed at the industrial end of the harbour", but Rick's "easy-to-miss" seaside chippy offers "superb" fish and "awesome" chips; in season, queues can be "long". / **Sample dishes:** battered oysters; lemon sole. **Details:** www.rickstein.com; 9 pm; no Amex.

PARK GATE, HAMPSHIRE 2–4D

Kam's Palace £ 36

1 Bridge Rd SO31 7GD (01489) 583328

"The food is better than anything I've had in Hong Kong or Beijing", insists a hard-core fan of this "jewel" of an oriental; even a less-impressed reporter concedes that it's a "good" all-rounder, with a "pleasant riverside setting". / **Details:** 10.30 pm.

PARKGATE, CHESHIRE 5–2A

Marsh Cat £ 31

1 Mostyn Sq CH64 6SL (0151) 336 1963

"Competent cooking" from an "eclectic menu", and "great views across to Wales too" – such are the virtues which make this "pleasant" and "cheerful" bistro quite a "haven" on the Wirral. / **Sample dishes:** scallop and garden pea risotto; best end of lamb, parsnip purée, lentil stock sauce and black pudding baignets; berry meringue. **Details:** www.marshcat.com; 10 pm.

PAULERSPURY, NORTHANTS 2–1D

Vine House £ 48

100 High St NN12 7NA (01327) 811267

It may look "ordinary" and "in need of updating", but this "cosy and relaxed" establishment is tipped for serving a "small selection of excellent dishes". / **Details:** www.vinehousehotel.com; 2m S of Towcester just off A5; 10 pm; closed Mon L-Wed L, Sat L & Sun; no Amex. **Accommodation:** 6 rooms, from £95.

Churchill Arms £ 36
GL55 6XH (01386) 594000
Leo & Sonya Brooke Little sold this popular Cotswolds inn shortly after
our survey closed, so no rating is appropriate; let's hope the new
régime maintains its "relaxed" style and "inventive" cooking.
/ **Sample dishes:** chicken and mushroom pancake with cheese glaze; monkfish
medallions, sweet & sour butternut; soft almond meringue with saffron poached
pear and apricot parfait. **Details:** www.thechurchillarms.com; off Fosse Way;
9 pm; no Amex; no booking. **Accommodation:** 4 rooms, from £70.

A

Cringletie House £ 54
Edinburgh Rd EH45 8PL (01721) 725750
The "intimate" dining room of this Baronial-style Borders country
house hotel continues to please most reporters with its "excellent"
cuisine; the chef has changed of late, but the cuisine "doesn't seem
that different". / **Sample dishes:** pan-seared foie gras, spiced lentils with apple
and fig; fillet and belly of pork caramelised apple purée and creamed Savoy
cabbage; Cringletie-style jaffa cake. **Details:** www.cringletie.com; between Peebles
and Eddleston on A703, 20m S of Edinburgh; 9 pm. **Accommodation:** 13
rooms, from £220.

A

Spotted Dog £ 33
Smarts Hill TN11 8EE (01892) 870253
"A lovely old pub in a beautiful setting"; city-slickers may find it "a bit
rustic", but fans say it's a "friendly" place with "excellent pub food".
/ **Sample dishes:** home cured gravadlax with a mustard & honey dressing;
pork chop served on a bed of garlic mash with vegetables & sage sauce;
home-made marmalade & chocolate bread & butter pudding served with custard.
Details: www.spotteddogpub.co.uk; near Penshurst Place; 9 pm, Fri & Sat
9.30 pm, Sun 7 pm; no Amex.

✪✪

The Abbey Restaurant £ 64
Abbey St TR18 4AR (01736) 330680
"New chef Michael Riemenschneider is taking the Abbey kitchens
to an even greater height", so it's "well worth a visit" to this
"acclaimed spot", just off the sea-front, to sample his "simple,
exquisitely prepared and very fresh" food; (the young Swiss chef,
incidentally, has subsequently acquired Juniper, near Manchester,
so let's hope he's not taking on too much). / **Sample dishes:** langoustine
with pearl barley, asparagus & burdock; turbot with razor clam marinière;
pumpernickel parfait with balsamic caramel and strawberries.
Details: www.theabbeyonline.com; 9 pm; closed Mon, Tue L, Wed L,
Thu L & Sun.

T

The Bay Restaurant £ 39
Britons Hill TR18 3AE (01736) 366890
A contemporary spot, tipped for its terrace overlooking town and sea,
and offering good all-round standards. / **Sample dishes:** braised oxtail and
wild mushroom risotto, garlic and herb croutons; roast chump of lamb, purée
of butternut squash, dauphinoise cake with a pearl barley and mint reduction;
vanilla roast rhubarb, goats cheese and Cornish cream ice cream.
Details: www.bay-penzance.co.uk; 9.30 pm; closed Sat L. **Accommodation:** 24
rooms, from £140.

Deans At Let's Eat £ 44
77-79 Kinnoull St PH1 5EZ   (01738) 643377

A city-centre restaurant, of some note locally; it's often tipped for its "good value", especially at lunch. / **Sample dishes:** *fine Arbroath Smokies & Parmesan cheese pastry tart with a spiced cucumber salad; pan seared fillet of halibut with carrot & coriander papardelle, saffron potato & smoked salmon sauce; warm ginger pudding with vanilla pod ice & caramel sauce.* **Details:** *www.letseatperth.co.uk; on corner of Atholl Street and Kinnoull Street, short walk from city-centre; 9 pm; closed Mon & Sun; no Amex.*

JSW £ 56
20 Dragon St GU31 4JJ   (01730) 262030

This well-discovered venture is much "less cramped" in its current "simple and spacious" setting, in a former coaching inn; there is the occasional gripe, but most reporters praise the "beautifully presented" food, and the wines are "fantastic" too. / **Sample dishes:** *scallops with truffle and cep risotto; honey roast duck with girolles; chocolate and olive oil delice with malt ice cream.* **Details:** *www.jsw.restaurant.com; 9.30 pm; closed Mon & Sun; no Amex; children: 7+.*

The White Swan £ 41
Market Pl YO18 7AA   (01751) 472288

"Always a delight" – this town-centre inn offers "a consistently interesting menu and a fine selection of wines". / **Sample dishes:** *grilled Iona dairy goat's cheese, pecan biscuit & caramelised red onions; slow roast belly pork, apple & radish relish, chive pesto potatoes & baby peppery leaf salad; chocolate cake, clotted cream & boozy cherries.* **Details:** *www.white-swan.co.uk; 9 pm.* **Accommodation:** *21 rooms, from £145.*

Friends £ 44
11 High St HA5 5PJ   (020) 8866 0286

A "lovely little restaurant", where you are "always welcomed as a friend"; even some fans, however, say standards "seem to be stalling", and some recent meals have seemed "mediocre". / **Sample dishes:** *terrine of pheasant with Cumberland sauce; escalopes of wild boar with red cabbage, civet sauce; orange bread & butter pudding.* **Details:** *www.friendsrestaurant.co.uk; near Pinner Underground station; 9.30 pm; closed Mon & Sun D.*

La Giralda £ 28
66-68 Pinner Grn HA5 2AB   (020) 8868 3429

"Unchanged in 40 years!" – this Spanish veteran still has the "same staff and the same menu", and remains "reliable and good-value"; perhaps inevitably, though, the "service is getting rather tired, and the décor is too". / **Sample dishes:** *melon slices with dried cranberries; beef riojana with mushrooms & button onions; warm frangipane tart of rhubarb & raspberry, white chocolate ice cream.* **Details:** *www.lagiralda.co.uk; A404 to Cuckoo Hill Junction; 10 pm; closed Mon & Sun D.*

L'Orient £ 48
58 High St HA5 5PZ   (020) 8429 8488

Locals still tip this prettily-housed pan-Asian as a superior and "romantic" destination (even if one long-term customer bemoans "declining quality over the years"). / **Details:** *www.lorientcuisine.com; 11 pm.*

Plockton Inn £ 30
Innes St IV52 8TW (01599) 544222
"Fresh and reasonably-priced seafood" is the highlight at this
"obliging", "cosy" and "busy" inn; "good real ale" too.
/ **Details:** www.plocktoninn.co.uk; 9 pm; no Amex. **Accommodation:** 14 rooms,
from £84 summer.

Perkins £ 36
Old Railway Station NG12 5NA (0115) 937 3695
"A long-established bistro now run by the second generation of the
same family"; quirkily-located in a former railway station, it's a
"very pleasant" operation offering "good value for money" – lunches,
in particular, are "a real bargain". / **Details:** www.perkinsrestaurant.co.uk;
off A606 between Nottingham & Melton Mowbray; 9.30 pm; closed Mon &
Sun D.

🅐⭐

The Barbican Kitchen Brasserie £ 29
58 Southside St, The Barbican PL1 2LA (01752) 604448
This very popular "modern brasserie" was closed for the first half
of 2008, owing to fire damage; it re-launches as this guide goes
to press – let us hope it arises, phoenix-like, as a destination for
"enjoyable" meals served in "interesting" surroundings.
/ **Details:** www.barbicankitchen.com; 9pm; no Maestro.

Chloe's
Gill Akaster House £ 47
Princess St PL1 2EX (01752) 201523
"Ideal for a romantic meal, or for pre- or post-theatre dining" –
this restaurant handily close to the Civic Centre is a "cosy" place,
serving "good local food, with a French twist, but without pretension".
/ **Sample dishes:** mussels in creamy saffron sauce; cassoulet of duck and pork;
clafoutis of hot griottine cherries pistachio ice-cream.
Details: www.chloesrestaurant.co.uk; 10 pm; closed Mon & Sun.

Tanners Restaurant £ 46
Prysten Hs, Finewell St PL1 2AE (01752) 252001
"By far the best restaurant in a city tragically short of good eateries";
the eponymous brothers' "friendly" and "intimate" venture – in an
historic building – is a "formal" sort of place, where the food is often
"beautifully presented" (if arguably on the pricey side for what it is).
/ **Sample dishes:** cannelloni of rabbit & tarragon, pancetta & girolles; fillet
of Atlantic halibut, crushed potatoes, young carrots, mussel velouté; tamar valley
strawberry, semi freddo, salad & soup. **Details:** www.tannersrestaurant.com;
9.30 pm; closed Mon & Sun.

🅣

The White Hart £ 34
Main St LS21 1LH (0113) 203 7862
A gastropub that's tipped as "a real find", with a "very decent menu",
"well-executed" cuisine and "first-rate" staff. / **Sample dishes:** sardines,
tomatoes, garlic and red onions bruschetta; rack of st louis babecue ribs, slaw and
frites; maple and walnut ice cream sundae, with honey, cream and Belgian waffle.
Details: www.thewhitehartpool.co.uk; in Poole village 2m from Leeds & Bradford
airport; 10 pm, Fri-Sat 10.30 pm; no booking.

Cafe Shore   **£ 46**   🅣
10-14 Banks Rd BH13 7QB   (01202) 707271
The food can be "a bit hit-and-miss", but this "stunningly-situated"
waterfront bar/restaurant is nonetheless tipped as "a great place
*to go on a beautiful summer night". / **Sample dishes:** dressed crab; baked*
*fillet of salmon; passion fruit panna cotta. **Details:** www.cafeshore.co.uk;*
10.30 pm.

Guildhall Tavern   **£ 38**   🅐🟊
15 Market St BH15 1NB   (01202) 671717
"A little bit of France in England" – this "warm and welcoming" spot
wins praise for its "excellent blackboard specials", among which fish
*dishes are the highlight. / **Sample dishes:** mussels cooked in white wine with*
garlic, onion & parsley, finished with cream; pan fried fresh fillet of halibut served
with champagne sauce; pear clafoutis served with clotted cream ice cream.
***Details:** www.guildhalltavern.co.uk; 9.30 pm; closed Mon.*

Andrews On The Weir   **£ 50**
Porlock Weir TA24 8PB   (01643) 863300
It's for the most part still hailed for offering "lovely food in a beautiful
setting", but some reporters find a "flat" ambience at this restaurant-
with-rooms, and sense a "creeping carelessness" in its approach.
*/ **Sample dishes:** fillet of Cornish pollock with sweet pepper stew, chick peas and*
chorizo oil; Exmoor lamb braised for eight hours with dauphinoise potatoes,
roast sweetbreads and rosemary; rhubarb and lemon possett with lemon and
*pistachio biscotti. **Details:** www.andrewsontheweir.co.uk; 9 pm; closed Mon & Tue;*
*no Amex; children: 12+. **Accommodation:** 5 rooms, from £100.*

Airds Hotel   **£ 65**   🅐🟊
PA38 4DF   (01631) 730236
It's not just the "pleasant and tranquil surroundings" (overlooking
Loch Linnhe) which make this old-fashioned hotel of note – it's also
*consistently praised for its "excellent" cooking. / **Sample dishes:** warm*
seafood salad with crispy artichoke, orange and thyme reduction; roast local
salmon fillets with a light broth of mussels and surf clams; vanilla mousse with
*poached rhubarb and ginger crumble. **Details:** www.airds-hotel.com; 20m N*
of Oban; 9 pm; closed Jan. 6 - 23; no Amex; no jeans or trainers; children: 8+ at
*D. **Accommodation:** 11 rooms, from £245.*

Pier House Hotel   **£ 46**   🅐🟊
PA38 4DE   (01631) 730302
With its "glorious" seafood and "a location to die for" (on the shores
of Loch Linnhe), this hotel dining room is a "brilliant" destination;
its appeal is undiminished under its new ownership.
*/ **Details:** www.pierhousehotel.co.uk; just off A828, follow signs for Port Appin &*
*Lismore Ferry; 9.30 pm. **Accommodation:** 12 rooms, from £90.*

Port Gaverne Hotel   **£ 40**   🅣
PL29 3SQ   (01208) 880244
"The best crab sandwich around" wins a 'tip' for the bar of this
comfortable hotel, near a cute fishing harbour.
*/ **Details:** www.portgavernehotel.co.uk; N of Port Isaac on coast road (B3314);*
*8.30 pm; no Amex; children: 7+. **Accommodation:** 15 rooms, from £52.50.*

The Shed   £ 47
SA62 5BN   (01348) 831518

A "pleasant" place offering "delicious fresh fish dishes in an outstanding location"; parents looking for a laid-back meal, however, should be prepared for notices warning families against disruptive behaviour... / **Details:** www.theshedporthgain.co.uk; 9 pm; closed Tue D & Sun D; no Amex.

Egerton Grey   £ 43
CF62 3BZ   (01446) 711666

This small country house hotel only attracts a few reports, but is sometimes tipped as a "stunning" destination, with "friendly" service, and good locally-sourced cuisine. / **Sample dishes:** caramelised red onion and goat's cheese tart, sorrel sauce; seamed turbot and John Dory, spinach and saffron boulangere potatoes, lemon and chervil glace; warm chocolate soufflé, chocolate sauce, vanilla bean ice cream. **Details:** www.egertongrey.co.uk; 9 pm. **Accommodation:** 9 rooms, from £140.

Yr Hen Fecws   £ 36
16 Lombard St LL49 9AP   (01766) 514625

A restaurant-with-rooms, beautifully located in Snowdonia, and tipped for its "consistently good cuisine"; even fans, though, aren't always sure the service measures up. / **Sample dishes:** pan fried scallops with crispy bacon tossed salad; Welsh fillet of beef with glazed shallots, port and thyme sauce; brandy snap baskets with bananas, ice cream and toffee sauce. **Details:** www.henfecws.com; 10 pm; D only, closed Sun. **Accommodation:** 7 rooms, from £62.

The Bluefish Restaurant & Cafe   £ 37
15-17a, Chiswell DT5 1AN   (01305) 822991

A "short but ever-changing menu focussed on fish" inspires high praise for this "restaurant housed in a traditional stone fisherman's house"; it's also an "excellent brunch venue". / **Sample dishes:** monkfish cake with china beef, chorizo and carrots; pollack, butternut squash risotto, mushroom duck salad and grain mustard; hot chocolate pudding, black cherries and amaretto chantilly. **Details:** 10 pm; closed Mon, Tue-Fri D only, Sat & Sun open L & D; no Amex.

Portmeirion Hotel   £ 53
LL48 6ET   (01766) 770000

With its "fabulous setting" – at the heart of Sir Clough Williams-Ellis' famous Italianate village, and with marvellous estuary views – this "wonderful" dining room is, on nearly all accounts, "a hidden heaven"; the food is sometimes "very good" too (though it arguably appears to best advantage at lunch). / **Details:** www.portmeirion-village.com; off A487 at Minffordd; 9 pm; no trainers. **Accommodation:** 14 rooms, from £188.

Knockinaam Lodge   £ 57
DG9 9AD   (01776) 810471
*We wish we had more reports on the "old-fashioned but comfortable" dining room of this country house hotel, which enjoys "wonderful sea views", and where the cuisine is tipped as being "imaginative, refined and exquisitely presented". / **Sample dishes:** cauliflower and wild garlic velouté with a softly poached quail's egg and white truffle oil; grilled fillet of salmon with potato wafer paysanne of leek and a red wine and star anise reduction; hot banana and galliano soufflé with double vanilla bean ice cream.*
Details: *www.knockinaamlodge.com; off A77 at Colfin Smokehouse, follow signs to lodge; 9 pm; no jeans or trainers; children: 12+. **Accommodation:** 9 rooms, from £230.*

Ramore   £ 33
6 The Harbour BT56 8BN   (028) 7082 4313
*The setting may be "almost canteen-like", but this "harbour-view" establishment is always "buzzing", thanks not least to its "tasty" and "creative" cuisine, which comes at "great prices".
/ **Details:** www.portrushharbour.co.uk; 10 pm, Fri & Sat 10.30 pm, Sun 9 pm; no Amex; need 10+ to book.*

Rosie's Vineyard   £ 31
87 Elm Grove PO5 1JF   (02392) 755944
*A town-centre wine bar, tipped for its "excellent fish and vegetarian main dishes" (in particular), and its "huge selection of wines"; live jazz is a regular feature too. / **Sample dishes:** crab, spring onion & ginger fritters with chilli pepper jam; lemon & oregano marinated rack of lamb, roast garlic & sauté potatoes, with fresh vegetables; peach tarte Tatin.*
Details: *www.rosies-vineyard.co.uk; due south from M275 towards Southsea. At roundabout with City Museum turn left into King's Road, which leads into Elm Grove. Rosie's on your left.; 11 pm, Sun 10 pm; D only, ex Sun open L & D.*

The Falcon Inn   £ 43
London Rd GL7 5HN   (01285) 850844
*An ancient inn, refurbished in recent times, and re-opened in the summer of 2008, under the same ownership as the Puesdown Inn, Cheltenham (which is a pretty good all-rounder). / **Sample dishes:** tiger prawn & black pudding salad; fillet of seabass; amaretto rice pudding.*
Details: *www.thefalconpoulton.co.uk; on A417 between Cirencester and Fairford; 10 pm; closed Sun D; no Amex.*

Hat Shop   £ 31
7 High St LD8 2BA   (01544) 260017
*Tipped for its use of truly local ingredients ("often grown in the staff's own polytunnels!"), this handy stand-by in a "lovely little town" is also of note for its "good teas and coffees". / **Sample dishes:** Moroccan-style stuffed peppers; crispy duck leg with salad & potatoes; chocolate charlotte.*
Details: *9 pm; closed Sun.*

The Crabmill £ 39
B95 5EE (01926) 843342

"Handy for the M40, and worth breaking a journey for" –
this "eclectic" pub-conversion in a "lovely old building" combines
"interesting but not way-out ingredients" in "novel and tasty ways".
/ **Sample dishes:** honey roast ham, black pudding and ratte potato terrine with
apple and calvados chutney; seabass fillets with sundried tomato pesto pappadella
and basil mascarpone; chocolate and almond tart. **Details:** www.thecrabmill.co.uk;
on main road between Warwick & Henley; 9.30 pm; closed Sun D; no Amex.

Bukhara £ 18
154 Preston New Rd PR5 0UP (01772) 877710

"Exceptional food, friendly and efficient service, and a buzzy
atmosphere" ("even without alcohol!") – that's the deal that makes
this "interesting" and "authentic" Indian very popular.
/ **Sample dishes:** chicken tikka; lamb and okra cooked with onions, ginger and
garlic; a centre of dark chocolate sauce surrounded in mint ice cream covered
in dark chocolate. **Details:** www.bukharasamlesbury.co.uk; 11pm; D only;
no Maestro.

Winckley Square Chophouse £ 42
23 Winckley Sq PR1 3JJ (01772) 252732

"Can be good, but also quite frequently lets you down" – a number
of reports attest to the "uninspiring" food and "indifferent" service
too often found of late at this outpost of the "Heathcote Empire";
shame – "it used to be one of the best bets".
/ **Sample dishes:** roast breast of wood pigeon with beetroot, lentils and cabernet
sauvignon vinegar; roast loin and braised leg of rabbit with golden raisins, toasted
pine nuts and sherry vinegar; bread and butter pudding, apricot compote and
clotted cream. **Details:** www.heathcotes.co.uk; 10 pm, Sat 11 pm, Sun 9 pm.

Butchers Arms £ 45
Church End CV47 7SN (01327) 260504

A "welcoming", "eccentric" and "delightful" village pub, whose
"random" menu and retro-styling – "the dessert trolley has to be seen
to be believed" – can make a visit here somewhat "bizarre"; prices,
though, are high. / **Sample dishes:** grilled goats cheese; fillet steak piri piri;
Swiss dairy ice cream. **Details:** www.thebutchersarms.com; 9.30 pm; closed
Sat L & Sun D.

Plas Bodegroes £ 61
Nefyn Rd LL53 5TH (01758) 612363

A beautifully-located and "welcoming" restaurant-with-rooms where
the menu may be "long", but is consistently realised to an
"outstanding" level; a "very interesting Welsh wine list" is also
a feature. / **Details:** www.bodegroes.co.uk; on A497 1m W of Pwllheli; 9.30 pm;
closed Mon, Tue-Sat D only, closed Sun D; closed Dec-mid Feb; no Amex; children:
10+ at D. **Accommodation:** 11 rooms, from £110.

RAMSBOTTOM, LANCASHIRE   5–1B

Ramsons   £ 38
18 Market Pl BL0 9HT   (01706) 825070
"Superlative cooking" and an *"intriguing"*, *"all-Italian"* wine list again
win the highest acclaim for this *"small and intimate"* gaff *"in a
picturesque village"*, north of Manchester; *"affably eccentric"* owner
Chris Johnson makes an *"ever-present, enthusiastic, passionate and
extremely knowledgeable host"*. / **Details:** www.ramsons.org.uk; 9.30 pm,
3.30 Sun; closed Mon, Tue & Sun D; no Amex; booking: max 10.

RAMSGILL-IN-NIDDERDALE, NORTH YORKS   8–4B

Yorke Arms   £ 62
HG3 5RL   (01423) 755243
"Picture-perfect from the outside, and it just gets better!" –
most reports on Frances and Gerald Atkins's *"excellent"* inn, and its
"amazing" and *"creative"* cuisine, are a hymn of praise;
it's undoubtedly on the pricey side, though, and the occasional
reporter finds it *"precious"*. / **Sample dishes:** *seared tuna, aubergine relish,
chorizo, tomato & squid; saddle of venison, oxtail pastry, wild mushroom,
leek velouté & juniper; apricot clafoutis, brandy ice cream.*
Details: www.yorke-arms.co.uk; 4m W of Pateley Bridge; 9 pm.
Accommodation: 14 rooms, from £150.

RAWTENSTALL, LANCASHIRE   5–1B

The Dining Room   £ 47
8-12 Burnley Rd BB4 8EW   (01706) 210567
Andrew Robinshaw's *"creative"* and *"expertly-executed"* cuisine
is making a big name for this unpromisingly-located two-year-old;
with its *"discreet"* and *"friendly"* service, it's already being hailed
as *"one of the best restaurants in the North West"*.
/ **Sample dishes:** *ballotine of slow cooked rabbit, trio of pickled beetroots, black
truffle mascarpone, toasted brioche; pan fried loin of venison, wild garlic crushed
potatoes, morel mushrooms, creamed curly kale, madeira sauce;
rhubarb soufflé, poached rhubarb, sauce anglais.*
Details: www.thediningroomrestaurant.co.uk; 9.30 pm; closed Tue.

READING, BERKSHIRE   2–2D

Forbury's Restaurant & Wine Bar   £ 48
1 Forbury Sq RG1 3BB   (0118) 957 4044
Fans hail this *"lovely French restaurant right in the heart of Reading"*,
but this ambitious, *"modern"* outfit left a fair few reporters
"underwhelmed"; as this guide went to press, however, ex-Cliveden
chef Daniel Galmiche was put in charge of the stove – he is also
to open a 20-seat fine dining room (Eden). / **Sample dishes:** *tián
of Cornish crab, confit tomato & cucumber; roast Barbary duck breast, puy lentils,
beetroot & cherries; bourbon vanilla panna cotta, chilled rhubarb & mandarin
soup.* **Details:** www.forburys.com; 10 pm; closed Sun.

London Street Brasserie   £ 44
2-4 London St RG1 4SE   (0118) 950 5036
"A safe bet" – this *"bustling"* spot has a nice setting (*"in the middle
of the town, by the River Kennet"*), and its *"interesting food and good
service"* make it *"a great place for a business lunch, or for dinner"*.
/ **Sample dishes:** *crispy fried salt and pepper squid oriental salad and chili
dressing; pink carved venison fillets and haggis, figs, baby spinach and port,
redcurrant and juniper sauce; hot chocolate fondant and Bailey's ice cream.*
Details: www.londonstbrasserie.co.uk; On the corner of the Oracle shoping centre;
10.30 pm.

The Cabinet at Reed £ 43

High St SG8 8AH (01763) 848366

*This 16th-century inn changed hands towards the end of the survey year, so we've left it un-rated; one clearly post-sale report, however, notes the new régime as satisfactory, rather than anything more. / **Sample dishes:** warm scallop & black pudding creamed potatoes; honey & soy duck, potato cake, garlic greens; rhubarb crème brûlée.* **Details:** *www.thecabinetatreed.co.uk; 9.pm; closed Mon & Sun D.*

La Barbe £ 45 🅐⭐

71 Bell St RH2 7AN (01737) 241966

*Local Francophiles are still very taken with this "lively" and "fun" bistro "gem", where "lovely staff" serve up "good cooking at reasonable prices". / **Sample dishes:** puff pastry case filled with mussels cooked in a red wine, shallot and cream velouté; stuffed guinea fowl leg served on a bed of vegetable medley and light mustard sauce; fresh strawberry and cream rolled in a light sponge biscuit, strawberry and rose syrup sauce.* **Details:** *www.labarbe.co.uk; 9.30 pm; closed Sat L & Sun D.*

Tony Tobin @ The Dining Room £ 58 ⭐

59a High St RH2 9AE (01737) 226650

*TV-chef Toby Tobin's food is "on a par with many top London restaurants", say fans of this "accommodating", contemporary-style town-centre spot. / **Sample dishes:** roast Parma ham wrapped figs, gorgonzola gnocchi, port wine reduction; spiced monkfish tail, marinated mushrooms, spinach, tomato vinaigrette; pot au chocolat, chocolate samosa, chantilly cream.* **Details:** *www.tonytobinrestaurants.co.uk; 10 pm; closed Sat L & Sun D; booking: max 8, Fri & Sat.*

The Westerly £ 40 ⭐

2-4 London Rd RH2 9AN (01737) 222733

*"Superb and imaginative food" features in most reports on the Coombs' "superb local restaurant", which also offers some "classy" wines (including "by the glass"); despite its iffy location and somewhat "austere" setting, it's getting ever more "popular". / **Sample dishes:** warm salad of salt cod, chickpeas, artichokes and romesco; roast rump of salt marsh lamb, crushed peas, boulangere potatoes; px and raisin jelly, crème catalane, caramelised peach sorbet.* **Details:** *www.thewesterly.co.uk; 10 pm; closed Mon, Tue L, Sat L & Sun.*

Fairyhill £ 53 ⭐

SA3 1BS (01792) 390139

*"On the lovely Gower Peninsula", this hard-to-find small hotel offers a "classy" experience offering "a real break from normality"; the food is "top-quality" too, and there's a "fantastically varied and extensive wine list". / **Sample dishes:** soft boiled duck egg, mixed leaves and toasted pine nuts; roast loin and faggot of Welsh lamb, leek and ginger mash, red wine sauce; spiced plum crumble, orange crème anglaise.* **Details:** *www.fairyhill.net; 20 mins from M4, J47 off B4295; 9 pm; no Amex; children: 8+ at D.* **Accommodation:** *8 rooms, from £165.*

RHIWBINA, CARDIFF 2–2A

Juboraj £311
11 Heol-y-deri CF14 6HA (029) 2062 8894
The "pick of the crop of Juboraj restaurants": this contemporary-style
HQ of a small chain is tipped for its sometimes "outstanding" results.
/ Details: www.juborajgroup.com; 10.30 pm; closed Sun.

RIDGEWAY, SOUTH YORKSHIRE 5–2C

Old Vicarage £ 53
Ridgeway Moor S12 3XW (0114) 247 5814
Tessa Bramley's "florally-decorated" Victorian vicarage inspires mixed
views; the food is clearly "pretty good" overall, and she has
a "fabulous" cellar – those who feel the décor "needs updating",
however, or who encounter "pushy" service may find the place
"very overpriced". / Details: www.theoldvicarage.co.uk; 10 mins SE of city
centre; 9.30 pm; closed Mon, Sat L & Sun; no Amex.

RIPLEY, SURREY 3–3A

Drakes £ 58
The Clock Hs, High St GU23 6AQ (01483) 224777
The "painstaking" cuisine Stephen Drake offers at this village-centre
outfit is "clever, inspired, delicious, seasonal and well-presented"; it's a
shame, then, that some reporters feel its "dreary" interior has "all the
ambience of a Travelodge". / Sample dishes: roast scallops, seaweed
tartare, cauliflower purée and sherry; lamb cooked in a herb crumb,
roast aubergine purée and braised fillet of lamb; crème renversée with Granny
Smith sorbet and dried apple tuile. Details: www.drakesrestaurant.co.uk;
just beyond the intersection of A3 and M25 (J10) heading towards Guildford;
9.30 pm; closed Mon, Sat L & Sun; no Amex; booking: max 6; children: 12+.

RIPON, NORTH YORKSHIRE 8–4B

Prima Pizzaria £ 22
33 Kirkgate HG4 1PB (01765) 6022034
Tipped, as you'd hope, for a "good selection of pasta dishes and
pizzas", this is the sort of destination that's "great for a family
outing".

RIPPONDEN, WEST YORKSHIRE 5–1C

El Gato Negro Tapas £ 29
1 Oldham Rd HX6 4DN (01422) 823070
"Wonderful tapas" – and "tremendous service, from Chris the
welcoming host" – have made a big name for this "totally relaxed"
hang-out, in a converted rural boozer. / Sample dishes: grilled hake with
samphire & salsa verde; roast belly pork with morcilla, pea purée & apple;
summer fruits with cava sabayon. Details: www.elgatonegrotapas.com; 9.30 pm,
10 pm Sat; closed Mon, Tue, Wed L, Thu L, Fri L & Sun D; no Amex.

RISHWORTH, WEST YORKSHIRE 5–1C

Old Bore £ 40
Oldham Rd HX6 4QU (01422) 822291
"Always full" – this ancient coaching inn serves an interesting menu,
that's consistently well-received by reporters.
/ Details: www.oldbore.co.uk; 9.30 pm, Sat 10 pm, Sun 8 pm; closed Mon & Tue;
no Amex.

ROADE, NORTHAMPTONSHIRE
3–1A

Roade House £ 44 ⭐

16 High St NN7 2NW (01604) 863372

"Imaginative" cooking *"of a high standard"* makes this *"unpretentious"* stalwart very popular; the *"functional"* décor however, clearly *"needs updating"* (post script: news arrived that they've 'fully refurbished'). / **Details:** www.roadehousehotel.co.uk; 9.30 pm; closed Sat L & Sun D; no shorts; booking essential. **Accommodation:** 10 rooms, from £75.

ROCKBEARE, DEVON
1–3D

Jack in the Green Inn £ 42

London Rd EX5 2EE (01404) 822240

This *"busy"* pub-cum-restaurant, just off the A30, is certainly *"easy to get to"*, and on most accounts it's a *"welcoming destination"*, with *"consistent"* standards; there's no denying, though, that the year also saw the odd disastrous report. / **Sample dishes:** terrine of smoked ducks and sundried tomatoes; roast loin and belly of pork and olive oil potato purée and carrots; blackcurrant mousse and apricot purée.
Details: www.jackinthegreen.uk.com; 2 miles from Exeter airport on the old A30; 9.30 pm; no Amex.

ROMALDKIRK, COUNTY DURHAM
8–3B

The Rose & Crown £ 38

DL12 9EB (01833) 650213

A *"traditional"* and *"cosy"* village coaching inn that offers an *"excellent"* range of *"hearty"* fare. / **Details:** www.rose-and-crown.co.uk; 6m NW of Barnard Castle on B6277; 8.45 pm; D only, ex Sun open L & D; no Amex; children: 6+ in restaurant. **Accommodation:** 12 rooms, from £135.

ROSEVINE, CORNWALL
1–4B

🅐⭐

Driftwood
Driftwood Hotel £ 48

TR2 5EW (01872) 580644

"A special place by the sea"; it's not just the *"fantastic views of the Roseland peninsular"* that make it popular though – this contemporary hotel dining room also attracts praise for *"beautiful food, exquisitely presented"*. / **Sample dishes:** Viennoise glazed pollack, tomato fondue, tapenade dressing; lamb, Jerusalem artichoke, fondant potatoes, sweetbreads & mint; gâteaux opera, honeycombe, clementine sorbet.
Details: www.driftwoodhotel.co.uk; Off the A30 to Truro, towards St Maees; 9.30 pm; D only; booking: max 6; children: 8+. **Accommodation:** 15 rooms, from £200.

ROSSETT, WREXHAM
5–3A

🅣

The Golden Lion £ 37

Chester Rd LL12 0HN (01244) 571020

"Neither too pubby nor too restaurant-like", this *"friendly"* gastropub is tipped as *"raising the bar for quality in the area"*.
/ **Sample dishes:** king prawn & monkfish with chilli sauce and dipping bread; surf and turf; sticky toffee pudding with vanilla ice cream. **Details:** 9.30 pm, 9 pm Sun; no Amex.

The Greyhound   £ 41   ⭐

Gallowstree Ln RG9 5HT   (0118) 9722227

Perhaps because he lives locally, Antony Worrall Thompson seems to give customers a much better deal at this poshed-up country pub than he does at the equivalent operations in the metropolis; an "honest-to-goodness" all-rounder, it inspires only positive reports. / **Sample dishes:** moules marinières; roast porchetta, apple chilli jelly, sage & onion stuffing; triple chocolate: chocolate brownie with chocolate ice cream with chocolate mousse in a chocolate cup. **Details:** www.awtrestaurants.com; 9.30 pm, Fri & Sat 10.30 pm; no Amex.

George & Dragon   £ 40   ⭐

High St SN10 2PN   (01380) 723053

It may be "off the beaten track", but this rural inn has long been known to "hit the heights" food-wise (particularly for fish), and real devotees insist that it is "one of the best out-of-town restaurants". / **Sample dishes:** grilled baked field mushroom with pesto; Cornish crab risotto; raspberry brûlée. **Details:** www.thegeorgeanddragonrowde.co.uk; on A342 between Devizes & Chippenham; 10 pm; closed Sun D; no Amex; booking: max 8. **Accommodation:** 3 rooms, from £85.

Chequers Inn   £ 43

RH12 3PY   (01403) 790480

A popular pub generally tipped for its "good food"; standards can drift in the chef's absence, though, which is perhaps why some reporters find the place "overpriced". / **Sample dishes:** goats cheese and caramelised red onion tart on salad; roast chump of lamb with dauphinoise potato, spinach, with a roast garlic jus; rose wine jelly with English rhubarb and vanilla syrup. **Details:** www.nealsrestaurants.biz; 9 pm; closed Sun D; no Amex.

Emperors   £ 32   🅐⭐

Bath Pl CV31 3BP   (01926) 313666

This smart Chinese may have been around for yonks, but it's certainly not slacking, and continues to win praise for its "wonderful food in exquisite surroundings". / **Sample dishes:** prawn toast; chicken in black bean sauce; banana fritter. **Details:** 11 pm; closed Sun.

Thai Elephant   £ 32   🆃

20 Regent St CV32 5HQ   (01926) 886882

A long-established oriental that's tipped as being "as popular as ever", thanks to the "continuing high standard" of its "beautifully-flavoured" fare. / **Sample dishes:** scallops stir fried with garlic, black peppercorns & fresh Thai herbs; grilled marinated breast of chicken with lemongrass, garlic & soy sauce, topped with a creamy curry sauce; mango mousse. **Details:** www.thaielephantrestaurant.co.uk; 10.30 pm; closed Sat L.

Landgate Bistro   £ 28
5-6 Landgate TN31 7LH   (01797) 222829
Something of a "hidden gem" – this "friendly" and long-established bistro is re-establishing its reputation for sometimes "excellent" fare, and at "good prices" too. / *Sample dishes:* tarragon and turbot fish cakes; selection of cuts of Romney Marsh lamb; lemon tart.
Details: www.landgatebistro.co.uk; below Landgate Arch; 9.30 pm; closed Mon, Tue, Wed L, Thu L, Fri L & Sun D.

Webbes at the Fish Café   £ 46
17 Tower St TN31 7AT   (01797) 222210
"Lucky Rye!"; Paul Webb's open-kitchen café, in a "well-converted warehouse building", offers "very good fish" – "much better than many more expensive and pretentious places". / *Sample dishes:* salmon ballotine and crayfish salad; wild seabass on a bed of spinach and scallion tagliatelle with basil cream; crème brûlée. **Details:** www.thefishcafe.com; 9 pm; closed Mon L; children: 12+ at D.

The Crown And Thistle   £ 33
High St CB10 1PL   (01799) 530278
A "very good gastropub", where all reports attest to the "high standards" of the "interesting" and "imaginative" cuisine. / *Sample dishes:* sticky toffee pudding. **Details:** 9.30 pm; no Amex.

Oyster Shack   £ 35
10-13 Island St TQ8 8FE   (01548) 843596
This year-old spin-off from the famous Bigbury institution "started badly, but has improved considerably"; feedback is still thin, but such as there is praises its "more reliable" performance and "sometimes outstanding" seafood. / **Details:** www.oystershack.co.uk; 9 pm; Reduced opening in winter.

Anokaa   £ 36
60 Fisherton St SP2 7RB   (01722) 414142
"Going from strength to strength", a "top-class Indian on a street where you wouldn't expect to find such a good place"; its "delicately flavoured and inventive dishes" please all who comment on it. / **Details:** www.anokaa.com; 10.30 pm; no shorts.

Jade   £ 33
109a Exeter St SP1 2SF   (01722) 333355
"Sometimes mixed, usually very good" - this long-established restaurant is tipped as "more authentic than most". / **Details:** www.jaderestaurant.co.uk; near the Cathedral; 11.30 pm; closed Sun; no Amex.

Salts Diner £ 30 **A**
Salts Mill, Victoria Rd BD18 3LB (01274) 530533
"A lively restaurant which shares a converted mill with a David
Hockney gallery"; the food is "fresh and of good quality",
and weekends can be "very busy". / **Details:** www.saltsmill.org.uk; 2m from
Bradford on A650; L & afternoon tea only; no Amex.

Cookies Crab Shop £ 15 ⭐
The Grn, Coast Rd NR25 7AJ (01263) 740352
It may be "a bit chaotic", but who cares? – for "great-value cold fish
and seafood platters", this shed-like spot is the way to go, and "great
value for money" too. / **Sample dishes:** royal salad; kipper and tomato soup;
apple crumble. **Details:** www.cookies.shopkeepers.co.uk; on A149; 7.30 pm;
Nov-Feb bookings only; no credit cards.

The Bell at Sapperton £ 46
GL7 6LE (01285) 760298
A "lovely" contemporary-style Cotswold village inn, which fans say
is "worth a journey for great food, beautifully presented and well-
served, in a lovely setting"; as ever, however, sceptics find
performance only "serviceable". / **Sample dishes:** deep fried goats cheese
in wheatgerm, balsamic roast onions & spiced avocado; crisp belly of old spot pork
with a pork samosa and sage and Parmesan polenta.
Details: www.foodatthebell.co.uk; 9.30 pm; no Amex; no booking at L; children:
10+ at D.

The Straw Hat Oriental £ 31 **T**
Harrow Rd CM21 0AJ (01279) 722434
A "lively and friendly" venue tipped for its "good oriental menu"
(and "excellent" sushi); the odd reporter thinks it "overpriced",
though. / **Sample dishes:** Japanese style king prawns with wasabi; chicken clay
pot with sweet basil, chilli & spring onion. **Details:** www.strawhat-oriental.co.uk;
On the A1184, 1m south of Sawbridgeworth; 11.30 pm, Sun 9.30 pm; no shorts;
children: No children after 9 pm.

The Spread Eagle £ 34
BB7 4NH (01200) 441202
"Fantastic" views over the River Ribble are "the main thing" at this
""always buzzing"" gastropub, where the food has typically been
"reliable rather than excellent"; we've foregone a rating, however, as it
changed hands in 2008, and is set for a full refurb inside and out.
/ **Sample dishes:** poached king prawns & crayfish tails, with green chilli &
tomato mayonnaise, on gem lettuce & granary bread; home-made pure English
beef burger, on an English muffin, baby gem, beef tomato, blue cheese with
hand-cooked chips & tomato relish; English pudding plate of jam roly-poly,
raspberry fool, sherry trifle and bread & butter ice cream.
Details: www.spreadeaglesawley.co.uk; NE of Clitheroe off A59; 9 pm,
Sun 7.30 pm; no Amex.

Bell Hotel £ 31
31 High St IP17 1AF (01728) 602331
On a good day you get "some of the best food in the area",
at Andrew Blackburn's small dining room; the setting is "gloomy",
though, and a number of reports hint at a fair degree of "unrealised
potential" all round. / *Sample dishes: terrine of pigeon and rabbit wrapped
in bacon served with salad and truffle vinaigrette; roast poussin with pearl barley,
spinach, rosti potatoes and a red wine sauce; white chocolate and lemon mousse
with shortbread biscuit.* **Details:** *www.bellhotel-saxmundham.co.uk; 9 pm; closed
Mon & Sun; no Amex.* **Accommodation:** *10 rooms, from £75.*

Lanterna £ 46 ⭐
33 Queen St YO11 1HQ (01723) 363616
"Lovely fresh fish" is the menu highlight at this "friendly" and
"reliable" Italian, which offers "much the best food in town".
/ *Sample dishes: handmade spaghetti with velvet crab; truffle risotto; zabaglione.*
Details: *www.lanterna-ristorante.co.uk; near the Old Town; 9.30 pm; D only,
closed Sun; no Amex.*

Pepper's £ 44 🅣
11 York Pl YO11 2NP (01723) 500642
A small restaurant of over a decade's standing, tipped for its
"consistent" culinary standards. / **Details:** *www.peppersrestaurant.co.uk;
10 pm; Mon-Thu D only, closed Sun D.*

Blue Elephant £ 26 🅣
Southport Road L40 8HQ (01704) 841222
An Indian restaurant tipped for its sometimes "superb" realisation
of "all the staples, plus some other dishes you wouldn't have thought
of"; "reasonable prices" too. / *Sample dishes: exotic duck; monkfish.*
Details: *10 mins from Ormskirk on the A570; 10.30pm, Sat 11pm; closed
weekday L; no Amex.*

White Room
Seaham Hall £ 65
Lord Byron's Walk SR7 7AG (0191) 516 1400
Von Essen – the voracious country house hotel group – snapped
up the North East's sexiest boutique-hotel (plus celebrated spa)
towards the end of our survey year; an appraisal of the new régime
will have to wait until next year. / *Sample dishes: crab, confit salmon,
avocado, passionfruit, caviar; wild seabass, onion purée, gnocchi, chanterelles,
Parmesan and truffle; banana parfait, pistachio cake, pistachio foam.*
Details: *www.seaham-hall.co.uk; 10 pm; booking: max 8.* **Accommodation:** *19
rooms, from £250.*

Artisan   £ 42   ⭐
32-34 Sandygate Rd S10 5RY   (0114) 266 6096
A "Sheffield favourite" – which includes both a ground-floor bistro and
a seafood restaurant upstairs – where the cooking is often "very good
value" (and occasionally "brilliant"); "patchy" service and iffy décor,
however, can let the side down. / **Sample dishes:** goats cheese, honey,
thyme parfait, glazed figs, candied walnuts, aged balsamic; slow braised pigs
trotter, creamed potatoes, bourguignonne garnish, rich red wine sauce; artisan
chocolate gâteaux, nougat ice cream, mocha sauce.
Details: www.artisanofsheffield.com; 10 pm.

Café Ceres   £ 18   ⓣ
390 Sharrowvale Rd S11 8ZP   (0114) 267 9090
A "small but perfectly formed café", which is "good for breakfasts
and cakes", but also tipped for "great French cooking"
(some evenings only). / **Details:** Fri & Sat 9.30 pm; Mon-Thu L only,
closed Sun.

Kashmir Curry Centre   £ 17   ⭐
123 Spital Hill S4 7LD   (0114) 272 6253
"A unique place that's casual in the extreme, but they create some
very fine curries indeed" at "very good value" prices; "BYO, or there's
some excellent beer at the adjacent pub". / **Details:** midnight; D only,
closed Sun; no credit cards.

Nirmals   £ 28
189-193 Glossop Rd S10 2GW   (0114) 272 4054
Fans of Mrs Nirmal's offbeat veggie veteran say its food is "utterly
reliable and very delicious", "even for confirmed carnivores"; sceptics,
though, couldn't disagree more – "with its pushy service and tired
cooking, it should not be in your guide!" / **Details:** near West St; midnight;
closed Sun L.

Rafters   £ 49   ⭐
220 Oakbrook Rd, Nether Grn S11 7ED   (0114) 230 4819
"A peaceful haven, accessed via a steep and narrow staircase" –
this contemporary outfit, in Ranmoor, is "still Sheffield's
best restaurant"; service, though, can be "mediocre".
/ **Details:** www.raftersrestaurant.co.uk; 10 pm; D only, closed Tue & Sun;
children: 5+.

Three Acres   £ 45   Ⓐ⭐
Roydhouse HD8 8LR   (01484) 602606
"Ever-popular with visitors from all over the north"; this "always-
crowded" inn – "with impressive views from the heights of Emlyn
Moor" – offers "a lovely blend of relaxed country pub and top-quality
food". / **Details:** www.3acres.com; near Emley Moor TV tower; 9.30 pm.
Accommodation: 20 rooms, from £120.

SHEPTON MALLET, SOMERSET 2–3B

Charlton House £ 75 ⭐
Charlton Rd BA4 4PR   (01749) 342008
This Mulberry-owned (and decorated) country house hotel induced only modest feedback this year, but all of it to the effect that it has "excellent" service, and that its "very fresh" cooking makes "interesting use of local produce". / ***Sample dishes:*** carpaccio of Devonshire red beef, white wine jelly and oxtail 'Scotch' egg; saddle of Wiltshire venison,fondant potatoes with shoulder of venison, creamed cabbage; mandarin mousse, mandarin and lemon thyme jelly, warm orange madeleines. ***Details:*** www.charltonhouse.com; on A361 towards Frome; 9.30 pm, 10 pm Fri & Sat.. ***Accommodation:*** 25 rooms, from £180.

SHERBORNE, DORSET 2–3B

The Green £ 43 ⭐
The Green DT9 3HY   (01935) 813821
Michael Rust's "comfortably elegant" restaurant doesn't inspire a huge amount of feedback, but his menu is consistently hailed as "very appealing", and his dishes are usually "beautifully cooked and presented". / ***Sample dishes:*** mackerel fillets with crayfish tails, apples, red onions, toasted almonds, dill mayonnaise and new potatoes; pink-roast loin of Dorset venison with celeriac mash, braised celery, butternut squash, and morel mushrooms; panna cotta with rhubarb and honey. ***Details:*** 9 pm; closed Mon & Sun.

SHERE, SURREY 3–3A

Kinghams £ 49 🅰
Gomshall Ln GU5 9HE   (01483) 202168
"A pretty cottage in a picture postcard village" provides a "cute" setting for Paul Barker's "cheerful" fixture; its style strikes the occasional reporter as a little "passé", but the cooking is "wholesome" and "fairly-priced". / ***Details:*** www.kinghams-restaurant.co.uk; off A25 between Dorking & Guildford; 9 pm; closed Mon & Sun D.

SHINFIELD, BERKSHIRE 2–2D

L'Ortolan £ 81 🅰⭐
Church Ln RG2 9BY   (0118) 988 8500

"A fantastic gastronomic treat every time" – this grand Gallic restaurant, in a former rectory, is a great showcase for Alan Murchison's "top-calibre" cuisine; "excellent" service and a "relaxed" atmosphere somewhat help soften the blow of the "steep" prices. / ***Details:*** www.lortolan.com; J11 off M4, take A33 towards Basingstoke, at first roundabout restaurant signposted; 9.30 pm; closed Mon & Sun.

SHIPBOURNE, KENT   3–3B

The Chaser Inn   £ 35
Stumble Hill TN11 9PE   (01732) 810360
"Classic pub fare with a bit of polish" helps win praise for this popular "family-friendly gastropub", which has a "nice garden and covered terrace"; critical reporters, however, say the food's no better than "OK", and that service is sometimes "non-existent".
/ **Sample dishes:** *potted smoked mackerel served with gooseberry chutney & toasted ciabatta sticks; roast chicken legs served on a bubble & squeak mash, with a thyme and garlic sauce; assorted ice creams.* **Details:** *www.thechaser.co.uk; 9.30 pm; no Amex.*

SHIPLEY, WEST YORKSHIRE   5–1C

Aagrah   £ 28   ⭐⭐
4 Saltaire Rd BD18 3HN   (01274) 530880
Even by the standards of the exemplary local chain of which it is a part, this is a superb subcontinental; the "marvellous" buffet attracts particular praise. / **Sample dishes:** *chucks of lamb marinated with coriander, mint, green chilli, lime juice, selected herbs and spices; marinated chicken cooked with garlic, ginger, yoghurt & fenugreek leaves.* **Details:** *www.aagrah.com; 11.30 pm; closed Sat L & Sun L.*

SKENFRITH, MONMOUTHSHIRE   2–1B

Bell   £ 42
NP7 8UH (01600) 750235
This riverside inn has quite a reputation, and inspires numerous – but mixed – reviews; fans vaunt "a country restaurant just the way you want it in the 21st century", whereas critics insist: "there are so many pubs better than this". / **Sample dishes:** *beetroot panna cotta, goat's cheese, spinach and walnut spring roll, dressed leaves, basil pest; assiette of spring lamb, lemongrass jus; passion fruit mousse on vanilla sponge, vanilla panna cotta, pineapple sorbet, citrus curd.* **Details:** *www.skenfrith.co.uk; on B4521, 10m NE of Abergavenny; 9.30 pm, Sun 9 pm; closed Mon (Nov-Mar only); children: 8+ at D.* **Accommodation:** *11 rooms, from £105.*

SLEAT, ISLE OF SKYE   9–2A

Kinloch Lodge   £ 62   🅐⭐
IV43 8QY   (01471) 833333
"A fortune has been spent, and to good effect", on the MacDonalds' family seat, run by various members of the clan; "with the appointment of Marcello Tully as head chef, it's returned to days of former glory" food-wise, and emerging as one of the Highlands' more "impressive" destinations. / **Details:** *www.kinloch-lodge.co.uk; 9.30 pm; D only.* **Accommodation:** *14 rooms, from £200.*

SNAPE, SUFFOLK   3–1D

The Crown Inn   £ 35
Bridge Rd IP17 1SL   (01728) 688324
"A cosy Adnams inn, offering surprisingly good pub grub" (including "glorious fish and chips"); we couldn't spot any change in the tenor of reports following a recent change in ownership, but we've left it unrated nevertheless. / **Sample dishes:** *pork terrine with piccalilli; roast skate wing with caper and raisin dressing; rhubarb and ginger trifle.* **Details:** *off A12 towards Aldeburgh; 9.30 pm, Sat 10pm; no Amex; children: 14+.* **Accommodation:** *3 rooms, from £75.*

Rose & Crown   £ 32   🆃

Old Church Rd PE31 7LX (01485) 541382
A classic "cold winter's day" destination, this village inn is tipped for its "really good pub food" (and a "log fire" too).
/ **Details:** www.roseandcrownsnettisham.co.uk; 9 pm; no Amex.
Accommodation: 16 rooms, from £90.

Beau Thai   £ 29   ⭐

761 Old Lode Ln B92 8JE (0121) 743 5355
A "friendly" family-run oriental, which is maintaining the reputation for "terrific Thai food" built up over many years by the previous owners. / **Sample dishes:** king prawns in filo pastry; king prawns with ginger and spring onions. **Details:** www.beauthairestaurant.co.uk; 10.30 pm, 11 pm Fri & Sat; closed Mon L, Sat L & Sun L.

Metro Bar & Grill   £ 39   🆃

680-684 Warwick Rd B91 3DX (0121) 705 9495
A top tip for a "quick lunch" – a "relaxed", "cheap and cheerful" place with "friendly" staff, where fish comes especially recommended.
/ **Sample dishes:** melon, Serrano ham and balsamic strawberries; fillet of pork chorizo, sweet potatoes and apple; baked egg custard.
Details: www.metrobarandgrill.co.uk; 2 doors down from "House of Fraser"; 11 pm, Thu-Sat midnight; closed Sun; no trainers.

Rajnagar   £ 33   🆃

256 Lyndon Rd B92 7QW (0121) 7424842
"As welcoming today as when it opened in 1987", this grand Bangladeshi restaurant is tipped for its "refreshing emphasis on subtle flavours and its memorable range of tandoori fish".
/ **Details:** www.rajnagar.com.

The French Horn   £ 85   🅰⭐

RG4 6TN (0118) 969 2204
It can seem like "a time warp", but this riverside stalwart (with a "beautiful setting in summer") is, on most accounts, simply "excellent in every way" – not least its celebrated spit-roast duck, and the "amazing" wines to go with it. / **Sample dishes:** asparagus with hollandaise; pan fried fillets of Dover sole with wild mushrooms and a cream and white wine sauce; raspberry soufflé. **Details:** www.thefrenchhorn.co.uk; M4, J8 or J9, then A4; 9.30 pm; booking: max 10. **Accommodation:** 21 rooms, from £160.

Le Cassoulet   £ 45   ⭐

18 Selsdon Rd CR2 6PA (020) 8633 1818
"Believe the hype!", it's worth a trip to Sarf London to check out Malcolms John's "extremely welcome addition to the wasteland that is Croydon's restaurant scene" – "a thoroughly French" newcomer, offering notably "correct" cuisine. / **Details:** www.lecassoulet.com; 10.30 pm.

Tinkers £ 37
299 High St CR0 1QL (0208) 6865624
"Excellent, if a little cramped" – especially on the food front,
this "charming" family-run operation is praised by all who comment
on it. / **Details:** *www.tinkersrestaurant.co.uk; 9.30 pm; D only, closed*
Mon & Sun.

SOUTH LEIGH, OXFORDSHIRE 2–2D

Mason's Arms £ 34 ★
Station Rd OX8 6XN (01993) 702485
"Good cooking in a relaxed atmosphere" – that's the gist of pretty
much all commentary on this "imaginative" gastropub, which is of
particular note for an "exceptional-value lunch".

SOUTHAMPTON, SOUTHAMPTON 2–3D

Kuti's £ 34
37-39 Oxford St SO14 3DP (023) 8022 1585
"Maybe it's not that different from other less well-known Indians",
but this "reliable" Bangladeshi has long been the leading destination
locally for a "top, tasty and authentic curry". / **Sample dishes:** *tandoori*
lamb chops; chicken bahar; gulab jamon. **Details:** *www.kutis.co.uk; near Stanley*
Casino; 11 pm.

SOUTHEND-ON-SEA, ESSEX 3–3C

Pipe of Port £ 33 T
84 High St SS1 1JN (01702) 614606
"A reliable old-favourite"; if you're looking for "good, traditional rustic
English food", this sawdust-strewn basement wine bar may be just the
place. / **Details:** *www.pipeofport.com; basement just off High Street; 10.30 pm;*
closed Sun; no Amex; children: 16+.

Michael's   £ 34   Ⓐ✪✪

47 Liverpool Rd PR8 4AG   (01704) 550886

Three years into its existence, this "cosy" and "unpretentious" Birkdale Village restaurant is beginning to make a real name for its "outstanding" food; service is notably "friendly" and "helpful" too. / **Sample dishes:** seared king scallops with tabbouleh, red pepper essence and balsamic reduction; Goosnargh chicken breast stuffed with asparagus and tarragon mousse, roast vegetables and herbed new potatoes; white and dark chocolate mousse with fresh raspberries and raspberry coulis. **Details:** www.michaelsbirkdale.co.uk; 3 minutes walk from Birkdale train station; 10 pm; D only, closed Mon & Sun; no Amex.

Warehouse Brasserie   £ 40   Ⓐ

30 West St PR8 1QN   (01704) 544662

"In a poorly-served area", this "buzzy, posy place" offers "a great night out" – "totally reliable" food and service that's "individual and friendly", in a "modern and stylish" setting. / **Sample dishes:** crispy duck spring roll; suckling pig with wild mushroom & spinach; rhubarb crumble crème brûlée. **Details:** www.warehousebrasserie.co.uk; 10.30 pm; closed Sun; no Amex.

The Swan at Southrop   £ 40

GL7 3NU   (01367) 850205

Re-launching as this guide goes to press, this popular inn is now in the hands of west London chef Sebastian Snow (of 'on the Green' fame); could be one to watch. / **Sample dishes:** foie gras, fried egg & balsamic vinegar with toasted brioche; crisp confit of pork belly with an artichoke and mushroom compote; fig tarte fines with mascarpone & lime chantilly. **Details:** www.theswanatsouthrop.co.uk; 10 pm; closed Sun D; no Amex.

The Crown
Adnams Hotel   £ 39

High St IP18 6DP   (01502) 722275

"For a no-nonsense bite", this "casual" and "attractive" Adnams inn – with its "excellent" wines and beer – is still "an obligatory stop when passing through"; the "straightforward" food is usually "very acceptable", but nowadays it can also be rather "variable". / **Sample dishes:** grilled roast of mackerel fillet with beetroot; braised shoulder and roast cutlet of spring lamb and grilled Mediterranean vegetables; orange cake with rosewater ice cream and orange crisp. **Details:** www.adnamshotels.co.uk; 9 pm; no Amex. **Accommodation:** 14 rooms, from £132.

Sutherland House   £ 34

56 High St IP18 6DN   (01502) 724544

In an ancient central building, a "stylish" hotel and restaurant hailed by fans as a "wonderful find", offering "interesting cooking"; the "food miles scheme" has the worthy aim of supporting local farms, but strikes some reporters as a bit of a "gimmick". / **Sample dishes:** pan fried scallops with apple & chillis; braised belly of pork with fondant potato; chocolate marquise with oranges, nougatine & sugared pestinos. **Details:** www.sutherlandhouse.co.uk; 9.30 pm. **Accommodation:** 4 rooms, from £100.

The Swan £ 48

The Market Pl IP18 6EG (01502) 722186

Adnams' "lovely old coaching inn" boasts an "elegant" (if slightly "hushed") dining room, which still generally pleases reporters with its "carefully-prepared", "traditional"-ish cuisine; nowadays, however, "it doesn't always deliver". / *Sample dishes:* Loch Duart salmon sashimi crayfish & lemon salad; roast Suffolk chump of lamb, niçoise style salad, rosti potatoes, sauce vierge; dark chocolate fondant, crushed honeycomb, hazelnut ice cream. *Details:* www.adnams.co.uk; 9 pm; closed Sat D; no Amex; children: 5+ at D. *Accommodation:* 42 rooms, from £156.

SOWERBY BRIDGE, WEST YORKSHIRE 5–1C

Gimbals £ 36 🅰⭐

Wharf St HX6 2AF (01422) 839329

"Increasingly popular, and justifiably so" – this "cosy restaurant in a terrace house" offers a range of "good, and ever-changing dishes", and some "decent and not too pricey wines" to go with 'em. / *Sample dishes:* saffron hommous with Anadalucian spiced ground lamb with coriander, toasted pine kernels, and sea salt flatbread; baked halibut fillet with a thermador gratin on a smoked salmon & vanilla cream; burnt crème caramel & vanillla panna cotta with carmelized oranges & hazelnut biscotti. *Details:* 9.15 pm; D only, closed Sun; no Amex.

The Millbank £ 37 ⭐

Millbank Rd HX6 3DY (01422) 825588

"A lovely setting and views" ("with the option of sitting out in good weather") is "matched by top-quality cooking", at this "imaginative" transformation of a "once-dead" Pennines pub. / *Sample dishes:* blue cheese fritters with pickled shitake mushrooms; shoulder of lamb, merguez sausage with roast vegetables and creamed potatoes; vodka and lime sorbet, coconut macaroon and mango. *Details:* www.themillbank.com; The M62, between junctions 22 and 23; 9.30 pm, Sun 8 pm; closed Mon; no Amex.

SPARSHOLT, HAMPSHIRE 2–3D

Plough Inn £ 20 ⭐

SO21 2NW (01962) 776353

A "spacious" and "comfortable" pub that's usually "busy", thanks to its "first-rate" choice of food, and its often "excellent'" value. / *Details:* 9 pm; no Amex; children: 14+ after 8.30 pm.

SPEEN, BUCKINGHAMSHIRE 2–2D

The Old Plow £ 47 ⭐

Flowers Bottom Ln HP27 0PZ (01494) 488300

This converted Chilterns pub now comprises a posh bistro, and a grander adjoining restaurant; it serves "consistently good" cooking at "excellent value" prices, but complaints of "arrogant" service are not unknown. / *Details:* www.yeoldplow.co.uk; 20 mins from M40, J4 towards Princes Risborough; 9 pm; closed Mon, Sat L & Sun D.

SPELDHURST, KENT 3–4B

George & Dragon £ 36 🅰

Speldhurst Hill TN3 0NN (01892) 863125

An ancient inn, full of "classic beam-y charm"; most reporters hail its "locally-sourced" gastropub cuisine as "brilliant" too, but the odd let-down is not unknown. / *Details:* www.speldhurst.com; 9.30 pm; closed Sun D; no Amex.

Asia £ 32

2 Beaconsfield Rd AL1 3RD (01727) 800002

"A very good Indian/pan-Asian, in an old post office" – the drift of pretty much all commentary on this "stylish" yearling. / **Sample dishes:** Thai fish cakes with a sweet chilli sauce; chicken with coconut, star anise, red chilli and peppercorns, honey-glazed baby carrots; caramelised sweetened mashed baby carrots served with vanilla ice cream. **Details:** www.asia-dining.co.uk; 11 pm, 11.30 pm Fri & Sat.

Barissimo £ 13

28 St Peter St AL1 3NA (01727) 869999

Tipped for "the best coffee in Herts", an Italian café that's an "ideal spot for a post-shopping recharge". / **Sample dishes:** pasta; pannini. **Details:** 5.30pm, Sun 4pm; L only; no credit cards.

La Cosa Nostra £ 33

62 Lattimore Rd AL1 3XR (01727) 832658

A "fun and busy" local Italian veteran still sometimes tipped for "the best pizza around". / **Sample dishes:** bruschetta with red peppers, olives, and goat cheese; fusili with mushrooms, spinach, goat cheese and double cream; tiramisu. **Details:** near railway station; 10 pm; closed Sat L & Sun; no Amex.

Darcy's £ 38

2 Hatfield Rd AL1 3RP (01727) 730777

Perhaps because it's "an oasis in an otherwise barren area", this "good local", in the town-centre, attracts a disproportionate amount of feedback; an alternative explanation might be that its aspirations used to be rather higher than they have often seemed of late. / **Sample dishes:** grilled halloumi & roast pear, watercress and aged balsamic; smoked lamb cutlets with ratatouille & salsa verde; white peach & red currant ice cream. **Details:** www.darcysrestaurant.co.uk; 9.45 pm.

Lussmans £ 32

Waxhouse Gate, High Street AL3 4EW (01727) 851941

"A serious rival to Darcy's" ("in what's otherwise a culinary desert") – a very popular local stand-by, "just by the Abbey". / **Sample dishes:** grilled squid with chilli and rocket; pork loin steak, sautéed in marsala and sage, with mash; sticky toffee pudding with toffee sauce and Minghella's vanilla ice cream. **Details:** www.lussmans.com; Off the High Street, close to the cathedral; 10 pm, 10.30 pm Fri & Sat, 9 pm Sun.

Mumtaj £ 25

115 London Rd AL1 1LR (01727) 843691

"For traditionalists", this "shabby"-looking curry house, near the Old Cinema Hall, is tipped as "the best Indian in town". / **Details:** midnight.

St Michael's Manor £ 51

Fishpool St AL3 4RY (01727) 864444

Hidden-away from the hustle and bustle, and with "a lovely setting", especially in summer – this long-established hotel is praised for its "good value" and "friendly service". / **Sample dishes:** potted salt beef, horseradish mousse, apple & mixed cress salad; whole roast red mullet, beetroot dauphinoise with watercress salad & raspberry dressing; black cherry panna cotta with dark chocolate roulade & coffee sauce. **Details:** www.stmichaelsmanor.com; near Cathedral; 9 pm. **Accommodation:** 30 rooms, from £180.

The Waffle House
Kingsbury Water Mill £ 18
St Michael's St AL3 4SJ   (01727) 853502
*"Sitting out with the ducks, eating your waffles" is tipped
as something of a "highlight" of summer for fans of this veteran
snackery; when it gets busy, though, service can be "slow".*
*/ Sample dishes: houmous & avocado waffle; pecan nut waffle with butterscotch
sauce.* **Details:** *www.wafflehouse.co.uk; near Roman Museum; 6 pm; L only;
no Amex; no booking.*

ST ANDREWS, FIFE 9–3D

Seafood Restaurant £ 61
The Scores KY16 9AB   (01334) 479475
*"How did they get planning permission" for this striking, "glass-
walled" box? – its cliff-side location is undoubtedly "awesome",
and the fish and seafood on offer are "unbeatable" (if undoubtedly
on the "pricey" side). / Details: www.theseafoodrestaurant.com; 9.30 pm;
no shorts; children: 12+ at D.*

Vine Leaf £ 41
131 South St KY16 9UN   (01334) 477497
*"Excellent fresh seafood" is a menu highlight at this "relaxed" –
and, to some, "romantic" – bistro favourite. / Sample dishes: Scottish
sea scallop with black pudding & rocket salad; 8-hour lamb with rosti potato;
brown sugar pavlova with fresh mango, passion fruit & cream.*
Details: *www.vineleafstandrews.co.uk; 9.30 pm; D only, closed Mon & Sun.*
Accommodation: *3 guest apartments rooms, from £80.*

ST GEORGE, CONWY 4–1D

The Kinmel Arms £ 42
The Village LL22 9BP   (01745) 832207
*"One of the best new places to eat in North Wales" – a revamped
inn, praised for its "lovely" atmosphere and "good food at reasonable
prices". / Details: www.kinmelarms.co.uk; 9.30 pm; closed Sun.*

ST IVES, CORNWALL 1–4A

Alba Restaurant £ 41
The Old Lifeboat Hs, Wharf Rd TR26 1LF   (01736) 797222
*"Up above the harbour, in an ideal setting to enjoy some fresh fish" –
all reporters agree that Grant Nethercott's establishment
is "very good, and worth a visit". / Sample dishes: diver caught scallops
wrapped in pancetta with grilled summer vegetables and basil pesto; pappardelle
pasta with Cornish blue lobster, tomato and basil; passion fruit tart with toasted
coconut ice cream and passion fruitsyrup.* **Details:** *www.thealbarestaurant.com;
10 pm.*

Blue Fish **£ 40**

Norway Ln   TR26 1LZ   (01736) 794204

"Excellent" fish and seafood provides the foundation for many positive reports on this arts-centre restaurant, which has the benefit of a panoramic terrace. / **Sample dishes:** *squid and chorizo, pan fried with tomato, chilli, garlic, white wine and basil; monkfish and scallops wrapped in Parma ham served with Parmasan mash, and a cream and tarragon sauce; chocolate and orange cheesecake served with chocolate sauce and fresh cream.* **Details:** *behind the Sloop Inn; 10 pm; no Amex.*

Peppers **£ 25**

22 Fore St   TR26 1HE   (01736) 794014

A top tip for family dining on a budget – a pizza-and-more establishment that *"can't be beaten for a cheap meal"*. / **Details:** *www.peppers-stives.co.uk.*

Porthgwidden Beach Café **£ 35**

TR26 1SL   (01736) 796791

"The quieter, smaller and less formal sister to the Porthminster Beach Cafe", tipped as *"excellent for a late breakfast overlooking the beach"*. / **Details:** *www.porthgwiddencafe.co.uk; 10 pm; closed end of Oct - mid December; no Amex; booking: max 10.*

Porthminster Café **£ 44**

Porthminster Beach   TR26 2EB   (01736) 795352

"Like being at my favourite restaurant in Greece" – this *"magical"* spot is *"perched right on the beach, and overlooks a beautiful bay"*; it also offers *"superb"* food, including *"much local fish"*, in *"laid-back"* style. / **Details:** *www.porthminstercafe.co.uk; near railway station; 10 pm; closed Nov-Mar; no Amex.*

The Seafood Café **£ 33**

45 Fore St   TR26 1HE   (01736) 794004

"Great fish, simply and freshly served with plenty of options" – not to mention *"inspiring ocean views"* – ensures this *"bustling"* eatery is often hailed as *"a real gem"*. / **Sample dishes:** *grilled scallops with lemon coriander olive oil; whole seabass with rocket mash and ginger & spring onion glaze; raspberry crème brûlée.* **Details:** *www.seafoodcafe.co.uk; map on website; 10.30 pm; no Amex.*

Tate Cafe
Tate Gallery **£ 29**

Porthmeor Beach   TR26 1TG   (01736) 791122

If it's hot, sit on the terrace (*"you get some great views"*), at this *"friendly"* café, which is located on the top floor of the gallery. / **Sample dishes:** *potted mackerel with toast; smoked haddock & salmon fishcakes, tartare sauce & pea sauce; Seville orange & pecan bread & butter pudding.* **Details:** *www.tate.org.uk; L only; no Amex.*

Juliet's Garden   £ 35

Seaways Flower Farm TR21 0NF   (01720) 422228

*Tipped for its "top view" – which you can appreciate al fresco in summer – this remote establishment, above Porthloo Beach, continues to inspire only positive feedback. / **Sample dishes:** torn chicken salad and kalamata olives, char-grilled and basil pesto dressing; lemon sole fillet and crab ravioli and tomato bisque sauce; chocolate parfait cups with roast strawberries. **Details:** www.julietsgardenrestaurant.co.uk; 8.30 pm; closed Tue D; no Amex.*

Hotel Tresanton   £ 60

27 Lower Castle Rd TR2 5DR   (01326) 270055

*"Just wonderful!"; "food and service now live up to the spectacular views" (especially from the terraces) at Olga Polizzi's "beautifully-situated" Chelsea-sur-Mer hotel – "lovely fresh fare by the sea, who could ask for more?" / **Details:** www.tresanton.com; near Castle; 9.30 pm; booking: max 10; children: 6+ at dinner. **Accommodation:** 29 rooms, from £230.*

Rising Sun   £ 42

The Square TR2 5DJ   (01326) 270233

*"What could be better on a summer's day than lunch on the Rising Sun's terrace ?"… especially as this harbour-side inn's "good-quality bar food" is its best feature; the restaurant, in comparison, has traditionally seemed "too ambitious and pricey", but (currently closed) it's to reopen this winter in a different part of the building. / **Details:** www.risingsunstmawes.com; 9 pm; D only, ex Sun open L & D. **Accommodation:** 8 rooms, from £120.*

Ripleys   £ 48

PL28 8NQ   (01841) 520179

*"Neither St Merryn's nor the restaurant's exterior is especially attractive", but Paul Ripley's "pleasant" venture near Newquay Airport wins consistent praise nonetheless for its "fresh and exciting" food (and "great fish" in particular). / **Details:** 9.30 pm; closed Sun & Mon, D only Tue-Sat; no Amex; booking: max 8; children: 6.*

Seafood Restaurant   £ 50

16 West End KY10 2BX   (01333) 730327

*"A delightful spot in a Fife fishing village"; Craig Miller's "light" and "bright" dining room, near St Andrews, wins little but praise for its "excellent" fish and other fare. / **Details:** www.theseafoodrestaurant.com; 9.30 pm; closed Mon & Tue Sept - May.*

The Crazy Bear   £ 49

Bear Ln OX44 7UR   (01865) 890714

*"So wild and wacky, but with good food thrown in"; this "stylishly" bizarre gastropub – with "a choice of Thai or British dining rooms" – goes down well when you want "something a bit different", and "is a hit with Londoners and locals alike". / **Sample dishes:** salad of goats' cheese & golden baby beets; slow-cooked rump & roast cutlets with pea shoots & broad beans; chocolate cake with lavender ice cream.*
Details: *www.crazybeargroup.co.uk; 10 pm.* ***Accommodation:*** *17 rooms, from £115.*

Endeavour   £ 39

1 High St TS13 5BH   (01947) 840825

*"A tiny restaurant-with-rooms" set in a cute coastal village, and serving "an innovative menu of fresh food, mainly fish"; all accounts say the food is "good", and some that it's "exquisite". / **Sample dishes:** local salt cod mousse with brandade of smoked cod; fillet of Whitby halibut on a Mediterranean butterbean ragu with black olive tapenade; rich lemon mousse with lemon curd ice cream.*
Details: *www.endeavour-restaurant.co.uk; 10m N of Whitby, off A174; 9 pm; D only, closed Mon & Sun; no Amex.* ***Accommodation:*** *4 rooms, from £80.*

Fratellis   £ 34

13 St Mary's Hill PE9 2DP   (01780) 754333

*"A good alternative to all the pizzeria chains – family-run, and it shows"; "very good pasta dishes" are the top tip. / **Sample dishes:** bruschetta; fresh pasta filled with lobster & ricotta cheese in a cream & saffron sauce; chocolate & almond cake.* ***Details:*** *www.fratellis.co.uk; 9.30 pm.*

The George Hotel   £ 52

71 St Martins PE9 2LB   (01780) 750750

*For sheer character, its hard to beat this vast and "beautiful" coaching inn – that's why it's always "unbelievably busy", despite food that's "expensive" and rather "relying on its reputation"; you can also eat in the cheaper Garden Room brasserie, or – in summer – have a BBQ in the "fabulous" courtyard. / **Sample dishes:** Galia melon with fresh figs & fruits; rump of lamb, courgette & rosemary pancake, roast plum tomato & sweet pepper essence; crème caramel.* ***Details:*** *www.georgehotelofstamford.com; off A1, 14m N of Peterborough, onto B1081; 10 pm; jacket & tie required; children: 8+ at D.* ***Accommodation:*** *47 rooms, from £130.*

Leaping Hare Vineyard £ 39 A✪

Wyken Vineyards IP31 2DW (01359) 250287

"Wonderful" food, "reflecting superb local ingredients", justifies the trip to this "oustanding" café-cum-restaurant, housed in a barn "in the middle of nowhere"; as you'd hope "there's an impressive range of their own wines" too. / *Sample dishes:* salad of seared scallops, smoked bacon and new potatoes; pork fillet, rosti potato and broccoli; strawberries and raspberries, organic Jersey cream, shortbread.
Details: www.wykenvineyards.co.uk; 9m NE of Bury St Edmunds; follow tourist signs off A143; 9 pm; L only, ex Fri & Sat open L & D; no Amex.

Red Lion Inn £ 37 ✪

2 Red Lion St LE14 4HS (01949) 860868

This "rustic", "shabby chic" hostelry, near Belvoir Castle, is a sibling to Clipsham's famous Olive Branch; the "gastropub fare" can be "uneven", but it's "generally good", and is accompanied by "a huge range of beers and good wine". / *Details:* www.theredlioninn.co.uk; 9.30 pm; closed Sun D; no Amex.

Clos du Marquis £ 44 A✪

London Rd SO20 6DE (01264) 810738

"Excellent" provincial-Gallic cooking and "genial" service make the (South African) Marquis family's "welcoming" pub-conversion popular with all who comment on it; a "massive, all-French" wine list plays a worthy supporting rôle. / *Sample dishes:* brioche of smoked eel and scrambled duck egg; fillet & braised cheek of beef served with a red wine & shallot sauce. *Details:* www.closdumarquis.co.uk; 2m E on A30 from Stockbridge; 9 pm; closed Mon & Sun D.

Greyhound £ 48

31 High St SO20 6EY (01264) 810833

Fans hail this "upmarket boozer" as "one of the best gastropubs in the South East", and praise its "honest country cooking"; for others, though, its performance is all a bit "ordinary". / *Sample dishes:* fish cake with poached egg & chive beurre blanc; pot roast marinated poussin with a fricassé of broad beans & peas, crushed new potatoes & roast vine tomatoes; dark chocolate fondant with tonka bean ice cream & banana tuile. *Details:* www.thegreyhound.info; 9 pm; closed Sun D; no Amex; booking: max 12. *Accommodation:* 8 rooms, from £90.

Vineyard at Stockcross £ 94 A✪

RG20 8JU (01635) 528770

A "massive" wine list – "mainly top-end Californian vintages" – and John Campbell's "stunning" cuisine combine to win all-round acclaim for this "luxurious" (if slightly "bland") contemporary country house hotel; some dishes are "minute" or "over-fussy", though, and not everyone likes the "Muzak". / *Sample dishes:* velouté of pumpkin, rabbit ravioli & Parmesan foam; venison with celeriac, bacon, sloe gin jelly; chocolate tiramisu. *Details:* www.the-vineyard.co.uk; from M4, J13 take A34 towards Hungerford; 9.30 pm; no jeans or trainers. *Accommodation:* 49 rooms, from £270.

The Wildebeest Arms   £ 34
82-86 Norwich Rd   NR14 8QJ   (01508) 492497
"A bright spot in a culinary desert" – that may be why *"you need to book"*, at this *"very popular"* and *"lively"* inn, which reporters praise for its *"imaginative"* cuisine. / **Sample dishes:** pan fried scallops with truffled potato purée and brown shrimps; honey roast Gressingham duck breast with alsace bacon, fondant potato, creamed cabbage, girolles, caramelised turnip and bigerade jus; vanilla and cardamom crème brûlée, with a pineapple and passion fruit granita. **Details:** www.animalinns.co.uk; from A140, turn left at Dunston Hall, left at T-junction; 9 pm.

The Crooked Billet   £ 43
Newlands Ln   RG9 5PU   (01491) 681048
This *"perfect"*-looking inn, *"deep in the Oxfordshire countryside"*, makes *"a particularly romantic location at night"* (*"especially in winter when the fires are ablaze"*); it serves *"great traditional dishes in huge portions"*. / **Sample dishes:** warm pigeon salad, wild mushrooms, roast garlic, frissee vinaigrette, pea shoots; whole lemon sole grilled on the bone, sugar snaps, hollandaise; Bakewell tart, custard sauce. **Details:** www.thecrookedbillet.co.uk; off the A4130; 10 pm; no Amex.

Angel Inn   £ 34
Polstead St   CO6 4SA   (01206) 263245
A popular 16th-century coaching inn, tipped for its *"large selection of interesting and well-cooked pub grub"*. / **Sample dishes:** chicken liver pâté with a red onion confit and toasted granary bread; griddled skate with salad and fries; hot chocolate fondue. **Details:** www.theangelinn.net; 5m W of A12, on B1068; 9.30 pm; no Amex. **Accommodation:** 6 rooms, from £75.

The Crown   £ 39
CO6 4SE   (01206) 262346
"Beautifully situated in Constable Country", this *"huge"* gastropub is a *"high-quality-all-round"* operation, whose main problem is that it's *"often too busy"*. / **Sample dishes:** wild rabbit schnitzel, quails egg, anchovy & caper butter; pan fried calves liver, bubble & squeak croquettes, crispy onions, sage gravy; steamed simnel pudding, vanilla custard. **Details:** www.eoinns.co.uk; on B1068; 9.30 pm, Fri & Sat10 pm, Sun 9 pm; no Amex.

The Sorrel Restaurant
Ston Easton Park Hotel   £ 64
Ston Easton   BA3 4DF   (01761) 241631
The overall experience can be a bit *"OTT"*, but this Palladian country house hotel (a Von Essen property) is tipped as offering *"good food"* nonetheless. / **Sample dishes:** goat's cheese & saffron panna cotta, pear & lavender compote, blackberry compote; roast loin of monkfish wrapped in Parma ham, provençale vegetables & basil jus; lemon meringue cream wrapped in chocolate, warm raspberry jelly. **Details:** www.stoneaston.co.uk; 11m SW of Bath on A39; 9.30 pm; no jeans. **Accommodation:** 22 rooms, from £195.

Carron £ 35

Cameron St AB39 2HS (01569) 760460

Any "faithfully-restored Art Deco restaurant" would be worthy of a tip for that very fact alone, but these converted tea-rooms also offer a simple but very satisfactory menu including "good local beef, venison and seafood". / *Sample dishes:* crab soup; twice cooked shank, set on a parsnip and thyme purée, with a mirepoix of root vegetables and a red wine jus; topped with a pineapple cream and a dark chocolate thin. *Details:* www.carron-restaurant.co.uk; 9.30 pm; closed Mon & Sun; no Amex.

Lairhillock Inn £ 40

Netherley AB39 3QS (01569) 730001

Tipped for "good hearty bar meals prepared with gastro-flair", this isolated pub seems to be thriving under its new ownership. / *Sample dishes:* grilled wood pigeon salad with toasted pine kernels and a redcurrant and mustard dressing; beef medallions and roast venison saddle, peppercorn sauce and port jus; miniature desert platter. *Details:* www.lairhillock.co.uk; 7m S of Aberdeen; 9.30 pm.

Marine Hotel £ 50

9-10 Shore Head AB39 2JY (01569) 762155

Now under the same ownership as the Creel Inn, Catterline, this "superb harbour-side pub" has been "much freshened up", and offers "simple but really good food" (in both bar and restaurant), and a "stunning list of real ales and bottled beers". / *Details:* www.britnett-carver.co.uk/marine; 9 pm.

The Old Butchers £ 38

7 Park St GL54 1AQ (01451) 831700

"A lively and bustling" main-street bistro, widely hailed as a "gem", thanks to its "well-prepared and imaginative" dishes from "locally-sourced" ingredients. / *Details:* www.theoldbutchers.com; 9.30 pm.

Café Chutney £ 33

Beaconwood Bordon Hill CV37 9RX (01789) 204427

Tipped for its "authentic Indian food", this "relaxing" curry house continues to attract only positive feedback.

Lambs £ 38

12 Sheep St CV37 6EF (01789) 292554

A "lovely" bistro, in a Tudor house, whose "swift and welcoming service" helps make it the town's most frequent nomination as "best place for a pre-theatre dinner". / *Sample dishes:* crispy duck and watercress salad; rack of Cotswold lamb provençale and dauphinoise potatoes; sticky toffee pudding and vanilla ice cream. *Details:* www.lambsrestaurant.co.uk; 9.45 pm; closed Mon L & Sun D; no Amex; booking: max 12.

The Oppo £ 37

13 Sheep St CV37 6EF (01789) 269980

"Consistently good, and excellent pre-theatre" – this "cosy" little place doesn't inspire the hugest volume of commentary, but it's all very positive: "good wines by the glass", "child-friendly" and "nice staff" too! / *Sample dishes:* crispy duck with watercress salad; breast of chicken roast with banana in lime butter; sticky toffee pudding. *Details:* www.theoppo.co.uk; 10 pm, Sun 9.30 pm; closed Sun L; booking: max 12.

Thai Kingdom £ 30
11 Warwick Rd CV37 6YW (01789) 261103
"A regular part of our Shakespeare experience"; we don't know what
the Bard would have made of the Thai cuisine on offer at this
townhouse restaurant, but reporters find it "consistently good"
(and occasionally "exceptional"). / **Details:** www.thaikingdom.co.uk;
Opposite the Grosvenor hotel; 10.45 pm.

The Vintner £ 35 Ⓐ⭐
4-5 Sheep St CV37 6EF (01789) 297259
"Decent brasserie food, in an appealing building" – such are the all-
day charms of this "olde-worlde" spot whose repertoire includes
"the best breakfast in Stratford" and some "excellent surf 'n' turf
options". / **Sample dishes:** tian of Cornish crab; grilled fillet of sea bass with
crushed potatoes, asparagus & lobster sauce; banoffi pie.
Details: www.the-vintner.co.uk; 10 pm, Sun 9 pm; no Amex.

STRONTIAN, ARGYLL 9–3B

Kilcamb Lodge Hotel £ 58 Ⓣ
PH36 4HY (01967) 402257
We wish we had more reports, but this "lovely" small hotel,
overlooking the Loch, is once again tipped for its "excellent
restaurant". / **Sample dishes:** pork and roast vegetable tureen, black pudding
bon bon, hot mulled wine jelly and walnut salad; organic salmon fillet with
watercress, seared scallop, pea purée and saffron foam; hot chocolate pudding,
tonka bean ice cream and white chocolate mousse.
Details: www.kilcamblodge.co.uk; At the top of the hill, on the left ; 9.30 pm;
no Amex; no jeans or trainers; booking essential; children: 12+ at D.
Accommodation: 10 rooms, from £130.

STUCKTON, HAMPSHIRE 2–3C

Three Lions £ 51 ⭐
Stuckton Rd SP6 2HF (01425) 652489
"Helpful service makes you feel welcome", say fans of this "relaxed"
New Forest venture where the "gastropub fare" is "a cut above";
the formula strikes some reporters as rather "static", though,
especially when it comes at "London prices". / **Sample dishes:** sautéed
scallops served on a bed of shrimps with sweet Thai dressing; dry cut Scotch fillet
of beef with salsify; hot chocolate pudding with home-made vanilla ice cream.
Details: www.thethreelionsrestaurant.co.uk; 1m E of Fordingbridge off B3078;
9 pm, Fri & Sat 9.30 pm; closed Mon & Sun D; no Amex. **Accommodation:** 7
rooms, from £75.

STUDLAND, DORSET 2–4C

Shell Bay Seafood £ 42 Ⓐ
Ferry Rd BH19 3BA (01929) 450363
You get "a jaw-dropping view", and some "good seafood" to boot,
at this "heavenly" waterfront spot, near the Sandbanks ferry; NB: the
full menu is no longer served at lunchtime... and as we go to press
we learn the restaurant is closed for a refurb, re-opening April 2009.
/ **Details:** www.shellbay.net; just near the Sandbanks to Swanage ferry; 9 pm;
children: 12+ at dinner.

Plumber Manor £ 42 ★

DT10 2AF (01258) 472507

"Nothing changes", at this *"homely"* country house hotel, for over 35 years in the ownership of the Prideaux family – standards remain *"very good"* all-round. / **Details:** www.plumbermanor.com; off A357 towards Hazelbury Bryan; 9.30 pm; D only, ex Sun open L & D. **Accommodation:** 16 rooms, from £110.

Fego Caffe £ 25 Ⓣ

Chobham Rd SL5 0DU (01344) 876464

Part of a chain with various branches in the leafy Thames Valley: a "good sandwich and snack bar" that's tipped as "great for weekend brunch". / **Sample dishes:** penne arrabiata; vanilla ice cream topped with espresso. **Details:** www.fegocaffe.co.uk; 5 pm; L only; no Amex.

The French Table £ 44 ★

85 Maple Rd KT6 4AW (020) 8399 2365

"In a surprising culinary desert", the Guignards' *"buzzy"* suburban spot makes an *"excellent local restaurant"*, with *"lovely"* food and a *"great wine list"*; *"it still struggles with the acoustics"*, though. / **Sample dishes:** poached breast of Anjou pigeon, braised leg and vegetable brochette; home smoked rack and rump of lamb with aubergine relish, courgette purée, red pepper coulis; caramelised pear coated in walnut crumble with ginger pain perdu, liquorice ice-cream. **Details:** www.thefrenchtable.co.uk; 10.30 pm; closed Mon & Sun D; booking: max 10, Fri & Sat.

Joy £ 37 ★

37 Brighton Rd KT6 5LR (020) 8390 3988

"By far the best Indian restaurant in the Kingston area"; this *"wonderfully different"* spot has a big following among reporters for its *"interesting"* and *"reliable"* cuisine. / **Details:** www.joy-restaurant.co.uk; 11.30 pm.

Anchor £ 40 Ⓐ

Bury Ln CB6 2BD (01353) 778537

With its "lovely setting" – albeit in "an odd corner of the Fens" – this isolated ancient inn is a top destination locally, and its food can be surprisingly "inventive"; "when they're under pressure, though, it often fails to deliver". / **Sample dishes:** asparagus wrapped in wild boar ham grilled with vintage cheddar; baked fillet of sea trout with crushed minted Jersey royals, watercress sauce and wild garlic pesto; almond-topped English rhubarb and ginger crumble with Cornish clotted cream. **Details:** www.anchorsuttongault.co.uk; 7m W of Ely, signposted off B1381 in Sutton; 9pm, Sat 9.30 pm. **Accommodation:** 4 rooms, from £79.5.

Olive Tree   £ 43

Sutton Green Rd GU4 7QD   (01483) 729999

"Good fish" is tipped as a menu highlight at this busy gastropub.
/ *Sample dishes:* tiger prawns; rack of lamb; treacle tart. *Details:* 9.30 pm;
closed Mon D & Sun D; no Amex.

SWANSEA, SWANSEA   1–1C

La Braseria   £ 38

28 Wind St SA1 1DZ   (01792) 469683
*A useful, city-centre Spanish bodega-style joint akin to Cardiff's
La Brasserie, with a similar you-choose-it-we-cook-it meat/fish formula;
on limited feedback, it's strongest on atmosphere, but with decent
food.* / *Details:* www.labraseria.com; 11.30 pm; closed Sun; need 6+ to book;
children: 6+.

Patricks   £ 35

638 Mumbles Rd SA3 4EA   (01792) 360199
*On the Mumbles, a crowded brasserie-with-rooms that's long been
a "locals' favourite".* / *Details:* www.patrickswithrooms.com; in Mumbles,
1m before pier; 9.50 pm; closed Sun D. *Accommodation:* 10 rooms,
from £110 .

SWINTON, SCOTTISH BORDERS   8–1A

The Wheatsheaf at Swinton   £ 37

Main St TD11 3JJ   (01890) 860257
"An oasis in a desert" – this *"charming former public house"* is again
winning consistent praise for its *"exceptional food generally,
but perfect fish in particular".* / *Sample dishes:* sautéed mushrooms
with bacon in a filo pastry case with glazed cheddar; whole Dover sole with fresh herb
butter; hot sticky ginger and pear pudding with fudge sauce and vanilla pod
ice-cream. *Details:* www.wheatsheaf-swinton.co.uk; between Kelso &
Berwick-upon-Tweed, by village green; 9 pm; Closed Sun D Jan & Feb; no Amex;
children: 10+ at D. *Accommodation:* 10 rooms, from £102.

TADCASTER, NORTH YORKSHIRE   5–1D

Aagrah   £ 27

York Rd LS24 8EG   (01937) 530888
"As ever with this chain, the food was interesting and good" –
this outpost of Yorkshire's excellent curry multiple continues to put
in a notably *"consistent"* performance. / *Sample dishes:* seekh kebab;
chicken mangalore; ras malai. *Details:* www.aagrah.com; 7m from York on A64;
11.30 pm, 11 pm Sun; D only.

Terrace
Cliveden House £ 81
Cliveden Rd SL6 0JF (01628) 668561
*The occasional reporter does proclaim it "exceptional in every way",
but the most striking aspect of feedback on the less formal dining
room at the Astors' impossibly grand former palazzo (now a Von
Essen hotel) is just how little of it there is – hence its inclusion as a
'tip'. / Sample dishes: langoustine ravioli & light bisque on a bed of saffron
potatoes, watercress salad; confit duck leg 'sautéeed minute' ratte new potatoes,
wild mushroom forestière, sorrel jus; amaretto soufflé marbled with bitter
chocolate, black cherry sorbet & compote. Details: www.clivedenhouse.co.uk;
9.30 pm; no trainers. Accommodation: 39 rooms, from £240.*

Waldo's
Cliveden House £102
Berry Hill SL6 0JF (01628) 668561
*If the setting is all-important, this grand basement dining room
is "certainly a place to take someone you want to spoil or impress";
food-wise, the year which saw a change of chef has inspired few
reports – such as they are are very mixed too.
/ Details: www.clivedenhouse.co.uk; M4, J7 then follow National Trust signs;
9.30 pm; D only, closed Mon & Sun; jacket & tie required; booking: max 6;
children: 12+. Accommodation: 39 rooms, from £360.*

The Castle Hotel £ 61
Castle Grn TA1 1NF (01823) 272671
*"A beacon of excellence"; this landmark hotel's dining room has had
its ups and downs over the years, but most recent reports are
of "lovely" food and "very helpful" service. / Sample dishes: seared
scallops with brocolli purée and candied lemon; fillet rib and flank of west country
beef; rhubarb vachrin. Details: www.the-castle-hotel.com; follow
tourist information signs; 9.30 pm; closed Sun D. Accommodation: 44 rooms,
from £185.*

Willow Tree £ 45
3 Tower Ln TA1 4AR (01823) 352835
*"Why did this consistently excellent restaurant disappear from your
guide?"; too few reports, sadly, but this "comfy" venue inspired a good
deal of praise this year for its "outstanding" food, "unobtrusive"
service and "warm" ambience. / Details: www.willowtreerestaurant.co.uk;
10 pm; D only, closed Sun & Mon; no Amex.*

Browns Hotel £ 50
80 West St PL19 8AQ (01822) 618686
*Especially "in the courtyard on a sunny day", this town-centre hotel
brasserie it tipped as a "'good place for a snack"; as a serious
culinary destination, however, its attractions are more moot.
/ Details: www.brownsdevon.co.uk; 10 pm. Accommodation: 20 rooms,
from £99.*

Hotel Endsleigh £ 57
PL19 0PQ (01822) 870 000
*Olga Polizzi sold this "fantastic hide-away of an hotel" just as this guide was heading to press (though chef, Nick Fisher, is to remain at the stove); it's drifted a bit of late – "new owners will have their work cut out to get it back on track". | **Sample dishes:** salad of red mullet, ratatouille, fettuccini of vegetables; roast monkfish, glazed pork belly, cauliflower purée, asparagus, bok choi; gâteau opera, honeycomb, dark chocolate sorbet.* **Details:** www.hotelendsleigh.com; 10.30 pm. **Accommodation:** 16 rooms, from £200.

TEFFONT EVIAS, WILTSHIRE 2–3C

Howards House Hotel £ 58
SP3 5RJ (01722) 716392
*"A real find!"; this small hotel is tipped for its "surprisingly good food" and its "very friendly staff" too. | **Sample dishes:** seared scallops with peas & crisp pancetta; breast of duck, pistachio & duck sausage & black cherry jus; trio of passion fruit with panna cotta & sorbet.*
Details: www.howardshousehotel.com; 9m W of Stonehenge off A303; 9 pm.
Accommodation: 9 rooms, from £155.

TETBURY, GLOUCESTERSHIRE 2–2B

Calcot Manor £ 47
GL8 8YJ (01666) 890391
*This child-friendly hotel (and spa) is a "heavenly retreat" (especially for stressed-out parents), with food that's "consistently good" (but stops short of being a 'wow'); for less formal dining, there is an in-house pub, the Gumstool Inn. | **Sample dishes:** pressed foie gras & apple terrine, pear & saffron chutney; roast Gressingham duck breast, crisp leg parcel, spiced yellow peas; kirsch cherry & almond clafoutis, clotted cream ice cream.* **Details:** www.calcotmanor.co.uk; junction of A46 & A4135; 9.30 pm. **Accommodation:** 35 rooms, from £220.

Priory Inn £ 38
London Rd GL8 8JJ (01666) 502251
*"Looking like a pub, but performing like a middle-range restaurant" – this "family-friendly" place (majoring in pizza) has quite a niche in this fashionable town, even if the occasional reporter feels it's "over-rated". | **Details:** www.theprioryinn.co.uk; 10 pm. **Accommodation:** 14 rooms, from £99.*

TEWKESBURY, GLOUCESTERSHIRE 2–1B

Abbey Refectory
Tewkesbury Abbey £ 19
Church St GL20 5RZ (01684) 273736
Even if the food can be a bit "ordinary", this self-service operation is still a "useful and convenient" tip, near the Abbey.
*| **Details:** www.tewkesburyabbey.org.uk; M5 motorway, exit junction number 9; L only; no Amex.*

THIRSK, NORTH YORKSHIRE 8–4C

Carpenters Arms £ 34
YO7 2DP (01845) 537369
*"A village pub taken over by a talented young chef and his partner" – all reporters put the food somewhere between "decent" and "super", and the setting is "lovely" too. | **Sample dishes:** queen scallops with lemon garlic; local free belly pork with garlic honey and spice; trio of crèmes brûlées with home-made shortbreads. **Details:** www.carpentersarmsfelixkirk.com; 9 pm; closed Mon & Sun D; no Amex.*

Bakers Arms   **£ 36**   Ⓐ
Main St LE16 7TS   (01858) 545201
This "quaint" and "buzzing" village pub is a "most welcoming" place;
its culinary style can seem "predictable", but results are usually
"enjoyable". / **Sample dishes:** goats cheese tart with red onion marmalade;
roast rack of lamb with butternut squash; sticky toffee pudding.
Details: www.thebakersarms.co.uk; near Market Harborough off A6; 9.30 pm;
D only, ex Sat open L & D & Sun open L only, closed Mon; no Amex;
children: 12+.

Stagg Inn   **£ 40**   ✪
HR5 3RL   (01544) 230221
"A Michelin-starred pub that hasn't lost its local feel" – a "quirky",
countrified sort of place, run with "friendly competence", and serving
"very good ingredients cooked with deceptive simplicity".
/ **Sample dishes:** crab cake with avocado salsa; duck breast with elderflower
sauce & perry potato fondant; chocolate meringue with blackcurrants.
Details: www.thestagg.co.uk; on B4355, NE of Kington; 9 pm; closed Mon &
Sun D; no Amex. **Accommodation:** 6 rooms, from £85.

Superfish   **£ 17**   ✪✪
25 The Broadway KT6 7DJ   (020) 83902868
A representative member of a small Surrey chain of "genteel"
chippies, offering "some of the best fish and chips round London".
/ **Sample dishes:** lemon sole fillet with chips, French bread & butter; Dutch
morello cherry flan. **Details:** www.superfishuk.co.uk; 10 pm; closed Sun.

Darts Farm Café   **£ 23**   Ⓣ
Clyst St George EX3 0QH   (01392) 875587
"Noisy but fun" – this largely al fresco café (part of a rural retail
complex) is particularly tipped for its "fresh fish 'n' chips, cooked
to order". / **Sample dishes:** grilled chicken with baby spinach garlic,
mushrooms, and fries; seasonal fruit crumble with clotted cream.
Details: www.dartsfarm.co.uk; L only; no Amex.

The Galley   **£ 52**   Ⓣ
41 Fore St EX3 0HU   (01392) 876078
Tipped as a "high-quality establishment with character", this small
restaurant-with-rooms is of particular note for its fish and seafood
cooking. / **Sample dishes:** seafood chowder with vegetables, light spices &
cream; fillet of halibut on seaweed mashed potatoes with seared scallops & chilli
ice cream masked with ginseng & caviar butter sauce; bread & butter pudding
using brioche, basil & mint. **Details:** www.galleyrestaurant.co.uk; 9.30; closed
Mon & Sun; booking essential; children: 12+.

La Petite Maison £ 44 **A ⭐**

35 Fore St EX3 OHR (01392) 873660

A "small" and "unpretentious" spot in a popular town, where
"very welcoming hosts" create "a charming atmosphere" –
"an intimate dining experience with great food and sensible prices".
*/ **Sample dishes:** goat's cheese soufflé on mixed leaves with pesto dressing;*
roast chump of local lamb, confit of shoulder, ratatouille, chive & parsley potato
cake; rhubarb crunchy walnut crumble, rhubarb jelly & ginger ice cream.
Details: *www.lapetitemaison.co.uk; Next to The Globe Hotel; 10 pm; closed*
Mon & Sun; no Amex; booking essential at L.

TORCROSS, DEVON 1–4D

Start Bay Inn £ 26 ⭐

TQ7 2TQ (01548) 580553

"Fresh, local fish and seafood, right on the sea-front" – that's the deal
that ensures that this "friendly" hostelry is always hailed as a "reliable
holiday treat"; at the height of the season, though, it can be "manic".
*/ **Sample dishes:** smoked mackerel; mixed seafood platter: smoked salmon,*
prawns, mussels, smoked mackerel a Marie Rose dip; spotted dick with custard.
Details: *www.startbayinn.co.uk; on beach front (take A379 coastal road*
to Dartmouth); 10 pm; During winter closing is earlier; no Amex; no booking.

TORQUAY, DEVON 1–3D

Elephant Bar & Restaurant £ 42 ⭐

3-4 Beacon Ter, Harbourside TQ1 2BH (01803) 200044

It's "a treat" to visit this ambitious establishment, where the food
is invariably "above average", and sometimes very fine indeed;
reporters seem to prefer the "buzzy" brasserie to the (Michelin-
*starred) dining room above. / **Sample dishes:** chicken liver parfait with tea*
soaked prunes and toasted brioche; braised moorland lamb shank with colcannon
mash and cooking liquor; sticky toffee pudding with vanilla ice cream.
Details: *www.elephantrestaurant.co.uk; 9.30 pm; closed Mon & Sun D; children:*
14+ at bar.

No 7 Fish Bistro £ 41 ⭐

Beacon Ter TQ1 2BH (01803) 295055

"The fish are so fresh they've barely stopped wriggling" at this "fun"
spot – still "THE place" locally, and with "fabulous" service too.
*/ **Sample dishes:** seafood broth; fillet of sole filled with prawns and baked under*
a cheese and wine sauce; treacle tart served with hot custard.
Details: *www.no7-fish.com; 9.30 pm; D only Sun-Tue, closed Sun & Mon*
in Winter.

Orchid Restaurant
Corbyn Head Hotel £ 50

Seafront TQ2 6RH (01803) 296366

Some reporters have "truly memorable" dining experiences at this
sea-view dining room; even a fan, though, says it "looks like your
mother-in-law's sitting room circa 1985", and dissenters find the
*culinary style "dated" too. / **Sample dishes:** confit belly of pork, cured foie*
gras, apple salad, parsnip cream; pave of halibut with chorizo, confit fennel,
pomme dauphine, Dijon foam; dark chocolate & lime fondant with coconut sorbet.
Details: *www.orchidrestaurant.net; 9.30 pm; closed Mon, Tue L & Sun; no jeans*
*or shorts; children: 5+. **Accommodation:** 45 rooms, from £120.*

Kingsbridge Inn   £ 36   ⓣ
9 Leechwell St   TQ9 5SY   (01803) 863324
*"A newly-refurbished" inn with "fresh food and friendly staff",
and tipped as a "very positive dining experience" all-round.*
/ **Details:** 9.30 pm; closed Mon.

Gurnards Head   £ 38   ★
TR26 3DE   (01736) 796928
*A "spectacular location" (near Land's End, with "views of the
Atlantic"), has helped this "lovely" dining pub (sibling to the Felin Fach
Griffin at Brecon) win a wide following; sometimes, though, it can
seem a touch "complacent".* / **Sample dishes:** red mullet escabeche with
golden marjoram & red peppers; grilled lemon sole with garlic, oregano, sautéed
potatoes & foraged leaves; stem ginger buttermilk pudding with rhubarb sorbet.
Details: www.gurnardshead.co.uk; on coastal road between Land's End & St Ives,
near Zennor B3306; 9.30 pm; no Amex. **Accommodation:** 7 rooms,
from £82.50.

Queen's Head   £ 34   Ⓐ
Townhead   LA23 1PW   (01539) 432174
*The secret's well and truly out about this "perfect" Lakeland "hide-
out", and it's often too "busy" for its own good; the "above-average"
food is generally "worth the wait", but some punters – even having
booked "weeks in advance" – end up feeling simply "ignored".*
/ **Details:** www.queensheadhotel.com; A592 on Kirkstone Pass; 9 pm; no Amex;
booking: max 8, Fri & Sat. **Accommodation:** 16 rooms, from £100.

Hotel du Vin et Bistro   £ 45
Crescent Rd   TN1 2LY   (01892) 526455
*The "lovely" atmosphere and "extensive and unusual" wine list are
the highlights you might expect at this boutique-hotel dining room;
however, "as with all the HdV's, it can be a bit hit-and-miss...
sometimes a big miss".* / **Sample dishes:** chicken & shitake mushroom
terrine & tomato dressing; shoulder of lamb with niçoise jus; treacle tart with
clotted cream. **Details:** www.hotelduvin.com; 10 pm, Fri & Sat 10.30 pm;
booking: max 10. **Accommodation:** 34 rooms, from £95.

Thackeray's   £ 52   Ⓐ★★
85 London Rd   TN1 1EA   (01892) 511921
*"What a fine chef Richard Phillips is" – his "dazzling" cooking
is renewing acclaim for this "very civilised" villa, which feels "quite
modern, despite retaining much of the old building"; "the set lunch
is the best bargain in the UK".* / **Sample dishes:** seared Cornish scallops,
confit tomato, baby leeks, celeriac purée, carrot & cumin foam; assiette of pork,
pomme purée, creamed cabbage, apple compote, ginger & clove jus; passion fruit
soufflé, coconut ice cream, pina colada 'foam'.
Details: www.thackerays-restaurant.co.uk; near Kent and Sussex hospital;
10.30 pm; closed Mon & Sun D.

TUNSTALL, LANCASHIRE   7–4D

Lunesdale Arms   **£ 33**   🅰⭐
LA6 2QN   (01524) 274203
*"Still the best in the area" ("though the competition is getting stiffer")
– Emma Gillibrand's "comfortably updated" and "very friendly" pub
continues to win praise with its "locally-sourced ingredients, skillfully
cooked and served".* / **Sample dishes:** *liver pâté with medlar jelly; sirloin
steak with a herby-stuffed tomato, herb butter, chips and vegetables; Seville orange
upside down cake and crème fraîche.* **Details:** *www.thelunesdale.co.uk; 15 min
from J34 on M6 onto A683; 11 pm; closed Mon.*

TURNERS HILL, WEST SUSSEX   3–4B

Alexander House Hotel   **£ 60**   🅰
East St   RH10 4QD   (01342) 714914
*"Superb" food and an "interesting" wine list in a "stunning" setting,
or just thoroughly "overpriced"? – this Jacobean country house hotel
has much to commend it, but even some fans note it "tends to be
pricey", and critics just find it "disappointing".* / **Sample dishes:** *terrine
of oriental spiced duckplum and five spice coulis, micro leaf salad; duo of lamb,
ballotine of the shoulder and noisettes, wilted spinach, warm potato and mint
mousse, pot au feu of baby vegetables; sweet pistachio tart, fresh grapefruit,
grapefruit sorbet.* **Details:** *www.alexanderhouse.co.uk; off M23 J10, follow signs
to E. Grinstead and Turners Hill, on B2110; 10pm; no jeans or trainers.*
Accommodation: *38 rooms, from £185.*

TWICKENHAM, MIDDLESEX   3–3B

Arthur's   **£ 37**   🆃
The Green   TW2 5AB   (020) 88933995
*"A nice little local" – a "quirky former loo block" – on Twickenham
Green; the food is "a bit variable", but the place is tipped for its "fun"
and "homely" style.* / **Sample dishes:** *grilled goat's cheese crostini with olive
tapenade; fishcake with crème fraîche & chives; apple & plum crumble with
custard.* **Details:** *www.arthursonthegreen.co.uk; 10 pm; no Amex.*

TYN-Y-GROES, CONWY   4–1D

Groes Inn   **£ 38**   🅰
LL32 8TN   (01492) 650545
*"The oldest pub in Wales" continues to please most reporters with its
"dependable" quality, and its "lovely fish dishes and puds".*
/ **Sample dishes:** *crispy lamb & Feta salad; local seafood platter; cinnamon &
honey ice cream.* **Details:** *www.groesinn.com; on B5106 between Conwy &
Betws-y-coed, 2m from Conwy; 9 pm.* **Accommodation:** *14 rooms, from £103.*

TYNEMOUTH, TYNE & WEAR   8–2B

Sidney's   **£ 40**
3-5 Percy Park Rd   NE30 4LZ   (0191) 257 8500
*"Good fresh fish" is a highlight of the "interesting" menu on offer
at this "grown-up" bistro.* / **Details:** *www.sidneys.co.uk; 9.30 pm; closed
Mon L & Sun.*

ULLINGSWICK, HEREFORDSHIRE 2–1B

The Three Crowns Inn £ 38
HR1 3JQ (01432) 820279
A "lovely" location is a key attraction of this half-timbered inn;
the food is "usually very good" too, but it "can be a little variable".
/ **Sample dishes:** leek and potato velouté with smoked haddock & poached egg;
peppered sirloin of Herefordshire beef with gratin dauphinoise; chocolate fondant
with pistachio ice cream & griottine cherries. **Details:** www.threecrownsinn.com;
1.5m from A417; 9.30 pm; closed Mon; no Amex. **Accommodation:** 1 room,
at about £95.

ULLSWATER, CUMBRIA 7–3D

Sharrow Bay £ 71 Ⓐ⭐
CA10 2LZ (01768) 486301
A "beautiful" Lakeland setting (and view), an "elegant" interior and
"cosseting service" still create a "top, old-school experience", at the
UK's original country house hotel (now a Von Essen establishment);
there is a growing band of sceptics, though, for whom the hearty
"gourmet" fare, while still "correct", seems rather "unexciting".
/ **Details:** www.sharrowbay.co.uk; on Pooley Bridge Rd towards Howtown; 8 pm;
children: 13+. **Accommodation:** 24 rooms, from £350.

ULVERSTON, CUMBRIA 7–4D

Ⓐ

The Bay Horse £ 46
Canal Foot LA12 9EL (01229) 583972
A "beautiful location overlooking Morecambe Bay" has helped make
a name for this "cosy" hostelry, complete with conservatory dining
room; the food is sometimes "really delicious" too.
/ **Sample dishes:** toasted goats cheese apples and black pudding with a balsamic
reduction; medallions of fillet steak pan fried and served with a green peppercorn
cream and brandy sauce; brown sugar meringue with fresh pineapple, mango and
cream. **Details:** www.thebayhorsehotel.co.uk; after Canal Foot sign, turn left &
pass Glaxo factory; 8 pm; closed Mon L; children: 12+ evening.
Accommodation: 9 rooms, from £100.

UPPER SLAUGHTER, GLOUCESTERSHIRE 2–1C

Ⓐ⭐

Lords of the Manor £ 75
GL54 2JD (01451) 820243
"Want to feel – or make your partner feel – like royalty?"; then head
for this "lovely" dining room in a picture book Cotswold village; as with
last year, however, there's the odd report suggesting "service lacks
attention to detail". / **Sample dishes:** warm terrine of ham hock, crushed
peas and marjoram, pea and ham mousse; honey roast breast of Gressingham
duck, white peaches, young leeks and duck jus; passion fruit soufflé, coconut
sorbet and pineapple purée and coconut tuille.
Details: www.lordsofthemanor.com; 2m W of Stow on the Wold; 9.30 pm;
no jeans or trainers; children: 7+ at D. **Accommodation:** 26 rooms, from £225.

UPPINGHAM, RUTLAND 5–4D

Ⓣ

The Lake Isle £ 38
16 High Street East LE15 9PZ (01572) 822951
In a small market town, a restaurant-with-rooms tipped for its
"careful" cooking of "well-sourced" ingredients. / **Sample dishes:** twice
roast pavé of pork belly and summer vegetable 'slaw', chilli cashews and apple and
anise compote; grilled fillet of sea bream and sautéed tiger prawns, artichokes,
sun blush tomatoes and pnk grapefruit; Greek yoghurt panna cotta and poached
apricots, pistachios and burned honey syrup. **Details:** www.lakeisle.co.uk; past the
Market place; 9 pm, Fri &Sat 9.30 pm; closed Mon L & Sun D.
Accommodation: 11 rooms, from £75.

Isinglass **£ 36**
46 Flixton Rd M41 5AB (0161) 749 8400
Sometimes tipped as a "hidden gem", this Urmston brasserie is praised for its "good-quality" cuisine, and its "commitment to locally-sourced produce". / **Sample dishes:** *breaded brie bubble and squeak, spiced beetroot chutney, damson and vodka jam; poached corn-fed tarragon chicken, mushroom and barley casserole, Parmesan and pancetta crisp and black truffle oil; seasonal berry profiteroles and bitter chocolate sauce and vanilla ice-cream.* **Details:** *www.isinglassrestaurant.co.uk; 10 pm; closed Mon, Tue-Fri D only, Sat & Sun open L & D.*

Restaurant Gilmore **£ 49**
Strine's Farm ST14 5DZ (01889) 507100
"In a quiet spot, but only minutes from the A50", this former farmhouse (run by refugees from Brum) is "the best restaurant in the area", and "well worth seeking out". / **Details:** *www.restaurantgilmore.com; 9 pm; closed Mon, Tue, Wed L, Sat L & Sun D.*

Percy's **£ 55**
EX21 5EA (01409) 211236
"Just the most perfect place to spend a weekend"; the Bricknell-Webbs' restaurant-with-rooms wins nothing but praise for its "lovely setting, friendly and welcoming staff, beautiful food and fantastic accommodation". / **Details:** *www.percys.co.uk; 9.30 pm; D only; no Amex; children: 12+.* **Accommodation:** *8 rooms, from £110.*

Five Arrows **£ 44**
High St HP18 0JE (01296) 651727
*"Elegant, if slightly starchy" – the dining room of this "traditional" inn on the Rothschild Estate is hailed for its "fine food", and sometimes even for its "great value for money"; you can guess about the key strength of the wine list... / **Sample dishes:** garden pea, broad bean & mint, poached egg & sorrel nest; roast pork loin, confit belly with apple compote, sage & onion rosti, buttered Swiss chard, morel mushroom sauce; dark chocolate tart with crème brûlée ice cream and amaretti biscuits.* **Details:** *www.thefivearrows.co.uk; on A41; 9.15 pm, Sun 7 pm.* **Accommodation:** *11 rooms, from £85.*

Aagrah **£ 27**
Barnsley Rd WF1 5NX (01924) 242222
"Cracking curry that's very fresh and original", and "great staff" too, win applause at this "unfailing" branch of the outstanding Yorkshire chain. / **Sample dishes:** *seek kebab; chicken mangalore; ras malai.* **Details:** *www.aagrah.com; from M1, J39 follow Barnsley Rd to A61; 11.30 pm, 11 pm Sun; D only.* **Accommodation:** *13 rooms, from £40.*

Anchor   £ 31
Main St IP18 6UA   (01502) 722112

Despite the menu offering "the usual staples", this rural relation to west London's famous White Horse offers "a big step-up on pub grub" – it's "worth the drive from Southwold", and "always busy". / **Sample dishes:** *moules marinière with home-made bread; beer battered local haddock with hand cut chips with jalepeno tartare sauce and pease pudding; lavender panna cotta.* **Details:** *www.anchoratwalberswick.com; 10 pm.* **Accommodation:** *8 rooms, from £45/person.*

Bell Inn   £ 35   🅰⭐
Ferry Rd IP18 6TN   (01502) 723109

"A lovely setting in a picturesque coastal village" is not the only attraction of this inn-on-the-green; it serves "delicious home-made food" (which includes a "classic" fish pie as well as a "very good" vegetarian menu). / **Sample dishes:** *Suffolk smokies; roast breast of duck with a chili, soy, honey, toasted sesame seed and lime glaze with egg noodles; sticky toffee pudding served with butterscotch sauce.* **Details:** *www.blythweb.co.uk/bellinn; off A12 on B1387 (no access from Southwold); 9 pm; no Amex.* **Accommodation:** *6 rooms, from £80.*

Angel Inn   £ 37   🆃
Upton Scudamore BA12 0AG   (01985) 213225

A cosy inn, tipped for offering "reliably good food in a peaceful setting"; local artworks on the wall are "a bonus" too. / **Sample dishes:** *pan seared Brixham scallops with a ginger beurre blanc; roast lamb chop on confit onion mashed potatoes; panna cotta with mixed berry and crème anglaise.* **Details:** *www.theangelinn.co.uk; 9.30 pm; no Amex.* **Accommodation:** *10 rooms, from £88.*

The Art Kitchen   £ 44   ⭐
7 Swan St CV34 4BJ   (01926) 494303

"Excellent Thai food, prepared and served by Thais, in a relaxed and informal atmosphere" – that's the deal that commends this great little spot to all who comment on it. / **Sample dishes:** *minced chicken, prawn, garlic and peppers in a rice paper 'money bag'; fillet of Aberdeen angus beef wok fried with fresh chilli and sweet basil; pandan and coconut pancake served with vanilla ice cream.* **Details:** *www.theartkitchen.com; 10 pm.*

Saffron   £ 26   ⭐
Unit 1 Westgate Hs, Market St CV34 4DE   (01926) 402061

The location, in a shopping centre, may not be great, but – for "the best curry in the area" – seek out this "welcoming" spot. / **Details:** *www.saffronwarwick.co.uk; 11.30 pm; D only.*

Saxon Mill   £ 40
Coventry Rd, Guys Cliffe CV34 5YN   (01926) 492255

"The most incredible waterside setting" helps this "stylish and popular" inn generate a fair volume of reports; the food can seem "expensive for what it is", though, and critics find the menu "boring and weirdly-presented". / **Details:** *www.saxonmill.co.uk; 9.30 pm, Sun 9 pm.*

Ⓐ

The Beach Hut
Watergate Bay Hotel **£ 37**
On The Beach TR8 4AA   (01637) 860543
*"A cheap alternative to Fifteen"; if your budget doesn't stretch
to Jamie's landmark restaurant, you might like to check out this self-
explanatory spot (just below), which has a "fantastic location right
on the beach" – "you can watch kite-surfing while you eat".*
/ **Sample dishes:** clam chowder with clams, cockles and smoked bacon; grilled
Cornish pollock with saffron aioli, white beans, tomato and fennel; organic Cornish
ice creams. **Details:** www.watergatebay.co.uk; 9 pm; no Amex.

Ⓐ

Fifteen Cornwall **£ 60**
Watergate Bay Hotel TR8 4AA   (01637) 861000
*"The superb panoramic view (get a window seat!)" and "relaxed" vibe
generally "make up for average food and service", at Jamie Oliver's
charitable seaside venture; more critical reporters, however, just find
it "overpriced and over-hyped".* / **Sample dishes:** bruschetta of mackerel
fillets, peperonata & herbs; chargrilled pork loin, smashed celeriac, spring
cabbage & salsa verde; rhubarb, cinnamon pudding & clotted cream custard.
Details: www.fifteencornwall.co.uk; on the Atlantic coast between Padstow and
Newquay; 9.15 pm; children: Age 7-12 welcome for early sittings only.

Ⓣ

Leeming House Hotel **£ 56**
Ullswater CA11 0JJ   (01768) 486674
*Overlooking the lake, a country house hotel tipped, in particular, as a
"good value-for-money lunch destination".* / **Sample dishes:** seared
scallops and braised chicken wing, Parmesan and apple; lamb served three ways
with dauphinoise potatoes and oregano jus; sticky toffee pudding soufflé and its
own ice cream. **Details:** www.macdonald-hotels.co.uk; directly off A592; 9 pm;
no jeans or trainers. **Accommodation:** 41 rooms, from £155.

Ⓐ

Sportsman's Arms **£ 42**
HG3 5PP   (01423) 711306
*"A very good foodie pub", where chef/patron Ray Carter has been
in charge for over 30 years; it has a "beautiful location" too, out in
the Dales.* / **Sample dishes:** king scallops on dressed leaves with roast pine
nuts, Parmesan & pancetta; roast local lamb on wilted spinach with roast garlic &
vine tomatoes; sticky toffee pudding with vanilla ice cream & toffee sauce.
Details: www.sportsmans-arms.co.uk; take Wath Road from Pateley Bridge; 9 pm,
Sun 8 pm; no Amex. **Accommodation:** 11 rooms, from £60/person.

Ⓐ

Fox & Hounds **£ 41**
Christmas Common OX49 5HL   (01491) 612599
*A "picture-book" Chilterns pub that's got the lot – "a garden for the
summer, a warm and cosy interior in the winter, good beer, a well
thought-out menu and generous portions"; eat in the bar or in the
"airy, barn-style" dining annex; (breaking news – it changed hands
just as we went to press).* / **Details:** www.thefoxandhounds.org; 10 pm;
no shorts.

Goodfellows   **£ 52** ⭐⭐

5 Sadler St BA5 2RR   (01749) 673866

"A high-quality restaurant, with a consistently growing reputation", thanks to Mr Fellows's *"very good fish and seafood"*, which is *"presented imaginatively and cooked to perfection"*… and to his wife's *"artisan pâtisserie"* (which can also be enjoyed at the adjacent café). / **Sample dishes:** chilled gazpacho with crayfish tails & baby artichoke; seabream with summer baby vegetables, samphire & bouillabaisse sauce; chocolate plate. **Details:** www.goodfellowswells.co.uk; Near the Cathedral and the Market Square; 9.30 pm; closed Mon, Tue D & Sun. **Accommodation:** 0 rooms, from £0.

Old Spot   **£ 41** ⭐

12 Sadler St BA5 2SE   (01749) 689099

"Why can't they all be like this?" – *"gourmet dining comes to the shires"*, at this (ex-Bibendum) chef/patron's *"relaxed"* yearling, praised by (nearly) all reporters for its *"exceptional food at reasonable prices"*. / **Details:** 10.30 pm; closed Mon, Tue L & Sun D.

The Wellington   **£ 38**

1 High St AL6 9LZ   (01438) 714036

An *"imaginative bistro menu"* is *"generally well prepared and presented"*, at this *"stylish"* inn (which benefits from a *"small riverside garden"*); however, its *"full range by the glass of d'Arenberg wines"* (a famous Aussie vineyard) is arguably an even greater attraction. / **Sample dishes:** salt and pepper squid with a watermelon and chilli salsa and peashoot salad; slow-cooked blade steak in a smoked garlic and tomato sauce on spring onion mash with baby spinach; white chocolate and raspberry cheesecake with a raspberry coulis. **Details:** www.wellingtonatwelwyn.co.uk; 10 pm; no Amex.

Chu Chin Chow   **£ 34** 🆃

63 Old Woking Rd KT14 6LF   (01932) 349581

A long-established Chinese restaurant awarded top marks for food by a more-than-local fan club. / **Sample dishes:** babecue spare ribs; crispy duck pancakes; toffee banana. **Details:** www.chuchinchow.com; 11 pm.

La Paz   **£ 29** 🆃

3 Banks Rd CH48 4HD   (0151) 625 7200

"Newly-opened and already popular", this *"friendly"* spot – open all day, but offering quite an ambitious menu by night – is already tipped as *"deserving to be one of the Wirral's more-frequented restaurants"*. / **Sample dishes:** oven baked Cornish sardines with garlic, vine tomato & anchovy; slow braised pork belly with onion tart and teriyaki glaze; rasberry & blueberry Eton Mess. **Details:** www.lapazrestaurants.co.uk; 9.30 pm, Fri & Sat 10 pm; closed Mon & Sun D.

Swan   £ 45   Ⓐ

35 Swan St ME19 6JU (01732) 521910

"A buzzy, stylish restaurant" – part of a (much) tarted-up former coaching inn, in a "lovely village" – where the cooking varies "from good to average". / **Sample dishes:** *crab mayonnaise, cucumber, crème fraîche; roast pork belly, glazed apple & sweet mash; strawberry & cream shortbread sandwich.* **Details:** *www.theswanwestmalling.co.uk; 11 pm, Sun 7.30 pm.*

The Thomas Lord   £ 37   Ⓐ⭐

High St GU32 1LN (01730) 829244

"An excellent gastropub", offering "innovative" cooking, with a strong emphasis on "local produce" ("no orange juice at the bar, but delicious apple & elderflower instead!"); "great staff" and "lovely atmosphere" too. / **Sample dishes:** *longhorn beef faggot & picalilli salad with strawberry spinach; beetroot & potato gratin, mixed beans, poached egg, Isle of Wight blue cheese sauce; lemon verbena panna cotta.*
Details: *www.thethomaslord.co.uk; 9 pm, Sat 9.30 pm; no Amex.*

The Company Shed   £ 16   ⭐⭐

129 Coast Rd CO5 8PA (01206) 382700

"I will never queue, especially to eat... except here of course"; this "grotty old shed", with "Formica tables and neon lights", is as "basic" as it gets, but still "worth the drive any day" for its "unsurpassed" seafood; "you have to take your own bread, wine, cork opener, etc...", BUT – "a radical step!" – "they now do salad!". / **Sample dishes:** *fresh seafood platter.* **Details:** *L only, closed Mon; no credit cards; no booking.*

The Wensleydale Heifer   £ 43   ⭐

Main St DL8 4LS (01969) 622322

Within a "popular Dales inn", this "excellent fish restaurant" ("miles from the sea!") is consistently hailed as one "not to be missed"; "better still, stay the night in one of their superb rooms". / **Sample dishes:** *chilli salt squid, lime marinated fennel & noodle salad, French beans and sweet chilli dressing; warm salad of maple roast lobster, king scallop and tiger prawns, with crispy bacon; snickerbockerglory.*
Details: *www.wensleydaleheifer.co.uk; 9.30 pm.* **Accommodation:** *9 rooms, from £110.*

Kinara
Pitts Cottage   **£ 32**
High St TN16 1RQ   (01959) 562125
"A treasure!"; you don't expect to find Pakistani food in the
"charming" and "quaint" surroundings of a "traditional English
cottage" (once owned by William Pitt), but here it's "fantastic",
and served by "the most charming staff".
/ **Details:** www.pittscottage.co.uk; 11.30 pm.

Napoli E   **£ 26**
18a-18b, Market Sq TN16 1AR   (01959) 561688
"Just like when I was in Italy"; this "excellent local" is tipped for its
"huge portions" of "really good" nosh.

The Wild Mushroom   **£ 42**
Westfield Ln TN35 4SB   (01424) 751137
"Unbeatable locally for delightful cooking, imaginative presentation
and caring service" – all reporters agreed that this restaurant
is "a joy", and "excellent value" too. / **Sample dishes:** warm red mullet,
potato and shallot salad with orange dressing; fillet of beef with port wild
mushroom jus and potato galette; apple mousse on an apple sorbet with
blackberry compote. **Details:** www.wildmushroom.co.uk; 9.30 pm; closed Mon &
Sun D; closed 2 weeks in Jan; children: 8+ at D.

Colony   **£ 35**
3 Balfour Rd KT13 8HE   (01932) 842766
A long-established Chinese restaurant, tipped for its "decent 'home-
style' cooking" and its "efficient service". / **Sample dishes:** sesame prawn
toast; crispy beef in chilli sauce; toffee apples. **Details:** on A317; 10.30 pm.

Perry's   **£ 38**
4 Trinity Rd, The Old Harbour DT4 8TJ   (01305) 785799
"A little place overlooking the harbour"; on practically all accounts,
it makes "a fantastic find", thanks to its "delicious food and
enthusiastic, knowledgeable service".
/ **Details:** www.perrysrestaurant.co.uk; 9.30 pm; no Amex; children: 7+.

Three Fishes   **£ 32**
Mitton Rd BB7 9PQ   (01254) 826888
"Arrive early!", if you want to eat at this mega-popular spin-off from
nearby Northcote – it's "always busy" and there's no booking; this is
"everything a country pub should be", with "simple, local dishes
of very high quality" – plus "regional ales" and "good wines" – served
in an "attractive" setting. / **Sample dishes:** potted brown trout, chives,
pickled beetroot, samphire; scallop of veal chargrilled with lemon crack wheat &
summer vegetables; vanilla junket, raspberries, Goosnargh cakes.
Details: www.thethreefishes.com; 9 pm, Sun 8.30 pm.

Greens £ 40
13 Bridge St YO22 4BG (01947) 600284
*Refurbishment and expansion seems to have done nothing to dent
the charms of the Greens' busy bistro, where top tips include its
"lovely roast beef, and local fish". / **Sample dishes:** paupiette of Whitby
smoked salmon with asparagus, watercress & a watercress dressing; carved fillet
of chargrilled beef with braised oxtail 'cappuccino,' fillet steak hash brown, shallot
confit and marrowbone jus; dark chocolate tart with iced hazelnut nougat with
orange cream. **Details:** www.greensofwhitby.com; 9.30 pm, Fri & Sat 10 pm;
no Amex.*

Magpie Café £ 28
14 Pier Rd YO21 3PU (01947) 602058

*"There are no better fish 'n' chips on earth" than at this "cosy"
("crammed") harbour-side classic – one of the UK's best-known
eateries; "who cares about the queue?" / **Sample dishes:** local smoked
kippers served with brown bread; portions of lemon sole and poached salmon
served in a white wine, chive and lemon butter sauce with king prawns; spotted
dick and custard. **Details:** www.magpiecafe.co.uk; opp Fish Market; 9 pm;
no Amex; no booking at L.*

Trenchers £ 36
New Quay Rd YO21 1DH (01947) 603212
*"It's as good as the Magpie but more comfortable", say fans of this
modern chippy; on average, it's actually rated less well than its rival,
but by any measure it serves "excellent fish 'n' chips" and is "always
a joy!" / **Sample dishes:** Mediterranean prawns; fresh halibut steak with
potatoes, lemon & tartar sauce; sticky toffee meringue with roast hazelnuts &
cream. **Details:** www.trenchersrestaurant.co.uk; opp railway station, near marina;
8.30 pm; no Amex; need 7+ to book.*

The White Horse & Griffin £ 48
Church St YO22 4BH (01947) 604857
*There's quite a lot of commentary on this handsome inn; supporters
say it's a "favourite" destination with "consistently high standards",
but doubters find it "over-rated" and "a bit overpriced".
/ **Sample dishes:** oysters; chateaubriand with hollandaise sauce, summer
vegetables & new potatoes; chocolate mocha tarte with amaretto & almond ice
cream. **Details:** www.whitehorseandgriffin.co.uk; centre of old town, on Abbey side
of river; 9 pm; no Amex. **Accommodation:** 10 rooms, from £60.*

Royal Oak £ 50 ⭐

Paley St SL6 3JN (01628) 620541

"Known far-and-wide as 'Parky's Pub'", the inn run by the son (Christopher) of the TV chat-show supremo is consistently praised for its "beautiful cooking" – but then, you'd rather hope so, as the chef used to run Heston Blumenthal's Hind's Head, at Bray!
/ **Details:** www.theroyaloakpaleystreet.com; 9.30 pm, Fri & Sat 10 pm; closed Sun D.

The Crown at Whitebrook £ 63 ⭐⭐

NP25 4TX (01600) 860254

"The best in South Wales"; it may be "tucked-away in the Wye Valley", but this "idyllically-located" and "relaxed" restaurant-with-rooms has won considerable renown for its "outstanding" cuisine.
/ **Sample dishes:** butternut squash, confit endive, artichoke and goat's cheese; roast loin of venison, sweet corn, hazelnut, celeriac and chocolate; baked fig soufflé, golden raisin, sherry and maple. **Details:** www.crownatwhitebrook.co.uk; 2m W of A466, 5m S of Monmouth; 9 pm; closed Mon, Tue & Sun D; no Amex; children: 12+. **Accommodation:** 8 rooms, from £115.

The Pear Tree Inn £ 44

Top Ln SN12 8QX (01225) 709131

An "out-of-the-way" former pub, "set in delightful gardens", often said to be "worth seeking out"; under new ownership, however, the fare is "more basic" than it was, and harsher critics say it's "getting worse on every visit". / **Details:** www.maypolehotels.com; 9.30 pm, Sat 10 pm, Sun 9 pm; no Amex. **Accommodation:** 8 rooms, from £90.

Crab & Winkle £ 45

South Quay, Whitstable Harbour CT5 1AB (01227) 779377

Right over the harbour-side fish market (and with "good sea views"), this "perennial" trippers' favourite serves up some "wonderful" seafood; for what it is, though, it can seem "quite pricey".
/ **Sample dishes:** baby pink fir apple potato salad; shellfish, red onion, fennel & saffron broth, scallops, mussels, crevette, cockles, baby wilja potatoes; vanilla & ginger burnt cream mini rhubarb crumble, rhubarb sorbet. **Details:** www.crab-winkle.co.uk; 9.30 pm; no Amex.

JoJo £ 22 ⭐

209 Tankerton Rd CT5 2AT (01227) 274591

"Exceptional fresh fish" and "superb tapas, cooked to order" are culinary highlights of this "cheap and cheerful" (BYO) spot, which enjoys a following disproportionate to its tiny size – "booking is essential". / **Details:** www.jojosrestaurant.co.uk; 10.30 pm; closed Mon, Tue, Wed L, Thu L, Fri L & Sun D; no credit cards.

Sportsman £ 37 ⓐ⭐⭐

Faversham Rd, Seasalter CT5 4BP (01227) 273370

"The produce is local (they even make their own sea salt!)", at this "adventurously-located" and "rather minimalist" gastropub, where Stephen Harris's "very imaginative" cooking regularly achieves "outstanding" results. / **Details:** www.thesportsmanseasalter.co.uk; 8.45 pm; closed Mon & Sun D; no Amex; children: 18+ in main bar.

Wheeler's Oyster Bar   **£ 33**   A ✪✪

8 High St CT5 1BQ   (01227) 273311

A "quaint" and "quirky" setting and "idiosyncratic" (but "super-friendly") service belie the "memorable" and "sophisticated" fish and seafood at this "miniscule" (16 cover!) "back-room restaurant"; "BYO keeps prices very reasonable". / *Sample dishes:* roast scallops, slow cooked pork belly with sweet potato purée, orange and star anise dressing; pan-fried wild seabass with lobster crushed potatoes, caramelised scallops, griddled asparagus and nantua sauce; lime and mango soufflé with coconut sorbet. *Details:* www.seewhitstable.com; 7.30 pm; closed Wed; no credit cards.

Whitstable Oyster Fishery Co.   **£ 50**   A

Horsebridge CT5 1BU   (01227) 276856

"Waiters who don't catch your eye" too often fuel a sense of "underwhelm-ment" at this "expensive" and "rather up-itself" destination on the beach; a shame, as the location is "fantastic", and the seafood – "straight from sea to plate" – can be "a delight". / *Details:* www.oysterfishery.co.uk; on the seafront; 9 pm, Sun 8.15 pm; closed Mon .

WILLIAN, HERTFORDSHIRE   3–2B

The Fox   **£ 39**   ✪

SG6 2AE   (01462) 480233

"Coming on by leaps and bounds", this "pleasant" gastropub pleases all reporters, not only with its "fish freshly-delivered from Norfolk", but also its "wonderful steaks"; "good value" too. / *Sample dishes:* pear, pecan nut and celery salad served with blue cheese beignets; roast crown of partridge wrapped in bacon served with a savory bread and butter pudding; caramelized pear pain perdu maple syrup drizzle and mascarpone. *Details:* www.foxatwillian.co.uk; /1 mile from junction 9 off A1M; 9.15 pm; closed Sun D; no Amex.

WINCHCOMBE, GLOUCESTERSHIRE   2–1C

5 North Street   **£ 46**   ✪✪

5 North St GL54 5LH   (01242) 604566

With Marcus Ashenford's "distinctive" and "faultless" cuisine, and wife Kate's "personable" and "efficient" service, this "attractive" venture is "something of a hidden treasure"; it is "tiny", though, and can seem "a bit claustrophobic". / *Sample dishes:* lung fish cheeks, chicken wings, bok choi, crisp artichoke, celeriac and horseradish purée with a five spice reduction; local duck breast, with confit ballotine, fig chutney chestnut choucroute with a bittersweet sauce; layers of dark and white chocolate, mango, rose wine jelly and Bailey's ice cream. *Details:* 9 pm; closed Mon, Tue L & Sun D.

Wesley House   **£ 52**   A ✪

High St GL54 5LJ   (01242) 602366

"A lovely experience from start to finish"; all reports sing the praises of this "light" and "elegant" inn, where the service is "efficient", and the food "delicious". / *Sample dishes:* juniper & fennel cured salmon, citrus and pea shoot salad; duo of Scottish beef, dauphinoise potatoes, with a forest mushroom, red wine and bay leaf sauce; dark chocolate and cardamom tart with a strawberry salad. *Details:* www.wesleyhouse.co.uk; next to Sudeley Castle; 9 pm; closed Sun D. *Accommodation:* 5 rooms, from £80.

The Black Rat £ 31
88 Chesil St SO23 0HX (01962) 844465

Reporters endorsed this revamped newcomer ("in a formerly run-down pub") as a "seriously excellent" gastropub, offering unusually "sophisticated" food at "bare, large oak tables"; we've left it unrated, though, as local-big-name chef Philip Storey left as the survey was drawing to a close. / **Details:** www.theblackrat.co.uk.

Chestnut Horse £ 44
Easton Village SO21 1EG (01962) 779257

On some reports, this Itchen Valley boozer is "the epitome of a lovely pub", offering "great food and good value"; it's "usually crowded", though, and – of late – critics too often find staff "trying in vain to keep everyone happy" too. / **Sample dishes:** *tomato consomme, confit tomatoes, truffle oil; open lasagne of Mediterranean vegetables, Dolcelatte cream sauce, tomato fondue, celeriac crisps; vanilla crème brûlée.*
Details: *www.thechestnuthorse.com; 9.30 pm, 8pm Sun; no Amex.*

Hotel du Vin et Bistro £ 45 🅐
14 Southgate St SO23 9EF (01962) 841414

Things are "still running smoothly", at the original branch of what's nowadays a nationwide boutique hotel chain; the "interesting and comprehensive" wine list and "always-enjoyable" atmosphere remain its "best assets", but the food is "good and reasonably priced" too. / **Sample dishes:** *guinea fowl, caramelised quince, red wine jus; fillet of turbot, sautéed gnocchi with wild mushrooms & cèpe foam; panna cotta with raspberries.*
Details: *www.hotelduvin.com; 9.45 pm; booking: max 10.* **Accommodation:** *24 rooms, from £130.*

Avenue ⭐
Lainston House Hotel £ 68
SO21 2LT (01962) 776088

An "elegant" country house, with a "lovely" location and a chef who is "trying hard", and where the food is often "excellent"… but which is still often judged to be rather "expensive" for what it is. / **Sample dishes:** *Portland crab ravioli, pak choi, grapefruit & vanilla dressing; roast saddle of venison parsnip purée, sweet potato fondant, red cabbage compote; apple crumble soufflé, vanilla ice-cream, custard.*
Details: *www.lainstonhouse.com; 9.30 pm, 10 pm Fri & Sat.*
Accommodation: *50 rooms, from £235.*

Wykeham Arms £ 38 🅐
75 Kingsgate St SO23 9PE (01962) 853834

This "super" candlelit boozer is a "romantic" sort of place, with a "great location between the cathedral and the College"; especially on the food front, though, it's "not as good as it used to be". / **Sample dishes:** *Stilton and mushroom tartlet with rocket pesto and toasted walnuts; roast herb crusted rack of lamb with dauphinoise potatoes, a panache of market vegetables and a redcurrant and mint jus; dark chocolate nemesis with a rum and banana purée and toasted almonds.* **Details:** *www.fullershotels.com; between Cathedral and College; 8.45 pm; booking: max 8; children: 14+.*
Accommodation: *14 rooms, from £115.*

The Ship Inn £ 40 🅐⭐
Barlow Hill SK11 0QE (01260) 227217

One reporter speaks for all on this "cosy and welcoming walkers' pub", which is "worth seeking out" for its "excellent home-cooking". / **Details:** *11 pm; closed Mon.*

★

First Floor Café
Lakeland Limited £ 26
Alexandra Buildings LA23 1BQ (015394) 47116
You "always have to wait", at the café above the famous kitchenware retailer's flagship store; it's "well worth going out of your way for", though – the food is "very good", and "nicely presented" too.
/ **Sample dishes:** tandoori-style chicken chargrilled tortilla wrap with apricot & apple chutney, cucumber raita; chocolate almond slice. **Details:** 6 pm, Sat 5pm, Sun 4 pm; no Amex.

A ★

Gilpin Lodge £ 65
Crook Rd LA23 3NE (01539) 488818
For "a truly first-class experience in a most picturesque location", it's hard to beat this "lovely" Edwardian country house hotel, which combines "sheer luxury", with "friendly", "family-run" service, and "expensive but good-quality" cuisine. / **Sample dishes:** crab ravioli with a crab and lemongrass flavoured bisque; best end of lamb with potato fondant, confit swede, shallot purée and a rosemary jus; hot prune and armagnac soufflé with its own ice cream. **Details:** www.gilpinlodge.co.uk; 9.15 pm; children: 7+. **Accommodation:** 20 rooms, from £270.

A ★

Holbeck Ghyll £ 73
Holbeck Ln LA23 1LU (01539) 432375
"A great experience, from the amuse-bouches to the petits-fours" – this country house hotel dining room continues to please most reporters with its "excellent" food and its "stunning" Lakeland views; the style can occasionally seem a mite "stiff", but the staff are "friendly" enough (including to kids). / **Sample dishes:** salad of warm Scottish langoustines with lobster & celeriac remoulade; best end of lamb with lentils, suede purée & haggis beignets; chocolate plate.
Details: www.holbeckghyll.com; 3m N of Windermere, towards Troutbeck; 9.30 pm; booking essential; children: 8+ at D. **Accommodation:** 23 rooms, from £220.

A ★

Jerichos at The Waverly £ 44
College Rd LA23 1BX (01539) 442522
The Blaydes shifted their outstanding restaurant to new premises (with rooms) at the start of 2008; early reports suggest the "beautifully cooked, fresh local food" is "as good as ever", likewise the "personal" service. / **Sample dishes:** roast grilled pepper and garlic crostini, aioli, rocket, olives, vinaigrette; chargrilled rib eye steak and cabernet sauce, grilled tomatoes, mushrooms, chips; lavender panna cotta and shortbread, raspberries and raspberry sorbet. **Details:** www.jerichos.co.uk; 9.30 pm; closed L; no Amex; children: 12+. **Accommodation:** 11 rooms, from £85.

A ★

Linthwaite House £ 62
Crook Rd LA23 3JA (01539) 488600
A change of chef seems to have done nothing to dispel the charms of this "classic country house hotel restaurant", where the food is "great" and the wine list "fantastically comprehensive"; the conservatory has "lovely lake-views" too. / **Sample dishes:** seared scallops and caramelised cauliflower, hazelnuts, baby leek and jerez vinegar; slow braised feather beef, forestière garnish, salsify, potato purée and red wine jus; strawberry soufflé, strawberry ice cream and shortbread biscuit.
Details: www.linthwaite.com; near Windermere golf club; 9 pm; no jeans or trainers; children: 7+ at D. **Accommodation:** 32 rooms, from £180.

The Samling £ 78

Ambleside Rd LA23 1LR (01539) 431922

As our survey year was drawing to a close, this "gloriously-located" contemporary country house hotel, overlooking Windermere, was snapped up by the ever-acquisitive Von Essen group; in the circumstances, a rating isn't appropriate.
/ **Details:** www.thesamlinghotel.co.uk; take A591 from town; 9.30 pm.
Accommodation: 11 rooms, from £200.

WINDSOR, WINDSOR & MAIDENHEAD 3–3A

Al Fassia £ 32 Ⓣ

27 St Leonards Rd SL4 3BP (01753) 855370

This "value-for-money" neighbourhood joint is tipped for its "pretty authentic" Moroccan fare. / **Details:** 10.30 pm, Fri & Sat 11 pm.

The Greene Oak £ 35

SL4 5UW (01753) 864294

"Now one of the best restaurants in Windsor" – this "really lovely pub" is beginning to get quite a name for its "honest" British cooking and its "relaxed but attentive" service. / **Sample dishes:** asparagus, grilled haloumi and aged balsamic; corn fed chicken breast with spinach and walnuts, cabbage, bacon and crushed purple potatoes; baked lemon cheesecake.
Details: www.thegreeneoak.co.uk; 9.30 pm; no Amex.

Spice Route £ 39 Ⓣ

18a, Thames St, Boots Pas SL4 1PL (01753) 860720

"A cut above your usual high street Indian", tipped for its "imaginative" cuisine. / **Sample dishes:** minced lamb with ginger, garlic, mixed herbs & spices cooked on skewers in a clay oven; chicken mallai tikka; rose scented panna cotta with spiced orange compote.
Details: www.spice-route.co.uk; 11 pm; D only.

WINKFIELD, BERKSHIRE 3–3A

Cottage Inn £ 48

Winkfield St SL4 4SW (01344) 882242

Critical reporters feel this potentially "lovely" village inn could "do with a bit of a facelift"; that said, its "great traditional pub food" still generally satisfies. / **Sample dishes:** smoked haddock crumble; fillet steak braised in red wine, shallots & mushrooms; panettone bread & butter pudding.
Details: www.cottage-inn.co.uk; 10 pm; closed Sun D. **Accommodation:** 10 rooms, from £100.

WINTERINGHAM, LINCOLNSHIRE 5–1D

Winteringham Fields £101 Ⓐ

DN15 9ND (01724) 733096

It's as "quaint and charming" as ever, but this remote country house hotel is still in decline following the Schwabs' departure three years ago; fans do say it's "still up there" – even after chef Robert Thompson's recent departure – but for too many reporters now it's "not the place I came to love", and critics find prices "outlandish".
/ **Sample dishes:** scallops carbonara, baby leek étuvée, crispy pancetta; rolled rack of lamb, aubergine purée, baby artichoke, fondant potato, anchovy tempura, sauce vierge; praline baked alaska, orange jelly and warm chocolate sauce.
Details: www.winteringhamfields.com; 4m SW of Humber Bridge; 9.30 pm; closed Mon & Sun; booking: max 8. **Accommodation:** 10 rooms, from £155.

Spooners Restaurant £ 42
61 High St MK17 8QY (01908) 584385
A "small and friendly" place where a number of locals say they've
"never had a bad meal"; it changed hands in late spring – hence
we've left it unrated – but an early report on the new régime says it's
"just as good as ever". / **Details:** www.spooners.co.uk; 2m from J13 on the
M1; 9.45 pm; closed Mon & Sun.

Birch £ 42
20 Newport Rd MK17 9HX (01525) 290295
A "very professional rural restaurant-cum-gastropub",
made "very popular" by its "spoiling" service, "cracking" atmosphere
and "consistently good" food; it's "safest to book". / **Sample dishes:** pan
fried halloumi cheese with chargrilled vegetables drizzled with balsamic and olive
oil; peppered griddled venison steak with gorgonzola potatoes, market vegetables
and an apricot chutney; Kahlúa scented cheesecake with armagnac soaked prunes.
Details: www.birchwoburn.com; 10 pm; closed Sun D; booking: max 12,
Fri & Sat.

Paris House £ 73
Woburn Pk MK17 9QP (01525) 290692
With its "beautiful setting in the Bedford estate", this "antique" Gallic
restaurant is naturally "a local institution"; it's the sort of place that
can so easily tip into being a "time warp", though (and one reporter
"couldn't recommend a place where one table was evicted for making
a gentle complaint about their starter!"). / **Details:** www.parishouse.co.uk;
on A4012; 9.30 pm; closed Mon & Sun D.

Inn @ West End £ 38
42 Guildford Rd GU24 9PW (01276) 858652
"Just two miles from J3 of the M3", an "outstanding" gastropub;
it "doesn't look anything from the outside", but attracts only very
positive reports, in particular for its service ("just about perfect") and
its wine list ("remarkable"). / **Details:** www.the-inn.co.uk; 9.30 pm,
Sun 9 pm; children: 5+.

Saracen's Head £ 37
NR11 7LX (01263) 768909
"Slightly eccentric, but always enjoyable" – this "romantic" inn pleases
all who comment on it; the sale of the property is mooted for some
time in 2009. / **Details:** www.saracenshead-norfolk.co.uk; 2m W of A140
through Erpingham; 9 pm; closed Mon L & Tue L; booking essential.
Accommodation: 6 rooms, from £85.

Trout Inn £ 36

195 Godstow Rd OX2 8PN (01865) 302071

"Refurbished and re-branded as quite a smart gastropub" – this well-known (if "off-the-beaten-track") inn has a "great location" (as immortalised on Inspector Morse), and "the food, atmosphere and internal environment are all better under the new régime"; now if they could just sort out the "very poor service"…

/ **Sample dishes:** asparagus, Cumbrian air-dried ham, poached egg & hollandaise; fillet steak with bearnaise sauce; apple & rhubarb crumble with fresh custard. **Details:** www.thetroutoxford.co.uk; 2m from junction of A40 & A44; 10 pm, Sun 9.30 pm.

Bilash £ 42 ⭐

2 Cheapside WV1 1TU (01902) 427762

"Many Londoners tell me this is as good as any Indian in the capital!" – not least in a "culinary desert", this innovative outfit pleases all who report on it; "how refreshing to see an owner so concerned that everyone enjoys their food". / **Sample dishes:** potato with turmeric, mango powder, green chilli; monkfish jhalfry. **Details:** www.thebilash.co.uk; opp Civic Centre; 10.30 pm; closed Sun.

Captain's Table £ 35

3 Quay St IP12 1BX (01394) 383145

"Unpretentious but welcoming" – Pascal Pommier's village-restaurant pleases most reporters, with its "good, local dishes" (and especially its "real home-made desserts"). / **Sample dishes:** twice baked goats cheese souflee with and onion marmalade and gratinated cheese sauce; slow roast duck leg confit with redcurrant sauce, mashed potato and organic vegetables; vanilla crème brûlée. **Details:** www.captainstable.co.uk; 100 yds from theatre; 9.30 pm, Fri & Sat 10 pm; closed Mon & Sun D; closed 2 weeks in Jan; no Amex.

The Riverside £ 40

Quayside IP12 1BH (01394) 382174

Book a dinner (or tapas) 'n' film package for top value, at this "smart but austere" dining room, attached to a cinema; its "careful and inventive" food makes it of some note locally.

/ **Details:** www.theriverside.co.uk; next to Woodbridge train station; 9.30 pm; closed Sun D.

Seckford Hall Hotel £ 41 Ⓐ

IP13 6NU (01394) 385678

A "comfortable" and "old-fashioned" hotel with an "amazing location", "wonderful grounds" and very good service too; the food is something of a supporting attraction, but never seems to disappoint. / **Details:** www.seckford.co.uk; off the A12, signposted from last Woodbridge roundabout; 9.30 pm; closed Mon L; no jeans or trainers. **Accommodation:** 32 rooms, from £140.

The Waterfront Cafe   **£ 38**

The Granary, Tide Mill Way IP12 1BY   (01394) 610333

Tipped for its "lovely location", this self-explanatory operation is a good, if slightly pricey, sort of place, and often "very busy".
/ **Details:** www.thewaterfrontcafe.co.uk; 5 pm.

WOODLANDS, NETLEY MARSH, HANTS   2–4C

Terravina
Hotel Terravina   **£ 46**
174 Woodlands Rd SO40 7GL   (023) 80293784

WINNER 2009

RÉMY MARTIN
FINE CHAMPAGNE COGNAC

On the edge of the New Forest, this "chic" new hotel/restaurant has been instantly hailed as "a find!"; with Gerard Basset – co-founder of Hotel du Vin – in charge, it's not surprising that the wines are "excellent", but the cuisine can be "wonderful" too.
/ **Sample dishes:** crab & leek lasagne; chargrilled rib-eye of beef with chateaubriand sauce; lemon tart with raspberry sorbet.
Details: www.hotelterravina.co.uk; 9.30 pm.

WOODSTOCK, OXFORDSHIRE   2–1D

The Feathers Hotel   **£ 48**
Market St OX20 1SX   (01993) 812291

It's hard to avoid the conclusion that this well-known inn trades on its location in the "glamorous" village by the gates of Blenheim Palace – reporters again too often describe its catering operation as "haphazard" or "pretentious". / **Sample dishes:** tomato and green olive risotto, Parmesan and rocket; paillard of spiced chicken, green bean salad; dark chocolate mousse with shortbread. **Details:** www.feathers.co.uk; 8m N of Oxford on A44; 10.30 pm; closed Mon L & Sun D; no jeans or trainers.
Accommodation: 20 rooms, from £169.

WOOLSTHORPE-BY-BELVOIR, LINCS.   5–3D

Chequers Inn   **£ 37**
Main St NG32 1LU   (01476) 870701

In a "lovely village" near Belvoir Castle, a pub that's still consistently tipped for its "good food". / **Sample dishes:** smoked loin of pork, saffron risotto; clam, squid & salmon risotto with Parmesan; peach melba, sable biscuit.
Details: www.chequers-inn.net; 9.30 pm, 8.30 pm Sun. **Accommodation:** 4 rooms, from £59.

Glasshouse **£ 43**
Danesbury Hs, Sidbury WR1 2HU   (01905) 611120
"It may say Shaun Hill is the chef", but the modern brasserie he co-owns "could be any regional restaurant" – many reporters do speak of its "original and well-executed food", but a few "very average" experiences were also recorded. / Sample dishes: warm artichoke heart, mushroom duxelle, hollandaise sauce; monkfish with mustard and cucumber sauce; Bakewell tart with vanilla and cardamom ice cream.
Details: *www.theglasshouse.co.uk; 9.30 pm; closed Sun D.*

Loftsome Bridge Coaching House **£ 34**
YO8 6EN   (01757) 630070
This ancient bridge-side inn is tipped as an "unfailingly good" destination; you "need to book". / Sample dishes: cocktail of prawns and smoked salmon on a bed of lettuce and a piquant seafood sauce; sautéed madallions of English pork simmered in a cider and calvados cream sauce, finished with sliced apple and toasted almonds; lemon tart with raspberries.
Details: *www.loftsomebridge-hotel.co.uk; On the main road to Selby, opposite the windmills; 9 pm; D only, ex Sun L only; no jeans or trainers.*
Accommodation: *17 rooms, from £67.50.*

Pant-yr-Ochain **£ 34**
Old Wrexham Rd LL12 8TY   (01978) 853525
With its "lovely setting", by a small lake, this small country house – run as an airy gastropub – had made itself a popular local destination; the food is pretty "good" too, but "prices are creeping up…". / Sample dishes: marinated tiger prawn salad; pan fried duck breast; orange panna cotta. Details: www.pantyrochain-gresford.co.uk; 1m N of Wrexham; 9.30 pm, Sun 9 pm; children: 13+.

Mulberry Tree **£ 42**
9 Wood Ln WN6 9SE   (01257) 451400
A pub-conversion near the M6, where "the bar is better value than the restaurant"; critics liken its ambience to "motorway services" but there's also praise for its "good choice of food". / Sample dishes: black pudding tart with a softly poached egg, hollandaise sauce and seasonal leaves; roast Cumbrian rump of lamb with basil and sun blush tomato jus, and pesto; cinder toffee meringue, butterscotch sauce and vanilla ice cream.
Details: *www.themulberrytree.info; 2m along Mossy Lea Rd, off M6, J27; 9.30 pm; no Amex; children: 14+.*

Simply Heathcote's
The Wrightington Country Club Hotel £ 42
Moss Ln WN6 9PB   (01257) 424500
This contemporary outpost of the Heatcote empire makes an unexpected tip in a sleepy village hotel; there is only a modest level of reports, but all suggest consistent good standards. / Sample dishes: potted trout & parsley, with capers & brown bread; roast breast of Goosnargh duck with peas, broad beans, potato dumplings & sage oil; lemon posset with raspberries & rosemary shortbread.
Details: *www.heathcotes.co.uk; Just off Junction 27 of the M6; 10 pm, Sat 11 pm, Sun 9 pm.*

WYKE REGIS, DORSET 2–4B

Crab House Café £ 40 ⭐
Ferrybridge Rd DT4 9YU   (01305) 788867
A "slightly ramshackle" place, overlooking Chesil Beach – "it's casual
and hard-to-find, but the seafood is brilliant and fresh".
/ **Sample dishes:** crab cocktail with fennel and orange; huss medallions with red
wine and bacon; raspberry panna cotta with mango sauce.
Details: www.crabhousecafe.co.uk; 9 pm, Sat 9.30; closed Tue; no Amex.

WYTHAM, OXFORDSHIRE 2–2D

The White Hart £ 38 🅐
OX2 8QA   (01865) 244372
"Off the tourist radar, a pub/restaurant that makes a lovely place for
a meal, especially in summer"; above the bar, there's a "more formal"
upstairs restaurant, but the atmosphere is "cheerful" throughout.
/ **Sample dishes:** fish terrine with dill crème fraîche & toasted baguette;
pink lamb rump with Mediterranean ratatouille & dauphinoise potatoes; chocolate
and hazelnut fondant with chocolate sauce & amaretto biscuit.
Details: www.thewhitehartoxford.co.uk; Off the A34; 10 pm; no Amex.

YARMOUTH, ISLE OF WIGHT 2–4D

George Hotel £ 50 🅐
Quay St PO41 0PE   (01983) 760331
"If the sun is shining, you can't beat the waterside dining", at this
popular hotel; its re-jigged dining arrangements seem to be settling
in nicely – "excellent fish and steak" are highlights of a menu that
seems to satisfy across the board. / **Sample dishes:** local steamed
asparagus with hollandaise; sea bass stuffed with herbs with potato rosti &
a tomato, caper & olive salsa; warm apple tart with honey & almond ice cream.
Details: www.thegeorge.co.uk; 9.30 pm. **Accommodation:** 17 rooms,
from £190.

YARPOLE, HEREFORDSHIRE 2–1B

Bell Inn £ 35
Green Ln HR6 0BD   (01568) 780359
"A real find, tucked-away in deepest Herefordshire"; this "top pub" –
run by the brother of the proprietor of Mayfair's Hibiscus – is a
"lovely old place", offering "beautifully prepared food without
pretension". / **Sample dishes:** Scottish smoked salmon rillettes, mixed leaves,
caper & shallot dressing; slow roast leg of Brittany rabbit, pommes boulangère,
glazed baby carrots, peas, mustard & basil sauce; rhubarb sherry trifle.
Details: www.thebellinnyarpole.co.uk; 9.30 pm; closed Mon; no Amex.

YATTENDON, BERKSHIRE 2–2D

Pot Kiln £ 47 ⭐
Frilsham RG18 0XX   (01635) 201366
"A great place... if you can find it"; despite its "really rustic" location,
Mike Robinson's "gem" of an inn has won itself an impressive
following with its "honest" food (including much locally-sourced game),
its "interesting" wines and its "great real ale". / **Details:** www.potkiln.org;
between J12 and J13 of the M4; 9 pm; opening times vary seasonally.

Royal Oak Hotel   **£ 48**
The Square RG18 0UG   (01635) 201325
*"It feels a bit like being in a Hugh Grant movie", at this "archetypical
English country pub"; it used to have quite a reputation, but can seem
like a "find" nowadays (though it isn't far from the M4).*
/ **Details:** www.royaloakyattendon.com; 5m W of Pangbourne, off B4009;
9.30 pm, Sun 9 pm. **Accommodation:** 5 rooms, from £130.

Bettys   **£ 35**
6-8 St Helen's Sq YO1 8QP   (01904) 659142
*"An institution" – this "quaint" and famous tea-room is "always busy"
(and you risk "a long wait for a table"); fans say that "if you want
a nice, sophisticated lunch or tea this is for you", but sceptics feel that
"though the food is good, it really is overpriced".* / **Sample dishes:** crab,
prawn & avocado salad; smoked chicken & asparagus rösti; lemon meringue
pancakes. **Details:** www.bettysandtaylors.com; down Blake St from York Minster;
9 pm; no Amex; no booking.

Blue Bicycle   **£ 48** Ⓐ
34 Fossgate YO1 9TA   (01904) 673990
*"Try a booth downstairs for extra romance and intimacy", at this
"popular" bistro ("once a brothel"); even fans note that it's
"not cheap", however – "it needs to move up a notch to compete
with J Baker's".* / **Sample dishes:** red mullet fillet grilled with basil salt, on
a tomato & olive salad; Moroccan fish curry with apricot & mint cous cous; apple,
sultana & brioche charlotte with custard. **Details:** www.thebluebicycle.com;
9.30 pm, Sun 9 pm; no Amex; booking: max 8. **Accommodation:** 4 rooms,
from £150.

Café Concerto   **£ 36** Ⓣ
21 High Petergate YO1 7EN   (01904) 610478
*By the Minster, a "lovely coffee shop", tipped for its "nice cosy
atmosphere" and its "kind and friendly service"… but "it's the cakes
that are worth coming for!"* / **Sample dishes:** hot duck confit salad with
redcurrant, orange & port sauce; satay beef stir-fry, fragrant rice and satay sauce;
sticky toffee pudding with fresh orange, caramel sauce.
Details: www.cafeconcerto.biz; by the W entrance of York Minster; 9.30 pm;
no Amex; booking: max 6.

City Screen Café Bar   Ⓣ
City Screen Picturehouse   **£ 24**
Coney St YO1 9QL   (01904) 612 940
*Tipped for its "lovely" riverside location (and terrace), a cinema café
where the food is sometimes "interesting" too.* / **Sample dishes:** salmon
and spring onion fishcakes, lemon mayonnaise & mixed leaf salad; grilled
chorizo & goat's cheese; Tunisian orange cake. **Details:** www.picturehouses.co.uk;
9 pm; no Amex; no booking.

J Baker's Bistro Moderne   **£ 43** ⭐⭐
7 Fossgate YO1 9TA   (01904) 622688
*"Definitely the top place to eat in York by a mile" – Jeff Baker's year-
old venture may look low-key, but you couldn't say the same of his
"avant-garde interpretations of traditional dishes", which are
"inspired" and "brilliant value for money".* / **Details:** www.jbakers.co.uk;
10 pm; closed Mon & Sun.

Masons Bistro £ 40

13 Fossgate YO1 9TA (01904) 611919

In a former city-centre boozer, a "quirky" bistro, universally commended by reporters for its "interesting" and "well-cooked" dishes. / **Sample dishes:** *wilted spinach, Feta cheese, parsley and nutmeg layered with crisp filo pastry; fennel and sea salt roast belly pork with caramelised apple and black pudding; drunken cherry clafoutis with home-made vanilla ice cream.* **Details:** *www.masons-bistro.co.uk; 9.30 pm; closed Mon L; children: 14+ at D.*

Melton's £ 42 ⭐

7 Scarcroft Rd YO23 1ND (01904) 634 341

"A credit to York" – this small venture, "in a rather unfashionable corner of the city", has "kept consistently high standards over many years", and fans still rate its "interesting" cooking as "the best in town". / **Sample dishes:** *York ham with herbs, peas and broad beans in a Parmesan crust; medley of seafood with Yorkshire lobster, greens and crushed new potatoes; red wine jelly with seasonal berries and crème anglaise.* **Details:** *www.meltonsrestaurant.co.uk; 10 mins walk from Castle Museum; 10 pm; closed Mon L & Sun; no Amex.*

Melton's Too £ 30 ❌

25 Walmgate YO1 9TX (01904) 629 222

This popular all-day café-bar-bistro continues to divide opinion; fans find it "reliable" and "atmospheric" – critics that it's "resting on its laurels" to a sometimes "appalling" extent. / **Sample dishes:** *grilled local goat's cheese with a walnut salad; fillet of sea bass with a crab cream sauce; vanilla panna cotta with a rhubarb compote.* **Details:** *www.meltonstoo.co.uk; 2 minutes from the City centre; 10.30 pm, Sun 9.30 pm; no Amex; need 8+ to book.*

Middlethorpe Hall £ 57 Ⓐ

Bishopthorpe Rd YO23 2GB (01904) 641241

On the fringe of the city, "an elegant country house hotel", offering "traditional cooking with a few modern twists"; the approach can seem a mite "pretentious", but most accounts this year were of "excellent" cooking. **Sample dishes:** *garden pea mousse, summer vegetable salad and crisp ham; roast halibut fillet, celeriac and fennel purée, baby leeks and roast chicken sauce; hot raspberry soufflé, raspberry sorbet and raspberry compote.* **Details:** *www.middlethorpe.com; next to racecourse; 9.30 pm; no shorts; children: 4+.* **Accommodation:** *29 rooms, from £190.*

UK MAPS

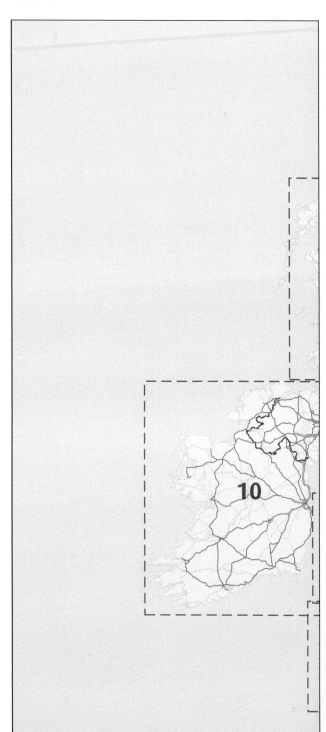

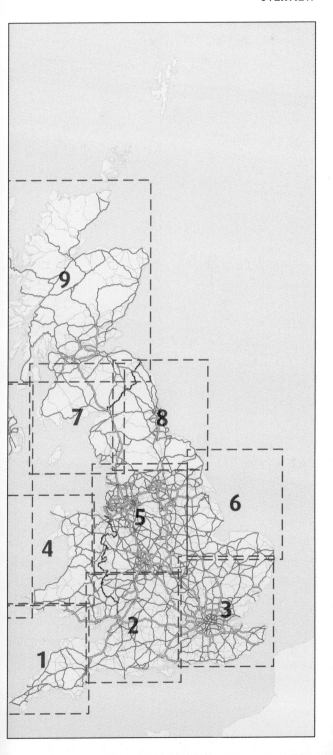

MAP I

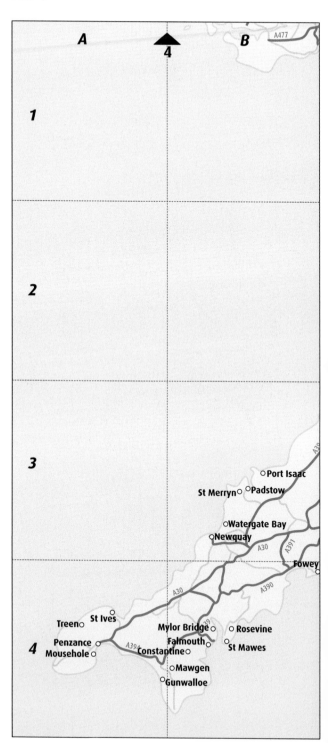

MAP 1

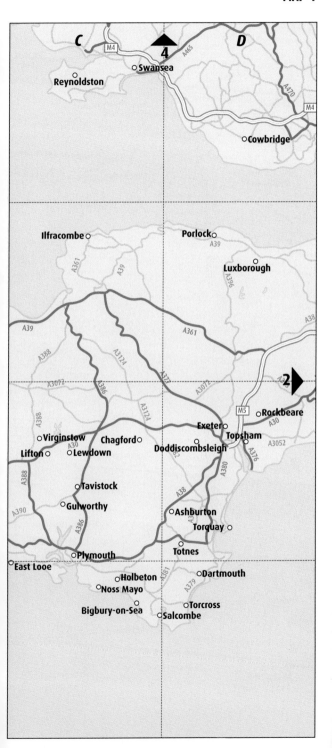

MAP 2

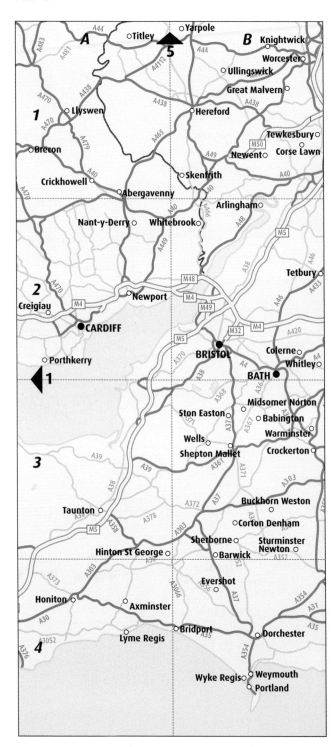

MAP 2

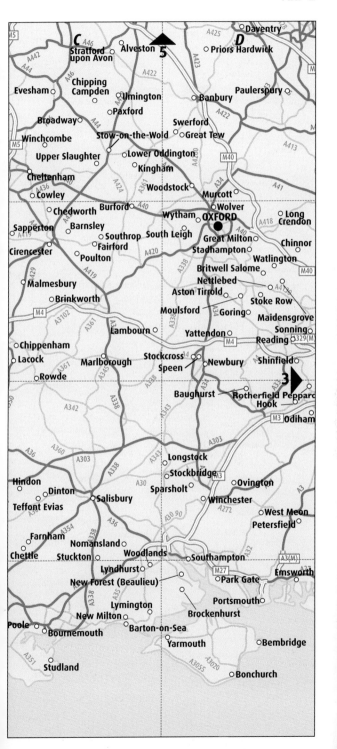

MAP 3

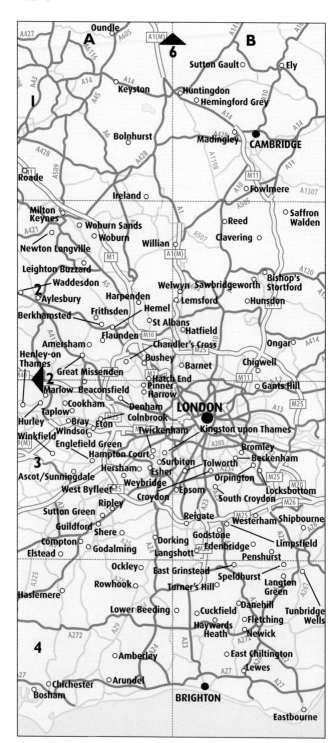

MAP 3

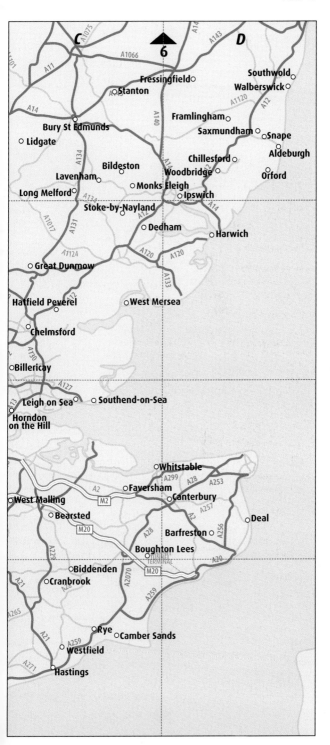

MAP 4

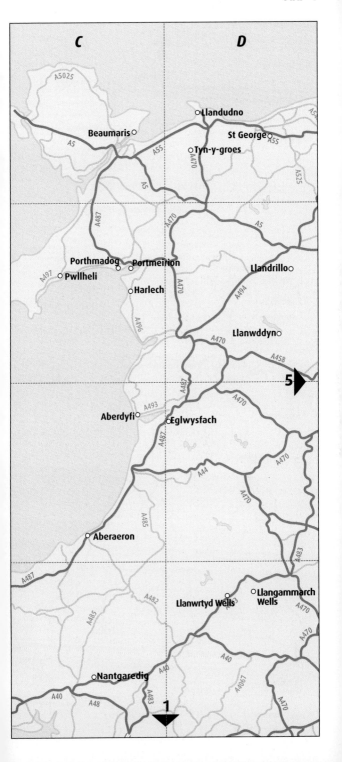

MAP 4

MAP 5

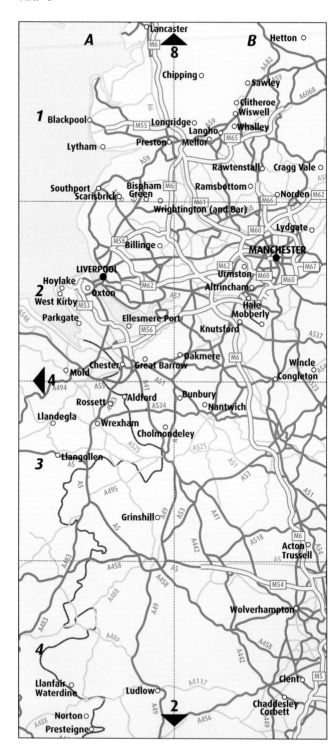

MAP 5

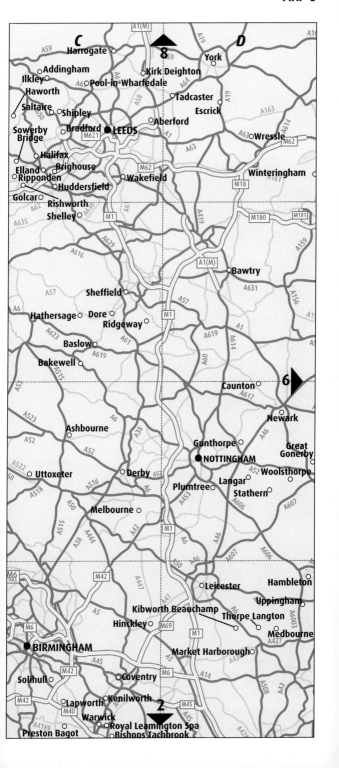

MAP 6

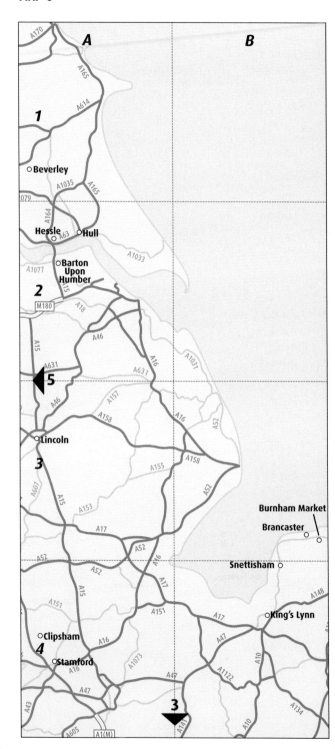

MAP 6

MAP 7

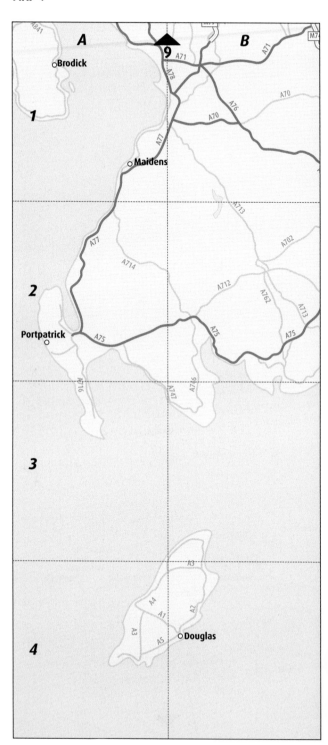

MAP 7

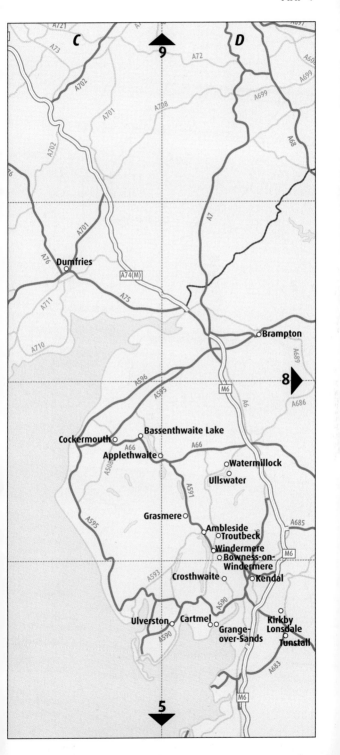

MAP 8

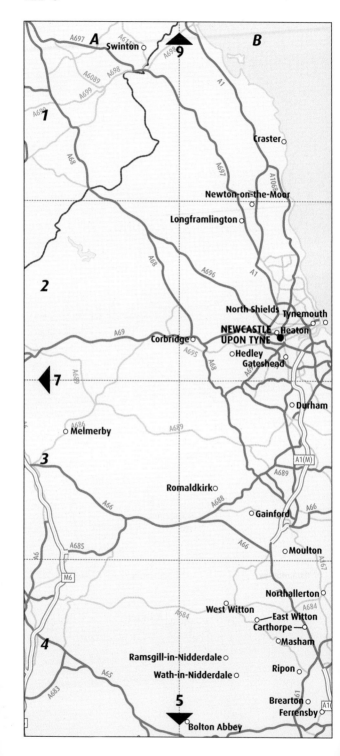

MAP 8

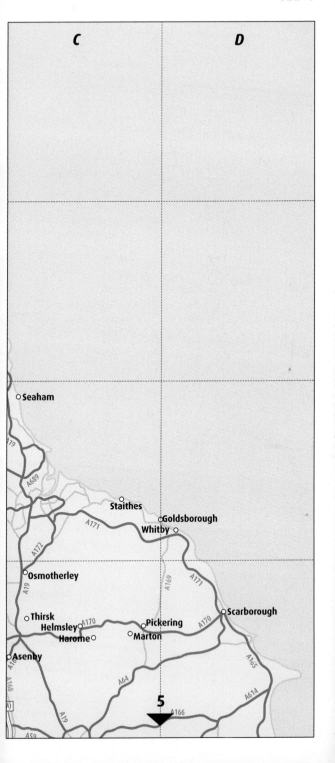

MAP 9

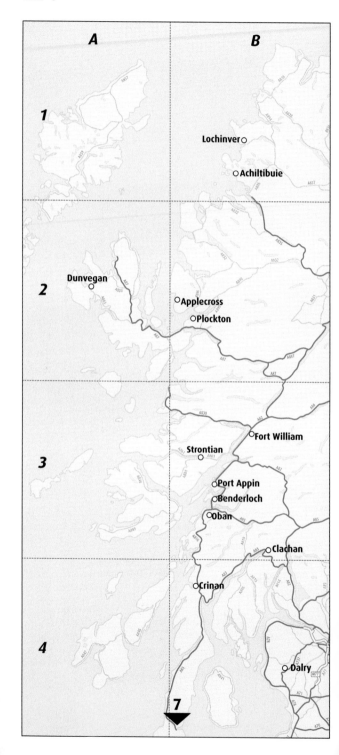

A   B

1

Lochinver ○

○ Achiltibuie

2

Dunvegan
○

○ Applecross

○ Plockton

3

○ Fort William

Strontian
○

○ Port Appin
○ Benderloch
○ Oban

○ Clachan

○ Crinan

4

○ Dalry

7

MAP 9

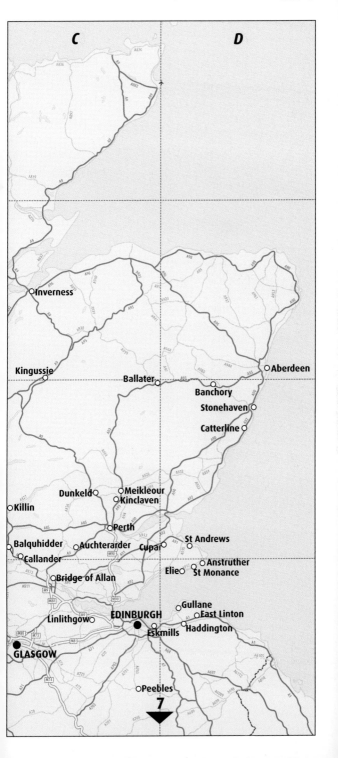

C

D

Inverness

Kingussie

Ballater

Aberdeen

Banchory

Stonehaven

Catterline

Dunkeld Meikleour
Kinclaven

Killin

Perth

Balquhidder Auchterarder Cupar St Andrews

Callander

Elie St Monance Anstruther

Bridge of Allan

Gullane

East Linton

Linlithgow EDINBURGH

Eskmills Haddington

GLASGOW

Peebles

7

MAP 10

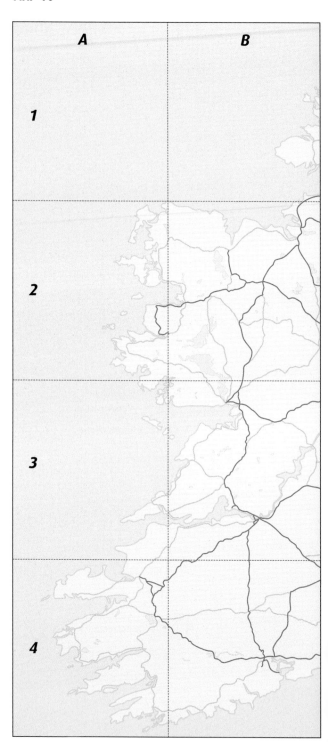

MAP 10

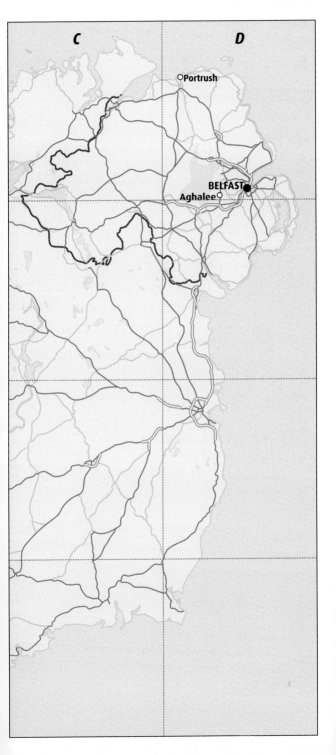

C

D

Portrush

BELFAST

Aghalee

ALPHABETICAL
INDEX

ALPHABETICAL INDEX

ALPHABETICAL INDEX

ALPHABETICAL INDEX

ALPHABETICAL INDEX

ALPHABETICAL INDEX

ALPHABETICAL INDEX

442